AS ABOVE

SO BELOW

# As Above
# So Below

# Star Wisdom, volume 3
## 2021

**EDITOR**
Joel Matthew Park

**ADVISORY BOARD**
Brian Gray ~ Claudia McLaren Lainson ~ Robert Powell, PhD
Lacquanna Paul ~ Robert Schiappacasse

Lindisfarne Books

LINDISFARNE BOOKS
an imprint of Steinerbooks/Anthroposophic Press, Inc.
402 Union Street, No. 58, Hudson, NY 12534
www.steinerbooks.org

With grateful acknowledgment to Peter Treadgold (1943–2005), who wrote the Astrofire program (available from the Sophia Foundation), with which the ephemeris pages in *Star Wisdom* are computed each year.

Disclaimer: The views expressed by the contributors in *Star Wisdom* do not necessarily reflect those of the editorial board of *Star Wisdom* or Lindisfarne Books/Anthroposophic Press, Inc.

Design by William Jens Jensen

ISBN: 978-1-58420-905-8 (paperback)
ISBN: 978-1-58420-906-5 (eBook)

Printed in the United States of America

# CONTENTS

# ASTROSOPHY

The Sophia Foundation was founded and exists to help usher in the new Age of Sophia and the corresponding Sophianic culture, the Rose of the World, prophesied by Daniel Andreev and other spiritual teachers. Part of the work of the Sophia Foundation is the cultivation of a new star wisdom, *Astro–Sophia* (*astrosophy*), now arising in our time in response to the descent of Sophia, who is the bearer of Divine Wisdom, just as Christ (the Logos, or the Lamb) is the bearer of Divine Love. Like the star wisdom of antiquity, astrosophy is sidereal, which means "of the stars." Astrosophy, inspired by Divine Sophia, descending from stellar heights, directs our consciousness toward the glory and majesty of the starry heavens, to encompass the entire celestial sphere of our cosmos and, beyond this, to the galactic realm—the realm that Daniel Andreev referred to as "the heights of our universe"—from which Sophia is descending on her path of approach into our cosmos. Sophia draws our attention not only to the star mysteries of the heights, but also to the cosmic mysteries connected with Christ's deeds of redemption wrought two thousand years ago. To penetrate these mysteries is the purpose of the annual volumes of *Star Wisdom*.

For information about Astrosophy / Choreocosmos / Cosmic Dance workshops
Contact the Sophia Foundation:
4500 19th Street, #369, Boulder, CO 80304
Phone: (303) 242-5388; sophia@sophiafoundation.org;
www.sophiafoundation.org

# PREFACE

## Robert Powell, PhD

This is the third volume of the annual *Star Wisdom* (formerly *Journal for Star Wisdom*), intended to help all people interested in the new star wisdom of astrosophy and in the cosmic dimension of Christianity, which began with the Star of the magi. The calendar comprises an ephemeris page for each month of the year, computed with the help of Peter Treadgold's *Astrofire* computer program, with a monthly commentary by Joel Park. The monthly commentary relates the geocentric and heliocentric planetary movements to events in the life of Jesus Christ.

Jesus Christ united the levels of the earthly personality (*geocentric* = Earth-centered) and the higher self (*heliocentric* = Sun-centered) insofar as he was the most highly evolved earthly personality (Jesus) embodying the higher self (Christ) of all existence, the Divine "I AM." To see the life of Jesus Christ in relation to the world of stars opens the door to a profound experience of the cosmos, giving rise to a new star wisdom (astrosophy) that is the Spiritual Science of Cosmic Christianity.

Star Wisdom is scientific, resting on a solid mathematical–astronomical foundation and a secure chronology of the life of Jesus Christ, while it is also spiritual, aspiring to the higher dimension of existence, expressed outwardly in the world of stars. The scientific and the spiritual come together in the sidereal zodiac that originated with the Babylonians and was used by the three magi who beheld the star of Bethlehem and came to pay homage to Jesus a few months after his birth.

In continuity of spirit with the origins of Cosmic Christianity with the three magi, the sidereal zodiac is the frame of reference used for the computation of the geocentric and heliocentric planetary movements that are commented upon in the light of the life of Jesus Christ in *Star Wisdom*.

Thus, all zodiacal longitudes indicated in the text and presented in the following calendar are in terms of the sidereal zodiac, which needs to be distinguished from the tropical zodiac widely used in contemporary astrology in the West. The tropical zodiac was introduced into astrology in the middle of the second century AD by the Greek astronomer Claudius Ptolemy. Prior to this, the sidereal zodiac was used. Such was the influence of Ptolemy on the Western astrological tradition that the tropical zodiac replaced the sidereal zodiac used by the Babylonians, Egyptians, and early Greek astrologers. Yet the astrological tradition in India was not influenced by Ptolemy, and so the sidereal zodiac is still used to this day by Hindu astrologers.

The sidereal zodiac originated with the Babylonians in the sixth to fifth centuries BC and was defined by them in relation to certain bright stars. For example, Aldebaran ("the Bull's Eye") is located in the middle of the sidereal sign–constellation of the Bull at 15° Taurus, while Antares ("the Scorpion's heart") is in the middle of the sidereal sign–constellation of the Scorpion at 15° Scorpio. The sidereal signs, each 30° long, coincide closely with the twelve astronomical zodiacal constellations of the same name, whereas the signs of the tropical zodiac—since they are defined in relation to the vernal point—now have little or no relationship to the corresponding zodiacal constellations. This is because the vernal point, the zodiacal location of the Sun on March 20–21, shifts slowly backward through the sidereal zodiac at a rate of 1° every seventy-two years ("the precession of the equinoxes"). When Ptolemy introduced the tropical zodiac into astrology, there was a nearly exact coincidence between the tropical and the sidereal zodiac, as the vernal point, which is defined as 0° Aries in the tropical zodiac, was at 1° Aries in the sidereal zodiac in the middle of the second century AD. Thus, there was only 1° difference between the two zodiacs. Thus, it made hardly any difference to Ptolemy or his contemporaries to use the tropical zodiac instead of the sidereal zodiac. Now, however—the vernal point having shifted back from 1° Aries to 5° Pisces owing to precession—there is a 25° difference, and thus there is virtually no correspondence between the two. Without going into further detail concerning the complex issue of the zodiac (as shown in the *Hermetic Astrology* trilogy), the sidereal zodiac is the zodiac used by the three magi, who were the last representatives of the true star wisdom of antiquity. For this reason, the sidereal zodiac is used throughout the texts in *Star Wisdom*.

Readers interested in exploring the scientific (astronomical and chronological) foundations of Cosmic Christianity are referred to the works listed here under "Literature." The *Chronicle of the Living Christ: Foundations of Cosmic Christianity* (listed on the following page) is an indispensable reference source (abbreviated *Chron.*) for *Star Wisdom*. The chronology of the life of Jesus Christ rests upon Robert Powell's research into the description of Christ's daily life by Anne Catherine Emmerich in her three-volume work, *The Visions of Anne Catherine Emmerich* (abbreviated *ACE*).

Further details concerning *Star Wisdom* and how to work with it on a daily basis may be found in the general introduction to the *Christian Star Calendar*. The general introduction explains all the features of *Star Wisdom*. The new edition, published in 2003, includes sections on the megastars (stars of great luminosity) and on the 36 decans (10° subdivisions of the twelve signs of the zodiac) in relation to their planetary rulers and to the extra-zodiacal constellations, or the constellations above or below the circle of the twelve constellations–signs of the zodiac.

Further material on the decans, including examples of historical personalities born in the various decans, as well as a wealth of other material on the signs of the sidereal zodiac, can be found in *Cosmic Dances of the Zodiac* (listed below). Also foundational is *History of the Zodiac*, published by Sophia Academic Press (listed under "Works by Robert Powell").

## Literature

*(See also "References" section)*

*General Introduction to the Christian Star Calendar: A Key to Understanding*, 2nd ed. Palo Alto, CA: Sophia Foundation, 2003.

Bento, William, Robert Schiappacasse, and David Tresemer, *Signs in the Heavens: A Message for our Time*. Boulder: StarHouse, 2000.

Emmerich, Anne Catherine, *The Visions of Anne Catherine Emmerich* (new edition, with material by Robert Powell). Kettering, OH: Angelico Press, 2015.

Paul, Lacquanna, and Robert Powell, *Cosmic Dances of the Planets*. San Rafael, CA: Sophia Foundation Press, 2007.

———, *Cosmic Dances of the Zodiac*. San Rafael, CA: Sophia Foundation Press, 2007.

Smith, Edward R., *The Burning Bush: Rudolf Steiner, Anthroposophy, and the Holy Scriptures* (3rd ed.). Great Barrington, MA: SteinerBooks, 2020.

Steiner, Rudolf, *Astronomy and Astrology: Finding a Relationship to the Cosmos*. London: Rudolf Steiner Press, 2009.

Sucher, Willi, *Cosmic Christianity and the Changing Countenance of Cosmology*. Great Barrington, MA: SteinerBooks, 1993. *Isis Sophia* and other works by Willi Sucher are available from the Astrosophy Research Center, PO Box 13, Meadow Vista, CA 95722.

Tidball, Charles S., and Robert Powell, *Jesus, Lazarus, and the Messiah: Unveiling Three Christian Mysteries*. Great Barrington, MA: SteinerBooks, 2005. This book offers a penetrating study of the Christ mysteries against the background of *Chronicle of the Living Christ* and contains two chapters by Robert Powell on the Apostle John and John the Evangelist (Lazarus).

Tresemer, David (with Robert Schiappacasse), *Star Wisdom and Rudolf Steiner: A Life Seen Through the Oracle of the Solar Cross*. Great Barrington, MA: SteinerBooks, 2007.

## ASTROSOPHICAL WORKS BY ROBERT POWELL, PhD

**Starcrafts (formerly Astro Communication Services, or ACS):**

*History of the Houses* (1997)
*History of the Planets* (1989)
*The Zodiac: A Historical Survey* (1984)
www.acspublications.com
www.astrocom.com
Business Address:
Starcrafts Publishing
334 Calef Hwy.
Epping, NH 03042
Phone: 603-734-4300
Fax: 603-734-4311
Contact maria@starcraftseast.com

### SteinerBooks:

Orders: (703) 661-1594; www.steinerbooks.org
By email: service@steinerbooks.org

*The Astrological Revolution: Unveiling the Science of the Stars as a Science of Reincarnation and Karma*, coauthor Kevin Dann (Great Barrington, MA: SteinerBooks, 2010). After reestablishing the sidereal zodiac as a basis for astrology that penetrates the mystery of the stars' relationship to human destiny, the reader is invited to discover the astrological significance of the totality of the vast sphere of stars surrounding the Earth. This book points to the astrological significance of the entire celestial sphere, including all the stars and constellations beyond the twelve zodiacal signs. This discovery is revealed by the study of megastars, illustrating how they show up in an extraordinary way in Christ's healing miracles by aligning with the Sun at the time of those events. This book offers a spiritual, yet scientific, path toward a new relationship to the stars.

*Christian Hermetic Astrology: The Star of the magi and the Life of Christ* (Hudson, NY: Anthroposophic Press, 1998). Twenty-five discourses set in the "Temple of the Sun," where Hermes and his pupils gather to meditate on the Birth, the Miracles, and the Passion of Jesus Christ. The discourses offer a series of meditative contemplations on the deeds of Christ in relation to the mysteries of the cosmos. They are an expression of the age-old hermetic mystery wisdom of the ancient Egyptian sage, Hermes Trismegistus. This book offers a meditative approach to the cosmic correspondences between major events in the life of Christ and the heavenly configurations at that time 2,000 years ago.

*Chronicle of the Living Christ: Foundations of Cosmic Christianity* (Hudson, NY: Anthroposophic Press, 1996). An account of the life of Christ, day by day, throughout most of the 3½ years of his ministry, including the horoscopes of conception, birth, and death of Jesus, Mary, and John the Baptist, together with a wealth of material relating to the new star wisdom focused on the life of Christ. This work provides the chronological basis for *Christian Hermetic Astrology* and *Star Wisdom*.

*Elijah Come Again: A Prophet for our Time: A Scientific Approach to Reincarnation* (Great Barrington, MA: SteinerBooks, 2009). By way of horoscope comparisons from conception–birth–death in one incarnation to conception–birth–death in the next, this work establishes scientifically two basic astrosophical research findings. These are: the importance 1) of the sidereal zodiac and 2) of the heliocentric positions of the planets. Also, for the first time, the identity of the "saintly nun" is revealed, of whom Rudolf Steiner spoke in a conversation with Marie von Sivers about tracing Novalis's karmic background. The focus throughout the book is on the Elijah individuality in his various incarnations, and is based solidly on Rudolf Steiner's indications. It also can be read as a karmic biography by anyone who chooses to omit the astrosophical material.

*Star Wisdom* (2019–); *Journal for Star Wisdom* (2010–2018) (Great Barrington, MA: Lindisfarne Books, edited by Joel Matthew Park, Robert Powell and others engaged in astrosophic research. A guide to the correspondences of Christ in the stellar and etheric world. Includes articles of interest, a complete geocentric and heliocentric sidereal ephemeris, and an aspectarian. According to Rudolf Steiner, every step taken by Christ during his ministry between the baptism in the Jordan and the resurrection was in harmony with, and an expression of, the cosmos. The journal is concerned with these heavenly correspondences during the life of Christ. It is intended to help provide a foundation for Cosmic Christianity, the cosmic dimension of Christianity. It is this dimension that has been missing from Christianity in its 2,000-year history. A starting point is to contemplate the movements of the Sun, Moon, and planets against the background of the zodiacal constellations (sidereal signs) today in relation to corresponding stellar events during the life of Christ. This opens the possibility of attuning to the life of Christ in the etheric cosmos in a living way.

## Sophia Foundation Press and Sophia Academic Press Publications

Books available from Amazon.com
JamesWetmore@mac.com
www.logosophia.com

*History of the Zodiac* (San Rafael, CA: Sophia Academic Press, 2007). Book version of Robert Powell's PhD thesis, *The History of the Zodiac*. This penetrating study restores the sidereal zodiac to its rightful place as the original zodiac, tracing it back to fifth-century-BC Babylonians. Available in paperback and hardcover.

*Hermetic Astrology: Volume 1, Astrology and Reincarnation* (San Rafael, CA: Sophia Foundation Press, 2007). This book seeks to give the ancient science of the stars a scientific basis. This new foundation for astrology based on research into reincarnation and karma (destiny) is the primary focus. It includes numerous reincarnation examples, the study of which reveals the existence of certain astrological "laws" of reincarnation, on the basis of which it is evident that the ancient sidereal zodiac is the authentic astrological zodiac, and that the heliocentric movements of the planets are of great significance. Foundational for the new star wisdom of astrosophy.

*Hermetic Astrology: Volume 2, Astrological Biography* (San Rafael, CA: Sophia Foundation Press, 2007). Concerned with karmic relationships and the unfolding of destiny in seven-year periods through one's life. The seven-year rhythm underlies the human being's astrological biography, which can be studied in relation to the movements of the Sun, Moon, and planets around the sidereal zodiac between conception and birth. The "rule of Hermes" is used to determine the moment of conception.

*Sign of the Son of Man in the Heavens: Sophia and the New Star Wisdom* (San Rafael, CA: Sophia Foundation Press, 2008). Revised and expanded with new material, this edition deals with a new wisdom of stars in the light of Divine Sophia. It was intended as a help in

our time, as we were called on to be extremely wakeful up to the end of the Maya calendar in 2012.

*Cosmic Dances of the Zodiac* (San Rafael, CA: Sophia Foundation Press, 2007), coauthor Lacquanna Paul. Study material describing the twelve signs of the zodiac and their forms and gestures in cosmic dance, with diagrams. Includes a wealth of information on the twelve signs and the 36 decans (the subdivision of the signs into decans, or 10° sectors, corresponding to constellations above and below the zodiac).

*Cosmic Dances of the Planets* (San Rafael, CA: Sophia Foundation Press, 2007), coauthor Lacquanna Paul. Study material describing the seven classical planets and their forms and gestures in cosmic dance, with diagrams, including much information on the planets.

## American Federation of Astrologers (AFA) Publications (currently not in print)

www.astrologers.com

*The Sidereal Zodiac,* coauthor Peter Treadgold (Tempe, AZ: AFA, 1985). A *History of the Zodiac* (sidereal, tropical, Hindu, astronomical) and a formal definition of the sidereal zodiac with the star Aldebaran ("the Bull's Eye") at 15° Taurus. This is an abbreviated version of *History of the Zodiac.*

## Rudolf Steiner College Press Publications

9200 Fair Oaks Blvd., Fair Oaks, CA 95628

*The Christ Mystery: Reflections on the Second Coming* (Fair Oaks, CA: Rudolf Steiner College Press, 1999). The fruit of many years of reflecting on the Second Coming and its cosmological aspects. Looks at the approaching trial of humanity and the challenges of living in apocalyptic times, against the background of "great signs in the heavens."

## The Sophia Foundation

4500 19th Street, #369, Boulder, CO 80304; distributes many of the books listed here and other works by Robert Powell.
Tel: (303) 242-5388
sophia@sophiafoundation.org
www.sophiafoundation.org

Computer program for charts and ephemerides, with grateful acknowledgment to Peter

Treadgold, who wrote the computer program *Astrofire* (with research module, star catalog of over 4,000 stars, and database of birth and death charts of historical personalities), capable of printing geocentric and heliocentric–hermetic sidereal charts and ephemerides throughout history. The hermetic charts, based on the astronomical system of the Danish astronomer Tycho Brahe, are called "Tychonic" charts in the program. This program can:

- compute birth charts in a large variety of systems (tropical, sidereal, geocentric, heliocentric, hermetic);
- calculate conception charts using the hermetic rule, in turn applying it for correction of the birth time;
- produce charts for the period between conception and birth;
- print out an "astrological biography" for the whole of lifework with the geocentric, heliocentric (and even lemniscatory) planetary system;
- work with the sidereal zodiac according to the definition of your choice (Babylonian sidereal, Indian sidereal, unequal-division astronomical, etc.);
- work with planetary aspects with orbs of your choice.

The program includes eight house systems and a variety of chart formats. The program also includes an ephemeris program with a search facility. The geocentric–heliocentric sidereal ephemeris pages in the annual volumes of *Star Wisdom* are produced by the software program *Astrofire,* which is compatible with Microsoft Windows.

Those interested in obtaining the *Astrofire* program should contact:

**The Sophia Foundation**
4500 19th Street, #369
Boulder, CO 80304
Tel: (303) 242-5388
sophia@sophiafoundation.org
www.sophiafoundation.org

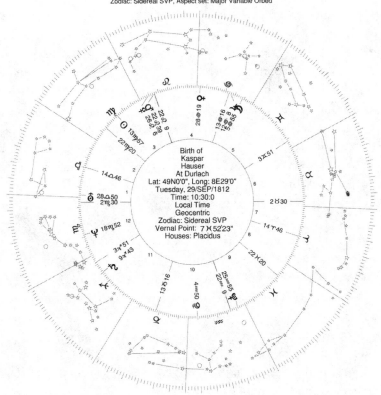

*A horoscope generated by the* Astrofire *program*

# THE SEVEN IDEALS OF THE ROSE OF THE WORLD
## *Robert Powell, PhD*

*In gratitude to Daniel Andreev (1906–1959), the Russian prophet of the Rose of the World as the coming world culture, inspired by Sophia—a culture based on Love and Wisdom.*

*Daniel Andreev, c.1957*

The Rose of the World is arising through the approach of Divine Sophia toward the Earth. Her approach is calling forth the following basic qualities or attributes of the new world culture that She is creating and inspiring:

1. First and foremost: *interreligion.* For Sophia all true religious and spiritual traditions are different layers of spiritual reality, which She seeks to weave together as petals of the Rose of the World. Sophia is not founding a new world religion as She approaches, descending from cosmic heights, and drawing ever closer to our solar system. On Her path of descent, approaching our planet to incarnate into the Earth's aura during the Age of Aquarius, She is bestowing insight concerning each religion and spiritual tradition, thus awaking interreligiosity, signifying a heartfelt interest in religious and spiritual traditions other than one's own. This signifies the blossoming and unfolding of the petals of the Rose of the World, creating brother–sisterhood between all peoples.

2. Sophia's approach toward our planet is bringing about an awaking of social conscience on a global scale, inspiring active compassion combined with unflagging practical efforts on behalf of social justice around the world.

3. Through Sophia a framework for understanding the higher dimension of historical processes is coming about: metahistory, illumining the meaning of historical processes of the past, present, and future in relation to humankind's spiritual evolution. This entails glimpses into the mystical consciousness of humanity such as may be found in the book of Revelation.

4. On the national sociopolitical level, Sophia's inspiration is working to transform the state into a community. The community of Italy, the community of France, etc., is the ideal for the future, rather than the political entity of the state representing (or misrepresenting) the people. And on the global scale Sophia is seeking to bring about the unification of the planet as a world community through bringing the different country communities into a harmonious relationship with one another on a religious, cultural, and economic level.

5. This world community, the Rose of the World, inspired by Sophia, will seek to establish the economic wellbeing of every man, woman, and child on the planet, to ensure that everyone has a roof over their heads and sufficient food to live on. Here it is a matter of ensuring a decent standard of living for all peoples of the Earth.

6. A high priority of the Rose of the World will be the ennobling of education. New methods of education are being inspired by Sophia to help bring out everyone's creative talents. To ennoble education so that each person's creativity can unfold is the goal here.

7. Finally, Sophia is working for the transformation of the planet into a garden and, moreover, for the spiritualization of nature. Humanity and nature are to live in cooperation and harmony, with human beings taking up their responsibility toward nature, which is to work for the spiritualization and redemption of the kingdoms of nature.

# EDITORIAL FOREWORD

## *Joel Matthew Park*

Dear Friends, as I write these words, the world is in great turmoil—since the early months of 2020, human beings have been engulfed in the threat of pandemic on the one hand—and the accompanying threat of technocratic over-reach of scientific and political authorities in the name of safety on the other hand. The result has been catastrophic—not only in terms of the loss of life, but in terms of the global economy, in terms of our trust in the presentation of so-called "facts" and "statistics," and the exercise of our civil liberties. We can imagine the primal gifts of Archangel Jesus and Christ as the inalienable rights of all human beings. The first sacrifice of Christ, related to our uprightness as human beings, bestows upon all human beings the right to *move*, to freely assemble. The second sacrifice, related to speech, bestows upon all human beings the right to *express*, to speak and communicate freely. The third sacrifice, related to thought, bestows upon all humans the right to *freedom of thought*. The fourth sacrifice—the Mystery of Golgotha—which gave the gift of the freedom of conscience to humanity, allows for the *freedom of religion*, the right to religious expression. And the fifth sacrifice, being gifted to human beings as you read these words, is related on one level to the unfolding of karmic knowledge. This karmic knowledge is both the "holiest of holies" in terms of the inner life of the human being at this time, and the "Supreme Court" in terms of the unfolding of an individual's destiny—our karma is an infinitely wiser judge than any human judge can be, both more severe and more merciful simultaneously. This fifth gift of Christ to humanity is related, then, both to the *right to privacy* (the "holiest of holies") as well as *absolute equality under the law*. We are well past the time when any special treatment should be given to those who have the resources to blackmail and bribe their way out of the legal consequences of their actions; conversely, the time is long past for the underprivileged, the minority, the disadvantaged, to be taken advantage of and unduly prosecuted.

Humanity has the tendency to wish for there to be *equality* in the spiritual/cultural life and *freedom* in the legal sphere. That is, there is a desire within each of us for everyone else to think the same way that we do—we do not truly wish for there to be absolute freedom of thought and expression. We assume, and hope, that others will be an echo chamber to our own precious precon-ceptions. When it comes to those in power, this wish is especially apparent—they will do what-ever they can, through whatever medium is acces-sible to them, to "level the playing field" of ideas. Equality in the spiritual/cultural life—that is, a lack of freedom of thought—makes for a much easier management of the mass of humanity. On the other hand, each of us harbors a secret wish for "special treatment" under the law. We do not want to experience shame or punishment for what we have done wrong—we would rather it just go unnoticed. Again, those in power express this more-or-less universal subconscious impulse in a much more blatant way. Those in power will find the way to escape justice, while those who are a threat to the powerful will be prosecuted much more severely than is justified under the law (one might think, for example, of Julian Assange).

But the time of the Etheric Christ is upon us. Each human being must be given as much support as possible in becoming a *free individuality*. The *sole purpose* of the State (i.e., of legal structures) is to protect one free individuality from infring-ing on the inalienable rights of another. There is no room here for law and order to be selective—Lady Justice is blind. We must leave the "indi-vidual adjustment" of the scales of justice up to *karma*—i.e., to Christ, the Lord of Karma.

This might seem like a great divergence, but all of the above is exactly what has come to be of greatest significance in the aftermath of COVID-19. All of what are supposed to be inalienable rights—to assembly, speech, thought, religion, privacy—have been partially or totally suppressed, whether directly or indirectly, as a result of the response of many authority figures and the media to this crisis. *Fear*—of the disease, of other human beings, of disobeying guidelines, of the loss of civil liberties, of the breakdown of economy, etc.—is the *actual* viral pandemic that infects the globe.

All of this created the pressure cooker in which *rage* could slowly build up and reach its boiling point, which it did in late May with the viral video of the death of George Floyd. The issue of "equal justice under the law" is, as I write these words, in the midst of a horrible struggle for survival. From above, humanity is victim to the tyrannical overreach of authority figures, too long given power without checks and balances—police brutality against unarmed and disenfranchised citizens being just one example among many of this tragic circumstance. Yet from below, the response (especially from an adequately goaded and prepared populace) is to respond to this tyranny with its equal opposite—rage-filled rioting and destruction. To find the "middle way"—the way that stands in a long tradition of Martin Luther King, Jr., Mahatma Gandhi, Tolstoy, and the Transcendentalists, all the way back to Jesus Christ himself—the way of non-violent protest, becomes increasingly difficult in our time. For the essence of nonviolent protest is always two-fold: its foundation is the deepest love for humanity—each individual human being, even those we protest against—and it moves through the world with the greatest expression of courage, to stand unflinchingly and unresponsively in the face of violence and hatred. In an atmosphere saturated with fear, rage, and mistrust, the free deed of love becomes increasingly difficult—and yet all the more refined in its nobility from this very fact, like a pearl in an oyster.

As I hope some of our readers may have noticed, from mid- to late March 2020, we experienced an extremely tight alignment of Mars, Jupiter, Saturn, *and* Pluto—with the Moon joining them briefly, as well. This is an incredibly rare alignment—one that, as far as I can tell, has not occurred since the 9th century (around January-February AD 849, albeit in Pisces rather than on the Sagittarius/Capricorn cusp). Not only that, but that same time period (Mar. 2020) saw the approach of the Comet Neowise, which became visible in July. What a year! A comet, conjunctions of Saturn and Pluto, Jupiter and Pluto, and finally Saturn and Jupiter to bring the year to a close…from an astrological perspective, it is no wonder that 2020 became such a battlefield! I write these words with no clear perspective on how the year will end, but I continue to have hope in the Great Conjunction, one which calls to mind the Changing of Water into Wine, the Visitation of the magi, as well as the future Age of Capricorn—the Age of Skythianos, of the transition from the Russian cultural epoch to the Anglo–American. May these gestating cultures in the East and West find their guiding archangels in the forming of their destinies—and may Europe be free to continue to unfold hers!

The influence of this alignment of Saturn and Jupiter will then extend into the early part of 2021. But, heaven be praised, the stars portend a much less turbulent year for 2021 vs. 2020! The key alignments that occur this year are the geocentric square of Neptune and Node on January 26, and the squares of both Jupiter and Saturn with Uranus. Jupiter squares Uranus geocentrically on January 17, and heliocentrically on February 2. Saturn squares Uranus geocentrically several times: first on February 17, then again on June 14, and once again on December 24. Heliocentrically they align on October 19. The squares of Neptune/Node and Jupiter/Uranus are brief, serving to transition us to the most dominant alignment of the year: the square of Saturn and Uranus, as these two are close to alignment for virtually the entire year. What does a square of Saturn and Uranus indicate?

Saturn and Uranus are in a way polar opposites. Saturn is generally concerned with constriction, restriction, limitation, order, conservation, death, harvest, solidification, darkness, etc. She is both the Angel of Death as well as the Most Holy Virgin, *Kore Kosmu*—the "Virgin of Black Perfection." Uranus, on the other hand, is concerned with freedom, liberty, revolution, ingenuity, creativity, brilliance, and light—he is "Prometheus Unbound," so to speak, Lucifer both unredeemed as Tempter, and redeemed as the faculty of *Imaginative cognition*. These two planets could be thought of as analogous to a "Sun" (Uranus) and a "Moon" (Saturn), going through a similar "lunar month" of New Saturn (Saturn conjunct Uranus)—First Quarter (Saturn ahead of Uranus by 90°)—Full Saturn (opposition)—Last Quarter (Saturn behind by 90°). However, while the lunar month lasts only 29 to 30 days, the Saturn-Uranus cycle lasts for approximately 45 years. This year, they are entering their "Last Quarter" equivalent, with Saturn in Capricorn square Uranus in Aries. Let's take a look back at the Saturn-Uranus cycles over the centuries to get some kind of a grasp of our cosmic orientation.

From the time of Christ up through the year AD 1296, there was not a great deal of regularity in terms of the overall gesture of the Saturn-Uranus cycle. A brief exception to this occurred between AD 365–639. During this time, Saturn and Uranus spent 92 years (two "cycles") during which "New" and "Full" Saturn occurred in Cardinal Signs and the two Quarters in Fixed Signs; then 91 years during which New and Full occurred in Fixed Signs and Quarters in Mutable; then 91 years of New and Full in Mutable Signs, with Quarters in Cardinal Signs. After AD 639, this pattern was lost. It became regular again from 1296 onward. One might wonder what potential the establishment of this regularity of rhythm between restriction (Saturn) and freedom (Uranus) has created for the development of modern occidental culture?

From 1296 through 1376, the Saturn–Uranus cycle saw New and Full phases occurring in Cardinal Signs, and Quarters in Mutable Signs. Then, from 1376 through 1467, New and Full occurred in Fixed Signs while Quarters occurred in Cardinal. From 1467 through 1558, New and Full were Mutable, while Quarters were Fixed. This cycle then repeated itself: 1558–1648 was akin to 1296–1376 (Cardinal and Mutable); 1648–1728 was akin to 1376–1467 (Fixed and Cardinal).

So the time period from 1296 through 1728 saw four approximately 90 year periods (each of two Saturn-Uranus cycles), moving sequentially from Cardinal/Mutable, to Fixed/Cardinal, to Mutable/Fixed, and so on. The fifth period was cut short: 1648–1728 is only 80 years (one full Saturn–Uranus cycle, and a portion of a second). It was in the midst of this fifth cycle that the pattern changed. After April 28, 1728, the pattern of the Saturn–Uranus cycle switched from Fixed and Cardinal to Mutable and Cardinal. This pattern of Mutable New/Full and Cardinal Squares lasted from 1728 through 1795—a pattern which had not occurred since the 12th century, during the time of the emergence of the Knights Templar (between 1114 and 1149). This re-emergence during the 18th century brought in its wake the establishment of Freemasonry, Hermetic Martinism, the life of the Count of St. Germaine, and the flourishing of the Enlightenment which set the stage for the time of Goethe, Schiller, Weimar Classicism, the Idealists and the Romantics—and the American and French Revolutions.

The next time period of two cycles held the pattern of New and Full in Cardinal Signs, while Quarters were in Fixed Signs. This time period lasted from 1795 through 1885, and can be split neatly into the two Saturn–Uranus cycles of this period: the first extending from 1795 through 1840 (focused around the German cultural movements listed above); and the second from 1840 through 1885 (the time of Wagner and King Ludwig II, a time that felt the *absence* and over-lighting of Kaspar Hauser more than his tangible presence on the world stage).

The next time period of two cycles falls under the pattern of New and Full Saturn in Fixed Signs, with Quarters in Mutable Signs; it too can be neatly split into two halves. The first half extends from 1885 through 1931—this is the time of Rudolf Steiner's entire adult professional career, up through the emergence of key successors such as Valentin Tomberg and Willi Sucher. The development of Goethean epistemology and the establishment of Anthroposophy are of key significance here. Specifically, this Saturn–Uranus cycle saw (heliocentrically):

December 10, 1885: Saturn 11°19' Gemini
    square Uranus 11°19' Virgo (Last Quarter)
April 24, 1897: Saturn conjunct Uranus,
    3° 26' Scorpio (New Saturn)
October 30, 1909: Saturn 26°51' Pisces square
    Uranus 26°51' Sagittarius (First Quarter)
June 8, 1919: Saturn 5°16' Leo opposite Uranus
    5°16' Aquarius (Full Saturn)
January 10, 1931: Saturn 20°38' Sagittarius
    square Uranus 20°38' Pisces (Last Quarter)

Notice that with the Last Quarter of 1885, Rudolf Steiner is only 24 years old, having just begun his work on the scientific writings of Goethe a few years prior. By the New Saturn in 1897, he has finished with this work, and within a few years will begin working in the context of the Theosophical Society. During the First Quarter in 1909, he is beginning to fully unfold the Rosicrucian (Christian) Theosophy that will become Anthroposophy; by the Full Saturn in 1919, he has not only established Anthroposophy, but is beginning to extend it practically into all realms. By the time we come to the Last Quarter of 1931, a new story is beginning to unfold...

The second cycle of this time period extends from 1931 through 1976, during which both Valentin Tomberg and Willi Sucher developed and elaborated Anthroposophy in new and exciting directions. Specifically, we see:

January 10, 1931: Last Quarter (see above)
April 22, 1942: Saturn conjunct Uranus
    6°51' Taurus (New Saturn)
June 8, 1952: Saturn 19°49' Virgo square Uranus
    19°49' Gemini (First Quarter)
November 16, 1965: Saturn 21°52' Aquarius
    opposite Uranus 21°52' (Full Saturn)
July 19, 1976: Saturn 11°46' Cancer square Uranus
    11°46' Libra (Last Quarter)

Already in 1931, both Valentin Tomberg and Willi Sucher were actively writing and lecturing on anthroposophic topics—Tomberg in Estonia, and Sucher in Germany. By 1942, each of them had begun to branch out into new ventures: Valentin Tomberg was in the midst of his Lord's Prayer Course in The Netherlands—on the verge of converting to Catholicism—and Willi Sucher had begun working in anthroposophic curative homes for children in the UK. By 1952, Valentin Tomberg had retreated fully into a meditative, devotional Catholicism, while Willi Sucher began publishing his full-length works on the new astrosophy. By 1965, both Tomberg and Sucher were engaged in enormous projects: Tomberg was in the midst of penning his 22 Letter-Meditations on the Tarot of Marseilles, while Sucher had established his own special school in California in 1961 and in 1965 began writing his *Monthly Star Journal*—the predecessor to the *Mercury Star Journal*. By 1976, once again, a new story began to unfold...

And now we finally come to our present situation. In the 18th and 19th centuries, we had the Cardinal/Fixed pair of Saturn–Uranus cycles. Then, from the 19th to 20th centuries, we had the Fixed/Mutable pair. The next time period of two Saturn-Uranus cycles extends from 1976 through 2067; once again, New and Full Saturn takes place in Mutable Signs, while the First and Last Quarter occur in Cardinal Signs—just as they did during the time of the Knights Templar and the Count of St. Germaine. This time period will also be split into two distinct cycles: the first running from 1976 to 2021, the second from 2021 to 2067. Specifically, we see:

July 19, 1976: Last Quarter (see above)
June 9, 1988: Saturn conjunct Uranus
    4°21' Sagittarius (New Saturn)
January 28, 2000: Saturn 21°58' Aries square
    Uranus 21°58' Capricorn (First Quarter)
September 1, 2009: Saturn 29°35' Leo opposite
    Uranus 29°35' Aquarius (Full Saturn)
October 19, 2021: Saturn 17°33' Capricorn
    square Uranus 17°33' Aries (Last Quarter)

It was around 1976 that a young Robert Powell was newly immersing himself in the work of Rudolf Steiner, Valentin Tomberg, and Willi Sucher. He had, in 1974, already taken over editorship of the *Mercury Star*

*Journal* (predecessor to this publication); within a year's time, he would have his first experience of karmic clairvoyance; within two years, he would be actively engaged in translating *Meditations on the Tarot* from French to English, and begin his eurythmy training in Dornach.

By 1988, he had finished translating *Meditations on the Tarot,* and was in the midst of publishing his three landmark volumes of *Hermetic Astrology.* By the year 2000, he had founded the Sophia Foundation of North America with his friend and colleague Karen Rivers, and that year established the School of Choreocosmos, a training in Cosmic and Sacred Dance. By 2009 (note that this "Full Saturn" deviates from the overall pattern by occurring in Fixed Signs), he had established the Grail Facilitator's Training, published his PhD thesis on the history of the zodiac, as well as results of investigations into metahistory (*Christ and the Maya Calendar*) and astrological karma research (*Elijah Come Again*). He had met and begun actively working with the modern visionary Estelle Isaacson, with whom he published several volumes of work. And between 2006 and 2012, he published *Cosmic Dances of the Planets, Cosmic Dances of the Zodiac,* and *Cultivating Inner Radiance*— the fruits of a life's work devoted to cosmic and sacred eurythmic movement.

This brings us to 2021. Is a new story beginning? During other "Last Quarters"—1885, 1931, and 1976—we have seen the emergence of young visionaries who carry on and further elaborate the work of their predecessors: Rudolf Steiner (age 24) with Goethean epistemology, Valentin Tomberg (30) and Willi Sucher (28) with Anthroposophy, and Robert Powell (29) with both astrosophy and Christian Hermeticism. Each of these individuals started to work actively and publicly in his respective stream one or two years prior to the "Last Quarter", and spent the subsequent decade dutifully expanding the work of his predecessor until, after the "New Saturn" (in 1897, 1942, and 1988 respectively) they struck out into their own independent cultural creations.

Thus, 2021 is a turning point. Of course, Robert Powell continues to be quite active. In 2016, he moved to Ecuador, and since then he has been developing a new, deepened form of eurythmic sacred practice called The Path to Shambhala— and yet the astrological gesture of our time speaks in particular to elders and the young. It is a time for young people to rise up, and for elders to "pass the torch" to a new generation. Speaking personally, I feel this is the essence of my relationship with Robert Powell, just as he had a similar relationship with his friend and mentor Willi Sucher. The elders do this in the confidence that for a time these young people will expand on and elaborate the work already begun—and young people can have the confidence that by acting in service to what has come before, a new fruit will be borne in time in their souls; that we need not tear up the old script and, in a revolutionary mood, attempt to recreate all forms overnight; that "the kingdom of God is as if a man should scatter seed upon the ground, and should sleep and rise night and day, and the seed should sprout and grow, he knows not how" (Mark 4: 26-27). The youth can have confidence that, by practicing obedience, chastity, and poverty toward whatever tradition to which we can adhere, we can sow seeds that, in good time, will sprout in a totally new and original creation. Therefore, to young people who might be reading this: *Seek out your elders!* To elders: *Be open to young people!* For now, in 2021, we straddle two generations; it is a time when proper hand-off is of key significance.[1]

*As Above, So Below*—the title for this year's edition of *Star Wisdom*—originates in the Hermetic axiom found in the *Tabula Smaragdina,* or *Emerald Tablet,* of Hermes Trismegistus:

---

1 There is much more that could be said here, and perhaps in good time I will elaborate on this theme on my website, www.treehouse.live. In the meantime, I direct the interested reader to my article "The Seven Miracles" in the Holy Nights 2019 edition of *Starlight,* available here: https://sophiafoundation.org/wp-content/uploads/2017/03/Starlight-Holy-Nights-2019-20sm.pdf

1. True it is, without falsehood, certain and most true.
2. That which is above is like to that which is below, and that which is below is like to that which is above, to accomplish the miracles of (the) one thing.
3. And as all things were by contemplation (meditation) of (the) One, so all things arose from this one thing by a single act of adaptation.
4. The father thereof is the Sun, the mother the Moon; the wind carried it in its womb; the earth is the nurse thereof.
5. It is the father of all works of wonder (*thelema*) throughout the whole world.
6. The power thereof is perfect; if it be cast on to earth.
7. It will separate the element of earth from that of fire, the subtle from the gross, gently and with great sagacity.
8. It doth ascend from earth to heaven; again, it doth descend to earth, and uniteth in itself the force from things superior and things inferior. Thus, thou wilt possess the glory of the brightness of the whole world, and all obscurity will fly far from thee.
9. This thing is the strongest of all powers, the force of all forces, for it overcometh every subtle thing and doth penetrate every solid substance.
10. Thus, was this world created.
11. Hence there will be marvelous adaptations achieved, of which the manner is this.
12. For this reason, I am called Hermes Trismegistus, because I hold three parts of the wisdom of the world.
13. That which I had to say about the operation of *sol* is completed.[2]

This title was chosen in part to commemorate the hundredth anniversary of Rudolf Steiner's third scientific course on astronomy, 18 lectures given in January 1921.[3] In particular, this title

commemorates the contents of the 10th lecture in this series, in which Rudolf Steiner elaborates the following:

> Our attention is drawn to what underlies the human metabolic system and to the forces active there, forces which are connected with the pole of earthly activity, and also with "radiality," with the radius. In seeking for the polar opposite, within ourselves, to that part of our constitution that provides us with knowledge, we are directed from the encompassing sphere to the Earth. The radii converge to the middle point of the Earth. In the radial element we have something by which we feel ourselves, which gives us the feeling of being real. This is not that thing which fills us with pictures in which we are merely conscious; rather, this is the aspect of our experience that allows us to appear real to ourselves. When we really experience this polarity, we always enter into that which we see as the mineral kingdom. We're led from something that's framed only for the image to something that is framed for reality. In other words: In connection with the cause and origin of our life of knowledge, we are led to the wide, encompassing sphere—we conceive it in the first place as a sphere—whereas, in following the radii of the sphere toward the middle of the Earth, we are led to the middle point of the Earth as the other pole.
>
> Thinking this out in more detail, we might say: Well, according to the Ptolemaic paradigm, for example, out there is the blue sphere, and here a point [fig. 1]—we would have to think of a polar point in the center of the Earth. When conceived in a simplified way, every point of the sphere would have its reflected point in the Earth's center. But, of course, it is not to be understood so simply. (I shall speak more in detail later on; to what extent these things correspond exactly is not the question for the moment.) The stars, in effect, would be here [fig. 2]. So that, in thinking of the sphere concentrated in the center of the Earth, we would have to think of it in the following way: The polar opposite of this star is here, of this one here, and so on [fig. 2]. We come, then, to a complete mirroring of what is outside in the interior of the Earth.

2   *Tabula Smaragdina*, 2; trsl. R. Steele and D. W. Singer, *Proceedings of the Royal Society of Medicine* xxi, 1928, p. 42.

3   Steiner, *Interdisciplinary Astronomy*.

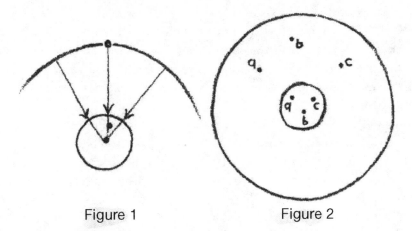

Figure 1                           Figure 2

Picturing this in regard to each individual planet, we have, say, Jupiter and then a "polar Jupiter" within the Earth. We come to something that works outward from within the Earth in the way that Jupiter works in the Earth's environment. We arrive at a mirroring (in reality it is the opposite way round, but I will now describe it like this), a mirroring of what is outside the Earth by the interior of the Earth. And if we think about the effects of this reflection in the forms of the minerals then we must also think about the effects of what works outside in the cosmic sphere itself in forming our capacity to understand the minerals. In other words, we can think of the whole celestial sphere as being mirrored in the Earth. We conceive the mineral kingdom of the Earth as a result of this reflection, and we conceive that what lives within us, enabling us to understand the mineral kingdom, comes from what surrounds us out in the celestial space. Meanwhile the realities we grasp by means of this faculty of understanding come from within the Earth.[4]

This lecture delves into the nitty-gritty details of the very basic premise, "As Above, So Below." Here Rudolf Steiner is proposing the (literally) radical idea that the periphery—the cosmos, the zodiac—radiates centrifugally *into* the very center of Earth and forms the Earth herself. Reaching this center point, it undergoes an inversion—it turns inside out, and radiates centripetally in this inverted form back out into the cosmos. One

is reminded with this imagery of one of Steiner's popular verses:

> The Stars once spoke to Humanity.
> It is World Destiny that they are silent now.
> To be aware of the Silence
> Can become Pain for earthly humanity.
> But in the deepening Silence
> There grows and ripens what
> Human Beings speak to the stars.
> To become aware of this Speaking
> Can become strength for spirit humanity.[5]

This gesture "As Above, So Below" has guided the arrangement of the proceeding articles in this year's edition of *Star Wisdom*. We begin in the farthest reaches of the cosmos—not only the encircling zodiac of the ecliptic, but all of the galactic entities above and below it—with Robert Powell's "Rama and Krishna Avatars: Karma Research and Star Wisdom," in which he unveils new research into the connections between the signs of the zodiac and the Great Teachers of humanity—particularly the Master Jesus. We then move somewhat closer with "Rudolf Steiner and the Christmas Conference: Astrological Aspects of the Laying of the Foundation Stone," which looks to both Sirius and Pluto for help in understanding this great event. With this piece, we welcome Krisztina Cseri, an astrosopher from Hungary. This is her first contribution to *Star Wisdom*.

Following Krisztina's piece, we come to a very timely piece by Julie Humphreys (written in early

---

4  Ibid., pp. 158–159.

5  Steiner, *Verses and Meditations*, p. 97 (revised).

spring 2020, *before* the worldwide protests of the summer that followed), "The Bellows of Ahriman: Pluto Reaches Capricorn." Next comes another article from a new contributor: "Anthroposophy, Astrology, Music," by Amber Wolfe Rounds—welcome Amber! In this article, she takes us beyond the realm of Pluto and to the regions of Neptune and Uranus, as well, to investigate the implications of a truly modern, anthroposophically inspired and astrologically guided form of music creation.

Next we feature another in the series of "Classics in Astrosophy," with this year's contribution from Robert Powell's articles on the Holy Grail and the Great Conjunctions of 1979—we have now moved from the zodiac, through the outer planets, and into the realm of Saturn and Jupiter. After this is a piece by Bill Trusiewicz, which considers the transition from the Age of Pisces to the Age of Aquarius—the precession of the Sun's position at the vernal equinox—and its relationship to the experience of the Second Coming of Christ, in "The Path from Pisces to Aquarius as Key to Meeting Christ in the Etheric: A Modern Reading of the Starry Script." Here we are brought into the realm of the Sun, and down into the etheric aura of the Earth, extending all the way to the orbit of the Moon. Bill is a new contributor to *Star Wisdom* as well—although some of our readers may recognize him as the author of many wonderful articles through the years in *Starlight*, the journal of the Sophia Foundation.

Finally, we come down to Earth with my piece "Finding Future Grail Sites: An Astrogeographical Investigation," which looks to practically apply the newly emerging science of astrogeography. It is the Hermetic axiom "As Above, So Below" that inspired Robert Powell in his quest to develop this new science of astrogeography, which he began investigating in 2005, culminating in the book *Astrogeographia: Correspondences Between the Stars and Earthly Locations*. But the Hermetic axiom is not limited to simply delineating the analogical relationship between above and below; it could also be phrased "As Without, So Within" or "As the Periphery, So the Point," taking Rudolf Steiner's words above as inspiration. It is this aspect—of moving from the periphery to the center, turning inside out, and radiating back to the periphery—that takes us into the sub-earthly with the final piece, my second offering for this edition, "The Tree of Life: Returning to the Origin of the Houses, Part II," which continues and deepens the perspective I began to lay out in the first part, "Saturn in Cancer," published in last year's edition of *Star Wisdom*.

We hope you enjoy this movement from periphery (the zodiac and megastars) to the point (the center of the Earth). To end, I want to express my gratitude to all of the contributors—you have each contributed such unique and fantastic articles—thank you! Thanks to the Advisory Board of *Star Wisdom* for all of their support, to Jens Jensen and Stephan O'Reilly for all their dedicated work at Lindisfarne/Steinerbooks in helping this come to print, and of course to all of our readers. To close, here is our first "Letter to the Editor," which for me radiated back so much warmth, beauty, and gratitude for *Star Wisdom*. To Sophia, who sent this letter and these beautiful displays of projective geometry, warm greetings and deep gratitude!

*Pax et Bonum,*
*Joel Matthew Park*

# A LETTER TO THE EDITOR

## *Sophia*

*Hello,*

Hoping all is well with you in these testing times. I am a Waldorf teacher in Australia, and an artist and projective geometer.

I would dearly like to thank all those who contributed to *Star Wisdom*, volume 2. And I was hoping someone might forward this email also to Joel Matthew Park.

While I have long had an interest in the stars, I have only very recently discovered astrosophy through Brian Keats (southern Hemisphere astro-calendar) with whom I recently co-presented a Projective Geometry workshop—before COVID restrictions. I was inspired to order your journal and learn more. In it I found an article by David Bowden, whom I have met a few times and who has peer reviewed one of my Projective Geometry articles.

I was wishing to share my Easter drawing and creative processes, which includes the resurrection horoscope I discovered in Joel Matthew Park's article in Volume 2. I will admit it was still quite a process for me to translate this into pictorial form and I had to do quite a bit of research and gain some clues from my Australian friends before I managed.

*Kind Regards,*
*Sophia*

## 2020 EASTER IMAGINATION

This year my meditations brought me an image for a Resurrection imagination that depicts the connection from horizon to horizon of the rising Sun aligned through the perspective of a witness (the viewer of the picture is in the position of Mary Magdalene) to the risen Christ.

The Moon is setting and the Sun has risen (it is the change of era from Moon to Sun). The placement of the elements draws on my experience of looking into deep water with the Sun behind me and seeing all the rays of the Sun as coming out of the shadow of my head deep in the water, like a halo (also the phenomenon of your own head always being in the line between the Sun and the center of a rainbow). The halo in the mist/ether is beautifully called a "sun glory." The Sun is risen, so the phenomena of the "glory" is formed BELOW the horizon line, symbolizing the Easter Saturday events within the Earth.

I felt the relationship between my experiences with Steiner's Easter lecture describing the pre-Christian autumn initiation rites—sinking a statue of Adonis beneath the waves (ether) and then retrieving it after three days of mourning.

The image in the ether (also a cross) is created in the shadow of the witness/viewer with the risen Sun shining through the witness's perceptions into the mist (ether). It is a two-way interaction—by becoming the cross formation of the image in the ether, the witness takes on the cosmic gesture (as happens in eurythmy)—the shape of the image depends on the viewer and vice versa.

I have depicted the landscape of Jerusalem, taken from a painting by David Roberts. It was drawn from the Mount of Olives and the Garden of Gethsemane. The cemeteries that extend along the slopes happen to be the burial places, according to the Jewish Prophets, from which the dead can be resurrected.

The cliffs either side of his hands are like the parting of Earth as he rises.

The underlying projective geometry construction is a spiroid field, which I have chosen as all the activity is created BELOW the horizon line. The focus of the spiral is the Sun point (center of head), and twelve rays come from the head and intersect the horizon. From these the spiroid field is created.

There is also the reflected form in the clouds above.

I am not trying to picture the risen Christ, but to create a visual etheric connection between the Sun, the Earth and the close atmosphere...

If you create an afterimage of what I have drawn by steadily staring at it and then looking into blank white paper it is a beautiful white cross with a solar halo around it...and the colors of the chakras are also transformed.

I have also included the constellations for the western sky of this morning (with the help of astrosophy).[1]

---

1   Sophia's beautiful images are much better in color. Please go to https://treehouse.live/2020/07/27/ letter-to-the-editor-images/ to see them.

# RAMA AND KRISHNA AVATARS
## KARMA RESEARCH AND STAR WISDOM

### Robert Powell, PhD

New reincarnation and karma research is presented in this article. And in a subsequent article, the astrosophical dimensions of this research will be explored by way of the comparison of conception, birth, and death horoscopes of the same individuality from one incarnation to the next or of great individuals who are closely connected spiritually with one another.[1] In the present article it is a matter of laying a foundation for the subsequent astrosophical research.

It is noteworthy that the only reincarnation reference we find in the Gospels, made by Jesus Christ, is that John the Baptist was previously incarnated as Elijah—"Elijah has already come, and they did not recognize him, but have done to him everything they wished. In the same way the Son of Man is going to suffer at their hands." Then the disciples understood that he was talking to them about John the Baptist (Matt. 17:12–13).

*Elijah* means "the way." Similarly, *Moses* means "the truth," and Jesus himself was "the life." When we think of these two great predecessors from ancient Israel who were preparing the Israelites for the coming incarnation of Jesus—Moses and Elijah: the *truth* and the *way*—we marvel at their connection, their close relationship with Jesus Christ, as revealed in the experience of the disciples Peter, James and John on the night of the Transfiguration on Mt. Tabor.

This event—the Transfiguration of Jesus Christ—was beheld by the three disciples, Peter, James, and John, who accompanied Jesus up Mt. Tabor on the evening of April 3rd in the year AD 31.[2] Jesus taught the disciples as they ascended the mountain, and he became more and more radiant as they approached the summit. It was around midnight from the night of the 3rd to the 4th of April AD 31, two years before Christ's sacrifice on Golgotha on Good Friday, the 3rd of April 33. At midnight, having reached the summit of Mt. Tabor, Jesus Christ appeared to the disciples as a radiant Sun. They beheld Divine Light pouring down from the heavens into and upon him—completely permeating him and radiating out from him.

In terms of the theme of this article, it is important to grasp that the vision of the three disciples of the Transfiguration was a glimpse vouchsafed to them into the realm of the bodhisattvas, where they beheld three great bodhisattvas—one could also say avatars—with the Avatar Jesus in the center, flanked by the Bodhisattva Moses at his right hand and the Bodhisattva Elijah at his left hand. This remarkable vision is the subject of Raphael's last painting, which one can see in the Vatican Museum in Rome (page 26).[3]

The realm of the bodhisattvas refers to the cosmic abode of the twelve great teachers of humanity who, on the spiritual level, form what is known as the White Lodge—appearing in a circle surrounding Christ in the spiritual realm. The twelve teachers of

---

1  See, for example, Powell, *Elijah Come Again.*

2  The true and exact dates of events in the life of Christ are given in Powell, *Chronicle of the Living Christ.* See also the three-volume work *The Visions of Anne Catherine Emmerich*, which, in terms of the dates of events in the life of Christ, is based on the research leading to the discovery of the exact dates presented in *Chronicle of the Living Christ.*

3  As indicated by Rudolf Steiner on various occasions (see his "final address," Sept. 28, 1924, included in *Karmic Relationships: Esoteric Studies*, vol. 4), he spoke of the great Renaissance painter Raphael (1483–1520) as a reincarnation of John the Baptist, who, in turn, was a reincarnation of the Old Testament prophet Elijah. Against this background, we can understand that Raphael was existentially connected with the theme of his last painting, since it was himself, as Elijah from an earlier incarnation, he was depicting. See also Powell, *Elijah Come Again.*

**The Transfiguration,** *by Raphael*
*(1516–20, Tempera on wood, 159 in. × 109 in. Pinacoteca Vaticana, Vatican City)*

the White Lodge are referred to in different ways in the various spiritual traditions of humankind. And in modern times in this connection one often hears the expression "Ascended Masters" applying to great teachers (bodhisattvas) such as the Maitreya and the Master Jesus—both of whom are discussed in some detail later in this article.

Just as Jesus Christ had twelve disciples on Earth, with whom he was very much connected, and who were very important for his earthly mission, so also does he have the twelve great teachers of the White Lodge around him in the spiritual world. These great teachers incarnate—not usually all together and at the same time, but generally at different epochs in history—as teachers of humanity sent by Christ (both before and after his incarnation) to bring the appropriate message for the unfolding of his work at that time when they incarnate, whereby their spiritual teaching is adapted in order to be presented in an appropriate way to the people to whom they are speaking. This is a remarkable subject in which I have been deeply interested over many years.

Rudolf Steiner refers to the realm of the bodhisattvas, and this is where he brings a most powerful image: that of Christ as a Sun—a Sun-like being—in the midst of the circle of the twelve great teachers of the White Lodge.[4]

Just as there is a connection of the twelve disciples with the twelve signs of the zodiac, so also there is a relationship of the twelve great teachers of humanity with the twelve signs of the zodiac, which we shall go into later in this article. In the Buddhist tradition these great teachers are called *bodhisattvas*, and in the Hindu tradition they are called *holy rishis*. And, moreover, those rishis who are directly in service to Vishnu[5]—such as Rama and Krishna—are referred to as *avatars*. We can consider that the great teachers of humanity, each in their own way, were preparing for the coming of Christ as the Messiah. In particular, in the

---

4 Steiner, *The Christ Impulse and the Development of Ego-Consciousness*, lect. 1, "The Sphere of the Bodhisattvas."

5 The Trinity in Hindu tradition comprises Brahma, Vishnu, and Shiva. In terms of the Trinity in Christianity, Brahma corresponds to the Father and Vishnu to the Son.

Hebrew tradition three outstanding bodhisattvas are highlighted—Abraham, Moses, and Elijah.[6]

As referred to above, Elijah reincarnated as John the Baptist, the prophet whose mission it was to prepare for Christ's coming in a physical body—first by proclaiming his coming, and then to "facilitate" his incarnation into the body of Jesus of Nazareth at the baptism in the River Jordan.

Let us contemplate again the vision of the disciples on Mt. Tabor on the night of the Transfiguration. They beheld their beloved teacher Jesus of Nazareth fully permeated with light, beholding the light permeating Christ extending all the way up through the spiritual hierarchies to the highest realm of heaven. Then they witnessed appearing on either side of him Moses and Elijah—Moses at his right, and at his left hand, Elijah. Of course, at that point in time the disciples did not know that Elijah had returned into incarnation upon the Earth as John the Baptist, the prophet of the coming of the Messiah.

The bodhisattva individuality who was incarnated as Elijah and then as John the Baptist had other incarnations that were indicated by Rudolf Steiner. Among the incarnations belonging to the post-Christian era, he referred to an incarnation of the Elijah individuality as Raphael (1483–1520), the great Renaissance painter, who subsequently incarnated as Novalis (1772–1801), the founder of the German Romanticism poetry movement. In 1924, Rudolf Steiner pointed out that this individuality—previously incarnated as Novalis—was at that time in the spiritual world, but would be incarnating later in the century to lead humanity through the great crisis that was coming.[7] Rudolf Steiner himself, as the reincarnated Moses,[8] had

a very close connection with the individuality of John the Baptist.

Rudolf Steiner described that Jesus, who himself was a great teacher of humanity, had held back in terms of his incarnations and had not incarnated at all prior to the incarnation as Jesus of Nazareth, but had worked in an inspiring, over-lighting way, in terms of what is referred to as the *pre-earthly deeds of Christ*.[9] So he was a pure soul, meaning he had not gone through the Fall—that is, he had not undergone the process of incarnating upon the Earth. His first—and only—incarnation was as Jesus of Nazareth.

There is, moreover, a further remarkable indication by Rudolf Steiner: Jesus, prior to his one and only incarnation on the Earth, over-lighted Arjuna as Krishna,[10] and through this over-lighting

on the spiritual path, having evolved a level of consciousness capable of bearing a folk spirit (archangel) and thus being recognized as the teacher of a people by virtue of being the bearer of the Folk Spirit of that people. Moses is widely recognized, not as the founder, but as the great teacher of ancient Israel—of whom the Archangel Michael was the folk spirit. See Steiner, *Freemasonry and Ritual Work: The Misraim Service* (CW 265): "The folk spirit that united with Moses at his initiation, and then dwelt in him, was Michael" (p. 419). See also Dionysius the Areopagite, *Mystical Theology and the Celestial Hierarchies*, p. 47: "Michael is called the Lord of the people of Judah." The Moses Bodhisattva, who is the bearer of the Archangel Michael in each of his incarnations, is the bearer of Truth. As the reincarnated Moses Bodhisattva, toward the end of his life Rudolf Steiner founded the School of Michael bearing the esoteric teachings of the Archangel Michael. That is, as the bearer of the Archangel Michael, Rudolf Steiner was empowered to found on Earth, for the first time in the history of humankind, the Michael School, the content of which was given directly by the Archangel Michael through Steiner. For further details regarding the hundred-percent-certain identification of Rudolf Steiner as the reincarnation of the Moses Bodhisattva, see Robert Powell and Keith Harris, "The Transition" (https://sophiafoundation.org/wp-content/uploads/2017/04/the-transition_final.pdf).

6  Steiner, *Esoteric Christianity and the Mission of Christian Rosenkreutz*, lecture of Nov. 5, 1911, "Jeshu ben Pandira," lecture 2.

7  Steiner, "The Last Address," Sept. 28, 1924, in *Karmic Relationships: Esoteric Studies*, vol. 4. See also Robert Powell, *Elijah Come Again*.

8  Moses brought the pre-Christian teaching of the seven days of creation in Genesis, the first book of the Bible, and Rudolf Steiner brought the Christianized teaching of the seven days of creation in his 1909 book *An Outline of Esoteric Science*. By definition, a bodhisattva is far-advanced

9  Steiner, *Approaching the Mystery of Golgotha*, lecture of Mar. 7, 1914, "The Christ Impulse across the Ages and Its Power in the Human Being."

10  See Tomberg, *Christ and Sophia*, appendix, "The Four Sacrifices of Christ and the Appearance of Christ in the Etheric"; see also, Steiner, *The Bhagavad Gita and the West: The Esoteric*

Krishna bestowed the content of the *Bhagavad Gita*, the great spiritual work of Hindu spirituality as, so to say, the "Bible" of the Hindu tradition. Through inspiration he transmitted the content of this great work by way of his over-lighting of Arjuna. This took place around the end of what in Hindu tradition is called the Dvapara Yuga, the third great Yuga, or Age, and simultaneously began then the Kali Yuga, the fourth great Age, also known as the Dark Age. A darkening was experienced by Arjuna when Krishna, who had been over-lighting him, withdrew from him at the beginning of the period of darkness, Kali Yuga.

It is important to hold all of this in consciousness when we consider some further discoveries in the process of karma research in connection with Rudolf Steiner's indications concerning the incarnation of Jesus of Nazareth. As is evident from this background, it is possible to refer to Jesus of Nazareth as the Krishna Bodhisattva.

Now, in Rudolf Steiner's description, he points to Jesus of Nazareth as descended from the line of Nathan, going back to King David, who had many sons; Nathan was the third son of David and Bathsheba. The genealogical line of Jesus of Nazareth is described in the Gospel of St. Luke, where Jesus of Nazareth can be traced back to Nathan.

Rudolf Steiner was one of the first to notice something in connection with this genealogy and he was the first to explain its significance in a deeper sense. It had been noticed by others previously, but no one had been able to explain it adequately. The central point here is that in the Gospel of St. Matthew there is a *different genealogy of Jesus*, which, although also going back to King David, does so via his son Solomon, the most well-known son of David, who later became king of Israel. Solomon was the fourth son of David and Bathsheba—that is, he was the younger brother of Nathan.

Rudolf Steiner referred to this Jesus child, whose birth is described in the Gospel of St. Matthew, as the *Solomon Jesus*, whereas the Jesus

child of the Gospel of St. Luke he referred to as the *Nathan Jesus*. The circumstances depicted in the Gospels surrounding the births of the two Jesus children are quite different. In the case of the Solomon Jesus child, he is born in his parental home—in a *house* in Bethlehem—and he is visited by the three magi. Whereas the parents of the Nathan Jesus come from their home in Nazareth to Bethlehem, where the child is born in a *cave* there and is visited by the shepherds. By way of analogy with the three magi it is often assumed that there were three shepherds, although the number is not specified in the Gospel (Luke 2:8–20).[11]

Thus, the genealogies and the circumstances of their births, described in the Gospels, are quite different. As Rudolf Steiner points out, these births took place at different points in time. In relation to the birth of the Solomon Jesus child we read in the Gospel of St. Matthew of the slaughter of the innocents in Bethlehem—all male children younger than two years of age were murdered at the command of King Herod the Great, whose goal was to have the Solomon Jesus child slaughtered, the birth of whom he had learned of from the three magi. Rudolf Steiner indicates that the birth of the Nathan Jesus child must have taken place sometime after that horrific event, which, because of the time that had subsequently elapsed, had consequently become more or less forgotten. Otherwise, Joseph and Mary, who was at an advanced stage of her pregnancy, would certainly not have made the journey from Nazareth to Bethlehem if the murderous event ordered by King Herod had taken place only a short time before.

I have gone into all of these details in my book *Chronicle of the Living Christ*, where I was able to determine the exact dates of birth of the two Jesus children—that were 4 years and 9 months apart. Interestingly, Rudolf Steiner also points out

---

*Meaning of the Bhagavad Gita and Its Relation to the Letters of St. Paul.*

11 Technically, there is similarly no mention of "three magi" in the Gospel of Matthew, only a mention of three gifts: gold, frankincense, and myrrh. The identities of the three magi have been passed down through tradition, however, as Melchior, Caspar, and Balthasar. The visions of Anne Catherine Emmerich confirm that there were three magi, and give their true names as Mensor, Theokeno, and Sair.

that, in both cases, these children are named Jesus, and both had parents named Mary and Joseph. Rudolf Steiner goes into some detail describing various events in connection with the two families, including the death at a relatively early age of the mother of the Nathan Jesus child, the date of which—as well as her date of birth—I was able to determine. Through my research I found that she died at the age of 28. Moreover, the father of the Solomon Jesus child also died within a timeframe not far removed from the death date of the Nathan Mary. Subsequently, the remaining two individuals: Mary, the mother of the Solomon Jesus child, and Joseph, the father of the Nathan Jesus child, both of whom were widowed upon the deaths of their spouses, then married each other. Thereby, the one known as the Virgin Mary, who was the mother of the Solomon Jesus child, through marriage became the stepmother of the Nathan Jesus child. Without going into further details here regarding these complexities, it suffices to point out that I have described all these circumstances in detail in my book *Chronicle of the Living Christ*.

Let us now reflect on the Solomon Jesus child. Through karma research, I found many years ago that this individual had a significant incarnation as a contemporary of Rudolf Steiner. Since the time of his incarnation as the Solomon Jesus child, according to Steiner this individual has been incarnated in every century and is referred to esoterically as the *Master Jesus*.[12] Steiner indicated that the Master Jesus has been incarnated in every century since the Mystery of Golgotha. As described in the following, Master Jesus incarnated in the nineteenth century, in 1864, approximately three-and-one-half years after Rudolf Steiner, who was

born in 1861. The Master Jesus individuality is the reincarnation of the Solomon Jesus, who in turn, as Rudolf Steiner discovered and made known through his karma research, is a reincarnation of Zarathustra, the founder of the ancient Persian culture in the Age of Gemini, around 6000 BC. This individual reincarnated in 1864 in Bulgaria as Peter Deunov (1864–1944), and later became known as the Master Beinsa Douno.

This great teacher of humanity was a contemporary of Rudolf Steiner, as referred to in the article "Prophecy of Peter Deunov," written by Harrie Salman and me.[13] That article refers to statements made by Deunov in a private conversation concerning his own previous incarnations/manifestations on Earth. He was responding to a question asked of him.

To understand the reincarnation indications given as follows concerning Peter Deunov, it is important to be familiar with the article "Prophecy of Peter Deunov," especially his own statements about his earlier incarnations.

By way of comparison, it is true to say that Rudolf Steiner began his mission at the start of the twentieth century as a great spiritual teacher of Western humanity—in particular, his activity was focused in western European countries, bringing Spiritual Science as the continuation of modern science that includes the exploration of spiritual realms.

In contrast, the individuality of Master Jesus—who (as indicated in the article "Prophecy of Peter Deunov") incarnated shortly after Rudolf Steiner—incarnated in Bulgaria as Deunov and later known as the Master Beinsa Douno, came as the great spiritual teacher of the Slavic people to awaken them to their mission for the coming Age of Aquarius, as well as to communicate to them the teaching of Divine Love. He began his teaching activity in Bulgaria about the same time as Rudolf Steiner commenced his teaching activity in Germany.

---

12 In response to a question (exact date unknown, but possibly 1917, and certainly prior to 1923) from Friedrich Rittelmeyer concerning the "Friend of God" (from the Oberland in the fourteenth century), Rudolf Steiner answered that he (the Friend of God) was an incarnation of the Master Jesus, who since the Mystery of Golgotha had been incarnated in every century. Regarding the further question whether he was presently (at that time) incarnated, the answer was that at the present time (i.e., shortly before 1920 or shortly after 1920) he was in the Carpathians, and Rudolf Steiner indicated that he was in purely spiritual connection with him.

---

13 Powell and Salman, "Prophecy of Peter Deunov," available on the Sophia Foundation website under "Articles" (https://sophiafoundation.org/wp -content/uploads/2020/06/Prophecy-of-Peter -Deunov-Beinsa-Douno.pdf).

Now let's look more closely at the karma research concerning Peter Deunov, which I was able to undertake with Harrie Salman, a friend who reads and speaks Bulgarian and was therefore able to contribute valuable input from the works of Peter Deunov for the article we wrote, "Prophecy of Peter Deunov." At the time of writing the first draft of this article in 2019, initially I did not bring to expression the finding (by way of exact karma research) that I had withheld for many years concerning the discovery of Peter Deunov as an incarnation of the individuality of the Master Jesus. However, in the new version (2020) of the article, I have indicated in footnote 3, near the end of that article, the reason for making known this finding of karma research in early 2020, only 75 years after the death/transition of Peter Deunov in December 1944—rather than waiting a full century, until 2045.[14]

Without going into all the details, which can be found in the article, it was extraordinary that, after publishing the article for the first time, a contact in Bulgaria, Emily Michael (who has written a wonderful book about the two great teachers Rudolf Steiner and Peter Deunov[15]), reported to me that there were indications from Peter Deunov himself concerning his previous incarnations. Those indications have now been included in the updated version of the article "Prophecy of Peter Deunov." The historical manifestation of this great teacher of humanity as Zarathustra, the founder of the ancient Persian cultural epoch in the zodiacal age of Gemini, was confirmed. This finding was also presented in various lectures by Rudolf Steiner on the basis of his highly advanced karma and reincarnation research. Among other previous incarnations, Peter Deunov also mentions Rama, whom we associate with the Hindu

spiritual tradition, and who in that Vedic tradition is referred to as the Seventh Avatar of Vishnu, whereas Krishna is spoken of as the Eighth Avatar of Vishnu. (As an aside, it is evident that Rama must have lived before the time of Krishna.)

Now, this is where it becomes very interesting in terms of karma research. First, however, I want to point out that for me it was a great affirmation that Peter Deunov did confirm his earlier incarnation as Zarathustra. What arose in addition to that were other incarnations, as indicated in the article written with Harrie Salman. The indication of the incarnation as Rama (obviously associated with the ancient Indian culture) needs further investigation, because Rama is outside our normal historical frame of reference; moreover, there are various ideas as to when Rama lived. The great epic of the Hindu tradition, *Ramayana* ("exploits of Rama"), offers a beautiful, poetic, and mythological recital of his life.[16] In this connection, we think of Rama and his bride, Sita—Rama accompanied by his beloved Sita.

The trinity of Brahma, Vishnu, and Shiva is referred to in the Hindu tradition. In the Christian tradition, Brahma corresponds to the Father and Vishnu to the Son. When we contemplate the communication handed down to us through the ages concerning the incarnation of Rama as the Seventh Avatar of Vishnu, this points to a great teacher—one of the twelve belonging to the White Lodge—who incarnated long ago in India in service to Christ (Vishnu).

Rama, as the Seventh Avatar in the Hindu tradition, had many subsequent incarnations; one of the most outstanding was Zarathustra, the founder of the ancient Persian cultural epoch. As indicated by Rudolf Seiner, later in the sixth century BC, Zarathustra incarnated as Zoroaster, who was born into the Persian royal family and traveled to Babylon. There, he was a great teacher of the Babylonian priesthood at the temple of Esagila, the temple of Marduk, whom Rudolf Steiner identifies with the Archangel Michael. The incarnation as Zoroaster during the sixth century BC was during

---

14 The rule of maintaining silence for one century—after death/transition—regarding the identity of great spiritual teachers, such as the Master Jesus or the Master Christian Rosenkreutz, is referred to by Rudolf Steiner in *Esoteric Christianity and the Mission of Christian Rosenkreutz*, lecture of Sept. 27, 1911.

15 Michael, *Sealed by the Sun: Life between Rudolf Steiner and Peter Deunov* (see http://www.emily-michael.info).

16 Dutt, *The Ramayana and the Mahábhárata: Condensed into English Verse.*

the early part of the previous epoch of Archangel Michael, which extended from 607 to 252 BC.

There would be more to say regarding the pre-Christian incarnations of the Rama Bodhisattva. However, let us keep our focus on the incarnations already mentioned (Rama, Zarathustra, and Zoroaster), followed, as indicated by Rudolf Steiner, by the incarnation as the Jesus child described in the Gospel of St. Matthew—the Solomon Jesus child. We connect Solomon with wisdom, and this is an appropriate quality in this connection, because Steiner described Zoroaster as the wisest human being of his time (the sixth century BC).[17] The Solomon Jesus child was an incarnation of Rama Bodhisattva, as is evident when we contemplate this incarnation against the background of this Jesus child being a reincarnation of Rama, the Seventh Avatar of Vishnu in the Hindu tradition.

In Hindu tradition, the Eighth Avatar of Vishnu is spoken of as Krishna, who, though he did not incarnate physically, over-lighted Arjuna and worked through him. In general, with the exception of some enlightened teachers (*rishis*) in the Hindu/Vedic tradition, there is not really an understanding in that tradition that Krishna did not incarnate physically. (In India, Krishna is usually regarded as having been incarnated physically.) This is a misunderstanding, which has been corrected through the indications of Rudolf Steiner, explaining that Krishna over-lighted Arjuna, as referred to earlier in this article. Unfortunately, though, Steiner's communications concerning Krishna are generally unknown in India.

To summarize, Rama is the Seventh Avatar and Krishna is the Eighth Avatar of Vishnu.[18] We see in the case of these two great avatars of the Hindu tradition that Rama reincarnated as the older Jesus child, the Solomon Jesus child, and Krishna as the younger Jesus child, the one we usually refer to as the Nathan Jesus child, or Jesus of Nazareth.

We see here two great teachers from the circle of bodhisattvas, or rishis, or avatars around Christ, who incarnated at the time of Christ's incarnation. They then worked together to prepare for the incarnation of Christ himself—the greatest event of earthly history.

Again, it is thanks to Rudolf Steiner that we have some understanding of what took place. At the age of 12, the younger Jesus boy came to Jerusalem with his parents for the feast of the Passover, as was the yearly custom. In AD 12, at the time of the Passover festival, the Nathan Jesus boy was twelve years of age. In the Gospel of St. Luke, it is explained that when the parents left Jerusalem after the feast of the Passover to return to Nazareth, to their dismay they noticed that their 12-year-old son Jesus had gone missing. Because they had come with a group of people from Nazareth, they had not noticed their son was missing. They had assumed he was part of the group from Nazareth. Discovering that he was missing from the group, the parents returned to Jerusalem to look for him. To their amazement they found him teaching the rabbis and scribes in the temple of Jerusalem.

Their 12-year-old son was an extremely loving boy. He poured out his heart but was not what one would call "developed" in terms of his ability to think and ask questions. Up to that point in time, he had not displayed much intellectual ability whatsoever. To the astonishment of his parents, their 12-year-old son was teaching the rabbis and scribes in the temple. He was teaching not just the mysteries of Old Testament theology related to the history of ancient Israel, with which he was conversant, but he was also conversing on the themes of agriculture, astronomy, weather, and many other things. This astonished the scribes and Pharisees, and the parents of the 12-year-old boy, as well. It is thanks to Rudolf Steiner's spiritual research that this sudden and extraordinary development in the life of the younger Jesus child can be explained. In the Gospel of Luke 2:52, it says simply, "Jesus grew in wisdom and stature," but that does not tell us much.

The older Jesus boy, the Solomon Jesus, was at that time 17 years and 1 month of age. As I describe in *Chronicle of the Living Christ*, he was

---

17  Steiner, *According to Matthew: The Gospel of Christ's Humanity*.

18  As indicated in footnote 5, Vishnu in the Hindu tradition corresponds to the Son in the Christian Trinity.

4 years, 9 months older than the Nathan Jesus. This great teacher of humanity, the Zarathustra individuality (one could also say the Rama Avatar) had an extraordinary ability to move consciously outside his body.

At 17 years, 1 month of age, he had gone through a very rapid development of consciousness. For most young people, the birth of the "I" (the self), takes place around the age of 21, in the case of this great teacher it had already taken place, shortly before he reached the age of 17 years, 1 month. Because of this, the "I" of the older Jesus boy was able to leave his body consciously and unite with the vessel provided by the younger Jesus boy, whose "I" at that point in time was not yet truly born. In other words, there was a merger of the two Jesus boys, whereby the "I" of the older boy united with the vessel provided by the younger boy. Effectively, the one who was speaking to the scribes and Pharisees in the temple was the Rama Avatar (the individuality of Zarathustra–Zoroaster, the Solomon Jesus entelechy), who had consciously united with the threefold organism of the younger Jesus boy, comprising his physical and etheric bodies and his nascent astral body, and was indwelling this vessel as the radiant presence of "I"-consciousness. This is who spoke through the vessel provided by the younger Jesus boy to the scribes and Pharisees.

The Rama Avatar–Zarathustra–Zoroaster–Solomon Jesus had many other incarnations in the pre-Christian era. Further, let us not forget that the three kings, or magi, who came to the Solomon Jesus bearing the gifts of gold, frankincense, and myrrh, were reincarnated disciples of Zoroaster, the great teacher who had founded the spiritual stream of the magi back in the sixth century BC.[19] Belonging to this spiritual stream—of which the three magi were perhaps the last true representatives—implies that the three magi

were initiated into the mysteries of the starry heavens, whereby they had come to know that their teacher had reincarnated on Earth on the evening of March 5, the night of the Full Moon in the middle of Virgo, in 6 BC, when Mars and Jupiter were in conjunction at 5° Aries.[20] As I have described elsewhere, it was Zoroaster himself who had brought knowledge of the true and authentic division of the starry heavens into twelve zodiacal signs, each 30° long, defined in relation to the Aldebaran–Antares axis.[21]

This great individuality consciously left his own vessel and transferred himself—a sacrificial deed of love—into the vessel of the younger Jesus boy, the Nathan Jesus, the Krishna Avatar. What we see here is that there was a union of two individualities from the circle of the great teachers around Christ in spiritual realms, both of whom were incarnated on the Earth as the incarnation of Christ was approaching. Two of the great teachers from the White Lodge merged—the Rama Avatar and the Krishna Avatar. We cannot really begin to understand Jesus of Nazareth without knowing this background of the union of these two great Avatar individualities underlying the manifestation of Jesus of Nazareth in earthly existence. Two questions arise that offer the possibility of a better understanding of the relationship between them: Which signs of the zodiac did these two avatars represent? And, does the answer help us to grasp the relationship between them if we know which signs of the zodiac these two great teachers from the White Lodge represented?

In my research I found that the Krishna Avatar is connected with the sign of Pisces, the last of the twelve signs of the zodiac. He came into incarnation as the last of the great teachers of humanity from the White Lodge. He held back, but then he incarnated. This incarnation as Jesus of Nazareth was his one and only incarnation on Earth. He

---

19 Concerning the "gold king" (the reincarnated Pythagoras), the "frankincense king" (the reincarnated Cyrus the Great), and the "myrrh king" (the reincarnated prophet Daniel): I am preparing an extensive work on the destiny stream of Zoroaster/Jesus and his disciples, the three magi, who were the first Christians.

20 Powell, *Chronicle of the Living Christ*, p. 146.

21 Powell, *History of the Zodiac*, regarding the Aldebaran–Antares axis. Concerning Zoroaster as the transmitter of this ancient knowledge of the zodiac, see Powell, *Christian Hermetic Astrology: The Star of the Magi and the Life of Christ*, pp. 15–25, 28–34.

was a pure being; he was pure love. The Rama Avatar, on the other hand, had incarnated many times—as Rama in ancient India, as Zarathustra in ancient Persia, etc., and through his many incarnations, in conjunction with his advanced spiritual faculties, he had gained a vast wisdom.

Fortunately, we have an indication from Rudolf Steiner who points out in his karma lectures that each human being is connected with a particular star in the heavens, and he speaks of the great initiates as those who, generally speaking, are connected with the brightest stars in the heavens. In the case of Zarathustra—known as the Master Jesus in the post-Christian era—Steiner indicated his star to be Sirius,[22] which for us is the brightest star in the heavens, given its close proximity to our solar system. This helps us understand the name Zarathustra–Zoroaster, which means "radiant star." At the time of Zarathustra's incarnation around six thousand years before Christ, human beings were still clairvoyant. Thus, many belonging to the ancient Persian culture he founded were able to behold a radiant star shining above the head of Zarathustra, which is how he received his name. It was this same star, the star of his higher self, that guided the three magi to the house where he was when they arrived in Bethlehem. The magi beheld the radiant star shining above the house. Hence, the name "Star of Bethlehem," whereby it is important to note that this is not the same as "Star of the magi."[23]

It is important at this juncture to clarify one significant point in discussing the brightness of a star—the *intrinsic* luminosity, or brightness,

of a star represents the degree of energy the star radiates per second. This is measured in two different (though related) ways in astronomy: (1) by a unit called *absolute magnitude,* and (2) by a unit called *luminosity*, which is always measured in relation to our Sun. For example, the luminosity of Sirius is 25 times that of our Sun. In other words, if twenty-five copies of our Sun were bunched together at a certain (specified) distance from our solar system, this would indicate to us the luminosity of Sirius.

On the other hand, there is also the *apparent* magnitude, or brightness, of a star, which is a measure of how brightly the star *appears* to the naked eye of an observer.

First-magnitude stars are those that are brightest in the night sky to the observer. Sirius is the brightest of the first-magnitude stars, given that it is so close, relatively speaking, to our Sun. Only one other first-magnitude star is closer to our Sun than Sirius: Alpha Centauri, in the constellation of the Centaur. Alpha Centauri is 4.4 light years from our solar system, and Sirius is almost twice that distance, 8.6 light years away. Sirius is the brightest star in terms of its apparent magnitude (the brightness of its visible appearance), and Alpha Centauri is the third brightest star in terms of the brightness according to its visual appearance. The second brightest star in terms of its apparent magnitude is the star Canopus, which is in the constellation known to the Greeks as the ship Argo—now specified as being located in the region of the keel of the ship (Latin = *Carina*), marking one of the ship's oars. Canopus is about 310 light years away, but in terms of its intrinsic luminosity it is some 10,700 times more luminous than our Sun. Because of its high luminosity, it appears so bright even though, relative to Alpha Centauri and Sirius, it is so distant from our solar system.

Sirius has an intrinsic luminosity 25 times that of our Sun, but at a distance of 8.6 light years, it is also very much closer than Canopus, so it *appears* much brighter to us in the night sky. Alpha Centauri, at a relatively close 4.4 light years from our solar system, has a luminosity 1½ times that of our Sun, yet it appears as the third

22 Von Keyserlingk, *The Birth of a New Agriculture: Koberwitz 1924* (Adalbert Keyserlingk, ed.), pp. 89–90.

23 Powell, *Christian Hermetic Astrology: The Star of the Magi and the Life of Christ,* pp. 28–41, describes the difference between the *Star of the Magi* (the actual stellar configuration at the birth of the Solomon Jesus child) and the *Star of Bethlehem,* the manifestation of Zarathustra ("radiant star") himself to the three magi some 7½ months after the birth, in order to guide the three magi to Bethlehem—*radiant star* (Zarathustra–Zoroaster) proceeding ahead of them, guiding their way.

brightest star in the heavens—because it is so close to our solar system, not because of its (relatively low) luminosity.[24]

The stars that are closest to our Sun—Alpha Centauri (third brightest at 4.4 light years), Sirius (brightest at 8.6 light years), and Procyon (the eightieth brightest, at 11.5 light years)—are all very close, relatively speaking, to our solar system and can be thought of as part of the "close family" of our Sun among the billions of stars in our Milky Way galaxy. Procyon's luminosity is 7—it is seven times more luminous than our Sun. These stars—our close neighbors—belong together, like a family.

What I found through astrosophical star meditation is that Alpha Centauri is like a sister star to our Sun. Alpha Centauri is the closest first-magnitude star to our solar system and has a close affinity to our Sun in terms of the quality of the energy of its radiance. It works on the human heart chakra, as does our Sun. The heart chakra is the central one in the human astral body. The astral organ of the heart, the heart chakra, corresponds to our Sun. When we explore various stars in the night sky through astrosophical meditation, we can come to experience that Alpha Centauri, like our Sun, also works on our heart chakra. In terms of radiance, however, whereas our Sun has a masculine, Christlike radiance, Alpha Centauri has a more feminine, Christlike quality. In other words, through Alpha Centauri, we are able (potentially) to connect with Divine Sophia on the heart level—Sophia being referred to as the *Bride of the Lamb* in Revelation. Egyptians addressed her as *Isis*, the Bride/Sister of Osiris. That is, for the Egyptians, Isis and Osiris were the pre-Christian manifestations of Sophia and Christ.

In terms of its radiance within our local family of stars, Alpha Centauri is experienced as a sister to our Sun, whereas Sirius is like an elder brother to our Sun. In contrast to the loving heart-energy radiance of our Sun, Sirius radiates the wisdom-filled energy of Divine Love. In comparison with the level of love and compassion in our contemporary civilization today, the loving radiance of Sirius is not only much more powerful than that of our Sun, but it is also very wise and mature in nature.

The (relatively) recent incarnation from 1864 to 1944 of the great teacher Master Jesus, the Rama Avatar, whose eternal star is the star Sirius—as was already recognized by the ancient Persian disciples of Zarathustra—was a great blessing for the Earth and for humanity. This blessing continues to work on, embracing the whole world. It is always a blessing when this great teacher incarnates on Earth.

Rudolf Steiner himself spoke with great reverence of the Master Jesus incarnated as his contemporary. He indicated that he was at that time—toward the end of World War I, or shortly thereafter—in inner contact with the Master Jesus, who was (according to someone reporting Steiner's words from a private conversation) incarnated in the Carpathian mountains.

Geologically, the Southern Carpathian Mountains end where the section of the Danube River Valley, known as the "Iron Gate," separates the Carpathians from the Balkan Mountains, stretching all the way across northern Bulgaria, from Serbia to the Black Sea. The Balkan Mountains, and the Rhodope Mountains farther south, are the largest (in length) of the mountain ranges of Bulgaria. However, the highest mountains of Bulgaria are Mt. Musala in the Rila Mountains and Mt. Vihren in the Pirin Mountains—two smaller mountain ranges in Bulgaria that connect to the Bulgarian part of the Rilo–Rhodope Massif, which includes the Rila Mountains, the Pirin Mountains, the Rhodope Mountains, the Slavyanka Mountains, and the Sturgach Mountains.

Peter Deunov, or Master Beinsa Douno, was active in the Rila Mountains of Bulgaria, holding a

---

24 See for example: Powell and Dann, *The Astrological Revolution*, ch. 5, in which the great importance of the stars of high luminosity is revealed in terms of such stars being aligned with our Sun at various miracles performed by Christ. There I refer to stars with a luminosity of more than 10,000 as *mega stars* ("great stars"). For example, Canopus, whose luminosity is 10,700, is a mega star. See also: Powell, *The Significance of Mega Stars* (https://sophiafoundation.org/wp-content/uploads/2017/04/significance-of-mega-stars.pdf).

summer camp there every summer, where there are a series of seven beautiful lakes that cascade down from one to the other. Peter Deunov spoke of this as a special location on our planet—this being the reason he was guided to be there.

This fact led someone to say that the Master Peter Deunov could not be an incarnation of the Master Jesus, who (according to Rudolf Steiner) was incarnated in the Carpathian Mountains. It could be that the source (Friedrich Rittelmeyer), who communicated the statement about the Carpathians, did not report Rudolf Steiner's words precisely. Steiner's coworker, Ita Wegman, reported that she knew of Rudolf Steiner's statement that "Bulgaria had its own spiritual teacher"[25] (a theme explored in depth by Emily Michael in her book on Rudolf Steiner and Peter Deunov[26]). In other words, Steiner clearly indicated the incarnation of a high spiritual teacher in *Bulgaria* as a contemporary. It is scarcely to be imagined that there was a great and well-known spiritual teacher active in the Rila Mountains as founder of the Bulgarian branch of the White Brotherhood, while another great teacher, the Master Jesus, also from the circle of twelve known as the White Lodge, was active at the same time but unknown in the nearby Carpathian Mountains.

Regardless of this element of confusion at the mention of the Carpathian Mountains, an astrosophical study comparing the horoscopes of conception, birth, and death of the Solomon Jesus with the

*Peter Deunov (Beinsa Douno)*
*July 11, 1864 – Dec. 27, 1944*

conception, birth, and death of Peter Deunov leaves no shadow of doubt that Deunov and the Solomon Jesus are incarnations of the same individuality: Rama Avatar–Zarathustra–Zoroaster–Master Jesus.

There is one incarnation of the Master Jesus in the 14th century mentioned by Rudolf Steiner—the individual referred to as the "Friend of God from the Oberland," *the upper land.*[27] We do not have a name by which we can identify this individual's 14th-century incarnation. However, the area of the "upper land" most likely refers to the mountainous region around Bern, the capital of Switzerland. That region is known as the *Berner Oberland*, an elevated mountainous region in the area of Bern. There are spectacular mountains and lakes in the region. This great teacher, the Friend of God, whom Rudolf Steiner identified as an incarnation of the Master Jesus, was incarnated in that region. So, we see the propensity of this individuality to incarnate in regions of mountains and lakes, connected with the pure essence of Mother Nature.

His teaching is very much about awakening within human beings love for one another and love for Mother Nature. This is a central task for the great teacher, who, according to the Zoroastrian tradition, will be with humanity until the end of Earth's evolution. In other words, he will continue to incarnate in each century.

Research reveals that this great teacher from the White Lodge[28] is connected with the sign of Gemini, marked by the twins Castor and Pollux. In Greek mythology, Castor and Pollux were earlier called Apollo and Hercules, the heavenly twin

25 Zeylmans van Emmichoven, *Who Was Ita Wegman: A Documentation, Volume 2: 1925 until 1943.*

26 Michael, *Sealed by the Sun.* "[Rudolf] Steiner advised [Boyan] Boev to return to Bulgaria, to find the Bulgarian Initiate, and to attend a powerful movement led by him.... In 1912 Boev met this Great Initiate, who was leading the Bulgarian Brotherhood.... Boev became the closest and one of the most faithful disciples and the future secretary and stenographer of Master Deunov" (p. 226).

27 See, Steiner, *Mystics after Modernism: Discovering the Seeds of a New Science in the Renaissance*, the chapter "The Friendship with God."

28 Peter Deunov founded the Bulgarian branch of the White Lodge. See http://www.everabooks.com; also http://www.beinsa-douno.net.

and the earthly twin, who we can take as images of the relationship between the higher self, Apollo, connected with the Sun, and the earthly self, Hercules, who has to fulfill certain tasks of will on Earth—with the help and guidance of the higher self (Apollo) that is united with the Sun. It is interesting to see in the birth horoscope of Peter Deunov, from the year 1864, that he was born when the Sun was in conjunction with the star Castor, connected with the heavenly twin Apollo.

It needs to be noted briefly here that there is a mix-up in Greek mythology, which often identifies the heavenly twin with Pollux and the earthly twin with Castor. However, this is a complete reversal of the facts, since Castor is depicted with a lyre, the musical instrument associated with Apollo, and Pollux is shown with a club, a weapon wielded by Hercules.

Peter Deunov is viewed as the great teacher who came to teach love—to awaken this impulse toward community for the Slavic people.[29] He held several thousand lectures, of which more than four thousand are extant. He also taught a form of movement, Paneurhythmy, to be done outdoors in nature as a means of connecting with natural living forces. Deunov's teaching focuses on awakening the heart and connecting with one another in spiritual community and with nature. It can be compared with Rudolf Steiner's teaching, which has a pronounced cosmic dimension to it, however. Steiner's central teaching concerns cosmic evolution—in particular, the seven stages of planetary evolution relating the evolution of humanity and Earth. As outlined in *Cosmic Dances of the Planets*, the stages of planetary

evolution are embedded in the structure of our solar system.[30] The teachings of these two great spiritual teachers clearly complement each other, as do the cosmic realm and the earthly world of nature. Of course, Rudolf Steiner spoke of many other things, as well, but the cosmic dimension he brought throughout his teaching was extraordinary in terms of breadth of detail, and he returned again and again to depictions of the cosmic realms of existence based on his direct experience of them.

This cosmic dimension of Rudolf Steiner's *Spiritual Science* is foundational for astrosophy, *star wisdom*—the wisdom of stars. When we begin to consider Steiner as the great prophet for the second coming of Christ, for the coming of Christ in the etheric realm, then we can begin to understand this incarnation of the Moses individuality, who brought the Christianized teaching of the seven days of creation.[31] First, looking back, we can see the great importance of bringing the Christian teaching of the seven days of creation when he did, during the first decade of the twentieth century, and published in 1909 in his great work *An Outline of Esoteric Science*. This teaching was to counterbalance the materialistic teaching through Darwin's book *Origin of the Species*, published in 1859, just two years prior to Rudolf Steiner's birth.

Historical events often provide a background to the incarnations of the twelve great teachers from the White Lodge, with Christ at their center. Thus, John the Baptist—one of the twelve from the White Lodge—was sent by Christ as the baptizer, the water bearer, to prepare for the coming of Jesus Christ as the Messiah. John the Baptist is connected with the sign of the Water Bearer, Aquarius.

---

29 These words describing Peter Deunov are more or less exactly the words used by Rudolf Steiner to describe the mission of the Master Jesus. For a hundred-percent certainty regarding the identification of Peter Deunov as an incarnation of the Master Jesus, it is necessary to see the comparison of the conception, birth, and death horoscopes of the Solomon Jesus child with the conception, birth, and death horoscopes of Peter Deunov. See also Robert Powell and Harrie Salman, "Prophecy of Peter Deunov," an article posted on www.sophiafoundation.org under "Articles."

30 Powell and Paul, *Cosmic Dances of the Planets*, appendix 2.

31 For details regarding the hundred-percent certain identification of Rudolf Steiner as the reincarnation of the Moses Bodhisattva, see Robert Powell and Keith Harris, "The Transition" (https://sophiafoundation.org/wp-content/uploads/2017/04/the-transition_final.pdf).

John the Baptist prophesied the coming of Jesus Christ during the middle of the fourth sub-race. Now, however, the individuality of the Master Jesus leads humanity from the fifth to the sixth sub-race—again to John the Baptist–Waterman [Aquarius].... Through the principle of brotherly love, represented by the Master Jesus, the unification of humankind to become the sixth sub-race is taking place and, founded on this principle, it will lead into the future.[32]

From a cosmic perspective, John the Baptist connected with the sign of Aquarius, the Water Bearer—was the one chosen to baptize Jesus in the River Jordan. After his capture by Herod Antipas, his subsequent death at the behest of Herod's wife Herodias, and his transition to spiritual realms following his beheading, he served on a spiritual level as the group soul of the disciples. This great teacher clearly has an ability to work on the level of community-building, an impulse strongly connected with the sign of Aquarius. We see this community impulse in his spiritual activity as a group soul over-lighting the community of the twelve disciples of Christ. Also, we see this community impulse revealed in John the Baptist's earlier incarnation as Rachel at the time of the Patriarchs and the founding of ancient Israel. Rachel was the mother of the two youngest sons of Jacob—Joseph and Benjamin, the two youngest patriarchs of the twelve tribes. Rachel died in childbirth, while giving birth to Benjamin, the youngest of the twelve. Through that death, this great individuality (incarnated then as Rachel) became the group soul inspiring the twelve sons of Israel as the founders of the stream of ancient Israel that had the mission of bringing forth, many generations later, the perfect human being, Jesus of Nazareth.[33]

We see the capacity to spiritually over-light the patriarchs of the twelve tribes of Israel as Rachel and then, in the later incarnation as John the Baptist, again this individuality after death was once more active on the level of a group soul as an inspiring spirit for the circle of the disciples around Christ. This individuality is the one Rudolf Steiner spoke of in his final address on September 28, 1924. That lecture focused on this great individuality, the Elijah Bodhisattva, who reincarnated as John the Baptist, and who had subsequent significant incarnations in the post-Christian era, whereby Rudolf Steiner mentions in his last address the incarnation as Raphael and Novalis. Steiner went on to speak in his last address about another incarnation of this great individuality from the White Lodge, whom he said would incarnate again toward the end of the 20th century—and presumably continue to be active into the 21st century—to work in bringing the teaching and the impulse needed to lead humanity through the great crisis of our time.

In my karma research I was able to determine that this individuality did indeed incarnate, exactly as Rudolf Steiner had prophesied, in the mid-1970s. Moreover, I was able to determine that this incarnation was in female form to serve as a vessel for the activity of Christ in the etheric realm—not appearing as a teacher outwardly in the world, but instead serving on an inner level to connect all human beings with Christ in the etheric realm—for those seeking this connection.

This spiritual mode of activity—which could be described, again, as an over-lighting of all those seeking Christ in the etheric realm—is brought out in a most beautiful way in *The Mystery of Sophia*, written by Estelle Isaacson and me. The very first vision of Estelle Isaacson in that book is a beautiful description of the mission at the present time of the Elijah–John the Baptist–Rachel individuality in our time as the *second* witness spoken of in the Book of Revelation, this being the theme of the book *Elijah Come Again*.[34] Moreover, Moses (that is, the reincarnated Moses) is clearly identified as the *first* witness (mentioned in Revelation, chapter 11) during this time of Christ's second coming. Moses and Elijah (the reincarnated Moses and the reincarnated

32 Steiner, *From the History and Contents of the Esoteric School*, Feb. 12, 1906, p. 182.

33 She was referred to by Jesus Christ, who spoke of "Rachel weeping for her children" (Matt. 2:18).

34 Powell and Isaacson, *The Mystery of Sophia*, ch. 1. For details concerning the various incarnations of the Elijah Bodhisattva up to the present time, see Powell, *Elijah Come Again*.

Elijah), as the *first* and the *second* witnesses, are thus now identified. Once we understand that we are in this time of the *second* witness, we can grasp the nature of the time during which we are living. It is the time of the coming of the Antichrist, as depicted in connection with the two witnesses in chapter 11 of Revelation.

In conclusion, it is appropriate now to mention briefly that—in terms of karma research from the domain of astrosophy—in addition to the incarnation of the Master Jesus individuality as Peter Deunov, there are also three teachers of the 20th century who deserve our special attention: John the Baptist (the Elijah Bodhisattva), who is mentioned by Rudolf Steiner in relation to the sign of Aquarius[35]; the Krishna Avatar, the Nathan Jesus, in connection with Pisces; and the Moses individuality Rudolf Steiner, in connection with the sign of Aries.[36]

As already mentioned in connection with Raphael's painting *The Transfiguration,* it provides a glimpse into the circle of great teachers around Christ that was vouchsafed to the disciples Peter, James, and John on the night of the Transfiguration. They were given a glimpse into the realm that Rudolf Steiner calls the sphere of the bodhisattvas. They beheld two bodhisattvas on either side of Jesus of Nazareth: the Elijah Bodhisattva, connected with Aquarius, to Christ's left (with Jesus of Nazareth, the Krishna Bodhisattva, connected with Pisces), and to Christ's right the Moses Bodhisattva, connected with Aries. In the scene of the Transfiguration the disciples were granted a vista of the three bodhisattvas—Elijah

(the way), Moses (the truth), and Jesus–Krishna (the life)—corresponding to Aquarius, Aries, and Pisces.

Moreover, Rudolf Steiner spoke of his successor, a bodhisattva who incarnated around the year 1900 and who would become noticeable—active in the public arena—during the 1930s, and who will be the future Maitreya Buddha.[37] He said much about this great teacher from the White Lodge, who is referred to as the Kalki Avatar in the Hindu tradition. This being is the same as the one in the Buddhist tradition known as the Maitreya Bodhisattva—that is, the bodhisattva who around AD 4500 will become the Maitreya Buddha—who is one-and-the-same as Kalki, who is awaited in the Hindu tradition as the Tenth Avatar of Vishnu.

This again points to one of the great teachers from the White Lodge, and he is connected with the sign of Taurus. Rudolf Steiner indicated that the Maitreya has the mission to spiritualize the power of the word, which is connected with the human larynx that is related to the constellation of Taurus. Thus, in the circle of the twelve great teachers from the White Lodge, next to the Aries bodhisattva, Moses ("truth"), who reincarnated as Rudolf Steiner, we see the Maitreya, connected with Taurus—that is, the bodhisattva designated by Rudolf Steiner as his "eventual successor"[38] just as the sign Taurus follows that of Aries. After Aries and Taurus, comes the sign of Gemini, the sign of Bodhisattva Rama–Zarathustra–Zoroaster–Master Jesus, whose star Sirius has a longitude of 19½° Gemini. Thus, now we have an expanded glimpse into the realm of the bodhisattvas, these great teachers of

---

35 Powell and Salman, "Prophecy of Peter Deunov," footnote 4 at end of article and the first Master Jesus quote from Rudolf Steiner (https://sophiafoundation.org/wp-content/uploads/2020/06/Prophecy-of-Peter-Deunov-Beinsa-Douno.pdf).

36 See these volumes by Steiner: *An Esoteric Cosmology* (CW 94); *Building Stones for an Understanding of the Mystery of Golgotha* (CW 175); and *Founding a Science of the Spirit* (CW 95). Rudolf Steiner also connects the symbol of the two-petal lotus flower (Moses) with the astrological hieroglyph for the sign of Aries, thus linking the Moses Bodhisattva, who incarnated as Moses in the Age of Aries, with the sign of Aries.

37 Robert Powell and Keith Harris, "The Transition" (https://sophiafoundation.org/wp-content/uploads/2017/04/the-transition_final.pdf).

38 Steiner, *Die Konstitution der Allgemeinen Anthroposophischen Gesellschaft und der Freien Hochschule für Geisteswissenschaft. Der Wiederaufbau des Goetheanum* (CW 260a, in German), p. 31, which goes through the statutes of the newly founded Anthroposophical Society. In connection with the seventh statute, he speaks of naming his "eventual successor." In English, see Steiner, *Constitution of the School of Spiritual Science* (G. Adams, ed.).

humanity, who are for us now as important at this time of Christ's second coming, his manifestation in the etheric realm, as the twelve disciples were two thousand years ago for the coming of Christ in a physical body.

Here is a summary relating to the five bodhisattvas from the circle of the twelve great teachers of the White Lodge:

> Elijah–John the Baptist–Aquarius
> Krishna–Nathan Jesus–Pisces
> Moses–Rudolf Steiner–Aries
> Kashyapa–Maitreya–Kalki–Taurus
> Zarathustra–Master Jesus–Gemini

*"The twelve Masters of the White Lodge have all taken part in the whole Earth evolution.... We have to raise ourselves to their level."*[39]

In a subsequent article, some of the horoscope comparisons referred to in the article will be considered as a striking contribution to the new star wisdom of astrosophy.

## POSTSCRIPT

Text of the vision of Estelle Isaacson previously mentioned concerning the behind-the-scenes spiritual work of the John the Baptist individuality at the present time, the time of Christ's coming in the etheric realm, the realm of life forces. At the time of the first coming of Christ two thousand years ago, John the Baptist emerged as the prophet who came to proclaim Christ as the Messiah—his manifestation in physical incarnation in Palestine, as prophesied earlier by prophets of the Old Testament. Now, near the beginning (relatively speaking) of the 2,500-year period of time (1933–4433) of Christ's second coming, this individuality is again very active, as the following vision indicates—whereby her spiritual activity now, even though she is currently (as of 2020) incarnated in a physical body, is hardly on the physical plane of existence, but directly supports Christ's activity in the etheric world.

This spiritual mode of activity, which could be described as an over-lighting (i.e., over-lighting all those seeking Christ in the etheric realm), is brought out in a most beautiful way in the first vision in *The Mystery of Sophia* by Estelle Isaacson and me.[40] It is a beautiful description of the mission at the present time of this Elijah–John the Baptist–Rachel individuality in our time as the *second witness* (the reincarnated Elijah) spoken of in chapter 11 of the Book of Revelation, just as the first witness spoken of in chapter 11 of Revelation is identified with the reincarnated Moses.

## THE SECOND COMING OF CHRIST AND THE DESCENT OF SOPHIA

In the beginning of the vision, I saw a ray of beautiful blue-violet light. I entered into the light and saw a sphere moving toward me. I felt enveloped by the love and peace of the Divine Mother. Soon I came to realize that I was experiencing this love through the essence of the individuality of John the Baptist. The living energy of Shambhala was within his being as a stream of radiant blue light that was constantly flowing through and raying out to the world. I experienced the silence of Divine Love at the very core of his spirit. I beheld the stars of his being and could see the power of creation that is in him—the seed forces. I entered into the "world that he is," where everything was imbued with blue-violet light, and silence pervaded the atmosphere.

In mystical communion with him, I received the following vision and message:

This is the time of the second coming of Christ. And the second coming of Christ is announced from Shambhala, which has been issuing forth this great announcement for almost a century. The beings that serve the Mother bear this message from the mineral kingdom to the plant kingdom, the animal kingdom, and humankind—to all who can hear the news: that He comes again in clouds

---

39 Steiner, *From the History and Contents of the First Section of the Esoteric School*, Oct. 22, 1906, p. 183.

40 The vision occurred Dec. 9, 2011. Reproduced here is a portion of the vision as published in Powell and Isaacson, *The Mystery of Sophia*, ch. 1.

of glory! He is here! His body is the Earth. His breath is the wind. He is holding the Earth in His loving embrace.

Shambhala is awakening. Beings that have had to hold their silence may now speak and act. There is a great stirring and awakening in Shambhala. Shambhala has been in a time of winter, as it were, a time of holding in, a time of withdrawal. But because more human beings are awakening to the Divine Mother, the beings at the center of the Earth are stirring and are beginning to rise up and prepare for the descent of Holy Sophia—the heavenly Daughter; and Christ is preparing the way for Her in his second coming.

His *first coming* was to prepare hearts to attune to the Father. His *second coming* is to prepare hearts to receive Sophia. He will bring Mother and Daughter together on Earth, thereby reuniting the Earth Mother and the Divine Daughter.

A great awakening is on the horizon for humanity as Sophia draws ever nearer to the spiritual sphere of the Sun. And through our Sun, She will ray out to the world a new sustaining life force. This is a life force that has been present in this world mostly within a very small number of mystics, prophets, and seers who have been able to find Sophia in the heavens; they have embodied this life force energy and rayed it out to others. With the descent of Sophia and Her entrance into the Sun sphere, this life force energy will ray out to the whole world. A great healing will occur; just as mystics ray out healing, so shall Sophia emanate healing to the entire world—even through the rays of the Sun.[41]

---

41 This is clearly a reference to the "woman clothed with the Sun" in Rev. 12:1: "Behold a great sign appears in heaven: a woman clothed with the Sun, with the Moon under her feet, and on her head a crown of twelve stars."

"Every earthly condition during a certain period of time is to be explained as a weaving and interplay of those forces that come into flower and those that die away, those that belong to the rising and those that belong to the falling line—sunrise and sunset—and in between, the zenith at noon, where the two forces unite and become one.

Seen from one's horizon, a person beholds the stars in the sky, rising in the east and climbing ever higher until they reach their highest point in the south. From then onward, they sink until they set in the west. And though the stars disappear from sight in the west, one must nevertheless say to oneself: The real place of setting lies in the south and coincides with the zenith, just as the true place of rising is in the north and coincides with the nadir.

Rising starts from the nadir. Through that, a circular motion is described that can be divided into two halves by a vertical line running south to north. In the part containing the eastern point, the rising forces are active. In the part containing the western point, the sinking forces are present. The eastern and western points cut the semicircle through the center. They are the two points in which, for our physical eye, vision of the forces begins and ends. They are one's horizon."

—Rudolf Steiner, *"Freemasonry" and Ritual Work*, p. 387

# RUDOLF STEINER AND THE CHRISTMAS CONFERENCE
## ASTROLOGICAL ASPECTS OF LAYING THE FOUNDATION STONE

### *Krisztina Cseri*

As we approach the hundred-year anniversary of the Christmas Conference, held from December 25, 1923, until January 1, 1924, by Rudolf Steiner in Dornach, new gates are gradually opening for our deeper understanding of the event.

Many memoirs were written by participants of the Conference and other researchers—who were deeply moved by what happened at the Conference and in the daily life of Rudolf Steiner himself— about events during and after the Conference, culminating in Rudolf Steiner's death. Instead of citing or going into details of the breathtaking descriptions of the Laying of the Foundation Stone, I would like to call attention to a few aspects that—as far as I know—have not been studied or published yet. I would like to give further stimulus for readers to enlarge their vista and go further into the depths of the mystery of this great deed. I hope that new questions will arise from my approach that allow the theme to be enlivened in everyone, attuning us to the "Cosmic Turning Point of Time" as we are *all* in the process of approaching the anniversary of this event that continues to have tremendous consequences for our evolution.

I would like to note that, as we are dealing with a very complex question, I cannot in the present context go too deeply into the complexity, even of my own view, to clarify its place in the complex astrological (or astrosophical) picture or its connection to other approaches. It would be a further task to find the connecting points between the theories that were created about the astrological background of the Laying of the Foundation Stone and regarding the timing of the birth and death of Rudolf Steiner to arrive at the wholeness—at least in astrological aspects—of this theme.

There are two main issues on which I wish to meditate. One is the cosmic background of the Laying of the Foundation Stone as an "astro-psychological process," a "cosmic initiation through the head" (to which I refer throughout what follows as a "Sirian initiation"), brought to a close by the death of Rudolf Steiner. The other is the preparation of the individuality of Rudolf Steiner for the Laying of the Foundation Stone.

## I. LAYING OF THE FOUNDATION STONE AS A SIRIAN INITIATION

Despite the fact that this study is one-sided, taking into consideration only a few elements of the cosmic situation, I feel it necessary to offer a short guideline that helps in following my line of thoughts.

I begin with a basic assumption: Rudolf Steiner's death has an essential relationship with a particular cosmic process in which the *movement* of Pluto plays the main role. The possibility of this kind of link between Steiner's death and the Laying of the Foundation Stone leads to an investigation of further elements participating in this cosmic process. The first is a star, Sirius, which has great influence on earthly evolution according to the descriptions of our higher guides. Then I study the movement of Pluto in its connection with the Sun and Earth, with a view to the "astro-psychological" process in the development of the soul in general, and in particular regarding the participants of the Christmas Conference. The section on Koberwitz points out that the timing of the events in Koberwitz suggests that this lecture course was also an organic part of the detailed "astro-psychological" process, as a kind of second step after the Christmas Conference and before the death of Rudolf Steiner. In the next section I try to handle the elements of the cosmic process in one unity, drawing the particular relationship of the Sun and Earth into the picture already established. With few additional notes, my aim is to expand the image and suggest further investigations for larger periods of time.

## The Movement of Pluto

In 2010, I was very interested in the meaning of the planet Pluto and tried to grasp and explain the effects coming from the region of this planet. That was also the year when I made an oil painting of Rudolf Steiner and was very engaged in the event of Rudolf Steiner laying the Foundation Stone at the Christmas Conference in 1923. It was a very deep period in my life, and soon with some higher guidance I discovered the writings of Willi Sucher and Robert Powell online. Looking backward it was my "turning point of time," when a new phase of my life began.

Returning to the theme, I recognized that the Laying of the Foundation Stone and the death of Rudolf Steiner are in close connection with each other through the movement of Pluto. When I looked at the painting, I often felt Rudolf Steiner's breathing; it was as if he had said *I endured until the last minute I could*. At the same time, I realized that this "last minute" coincided with Pluto's return to direct motion after having stationed direct, *returning to the positions it last occupied on the dates of the Christmas Conference.*

More precisely, when Rudolf Steiner died, *Pluto was just turning to direct movement, at 17°43' Gemini*. Pluto had stationed for a few days, as it always does around its turns. Its direct motion started exactly on March 26, 1925, according to the Ephemeris. This turning into direct motion alone would be remarkable in relation to the death of Rudolf Steiner.

When Rudolf Steiner died, *Pluto was aligned with its position on December 30, 1923, during the Christmas conference—i.e., 17°43' Gemini.* It will not return to this position for 248 years. Over the course of 1923–25, Pluto was aligned with 17°43' Gemini four times—first on July 30, 1923, moving direct; then on December 30, 1923, moving retrograde; again on June 15, 1924, moving direct once again; and finally, from March 18 to April 3, 1925, while stationing direct. Owing to turning direct at 17°43' Gemini in 1925, it did not retrace the complete course it took during the entirety of the Christmas Conference, but only where it had been from December 25–30, 1923.

(Had Rudolf Steiner died on either March 3–4 or April 17–18, Pluto would have been conjunct 17°49' Gemini, its position on December 25, 1923.) The important factor here is that Rudolf Steiner died when Pluto (at its turn to direct motion) *was for the last time at any degree* it was during the Christmas Conference.

Over the years it has become increasingly clear for me that Rudolf Steiner in his weakened physical condition had to wait for the time when his death would not disturb the "astro-psychological" process in which the Foundation Stone was planted into the hearts of his followers. *During those days, the dark side of Pluto, working through people around him, was so strong that Rudolf Steiner could no longer live, but as a good shepherd he could not cross the threshold any earlier, as he had to wait until "it was fulfilled."* The process of the Laying of the Foundation Stone in the souls of the students was not finished until that time, and this was of primary importance.[1]

I think Rudolf Steiner's death is bound *primarily* to this cosmic deed made during his life and not to any of his horoscopes from the past. He had to endure until "it was fulfilled," otherwise his death would have had a negative impact on the initiation process of the students—and in a certain sense on his own initiation, as well. There is a strong image within me regarding Steiner as a servant of humanity and as an adept whose death should be handled in a unique way, versus those

---

1 Maybe it was very important for him to die on a day that is aligned astrologically—in terms of the Sun's position—with the birthday of the Solomon Jesus, and on those few days after the turn of Pluto, this is why he chose precisely that day to pass away, but the possibility of passing on the date of March 30 in itself was open for him in each year. Saturn was very close to Steiner's Ascendant on the day of his death, but if we assume that Steiner should have lived at least until 1933, this conjunction could not be the primary astrological factor in his death without other, more significant effects coming from his deeds in his life. Had he lived until 1933, perhaps this Saturn–Ascendant alignment would have marked a new phase of life, ideally at an even higher spiritual–soul level than he was at before, and this level would have served as a source for new ideas to introduce on the horizontal plane (the main aspect of the ASC–DESC axis).

of others, this is why I emphasize primarily the condition of the people around him and not his own destiny.

### The Influence of Sirius

*"Always have a look at the place where the planet turns retrograde!"* This was an important saying of my astrology teacher, one that I really put to good use in my studies. Wherever a planet turns to retrograde motion, a spiritual influence or a "spiritual message" is transmitted toward the human being from a certain star by the planet.

When we study the Christmas Conference, we find it very striking that Pluto reached the orb of the ecliptic meridian of Sirius in September 1923, before the Laying of the Foundation Stone. Furthermore, it might have reached it one year earlier, before the burning down of the first Goetheanum. It depends on experience (or perhaps more precisely on intuition) exactly what we accept as the orb of Sirius.[2] Therefore, we should ponder further on the question of how and when the effects of Sirius began to make themselves felt by Rudolf Steiner and his followers, and how the consequences of the effects of Sirius are linked to each other. It is certain that the two significant events happened in the same phase of the Pluto–Sun–Earth relationship—namely, at the opposition of Pluto and the Sun. The former opposition brought the Hades side of Pluto's influence; the latter brought the Phanes side (but we must not forget the poisoning of Rudolf Steiner on January 1, 1924, as a dark effect).[3] Both events were a kind of

"explosion" that characterize the opposition phase of the direct–retrograde movements (see later).

Remaining with the Christmas Conference, there was about 1.5° distance between the locations of Sirius and Pluto projected to the ecliptic at the Conference, and there was only a bit more than 0.5° distance between their locations when Pluto turned retrograde before the Conference. Taking into account the size (and orb) of Sirius, I think we can say that, in the case of the Conference, it is certain that Pluto reached the sphere (ecliptic meridian) of Sirius when it turned retrograde before the Conference; or we can even say that it remained in this influential region for the Conference, as well.

What can we know about Sirius? I would refer here briefly to five sources with which I could get acquainted and regard them as being important to our theme: Rudolf Steiner, Peter Deunov, H. P. Blavatsky, Alice Bailey, and Robert Powell. They all have in common the fact that they emphasize—in different ways or with different contents—the *special role of Sirius* among the stars.

There is a remarkable indication about Sirius, told by Rudolf Steiner to Countess Johanna Keyserlingk, in the book *Koberwitz, 1924 and the Introduction of Biodynamics*:

> "Sirius is the heart of Jesus–Zarathustra and is in the depths of the Earth.... Sirius is the world-thought that Christ produces out of his heart—therefore it is to be found within the Earth." He drew a curve to represent the Earth and wrote

---

2  An opinion from astrologer Anne Wright: "Most people give about 1° to fixed stars of 1st magnitude. I would give Sirius a maximum of 2°. Sirius is by far the brightest star. I give a 1st magnitude star about 1°15', gradually decreasing to 15' for a 6th magnitude star." (http://www.constellationsofwords.com/categories/natalrobson.htm).

3  Here there is not enough space to elaborate the entity of Pluto. The reader can get abundant information on it from elsewhere—for example, from the previous articles of the issues of *Star Wisdom*, or from Robert Powell, *Hermetic Astrology*, vol. 2, "Uranus, Neptune and Pluto." I would emphasize regarding Pluto in the context of this article.

a.  Even if Pluto is a trans-Saturnian planet and therefore represents qualities that are superhuman, the forces of the Pluto sphere pervade the cosmic existence in which humanity is embedded, and astrological researches have already shown that these forces play a significant role in the shaping of human destiny regarding the development of *higher human spiritual faculties, especially Intuition*.

b.  As the furthest astrologically significant planet, it has connections both with the *furthest* realms of the cosmos and with the *deepest* realms of the Earth—"as experience has shown that the spheres of the planets are reversed in their 'reflection' in the Earth" (Sucher, *The Drama of the Universe*, p. 64).

c.  Although the beings of the Pluto-sphere have great affinity to the evil forces (i.e., the Hades side of Pluto), Phanes, the Father of Existence, can give a truer image of Pluto as the planet of *Life* (*Love-Will*) of the cosmos.

on it, "metabolism and fulfilment," as though the thoughts issuing from the heart of Christ—that is from the Sun—are sent through Sirius to the center of the Earth, where they obtain their fulfilment by means of metabolism.[4]

In addition, there is another passage written by Countess Johanna Keyserlingk in her introduction to the 1952 English edition:

Rudolf Steiner spoke wonderful words to me of the divine heart of the Nazarene in the depth of the Earth, which hears all that stirs the human soul, where all human sorrow and human joy are received, and the prayer of the petitioning soul is accepted. "May there ascend from the Depths the prayer that is heard in the Heights"—are words from the Christmas Meditation of 1923. We may therefore pray to the heart in the Earth's depths. Thence come helping rays for Earth and humankind.[5]

It is interesting that the dialogue between Rudolf Steiner and Countess Johanna Keyserlingk occurred *on June 17, 1924, when Pluto had returned (in its direct movement) to its position on December 27, 1923, during the Christmas Conference.*

Quotations from Peter Deunov show that there is a culture of spiritual beings on Sirius that is more sublime than ours, and we are moving in our evolution toward that culture:

Often go out to watch Sirius. In July and August, it rises in the east some time before the sunrise, and in the spring—in the evening. And anyone who is sensitive will feel in stars trembling a quiet joy. This joy is a presentiment of that great happiness that awaits man when he goes to live on Sirius. In Sirius there is a harder life than in the solar system because it is more advanced as a system. In the distant future, leaving the solar system you will go to Sirius.

All the planets have their purpose. On them live advanced beings. They are more advanced in age and in wisdom than we are because they have emerged from God much earlier than we have. Their wisdom is so great that the culture of the modern world, in comparison with the culture of Sirius, is in its infancy. One day, when our solar system will finish its development, it will go the way of Sirius and then we will have completely different conceptions of things.[6]

Sirius has a culture twice as sublime as the one on the Sun....[7]

We can also enlarge our knowledge about Sirius from Hindu esoteric astrology and theosophic literature (e.g., H.P. Blavatsky and Alice Bailey), which latter has its roots in Trans-Himalayan esoteric occultism. These theories do not handle the event of Golgotha and the Second Coming of Christ (among other aspects of spiritual teachings) in their right place, but from the viewpoint of our theme it is important that they seem to agree with Western spiritual teachers that Sirius has a *prominent role in the evolution of humanity*. Alice Bailey characterizes Sirius as a kind of *cosmic heart center* and says that it is a *transmitter of the Cosmic Son* (or *Cosmic Christ*) *principle*. One can find much useful information about Sirius's link with the universal and cosmic principles, such as the laws of karma and periodicity, the principle of freedom, its function as the Great Star of Initiation, as a source of manas, as a star of Love and Wisdom, or its operation through an intricate system of astrological intermediaries, and so on in the book *Sirius*, written by a follower of Alice Bailey, Maureen Temple Richmond; however, it is not easy to make the bridge (i.e., to transpose the concepts) to Christianity-centered, anthroposophic–Sophianic concepts and terminology or to understand at all the views in their complexity.[8]

I quote here only a few sentences from this book, which might be relevant to our considerations:

...according to the Tibetan, the energies of Sirius are the agencies of the Cosmic Christ. These Sirian energies allow the Cosmic Christ to awaken the Christ principle in our solar system, on our planet, in the human kingdom, and in the subhuman kingdoms.

---

4  Von Keyserlingk: *The Birth of a New Agriculture*, p. 89.
5  Ibid., p. 18.

6  Beinsa Douno: *Astrology*, p. 168.
7  Ibid., p. 171.
8  Richmond, *Sirius*.

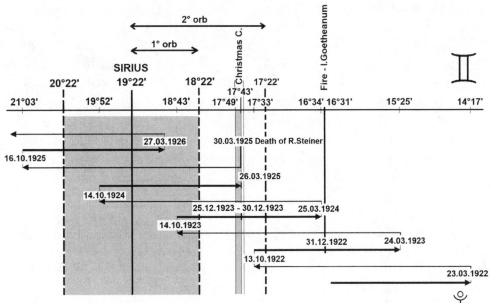

*Figure 1. Schematic drawing. The movement of Pluto between 1922 and 1926, around the ecliptic meridian of Sirius*

This power was demonstrated through the medium of the historical Christ who, the Tibetan says, "is...the expression, *par excellence*, of a Sirian initiation"...the energies of Sirius are the agencies of the Cosmic Christ, or the second person of the Divine Trinity....

It is evident that Sirian influence is behind the most outstanding of evolutionary developments on our planet.[9]

Robert Powell also emphasized the central role of Sirius in 2018 in Roncegno Terme, Italy, saying that Sirius has an important role in relation to our chakras, inasmuch as it *influences all of our chakras*, while the other stars influence only one of our chakras. He added that it also has a serious role in the transformation of our astral body into manas, which means that *it has much to do with the foundation of the Jupiter phase of evolution*—which in turn has a serious connection with the Laying of the Foundation Stone, as Valentin Tomberg also indicates in his *Studies on the Foundation Stone Meditation*.

### The Astro-psychological Process of Laying the Foundation Stone in Light of Pluto's Direct and Retrograde Movements

When I say "astro-psychological process of Laying the Foundation Stone" I mean the

relationship between soul development and the stellar framework (the guidance of Pluto in particular) of implanting the Foundation Stone into the members' hearts. Surely Steiner himself experienced the direct and retrograde phases of the movement of Pluto, bringing to earthly realization key points in this movement. Just as important, however, was the collaboration of the community gathered around him with the stellar–planetary changes (i.e., with the interplay of Pluto, Sun, and Earth) to form a cup out of their souls, receiving consciously the essence of the Foundation Stone—to prepare for it, to absorb it, and to "metabolize" it in the right way in their souls, in order to continue on their way in the world, manifesting the essence of the Foundation Stone in their deeds. The viewpoint of the development of the soul is the *psychological* perspective.

Rudolf Steiner indicated that the Christmas Conference is not something that ended with the last day of the Conference.[10] It might seem counterintuitive, therefore, to connect planetary movement with any kind of end to the Christmas Conference. However, from a particular

---

9  Ibid., pp. 159, 162, 181.

10  "...this Christmas Conference should actually never be finished, but always continue on in the life of the Anthroposophical Society" (Rudolf Steiner, Jan. 18, 1924).

viewpoint, there was actually a time that might indicate a point in the development of the Foundation Stone in the members' hearts when one aspect was fulfilled and something else began on its foundation. It is similar to the treatment of a plant seed that we put into the soil and, for a while, we water each day. The time then comes when it is enough to water it weekly, and we see that the plant feels good in our environment, so we do not have a look at it each day. We should think in *processes, or phases of processes*, and not in one action—at least not in the case of the psychological operations of the soul, which are interwoven with the further destiny of a particular event in one's life.

The direct vs. retrograde movements of the planets have significant effects on the operation of our souls. We speak of Aristotelian and Platonic souls, but obviously all of us have to take on both Aristotelian and Platonic attitudes in life, even if somebody is more karmically related to one of these two groups. *The direct motion of a planet can be associated more with an Aristotelian attitude, and the retrograde motion of a planet with a Platonic attitude.* Without changing these states, without the collaboration of these attitudes, there is no sense in speaking about development; they are both just as necessary as the direct and retrograde motions of the planets are a necessity in the cosmos. The direct motion indicates *attention*, when the observed and the observer are separated and the soul participates consciously in its environment. The retrograde motion indicates *awareness*, when the soul perceives the wholeness of, and fundamental unity with, its environment. "While awareness without attention gives rise to an overall sense of meaning, it cannot provide a differentiated understanding of the details of particular explicit [i.e., external] objects and their behavior. On the other hand, attention without awareness would consist of isolated, explicit forms without any sense of their overall context or meaning."[11] Thus, the development of the soul depends on the rhythm of *both* these processes.

Clearly, this is a very general approach, showing only two features of a much more complex web. What lies behind the development of the soul reveals itself in *different* aspects of astrology. When we try to grasp the processes in our soul in accordance with the cosmic constellations, a vast picture can appear before our eyes—from the viewpoints of the various astrological aspects. The collective imaginative visions are analogous to the wholeness of processes in the soul. The translation of the cosmic movements into soul processes can sometimes result in over-simplification, but inevitably something evolves that can unveil a greater complexity, though maybe it cannot be expressed properly in words.

One of the different astrological aspects within the phase-oriented (or evolution-oriented) view is the *power* of the planet. Here we no longer focus on the planet's position in a sign or in a house. The power of a planet lies partly in the fact that it *is* direct or retrograde—i.e., it is implicitly in aspect to the Sun—in the sense that the phenomenon of retrogression is meaningless without taking the Sun into consideration (in the geocentric view). Moreover, experience shows that, within the direct and retrograde relationships of the planet to the Sun–Earth reality, the power of the planet depends greatly on whether it has an *exact aspect with the Sun* or not. In other words, the collaboration of the planet and the Sun (as a vehicle of the Self, or "I") seems very important in the soul processes, in the intensity of the inner experience of the planet, during the direct and retrograde phases. This is especially true for the planets that are more distant from the Sun, such as Pluto. Pluto's retrograde and direct motion can be experienced as exhausting, but its significance and meaning are generally not felt in a conscious way, as Pluto transfers very unfamiliar contents. Exact angles of Sun and Pluto help the soul to grasp these unfamiliar contents.

From this point of view, it follows that, if we focus on Pluto (and follow the path of Pluto on the following diagram), we can see that *certain ecliptic points are more emphasized* than others; sextiles, squares, and trines with the Sun occur around the "turns" of the planet, whereas conjunctions and

---

11 Sullivan, *Retrograde Planets: Traversing the Inner Landscape*, p. 53.

oppositions with the Sun occur at "midways" of the planet between the turns. Thus, on the one hand all of the aspects of Pluto and the Sun have different power (depending on the type of the angle), and on the other hand they operate with slightly different spiritual forces as time (and the planet) goes on, drawing into operation the flow of four main ecliptic lines in one cycle (conjunction, around stationary retrograde, opposition and around stationary direct). In other words, there are two ecliptic *zones* around the turns, and two ecliptic *points* at conjunction and opposition that promote—like cornerstones—the phases of the soul's development.

Among them, the most crucial zone must be that at which Pluto stations retrograde, especially regarding the *spiritual evolution* of the soul; this line transmits the *main* cosmic impulse to integrate. In my imagination, the ecliptic lines are similar to the vertical warps of a weaving loom through which a carpet is woven, going with the thread and the shuttle from one direction to the other and then backward. The carpet is the life of the soul, growing into the life of the cosmos; the thread is the impulse, and the shuttle is the planet. At the turn, we sometimes introduce a new thread to have a diverse streak in the carpet. The ecliptic lines give structure and continuous support to the carpet, but the thread in the rows gives a new color, which on the two sides gives some new influx into the carpet—i.e., into the life of the soul. The ecliptic meridian, whereby the planet stations retrograde, indicates a cosmic infusion, and it seems that, on the other side where the planet turns direct, there is something that human beings start to add to the whole interaction through their thus illumined (during the retrograde phase) soul and consequent earthly deeds. Obviously, every influence, every inflow of forces of the stars, is important; I am speaking of primary and secondary messages, which can even accumulate in a certain way and in a certain sense by means of the planet(s) to eventually find points of release in humankind during the phases of the process. Astrology of the future will probably shed light to the further details of this question.

This example of the weaving loom, obviously, can be a simple and superficial reflection of the whole process, as conjunctions and oppositions (or the other angles) do not appear in it. I thought it suitable to imagine the new colors of influxes at the turns into the operation of the soul—from the stars and from humanity.

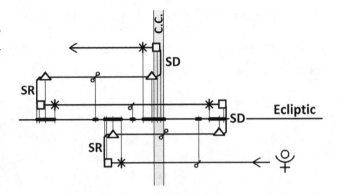

*Figure 2. Schematic drawing. Emphasized ecliptic meridians on the path of Pluto covering two cycles (around the Christmas Conference). Pluto certainly did not cross the ecliptic, the ecliptic was placed in the middle to emphasise the points and zones on it.*

The general process is the following, in terms of one cycle:

1. *From conjunction to station-retrograde:* At the conjunction, the planet [Pluto] is moving most quickly. It is a seed-period, when a cycle of activity begins. At sextile, the planet's motion is average. At square, the planet seems to slow down.

2. *Station-retrograde:* The planet is at a virtual standstill and has appeared so for a couple of days or weeks. Its power has become concentrated, and its apparently inert station creates a sense of impending change, but the quality of the change is unknown. The mood of a station-retrograde is one of suspense. The few days just prior to the station are often eventful or psychologically tense. The planet begins to deviate and develops acentrically, often operating in the individual in deeply unconscious ways that become conscious later, at opposition, and again at the station-direct point.

3. *From station-retrograde to opposition:* At the trine, the suspense of the station is

broken, and the trine often acts as the trigger for events. The Sun collects the energy of the stationing planet and manifests it. After the trine has passed, the retrograde motion has been absorbed and the effects are stabilized.

4. *Opposition:* This is the fastest motion of the retrograde cycle. The Sun and the planet meet to confront issues that have been suspended since the station.

5. *From opposition to station-direct:* At stationary direct trine, the planet is again at a virtual standstill, but retrogressing by minutes of arc. The Sun collects the product of the retrograde cycle and loads the stationed planet with restrained energy. Tension then builds up around the release at the station itself, unconscious mobilization of forces to prepare for direct motion. The mood around the stationery direct trine is one of suppressed intensity—compulsion with no direction—and one has the feeling of captivity. The tension is subjugated excitement that sets the tone for what will be released or revealed at the station-direct.

6. *Station-direct:* The planet appears to stop. As it turns direct, the mood is one of disorientation, of liberty with no direction. Gradually, over the subsequent days of direction, issues become clear. The manumission of the planet from the Sun's domination can create a sense of hysteria around events and in psychological responses. This is a highly reactive phase, which can discharge erratic energy and temporarily create chaos. The planet is liberated, but with no containment.

7. *From station-direct to conjunction:* At this point the planet is accelerating in direct motion. It receives the sobering square from the Sun. The subsequent period is the result of the entire retrograde phase, when the practical aims of the annual review become incorporated into the daily streams of life. The sextile of the planet and the Sun foreshadows the seeding at the next conjunction.[12]

There is a very complex procedure in the development of the soul behind the phases of the retrograde and direct movements of the planets. *Sometimes the internal or external occurrences are quite evident, sometimes not at all*, and the soul can construct a view about its development at a later time—in reverse, so to speak. The quality of the development depends on the planet in question and on the soul itself, which is at a certain point of its own development. Therefore, there can be only a few guidelines about the general occurrences at the phases of the direct-retrograde movements of the planets, which must be individualized.

In the case of the Laying of the Foundation Stone, we speak of Rudolf Steiner himself and his students. There are two points here. On the one hand, we can say that the sequence of the direct–retrograde movements of Pluto in relation to the culminating point of the Laying of the Foundation Stone started earlier regarding Steiner than regarding the other people. So, it must be decided what we try to examine—events from prior to the greatest event or events since the greatest event. On the other hand, it is evident that Rudolf Steiner was at a much more advanced spiritual level than the others behind him, as students; thus, it is a question as to how differently he recognized and metabolized the effects of the changes of the cosmic constellations.[13] I would also refer here to what I said previously about the perception of the streams from planets far distant from the Sun, which are probably felt more consciously by an initiate—without any additional angles to the Sun (or other planets).

If we try to imagine the effects of the retrograde–direct movements in the soul before our eyes, we can describe it with additional pictures.

---

12 Summary on the basis of Sullivan, *Retrograde Planets*, pp. 119–122. The description is generally valid for all of the outer planets.

13 Although he strode ahead of humanity in paving the way for the others, he was a man, with his own motions in his soul. This is why I think he was also subordinated in a way to the changes in the constellations, even if his reactions to them might be different from the others' reactions.

For example, with a broom sweeping to the left (direct phase) and to the right (retrograde phase) in the soul, inching forward gradually; or with a sandpaper polishing with left and right motions a stone in the soul.[14] And there must be few "hammerlocks" in the process to move some tough drosses or to force one's way to a noble metal in the stone—this would be the development of the soul through generally painful, often cathartic periods. (These pictures are, in a certain sense, the opposite of the weaving of a carpet, which shows "growing" regarding an object, a kind of enrichment of the soul by the stars and the world by the soul, while here the soul enriches in the opposite direction, eliminating the upper layers, mining to its core and to its future possibilities. In the former case, the emphasis was on the question of the streaming of forces through the ecliptic lines toward and away from the soul; in this latter case, the focus is on the inner *work* of the soul along events that bring breakthroughs into the layers of the soul.)

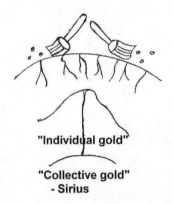

"Individual gold"

"Collective gold"
- Sirius

The phases build upon one another. The "polishing" leads to the innermost treasure of the soul, which is generally unconscious in ordinary life, veiled by certain activities or layers of the soul. This treasure consists of the intentions of the "I," coming from the life before birth and the embryonic period, when certain seeds were planted within the etheric body. At the turning points of the movement, there is always a breakthrough via the borders of the soul; either there is something that comes to light from the unconscious layer

---

14  I remain here with Pluto, but the mechanism of the movements of the trans-Saturnian planets and the outer planets are similar to it.

(after turning retrograde), or there is something that sinks from the conscious layer (after turning direct). *Turning inside or outside can be so exhausting that the effect can appear in the physical body as an illness, as well.*

At oppositions and conjunctions, there are also remarkable crossings within the layers of the soul, but departing from a more stable position—either from an introverted state in the retrograde phase or from an extroverted state in the direct phase. At opposition, the soul can reach its deepest point and, with the help of the cosmic infusion, integrate something (or allow it to arise) into the conscious part of the soul. Generally, an earthly event triggers the confrontation between the higher Self and the unconscious, provoking into consciousness what has been in rumination and reflection. At the same time, oppositions as the start of the "full phase" of the cycle may show where the fruit of the cycle is most likely to emerge. The issues that become apparent at the opposition are a key to understanding what the second half of the cycle is about. At conjunction, after completing the second half ("full phase") of the cycle, the weaving within the layers of the soul is quite conscious, as the planet and the Sun walk hand in hand, and the meaning or effect of the planet can manifest and prove itself through earthly deeds for conscious recognition. It marks the "inseminating" point, or beginning of a new cycle, after the conscious recognition and application of the fruit of the last retrogression period.

Everyday astrology generally speaks of the planet and house positions of the birth chart, and examines the transits (including the direct–retrograde aspect) in relation to these natal planets as a general rule. These natal planets and the axes, or houses, are the "sensitive points" where the transit has a soul-activating effect. Advanced astrology should go further into the gold mine of the "I," reaching the deepest characteristics of an individuality with the help of an examination of the embryonic period and past lives (when possible).

In the case of the Laying of the Foundation Stone, a kind of collective polishing occurred (in addition to Rudolf Steiner's own individual

process), something that does not lead back to personal traits but to something that is generally valid—a collective path. It is below the individual "gold mountains"; it is a collective "gold basement" beyond the individual. Here it is not only the "I" in question, but any further aspects of one's being—higher bodies that might be in only a seed condition at the moment. The marker of this collective path to the inner core was not a personal transit (e.g., a Pluto transit to a natal planet). Instead, the representative of this "collective gold" was Sirius. *Sirius was the trigger point from outside and the focal point from inside of this evolutionary step for these souls.* Sirius helped Rudolf Steiner, and Steiner helped others to find Sirius, and thus the next possible evolutionary step in their souls—a step that, once taken by Steiner, becomes possible for others.

In individual cases (as in the case of Rudolf Steiner himself) the motions should be handled in a sequence. For example, it seems that the burning of the first Goetheanum was a "hammerlock" at the previous Sun–Pluto opposition, a sign that something too bright for the dark forces was in preparation, and laying the Foundation Stone must have been done just before the next "hammerlock." In terms of Steiner's physical condition, it seems evident that his illness emerged and then worsened around the turning of Pluto, as those turns always induce some shifting in energy patterns.

However, the "sensitive point" was neither a personal transit of Rudolf Steiner (or anyone else's), nor was it the turns of Pluto and its conjunctions or oppositions with the Sun; rather, it was *the position of Pluto on the ecliptic at the time of the Laying of the Foundation Stone. The sensitive point was born at the time of the Laying of the Foundation Stone, and no earlier.* In the constantly ongoing sequence of direct and retrograde motions, after reaching Sirius, Pluto was in a position to brand into the universe a sensitive point (the cosmic Turning Point of Time). It was such a great event in the sequence of the movements of Pluto that it marked a sensitive point for Steiner, as well as for his students. This sensitive point becomes the point of orientation in our study of

Pluto's movements in relation to the events of that time.

Star Wisdom approaches "retrograde" as a time of emphasis and increased intensity of that planet's activity. With multiple crossings, each passing has a different flavor. The first crossing initiates the issues that require resolution. The second retrograde crossing deepens the issues, and can often be the most challenging. The third and final pass shows *how the resolution has been achieved* over the issue at hand.[15]

The number of crossings depends on the planet in question and its position in relation to the zodiac. The crossings always deepen the issue represented by a natal planet or axis—in this case the "cosmic Turning Point of Time." Here it was valid in a collective sense, and so Steiner's *death waited until the last crossing—the last possibility to go deeply into the "collective gold mine" and strengthen the connection with it.*

Here I quote a few passages regarding the general character of the Sun–Pluto opposition and the final pass, which can deepen the understanding for our study:

*Opposition*:
During the retrograde passage, the potential for transformation is internalized, insinuating itself into all facets of one's being, becoming organic. One's ego becomes defenseless, permeable, while boundaries drop, or at least blur. The grip of the ego weakens and becomes available to alternatives, opposing even. Extreme polarities begin to constellate, resulting in an interior split and creating tension that still remains free-floating and amorphous. The split eventually surfaces in the form of alternatives, decisions and crossroads. A strong feeling of fatedness normally accompanies the period around the Sun opposition to the retrograde planet. The ego becomes spongy, *absorbing increasing amounts of "new" energy from the unconscious*, rendering it incapable of relating to the environment in its accustomed way.... The opposition occurs mid-cycle and *has a powerful illuminating effect.* What is in

---

15 Tresemer and Schiappacasse, *Star Wisdom and Rudolf Steiner*, p. 37.

development often becomes manifestly active, either psychologically and intellectually, or by experiencing the inner drama in the environment through events, circumstances and happenings through other people.... [Opposition is] the *explosive turning point* at which one confronts issues needing to be integrated.

*Final passage:*

...(after the transiting retrograde planet has turned direct, moving past the natal degree): ...*It is the "birth" of what has been in development* for the last...period. Although we might be consciously aware of what the cycle has produced by this last passage, still to come is the digesting of the new knowledge before it becomes fully integrated. It is useful to "work" the unconscious in an active way, through association and self-analysis of thoughts, images, dreams and fantasies during phases of the cycles, remaining acutely conscious of behavior patterns, seeing if they are relevant to current needs.... The real work is done during the retrograde phase, and the implementation of new skills, perceptions and knowledge and the subsequent experimental phase of life begins at the direction.... The station-direct collects the unconscious process as much as possible and expels it, to externalize and manifest what one has been gestating. When it passes back over the degree in the natal chart, it is the end of the most intense change. Gradually, life stabilizes, but with infinitely more appropriate perspectives and irrevocable new direction.[16]

There is no astrological literature that would describe the process of initiation of the human soul, as in the case of the Laying of the Foundation Stone. It is our task to integrate the Laying of the Foundation Stone into a process that generally works with the ordinary contents of the human soul.

### Koberwitz and Laying the Foundation Stone

The exact conjunction of Pluto and the Sun (after their opposition on January 3, 1924) occurred on July 4, 1924, two to three weeks after the lectures on agriculture in Koberwitz.[17]

However, from June 12 until the end of the Koberwitz lectures on June 17, Pluto returned to its positions on the ecliptic, as in the time of the Christmas Conference, drawing the two events close to each other. Perhaps the events in Koberwitz demonstrate a kind of deepening of the Laying of the Foundation Stone. At the Christmas Conference, Rudolf Steiner was the spiritual teacher who, in the retrograde phase of Pluto, effected an impact through the heads of the students and into their hearts. In Koberwitz, he was a farmer who, in the direct phase of Pluto, stimulated directly the limbs to take actions—even if also through teachings.

In this high-level sequence of events, Koberwitz seems to be a fruit, a response, to the Laying of the Foundation Stone, which on the other hand is certainly a part of soul development and cannot be separated from the whole process of the initiation of souls. The healing of Earth and the physical future of humankind and the beings of nature could appear as a conscious recognition in souls reaching their *will* to begin the tasks. From the more theoretical fields of the soul, the emphasis was put to real actions in the physical sphere. The spiritual teacher became a farmer for that particular time. The emphasis on the head and the heart (in the retrograde phase) went to the limbs (in the direct phase).

Koberwitz is mentioned in memoirs as a Pentecostal impulse. Indeed, this was the last Pentecost of Rudolf Steiner on Earth. It seems it should be added that it was the second step after the Laying of the Foundation Stone in the sequence of Pluto's transition of its positions at the Christmas Conference, between the Laying of the Foundation Stone and Steiner's death, emphasizing the start of a new or renewed connection with the Earth, with goddess Natura. From this viewpoint, it can be seen as the Sophianic pair of the Laying of the Foundation Stone. What a vivid circumstance there—beautiful gardens showing the radiating life of Mother Earth and, according to the descriptions, even Steiner was much better by the end of

---

16 Sullivan, *Retrograde Planets*, pp. 319, 364, 365.

17 Steiner held his *Agricultural Course* from June 7 to 17, 1924, in Koberwitz, where he laid the

foundations for a new and conscious relationship to Earth Mother through the spiritually based form of agriculture known as the biodynamic method.

the conference. If we take also consider the next section, regarding the elliptical orbit of the Earth, the Tree of Life aspect appears before our eyes, giving an additional emphasis to the extroverted approach of the soul in this direct phase of Pluto.

Not by chance, key themes also came up in conversations with Johanna von Keyserlingk—for example, regarding Shambhala and Sirius, which can give indications for the further deepening into the mystery of the Christmas Conference and Rudolf Steiner.

### The Aphelion–Perihelion Axis of the Earth

Further spiritual points might come into focus if we examine the cosmic background of the Laying of the Foundation Stone. Pluto is in opposition to the Sun every year, but in 1923–24 this opposition took place very close to the axis of the perihelion and aphelion points of the Earth. I quote here two paragraphs from Willi Sucher's *Cosmic Christianity and the Changing Countenance of Cosmology* that can help turn our thoughts to this grand image:

The planets move, according to the heliocentric point of view, around the Sun. They do not move around the Sun in circles but in ellipses. The Sun is in one of the two foci [see the image]. The ellipse is the orbit of the planet. It is overdone in the figure for the sake of demonstration. In some cases, the differences are much smaller. The perihelion is the position where the planet is closest to the Sun, whereas in the opposition it is in the aphelion is the position where it is furthest away from the Sun. This orbit indicates the sphere of the planet.

If we want to come to a deeper comprehension of cosmic events, we must enter an investigation of the spheres. The spheres are contained within the orbit of the planets. With this concept we come closer already to the perception of the cosmos as a living organism. This endeavor is most important just in our time. We know that men have landed on the Moon, and there was much speculation on what this means for our knowledge of the cosmos: How this will affect the Moon, and so forth? However, we must not forget that the Moon is only a reflection. The Moon that we see in the sky is only the visible indicator of the whole invisible sphere contained within the orbit of the Moon. This sphere is the more important element. It is, so to speak, the workshop of divine hierarchies. This is where they work. Thus, for instance, the beings connected with Venus have their workplace, so to speak, in the sphere of Venus. The beings of Mars work in the sphere of Mars, and so forth.

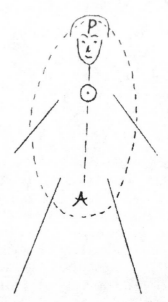

For our work, *it is important to know the difference between perihelion and aphelion. They are deeply connected with what was introduced into the universe and evolution around the time of the Fall in Paradise.* Before the Fall, the cosmos was, so to speak, an integrated whole, and human beings lived in this wholeness. At the moment of the Fall, humanity came apart. On the one hand the head forces developed. In other words, humanity "ate from the Tree of Knowledge." It is really the Tree of Knowledge that grows into the body. We need only to imagine the central nervous system, the brain as the root system of that Tree and the nerves that spread like branches into the whole body. One thing was then withheld from humanity: the Tree of Life, which is the opposite, the other polarity, of the human form that then developed. If we imagine the heart and the arteries going out from the heart, we have a picture of the Tree of Life, which spreads through the organism against the Tree of Knowledge, the Tree of the nerves. Actually, the human form was thus distorted. The gods had created it differently.

*This polarity was even introduced into the life of the spheres of the planets. Somehow all the spheres of the planets are involved in this.* We recall again, for instance, the workings of Saturn—Saturn forming the skeleton. Here we can quite clearly get an impression of the polarity. On the one hand, the skull is built by Saturn to enclose the brain. And on the other hand, the skeleton of the limbs supports the muscular substance and so forth from within. This is connected with the stage of evolution around the time of the Fall. Thus, we can say that *at the perihelion the planetary sphere is really integrated into our solar system. The spiritual beings who are connected with the perihelion within a particular sphere are interested in this solar system.* They combine with it; they identify themselves with it. In other words, we have something like the cosmic equivalent of a head [fig. 1.3]. It is an activity, somewhat faintly similar on a cosmic level with what otherwise every human being does with the head when observation combines with perception. *In the opposite part, at aphelion, the planet and its sphere almost look as though they were intent on going off on a rampage in the greater cosmos.* It expresses at least the tendency for this, whereas at perihelion the Sun would hold it back within the solar system. In a certain sense, an element of stagnation is involved in this polarity; an element, however, that facilitates a certain evolution until such times in the future when a breaking out of this state of stagnation will be necessary.

*The perihelion of the Earth, the point where the Earth comes closest to the Sun in its yearly orbit, is associated with the Fall of man in Paradise.* We have already referred in chapter 1 in detail to the perihelion–aphelion element, or line of apsides, and their manifestation in the human form. *As a consequence of the Fall, the human being developed a corporeally polaric entity, head and limbs,* and developed into a being that carried within the two trees, *the Tree of Knowledge as his head-formation and the Tree of Life, all that is connected with the metabolism and with the limbs, particularly*

*with the sphere of propagation.* The two poles were separated.[18]

In ordinary astrological research, we are constrained to simplify many aspects of the cosmos. It is enough to think of the circle of the horoscope. We use a circle as a "common denominator" to which we draw the planets (from "inside") and the zodiacal signs (from "outside"). The planets and the stars of the constellations are shown as if they were in equal distances from us (or from the Sun heliocentrically). In addition, they are drawn onto a two-dimensional plane and are arranged in the form of a circle. On the one hand, it is a necessity for our mind to determine a certain framework if we would like to detect and express the various lines of forces that can meet in different points in the cosmos and have an influence on us; however, this process of casting horoscopes of any kind often does not help, or even hinders our imaginations and evolutionary thinking as we do not ponder the subtle details *lost* in the process, taking the components of the charts as "absolute" things whereby the final products become points of departure.

Although in nature (in the universe), there are no such things as a *perfect* circle or a *perfect* ellipse, as they are mathematical forms, yet it is necessary to take into account the elliptical orbit of the planets and differentiate the properties of the ellipse from those of the circle in certain astrological researches to get closer to understanding human evolution (either for humanity as a whole or for individualities). In the field of contemporary astrology (I mean, in the previous three to four or even more decades), this issue and viewpoint of observation has come to the surface, and many astrologers began to research the elements of the ellipses of the planets, though I think not always with a sound spiritual background, such as Willi Sucher had, and (as far as I know) only regarding the orbit of the Moon (Black Moon Lilith) and the orbit of the Earth (Black Sun). Nevertheless, this approach could emerge into the *unlight*, and astrological literature evidently indicates a growing interest in this direction.[19]

---

18 Sucher, *Cosmic Christianity*, pp. 144–146, 186–187.

19 See for example a long chapter regarding Lilith

Willi Sucher, the first pioneer of astrosophy in the twentieth century, already in the 1960s strongly emphasized the importance of this viewpoint in studying *Cosmic Christianity,* saying, for example, in connection with Saturn's crossing the perihelion of Venus, that "this is one of the most important aspects of the story, and this can give also an idea, how one can combine, how one can make the geocentric and the heliocentric cooperate."[20] He called attention to the fact, in relation to the "Three years" of the Christ events, that "Saturn moved through the cosmic expression, the perihelion of the Impulse of Love [the 'head part' of the sphere of Venus] with regard to all future Earth evolution," adding, "It is really that impulse of love and compassion, communication with all existing things, that was introduced and practiced by true Christianity."[21]

Elsewhere, in another context, in harmony with the longer quotation, he also points out that the polarity of the head and body of the human organism is not a product of freak development, but it's a reflection of great cosmic stages of evolution.

Thus, the perihelion can be regarded as "head" of a planetary sphere, where one is more inclined to "contemplate" and adopt the affairs of the solar universe as its own, like the head organism of a human body receives the facts existent in its environment through perception. The aphelion of the sphere, distantly akin to the will in the limbs of our body, aims at developments and goals "outside" the "status quo" of the solar world.[22]

Nevertheless, it seems still quite difficult to determine the meaning of the apsides. It can be said that the polarity of the planet as a body, and the sphere as a field of energy, ensures the *possibility* of evolution. The planet as the representative of matter attempts to retain the material–physical in its present condition and to conserve and perpetuate the present; the sphere as the representative of forces of universal progress is inclined to transform substances and provides planetary movement—the foundation of time—to ensure evolution through constant change. The two great cosmic principles hold a balance against each other and in this way provide the basis for standard existence in the solar system. Within this wider context, the points of the line of the apsides ensure the *dynamics* of evolution, which is a particular setting of necessity (for a while). At the apsides, a particular shift comes into being in the cosmic balance, as if a breaking out of the balance would be possible toward conditions *beyond space and time.* As this shift is due to a kind of "inner change" in the realm of the sphere—i.e., in the realm of the spirit—the manifestations of the encounters of the apsides and planets in themselves (without alignments with Nodes or Solstices and Equinoxes) are generally more likely on the spiritual–thought level than on the material side of existence (e.g., in the form of natural catastrophes). Contemporary astrological literature also recognizes these dynamics and associates the encounters with this shift with a movement between earthly consciousness and cosmic consciousness, lower level of consciousness and a higher level of consciousness, cultural knowledge and supra-cultural knowledge. It is certainly still a question (among others) how we can regard the two focal points in the given sphere in relation with the human being. What can be the relevance of the "empty" focal point of the elliptical orbit, even though it seems to have no physical significance regarding the phenomenon of orbiting? And how can human beings regard (find the seeds of evolution of) their own corporeally polaric entity

and the Black Sun in a contemporary astrologer's book: Sebastian van Wingerden, *The Northern Moon Node: The Message from the Beyond.* The studies regarding Lilith are more widespread worldwide; the studies regarding the Black Sun are more limited to astrologers working in France and the Netherlands. The research was begun in France by Dom Néroman and later by Jean Carteret. "Black Sun" is an expression that characterizes the Sun in its farthest position from the Earth, as a "cosmic Sun," a "transparent Sun," or a "black Sun," as a distinctive character of the Sun in the imagination of astrologers.

20 Sucher, *Cosmic Christianity*, p. 144.

21 Ibid., p. 147. It should be noted that Willi Sucher used the elongated line of apsides of the planets, which reach the spheres of the more outer planets.

22 Sucher, "Practical Approach II": *Star Journal 11*

(2006), p. 122. Sucher referred to the apsides sometimes as a head–limb polarity, sometimes as a head–body polarity; in the latter case, he interpreted the region of the heart as part of the "body."

in connection with their evolution toward a *non-material existence* in the future?

Sucher indicated two "elements," two spiritual point-pairs, whereby he perceived life in the big machine of the Copernican system. These were the Nodes and the line of the apsides of the planets. Although both of them point to evolution owing to the shift of the Nodes and the Apsidal lines, pointing gradually to different stellar directions, their meaning is different. In the case of the apsides, it is not the *communication within the spheres* by a planet that promotes this evolution, as in the case of the Nodes, but instead a planet *enters the dynamics of a sphere* (*mentioned above*), where it seems that the strongest manifestation of the principle of the polarity of spirit and matter serves as a driving force of evolution. Remaining with the Sun–Earth context, the Sun and Earth creates a plane, the sphere of the Earth, to which planets can enter *at different points* (in the Nodes). *Within* this plane, there is an additional relationship of the Sun and Earth along the line of the apsides, which can be crossed by the planets *only at two points*.[23] Therefore, in this sense, it is a more special perspective, where, furthermore, it is as if an additional element would be perceivable in the special "empty" point: a "sphere" within the sphere. [24]

It is not by chance, that Willi Sucher referred to this line (and not to the Nodes) when he described the evolution of the Earth and humankind in the context of the streams in the planetary system from the periphery toward the Sun, which is featured by densification of sidereal ingredients progressing toward the Earth, and dissolution and spiritualization of matter progressing from the Earth toward the Sun (he called this the *solar process*). He said,

> On the Earth, we can, standing between the impacts of physical–material creation and dissolution, develop ego ["I"]-consciousness.

---

23 We speak of the elongated ecliptic plane and the elongated line of apsides.

24 Obviously, the theme of the apsides and the Nodes would require another article. Briefly and generally, I perceive the occurrences regarding the apsides as the *core-events* of evolution and the occurrences regarding the Nodes as elements of the *wider framework* of evolution. In the case of the apsides, only *one* sphere is directly involved and the primary aim seems to be the *individual evolution* of the given sphere; in case of the Nodes, always *two* spheres are directly involved and the primary aim is *mutual evolution* of the spheres executed by the interactions (exchange of impulses) within the spheres, which encounters eventually lead to the permeation of the whole solar system. (The planet itself is meant as a body and not as a sphere in this context.)

In the whole evolution of our solar system it is obviously the Earth that is in our focus and the question is: How can any occurrences in the planetary system make themselves felt on the Earth? I think that the "structural encounters" in

themselves (the encounters of the Apsidal and Nodal lines of the planets), the interplanetary relations (when a planet enters the apsides of another planet or the Node of another planet—the Node within spheres not including the Earth), and a part of the planet–Earth relations (when a planet enters its own apsides) are in quite *indirect* relation with the Earth where the *projection* is very stressed and the relation affects the plane of the Earth *generally*. In case of the other part of the planet–Earth relations (when the planet enters the apsides of the Earth or the Node of another planet), despite the still existing projection, the relation with the Earth seems *more direct*. (This is the case for the Christmas Conference, where Pluto was around the apsides of the Earth.) And when a planet enters its own Node we can speak about the *most direct* relation. Theoretically, the more direct a relation is with the Earth, the stronger and more perceptible the effects should be. However, practically, it is impossible to concretize the precise extent or expression of the effects of these encounters.

If we go beyond the planetary relations (inward) and arrive at the core relation of Sun and Earth, the encounters of the apsides of the Earth and the points of the Solstices and Equinoxes represent the *most direct* relations, where it seems that extreme manifestations appear penetrating to the depths of our material–spiritual existence. Such events are connected with the great geographical changes of the Earth (e.g., the destruction of Atlantis by the Flood)—as Elisabeth Vreede and Willi Sucher wrote, continuing the thoughts of Rudolf Steiner. These researches appear very interesting as this most intimate relation of Sun and Earth gets into close contact *purely* with the *world of the stars* (i.e., not involving any other planet) through the shift of the apsides and through the precession of the Equinoxes, probably carrying all the consequences of the interactions within the solar system (including human activity) into the crucial points of the encounters.

Through the activity of this ego, working through thinking, feeling, and willing, we will eventually be able to lift up external creation to a level where it becomes power of spiritual creation. In that moment, when this will have been achieved, the Earth will have fulfilled its task. This present universe will dissolve, and evolution will move on to the next stage, to future Jupiter. Future Jupiter will no longer consist of physical–material substance.[25]

After describing the solar process through the spheres of the planets he arrived at the Sun–Earth relation in the same chapter:

> The planet Earth is the qualitative center of the sphere of the Sun. There the highest degree of densification and the inauguration of the dissolution take place. Thus, we can see in the "elements" of the Earth orbit an indication of the life of the Sun sphere. These are the perihelion and aphelion of the Earth. *This means that we can see in the line of the apsides of our planet an expression of potentials toward realizing and lifting up to "I"-experience what is inaugurated by the sphere of Saturn as cosmic–psychic challenge.*[26]

Willi Sucher concentrated here on human evolution starting with the sphere of Saturn and leading to three-dimensional forms. He associated Saturn with a portal where sidereal substances enter first in a cosmic–psychic astral form and where a process of densification of these substances begins progressing toward the Earth. He regarded the spheres of the trans-Saturnian planets as "bystanders" who try to speak to the human being about the spiritual worlds of the divine hierarchies, of all that is of absolutely non-material, even nonspatial, nature. These spiritual spheres bring human beings to a realization of the spiritual origin of all beings. He speaks of sidereal substances that are in an even *higher spiritual–archetypal* form. I think it is precisely these substances in higher, spiritual–archetypal forms that helped to carry out the Christmas Conference and can help in understanding in

its wholeness. These higher spiritual substances can ensure the lifting of human consciousness to understanding our place in the divine hierarchies, and thereby toward beginning the task of transformation. These higher spiritual substances have to permeate human consciousness so that we can transform our astral body eventually into manas as progress toward Jupiter existence. Clearly, part of the trans-Saturnian spiritual substances cannot be inaugurated as a cosmic–psychic challenge, and they do not take part in the process of densification, but remain as a *cosmic–spiritual challenge* as they relate to the higher human bodies that do not densify into matter in the human being. These substances can enter human *cosmic-"I"* experience. From that experience, they can then work through the astral body in a positive sense—generally with the help of our relationship with the Sun.

Perhaps the reader thinks that the questions regarding the elements of the ellipses here, and that the study of the direct–retrograde movements (i.e., the loops) in the other section of the article are out of date, since Rudolf Steiner explained the movements of the planets as lemniscatory movements. According to my present knowledge, it seems that the lemniscatory movements are like a "superimposed layer" on the "existing layer" of the Copernican–Keplerian system, the latter of which does not lose its validity, either in astronomy or in the reflection in our consciousness. The movements in the ellipses and the loops can represent a *strong dynamic* as an "outside frame" into which the lemniscatory system brings *balance and harmony*. The complexity of these lemniscatory movements of the planets brings peace finally into the ellipses, which otherwise draw us in two directions regarding our consciousness dynamics, and to the loops, which again and again lead us toward new physical–spiritual experiences reflected in the directions of our soul life. Lemniscates draw us toward a *central point* within the figure-eight shape, while keeping the principle of evolution—i.e., never closing the figure (nor in the case of seeing from above, projected to a two-dimensional plane).

25 Sucher, *Cosmic Christianity*, pp. 99–100.
26 Ibid., p. 106.

Similarly, an ellipse never closes itself (which can be seen in the shift of the Nodes), and the loops never close themselves (which is an essential feature of them not to turn back to their "starting points"). Remaining with the elements of the ellipses here, it seems a necessity that the focal points of the ellipses give weight to the lemniscatory system, thus modifying either the speed of the heavenly bodies or the distances of their paths (or both of them), thus distorting either the constancy/uniformity of the dynamics within the lemniscates or the symmetry of the lemniscates (or both of them). The Copernican–Keplerian system and the lemniscatory system exist together as reality, nevertheless it must have great significance that Rudolf Steiner introduced the knowledge of the lemniscatory movements at that particular time into the development of consciousness.[27]

Turning to the Christmas Conference and continuing on the basis of the elliptical movement: The Earth revolves around the Sun, loses speed as it orbits away from the Sun, turns around and falls back toward the Sun. We can imagine the Earth as approaching slowly the farthest point from the Sun, which, according to Willi Sucher, the representative of the Tree of Life is the farthest point from that associated with the Tree of Knowledge.

On July 3, 1923, in close proximity to the perihelion–aphelion axis,[28] Earth was farthest from the Sun, while the Sun and Pluto conjoined, and a "seed period" as a cycle of activity began in their relationship (taking into account the direct and retrograde movements of Pluto).

During the next half-year, the Earth came into contact with Sirius through Pluto and eventually approached the position exactly between the Sun and Pluto on January 3, 1924, during the Christmas Conference. At that time, the Earth was standing between the two farthest astrologically accepted celestial bodies in our solar system (Pluto and the Sun), experiencing the greatest span that can occur in our solar system, which can mean the greatest inner tension in human beings and the expansion of consciousness. Additionally, the Earth was at its closest approach to the Sun, which gives an additional "color" to this span.

When Pluto and the Sun were in conjunction, the Sun was in the background becoming more star-like than Sun-like, and the greater cosmos came into the fore from the viewpoint of the Earth. When Pluto and the Sun were in opposition, the Earth took on the perihelion position and the Sun came to the fore while the greater cosmos went into the background from the viewpoint of the Earth—from the perspective of the Sun–Earth ellipse.

We can assume that the occupied focal point represents the culture, the culture of the material world, where "spiritual beings combine with it, identify themselves with it" (Sucher), and being close to this point (perihelion or close to perihelion) is to be at a level of consciousness associated with this present culture. The empty focal point may represent spiritual forces that pull people's consciousness to a higher level—generally speaking. Being close to the Sun means being close to our present culture. Being farther away from the Sun opens the possibility to receive impulses from spiritual forces who may serve a higher cosmic purpose. These higher elements of consciousness can be absorbed around aphelion and introduced

---

27 The further elaboration of these considerations would lead out from the main scope of this article on the one hand, and would require greater understanding and experience from me on the other hand. I recommend an interesting study to the reader for further investigations: Roland Schrapp: *The Lemniscatory Path System*, finalized in 2012 and appearing in parts in the German Journal *Jupiter* of the Anthroposophical Society in Dornach. Full text is at www.rolandschrapp.de/lemniskaten.html.

28 There is a slight change in the aphelion–perihelion points each year. "Dates change over time due to precession and other orbital factors, which follow cyclical patterns known as Milankovitch cycles. *In the short term, the dates of perihelion and aphelion can vary up to 2 days from one year to another*[13]. This significant variation is due to the presence of the Moon: while the Earth–Moon barycenter is moving on a stable orbit around the Sun, the position of the Earth's center, which is on average about 4,700 km (2,920 mi) from the barycenter, could be shifted in any direction from it—and this affects the timing of the actual closest approach between the Sun's and the Earth's centers (which in turn defines the timing of perihelion in a given year)" (https://en.wikipedia.org/wiki/Apsis).

later around perihelion into earthly culture.[29] If we take into account the unique dynamic constellations with Pluto and Sirius at the time of the Christmas Conference, it can be assumed that the Sirian influence was added from the greater cosmos to this transmission to earthly culture (Pluto turned retrograde within the region of the Sirius-meridian on Oct. 14, 1923).

Perhaps we can say that Rudolf Steiner and his students were standing under the impacts of such dynamic celestial constellations that could help the introduction of a next phase of Earth evolution: they could help to lift to cosmic "I"-experience the cosmic–spiritual challenge, or spiritual knowledge, that originates in Sirius. The situation could be a very favorable time–space constellation to experience the evolutionary step toward a new existence. The main target of the Foundation Stone was the heart of the students, but the initiation had to have its way through the head, so that they could *consciously* grasp the lines of "The Foundation Stone Meditation," and to establish a foundation for a society and a central building as its home in earthly circumstances.

This introduction also means an opening to other cosmic forces *beyond* the 12 zodiacal forces (like Sirius). Implanting the dodecahedron of, and for, the 12 zodiacal forces into the hearts of the students brought about a widening of the horizon toward the whole starry world. This is partly because the outer became inner, and in this way human beings found themselves in a greater outer world; and partly because the 12 zodiacal constellations can better serve with this focused action as transmitters of other cosmic forces of stars, which now can be consciously felt and responded to by human beings after absorbing the Foundation Stone. It is also remarkable that the dodecahedron is a three-dimensional form (and is not a ring or circle), which may mean an opening also toward multidimensionality (multidimensional structures of the universe that contain our spatial universe),

for which the 12 signs of the zodiac can represent focal points.

The exact opposition between Pluto and the Sun occurred on January 3, 1924, 12:25 a.m., in Dornach, with Pluto at 17°38' Gemini and Sun at 17°38' Sagittarius. The Earth reached its perihelion on January 2, 1924, 2:53 a.m., in Dornach, with the Sun at 16°44' Sagittarius.[30] Pluto reached the last perihelion-point of Earth (where the Sun was at 17°54' Sagittarius one year earlier on January 2, 1923), on December 21, 1923, geocentrically and on March 25, 1924, heliocentrically. As can be seen, these events did not occur exactly on the days of the Christmas Conference, but were in a close approximation. The Conference itself took place over the course of a week; therefore, other transits, and the importance of Christmas and the Holy Nights themselves, had an impact on Rudolf Steiner choosing the days from December 25 to January 1 for the Conference. It would divert from the main theme to elaborate fully how forces come into operation and manifest themselves one or two weeks earlier than their exact alignments. However, it probably would not necessarily have been more potent in a spiritual sense if the Earth had reached the Pluto–Earth–Sun–perihelion–aphelion axis on December 25, in which case the whole Conference would have occurred *after* the turn of the Earth on its way away from the Sun.

The Earth reaches perihelion (and aphelion) on different days each year, therefore there can be a plus or minus 1 to 2° difference in the Sun's positions in the zodiac year by year. It does not matter too much in the case of the Sun–Earth relation, but in taking into account Pluto's alignment with this axis, it is quite difficult to determine an exact date. I used the latest perihelion point (valid for January 2, 1923), as it was the latest day when the Earth reached this point—taking into account the possible interactions between the planets.

Regarding Sirius, at the Christmas Conference the elongated perihelion was not in exact conjunction with the meridian of Sirius, but it was in close alignment with the Pluto–Earth–Sun line that

---

29 "If there are conjunctions with the Black Sun, friction with culture ensues, because the planet or point that makes this conjunction has been designed to manifest itself" (van Wingerden, *The Northern Moon Node*, p. 49).

30 http://cococubed.asu.edu/data/perihelion_earth.dat.

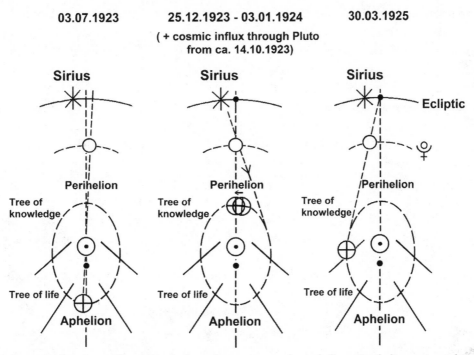

*Figure 3. Schematic drawings. Pluto–Earth–Sun alignments at the Aphelion–Perihelion axis within 2°20' orb (July 3, 1923) and within 1°44' orb (Jan. 3, 1924) of the ecliptic meridian of Sirius. The dashed arrow indicates the encounter with Sirius through Pluto. The situation for the date of Rudolf Steiner's death is also included.*

planetary cooperation I propose took part in the transmitting of the Sirian forces toward humanity.

Again, the Earth reaches perihelion and aphelion once *each* year and Pluto is in conjunction and in opposition with the Sun once *each* year. However, *considering both perspectives, it is only once in approximately 248 years that the Pluto–Sun conjunction/opposition takes place at the perihelion–aphelion axis, with Pluto in conjunction with the elongated perihelion position of the Earth; and as the perihelion–aphelion axis and the position of Sirius are gradually shifting, it is in a much longer time that this conjunction can take place (if it can at all) in the same relation with Sirius (in close conjunction with the meridian of Sirius).* This is why it is worthwhile to examine this situation regarding the Laying of the Foundation Stone.

The next remarkable year—from this perspective—is 2014. On the one hand Pluto reached the aphelion of the Earth and was in opposition with the Sun on July 4, 2014 (Pluto being at 17°21' Sagittarius and Sun being at 17°00' Gemini at the time of the exact aphelion). On the other hand, Pluto

was for the first time in sidereal opposition to its own place at the Christmas Conference, Koberwitz, and Rudolf Steiner's death on February 12, 2014 (at 17°43' Sagittarius in direct motion) and on June 20, 2014 (at 17°43' Sagittarius in retrograde motion), looking at the cosmic "memories" from the other side of the zodiac.[31]

It is also remarkable that at the time of Christ, Pluto turned to retrograde motion on March 17 AD 33 and the entry of Jesus Christ into Jerusalem occurred on March 19 AD 33, when Pluto was at 17°20' Sagittarius. This way, in 2014, through being at 17° Sagittarius, Pluto entered into contact both with the cosmic "memory" of the beginning

---

31 It is also worthwhile pondering that in the year of the exact opposition of Pluto and Sirius (2015), the first photo of Pluto was taken by NASA's New Horizons spacecraft (on July 14, 2015) during its closest approach to the planet. (On July 14, 2015 there was only 12' difference from the exact *opposition* of Pluto and Sirius, and only 7 days difference from the exact *conjunction* of Sirius and the Sun at the perihelion-aphelion axis of the Earth. At the time of the Earth's exact aphelion position on July 6, 2015, the Sun was at 19°26' Gemini, Pluto was at 19°18' Sagittarius and Sirius was at 19°21' Gemini.)

of the most decisive Christ events and beginning of the event of the Christmas Conference—in conjunction and in opposition, respectively.[32]

From the perspective of the apsides it is very important that 2014 was the *first* year that Pluto initially crossed the elongated aphelion of the Earth after its discovery in 1930—i.e., *after it appeared in our consciousness*. The Plutonic forces now should more easily contribute to our expansion to spiritual–cosmic dimensions to understand the place of the Laying of the Foundation Stone and the coming of Christ and of Sophia *in the largest contexts*, if we believe that the aphelion of the Earth is in connection with the "greater, apocalyptic implications of cosmic evolution, beyond the mere temporal solar setting,"[33] that is reaching to remote times when the Sun and the Moon were or will be in unity with the Earth, and we do not speak about their ellipses or lemniscates, or at least to the times of the Fall when the Earth was in a central position and to the times when it will be again in a central position in the cosmos. If both the whole dynamics of the apsides and the loss of the central position of the Earth originates in the Fall, and if the aphelion is in connection with a cosmic evolution that has the tendency to leave the present solar system, at least the present "setting" of the solar system, Pluto in and around the aphelion has to show in our esoteric Christian evolution *further steps regarding the identification with the Christ event* to heal the Fall, and show the way toward the establishing the rightful position of the Earth in the cosmos.

Thinking in the head–limb polarity, Rudolf Steiner gave the Foundation Stone when Pluto was at the perihelion of the Earth, that is, Pluto promoted the evolution of the head. It means that we speak not only of the "culture" where the physical traces (like a society or a building) can preserve and maintain an impulse, but of the introducing of a *type of thinking* in the evolution of consciousness. We call it *intuitive thinking* through the development of moral imagination, which is based on the expansion of consciousness and its orientation toward the spiritual world, while it requires carrying the thought streams through the heart. Steiner indicated the way for the head—how it can find life through a new type of thinking and how this thinking can lead the Earth and humankind, along spiritual creation, closer to its central position, eventually to become a new Sun-center of the universe.

Now, when we live in the opposite segment, symbolically in connection with the Tree of Life, we can have access also to the works of other spiritual teachers since Steiner, who deepened the way that was started by him. They further interwove and drew the link closer between the head and limb elements of our being through the *heart*, pumping additional wisdom through the web of veins to the last cells in the *periphery* of our body. If we think of *sacred eurythmy*, or *Choreocosmos*, we see the limbs in a spiritualizing process, raising the whole body to the edge of the physical and spiritual worlds, so to speak. The Foundation Stone went through the head to the heart to reach the limbs and reproduction system, whose function should finally be lifted to the capacity of spiritual creation. Around 2014 onward, the focus is on the limbs in the process—from the perspective of Pluto and the line of the apsides.

Remaining with the perspective of the evolution of the head forces, it is also an interesting viewpoint how this evolution receives stellar forces during longer periods of time as the perihelion gradually shifts through the zodiac. Willi Sucher called attention to Abraham, in whom the first traces of *independent thinking* (or brain-bound thinking of the intellect) had awakened around the time when the perihelion of the Earth entered from Taurus to Gemini, saying,

> The earthly Twin, our mortality, was on the
> road of emancipating its intelligence from the

---

32 At the time of the Christ events, at the last perihelion on Dec. 3 AD 32, the Sun was at 12°45' Sagittarius and at the next aphelion on June 3 AD 33, was at 12°25' Gemini. Earlier, from the Baptism of Jesus Christ, Pluto went through in close conjunctions the actual yearly aphelions of the Earth, starting its path from 6°54' Sagittarius on Sept. 23 AD 29 (http://cococubed.asu.edu/data /perihelion_earth.dat and http://cococubed.asu.edu /data/aphelion_earth.dat).

33 Sucher, *Star Journal II*, p. 122.

heavenly Twin, the old cosmic intelligence, which humanity of old had received as a gift in a state of dependence.... However...as much as we needed the development of spiritual freedom, so much was there also the danger of carrying emancipation too far.... There is the possibility that we completely separate from the course of divine evolution.... The perihelion of the Earth is still in Gemini...the final crisis, with regard to the destiny of the human intellect will come when the perihelion of the Earth will have entered the constellation of Cancer. Cancer, if it is not met by us with the power of the Christ Impulse of Love, becomes the cosmic expression of the abyss of utter destruction and oblivion.[34]

It seems that, when the perihelion reached the stellar forces of Sirius within Gemini, Rudolf Steiner inaugurated the Christ impulse of Love into the human intellect, culminating in the Laying of the Foundation Stone when Pluto entered the interplay of the approaching points or axes (perihelion progressing toward Cancer and Sirius-meridian regressing toward Taurus).

However, a few points are surely important to mention here. Willi Sucher did not use the same frames of the sidereal signs that Robert Powell introduced later into Western astrology; therefore, his intentions must be handled with attention. The sidereal apsidal precession amounts to about 110,000 years, according to present-day astronomy. It means that it takes about 9,200 years for the Apsidal line to go through one zodiacal sign. According to my calculations, it did not enter Gemini but was about 5° Gemini at the time of Abraham (2100-2000 BC) since Sucher positioned the start of the constellation of Gemini about 5° later than the real start of the sidereal sign of Gemini. He mentions elsewhere the beginning of Kali Yuga regarding this issue. According to my calculations, at the beginning of Kali Yuga the perihelion was around 2° Gemini.

Another point is that not only the gradual shift of the axis is slow, but also the oscillation mentioned earlier can cause variations between close degrees, even for longer periods of time. This way

the line of the apsides is also in a close orb of the meridian of Sirius in ± 248 years (or even more) to 1923–24, this way the Pluto–Sun–Earth–aphelion–perihelion–Sirius–meridian alignment occurs at least three times in a millennium. How we regard the orb of the meridian of Sirius, what we consider important in this orb, depends on our "sensitivity" (approaching the meridian or being exactly at the meridian), as well as how we handle the oscillation of the axis (for example by calculating "mean values" to see a gradual shift). It is also interesting to see that the perihelion–aphelion axis moves toward Cancer, but the position of the meridian of Sirius moves toward Taurus. According to astronomical data the first *exact* encounter of the aphelion–perihelion with the meridian of Sirius occurs *between* the Christmas Conference (1923–1924) and 2171 to 2172 (remaining with the alignments of the perihelion with Pluto).[35] The first occasion that, remarkably, the perihelion approached the meridian of Sirius was on January 4, 1903 (perihelion at 19°06' Gemini and Sirius at 19°22' Gemini), and the first time it had already intersected it was on January 4, 1952 (perihelion at 19°23' Gemini and Sirius at 19°21' Gemini).[36]

In the following schematic drawing (page 62), I try to demonstrate different positions of Pluto, within Gemini and Sagittarius, for the last 248 years.

Pluto completed seven cycles since AD 33 and arrived then at the perihelion of the Earth in 1923. Completing its eighth cycle, it arrived again at the aphelion of the Earth in 2014. In my view, the forces of the Pluto sphere produced a linkage between the "initiations of the Earth," the First and the Second Coming of Christ, and they promote further steps on the path of initiation of

---

34 Ibid., p. 123.

35 On Jan. 7, 2172, the Earth's perihelion position will be at 19°28' Gemini while the meridian of Sirius intersects the ecliptic at 19°19' Gemini. Although they will be very close, earlier they will have entered a period of moving away from each other.

36 According to Sebastian van Wingerden, for example, "this conjunction [Sirius and the perihelion point of the Earth] began around 1945 and it will end in 2085. This conjunction has an enormous impact upon the collective world consciousness." *The Northern Moon Node*, p. 50.

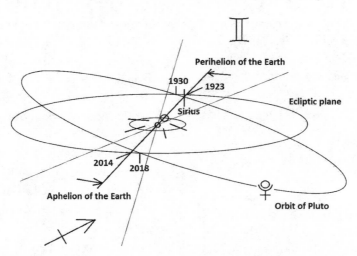

*Figure 4. Schematic drawing of Pluto's movement for one cycle.*
*The elongated line of the apsides of the Earth and a part of the meridian of Sirius are indicated.*

humanity after the Christmas Conference, *now as participants of our consciousness,* since Pluto was discovered in 1930. In this respect, as having been raised to our consciousness, Pluto's first encounter with the line of the apsides occurred in 2014, which must also mean that we *can* and *must* now take *more conscious steps* in making *right* connections with the beings of the Pluto sphere who can help our way on the path toward Shambhala in the depths of the Earth and toward the remote realms of the stellar cosmos.[37]

In a sense a kind of scissors closed in the cosmic space during the 20th century. If we interpret the Sirian meridian as an axis reaching from

---

37 It would lead out of the scope of this study to elaborate my thoughts on the COVID-19 coronavirus epidemic, which is a significant event regarding the sphere of Pluto. However, I would like to call attention here to the end of Oct. 2018, when Pluto crossed the ecliptic in its South Node viewed from the Earth, which I also marked on the diagram. I am convinced that, as beings of the Pluto sphere also have great affinity to evil forces, the *communication* of the Pluto sphere and Earth sphere in the Node had a trigger effect on the dark events afterward. Sucher says in the conclusion to *The Drama of the Universe* (p. 180) regarding the Nodes: "If planets step into these nodes, it appears as a rule that cosmic energy is precipitated into matter." It seems that in this "Plutonic case" virus material appeared in the invisible material field—hypothetically, as a consequence of the longer interplay of humanity and this sphere. (Pluto in its South Node in Sagittarius also may point in a dramatic way to the improper employment of the cosmic forces of the half-human and half-animal Sagittarius–Centaur, who is aiming at individualization and freedom—i.e., the development of the human

"I.") As we know, the illness affects especially the lungs–heart system of those who catch it, yet it is important how the epidemic restricts the *limbs* of *everybody* ("Stay at home!"), suggesting the image of Pluto still around the aphelion position of the Earth. And if we take into account the image regarding the aphelion, where the planets can get into contact with realms beyond the "present solar setting," it is also possible that beings appeared in the "gate" who connect us with other phases of cosmic evolution.

The picture might be widened, as it happens in an extremely large period of time when Saturn can also step in Pluto's South Node within one year after Pluto. Saturn stepped in Pluto's Node on Oct. 28, 2019, heliocentrically ushering the events further. I think that the crossings of Pluto's Node by Pluto and then Saturn is the *crucial hidden factor* behind the events—from an astrological viewpoint.

It is also necessary to consider that on June 17, 1924 (12:00 a.m.), at the *beginning* of a new connection with Earth Mother (in Koberwitz), Mars was in Pluto's South Node heliocentrically within 1° orb (at 24°43' Sagittarius). Mars was around the aphelion of the Earth and in exact opposition with Pluto on June 6, 1924, and it reached exactly the South Node of Pluto on June 18, 1924. It is as if through Mars, Steiner put the sword of Michael into the "soil" of the cosmos, into a gap, or niche, where the sphere of Pluto and the sphere of the Earth encounter each other. Now Pluto, as an "executor," raises the question: How has this enriched "soil" been prepared and cultivated by generations of humanity since then?

Gemini to Sagittarius, the two axes (line of the apsides and Sirius) entered into exact conjunction, which should mean a cosmic turning point in our spiritual history. These axes were also in a wide orb at the time of the First Coming, but the orb decreased to zero at the time of the beginning of the Second Coming.

In my image, the fuller meaning of the First Coming could enter the consciousness soul through Steiner by bringing the Fifth Gospel from the radiating field of Sirius as an echo of the four historical Gospels, and I think he could proclaim the Second Coming of Christ, mainly with the help of Sirian forces. Then our knowledge was deepened and is deepening by the guidance of the other great spiritual teachers, who I think also had and still have Sirian connections—i.e., they are committed to the work of the spiritual beings belonging to Sirius. The "scissors shut" during the first half of the century, in which period the time of the Laying of the Foundation Stone is most remarkable in the physical–spiritual world if we attribute great significance to the position of Pluto. Maybe we can say that it is the central point of this "closed state."

After this cosmic Turning Point of Time, a new phase began, with the scissors very slowly opening, in which the Second Coming of Christ is the most important ongoing event, and with which we should *identify ourselves* in order to be able to face the onslaughts of the evil forces and restore access to the "Lost Paradise" known as Shambhala, and through the redemption and spiritualization of the present Earth finally create a "new Earth" in the universe in the remote future.

In the next part of this study I plan to concentrate on the individuality of Rudolf Steiner and his preparation for the Laying of the Foundation Stone—certainly again from an astrological (or astrosophical) viewpoint. A new element drawn into the picture will be the connection of Rudolf Steiner's embryonic life and actual life, focusing on his "time organism," permeated at certain points with the interplay of forces that then could provide background for the Christmas Conference.

An additional perspective will be the possible influence of a star, Dubhe, which seems to produce links among St. Thomas Aquinas, Rudolf Steiner, and the event of the Laying of the Foundation Stone. Hopefully, the second part can also provide an additional certainty about the significance of the leading participants in the first part (Sirius and Pluto) and can enhance further studies toward a more complex understanding of the possible interplay of stellar forces that could have an important role in the background of the cosmic deed of Rudolf Steiner.

I would like to express my acknowledgements and gratitude to Joel Matthew Park, who allowed me to publish my thoughts here, and who helped the correction of my English writing to make the text more understandable.

---

*A star is above my head.*
*Christ speaks from the star:*
*"Let your soul be borne*
*Through my strong force.*
*I am with you.*
*I am in you.*
*I am for you.*
*I am your 'I.'"*
—RUDOLF STEINER

# THE BELLOWS OF AHRIMAN
## PLUTO REACHES CAPRICORN

### *Julie Humphreys*

*The idea of human freedom is the yardstick against which must be measured everything that human beings meet during this fifth post-Atlantean period. For, were their forces to weaken, this could cause everything to turn out for the worst.[1]*

This year a momentous shift is underway as Pluto enters the zodiacal constellation of Capricorn. As the long, slow orbit of Pluto around the Sun takes 248 years, its return to Capricorn requires that we consider world events, past and present, from the vantage of a goat atop the highest crag; only from this height will we be able to evaluate these events against the backdrop of human evolution.

It was when Pluto last traversed Capricorn (1773–1792) that the American colonists were able to wrest control of their destiny, as they saw it, from the British Crown, which stood at odds with their ideals of personal liberty and limited power of government. An entirely different revolution took place in France roughly fifteen years after the start of the American Revolution in 1775; much of the French Revolution (1789–1799) transpired under Pluto in sidereal Capricorn.

In addition to investigating the possibilities that may be in store for Pluto's return to Capricorn—the completion of a full cycle—we'll be looking at the crucial phases of Pluto during its counter-clockwise movement against the background of the stars of the zodiac between the evolutionary period and the current time: when did Pluto form the first square aspect, the opposition, and the final square aspect in relation to its entry into Capricorn in 1773?

A number of remarkable individualities were born around this time of revolutionary impulses.

The lives of Beethoven (b. 1770), Novalis (b. 1772), Anne Catherine Emmerich (b. 1774), and J. M. W. Turner (b. 1775) are particularly relevant to our theme. Additionally, Goethe (b. 1749) and Mozart (b. 1756) did their most important work during those years.

Pluto rules the underworld and, as such, is the planet of death and rebirth. Because this subterranean kingdom holds precious metals and stones, Pluto was to the Greeks the provider of wealth. In mythology he is known as the violent abductor of Persephone, as well her stern and loving husband (Eleusinian mysteries); in Orphic mythology, as Phanes, he is the deity of new life. He can be seen, then, as the Divine Father of All, whose orbit embraces his beloved creation.

It is through Pluto's influence, which moves like a heat-seeking missile toward *all that lies beneath,* that the dark underbelly is revealed—of the self, community, society, or civilization. Pluto is the individual and collective shadow, and as such its nature is disruptive. Because of this, fear is its hallmark—fear of the unknown, fear of the subconscious, fear of change and upheaval. Fear paralyzes the will; when we give fear entry to our soul and refuse to stand up to it we become the prey of the adversarial beings of the underworld who seek to obscure all the love in our heart, for they know that a heart filled with love allows no room for fear:

> God is love, and he who abides in love abides in God, and God abides in him. In this is love perfected with us, that we may have confidence for the day of judgment, because as he is so are we in this world. There is no fear in love, but perfect love casts out fear. (1 John 4:18)

---

1 Steiner, *Secret Brotherhoods*, p. 165.

Pluto works behind a curtain, influencing our souls in ways we cannot understand without the courage to look behind it—to the dark places where spiders freely spin their webs. When we stand up to fear, Pluto supports our efforts toward inner (and societal) transformation. A representative of the magical agent of fire, it allows us the opportunity to rebuild anew, provided we have established the proper moral foundation for our work. In other words, the metaphoric fires of Pluto can be tended in a conscious way, allowing us to control and direct its revolutionary influences in service of *purification*; alternatively, when we leave the "brush" unattended for too long, Pluto unleashes inevitable forces of destruction that cannot be opposed, much like a brushfire that has raged beyond our control.

Associated with ambition, sex, and violence, Pluto can seek domination over others. As human beings, we stand between the will of the hierarchies above and what lives in the subearthly layers below. Pluto forces us to choose: we are placed before the temptation of will-to-power, compelling us to make it our North Star. Robert Powell explains:

> The phenomenon of atomic power, which can burst forth like a volcanic eruption, gives an external picture of the way Pluto works in the human being. Here the primal life will is at work; cosmic love within the human being can become released, drawing him into union—oneness—with higher beings. On a lower level, this can manifest as erotic sexuality and even as violence (uncontrolled will impulses). The obsession with sex and violence in our culture is a negative aspect of Pluto forces in our time, as the atomic age is on the technological level.[2]

Under the influence of Pluto, we can become obsessed with the will-to-power to such an extent that reason and conscience play no part. By 1930, the year of Pluto's discovery, both Stalin's and Hitler's consolidations of power were well under way. Following that year, the murders committed accelerated at a staggering pace.

How are we to overcome this, when our culture assures us that power and money are its highest priorities? The quest for valuable metals is particularly apt for our theme, because they exist underground, in the realm of Hades. In modern times, some of the most egregious sins of mining are occurring on behalf of *technology* (coltan, worldwide, including Democratic Republic of the Congo [DRC], used in cell phones and other electronic devices), as well as *environmentalism* (cobalt for electric-car batteries, 60 percent of which is in DRC). Exposure to cobalt causes severe health damage, even death. At the time of this writing, 40,000 children are being exploited to mine it—some as young as four years of age.[3] Violence and sexual exploitation are endemic, and yet we hear nothing of this when we are encouraged by governments to "drive electric." Technology has indeed woven a tangled, multinational web.

Will-to-power can be overcome through the practice of the sacred vow of obedience. When the word "obedience" reaches contemporary ears, it is often understood as the subjugation of one's will to another (or to what Rousseau termed the *common will*), but this is not the case. It is, instead, the faculty of knowing and recognizing the *truth*, or spontaneous obedience to God. In obedience, one sets aside the personal will in order to serve. This practice rivets will-to-greatness, or the inclination to usurp what does not belong to one. As for a longing for money, its importance is properly minimized through our loving connections with others and with nature, domains in which one holds no power.

What is the significance of Pluto's movement from Sagittarius to the zodiacal sign of Capricorn? The task of the Archer—half animal, half human—is to overcome our lower instincts by permeating them with the higher faculties of conscience and reason. The Sagittarian arrow demands that we develop a taste for the *truth*, as it is only upon truth that the structures formed under Capricorn will be sound. This is increasingly difficult, as lies

---

2  Powell, *Hermetic Astrology* vol. 2, p. 306.

3  See https://www.dailymail.co.uk/news/article -4764208/Child-miners-aged-four-living-hell-Earth .html.

can be sent electronically 'round the world in an instant. Steiner said, *in 1917*:

> But how, exactly, are we so well informed? With all due respect—as one says nowadays when one intends to say something impolite— with all due respect, it is the press that informs us by disguising the very aspects that are essential, true and real, in other words: the aspects that matter.[4]

The disguises worn by evil (the costume of truth, the costume of empathy, the costume of social conscience—even the costume of environmentalism) are elaborate in detail. But identify them we must, as this is the task of our age. These disguises can fall away before our eyes if we follow the path of the Hermit:

> Then you will understand the role played by the mantle enveloping the Hermit, when he employs his lamp for seeing clearly into particular problems, and when he employs his staff for probing his terrain. The "mantle" is the presence at a deeper level of consciousness of the *whole truth*, and it is this which envelops and inspires all intellectual work relating to particular problems that is carried out by the conscious self with its lamp and staff. [This] sees to it that each solution to each particular problem is in harmony with the whole.[5]

Capricorn supports the continuity of tradition and of evolution. It demands order. The arcanum to which we turn to understand Capricorn is The Star, the "Arcanum of the Mother," or the "Arcanum of Eve."

> This is why the [Star] Card... represents a woman, the maternal principle, between the constellation of hope above her and the flow of continuity of biological life beneath her. Because every mother professes a double faith— the faith of celestial hope that the future will be more glorious than the present and the faith of terrestrial continuity that the flow of succeeding generations will go forward.... In other words, each mother professes—by the very fact that she is a mother—the divine origin of

the world and the divine aim of the world. If it were not so, she would refuse to give birth.[6]

The virtue of courage that streams from the Goat bestows upon humanity the ability to meet and take up our evolutionary tasks on behalf of the future. Capricorn, the earth sign, brings stability and endurance; Capricorn, under the rulership of Saturn, suggests form, structure, and direction; a cardinal sign, Capricorn works particularly on the human will to create firmness, resolve, and perseverance.

Steiner identifies the worldview streaming from the beings that work within the constellation of Capricorn as *spiritism*, or an inclination toward the spirit; the upward climb of a mountain goat helps us understand this, since it is to the mountaintop that we go in search of higher teachings— Mount Sinai, Mount Carmel, The Temple Mount, Mount Attarus, Mount Tabor, or The Mount of Olives. As we climb, we reach toward God and spirit, toward their life-giving waters: *the universal sap of life*. Both the fish's tail of the Sea Goat, (as Capricorn is sometimes depicted) and the watery "L" eurythmy gesture associated with it recall this. Through the influence of its ruler, Saturn, Capricorn bestows an instinctive sense for goodness, truth, and beauty, as the glorious accomplishments of the individualities mentioned. Having scaled the Seven Summits, they descended to bless humanity with all they have seen, heard, and touched.

It is through the forces of Capricorn that our knees and elbows are formed—the joints that allow us flexibility as well as the ability to absorb shock; through the influence of Capricorn, we are able to weather life's blows and work around any obstacles that we find in our way. It is taking up the courage of the Goat that makes this possible. When we bend the knees, it is impossible to lean back, into the past, into fear; bending this way—maintaining flexibility—overcomes the Capricorn tendency to adhere unproductively to the past. The movement of the knees also allows us to *genuflect*—to bow in reverence, in absolute

---

4   Steiner, *Secret Brotherhoods*, p. 72.
5   Anon., *Meditations on the Tarot*, p. 221.

6   Ibid., p. 473.

humility, to what we know to be of higher spiritual authority. The knees *will* bend, either voluntarily or involuntarily.

How does Pluto interpret the forces of Capricorn? While moving before the Goat, Pluto's influences can be channeled into a reasoned, well-planned course that meets the needs of the future—the course of evolution. If we remain flexible, we have the potential to identify missteps, and, with order, lawfulness, and an unbending will, bring about required changes. Capricorn, the disciplinarian of the zodiac, provides firm loving guidance, if only we have the eyes to see it: cosmically mandated restrictions hold spiritual gifts. Pluto in Capricorn says: "I revere God and I serve the future. My actions must be consistent with moral law."

Alternatively, lower Pluto forces combine with those of lower Capricorn to produce the potential for "the hammer to fall" like no other combination. The respect for natural hierarchy, a gift from Capricorn, can be distorted, in the absence of love of God, into lust for power and wealth. Without God, there is no reason to climb to the mountaintop. Fallen Goat forces can inspire cruelty, violence, and a craving for exposing the weakness of others. Pity and mercy are forgotten. When working together in this way, Pluto in Capricorn instills fear, saying, "You are my helpless captive and will do as I demand."

As the bellows of Ahriman works furiously to spread the embers of revolution, will we manage to tend the fire so that constructive, measured transformation is possible, or will we allow it to roar beyond our control, consuming all in its path? The American and French revolutions illustrate these two very different possibilities; as Pluto enters Capricorn this year, they are archetypes for our time. Spiritual evolution, or immolation?

### The American Revolution

As 1770 dawned, troops of the British Crown were still able to maintain discipline despite the dissatisfaction of the colonists. A longing for freedom was growing in the hearts of the colonists, however; they resented the authority of the Crown and the increasingly onerous taxes imposed by it. On March 5 of that year, a mob of Bostonian colonists formed around a soldier of King George III. Eight other soldiers came to his aid. The mob began by hurling snowballs, but soon moved on to clubs and stones, shouting (according to John Adams), "Kill them! Kill them!"[7] The British fired into the mob, resulting in five deaths. The well-known monument to this event now stands in the Boston Common.

It is important to understand that the Massacre did not serve as a rallying cry to the founders. As a lawyer, John Adams defended the *soldiers*, most of whom were acquitted by the American jury, and Paul Revere testified on their behalf. They believed that the Redcoats' attack was justified because they had been set upon by a *mob*. Even though

---

7  McCullough, *John Adams*, pp. 66–68.

they shared the frustrations of that mob, they definitively denounced mob violence as the culprit behind the shootings.

Three years later, colonial rebellion erupted again, this time at Boston Harbor. On December 16, 1773, as the little boy in Germany who would become Beethoven was turning three, chests of imported tea belonging to the East India Company (founded in 1600) were chucked into the harbor in protest of what the rebels deemed to be unfair taxation under the yoke of the Crown. Parliament had recently passed a measure that allowed the Company to sell tea at prices so low that the colonial merchants could not compete. The rebellion resulted in Parliament's closure of the port and martial law.

It would be well into the next century before this event acquired the sheen of respectability that it still carries. Because of the damage to private property—the tea—the founders largely disapproved of it, even though they were sympathetic to the cause, and no injuries had resulted from the protest. Benjamin Franklin was adamant that the lost tea should be paid for; a collection was subsequently taken up.

The First Continental Congress convened in Philadelphia in 1774; not yet convinced of the need to declare their independence, the delegates settled on boycotts intended to limit the reach of the Crown. Half a year later, as colonial discontent continued to grow, the great Virginian lawyer, Patrick Henry, encouraged his fellow patriots to take up arms in their defense, uttering the famous words, "Give me liberty or give me death."

By the time of the first military conflict of the Revolutionary War, which occurred less than a month after Henry's call to arms, Paul Revere had made more than a dozen rides to Philadelphia to bring Congress news of the brewing conflict in Massachusetts. His famous "Midnight Ride," immortalized by Henry Wadsworth Longfellow, alerted the colonists and its Minutemen to the movement of British troops. It was understood that the British sought seizure of American military supplies at Concord, as well as imprisonment of Adams and Hancock. The battles of Lexington and Concord began with what Emerson called "the shot heard round the world." Since then, the cause of the greatly outnumbered Minutemen lives on in the hearts of all oppressed peoples of the world as the archetype of the longing for liberty—and the power of ordinary people to achieve it. Of astrological interest is the position of Mars at this event: conjunct *Regulus*—the heart of Leo, symbol of moral courage, daring, and right action. (Five days later, J. M. W. Turner was born).

Following the colonists' loss at Bunker Hill in June 1775, at which the militia were nonetheless a formidable presence, Congress appointed Washington Commander in Chief. The Declaration of Independence was signed on July 4, 1776, when the Sun, at 21° Gemini, was closely aligned with *Sirius*, the eternal star of Zarathustra—and the star of Isis–Sophia.

The fighters for the fledgling nation then endured quartering at Valley Forge through the brutal winter of 1777–78. Nearly two dozen battles lay before them before it would be over. The Articles of Confederation—the document that first referred to the colonies as the United States of America—were finally ratified by all thirteen colonies on March 1, 1781. In use until the creation of the Constitution, the Articles maintained the sovereignty of the states and denied a central authority the right to tax them. Uranus, the planet of reform, was discovered twelve days later.

The final surrender of the British followed their loss at Yorktown, Virginia, on September 28, 1781. All told, fewer than 40,000 souls were lost during the Revolutionary War, one third of them American. The Treaty of Paris, negotiated by Benjamin Franklin (ambassador to France at the time), as well as John Adams and others, made the British retreat official. It would take another six years before the Constitution of the United States would replace the Articles of Confederation. As the founders signed the Constitution on September 17, 1787, the Sun (at 2° Virgo) stood before the zodiacal degree that was rising at the fulfillment of Christ's mission on Earth; the North Node (9° Sagittarius) on this day in '87 recalled Christ's confrontation with the Antichrist during the 39th day in the wilderness of Attarus.

This article does not address the matter of the personalities and personal failings of the founders, most notably their reliance on slavery as the basis of their economic success. Many revelations have been brought forward recently; the "1619 Project," underway at the time of this writing, is an effort by the *New York Times Magazine* to establish a race-themed narrative of the Revolution. Were the seventy farmers and shopkeepers—ordinary people of uncommon bravery—who opposed more than 700 Redcoats on Lexington Green seeking only to advance personal gain at the expense of others?

It is of undeniable value to seek a deeper understanding of the character of the time, yet important to remember is the danger of viewing events through a single lens, as does, for example, Marxism (the lens of capital—its viewpoint is purely and utterly materialistic). A single lens, used exclusively, distorts human consciousness. All selective viewpoints pose a danger in the form of their inevitable arbitrariness—in this case, its failure to condemn modern slavery, which is still common and thriving in many cultures. Additionally, the limited scope of inquiry risks a total eclipse of the Sophianic impulse that did indeed guide the founders, and of their sincere endeavor to establish laws that were a reflection of divine, moral law. Perhaps this is an underlying motive. Tomberg cautions:

> The death of tradition manifests itself in the degeneration of its constituent elements, which become separated. Then, Hermetic philosophy separated from magic, gnosis and mysticism becomes a parasitic system of autonomous thought which is, truth to tell, a veritable psychopathological complex, because it bewitches or enslaves human consciousness and deprives it of its liberty. A person who has had the misfortune to fall victim to the spell of a philosophical system (and the spells of sorcerers are mere trifles in comparison to the disastrous effect of the spell of a philosophical system!) can no longer see the world, or people, or historic events, as they are; he sees everything only through the distorting prism of the system by which he is possessed. Thus,

the Marxist of today is *incapable* of seeing anything else in the history of mankind other than the "class struggle."[8]

Karl Marx—being impressed by the partial truth (reduced to its simplest basis) that it is first necessary to eat in order to be able to think—raised the economic interest to THE principle of man and the history of civilization.[9]

The founders were deep thinkers and students of history who cast a wide net for guidance.

An entire volume of Franklin's collected works is devoted to the notes he took at a conference held in Albany, New York, in 1745. At that gathering, the tribal leaders of the Six Iroquois Nations (Mohawk, Cayuga, Onondaga, Oneida, Seneca, and Tuscarora) shared their ideas on proper governance. Franklin's insights into the wisdom and spirit of the Iroquois arguably influenced the creation of the Articles of Confederation and the Constitution, whose substance mirrors the six principles of the Iroquois League. In fact, many early depictions of Columbia show her dressed as a Native American Princess.

The establishment of a threefold government, represented in the executive, legislative, and judicial branches, was intended to create an ideal balance among them, in which each branch has a restraining effect on the other two. The ideal of threefold balance was, of course, taken up by Steiner as well, who spoke of the importance the harmonization of the thinking, feeling, and willing aspects of soul, which bring health to the human organism, and of the need for the proportional give-and-take among the economic, political, and cultural elements of society, which bring health to the societal organism.

The founders saw human rights as gifts of the Divine, not something that could be portioned out by government. They carefully defined rights as principles that are upheld not through the acts and sacrifices of others (or of government), but by their lack of interference in one's law-abiding life. Underlying this principle is the notion that no one has the authority to demand a sacrifice of another;

---

8  Anon., *Meditations on the Tarot*, pp. 42–43.

9  Ibid., p. 128.

it must be freely given. In this way the founders laid the cornerstone of individual rights over that of the collective; they regarded citizens as the source of government's power, not the other way around. They rejected the notion of monarchy; their common sense told them that the *principle* of kingship dwells in each human soul. In this light, the institution of monarchy was considered absurd by the founders, as they believed that it was not an instrument of God. Instead, hard work and prayer were. *Ora et labora.*

> In fact, Washington himself received letters suggesting that the only hope for saving the country from corruption and collapse was the establishment of a monarchy, bolstered by the army—with Washington serving as king.[10]

Washington repudiated all personal glory, reminiscent of Christ following the fourth healing miracle—the Feeding of the Five Thousand. From Anne Catherine Emmerich's account of the miracle:

> Jesus now dismissed the multitude, who were deeply moved. Scarcely had he left the spot upon which he had been teaching when the shout arose: "He has given us bread! He is our king! We will make him our king!" But Jesus disappeared into the solitude, and there gave himself up to prayer.[11]

In his farewell address to Congress in December 1784, General Lafayette (the French aristocrat who commanded the American troops at Yorktown) offered a benediction that "this immense temple of freedom Ever Stand a lesson to oppressors, an Example to the oppressed, a Sanctuary for the Rights of Mankind." In 1787, the year the Constitutional Convention drafted the plan for the new government, a congressman from Pennsylvania prophesied that American's federal government would "lay a foundation for erecting Temples of Liberty in every part of the Earth."[12] What was this Spirit of Liberty that united the founders and gave the struggles and ordeals a common purpose?

> This spirit was called by various names: sometimes Liberty, or the Statue of Liberty; other times Independence...even Columbia. She appeared in hundreds of poems and paintings.... The goddess with the flowing hair...often attended by an eagle, had a ubiquitous presence.[13]

> "As soon as the spark of Patriotism began to kindle, it flew like Lightning from Breast to Breast—it flowed from every tongue. and Pen. and Press. 'till it had diffused itself through every Part of the British Dominions in America; it united us all."[14]

Robert Powell, in a review of *A Sanctuary for the Rights of Mankind*, states further:

> The goddess Columbia was deemed appropriate by the Founding Fathers of the United States to represent America, especially in her aspect "as Liberty, protectress of the Republic and defender against tyranny and discord" (p. 63). The goddess Columbia, standing for Liberty, Justice, and Peace appears with hindsight to have been a reflection of Sophia, mirroring certain aspects of Sophia on Earth.[15]

Isis–Sophia is a God-born being, as is Christ. Sophia was present with God and the Logos at the beginning of time; she is Wisdom, the light of creation. Like the Christ spirit before her, Sophia is descending toward Earth in stages. The first stage of this descent from the Central Sun is to our part of the galaxy, the Orion Arm of the Milky way. (The Christ Spirit reached the level of the Sun during the Persian Epoch, about 8,000 years ago; it descended further to the level of the Moon during the Egyptian Epoch, to the elemental level in ancient Israel, and to the body of the Nathan Jesus in the year 29 CE.)

At the time when Dante wrote *The Divine Comedy* and had his vision and saw the snow-white rose, the celestial image of Divine Sophia united with the Throne of God in the

---

10 Spaulding and York, *A Sanctuary for the Rights of Mankind*, p. 46.

11 Emmerich, *Visions of the Life of Christ*, vol. 2, p. 301.

12 Spaulding and York, *A Sanctuary for the Rights of Mankind*, p. 73.

13 Ibid., p. iv.

14 Ibid., p. 6 (quoting *The Pennsylvania Journal*).

15 See *Starlight*, vol. 13, no. 2.

Empyrean, the highest divine realm, when Dante had this vision, at that time Sophia was still united with the Central Sun. She was at that time still dwelling in this highest sphere, the Empyrean, the divine realm united with the Throne of God. Since approximately 1775, Divine Sophia has become connected with the local part of our galaxy, the Orion Arm, and is now working especially through the twelve constellations of the zodiac....

The point in time of Sophia's entrance into the local part of our galaxy coincides with the founding of the United States of America in 1776. There is a very deep connection between these two events.[16]

Powell's work shines a spiritual light on the events surrounding the independence of the United States, under which its founding can be understood within the overarching intention of our evolution. The Pluto return is requiring of us that we reconsider the essence of the *Sophianic values* that inspired the American Revolution, no matter which country we call home, no matter which politicians we put our faith in. Under the current regency of the Archangel Michael, who is particularly associated with the Sun—indeed, works out of the Sun, according to Steiner—we *must not* limit our worldview due either to nationalism or to political party affiliation. It is in Ahriman's interest that we continue to distrust and denigrate each other. After all, it was during the previous regency of Michael (607–102 BCE) that there developed among various cultures an unprecedented exchange of ideas; these were the years of the ascension of the Gautama Buddha, of the great Greek thinkers—Pythagoras, Socrates and Plato among them—and of the enormous cultural exchange that took place under the rule of Alexander the Great.

In the modern day, this glorious interchange is *claimed* by what is now called globalism, which purports to promote universal brotherhood, fairness, and equality, perhaps in advance of their true time in evolution. The mantle worn by globalism

positively glitters with these jewels. But globalism may serve evil as well as good. Does it encourage a respectful exchange of ideas, or fundamentally consolidate power among those seeking wider domination? Does it offer hope, or merely a metastasis of centralized control? Does it claim to protect you, only to make itself scarce when trouble comes? Mass migration may promote respect among strangers, or it may result in destabilization so severe that world brothers tear at each other's throats. Who is being exploited? Why are refugee contractors getting rich? Steiner lectured on what he termed a colonization of ancient times, from Asia Minor to the special, almost paradisiacal land of Ireland:

> So when you hear historians...describing those people of ancient times, you must always be aware that such colonizations were imbued with a profound spiritual wisdom. They were guided and steered always with an eye to what was to take place in the future.[17]

The bridges that world organizations seek to build might uplift all, or might sow the seeds of chaos and destruction. Can unity last when crafted by political elites? What happens to those who openly oppose globalism's aims?

Lucifer and Ahriman (Satan) reveal the full spectrum of human behavior, from egoistic heat that seeks to lift oneself above every other, to the cold, fear-driven heartlessness of Ahriman, the adversary of Christ who chains us to the material by telling us that there is no God. Our task is to remain centered, between the two forces, through dynamic, active effort; we must choose where we want to be at every moment. It was Satan who came to Christ during his last temptation in the wilderness; this encounter is represented astrologically by the conjunction of the Sun (Christ) and Pluto (Ahriman) at 9° Sagittarius on that day.

Even mightier than Lucifer and Ahriman is the Sun Demon, the two-horned beast of Revelation known as Sorath. This is the Beast of the Apocalypse who seeks nothing less than the negation of humanity by inclining us toward

---

16 Powell, "Sophia and the Coming World Culture, the Rose of the World" (lecture, Durham, NC, July 29, 2005).

17 Steiner, *Secret Brotherhoods*, p. 170.

violence and depravity of every kind; Ahriman receives both inspiration and fuel for his resolves from this demon. The Sun Demon works against both Christ and Sophia, as they were both born of God. There has long been a movement afoot that seeks to replace Christ with another being (who will look like Christ, and possibly even use his name), and to put in Sophia's place the companion of the Beast, the Woman of Babylon. The most potent method of attack against Sophia is the splintering of family and community, as this is where she is felt most deeply. Pluto's return to its placement during the revolutionary period of the eighteenth century is giving us another opportunity to place her again at the center of our lives. Refusal to do so will result in graver consequences in the future.

### The French Revolution

The French Revolution tells a different story than that of America, though it began with a similar longing for freedom. The so-called Third Estate in France (the ordinary people) struggled with onerous taxes, food shortages, and complete lack of representation in the face of a profligate monarchy that well knew how to enrich itself at the expense of the people. A significant wellspring of this growing discontent was the writing and philosophy of Jean Jacques Rousseau. His worldview lives at the core of the French Revolution, Marxism, and communism.

The Swiss-born Rousseau believed that society was the source of all of humanity's ills, and that by making changes to it we can eradicate evil in the world. He considered the "savage" condition (to use a word from his time) to be idyllic, as he believed that there is no original perversity in the human heart.

This was certainly the condition of humanity before Adam and Eve partook of the fruit of the Tree of Knowledge of Good and Evil, a time when we had not yet acquired the physical body. Before the Fall, we were at one with the spiritual world, absent need and desire. It is the intention of our Creator that we eventually return to him; now past the midpoint of humanity's earthly condition,

we can feel the long, slow inbreath of creation that is drawing us back to the spirit.

One obvious danger of this denial of what is generally called Original Sin is the elimination of the need for personal redemption through labor (both physical and spiritual), as all troubles can be viewed as the fault of the social structure. In reality, we are called on to evolve spiritually, regardless of our circumstances and those of the society in which we find ourselves incarnated. More troubling still is the denial of the spiritual reality of the Fall. When the forbidden fruit was eaten, our three lowest members (physical, etheric, and astral) were defiled with desire and egoism. At the same time, the purified astral (*manas*), etheric (*buddhi*), and physical (*atma*) bodies were held back and protected from us in spiritual realms until we have evolved sufficiently to don those shining mantles again. The final stage of Earth's evolution—the attainment of the purified, or resurrection body, which occurs when one is so love-filled that even the physical body is transformed—has been achieved by only one individual.

In Jean Jacques Rousseau's worldview, there is only societal evolution; this, however, requires an elite to implement it—presumably (but not necessarily) on behalf of ordinary citizens. Who would be tasked to make these changes to society? What positions would such a person hold? What principles would be the guide? Which liberties would be trampled underfoot?

For Rousseau, the origin of our corruption is private property. Imagine living in an idyllic, Edenic condition in which private property does not exist: if you're hungry, you take a pear—just one, for that will satisfy you. There is no need to take another or to plan for the time you might be hungry again, for in this natural paradise there is always enough for all. From Rousseau's perspective, the trouble begins with the longing to acquire land and other property; once we put a fence around an orchard, for example, we have more pears than we need, and this, he believed, is always at the expense of others.

Rousseau's contribution to political philosophy includes the *Discourse on the Origins of*

*Inequality* (1755) and *The Social Contract* (1762). His central thinking in politics was that a state must be guided by the "general will," the collective will of its citizens.

A brief remark is called for here on the difference between what is known in Western civilization as the "greater good" and Rousseau's general [collective] will. In the former, sacrifices on behalf of others are freely given by the individual; in the latter, what is to be sacrificed is determined by those in power.

Rousseau argued that creating a system based on the general will would create a more equal and just society and must therefore be the sole source of the law. This concept became the basis for the consolidation of power by Robespierre, Stalin, and Hitler (as well as countless others), resulting in the inevitable need to silence or remove all who opposed them. It requires little imagination to understand that, if one's condition is not seen to depend on one's character or effort but instead on the failings and greed of one's fellows, one is more easily subject to fervent hatred for *the other*. Indeed, the French Revolutionaries cheered jubilantly around the guillotine, often running about joyfully with nobles' heads on their spikes. The French Revolution promoted hatred for the nobility and the clergy; Marxism, the bourgeoisie; Stalin, the kulaks: Hitler, the Jews. *You* are my problem. Without *you*, I will thrive.

Before the storming of the Bastille in 1789, which is widely regarded as the beginning of the revolution, discontent was fomenting among the largest sector of society, the Third Estate. Though ordinary citizens were highly taxed, they were shut out of positions of power, which were reserved for the clergy (the First Estate) and the nobility (the Second Estate), both of whom paid no taxes at all. Understandably, the Third Estate wanted representation; by June of 1789, the classless National Assembly was formed, asserting that it alone had legislative power. A victory was achieved in the recognition of this body by King Louis XVI. The *Ancien Régime* was, in a sense, overthrown. However, their request for a written constitution from the King was not yet granted. Tensions mounted further, precipitating many conflicts between royal forces and the revolutionaries.

On July 14, 1789, the jail known as the Bastille (formerly a fortress) held six (or seven—accounts vary) prisoners. Throughout Paris, as many as 60,000 citizens with pikes and axes moved between the town hall and the *Invalides,* searching for weapons and ammunition and finding only the former. About a thousand of those citizens gathered around the Bastille, agitated by whispers of torture within its walls and the superiority of the firepower at the king's disposal. As the crowd demanded ammunition, the Bastille's commander, Marquis de Launay, invited some of the crowd inside to discuss demands, and then closed the drawbridge. When their exit was delayed, the crowd outside became even more frenzied, fearing harm had befallen their fellows. The mob secured its own cannon and began firing. They swung their pikes and axes at the drawbridge and scaled the walls. De Launay offered total surrender and begged for a bloodless takeover—to no avail.

The prisoners were released, and many guards were taken into custody. De Launay himself was hacked to pieces while being paraded through the streets. Following his death, the crowd continued to mangle his corpse, eventually displaying his head on a pike. The bloodless takeover had been roundly rejected. Alexander Hamilton said to the American Revolutionary hero, Marquis de Lafayette:

> I dread the vehement character of your people, whom I fear you may find is more easy to bring on than to keep within Proper bounds, after you have put them in motion.[18]

In that same bloody summer, however, a ray of light appeared through the clouds in the form of the *Declaration of the Rights of Man and the Citizen,* which both Lafayette and Jefferson helped to draft. Completed just weeks after the National Assembly abolished the rights of the nobility and the clergy, this important document remains the foundation of French law today. In essence, it describes the citizens' duties to the government.

---

18 Hamilton. *Writings*, p. 521. Letter, Oct. 6, 1789.

It enumerates many rights—to liberty, property, resistance to oppression—but the origin of these rights is unnamed, and therefore open to interpretation. It claims to support an individual's right to disagree, for example, but this is undercut by the ability of the state to do what it feels it must in support of the common good. Three years later, this "good" was enforced by the appearance of the guillotine.

Where the French Declaration identifies the sole cause of public misery and government corruption as the turning away from the "rights of man," its American counterpart acknowledged that individuals are more likely to oppress one another (history had shown them this) than to cooperate toward a common good. In other words, it claimed an understanding of the Fall of humankind—thus leaving people as free as possible to work things out themselves, however imperfectly. It understood that people would always disagree, even vehemently, and that by coming together to seek the truth, opposing sides would be elevated.

In France, tyranny was waiting in the wings.

Maximilien Robespierre (1758–1794), inspired by Rousseau, was a highly effective statesman, known by his peers as "The Incorruptible" because of his lack of interest in money and women. The benefits of power, however, interested him greatly. Robespierre led the Jacobin Club, an organization born of the Revolution that sought change through the overthrow of the monarchy. As president of the Jacobins, Robespierre vigorously fought for and eventually achieved universal male suffrage, as well as an end to slavery in France, albeit for only eight years. (This was reversed by Napoleon in 1802.)

Robespierre was born under a conjunction of Mars and Neptune, which can bestow both the capacity to manifest one's ideals on Earth, or the possibility of being deluded by them. (Napoleon, too, came into the world under this conjunction.) Perhaps his hatred of the monarchy was a perversion of the story "The Healing of the Nobleman's Son," which also occurred under this aspect; the

miracle warns us that we should never cede our individual authority, as the nobleman did, even to a king. The nobleman's weakened "I" resulted in the illness of his child.

As the storming of the Bastille began the revolution, Robespierre was months away from his Saturn return. *His mission was thus formed.* His heliocentric astrological birth chart shows us what might have been: an opposition between Mars and Uranus offered the possibility that the rebellion he crafted might have been forged into peaceful reforms.

By the end of summer 1789, King Louis XVI had been kidnapped. His Austrian-born wife, Marie Antoinette, once beloved by the French people, suffered the same fate the following year. They were held at the Tuileries Palace. The Revolution still gained momentum. In 1790, it was demanded that the clergy swear allegiance to France alone, and by 1791 a new constitution was ratified with the support of King Louis. Robespierre, now the Secretary of the National Assembly, delivered a speech on the abolition of the death penalty; it would soon be overlooked.

In 1792, the year in which the guillotine was introduced, an angry August mob stormed the Tuileries, forcing the captive royal family to flee to the National Assembly for safety.

The king submitted to the mob by ordering the hundreds of the Swiss guards who were protecting them to surrender. But this was not enough for the revolutionaries, who—women and children among them—hacked the guards to pieces until no life remained in the Tuileries. King Louis XVI thus became an ordinary citizen.

The following month, an armed mob, breathing hatred, surrounded a caravan of clergymen who were being transported—as they represented Christ—to prison. The clergymen who managed to survive the first attack by this bloodthirsty group were killed as they arrived at the prison. Another Parisian gathering besieged a Carmelite convent, demanding that the clerics pledge loyalty to the state; they unanimously refused. The lone survivor, Abbé Sicard, described the butchery as the clerics were sliced to pieces and strewn into the fields and into wells. There were five more days of savagery, during which priests, prisoners, and the mentally ill were sacrificed on the altar of liberty, fraternity, and equality, the motto coined by Robespierre. Body parts were held up for display to the jeering crowds. From this womb the French Republic was born, with the Jacobins in control of the National Convention. The Convention established France's first government without a monarchy. The two-year Reign of Terror would shortly begin.

The years 1793–34 stretch beyond our designated period, as Pluto moved into Aquarius during the Terror, but a further look at the events of those years is called for here, as the Reign of Terror was the direct result of the handling of the revolutionary impulses felt during the Capricorn period.

January, 1793: Louis was taken to the guillotine; Marie Antoinette met the same fate nine months later. With the ascension of the Jacobins to power, Robespierre founded and led the Committee of Public Safety, a body designed to protect the republic from without and within. It quickly gained dictatorial powers, birthing the Reign of Terror to further its political aims. The Committee for Public Safety might provide the first historical example of a long line of organizations that have cloaked themselves in benevolent names in order to serve evil. Examples abound: to name a few: *Pravda* ("truth"), established in 1917 to distribute propaganda and cloud the tyranny of the Soviet Union; the Nazi Protection Squadron, or SS; President Obote's Public Safety Unit in Uganda.

One of the aims of the Jacobins, inspired by Rousseau's concept of *religion civile*, was the eradication of Christianity in France, in service of the establishment of their state religion; seeking a religion with social utility, Robespierre ultimately settled on the Cult of the Supreme Being. A huge festival (the Festival of the Supreme Being) was staged by Robespierre in June of 1794, on the human-made hill known as the Champs de Mars. One wonders if it served as inspiration for Hitler's Nuremberg Rallies.

The revolutionaries' destruction of churches and their works of art and artifacts across France is well known: stained-glass windows of the Cathedral of Notre Dame, created in the thirteenth and fourteenth centuries, were smashed. Hundreds of its sculptures were defiled and tossed into the Seine. Many churches fared even worse, losing treasures dating from the seventh century. Church bells—church bells!—were forbidden, some of which were melted down for armaments. Religious holidays were banned, of course, in favor of *"les fêtes de la raison."* Notre Dame was renamed *Temple de la raison* (in which Napoleon was crowned), and its altar, *Autel de la raison.* Celibacy was denounced (without God, there is no morality), and pagan rituals abounded, many featuring obscene depictions of the clergy.

The Reign of Terror oversaw the arrest and execution by guillotine of approximately 40,000 political enemies, some of whom were former close friends of an increasingly paranoid and desperate Robespierre. The Terror was supercharged by a 1794 measure issued by the Committee of Public Safety, known as *"La loi de la Grande Terreur,"* or 22 Prairial (named for the date of its passage on the bizarre calendar adopted by the revolutionaries in 1793). This law, which roughly translates as "22 Meadow," was tyranny's dreamchild, essentially making accusation sufficient for guilt. As the subjective view of another's character was all that was on trial, it greatly streamlined executions. Fearing a purge within the National Committee itself, Robespierre himself was guillotined in July 1794, *just one day after his arrest.*

It is not surprising that stability in France would remain elusive; soon they put their faith in Napoleon, crowning him Emperor in 1804.

The following comparison was made between the nature of the American and French revolutions:

> The French Revolution in fact produced something like the opposite of its American predecessor. The soil of democratic institutions had nurtured the growth of freedom in the States, yet it seemed only too apparent across the sea that the demand for the rights of man in the stony absence of such institutions led only to anarchy and tyranny.[19]

---

19 Spaulding and York, *A Sanctuary for the Rights of Mankind*, p. 89.

In France, hatred spread among the mob like a wildfire, igniting the sentient soul of France into an uncontrollable movement toward hatred (Pluto) of tradition and continuity (Capricorn). What began as the natural sentiment of a humanity longing for a more just society became an engine of terror. We can be grateful that the Cathedral at Chartres suffered as little as it did.

## BEETHOVEN, NOVALIS, EMMERICH, TURNER, AND GOETHE

Yet, from these same disruptive forces, many exceptional individualities received divine inspiration that completely transformed their fields of activity.

### Beethoven

For many admirers of the music of Beethoven, there has never been, nor will there ever be, anything as exalted as his compositions. Born into common circumstances of a chaotic nature (his father was a drinker), Ludwig van Beethoven (unlike Mozart) did not enjoy steady tutelage. Yet this background was the soil from which his Ninth Symphony came to life. His music is monumental, ambitious, and passionate, featuring broad strokes of wildness. In my own experience, only Beethoven is able to take me to the edge—the point at which I can bear no more glory—then pull me back in the nick of time.

The Sun at his birth (2° Sagittarius), was aligned with the Central Sun, the throne of the Creator. He all but names the Galactic Center as his source of inspiration, his spiritual hearing. Even deafness did not interfere with his ability to hear the harmonies of the cosmos:

Whence do I receive my ideas? When I gaze astonished in the evening upon the sky and the host of shining bodies resonating within its bounds, what we call suns and earths, my spirit soars across all those stars, millions of miles distant, to the archetypal fountain of them all from which flows all created things and from which new creations will continue to flow in all eternity.[20]

### Novalis

Great poetry unites the upper, spiritual waters with the lower waters in which we live; it reflects the Divine and therefore elevates our souls. Novalis was born in 1772, and though he died before his first Saturn return, he was an impressive polymath whose encyclopedic knowledge included the subjects of philosophy, science, law, religion, art, and politics. During much of his short adulthood, he managed salt mines; this is quite interesting in relation to the inspiration he so clearly found in Mary—for sodium is the element associated with the constellation of Virgo. He wrote:

In countless pictures I behold Thee
Maria, clothed in form divine;
But none so wondrously enfold Thee
As in my soul I see Thee shine.
I only know the world is flowing
Away from me like restless dreams;
A Heaven more sweet than mortal knowing
Within my soul forever gleams.[21]

The position of the Sun at the conception of Novalis (25° Cancer) is indeed an indication of the way that Mary shone in his soul, as the Sun also passed this degree at the birth of the Nathan Mary. Perhaps the "countless pictures" he beheld refer in part to the paintings of Raphael? For Robert Powell's astrological karma research has established that Novalis and Raphael are the same individuality (and before Raphael, St. Elisabeth and John the Baptist).[22] Raphael, in the opinion of this author, best depicted the pure sweetness of Mary, who was always shown with the infant Jesus, and often with his cousin, John the Baptist. In Madonna of the Goldfinch (1505 or 1506), Mary holds a book entitled *Sedes Sapientiae*, or *Throne of Wisdom*. Mary is the High Priestess, the Saturn being living within the second arcanum of *Meditations on the Tarot*.

Novalis' devotion to Christ radiates from his poetry, reflected well by the position of his natal

---

20 Warm, *Signature of the Celestial Spheres*, p. 73.

21 Novalis, "Sacred Song XV" (trans. by Eileen Hutchins).

22 See: Powell, *Elijah Come Again*.

Moon—for it occupied the same zodiacal degree (15° Aries) as the Sun at the Resurrection.

Robert Powell describes the effects of an initiatory experience had by Novalis at the grave of his first beloved, Sophie, who had died at fifteen:

> Novalis was lifted into a beholding of Sophie von Kühn as an aspect of Sophia, the Divine Feminine—leading to a single diary entry…: "Christ and Sophia." This realization found expression later in his *Hymns to the Night*…and was central throughout the creative outpouring that followed.[23]

### Emmerich

Anne Catherine Emmerich's visions of the life of Jesus began at the age of four and continued throughout her life. The extraordinary detail provided in these visions, including Hebrew dating, the phases of the Moon on which it depended, days of the week, and descriptions of the Holy Land (which she had never seen) established the foundation of the chronology of the life of Christ revealed by Robert Powell.[24] In addition to the inspiring nature of a life devoted entirely in service to Christ, Anne Catherine gave us a *living* portrait of Mary, one veiled for centuries by the Bible. Now that we can better understand her own joys and sorrows, we can also know how she has held those of humanity so close to her heart since the Turning Point of Time.

This devotion is a reflection of the starry script at her birth and death; as she came into the world in 1774, the Sun was conjunct Neptune (the Mother), bringer of inspiration; as she rejoined the angels, both Venus and Neptune were together at 16° Sagittarius, the position of the Sun at the birth of the Nathan Jesus child who would die on the cross at Golgotha.

### Turner

J. M. W. Turner was a painter and printmaker known for his unique interplay between darkness and light. Born under a Mars–*Regulus* alignment, Turner painted in an impossible array of bold

colors. Indeed, no matter what the subject of his art, we seem to be looking at the Sun. How was he able to bring forth such luminous forms?

Extraordinarily talented by any standard, he painted in a way that might seem contemporary even today, were it not for the less modern subject matter, including mythological scenes, naval battles, stormy seas, and angels. One of his most remarkable pictures is *The Angel Standing in the Sun* (a detail of which is shown above), revealing an angel from Revelation wrapped in gold, holding aloft a sword as if guarding Paradise itself; a chained serpent and many of the damned lie at her feet. Perhaps the painting represents a prefiguring of Sophia's descent to the Sun.

Later in his life, his style was so bold, so outrageous for the time, that many considered him to

---

23  Powell, *Elijah Come Again*, p. 42.
24  See: Powell, *Chronicle of the Living Christ*.

be deranged and thought him likely to be suffering from a mental illness! But there is no evidence for this. He saw what others could not. It is said that he loved to gaze at the Sun. In one account of his death at the fine age of 76, it is claimed that his final words were "The Sun is God."

### Goethe

The work of Goethe, described by Rudolf Steiner as the leading light of his age, represented a substantial focus of Steiner's early inquiries into the life of spirit. Goethe was a philosopher and writer of stunning multiplicity, who displayed, in the words of Emerson in *Representative Men*, a habitual reference to interior truth.[25] His work enriched every facet of intellectual life.

He refutes the notion that the microscope can reveal more than the eye. Emerson said of Goethe, "There is a certain heat in the breast, which attends the perception of a primary truth, which is the shining of the spiritual sun down the shaft of the mine."[26]

Born as Mercury was aligned with *Regulus*, the heart of the Lion—which begins to explain his abiding interest in the throbbing nature of life itself—Goethe saw inner radiance behind scientific observation, and unity in all of creation. He sought insight into the evolution of our world, understanding well that spirit and matter exist together.

### Mozart

Mozart is widely regarded as the most gifted musical prodigy in history. His father, Leopold, also a musician, longed for greater social stature, and made it his life's mission to nurture and to make public his son's extraordinary gifts. At Mozart's birth, Neptune, planet of spiritual hearing, was conjunct his Earth sign, Taurus. The star that marks the eye of the Bull, *Aldeberan*, is aligned on Earth with the city of Vienna[27]—that of Haydn, Mozart, Beethoven, and Schubert. Through this correspondence, the music qualities inherent in the forces of Taurus are obvious. (Taurus is ruled by Venus, planet of harmony.)

Wolfgang was exposed to the best musicians in Europe through the arduous tour arranged by his father when Wolfgang was seven. What the boy learned on this three-and-a-half-year tour was, in the words of his father, "beyond conception."

Writing his third opera at fourteen, Wolfgang may well have been the hardest working composer of all time, if this can be measured by the volume of compositions created during his thirty-five years of life. He was so consumed by his music that he had little time for anything else! Letters home while away on tour describe all that he heard but nothing of what he saw.[28]

Though he composed a wide variety of music, operas and piano concertos claimed most of his attention. Pieces seemed to come to him fully formed.[29] One can imagine, having been thus blessed by the Holy Spirit, how dull transcribing these compositions must have seemed to him. The beloved lightness, joy, and intricacy of his music endures. Its nature is eternal, reflecting as it does the glory of the spiritual world.

Which gurgling infants will become our Beethoven, our Anne Catherine, our Goethe? What might we offer today's musicians, painters, poets, and visionaries to nurture their gifts?

The Pluto return of the founding of the United States comes at a time in history when the being of Sophia is being experienced by more and more people in advance of the Slavic culture that will come to flower in 3574, the cultural Age of Aquarius. As she is drawing nearer, so, too, is the path to the Mother in Shambhala calling to more of us, as the presence of the Etheric Christ nears its centennial. More of us are seeking the golden thread that is our connection to the source of all that is loving and lawful. Is it not entirely predictable that we are experiencing such opposition to the remembrance of the founding of the nation inspired by Sophia's ideals? For the intent of the dark forces

---

25 Emerson, *Essays & Lectures*, p.756.

26 Ibid., p. 748.

27 See: Powell, *Astrogeographia*.

28 Tommasini, *The Indispensable Composers*, p. 124.

29 Ibid., p. 127.

to obliterate all traces of Christ and Sophia in all three social realms (economic, political, and cultural) has been steady all along. Much damage has been done.

The return is an echo of the original event, a homecoming to the same point along the circle. If we imagine this circle as a closed one (its image is the serpent biting its tail), confined to a single horizontal plane, we are left with *repetition*. This is the source of the fatalistic view that there is "nothing new under the Sun," that nothing we do can affect what is to be. In the closed circle there is no growth.

But when we allow radiance to shine upon us, down to our toes, the circle is opened to worlds above. We can then imagine the Pluto return as two points on a spiral, one directly above the other, implying movement both forward and *up*. This is the principle of growth, the constant, flowing universal sap of life that gives us the power to transform the ideal into the real. It allows for continuously flowing transformation that precludes the fiery fits of bloody revolution.

> It is not to be wondered at that Goethe, although he admits the reality of the magical agent or fire, ranges himself on the side of the agent of growth or water—for he was the author of four works on *metamorphosis*, the principal theme of his life, namely on the metamorphosis of light or color (*Farbenlehre*), on the metamorphosis of plants (*Metamorphose der Pflanzen*), on the metamorphosis of animals (*Metamorphose de Tiere*), and on the metamorphosis of man (*Faust*), which is his principal work. His faith was that of transformation, evolution, the tradition of cultural progress without revolution—in a word, Goethe himself believed in and attached value to all that *flows*, all that grows without leaps and bounds. He ranged himself on the side of the principle of *continuity*.[30]

Steiner stated that humanity needed to go to sleep spiritually so that spirituality could reappear in a new form. The time for burying one's head under a pillow is past.

---

30 Anon., *Meditations of the Tarot*, p. 466.

## THE STARS HAVE BEEN SPEAKING

The Saturn–Pluto conjunction of 2019 was a particularly relevant event, as Saturn rules the astrological sign (Capricorn) that Pluto is now entering. This combination can precipitate events that resound for decades to come. Saturn is always exhorting us to look to spirit—to seek and take up our individual mission to serve evolution. When we collectively ignore the relatively gentle reminders of spirit and divine law, Pluto will see to it that less subtle consequences will follow: *the knees will bend, either voluntarily or involuntarily.*

In 2020, the conjunction of Jupiter and Saturn brought to us the impulses that will serve us until their next meeting in 2040 (in Virgo); the union of these forces, in Capricorn, marked the start of a long series of these conjunctions in earth signs. The last such period encompassed the unfolding of the missions of the School of Chartres and the Knights Templar—movements inspired by the Divine Feminine, and deeply protective of the memory of the Turning Point of Time.

Also of great significance within the current Pluto–Capricorn period is the coming American solar eclipse of 2024, which will take place on April 8 of that year. This solar eclipse is the second of two so-called Great American eclipses, the first of which occurred on August 21, 2017. The path of the 2017 total eclipse swept southeast from Oregon to Georgia while the Sun and Moon were together at 4° Leo. The Moon's eastward movement across the face of the Sun provides an imagination of the potential of a total solar eclipse—i.e., for the "Sun" nature in the human being to be blotted out by lower, personal will forces. This is a challenge on a large scale that can be countered by our obedience to the will higher than our own, or the strengthening of the "I" forces in each of us. The American solar eclipse of 2017 recalled the Raising of Lazarus (Sun 3° Leo, Moon 4° Leo), the miracle in which light was called out of darkness—a darkness from which only Christ can rescue us. "Lazarus, come forth!" was the call of the total solar eclipse of 2017.

The path of the 2024 eclipse will move north-east from Texas to Maine and cross the path of the 2017 eclipse; the two paths form an "X" across the continent—indeed, very close to the longitude that (according to the celestial correspondence established by Robert Powell and David Bowden[31]) is associated with the first degree of the Aquarius constellation, the position of the Sun at the Healing of the Paralyzed Man. Aligned with this zodiacal degree is the star *Sadr*, which marks the breast of the Swan, also seen as the center of the Northern Cross. The intersection of these pathways can be seen as a warning to overcome our own paralysis in the face of the world's ever-growing mechanization and tyranny—or ignore their advance at our collective peril.

The degree that the Sun and Moon will occupy together during the 2024 eclipse—24° Pisces—is very powerful indeed, and can therefore be predictive of an especial assault by adversarial beings:

*Jupiter* (25° Pisces) and *Saturn* (24° Pisces) were conjunct at the conception of the Solomon Jesus. This conjunction is the "star" that drew the magi to Bethlehem.

*Uranus* reached 24° Pisces at the conception of the Nathan Jesus.

*Venus* reached 24° Pisces at the Crucifixion.

*Mercury* graced this degree at the Appearance of the Risen One at Emmaus, at which he broke the bread of eternal life for the disciples.

The span of this timeline runs from June 7 BCE to April 33 CE, nearly the entirety of the Christ Event on Earth. As the eclipse will be a time when the memory of all of these events will be enlivened, it will require all of our attention to oppose the anti-Christian sentiment that will inevitably gain force at this time. Comfort can be drawn from the fact that, on April 8, 2024, Pluto will have reached 7° Capricorn, the position of the Moon at the birth of Valentin Tomberg, and the position of Mars at the Cleansing of the Temple. We will need the dispassionate resolve and courage of Jesus to overturn the vendors' tables of our day.

It is essential, too, to be aware of another aspect of the coming years, during which Pluto will be in Capricorn. Pluto will touch into Aquarius in 2039 and then leave Capricorn for good in 2040—the year in which the "I" of Christ will complete its subearthly descent toward the Mother. This signifies that, until then, the placement of Pluto in Capricorn will be the constant companion of what remains of the descent of the Christ "I" through the eighth subearthly layer (ending in 2028), followed by the ninth (2028–2040). These two layers represent the repositories of our most severe transgressions, and the movement of the Christ "I" through them causes what lurks in their darkness to scatter in the presence of his light. As the demons make their way upward, they search for receptive souls.

The eighth subearthly layer, known as the "Earth Severer," is the source of all strife and conflict, murder and suicide. It has the capacity to tear us apart from one another, as recent world events clearly reveal. The effects of this layer will only be overcome when we unite in love and community, rejecting the false dichotomy of *us vs. them* and *me vs. you*. The cherubim assist us particularly in this endeavor.

Between the eighth layer and the golden dwelling place of the Mother, Shambhala, festers the ninth—the layer of pure hatred of everything good and beautiful. What in us will allow refuge to the beings of that sphere? Those beings never rest, as their aim is to keep Christ and Sophia unnoticed by us all. Indeed, without Christ and Sophia, we are unable to look into the abyss—the collective karma of humanity. In the third arcanum of *Meditations of the Tarot*, the anonymous author says,

Resist the devil, and the devil will be your friend. A devil is not an atheist; he does not doubt God. The faith which he lacks is faith in man. And the act of sacred magic with respect to such a devil is that of reestablishing his faith in man. The purpose of the trials of Job was not to dispel the doubts of God, but rather those of the devil. These doubts once dispelled, who was it then who labored to give Job all that he had lost, if not the same being who had formerly deprived him of everything? Job's enemy became

---

31 See Powell, *Astrogeographia*.

his voluntary servant—and "voluntary servant" means to say *friend*.[32]

We cannot become practitioners of sacred magic without first accepting our burdens as just, as Job did. His faith in God rendered him obedient to God's will. Following the Mystery of Golgotha, we can now understand those burdens as our *freedom*: as meeting our karmic necessity in order to pay our debts. We might even endeavor to pay the debts of others: *Bear one another's burdens and so fulfill the law of Christ* (Gal. 6:2).

It is in this way that saints practice sacred magic. They would not project their forces, their vitality or their fluids into someone else, but on the contrary would rather *take* from him that which was unhealthy in him.[33]

## THE CARDINAL CROSS OF PLUTO

Lastly, let's examine the movement of Pluto from the perspective of *phase*—when Pluto formed hard aspects (squares and the opposition) to its passage through Capricorn in the eighteenth century.

The cross, or *crux*, formed by Capricorn, Aries, Cancer, Libra, is cardinal in nature, relating in particular to the will forces of the human being. This cross is particularly relevant to the position of Pluto, as it is the will forces upon which Pluto acts most strongly; its forces find expression through the four elements—earth, fire, water, air—bringing to the human will firmness, intensity, adaptability, and scope. The zodiacal points of the cross reveals to us the four *crucial* moments in time when tensions escalate and decisions and restorative measures need to be considered. They mark points in history upon which much depended. It is true that these were moments in time when waves of opposition to the principles of our founding arose. However, as light stands beside darkness, these were also periods during which the potential for positive transformation was great, as well.

Let's spin this out further, keeping in mind that whereas the duration of the orbit of Pluto is consistent over time, the speed at which it travels is not:

---

32 Anon., *Meditations on the Tarot*, p. 63.
33 Ibid.

Pluto entered Capricorn: 1773
Pluto entered Aries: 1843–44
Pluto entered Cancer: 1933–34
Pluto entered Libra: 1981–82.

A brief examination of these years will serve to reveal the profound changes that have occurred within the threefold realm of economics, politics, and culture. These changes continue to accelerate at a speed that makes them very difficult to assimilate. The fantasy of the brotherhoods behind these changes is that our hopelessness will eventually render us unable to do so.

## *Pluto moved into Aries, 1843–44*

The year 1843 dawned just two years after the beginning of the struggle in the cosmos that would lead to what is known as the Fall of the Spirits of Darkness. The struggle, ultimately won by the Archangel Michael, arose when certain fallen angels sought to obscure spiritual knowledge from humankind. (Because of Michael's victory in 1879, the nefarious aim of the adversarial beings was not achieved in full, but as a consequence those beings now surround us on Earth, cultivating what Steiner referred to as the clientele of the dead.)

The first attack of the Beast against the founding principles of the United States was an economic one, as this was where the country was most vulnerable; prosperity reliant on slavery made economics its Achilles' heel. Although socialistic ideals had earlier found their way into the dreams of Rousseau and others, when Marx and Engels met in Paris in 1844, the concept of communism (the word used by Marx himself) was conceived—the government structure through which socialism can be imposed. Deeply affected by the exploitation of workers during the Industrial Revolution of the previous decades, Marx dreamed of what would now be called social justice. He imagined the elimination of a power- and money-hungry ruling class through the revolt of the proletariat, by the destruction of the market economy, and through central control of the means of production. Just as Marx was supported by the wealth of his wife's family, so can communism thrive for a time in a society previously fattened by the benefits of capitalism. But human nature inevitably makes it unsustainable, for men and women have lost none of their appetite for power, and great work has been so rarely in evidence absent a reward. Communism claims to free humanity from one set of chains, but leads it to another—the loss of individual freedom. At the time, socialism in the United States had no foothold, but the seed was planted; its roots would be deep and strong.

During the same year, the first long-distance Morse-code telegram was sent from Baltimore to Washington DC. It transmitted words from Numbers 23:23: "What hath God wrought?"—a question that received no serious answer at the time. *For the first time, subearthly forces were able to interfere with our communications to our fellow human beings.* It was a marvel that resulted eventually in the darkening of city skies with the crisscrossing network of transmission wires.

The year 1844 also marked the midpoint between the embarkation of Darwin's *Beagle* and the publication of *On the Origin of Species* in 1859. Although natural science had first worn the blush of materialism around the dawn of the 17th century, Darwin's work was revolutionary in that it drove a wedge between creation and evolution. The purely material concept of survival of the fittest depicts the course of humanity as devoid of spiritual intent, as if life came into being on its own. Darwinism without spirit is devoid of hope, trapping us inside the closed circle of the serpent.

Darwin's worldview has since evolved into a repudiation—even ridicule—of creation as described by Moses, and repudiation of the Christ Mystery. Not surprising, Steiner was concerned with the bleeding of Darwinism beyond biology, into other fields of life—for example, in the production of goods, if the speed of work were eventually to take precedence over its quality.

### Pluto moved into Cancer, 1933–34

Hitler became Chancellor in 1933 and Führer in 1934. In the USSR, Stalin's ambition to starve millions in Ukraine was underway. Gulags—prisons for all who stood in Stalin's way—were up and running. The gross travesty of justice referred to as show trials that would fill the gulags was still a few years off. By 1933, both tyrants had established totalitarian control of their governments—one socialist, one Communist—through propaganda, surveillance, snitching, fear, violence, and manipulation of their justice systems. Cruelty and hatred were the coin of their realms.

The explanation for how these students of the Sun Demon came to power at the same time lies in the realization that they represented a desperate attack on the appearance of Christ in the etheric in 1933. This attack is, at the same time, against the Mother, as awareness of her presence has been quickening as a result of the Christ presence around and throughout the globe. It can certainly be said that the Earth's travails have grown steadily since then.

Totalitarianism was, in 1933, abhorrent to the Americans, at least in regard to Adolf Hitler's Nazism. The little pro-Nazi sentiment that existed was usually connected with the idea that Soviet Russia a greater threat to the Western principles of freedom. Pro-Soviet and pro-Communist propaganda, on the other hand, was everywhere and was later adopted enthusiastically by countless writers and filmmakers.

In the throes of the misery and uncertainty of the Great Depression, the New Deal was launched in 1933. Opinions of economists differ widely about the ultimate efficacy of the ballooning federal government's aid in ending the Depression, but balloon it did—by a factor of seven, by some accounts. The West ultimately decided that it had to work with Uncle Joe (as FDR called him) in order to end the brewing world war. By this calculation, Stalin was an ally, and therefore ultimately the recipient of at least a billion taxpayer dollars of Lend–Lease aid. Their nuclear program did not suffer.

As a result, a rent in the Western political fabric allowed entry of the most foundational concept of communism—no limit to the reach and power of government.

Another precedent set at this time was the turning of the normal election process on its head, in service of continuity. (FDR, of course, died before completing his fourth term). Efforts to undermine this process have gained considerable strength in recent years. Subverting lawful voting is universal among totalitarian regimes, as it is essential to the preservation of their power.

### Pluto moved into Libra, 1981–82

As Pluto found Libra, efforts to damage the social fabric were begun in earnest. November, 1980 marked the entry of Christ's "I" into the Form Earth, the layer associated with beings that directly attack the sentient, or the feeling aspect, of the human soul. When one's feelings produce actions that are guided by neither reason nor conscience, one is unable to be sensitive to anything that is outside one's own wellbeing; righteousness is set aside in favor of "feeling good" and "whatever!" I would argue that the subsequent years were those in which the lid was ripped off of what might be called the counter- or subculture. Surely, depravity of all kinds has been with humanity always, but around this time there was a dramatic bleeding of this world into the one above it. Though the establishment of the internet and the attendant explosion of accessible pornography was nearly a decade off, around 1980 we began to see the strong cultural foundations of our world (the importance of the nuclear family, God, law and order, the majority striving toward decency) begin to melt beneath our feet. Since then we've been jumping from ice floe to ice floe—each one smaller than the last—praying that the last of the continuity of innocence and purity does not melt away altogether.

The Great Conjunction of 1980 took place at 15° Virgo, just 1° from the Sun's position at the birth of the Blessed Virgin. The cherubim were looking toward humanity, bestowing light-filled wisdom and self-awareness on those souls who made an effort to receive it. The seraphim sought to arouse our conscience to a higher level—one that would result in greater care for the innocent and for the Earth. These angels offered us the spiritual seeds of purity that might come to flower in the future, but many were left untended.

In September of 1981, Pluto passed *Spica* (29°), Virgo's brightest star. The Virgin teaches us of unfallen nature, or the act of bending to a force greater than our own. Pluto warned against being swept away by the fast-moving waters of the serpent's world, the currents of which cause fatigue and exhaustion. As the Virgin, who never tires, tends the garden of humanity, so must we learn to improve our tending of others, animals, and the whole of the natural world.

Saturn and Pluto found each other before the same zodiacal degree (3° Libra) in 1982, thus beginning the Saturn–Pluto cycle that would end in 2019. It is through the first half of the stars of Libra that the Moon passed between the Last Supper (3° Libra) and the Crucifixion (13°). The lines of the Libra glyph itself suggest an upper world and a lower world, identical but for the raised center of the upper line. This region represents the fulcrum of the Scales, where justice is served, and it is interesting that the brightest star of the Southern Cross is aligned with it. (The Southern Cross, connected to the Northern Cross, or the Swan, by the Milky Way, is described by Robert Powell as a portal to the Mother). To clairvoyant vision, the Scales are held by the Archangel Michael, assuring us that all transgressions will eventually be redeemed. It is through the sacrifice of Jesus at the Crucifixion, when the Moon had reached this fulcrum point, that this atonement can be achieved. Another imagination of the raised portion of the glyph is offered in *Meditations on the Tarot*:

> What is the *eighth* force which puts the seven forces of the astral body in equilibrium? For it is this eighth force which works in judging and weighing up by means of the balance of Justice, in the inner forum of consciousness.... The word *conscience* ("con-science") contains the idea of balance, for it implies "simultaneous knowing," i.e., knowledge of the facts of the *two scales* suspended at the extremities of the beam of the balance. Conscience is neither a product nor a function of *character*. It is above.[34]

---

34 Ibid., p. 196.

The unknown author tells us that balance, keeping extremes in check, is the basis of spiritual health. The scales of the spiritual world weigh truth, goodness, and beauty; the fallen scales, which represent an abdication from conscience, care only about measurable quantities—how much, how many, how far? These were the scales of Judas at the Last Supper, the scales that put a greater value on thirty pieces of silver than on the Son of God himself. Anne Catherine Emmerich saw Judas at the Last Supper, "interiorly inflamed with rage. During the whole meal I saw sitting at his feet a little monster, which frequently rose to his heart."[35]

As Saturn met Pluto at 3° Libra, did we take up the sword to fight for moral goodness? Or did we lay it down and allow events to sweep us away?

It may be appropriate to take a turn (unanticipated by the author at the outset of penning this article) toward the viral pandemic that has swept the world and remains unresolved at the time of writing. Clearly, the fact that we are at the moment unable to move freely and unable to interact with many of our loved ones (other than through easily surveilled devices) points to the evil intent behind the reaction to the pandemic, if not to the spread of the virus itself. So-called experts lie daily. Pornography sites waive subscription fees. The sale of marijuana, the *soma*[36] of our time, is deemed essential. The common will dictates that a lone paddle boarder is arrested in Los Angeles, and that a basketball hoop in rural America is removed because a single 12-year-old girl is seen using it. Unelected bureaucrats, who are not among the 26 million unemployed to date in the US, are suggesting that we might have to stay indoors until a (mandatory) vaccine is developed. Armbands, like those worn by Jews in Nazi Germany, are discussed. Apps are developed that track the infected. Can we not feel the quickened breath of the power-hungry? We

might call it madness, but this is not so. It is the blueprint of Ahriman. Can we not envision what he longs to create?

Once the pandemic resolves, whenever that may be, we can be certain of one thing; another crisis will appear to test our tolerance for the dictates of the Ahriman's will. The pandemic is merely a trial run. Ahriman is watching and learning. What will we tolerate?

This is a revolution without cannons, guns, grenades, or tear gas. The armory of the Beast holds satellites, money, lies, vaccines, opioids. The revolution of the Beast stalks the tender-hearted and the *aggrieved*. It is the culmination of more than a century of the anti-life, anti-Christian attacks on our financial health, our political health, and our cultural health. As Pluto returns to Capricorn, will our blindfolds come off? Will we turn in earnest to the only viable path forward, shown to us by Christ himself, our emissary from the Central Sun? Can we awaken to the love that is streaming from the center of the Earth?

### Pluto Enters Capricorn in 2021

As Pluto completes its cycle—from Capricorn in 1773 to Capricorn this year—we have an opportunity to *rise*, to achieve a higher level of devotion to Christ and Sophia, one proper to our time. For it is through Sophianic principles alone that we will eventually unite, not through the efforts of the UN, or the EU, or the WHO.

The forces of Capricorn sculpt and restructure our lives, retuning us to essentials. Capricorn reveals the frivolous for what it is. The stars of the Goat remind us, forever and always, that within each of us is the spirit that created the world, and that we stand between the constellation of hope above us and the flow of continuity of biological life below. A spiritual (Capricorn) transformation (Pluto) is at our threshold, urging us to climb. Those who serve Ahriman will continue to ridicule what we seek on the mountaintop. May we have certainty that the difficulties and challenges we encounter will only enhance our transformation; obstacles and deprivation mean nothing to a goat. He always perseveres.

---

35 Emmerich. *The Visions of Anne Catherine Emmerich*, vol. 3, p. 77.

36 See Huxley, *Brave New World*.

We can feel the earth rumbling beneath our feet. Evolution is demanding transformation, and resistance to it will result only in more chaos.

How do we re-evolve into the early promise of the United States? How do we transform that promise into our future? We have a stark choice this year; we can continue to ignore (and therefore serve) the brotherhoods, or we can stand up to them. It is our task to unmask evil and to name every manifestation of its corrupting work—while we still have the freedom to do so. Christ's passage through the subearthly layers will assist us. *Fighting* against evil, however, is not our burden at the present time. The unknown author reminds us:

> For good does not *fight* evil; it does not struggle against it. The good is only present, or it is not.[37]

We must not feel fear, as this is what Ahriman desires—paralysis of our collective will. Fear leads to hopelessness and to disharmony in the soul; it is essential that we strive toward *balance of soul*, as we can be sure that the task before us is the proper one, however difficult it might seem.

Nor should we allow ourselves to sink into indifference in the face of the metastasis of abstract, materialistic thinking, of political overreach, and of the constant grave-digging for the new corpses of lost innocence. And we must ask what we have betrayed for our own thirty pieces of silver.

Have we yet heard our "shot heard round the world"? Perhaps it was already fired by Li Wenliang, the Chinese physician who first raised the alarm on the pandemic in December 2019. We need to listen closely. Whether or not it has yet been fired, it will almost certainly take the form of an electronic report, a sharing with the world that will, like the musket shot of 1773, unite us in our resolve to preserve what remains of our freedoms. We will be lost if not united.

We must beware the Robespierres of our time, those who will claim to stand for reform as they serve Ahriman as instruments of violent destruction. Will we simply stand by as they seek to sever our continuity to the past?

Hope is the blood of the spiritual world. May we share the hope of all expectant mothers—the hope that the future will be even more blessed than the past.

---

37 Anon., *Meditations on the Tarot*, p. 114.

---

"When the Christ impulse entered the evolution of humanity in the way known to us, one result was that the chaotic forces of the sibyls were thrust back for a time, as when a stream disappears below ground and reappears later on. These forces were indeed to reappear in another form, a form purified by the Christ impulse.... Yes, a time is coming when the old astrology will live again in a new form, a Christ-filled form, and then, if one can practice it properly so that it will be permeated with the Christ impulse, one may venture to look up to the stars and question them about their spiritual script."

—RUDOLF STEINER (*Christ and the Spiritual World and the Search for the Holy Grail*, pp. 94, 122)

# ANTHROPOSOPHY, ASTROLOGY, MUSIC

## Amber Wolfe Rounds

Ancient Greek mythology accredits the Sun God Apollo with creation of the first lyre. Meanwhile, Athena, Goddess of Wisdom, invented the aulos, a double-reed instrument. Athena soon cast her creation aside, allegedly perturbed by how distorted her face became while playing the aulos. Marsyas, a wise Phrygian satyr who served as minister to the nature god, Dionysus, discovered and mastered the aulos. Apollo and Marsyas engaged in a legendary musical competition to determine the virtues of each instrument.

Marsyas was winning, until Apollo suggested they play with their instruments turned upside down. Apollo could perform equally well with his lyre reversed, but Marsyas could not possibly play the aulos upside down. The victor chose the mode of punishment for the loser. Apollo flayed Marsyas for his hubris in attempting to compete with a god. Blood from Marsyas's hide flowed down to form the river named in his honor.

Rivalry between lyre and aulos reflects a schism in ancient musical traditions. The lyre symbolized a microcosm of a divine, rational cosmos: each of the seven strings represented one of the seven planets. The music that came from the lyre conjured reverence and peace and was preferred by the aristocracy. The aulos, in contrast, represented the complicated human reality of mysterious, chthonic Earth and was a reminder of an earlier, matriarchal era. The music of the aulos evoked emotions, dancing, and passion. The common people of Rome used the tale of Marsyas as a symbol for their mistreatment by the ruling class, depicting the treachery of noble Apollo as a reminder not to trust those in power.[1]

The myth of Marsyas also evokes a primal belief that, due to the formative power of sound, divine beings were the source of all music. *Nadam brahmam* is a Sanskrit expression of a fundamental Vedic message from the Divine: "Sound is God. I am the sound that is God."[2] Judeo–Christian tradition acknowledges this spiritual truth in a corresponding manner: "In the Beginning was the Word" (John 1:1). Both sayings reflect the concept that sound is formed of vibration, and all vibration is a product of divine intent. The musicality of the human thus indicated a sacred interconnection between human, environment, and cosmos.

Rudolf Steiner renewed these ancient relationships between cosmos and music, inspiring avant-garde composers and musicians in his era. However, Anthroposophy has largely avoided engaging with experimental impulses in music since Steiner's death. This essay will provide historical examples of musicians who composed from Anthroposophy as a means of beginning to analyze new musical impulses that have arisen in the last century.

First, I will share how Steiner encouraged musicologist Kathleen Schlesinger and composer Elsie Hamilton to create avant-garde music that corresponded to the seven planets of antiquity. Astrological perspective on the modern planets, Uranus, Neptune, and Pluto will then be provided as a framework for understanding massive musical changes that occurred in the 20th century. Thereafter, I will introduce the work of experimental musician, David Tudor, to illustrate how Anthroposophy continues to influence avant-garde music. Next, I will discuss ruptures between material and spiritual approaches to music composition that

---

1 Ellen Van Keer, "The Myth of Marsyas in Ancient Greek Art," *Music in Art* 29, pp. 20–37.

2 Alexander Keefe, "Lord of the Drone: Pandit Pran Nath and the American Underground" (https://www.bidoun.org/articles/lord-of-the-drone).

continue to the present day. I will conclude with an introduction to my own research, which proposes to heal the schism in contemporary music through anthroposophic holism.

## Musica Universalis

Rudolf Steiner drew inspiration from an ancient concept known as the harmony of the spheres or *musica universalis*. The harmony of the spheres described three types of music, "*musica mundana, musica humana,* and *musica instrumentalis.*" The first was cosmic music, or the inaudible sound of the planets moving through the signs of the zodiac.[3] *Musica humana* was defined as the music that occurs from the multifaceted nature of the human personality. Musica humana was reflected in sympathies and antipathies of the astral realm, and in the drama of human social exchanges. *Musica instrumentalis* was the instrumental music that humans were able to create as receivers of cosmic music. Humans fashioned instruments out of natural materials, thus transmitting cosmic tone through chthonic environment.[4]

In *The Inner Nature of Music and the Experience of Tone,* Steiner reveals that what are perceived as the fixed stars and planets are, in fact, spiritual entities. Humans engage with stars and planets after death as the soul passes through various spheres during excarnation from earthly existence. Souls observe the spiritual entities of the planets and zodiac in a manner more akin to hearing than seeing. The planetary entities resound with what can be experienced as a "soul–vowel" sound, while the "fixed stars…ensoul this song of the planetary sphere with consonant elements," Cosmic music occurs as the planets pass through the different fixed stars in the zodiac, causing them to resound differently: "You have in the fixed stars a wonderful cosmic instrument, and the players of this instrument of the zodiac and fixed stars are the gods of the planets beyond."[5]

In earlier stages of evolution, humans were more aware of the archetypal music; therefore, music was intimately associated with primordial closeness to the divine. Gods spoke through the planets and the musical nature of the human being reflected divine communications. The word *music,* as used today, tends to refer only to *musica instrumentalis,* yet from the view of *musica universalis,* astrology is actually a musical discipline. Astrology shows where *musica mundana* impacts *musica humana.* This essay thus speaks of astrology and music as differing manifestations of the same principal.[6]

Steiner spoke of astrology most directly when explaining how the heavens are a macrocosm for the microcosm found on Earth. The human organism reflects the blueprint of the heavens in the makeup of the physical body. Steiner believed that similar to planetary music occurring on the macro level, music occurs on a micro level within the formation of the human being. The divine instrument that the ancient Greeks called "the lyre of Apollo" is actually the human body. In the lecture compilation *The Arts and Their Mission,* Steiner states:

What is experienced musically is really man's hidden adaptation to the inner harmonic–melodic relationship of cosmic existence out of which he was shaped. His nerve fibers, ramifications of the spinal cord, are marvelous musical strings with a metamorphosed activity. The spinal cord culminating in the brain and distributing its nerve fibers is the lyre of Apollo. Upon these nerve fibers the soul–spirit man is "played" within the earthly sphere. Thus, man himself is the world's most perfect instrument; and he can experience artistically the tones of an external musical instrument to the degree that he feels this connection between the sounding of strings of a new instrument, for example, and his own coursing blood and nerve fibers. In other words, man, as nerve man is inwardly built up of music, and feels it artistically to the degree that he feels its harmonization with the mystery of his own musical structure.[7]

3  Godwin, *Cosmic Music,* p. 77.
4  Stebbing, *Music: Its Occult Basis and Healing Value,* p. 54.
5  Steiner, *The Inner Nature of Music and the Experience of Tone,* p. 43.
6  Ibid., p. 3.
7  Steiner, *The Arts and Their Mission,* p. 37.

"Nerve man" as described in the passage above is one side of a polarity, with "breath man" as the other end. The nervous system, with its connection to thinking, moves toward a process of separation and hardening. Nerve man is related to the etheric body moving into the physical body. Breath man, however, is connected to the expansiveness of cosmos and is related to the etheric moving into the astral body. A healthy human being exists in balance between these polarities, but the two forces constantly pull in opposite directions. The nerve man impulse is dominant in the modern era, encouraging humans to be more rooted in materialism at the expense of spirituality.[8]

Steiner differentiated between sound and tone. He considered the vibrations that comprise sound wholly physical. Air provides the medium for speaking and singing on Earth, but this physical manifestation of sound is merely a shadow of the "soul–spiritual element" of tone. *Sound* is connected to an outer, physical experience, while *tone* is an inner spiritual experience.[9] Steiner critiques the burgeoning field of acoustics as relevant to only physics, claiming, "A tone physiology that would have significance for music itself does not exist."[10] He was, however, very engaged with new musical impulses that acknowledged the tone, or spiritual nature, of music.

### Musica Mundana

*Thus, in using the ancient modes as a new language of music, we have a perfectly open field where no modern laws of melody or harmony need exist to disturb the composer in his own untrammeled inspirations. Who can tell whether they may not lead to a new revelation in the music of the future?*[11]

British musicologist Kathleen Schlesinger (1862–1953) dedicated her career to pursuing the interrelations between the planets and music through comprehensive study of musical modes across ancient cultures. Australian pianist and composer Elsie Hamilton (1880–1965) joined Schlesinger in her studies, helping the research come alive by creating unique compositions. Steiner championed their research, for their studies illuminated the ancient link between cosmos, human, and music while also contributing to the modern field of microtonal music composition.[12]

Schlesinger visited museums throughout the world to examine relics of the ancient Greek *aulos*, a double-reed instrument similar in design to an oboe or Armenian duduk and thought to sound like a bagpipe.[13] Schlesinger was inspired by the rich musical tradition and mythology of the aulos. She observed that each type of Greek aulos had a different interval structure based on the distance between the finger holes on the aulos, producing distinct modes for each individual aulos. Each mode came from a different region of Greece and was therefore intimately associated with the folk soul or tribal spirit of that place. Furthermore, each mode, called *harmonai*, was associated with the ruling god of each region and therefore one of the seven planets. Schlesinger investigated the harmonic structures of these modes through experiments on the monochord. The monochord is a simple instrument with one string and a moveable wooden block that is slid under the string to change the string ratio and thus, the intervals.[14]

Pythagoras famously standardized intervallic associations and introduced formal mathematical laws into music using a monochord. The monochord enabled Schlesinger to derive modes from the harmonics that became apparent with adjustments of string length.[15] Pythagoras's monochord research did much to standardize intervallic associations, bringing mathematical coherence into music. According to Schlesinger, however, this approach was not necessarily a musical one but

---

8  Ibid., p. 17–25.

9  Steiner, *The Inner Nature of Music and the Experience of Tone*, p. 40.

10  Ibid., p. 70.

11  Hamilton, *Writings*, p. 5.

12  Lee, "Kathleen Schlesinger and Elsie Hamilton: Pioneers of Just Intonation" (http://www.anaphoria.com/lee.html).

13  West, *Ancient Greek Music*, pp. 83–34.

14  Schlesinger, *The Greek Aulos*, p. 1.

15  Hamilton, *Writings*, p. 16.

one born out of rational, mathematical convenience. Schlesinger explaines:

> …from their pseudo-musical speculations there grew the doctrine of the Harmony of the Spheres, according to which Sun, Moon, and planets, as they went along their orbits, were supposed to make sounds which could be identified with the notes of the Dorian scale; and such guesses at the foundations of the cosmos did more than the legitimate mathematical investigations to withdraw the study of music from its proper track.[16]

While Schlesinger was inevitably influenced by the concept of Harmony of the Spheres, she did not illumine the planetary connection to the Greek modes with the intention of proving a rational cosmic order. Instead, the *harmonai* demonstrated a subtle, qualitative link between cosmos and music. Schlesinger saw that the reduction of the world to mathematical principles through the harmony of the spheres was a form of early rationalism. She advocated for an organic, as opposed to idealistic, approach to music instead of adherence to reductionist systems.[17]

Australian composer Elsie Hamilton first met Schlesinger in 1916 at a Theosophical Society summer school. Hamilton was profoundly affected by Schlesinger's demonstration of the modes. The two women became fast friends, and Hamilton devoted herself almost exclusively to composing with the modes from that point forward. Hamilton began to conduct groups of lyre players and composed less with the piano. In 1921, both women became members of the Anthroposophical Society and soon met with Rudolf Steiner. He encouraged them in their pursuit to revitalize the modes. He was particularly interested in the connections between the modes and the planets. Hamilton and Schlesinger's compositions were shocking to mainstream audiences owing to the unusual modal and tuning structures, but they were well received by anthroposophic circles.[18]

Schlesinger did not publish writing about the connection between the *harmonai* and the planets. Hamilton learned of this connection from her personally and later wrote about the links. Schlesinger was careful about sharing such knowledge; she "was up against the most hardened and materialistic thinkers of the day who might have considered such knowledge as mere charlatanism, which would have been highly distasteful to someone of her scientific way of thinking," explained Hamilton. However, the planetary associations of the *harmonai* were essential for their compositions. For example, "Hymn to Ra" (the Egyptian Sun God) was written in the Dorian mode, associated with the Sun.[19]

One of the many reasons the Planetary Modes appealed to Hamilton as a composer was because of their variety in tone color, or timbre. As Hamilton explains, "If you play the same melody in the seven different Modes, you experience a distinctly different atmosphere each time, whereas in our modern well-tempered system it does not make much difference if we play the same melody in any or all the keys."[20] Although she was a pianist by training, Hamilton recognized the limitations of the piano. The piano standardized intervals by adjusting perfect thirds and fifths in order to fit them consistently across seven octaves. Hamilton and Schlesinger advocated for *just intonation*, the practice of playing instruments with true thirds and fifths rather than the standardization of 12 tones necessary to create the piano.[21] Steiner may have informed this perspective, for he too was a proponent of just intonation, calling the piano a "philistine" instrument.[22]

16 Kathleen Schlesinger, "The Return of the Planetary Modes," *Anthroposophy*, vol. 2. 1923, p. xxi.

17 Brian Lee, "Kathleen Schlesinger and Elsie Hamilton: Pioneers of Just Intonation," (https://www.yumpu.com/en/document/view/52208881/kathleen-schlesinger-and-elsie-hamilton-pioneers-of-naked-light).

18 Talisha Goh, "Australia's microtonal modernist: The life and works of Elsie Hamilton (1880–1965)" (https://ro.ecu.edu.au/theses_hons/194).

19 Renold, *Intervals, Scales, Tones: And the Concert Pitch c = 128 Hz*, p. 28.

20 Hamilton, *Writings*, p. 5.

21 Renold, *Intervals, Scales, Tones: And the Concert Pitch c = 128 Hz*, p. 43.

22 Steiner, *The Inner Nature of Music and the Experience of Tone*, p. 75.

Hamilton and Schlesinger conferred with Rudolf Steiner the second time in 1923. This encounter inspired the concept of *modal tone eurythmy*, a practice that would incorporate the Greek *harmonai* into the burgeoning art form of eurythmy created by Rudolf Steiner and Marie Steiner-von Sivers. Hamilton spent most of her life moving among various European cities and sharing her compositions with anthroposophic circles. She directed orchestras devoted to the modes on some occasions and collaborated with Eugen Kolisko (one of the pioneers of anthroposophic medicine) on how to use the modes in therapeutic practice. Schlesinger dedicated her book, *The Greek Aulos*, to Hamilton, and the two continued their collaboration until Schlesinger's death in 1953. Hamilton worked for the rest of her life in England and Australia to further Anthroposophy and music.[23]

As Talisha Goh asserts in her thesis "Australia's Microtonal Modernist," Hamilton was a cutting-edge, female, modernist composer who has been unjustly neglected within scholarly circles. One aspect that positioned Hamilton within the ranks of other modernist composers was her employment of microtonality. Hamilton explored microtonality from a unique vantage point: the Greek modes were all completely based on the overtone series. Hamilton herself best describes the overtone series in *The Modes of Ancient Greece*:

Now we all know that any musical sound gives forth a series of harmonics or overtones, which do not correspond with the tones of our modern keyboard. I used to listen in Paris to an aeroplane which flew over my studio about noon each day, and which produced the most beautiful harmonics from a deep fundamental tone of F. This is what is called the Harmonic Series, which we all learn about, but then put away in a pigeon hole in our brain, perhaps never to be called forth again, as we have no further use for it. Nevertheless, this Harmonic Series is the only musical law which is given to us by nature herself, and it rises first of all at the distance of

an octave from the fundamental tone, then on to a perfect fifth, a fourth, a third etc., until we get such tiny intervals, called microtones, that the ear can no longer distinguish them.[24]

Hamilton was not the only composer to work with microtones. She and other composers who were her contemporaries, such as Alois Hába (1893–1973), and Harry Partch (1901–1974), were inspired by local and global folk traditions to emphasize timbre and feature microtonality in their compositions.[25] Anthroposophy provided the spiritual and scientific basis from which Hamilton composed.[26]

In *The Inner Nature of Music and the Experience of Tone*, Rudolf Steiner indicated that each era of human development prefers certain musical intervals. In other words, the concept of harmony is subjective and dependent on epoch and culture. The interval of the fifth was considered the most harmonious in the ancient past, while the experience of the third has defined Classical Western music. Composers such as Arnold Schoenberg (1874–1951) increasingly emphasized the interval of the minor second or "semitone" during Steiner's lifetime. Furthermore, microtonal composers such as Hamilton highlighted intervals within the semitone. Thus, Hamilton helped listeners of the 20th century grow toward greater appreciation of singular tone by demonstrating the increased diversity and abundance of subtle intervals.

### Musica Humana

Steiner stated that, in the distant future, "a single tone will be experienced as something that is musically differentiated,"[27] enabling perception of the melody present within one tone. As music listeners grew more self-aware, their preference for smaller and smaller intervals would result in holistic appreciation for the octave and tonic as

---

23 Talisha Goh, "Australia's microtonal modernist: The life and works of Elsie Hamilton (1880–1965)" (https://ro.ecu.au/theses_hons/194).

24 Hamilton, *Writings*, p. 3.

25 Wolf, "Harry Partch" (https://marcjwolf.com /articles/harry-partch-america-s-first-microtonal -composer).

26 Goh, "Australia's Microtonal Modernist"; Hamilton "The Modes of Ancient Greece."

27 Steiner, *The Inner Nature of Music and the Experience of Tone*, p. 71.

one.[28] This appreciation would only be possible with greater spiritual evolution. Evolution toward unity of the tonic and octave is mirrored in the rapidly expanding awareness of the macrocosm and microcosm in the 20th century.

Although understanding of the macrocosm had expanded to include both Uranus and Neptune by the time Steiner was alive, he did not incorporate the two more recently "discovered" planets into his philosophy. Therefore, the astrological systems evoked by Steiner and the Planetary Modes of Schlesinger and Hamilton only acknowledge the five classical planets and the two luminaries. Steiner explained his reasoning in the following quote:

> Uranus and Neptune—did not originally belong to our solar system. They came flying into the sphere of attraction of our system much later. They then joined company and remained within it. They cannot therefore be reckoned as belonging to our system in the same sense as the other planets from Saturn onward, which, so to speak, belonged to it from the beginning.[29]

Modern astrologers, including Robert Powell, consider the newer planets Uranus and Neptune, and the dwarf planet, Pluto, valuable. This article follows suit, contending that contemporary reality is best analyzed from a viewpoint that encompasses the newfound heavenly bodies. Unlike the classical planets, the exact times of the first observation of these newer heavenly bodies are known. The social context of their discovery indicates the particular significance of Uranus, Neptune, and Pluto.[30]

Uranus is named after the Greek titan and god of the sky, Oranos. Uranus is considered "a higher octave of Mercury" due to the brilliant, intuitive intelligence that it represents.[31] Uranus is the "sun behind the Sun," representing the forces that the self cannot ever control.[32] Uranus is associated with individuality, freedom, unpredictable changes,

rebelliousness, and electricity. The discovery of Uranus in 1781 fits perfectly with these associations. The Enlightenment occurred throughout the 18th century, leading to intellectual individualism. Electricity also became a force that humans could understand and harness shortly after the discovery of Uranus.[33]

Paralleling the correspondence with Uranus and electricity, the discovery of Neptune coincided with the understanding of electromagnetism. Electromagnetism led to the ability to control and measure electricity. Neptune is associated with the ability for the feeling life of the social organism to be manipulated. Neptune is named after the god of the ocean, Poseidon. Powell suggested that Neptune was named incorrectly, however, and should have been named *Night* after the goddess of darkness that preceded the birth of the sky, Uranus, in Orphic cosmology. Regardless of the name of this planet, associations with the unconscious, the feeling life, and mystery are appropriate to the mythology of both Night and Neptune.

The dwarf planet Pluto was first observed in 1933, less than a decade after Steiner died. Pluto is named after the Roman god of the underworld, modeled after the Greek god, Hades. Powell again refers to Orphic cosmology and suggests that a more apt name for Pluto would have been Phanes, an androgynous deity that the Greeks believed was the source of Night, Uranus, and all later generations of gods. As symbolic of Hades and Phanes, Pluto is thus associated with both the primal spark and the depths of the underworld. On a cosmic scale, Pluto signifies the "Big Bang" or on the microcosmic scale, the tremendous power within a single atom. The discovery of Pluto accompanied advances in nuclear power and atomic warfare.

Steiner did not address Uranus and Neptune in his astrological schema, yet his development of Anthroposophy responded to the negative risks of these new forces and provided ways for human beings to overcome the dangers of Uranus and Neptune influences. Anthroposophy tends to view the technological advances represented by Uranus, Neptune, and Pluto with skepticism. The freeing

28 Ibid., pp. 47–52.

29 Steiner, *Spiritual Beings in the Heavenly Bodies and in the Kingdoms of Nature*, p. 151.

30 Powell, *Hermetic Astrology*, vol. 2, p. 287.

31 Hickey, *Astrology: A Cosmic Science*, p. 36.

32 Ibid.

33 Powell, *Hermetic Astrology*, vol. 2, p. 287.

of *subnatural* forces such as electromagnetism and nuclear energy has had devastating repercussions on the health of the planet. Steiner was very clear, however, that Anthroposophy did not advocate for a return to earlier states of civilization. Humans must rise, in full consciousness, to meet the challenges of these and future forces.[34]

In *Hermetic Astrology*, volume 2, Robert Powell interprets the recent three celestial figures as representatives of modern manifestations of evil. Uranus was discovered in 1781, barely preceding the French Revolution. Neptune was discovered in 1846 and the socialist revolution began two years later. Pluto was discovered in 1930, nearly congruent with rise of the Nazi movement. Each of these social movements brought out a new expression of evil but also illuminated a corresponding virtue that could combat the negative manifestation of power.[35]

Powell associates Uranus with the cosmic force of *Light*, leading to the virtue of *Illumination* and the capacity for *thinking*. Pluto represents the cosmic force of *Life*, the virtue of divine *Union*, and the capacity of *willing*. Neptune corresponds to the cosmic force of *Sound*, the virtue of *Inspiration*, and the capacity for *feeling*.[36] By cultivating these higher faculties, humans can rise to meet the challenges presented by the modern forces of evil. Where the seven classical planets represent aspects of individual spiritual development, Powell contends that Uranus, Neptune, and Pluto represent the challenges that must be met by collective societal evolution.

Contemporary music, like all aspects of society, is inseparable from the subnatural forces associated with the modern planets. In music technology, Uranus corresponds most directly to amplification, Neptune corresponds to the capacity to record and edit sound, and Pluto with the ability to perform with electronic musical instruments. The consciousness of the outer planets represents a corresponding movement into the Earth, evidenced

by reliance on subnature and rare-earth metals in music and instrument creation. The simultaneous inner and outer awareness corresponds to the holism of both the tonic and the octave, which Steiner states will be understood as humans develop their spiritual self-awareness.

Music creation and dissemination has changed at an unprecedented rate throughout the century since Rudolf Steiner's death. Recording technology and broadcasting has made the creation of pop and rock *stars* possible. Globalized music media has contributed to an erosion of folk traditions, and the rarefaction of musical ability. Awareness of the inherent musical capacity of the human being has been mostly lost, replaced by the belief that only musicians elevated to superstardom are worthy of expressing themselves musically. Most anthroposophists, rejecting the commercialization and denigration of human creativity in popular music, turned away from engagement with contemporary music.[37] Unfortunately, Anthroposophy has largely also avoided engagement with avant-garde and underground streams of music creation since Steiner's death. Musical evolution reflects changing spiritual consciousness, according to Steiner. Therefore, this article will next address several major changes to the conception of music in the second half of the 20th century and begin to explore spiritual implications for these developments.

### Musica Instrumentalis

*We must understand subnature for what it really is. This we can do only if we rise, in spiritual knowledge, at least as far into extra-earthly supernature as we have descended, in technical Sciences, into subnature. The age requires knowledge transcending nature, because in its inner life it must come to grips with a life content that has sunk far beneath nature—life content whose influence is perilous. Needless to say, there can be no question here of advocating a return to earlier states of civilization. The point is that human beings shall find the way to bring the conditions of*

---

34 Steiner, *Anthroposophical Leading Thoughts*, "From Nature to Subnature."

35 Powell, *Hermetic Astrology*, vol. 2, p. 287.

36 Ibid., p. 290.

37 Stebbing, *Music: Its Occult Basis and Healing Value.*

*modern civilization into their true relation-ship—to ourselves and to the cosmos.*[38]

David Tudor (1926–1996) created music from Anthroposophy that reflects the modern consciousness of Uranus, Neptune, and Pluto. Whereas Hamilton and Schlesinger revitalized cosmic influences to compose avant-garde music accepted by Steiner, Tudor transfigured chthonic inspirations to collaborate with electronic instruments, generally rejected by anthroposophists. Tudor harnessed the creative potential of loudspeakers and microphones (Uranus), recording media (Neptune), and electronic instruments (Pluto) to create supernatural sonic environments. Electronic instruments enabled Tudor to explore timbral nuances while also allowing him to externalize his inner imagination of tone. Tudor's sound environments were a product of exploring the depths of subnature for the purpose of intoning what Steiner (2002) describes as "extra-earthly supernature."[39]

David Tudor was taught an esoteric physiological method of piano based on the teaching of Emil Jaques-Dalcroze (1865–1950) by his teacher, Irma Wolpe (1902–1984). Tudor's esoteric foundation in music allowed him to become one of the most sought-after pianists of his generation. In the 1950s, Tudor applied his prodigious talents on the piano toward performing works by contemporary composers including John Cage (1912–1992), Morton Feldman (1926–1987), Karlheinz Stockhausen (1928–2007), and Christian Wolff (b. 1934). Christian Wolff recalled, "a lot of piano music was written in those years...precisely for an instrument that one might call David Tudor."[40] Tudor moved away from performance of any classical piano pieces once he began to collaborate with John Cage.

Cage and Tudor shared interests in both Eastern and Western forms of occult traditions. Tudor studied astrological texts, including *An Astrological Guide to Character* (1907) by Isabel M. Pagan, and had his own natal chart read on at least one occasion. Cage coined the term *chance operations* to describe the practice of linking musical notes to divination tools such as the I-Ching. Chance operations used the results of divination to determine musical compositions, a practice that has become known as *indeterminacy*. Tudor was inspired by the astrological symbolism of the Tarot and used the Major Arcana as his chance operation composition tool of choice.[41]

John Cage and David Tudor sought to remove subjective preferences of the composer through indeterminacy, allowing themselves to be surprised by the outcomes. Cage was one of the first composers to describe his own musical practice as *experimental*, a term that has since been associated with unorthodox approaches to music composition and performance. The practice of indeterminacy has since become a key component of experimental music.[42] Neptune can be seen as the astrological reflection of indeterminacy as a music composition tool. Neptune sublimates the clarity of the ego (Sun) to mimic nature in its mode of operation.[43]

Uniting Neptunian indeterminacy with the electric impulses of Uranus, Tudor developed his own experimental practice of working with loudspeakers within the piano. The variability of electronic components introduced another type of contingency into his performances. Feedback generated by the close proximity of loudspeakers to microphones inside of the piano completely changed the nature of the instrument. By the 1960s, Tudor had stopped working with the piano altogether and started building custom electronic instruments, often in collaboration with musician Gordon Mumma ((b. 1935). Their modular electronic instruments were arranged in complex signal chains intentionally designed to produce large amounts of feedback. "Tudor placed himself as a

---

38 Steiner, *Anthroposophical Leading Thoughts*, "From Nature to Subnature," p. 218 (trans. revised).

39 Ibid.

40 Quoted in You Nakai, "David Tudor and the Occult Passage of Music" (https://www.academia.edu/35233758/David_Tudor_and_The_Occult_Passage_of_Music).

41 Smigel, *Alchemy of the Avant-garde*, p. 218.

42 Steve Marshall, "John Cage's I Ching Chance Operations" (https://www.biroco.com/yijing/cage.htm).

43 Hickey, *Astrology: A Cosmic Science*, p. 43.

component within the network of modular instruments," manipulating and channeling feedback to create unpredictable results.[44]

Tudor sought to reduce the hierarchical nature of the human as composer by involving his instruments as partners in the process of composition. He befriended his electronic components and tried to help the instruments express their unique personalities. One approach to helping the instruments reveal their characters was through customizing or modifying equipment in nonstandard ways:

> ...an electronic component can seem to have a personality very much in the same way I try to make loudspeakers have a special voice. If you really examine a device that you might buy, like a filter or a small mixer, and you actually try to experience its capabilities, you have to push it, to ask it to do something that it's incapable of doing. When you make those experiments you find out that unique things are happening because you are influencing the electronics. I mean, take the classic experiment of using ordinary feedback: just take the output of something and feed it back into the input. Those of us who do that have had really rich experiences.[45]

David Tudor uncovered the hidden personality of his instruments by pushing at the limits of his own control as a creator, demonstrating the self-suspension of Pluto. He was not only collaborative with composers and electronics, however. The work of Tudor was eventually contextualized within the burgeoning genre of sound art, a field that originated as a byproduct of interdisciplinary creative ventures. For example, Tudor created *Rainforest I* in 1968 as a "sound score" for the Merce Cunningham dance piece of the same name.[46] The term *sound art* became increasingly common from the 1970s onward to describe the extra-musical pieces that many composers created, often in conjunction with other art forms.

A lifelong involvement with Anthroposophy informed Tudor's radical approach to experimental music, a fact that he kept quite private during his lifetime.[47] Despite having publicly renounced conventional piano performances, Tudor regularly traveled to Europe and performed private classical recitals for the Anthroposophical Society. Although leaders of the anthroposophic movement knew of the sonic experiments for which Tudor was famous, they were not interested in hearing these works performed. Music with any electronic component was anathema to Anthroposophy. In the words of Marie Steiner-von Sivers, "the mechanical musical instruments exercise their powerful, soul-deadening forces, doing away with all atmosphere and feeling."[48]

Anthroposophic circles rejected David Tudor's sound experiments, even as they celebrated his virtuosity as a classical pianist. Ironically, Tudor felt that his work with electronic instruments was more aligned with his spiritual viewpoint than the classical piano pieces requested by the Anthroposophical Society. For example, subtleties between noise, sound, and tone were of particular interest to Tudor.[49] Writings on the topic by Karl König (1902–1966), the anthroposophist who founded the Camphill movement, influenced Tudor in his radical approach to music composition:

> König's lecture on the "Twelve Senses" drew a distinction between three levels of aural perception: noise, sound, and tone (or music). Interpenetration of these levels may occur as, for example, when an uninvited car horn (sound) and the screeching of brakes (noise) interrupt a solo violin recital (tone), but the level to which a given stimulus belongs typically remains distinct. Cage advocated such interpenetration in his compositions, and Tudor was not disapproving, although this was not the primary interest of either. Rather...it is the moment of poetic conversion, the process by which one experiences the movement from

44 You Nakai, "David Tudor and the Occult Passage of Music."

45 Tudor, Interview with Teddy Hultberg. Dusseldorf, Germany (http://davidtudor.org/Articles/hultberg .html).

46 Ibid.

47 You Nakai, "David Tudor and the Occult Passage of Music"; Smigel, *Alchemy of the Avant-garde*.

48 Quoted in You Nakai, "David Tudor and the Occult Passage of Music."

49 Smigel, *Alchemy of the Avant-garde*.

one level of perception to another that seems to have fascinated Tudor. That is, at what point in the listening experience does one's perception of sound or noise register as music? [50]

Tudor created noise compositions in order to encourage listeners to find the musicality, or tone, that is ever-present in quotidian, noisy sound. For this reason, Tudor was fundamental in the formalization of *noise* as a genre of music. The genre of noise can be understood to embody the spirit of Pluto, questioning the validity of distinctions between music and noise, and even sound and silence.

John Cage and David Tudor, for example, revolutionized the classical world with the now infamous piece, *4'33"* (1952). In *4'33"* the prodigious instrument, David Tudor, walked on stage, sat in front of a piano, opened the lid, and sat silently for four minutes and thirty-three seconds. A full audience listened to the sounds of Tudor opening and closing the piano lid and turning the pages in the score, as well as to their own breathing, movements in a chair, and ambient sounds in the concert hall. By creating a "silent" piece, Cage and Tudor exposed the impossibility of such a construct. [51] By acknowledging the musical potential of noises as well as the impossibility of silence, Tudor harkened to *Musica mundana,* or the idea that humans are perpetually surrounded by the "ocean of tones" described by Steiner. Electronic instruments enabled him to explore new facets of timbre, illuminating the musical color within single tones.

Few people understood, however, that Tudor's exploration of noise was driven by an understanding of spiritual tone. Tudor investigated *musica humana,* the point at which the musicality of the human being allows one to be a bridge between macro and microcosm. In his personal notes, Tudor frequently refers to the anthroposophic concept of the human being as a divine instrument. He recognized himself as nerve man, a human

instrument of the cosmos, with electronic instruments forming his extended nervous system.

Beginning in the 1970s, Tudor created complex installations whereby electronics and field recordings interacted with sounds from surrounding environments to produce interactive soundscapes. For example, the "collaborative environmental work" *Rainforest IV* mixed the "live sounds of suspended sculptures and found objects, with their transformed reflections in an audio system." [52] In other words, Tudor worked with the sculptures as both loudspeakers and microphones, mixing a matrix of feedback from multiple sources back to multiple sources. Audio recordings of *Rainforest IV* document a synthetic tropical rainforest, replete with calls of birds and insects, noises from electronic instruments, and the voices of humans exploring the performance installation. Thus, Tudor performed, not only as nerve man, but also as synapse passing electrical signals throughout the nervous systems that were his compositions. [53]

Tudor's interest in "nerve man" extended from his earliest collaborative installations to his final works. For example, in *Neural Network Plus,* composed in 1992, Tudor performed with a synthesizer specifically designed to behave like neurons. [54] Tudor embraced the Uranus impulse represented by electricity, the Neptune impulse represented by recording media, and the Pluto impulse represented by electronic instruments because these subnatural forces allowed him to create a supernatural extension of the Lyre of Apollo. Where anthroposophists saw electricity as a negative element of subnature, Tudor illuminated the positive, supernatural potential of telluric forces. Tudor brought a profound understanding of the spiritual to the mechanical and was not deterred by anthroposophic distinctions between the two categories.

In summary, David Tudor brought spirituality into the art–science of experimental music

50 Ibid. p. 251.

51 Will Hermes, "The story of 4'33"," National Public Radio, May 8, 2000.

52 David Tudor, Interview with John Fullemann (https://davidtudor.org/Works/rainforest.html).

53 Ibid.

54 Mark Thorson et al., "A Neural Network Audio Synthesizer" (https://www.warthman.com/images /Dr.%20Dobbs%20-%20A%20Neural-Network %20Audio%20Synthesizer.pdf).

through occult explorations into the nature of tone. Tudor refers to Rudolf Steiner throughout his personal notes, which reveal that Tudor's life work was informed by Anthroposophy. Tudor read the work of Rudolf Steiner as art rather than as dogma. If Tudor had interpreted Steiner dogmatically, he would have rejected both the "abstract," "philistine" piano and the mechanical, "soul-deadening" music of electronic instruments.[55] Instead, Tudor innovated on the piano and revolutionized electronic music composition and performance through spiritual self-development. Thus, Rudolf Steiner, via the instrument of David Tudor, has indirectly influenced generations of experimental musicians.

### Tone, Noise, Sound

Rudolf Steiner distinguished between the physical vibration of sound and the spiritual reverberation of tone. The contemporary genre of New Age music has taken inspiration from sources similar to Anthroposophy to focus on the astral, healing properties of tone, often at the expense of acknowledging the challenges of the physical world. David Tudor helped codify *noise music* and establish *sound art*. Tudor's revolutionary contributions to both genres were born out of spiritual insight, a fact that has been lost to subsequent generations of artists. Both noise and sound art currently tend to focus on the physical reality of sound at the expense of acknowledging spiritual qualities of tone. Sound art from Anthroposophy, as Tudor originated it, could be a rhythmic practice, functioning as the soul to mediate between spirit and physical. Could sound art from Anthroposophy bring balance to this schism?

Thanks to the New Age movement, Anthroposophy experienced a surge in popularity during the late 1960s. New Agers popularized Eastern practices designed to transcend the limitations of the physical realm, in a manner that could be said to accentuate breath man. Many New Age musicians turned toward global folk traditions to find spiritual truths much as Hamilton and Schlesinger revitalized the Planetary Modes. New Age composers frequently combined folk instrumentation with electronics and field recordings to promote health and optimism. New Age music continues to be promoted in conjunction with other wellness practices, although many artists dismiss the label as a marketing ploy, rather than an authentic genre. New Age musicians had high aspirations for the healing possibilities of tone, yet the resulting music often lacked soul, overemphasizing the spiritual.[56]

The new definition of music inspired by noise radically changed how composers made music from the mid-twentieth century on. Unlike the earnest spiritual explorations of Tudor, the experimental noise music of the 1980s onward has become fundamentally agnostic, if not altogether nihilistic. Tudor exposed the hidden musicality within noise to show the omnipresence of tone. He consciously imagined himself as nerve human, extending his nervous system and, thus, his unique human capacity through electronics. Subsequent noise artists have placed increased emphasis on the physicality of sound without the same attention to tone. Deep materialism is often reflected in the emphasis on electronic instrumentation over the creative vision of the performer, themes that continue to the present day.[57]

Contemporary sound art also avoids spiritual affiliation, focusing on acoustics and the interaction between frequencies within installation spaces rather than on esoteric significance. Sound artists provided revelatory sonic experiences through calculated scientific research into resonant properties of a given physical space. Steiner anticipated that the understanding of sound and visual arts would become more interconnected in the future.[58] Sound art began to actualize his premonition, creating a framework for music to be analyzed in terms similar to the

---

55 Steiner, *The Inner Nature of Music and the Experience of Tone.*

56 Harley Brown, (Oct. 2, 2019), "The State of New Age Music in the Always-on 'Wellness' Era," *National Public Radio.*

57 J. Whitehead, "An Idiot's Guide to Noise" (http://www.jliat.com/txts/Anidiotsguidetonoise.pdf).

58 Steiner, *The Inner Nature of Music and the Experience of Tone.*

visual arts. While the progenitors of sound art are largely considered to be the same as noise music, the two streams differentiated themselves after the 1970s. The chief distinction between the two genres is the *context* of presentation: sound art has become institutionalized through installations at galleries and museums, whereas noise music is relegated to underground realms of basements and bars. Sound art installations are often site-specific, while noise music emphasizes performance.[59]

David Tudor could have shared Anthroposophy with future generations of musicians. Instead, like Kathleen Schlesinger, Tudor kept his spirituality private, fearing condemnation or dismissal from academics who disdain such "nonscientific" thinking. Anthroposophists chose not to engage with the experimental music of David Tudor, missing an opportunity to maintain relevance in the contemporary art world. Today, overt references to Anthroposophy in music are most likely to be found within the context of New Age rather than academic art circles. Thus, both anthroposophists and experimental musicians contributed to a growing schism between physical and spiritual sound practices that continues to this day.

Sound art practices informed by Anthroposophy could provide a harmonizing balance to the schism between physical and spiritual music, most extremely demonstrated in the polarization between New Age and noise music. A type of sound art that acknowledges the spiritual component of music as well as site specific occurrences could be distinguished by the term "tone art." Tone art could form a bridge between physical acoustics and spiritual sound similar to how the soul mediates between the physical and spiritual bodies. Tone art could incorporate new technologies with traditional practices to translate ancient wisdom to a new generation of musicians.

## Tone Art

I first began to explore the interconnections between Anthroposophy, astrology and music through collaborations with the ecological sound artist and pollinator conservationist, Jarrod Fowler. My background in astrology connected naturally with Fowler's work with phenology, "nature's calendar."[60] Our musical practice unfolded accordingly: Fowler offered organic wisdom; I provided cosmic insight. We called our project *Zizia,* after a North American native plant genus in the carrot family and host for butterflies and pollen-specialist bees.[61] Zizia creates contemporary sound art inspired by Anthroposophy.[62]

Fowler has performed ecological sound art for nearly 20 years. Ecological sound art is a contemporary movement within the genre of sound art that reflects "ecological concerns and exhibits an inherent ecocentricism in conception and realization."[63] Fowler's ecological sound art practice guided him to conservation and enhancement of habitats for non-humans. He actively addresses the insect apocalypse, while establishing habitats for future field recordings. His work exhibits an ecosystem of interactions between minerals, plants, animals, and humans, while creating embodied experiences of interconnectedness, and highlighting the vibrant agency of non-humans.[64] Fowler learned about Anthroposophy during professional pollinator habitat consultations for biodynamic farmers. Anthroposophy provided Fowler with a Goethean science vital for the transdisciplinary practice of ecological art, science, and spirituality.

My rediscovery of Anthroposophy as an adult coincided with the beginnings of Zizia. I was

---

59 LaBelle, *Background Noise*; Cox, *Sonic Flux.*

60 National Phenology Network, n.d., p. 1.

61 Fowler, Jarrod Fowler, "Specialist bees of the northeast: Host Plants and Habitat Conservation" *Northeastern Naturalist* 23, 305–320.

62 See Zizia's website http://zizia.xyz.

63 Gilmurray, Jonathan Gilmurray, "Ecology and environmentalism in contemporary sound art" (http://ualresearchonline.arts.ac.uk/13705/1 /Jonathan%20Gilmurray_PhD%20Thesis_FINAL %20SUBMISSION.pdf).

64 Ibid.

homeschooled in the Waldorf method until the 3rd grade, after which I studied at the Washington Waldorf School through 12th grade. My New Age upbringing included education inspired by Anthroposophy, as well as early training in astrology and contact improvisation.[65] As a child, I frequently attended contact improvisation retreats at Claymont Court, a historic mansion in West Virginia, where guitarist Robert Fripp taught Guitar Craft workshops in the 1970s. As an adult, I wrote and performed original musical compositions with guitar and voice most easily classifiable as folk. My performances became increasingly improvisational and experimental by the time I began to read Steiner. Anthroposophy offered me a living philosophy for what I already embodied through transdisciplinary practices in astrology, improvised dance, and folk music.

I asked: *What constitutes an authentic folk music of contemporary New England?* All aspects of a given folk culture can be traced to the environment from which a people derive their shared identity. Contemporary folk music composition necessitated a conscious understanding of the astral and terrestrial forces shaping culture. Observation of ecological occurrences and meditation on cosmic patterns became central to music making. Zizia did not want to perpetuate an extractive attitude toward nature by taking field recordings and instruments from a landscape without returning something to the environment. Thus, habitat establishment and restoration became part of our musical practice.

Zizia composed with environmental recordings and folk instrumentation, similar to many New Age musicians, while also emphasizing noise and silence. We have found further inspiration in ambient music, a genre that often bridges the divide between noise and New Age. Ambient musicians create atmospheric, tonal environments that do not put traditional melodies or rhythms in the foreground. Brian Eno, a foundational ambient musician, self-identified as a "non-musician," despite being one of the most influential creators and producers of modern music.[66] Correspondingly, our stance toward music might be considered "non-musical," suspending apparent differences between noise and music, astrology and ecology.[67] Zizia drew inspiration from *Frippertronics*, an ambient guitar technique pioneered by Fripp in the 1970s. Similar to Fripp, Zizia composes according to complex polyrhythms, thus emphasizing metric structures as well as tonal soundscapes.

Zizia grew into a tone art practice as Fowler and I deepened our anthroposophic studies. The understanding of a sevenfold human being guided our compositions as we acknowledged the holism of mineral, plant, animal, human, and spirit. Breath determined the meter for all of our performances, allowing for etheric attunement and flexible metrics. Electronics and stringed instruments formed extended nervous systems, helping us create unique sonic organisms within each performance space. Zizia mediated between cosmic and chthonic influences to provide "extra-earthly, supernatural" music as described by Steiner.

For my master's project, *Tone Art: Anthroposophy, Astrology, and Music* (2020), I sought to answer the question: *How does one create contemporary sound art from Anthroposophy?* Schlesinger and Hamilton inspired me to find new ways of composing from ancient associations between astrology and music. Tudor provided a framework of conscious collaboration with electronic musical instruments and inspired me to use astrology as a tool for indeterminate music composition. My action research involved two components. First, I collected feedback from listeners at a series of concerts that Zizia performed in 2018. Next, I composed music based on the natal charts

---

65 Steve Paxton first developed Contact Improvisation as an "art–sport" in the 1970s (see https://contactquarterly.com/index.php). Contact Improvisation reduced gender roles and performer–audience division and was highly influential in the dance world. Contact Improvisation parallels the radical nature of sound art in the music world.

66 "Lester Bangs interviews Eno." *Musician* (http://music.hyperreal.org/artists/brian_eno/interviews/musn79.html#musician). See also, Eno, *A Year with Swollen Appendices: Brian Eno's Diary*.

67 Jarrod Fowler, et.al., Non-musicology blog (http://nonmusicology.blogspot.com).

of 21 individuals and asked participants to share their experiences listening to melodies created from astrology.

The first element of research provided me with an opportunity to gather feedback on the experience of Zizia concert attendees. I sent a survey asking listeners to recall how listening to Zizia impacted their willing, thinking, feeling, and physical body. Despite the tendency to view sound art as overly intellectual, most survey respondents reported more feelings than ideas. Respondents reported vivid imaginations of nature, and often expressed having the desire to create their own art or music while at the Zizia performance. While we made no overt references to spirituality, many respondents reported the concerts being a meditative experience. Collecting feedback from audiences was a unique experience that allowed me to combine a scientific method with my art practice and empowered concert audiences to actively reflect on their listening experience.

The second aspect of my research provided even greater insight into the impact of astrologically composed melodies. I first analyzed the astrological makeup of my study group, using a multi-composite astrological chart of respondents to predict responses. I then translated 360° natal charts into a 36-beat melody comprised of three measures of 12/8 time. The planets and signs were thereby located within the 36-beat structure as a unique melodic pattern. I recorded the melodies on a harp tuned to specific astrological frequencies determined by Schlesinger and Hamilton. Respondents had widely varied experiences listening to each of the sparse, microtonal melodies. Many reported vivid imaginations of nature and water, although the only sounds were tones from the harp. My predictions based on the multi-composite also proved surprisingly accurate for determining how respondents answered questions related to thinking, feeling, and willing.

Research on Schlesinger, Hamilton, and Tudor together with the findings from my own studies inspired my definition of sound art inspired by Anthroposophy as "tone art." To summarize my working definition, tone art

- acknowledges the soul and spirit, as well as the physical properties of sound;

- is always transdisciplinary, working toward holism through art, science, and spirituality;

- reveres nature and collaborates with sub-nature to strive toward music creation that reflects extra-earthly supernature;

- as a methodology, not a genre, invites transformation of the composer–performer through cultivation of the higher faculties of imagination, inspiration, and intuition.

Rudolf Steiner once stated that he would change the name *Anthroposophy* every day if he could in order to keep the philosophy from becoming dogmatic. Similarly, tone art is a living, mutating term for anthroposophic sound art.[68]

Tone art continues to provide a creative framework for my practice as an astrologer and musician. For example, I now compose unique scores for every Zizia concert based on local apparent astrology. As my compositions have become more astrologically specific, Zizia performances also include more explicit ecological restoration. Zizia sustainably gathers plant bodies from around each performance venue and harvests native plant collaborators from our habitat restoration projects. Our restoration practice is inseparable from our musical performance: during a 2019 U.S. tour, Zizia sowed wildflowers in degraded habitats around each venue. The wildflowers will feed wild pollinators, who in turn will perform buzzing, rasping, rubbing, scraping, and tapping noises, sounds, and tones.[69]

One of the most exciting things to emerge from my action research was the predictive accuracy of casting a multi-composite chart for all participants in my natal chart study. Multi-composite charts provide beautiful symbolism for understanding and harmonizing group dynamics. I continue to work with composite astrological charts

---

68 Steiner, *The Child's Changing Consciousness*, pp. 21–22.
69 See http://zizia.xyz.

for composition and improvisation. For example, *Asteraceae* (2020) is a composition based on the multi-composite astrological chart for the group, Pisaura, a collaboration among Jarrod Fowler, composer Michael Pisaro-Liu, and me.

Pisaura layered a celestial map of our multi-composite astrological chart over a terrestrial map of greater Los Angeles. We gave site-specific performances, made field recordings, and took collections of natural objects at each planetary location from December 2018 to February 2019. Track contents were based on both site-specific materials and planet–sign–element–modality–specific archetypes. Our multi-composite chart presented patterns from which Pisaura created melodies and determined the duration of each track. Patterns and processes derived from layering a celestial map over a terrestrial map provided productive methods of indeterminacy in *Asteraceae*.[70] *Asteraceae* is one example of how tone art continues to evolve and transform through my work with Zizia.

Finally, the symbolic importance of the modern planets, Uranus, Neptune, and Pluto were essential in the imagination of tone art. Uranus, Pluto, and Neptune represent distinct modern approaches to music listening and music creation. I concluded that Uranus symbolizes both the intellectual idealism of sound art and the spiritual idealism of New Age music. Mysterious and confrontational Pluto suits the subversive nature of noise music. Neptune, positioned between the two, best represents my own exploration of a rhythmic tone art practice.

### Modern Planets

The astrology of 2020 and 2021 highlights the necessity of dialoguing with the modern impulses symbolized by Uranus, Neptune, and Pluto. Massive social changes are underway as evidenced by the conjunctions of Jupiter, Saturn, and Pluto in 2020. Revolutionary urges will be further activated through Jupiter and Saturn both squaring Uranus during 2021. Uranus activity in the 1960s, 1990s, and the present affirm that we are in the gateway toward the next astrological age;

the spiritual nature of humanity is changing rapidly. Possible polarization from Uranus and Pluto forces can be harmonized through embracing the attributes of Neptune in society.

In modern astrological interpretation, the planet Uranus is associated with revolutions, including the cultural revolution of the 1960s. Uranus thus represents the transcendent utopian ideals of the New Age movement. Uranus also epitomized the revolutionary, individualized thinking of the Enlightenment, out of which grew scientific analysis of the physical properties of sound and eventually inspired the discipline of sound art. Thus, from my perspective, Uranus represents both the idealism of New Age music and the academic abstraction of sound art. Uranus inspires musicians to evoke the spiritual foundation of tone, using higher faculties to compose illuminating music. Simultaneously, Uranus encourages musicians to embrace the scientific aspects of music, using the intellect to elucidate the nature of sound.

Pluto is, by far, the noisiest of the three outer planets. Pluto defies description, changing from planet to dwarf planet, yet still occupying a powerful role in astrological interpretation. Noise music similarly defies categorization. In its best form, the genre of noise wills modern people to listen closely to the quotidian song of creation. The Pluto impulse for divine union is expressed in the open-eared listening to the world that is deeply embedded within the genre of noise. In 4'33" Cage and Tudor encouraged an audience who had dulled their hearing to truly listen to the world. They willed listeners to be entertained, not by a performer, but by the environment and their own creative listening capacities.

Attributes of Neptune were most clearly reflected in responses to both studies in my action research, leading me to conclude that Neptune corresponds to tone art. Neptune provides a flowing rhythmic system between the materiality of noise and the spirituality of New Age music for soulful tone art. Similarly, Neptune provides a balance between the reality of Pluto and the ideals of Uranus. Neptune is considered a higher octave

---

70 See http://zizia.xyz/aster.html.

of Venus, thus sharing associations with aesthetics and love. Furthermore, Neptune shares many attributes with the Moon: they are both associated with feelings, water, and the unconscious. Responses to my studies reflected Neptune associations with feelings, the unconscious, water, and the virtue of inspiration.

Neptune is associated with the ways that modern technology impacts the emotional life, for better and for worse. Neptune encourages society to evolve toward "divine compassion," understanding that we "love because it is the nature of love to love."[71] Yet Neptune also offers the temptation to escape from the complexities of the emotional life through the illusions of virtual reality. For example, electronic instruments can function as substitutes for human performers, thus reducing musical community. I sought to uncover positive uses of electronic instruments, utilizing Neptunian impulses, not to distract from the feeling life, but to deepen possibilities for feelings via sounds.

David Tudor provided a positive model of electronic instrument composition. Although Tudor often performed as the only human mediator in his web of electronics, he was always collaborating with many artists. He might compose a piece with John Cage, create an instrument with Gordon Mumma, or collaborate on a performance with Merce Cunningham involving a dozen dancers. Electronic instruments as used by Tudor were actually transdisciplinary agents, enabling more communication across the arts. Tudor modeled a way to create art that moves toward supernatural artistic collaboration from the conscious use of subnature.

Although I was initially wary of collaborating with subnature, David Tudor demonstrated ways that technology can be used as a positive tool for connection rather than isolation. I now perform with more electronic instruments than I did before undertaking my research. Understanding how Tudor collaborated with electronics as agents of indeterminacy encouraged me to embrace the synchronicity of subnatural instruments. Moreover, studying the work of Tudor helped me to

appreciate the possibilities for tone creation made possible by electronic instruments. I have been able to transcend the fear that my music is valid only if I have a certain level of technical skill on an instrument, and instead realize unique possibilities of sharing my inner tone with others thanks to electronics.

The myth of the satyr Marsyas reveals the musical forces growing upward in nature toward the cosmos via the reed instrument of the aulos, and simultaneously the cosmos streaming down toward nature through the abstraction of the lyre. Both musical impulses are equally valid and necessary, however balance is essential. Hamilton, Schlesinger, and Tudor eschewed the stark division between the aulos and lyre traditions in music composition and performance. Schlesinger studied the aulos, yet Hamilton composed and performed on the lyre or piano—an abstracted string instrument. Tudor performed with the piano, yet he attributed his virtuosity with this idealized string instrument to his early esoteric training in breathing. Learning to breathe properly enabled Tudor to perform complex piano pieces. These musicians provided pathways toward imagining holistic music creation from astral and terrestrial, as well as breath and nerve impulses.

The tale of Marsyas affirms the value of diverse modes of musical expression. Apollo provides comforting form to the music of life, while Marsyas reminds us of the precious nearness to chaos. I view Hamilton and Schlesinger as affiliated with cosmic Apollo, while Tudor represented a chthonic Marsyas to the world of classical music. Hamilton and Schlesinger were lauded within the Anthroposophical Society, while the experiments of Tudor were rejected because they did not reflect the type of traditional music and classical virtuosity that anthroposophists celebrated. Hamilton and Schlesinger worked within established musical tradition and upheld a rational cosmic order, no matter how radical their compositions seemed at that time. Tudor embodied Anthroposophy in a unique manner, applying spiritual science to music creation. Tudor created geocentric, chthonic environments, with human as mediator rather than

---

71 Hickey, *Astrology: A Cosmic Science*, p. 191.

master over nature. Unlike Marsyas, however, Tudor was able to "invert the aulos," transforming self-as-instrument and instrument-as-self to make contemporary music from Anthroposophy.

As understanding of the cosmos continues to expand, Apollonian cosmic order seems increasingly mythological. While anthroposophic musicians have embraced tone, and a certain degree of silence, Tudor's explorations of noise were too radical for his spiritual community. Perhaps as Anthroposophy reaches the second century of existence, more anthroposophists will see the value of exploring the spiritual value of noise and the nuanced timbre of electronic instruments. If so, then anthroposophists will find themselves collaborating with some of the most radical contemporary composers and musicians, as Steiner once collaborated with Elsie Hamilton.

My research reflects the notion of *musica mundana,* cosmic music, by demonstrating that astrology is a form of music. The pattern of an astrological chart reminds us of spiritual origin and destiny, as does musical tone. The sevenfold nature of the human being corresponds to the seven planets; the four members of the human body correspond to the four elements; and the trinity of body, soul, and spirit reflects the three qualities of astrology. While the framework of the modern planets has helped me analyze *musica mundana* from a modern perspective, I recognize that including the modern planets has spiritual repercussions.

One might worry that incorporating Uranus, Neptune, and perhaps even dwarf planet Pluto would disrupt the astrological schema that Steiner referred to in his portrayal of the human being. In fact, the template for a ninefold system exists within the sevenfold system. Steiner collapsed a ninefold into a sevenfold system by overlapping the sentient soul with the astral body, the intellectual soul with the "I"-body, and the consciousness soul with the spirit self. Steiner explained that he could never have written about the sevenfold system during the time when the fifth was the dominant interval. Instead, because he was writing during the era of the third, Steiner had to overlap

the sentient soul and the sentient body, which represented the major and minor thirds, respectively. "The facts of human evolution are expressed in musical development more clearly than anywhere else," Steiner explained.[72]

Musical appreciation of the interval of the second, and movement toward the octave suggest that human spirituality is also changing. The collapsing of a ninefold into a sevenfold human being was necessary for Steiner to explain his conception of spiritual physiology during his lifetime.[73] Yet, he suggested that changing musical development reflects evolving human consciousness. The incorporation of Uranus and Neptune form a ninefold system, with noisy Pluto reminding us that definitions and perceptions of reality are ever fluctuating. Truth lies in a balance between the orderly cosmos of the lyre and the mysterious chthonic wisdom of the aulos.

The beauty of astrology lies in the music it provides through harmonization of distinct impulses. The complexity of astrology, like music or any other art, is what prevents astrologers from becoming dogmatic. Steiner frequently inverted his philosophies and contradicted himself, a reminder that Anthroposophy has always been a living path of inquiry motivated by inner spiritual growth. Steiner encouraged his followers to reevaluate the philosophy based on their own human-wisdom. The tale of Marsyas cautions authority figures against castigating the other or rejecting new impulses. Uranus, Neptune, and Pluto remind us that changes in music reflect changes in spiritual development that must be acknowledged. Anthroposophy invites constant reevaluation of new information in the light of inspiration, imagination, and intuition.

---

72 Steiner, *The Inner Nature of Music and the Experience of Tone,* pp. 60–70.

73 See, for example, Steiner, *Anthroposophy (a Fragment): A New Foundation for the Study of Human Nature.*

# CLASSICS IN ASTROSOPHY, PART IV
## THE HOLY GRAIL AND THE GREAT CONJUNCTIONS

### *Selections from early articles by Robert Powell, PhD*

Although the Great Conjunction of Jupiter and Saturn in Capricorn occurred heliocentrically in November 2020 and geocentrically in December, still for much of 2021 the two planets remain close to each other. In light of this, the "Classics in Astrosophy" portion of *Star Wisdom* this year features selections from Robert Powell's contributions to the Easter 1979 edition of the *Mercury Star Journal*. This work is of interest from two perspectives: first, it gives illuminating background information to the cycle of Great Conjunctions in human history. Second, it represents some of the earliest examples of Robert's lifelong research into the historical reality of the Grail legend *Parzival*.

However, some of the information in his article "Grail Research at the Goetheanum" is no longer accurate (for example, the birthdate of St. Guillaume being unknown). I have added my editorial to this article in certain places to clarify and update as needed in [brackets]. See my article "First Steps toward a Grail Timeline" in *Cosmology Reborn: Star Wisdom*, vol I (2018) for further exploration of these themes.—JMP

### Excerpts from the Editorial Foreword, Easter 1979:

> *He said there was a thing called the Grail*
> *Whose name he had read clearly*
> *In the constellations.*
> *A host of angels left it on the Earth*
> *And then flew away up over the stars.*[1]

These words—communicated by the heathen Flegetanis—inspired Kyot, the well-known master on the quest for the Holy Grail. Who was Flegetanis? And who was Kyot? What is the Grail?

And what relevance does it have for humankind in the twentieth century?

The *Mercury Star Journal* cannot pretend to give definitive answers to these questions, but rather—and perhaps more important—there is the hope that something of the *spirit* of the Grail can be communicated through the contents of the *Journal*. The Grail symbol is depicted on the cover of the *Mercury Star Journal*, and the contents—whether or not this is attained, at least the aspiration is present—aspire to be permeated with the sacred presence of the Grail. The spirit of the Grail seeks to breathe through the pages of this *Journal* and to be reborn in the hearts and minds of the readers—in the sense of reading behind and beyond the dead letters of the printed word. In this way the *Mercury Star Journal*—albeit among only a small circle of present-day humanity—seeks to be the bearer of an impulse of cultural renewal, an impulse that could be designated by the words "culture of the heart"—for this is what the Grail impulse is—it is *love*. It is the life of the human heart awakening to the love that underlies all existence.

The New Age that is dawning for humankind is an Age in which the spirit of the Grail will begin to awaken in an ever-increasing number of people. More and more a true seeking for "heart culture" is stirring in the depths of human souls. The Grail impulse, centering in the Mystery of Christ, speaks to the deeper, spiritual nature within each human being—to what lives in his "heart of hearts." Breathing, as the spirit of love, in the inmost depths of his soul, the Grail calls forth in man a longing to become conscious, to attain self-realization. Along the path of self-realization, in the light of the Holy Grail, definite inner knowledge can be attained—knowledge

---

1   Von Eschenbach, *Parzival*, p. 244.

that can give new purpose and direction to the life of he who acquires it.

One aspect of Grail knowledge that human beings can win for themselves along the path of initiation is the knowledge needed to help us further the development of our destiny. In other words, this aspect of the knowledge of the Grail is *practical*—specific to each person, relating to one's individual karma, acquired through inner communion with the Lord of Karma, the source of all Grail knowledge. This personal, specific knowledge that streams by way of a process of spiritual radiation to individuals when they direct themselves toward the Grail might be called "knowledge of the night"—i.e., belonging to the "nightside" of existence. This nightside of knowledge of the Grail is private and individual to each human being, concerning one's destiny or karma.

On the other hand, there is a "dayside" to knowledge of the Grail. This knowledge is of a universal, general nature. It applies to everyone. For example, knowledge concerning the origin and destination of the Earth and humankind could be called "knowledge of the day." The cosmic history of humankind, traced through various stages of planetary evolution (*manvantaras*) as described by Rudolf Steiner in *An Outline of Esoteric Science* exemplifies the universal, general knowledge of the Grail, which could be described (because of its universal, general nature) as a "science of the Grail." This "dayside" of knowledge of the Grail can be acquired in the first instance through *study*, which is the first step on one's path of initiation. It leads to a widening of objective consciousness, opening up new and far-reaching perspectives—e.g., when knowledge of cosmic history is acquired as supplementary to the evolutionary perspective available through conventional, exoteric sources at the present time. Through study, our ordinary, waking consciousness has its first access to the "dayside" of Grail knowledge.

The two sides to knowledge of the Grail—the "dayside" and the "nightside"—are supplementary. The more that "science of the Grail" is allowed to flow into waking consciousness through study,

the more that personal, intimate knowledge of the Grail can radiate spiritually into "night" consciousness. The two sides of Grail knowledge reciprocate each other. Thus, the more that individuals awake to their destiny, the more they will realize what is valid in a general, universal sense. The more we truly grasp what is of a universal nature, the more we open up the possibility of understanding our own destiny. Hence, the significance of knowledge of the Grail for each individual can be realized, and the value of its "spreading abroad" for humankind as a whole can be seen. The healthy unfolding of the future history of humanity depends on the increasing influx of knowledge of the Grail into modern culture. For knowledge of the Grail holds power that can heal the sickness of present-day civilization and can redirect humankind along paths that are beneficial and in harmony with the perspective of cosmic evolution. The New Age depends on realizing of the Grail impulse—with its path of Initiation, the Grail Initiation, and with its knowledge, the knowledge of the Grail.

> Symbolically, this hidden knowledge, which is taking hold of humanity from the other side and will do so increasingly in the future, can be called "the knowledge of the Grail." If we learn to understand the deeper meaning of this symbol as it is presented in stories and legends, we will discover a significant image of what has been described as the new initiation knowledge with the Christ Mystery at its center. Therefore, modern initiates can also be known as "Grail initiates."
>
> The path to suprasensory worlds, whose first stages have been described in this book, leads to "the science of the Grail."... To the extent that human evolution will absorb Grail knowledge, the impulse supplied by the Christ event can become ever-more significant. Increasingly, an inner aspect will be added to the external aspect of Christian evolution. What we can recognize through imagination, inspiration, and intuition about the higher worlds in conjunction with the Christ Mystery will increasingly permeate our life of ideas, feeling, and will. "Hidden" Grail knowledge will become evident; as an inner

force, it will increasingly permeate the manifestations of human life.[2]

The first stages of the Grail Initiation, following that of study, correspond to the higher stages of knowledge known as Imagination, Inspiration and Intuition. In volume 4 (1978) of the *Mercury Star Journal*, where the theme was the reformation of astrology, it was described how the development of the faculty of Imagination can lead to a true astronomy, to a perception of the etheric cosmic that underlies the physical world of objective consciousness. It was described also how the attainment of a real astrology—i.e., of the ability to read the inscriptions made by the human being in the planetary spheres before entering the physical world through conception and birth, depends upon the faculty of Inspiration. It is by way of the faculty of Inspiration that the "birth chart"—portraying the planetary configuration at the moment of an individual's birth—can begin to be understood. The reading of a birth chart, if it is true—i.e., if it is not simply a stringing together of traditional interpretation—requires Inspiration to decode the planetary configuration in terms of what it signifies as a "summing up" of the life of the soul in the planetary spheres prior to conception and birth.

But even an astrology based on Inspiration—profound though it may be—gropes in the dark without the still higher level of knowledge that is yielded by the faculty of Intuition, namely knowledge of reincarnation. This is the shattering realization that penetrates the consciousness of every astrologer—if he is honest with himself—that, with respect to the person facing him, who has come to seek his advice, he is in the dark as far as the other's destiny is concerned, if he does not know the other's former incarnation. The faculty of Intuition is what is required in order to penetrate the mysteries of reincarnation, and the knowledge yielded thereby leads beyond astrology to astrosophy—i.e., by way of Intuition, knowledge of former incarnations is added to that which can be read from a birth chart through Inspiration,

and this is what essentially distinguishes astrosophy from astrology. The Grail path of Initiation thus has the potential to lead to higher stages of knowledge—e.g., from astronomy to astrology, and from astrology to astrosophy. What distinguishes astrosophy from astrology is that whereas the latter (if it is truly astrology) endeavors to read the inscriptions made by the soul in the planetary spheres prior to conception and birth, the former seeks to take account of the former incarnation(s) of the individual.

At this point, although it is a slight digression, some light may be shed on the meaning of the terms "astrology" and "astrosophy." Astrology is a "science of the soul," i.e., science that studies the mysteries of the soul's existence in the planetary spheres during the life between death and rebirth. Astrosophy, however, is a "science of the spirit"—i.e., science that studies the mysteries of reincarnation, or the passage of the human spirit from one earthly life to the next. Just as astrologers seek insight into the human soul—by endeavoring to read the inscriptions in the planetary spheres through Inspiration—so do students of astrosophy aspire to knowledge of the human spirit by studying how the human spirit manifests in successive lives on Earth through the faculty of Intuition. Hence, astrosophy in no way replaces astrology, just as astrology does not replace astronomy. Rather, astrosophy aspires to supplement astrology by *adding* to what the latter can bring to light concerning the soul—namely, by adding knowledge from a hitherto unexplored dimension, knowledge of the stages of development of the human spirit from one earthly life to the next. Astrology and astrosophy are complementary and supplementary spheres of knowledge pertaining to the human soul and the human spirit, respectively.

Both astrology and astrosophy are dependent on astronomy, however. As had always been emphasized in the *Mercury Star Journal*, astronomy is the starting point on the path of knowledge leading to astrology and astrosophy....

Since the founding of the [Mathematical–Astronomical] Section at Christmas 1923, when

---

2  Steiner, *An Outline of Esoteric Science*, pp. 388–389.

the Dutch astronomer Elisabeth Vreede (1879–1943) was appointed by Rudolf Steiner to lead the Section, much valuable work has been accomplished, of which little is known in the English-speaking world.[3] The formulation of three higher levels of knowledge of the cosmos—astronomy, astrology and astrosophy—given by Elisabeth Vreede (cf. the introduction to her book *Anthroposophie und Astronomie*[4]) is founded on insights derived from Rudolf Steiner's Spiritual Science. The bulk of the work of the Section has been concerned with the first of these three higher levels of knowledge of the cosmos—namely astronomy. As an example of this work, Joachim Schultz's book *Rhythmen der Sterne* (Dornach, 1977) may be mentioned. Schultz succeeded Elisabeth Vreede as leader of the Mathematical–Astronomical Section, and worked intensively to establish a new, phenomenological approach to astronomy in order to raise it to the level of Astronomy—that is, to rise from astronomy of the physical universe, based on objective consciousness, to Astronomy, a level of knowledge corresponding to the etheric cosmos, the attainment of which depends on the faculty of Imagination.

The phenomena of the *rhythms* of the planets is all-important in this endeavor—in the attempt to get beyond a physical perspective to an understanding of the *inner working* of the solar system. The book *Rhythmen der Sterne* ("Rhythms of the Stars") is thus a landmark in the development of astronomy, the first of the three higher levels of knowledge of the cosmos. Many other examples of work established in the sphere of astronomy could be mentioned, the most well known (in association with, although not sponsored by, the Mathematical–Astronomical Section) being that of Maria Thun in the realm of agriculture, where insight into the relationship between the etheric cosmos and the plant world—given by the passage of the Moon through the various sidereal signs or constellations of the zodiac—is utilized to enhance plant growth....

The farsighted ideal of Elisabeth Vreede—the development of astronomy, astrology, and astrosophy—has thus to a certain extent, at least with respect to the first higher level of knowledge of the cosmos, been realized—albeit in the sense of laying a foundation for new knowledge of the cosmos. Parallel with the encouragement that she extended to Joachim Schultz in his pioneering, phenomenological work toward a new astronomy, Elisabeth Vreede also assisted and actively encouraged Willi Sucher, who was concerned with the development of a new astrology (and who has subsequently worked at laying the foundations for astrosophy). The early fruits of Willi Sucher's work in the sphere of astrology were published by Elisabeth Vreede, on behalf of the Mathematical–Astronomical Section, in [1934–]35. These *"Astrologische Betrachtungen"* ("Astrological Studies")...offer a completely new foundation for astrology (in the sense of astrology as a stage of higher knowledge of the cosmos). They are, therefore, valuable—as indeed is the whole of Willi Sucher's work—as a foundation for astrology and astrosophy. Thus, at the present time, a little over half a century after the founding of the Mathematical–Astronomical Section at the Goetheanum, the realization of the ideal of astronomy, astrology, and astrosophy is present in the world in seed form, thanks to the work of Joachim Schultz, Willi Sucher, and others.

Since the development of astronomy, astrology, and astrosophy depends up on the unfolding of higher faculties—Imagination, Inspiration and Intuition—that may be attained on the path of Initiation, it is in the measure to which these faculties are developed that the knowledge of the Grail will manifest itself in the world. That astronomy, astrology, and astrosophy (as aspects of the knowledge of the Grail) are present in modern culture only in seed form is indicative that the higher faculties upon which the knowledge of the Grail depends are as yet largely undeveloped. Nevertheless, it is important that the attempt is made to create a new culture—a "heart culture," manifesting the Grail impulse, and based on the knowledge of

---

3 See Selg, *Elisabeth Vreede: Adversity, Resilience, and Spiritual Science.*

4 Vreede, *Astronomy and Spiritual Science: The Astronomical Letters of Elisabeth Vreede.*

the Grail. The far-reaching ideal of a culture of love, sustained by the knowledge of the Grail, is one individual living in harmony with the cosmos, or, as Willi Sucher has expressed it, experiencing oneself as a citizen of the whole cosmos. This ideal can be realized in the extent to which human beings transform their self, on the one hand, and acquire knowledge of the cosmos, at ever higher levels, on the other. Hence, the manifestation of the Grail impulse depends as much on the individual's path of spiritual–moral development (the "nightside" of the Grail seeker's path) as on establishing the knowledge of the Grail (relating to the "dayside" of the Grail impulse) in the world....

It cannot be emphasized enough that the Grail is something that concerns *every* human being, and not just the group of people who lived in the [eighth to the] ninth century that are portrayed in the Grail epic. What the Grail symbolizes—as is evident from the text quoted above from Wolfram von Eschenbach—can speak to everyone who turns his gaze to the stars. Indeed, it was a "heathen," Flegetanis, who first awakened in Kyot the impulse to search for the Grail. Kyot was stimulated by the newly arising Arabic astrology of the eighth/ninth centuries. In the twentieth century there is again a newly arising interest in astrology, and all those who are inspired by modern astrology to seek its deeper meaning, to seek out the truth concerning humanity's relationship to the stars, are "Kyots" in a modern sense.... The *Mercury Star Journal* seeks to address itself to all who are seeking a deeper perspective concerning the world of stars, and the pathway outlined here—from astronomy to astrology, and from astrology to astrosophy—is envisaged as an ideal that can speak to all such seekers in the spirit of the Grail quest.

At Easter time, something occurs in the Earth's spiritual aura that can be expressed in the symbolic language of the Grail; it is with this thought that I would like to close this foreword to the new, fifth volume of the *Mercury Star Journal*, belonging to the year 1979. Words conveying this thought are spoken by the wise hermit Trevrizent to the young Grail seeker Parzival: these words might help to

awake something of the meaning of Easter for and within everyone:

> The stone is...called the Grail. This very day there comes to it a message wherein lies its greatest power. Today is Good Friday, and they (the Grail family) await there (at Munsalvaesche) a dove, winging down from Heaven. It brings a small white wafer, and leaves it on the stone. Then, shining white, the dove soars up to Heaven again. Always on Good Friday it brings to the stone what I have just told you, and from that the stone derives whatever good fragrances of drink and food there are on Earth, like to the perfection of Paradise. I mean all things the Earth may bear. And further the stone provides whatever game lives beneath the heavens, whether it flies or runs or swims. Thus, to the knightly brotherhood, does the power of the Grail give sustenance.[5]

### Grail Research at the Goetheanum, Easter 1979

In 1974 the School of Spiritual Science (Goetheanum) published Werner Greub's book *Wolfram von Eschenbach and the Reality of the Grail*.[6] This book contains the fruit of many years' research by Werner Greub into the historical background of Wolfram von Eschenbach's books *Parzival* and *Willehalm*.[7] The main theme of his research is that Wolfram von Eschenbach

---

5  Von Eschenbach, *Parzival*, p. 252.

6  Werner Greub, *Wolfram von Eschenbach und die Wirklichkeit das Grals* (Dornach, 1974).

7  Wolfram von Eschenbach is the best-known German poet of the Middle Ages. He wrote *Parzival* during the first dozen years or so of the thirteenth century, as a poet at the court of Hermann of Thuringia (died 25 April 1217). After the completion of *Parizival*, Wolfram began work on *Willehalm* at the request of Hermann of Thuringia. Only nine books of *Willehalm* are extant; the tenth book was either never written or lost. Based on his research, Werner Greub wrote a modern version of the missing tenth book (cf. ch. 4 of *Wolfram von Eschenbach und die Wirklichkeit das Grals*). Wolfram began the third work, *Titurel*, but it was not finished; only two books of *Titurel* are extant. (cf. the edition by Karl Lechmann of the complete works of Wolfram von Eschenbach, Berlin-Leipzig, 1965).

can be regarded as a historian, and that *Parzival* and *Willehalm* are not only poetic creations but also are historically authentic. In support of this theme, he adduces evidence that the personality known as "Kyot" in *Parzival* is the same figure as "Willehalm" in *Willehalm*, and that this individual "Kyot-Willehalm" was none other than Count Guillaume de Toulouse, who is mentioned in the Carolingian annals as having checked the violent Saracen offensive at the gates of Narbonne in 793.[8]

It is well known that Wolfram's book *Willehalm* is based on the life of Guillaume de Toulouse, who was also the subject of the French hero epic "Guillaume."[9] Werner Greub's thesis, however, is that Kyot (in *Parzival*) is identical with Willehalm. On this basis not only is *Willehalm* based

on historical reality, but also the Grail book *Parzival* may be regarded as historically authentic. If Kyot is identical with Willehalm—and therefore with Guillaume de Toulouse—the possibility is given of identifying other characters in *Parzival*, in addition to the previously known identification of many of the figures depicted in *Willehalm* (e.g., Willehalm's friend, King Loys) is clearly Louis the Pious, Charlemagne's third son, who was Holy Roman Emperor between 814 and 840, and Willehalm's sister, who is married to Loys, is clearly Queen Ermengarde, the first wife of Louis the Pious. Werner Greub's identification of Kyot as Willehalm (and therefore as Count Guillaume de Toulouse) may thus open the way for a new understanding of *Parzival*, since through his marriage to the "Grail-daughter," Schoysiane, Kyot became a member of the "Grail family" (more specifically, he was Parzival's uncle). Rereading *Parzival* with an awareness of the possible historical background underlying it gives an added dimension to Wolfram's poetic epic, and also gives the possibility of identifying other figures in the Grail epic, as will be attempted later in this report.

Making use of the astronomical references in *Parzival*, Werner Greub endeavors in the second half of his book to give a chronology of the events in *Parzival*. This chronology is based on the Saturn–Jupiter conjunction that took place on Whit Sunday (May 13) in the year 848. Assuming that Count Guillaume de Toulouse was born in the 770s (since he was a close contemporary of Louis the Pious, born in 778), he would have been in his seventies in 848, which corresponds to Wolfram's description of Kyot as an "old man" in the last chapter of *Parzival*. Moreover, Wolfram's epic account of the life of his hero (Parzival) culminates with the event of Parzival becoming Grail King (the so-called Parzival initiation) *on a Pentecost Sunday*. If this event did indeed coincide with a Saturn–Jupiter conjunction, then this would correspond to Whit Sunday in the year 848.[10]

---

8   The significance for Grail seekers of Werner Greub's research concerning the historical identity of Kyot can be inferred from Rudolf Steiner's statement: "(Kyot) received a book in his hand from Flegetanis in Spain. This was an astrological book. Without a doubt one can say: Kyot is the one who, inspired by Flegetanis—one whom he named 'Flegetanis' and in whom to a certain extent something of the knowledge of the starry script lived—saw something; thus, stimulated by this newly arising astrology, he saw something that is called the Grail. Then I knew that Kyot is not to be given up (as nonexistent), that he directly opens up an important trace if one undertakes spiritual–scientific research; that he, at least, has seen the Grail." (Rudolf Steiner, *Christ and the Spiritual World. The Search for the Holy Grail*, 6 lectures given in Leipzig, 1913/14, lecture 5). Thus Werner Greub's research supports Rudolf Steiner's statement that Kyot was a historically real person and not a figment of Wolfram's imagination. While most historians assume that Wolfram invented Kyot as a source for his work, there is one academic historian, Herbert Kolb, who, some ten years before Werner Greub's book appeared, sought to show that Kyot actually existed, cf. Herbert Kolb, *Munsalvaesche, Studien zum Kyot-Problem* (Munich, 1963).

9   A new recension of "Guillaume" in modern French has been made by Professor Liege. Cf. Jeanne Wathelet-Willem, *Reserches sur la chanson de Guillaume* (2 vols; Paris, 1975), vol. 2. pp. 730–1073. In vol. 1 Prof. Wathelet-WIllem studies the principal characters in the "Guillaume" epic and considers their possible historical prototypes among the friends and relatives of Count Guillaume de Toulouse.

10  There are several problematic pieces in the prior paragraph. Note that the current historical understanding of St. Guillaume is that he was born around AD 755 and died on May 28 in either AD 812 or 814 Robert Powell's personal feeling as

In the introduction to his book, Werner Greub expresses his hope that, through the publication of his findings, a circle of people would become interested in Grail research. Since the publication of the book in 1974, this has indeed happened, and several people have been stimulated to further research, including the author of this brief report.

One of those who have been inspired to devote themselves to Grail research is Robert Schmidt, a teacher at the Goetheanum School of Speech Formation and an actor in many of the plays that are produced regularly on the Goetheanum stage. Shortly after the publication of Greub's work, Schmidt discovered that the anonymous hero epic known as "Fierabras" is concerned with the same theme as Wolfram's *Willehalm*. The manuscript tradition of "Fierabras" has been traced to the second half of the twelfth century, but undoubtedly stems from a much earlier time since it is concerned with Charlemagne's fight against the Saracens.

The theme of the "Fierabras" epic begins with the flight of the Saracen king Balan with his son to Spain. Charlemagne and his army are also led to Spain in order to regain the plundered Passion Relics. His troops succeed in capturing Balan's son, the mighty Fierabras, although more French knights, including Oliver and Gui de Bourgogne, fall into the hands of the unbelievers. Floripas, the daughter of Balan, into whose custody the captured knights are entrusted, out of love for Gui seeks to alleviate his plight. Eventually she is even instrumental in the freeing of the knight and the winning back of the relics. After a series of adventurous encounters and romantic occurrences Balan is besieged and killed in the last, decisive battle with Charlemagne. The Emperor divides the newly won kingdom between Fierabras, who is won over to the Christian faith, and Gui de Bourgogne, who marries Floripas. The regained relics are returned to France in a triumphant march, where they are preserved in the abbey of Saint-Denis.[11]

Robert Schmidt, having read Werner Greub's book, realized that the "Fierabras" epic is in close agreement with *Willehalm*, if Gui de Bourgogne is identified with Count Guillaume de Toulouse. In Wolfram's telling, Willehalm is taken into captivity by the Arabs (in Spain) but is freed by Arabel, the daughter of the governor of Baghdad, who falls in love with him. After their escape they marry, and Arabel, who is converted to Christianity through her love for Willehalm, changes her name to Gyburc. Gyburc–Arabel's brother is Rennewart, son of Terramer of Baghdad. Thus, the equation between the "Fierabras" epic and the theme of *Willehalm*: Fierabras = Rennewart; Balan = Terramer; Floripas = Gyburc–Arabel; and Gui de Borgogne = Willehalm.[12] It is interesting that the composer Franz Schubert, at the age of 26, composed his opera *Fierabras*, based on the epic of the same name.[13]

---

of a few years ago is that May 28, 812 is the more likely date of death. Since Kyot (St. Guillaume) was present at the coronation of Parzival as Grail King at the conclusion of Eschenbach's *Parzival*, it is impossible that this could have occurred in AD 848. Additionally, there is no indication in the text of *Parzival* that this coronation occurred on a Pentecost Sunday. On the contrary, the text seems to indicate that the coronation occurred seventeen days after Ascension Thursday—the Feast of the Holy Trinity, one week after Pentecost (cf. Joel Matthew Park, "First Steps toward a Grail Timeline," *Star Wisdom*, 2018, p. 71) It would seem that while Werner Greub had a certain level of "spatial clairvoyance" in identifying the location of Grail settings and identities of Grail characters, he lacked a "temporal clairvoyance" that would pinpoint the timing of the Grail story. This is the reason for calling my article of a few years back the "*First* Steps toward a Grail Timeline," since prior to my article, as far as I could tell, there had only been unsuccessful attempts to set a date for the coronation of Parzival, and not to find precise dates for multiple events throughout the Grail legend. —JMP

11 Cf. *Kindlers Literatur Lexikon* (1965), vol. 2, p. 2898.

12 The "Fierabras" epic is the subject of a fresco at Roncesvalles. The conversion of Floripas to Christianity is commemorated each year during the month of August at Viana de Castelo, not far from Brage, by the presentation of a pageant "Auto de Floripes." Cf. Barton Sholod, *Charlemagne in Spain* (Geneva, 1966), p. 217.

13 A noteworthy fact is that Rudolf Steiner in his karma research indicated an earlier incarnation of Franz Schubert in the 8th/9th centuries as an Arab personality in Spain (cf. *Karmic Relationships*, vol 1, lectures 7 and 8). Rudolf Steiner depicted that this personality had experienced the war between the Arabs and the Franks, which is the theme both

My own Grail research has been concerned with the role of astronomy in the Grail events. Therefore, I was particularly interested in Werner Greub's conclusion that the Parzival initiation coincided with a conjunction of Saturn and Jupiter, and that Kyot had prior knowledge of the conjunction from Islamic sources. Through my research in the history of astronomy, I have discovered independent evidence in favor of this aspect of Werner Greub's thesis. The evidence is provided in a book by Masha'allah, an Islamic astrologer who flourished in Baghdad from the time of the city's founding in 762 until his death around 815.[14] Masha'allah's book, an astrological world history titled "On Conjunctions, Religions, and Peoples," has not survived intact, but a large fragment of it is embedded in a work by Ibn Hibintā, a Christian astrologer who lived in Baghdad in the tenth century. This fragment, together with an English translation and commentary, was published in 1971 by E. S. Kennedy and David Pingree as *The Astrological History of Masha'allah*.[15]

Masha'allah was one of the most famous astrologers in Baghdad in the eighth/ninth centuries.[16] He was born in Basra, of Jewish stock, but spent most of his life in Baghdad. In fact, he was involved with the astrological reckoning which led to the founding of the city in 762 (on July 30),

and he was active there until his death in ca. 815. Among his many literary accomplishments is *De elementis et orbibus coelestibus* (the title of the Latin translation by Gerard of Cremona of the lost Arabic original), which is apparently an exposition of doctrines and beliefs adhered to by the star-worshipping Sabians of Harran. Masha'allah was also a scholar, with knowledge of Greek astrological material, and he was possibly acquainted with Indian science through Kanaka, an Indian astronomer and astrologer who visited the courts of al-Mansur and Harun al-Rashid.[17]

Additional evidence for the historical authenticity of *Parzival* is the fact that Wolfram mentions the wise men "Kancor" and "Thebit" (*Parzival* 643), who may be identified tentatively with Kanaka and Masha'allah, both well-known sages in Baghdad. Identification of Kancor as Kanaka is evident in a philological sense, but identification of Masha'allah as Thebit requires further elucidation.

In his book, Werner Greub identifies Thebit with "Flegetanis," from whose writings Kyot first learned of the Grail (*Flegetanis* means simply "astrologer").

> The heathen Flegetanis could tell us how all the stars set and rise again and how long each one revolves before it reaches its starting point once more. To the circling course of the star's, man's affairs and destiny are linked.[18]

Flegetanis is clearly an astrologer with a good knowledge of astronomy, and according to Wolfram he wrote about these things. The designation "heathen" means that he wrote in Arabic. Moreover, Wolfram states that Flegetanis "had achieved high renown for his learning. This scholar of nature was descended from Solomon and born of a family which had long been Israelite."[19] Masha'allah was not only a scholar who wrote many astrological works in Arabic and was famous for his astrological wisdom, but also he was born into a Jewish

---

of Wolfram's *Willehalm* and Schubert's *Fierabras*. That there were definite relations between Count Guillaume de Toulouse (Willehalm) and the nobility in Spain is known from the "Astronomer" who writes in his *Vita Hludowici* that in the spring of 798 an embassy from the Asturian court of Alfonso II arrived at the general assembly at Toulouse to pay homage to Guillaume and Louis, cf. Barton Sholod, *Charlemagne in Spain* (Geneva, 1966), pp. 53–55. [Robert has updated this research into Franz Schubert in *The Astrological Revolution*, written with Kevin Dann and published in 2010. He builds on the research and conclusions of Richard Zienko that Schubert's prior incarnation was in the 13th century as Abu Yusuf Yaqub, ally of King Alfonso X.]

14 Cf. David Pingree, "Masha'allah," *Dictionary of Scientific Biography ix* (New York, 1974), pp. 159–162.

15 E. S. Kennedy and David Pingree, *The Astrological History of Masha'allah* (Harvard University, 1971).

16 Cf. Pingree, op. cit. (note 10) for biography of Masha'allah.

17 Kanaka is mentioned by al-Biruni in *The Chronology of Ancient Nations* (London, 1879), p. 129. Cf. David Pingree, "Kanaka," *Dictionary of Scientific Biography vii* (New York, 1973), pp. 222–224.

18 Von Eschenbach, *Parzival*, p. 244.

19 Ibid.

family. Most important of all, however, is that Masha'allah, through his work "On Conjunction, Religions, and Peoples," was the transmitter of the tradition concerning Saturn–Jupiter conjunctions.

*The Astrological History of Masha'allah* contains sixteen horoscopes cast by Masha'allah. All the horoscopes are for the time of the vernal equinox in the year of a conjunction between Saturn and Jupiter. As an explanation for the reason as to why these horoscopes were cast, Professor Kennedy writes:

> The astrological basis of Masha'allah's approach to world history is provided by a Sasanian theory that important religious and political changes are indicated by conjunctions of the planets Saturn and Jupiter, which recur at intervals of about twenty years. Successive conjunctions tend to stay in the same astrological triplicity. After a long time, however, over two centuries, they move along into another triplicity. Any such "shift" of triplicity indicates changes of a more sweeping nature than a simple conjunction—the rise of a new nation or dynasty. The advent of a major prophet, an event most portentous of all, is heralded by the completion of a cycle of shifts through all four triplicities. Predictions are made by casting the horoscope for the instant of the vernal equinox of the year in which this conjunction or shift occurs.[20]

Not only Masha'allah but also Kanaka was occupied with astrological history based on Saturn–Jupiter conjunctions, since according to Ibn al-Nadim's *Fihrist*, Kanaka wrote two books on Saturn–Jupiter conjunctions.[21] Thus, the possibility exists that it was Kanaka who transmitted the traditions of Saturn–Jupiter conjunctions to Masha'allah, although it is difficult to date Kanaka's life from historical sources. According to David Pingree: "One may tentatively conclude that Kanaka was in Baghdad during the reign of Harun al-Rashid and was an associate of Masha'allah."[22] In his dating of Masha'allah's book "On Conjunctions, Religions, and Peoples," David Pingree concludes that it was written in ca. 810, since the

first ten horoscopes of Saturn–Jupiter conjunctions refer to past events with the last of these, i.e., the tenth horoscope, referring to the accession of al-Ma'mun to the Caliphate in 809. However, the horoscopes may well have been cast long before 809, and the interpretation of the 809 horoscope could have been added later—i.e., after the event. The remaining horoscopes refer to the future (i.e., after Masha'allah's death), to the Saturn–Jupiter conjunctions in 829, 848, 868, 888, 907, and 928.

Thus, Masha'allah's book gives partial confirmation to Werner Greub's thesis, since it provides evidence (1) that there was a tradition (of Sasanian–Persian origin) which maintained that important events are heralded by the conjunctions of Saturn and Jupiter, and (2) that the conjunctions for the ninth century had been reckoned in advance, at least as early as ca. 810. If Masha'allah is identified with Flegetanis (Thebit), then Kyot could have learned of the coming great conjunctions in 829 and 848 from Masha'allah's book, either directly or indirectly (e.g., through Gyburc–Arabel) especially in view of the fact that he was a prisoner of the Arabs in Spain. Once having learned of this tradition Kyot became alerted to the significance of the conjunctions of Saturn and Jupiter, and would have looked to the coming conjunctions in 829 and 848. According to Werner Greub, the first of these (in 829) occurred a short while after the birth of Parzival (which he places tentatively in 827), whilst the second coincided with the event of Parzival becoming Grail King.[23]

---

20 Kennedy and Pingree, op. cit., p. vi.

21 Ibn al-Nadim, *Fihrist* (Cairo, n.d.), p. 392.

22 Pingree, *DSB* vii, p. 222.

---

23 This paragraph is problematic; neither Robert Powell nor Werner Greub were aware of the approximate birth and death years of Kyot (AD 755–812/14). However, this does not render the basic premise irrelevant. In my article "First Steps toward a Grail Timeline," I make the case for Parzival's birth being close to the Saturn–Jupiter conjunction in Pisces in AD 789. The subsequent Saturn–Jupiter conjunction was 25° Scorpio in Oct. 809; Parzival's coronation as Grail King would have occurred shortly after (May 26 AD 810). So it is still possible that the astrological works of Masha'allah–Flegetanis directed St. Guillaume–Kyot's gaze to this very significant time of transition from Anfortas to Parzival as Grail King. —JMP

As indirect support for his thesis that the Saturn–Jupiter conjunction in 848 holds the key to the chronology of *Parzival*, Werner Greub points out that the conjunction of 848 occurred in the same region of the zodiac (near the middle of sidereal Pisces) as the triple conjunction between Saturn and Jupiter in the year 7 BC, which latter conjunction has been associated with the "Star of Bethlehem."[24] The relationship between the Saturn–Jupiter conjunction of 7 BC and that of 848 is based on the ratio of the periodic times of Jupiter's and Saturn's orbits of the zodiac, which are very nearly in the proportion of 2 to 5, i.e., 5 Jupiter revolutions (each just under 12 years) are approximately equal to 2 Saturn revolutions (each a little less than 30 years). If the ratio were exactly 2 to 5, then successive conjunctions of Saturn and Jupiter would take place at exactly 240° intervals around the zodiac, thus forming an equilateral triangle (fig. 1)

Figure 1

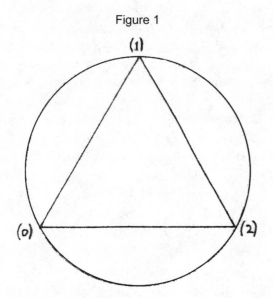

The mathematical solution to the sequence of conjunctions in figure 1 is as follows:

24 Cf. astronomer David Hughes' article "The Star of Bethlehem" in *Nature* vol. 264, Dec. 9, 1976, where he concludes that "the Star of Bethlehem was probably a triple conjunction of Saturn and Jupiter in the constellation of Pisces, the significance of which was only obvious to the magi of Babylonia....this occurred in 7 BC." [See Powell, *Chronicle of the Living Christ*, for a more up-to-date and thorough examination of the star of the magi.]

If 5 Jupiter revolutions = 2 Saturn revolutions, then 3+2 Jupiter revolutions = 2 Saturn revolutions; therefore, 1 + ⅔ Jupiter revolutions = ⅔ Saturn revolutions.

Thus, starting out from conjunction (0) in figure 1, after ⅔ of a revolution of the zodiac by Saturn point (1) is reached and simultaneously Jupiter reaches point (1) having made one and two-thirds revolutions of the zodiac. Therefore Jupiter and Saturn first come into conjunction at point (1), which is ⅔ of the zodiac from point (0), i.e., 240° (=⅔ x 360°) ahead of (0) in the zodiac. Similarly, starting out from conjunction (1), the next (second) conjunction would occur at point (2) lying 240° ahead of (1) in the zodiac. It follows that the next (third) conjunction, lying 240° ahead of (2), returns to the starting point (0), i.e., after three conjunctions the cycle of Saturn–Jupiter conjunctions is complete and a new cycle begins. This can be derived from the above equation: (1 + ⅔) Jupiter revolutions = ⅔ Saturn revolutions, since multiplications throughout by 3 gives whole numbers of revolutions for both Jupiter (5) and Saturn (2)-—i.e., after three conjunctions, Jupiter has made 5 revolutions and Saturn has made 2 revolutions of the zodiac. However, the ratio of the periodic times of Jupiter and Saturn is not exactly 2 to 5, and therefore the cycle is not completed (exactly) after three conjunctions.

In fact, the ratio of periodic times of Jupiter's revolution to Saturn's revolution is nearer 29 to 72. Therefore a more precise solution to the problem is as follows:

If 72 Jupiter revolutions = 29 Saturn revolutions, then (43 + 29) Jupiter revolutions = 29 Saturn revolutions; therefore, (1 + 29/43) Jupiter revolutions = 29/43 Saturn revolutions.

Thus, starting out from conjunction (0) in figure 1, Jupiter and Saturn first come together after Saturn has progressed through 29/43 of his revolution of the zodiac (with Jupiter having made one complete revolution plus a further 29/43 of a revolution of the zodiac). Since 29/43 x 360° = 242.79° = 242°47'26.5", it follows that conjunction (1) lies 242.79° ahead of conjunction (0) in the zodiac. In other words, the conjunctions between Saturn and Jupiter do not form an exact equilateral triangle as in figure 1, but the point of the triangle at (1) is displaced forward in the zodiac by approximately 2 x 2.79° = 5.59°. Likewise, the third conjunction between Saturn and Jupiter is displaced by approximately 3 x 2.79° = 8.37° ahead of the starting point (0°) in the zodiac. Thus, after three conjunctions between Saturn and Jupiter the triangle has rotated forward in the zodiac by approximately 8.37° (see fig. 2, showing the points of the triangle displaced forward in the zodiac by 8.37° every third conjunction).

It can be seen that the points of the triangle marked by conjunctions (1), (4), (7)...(see fig. 2) steadily advance toward the starting point (0). The question is: after how many conjunctions is the point (0) reached, thus indicating the commencement of a new cycle? From the equation: (1 + 29/43) Jupiter revs. = 29/43 Saturn rev. the answer follows that 43 conjunctions are required for the completion of a cycle, since multiplication throughout by 43 gives whole numbers of revolutions for both Jupiter and Saturn. Thus, in relation to figure 2, the points (1), (4), (7)...advance until (43) = (0). In actual fact, conjunction (43) does not fall *exactly* at the starting point (0), since the ratio of the periodic times of Jupiter's revolution to Saturn's revolution is not exactly 29 to 72, but is nearer to 60 to 149. Nevertheless, the ratio 29 to 72 suffices for the level of accuracy with which we are concerned.

From this ratio we have the equation: 72 Jupiter revolutions = 29 Saturn revolutions, i.e., with the occurrence of conjunction (43), Jupiter has completed 72 revolutions and Saturn has completed 29 revolutions of the zodiac. The length of time required for the completion of this cycle of 43 Saturn–Jupiter conjunctions is ca. 854 years. In fact, 72 Jupiter revolutions take ca. 854.08 tropical years, and 29 Saturn revolutions take ca. 854.27 tropical years, which yields a difference of ca. 0.19 year, or a little over two months. Given this slight difference due to the incommensurability of the revolutions of Jupiter and Saturn, it is nevertheless true to say that after 854 years the conjunctions of both Saturn and Jupiter return to the same region of the zodiac.

Thus the "Star of Bethlehem" signified by the conjunction of Saturn and Jupiter in Pisces in 7 BC, recurred 854 years later in AD 848, when Saturn and Jupiter were again in conjunction in the same region of Pisces. Werner Greub in his book refers to this latter conjunction as the "Star of Munsalvaesche" (Munsalvaesche is Wolfram's name for the Grail Castle), i.e., just as the meeting of Saturn and Jupiter in 7 BC proclaimed to the magi the birth of the Savior in Bethlehem, so did the recurrence of the conjunction of Saturn and Jupiter in Pisces in 848 announce the coming of the new Grail King, Parzival, to Munsalvaesche.[25]

Whether or not one accepts Werner Greub's thesis concerning the "Star of Munsalvaesche," it is a fact that the Saturn–Jupiter conjunction in the year 848 was the 43rd conjunction following the "Star of Bethlehem," and therefore occurred in the same region of the zodiac as the conjunction which heralded the birth of the Messiah. The determination by Werner Greub of the year of the Parzival Initiation as 848 therefore has a "cosmic validity," but it is clear that full confirmation of this date can be given only by more "earthly data" such as the dates of birth and death of the historical

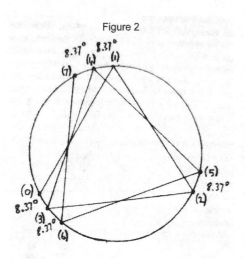

Figure 2

---

25 Again, while something significant certainly may have happened in the life of Parzival—or, for that matter, his son Lohengrin or his nephew Prester John, who would have been around 40 years of age in AD. 848—it was *not* his coronation as Grail King at Munsalvaesche. —JMP

personalities represented as various characters in *Parzival*. The reckoning of the finer details of the chronology of *Parzival* must be suspended until more of the figures in *Parzival* are historically identified. If dates of birth or death for any of the historically identifiable characters in *Parzival* are retrievable, this might enable the precise chronology of Wolfram's epic to be determined.[26]

Werner Greub's chronology rests implicitly upon the identification of Kyot as Count Guillaume de Toulouse, whose death date unfortunately is unknown [now said to have died in 1094]. On the basis of this identification, the possibility is given of assigning approximate boundaries to the historical periods for *Willehalm* and *Parzival*. *Willehalm* refers to the earlier, exoteric period of Count Guillaume's life, until the time of his exclusion from the service of Loys (Louis the Pious).[27] The *Parzival* epic coincides historically with the second period of the life of Count Guillaume de Toulouse, when he left the exoteric knighthood (in the service of the Carolingian dynasty) to become a knight in the service of the Grail.[28] This

transition is designated by Wolfram's use of the esoteric name "Kyot" to replace the exoteric name "Willehalm." Is it possible, however, to date historically Count Guillaume's transition from "Willehalm" to "Kyot," from exoteric knighthood to the Grail knighthood?

Very little is known from historical sources of the life of Guillaume de Toulouse. The *chanson-de-geste* "Guillaume" is a highly poetic and fanciful account of his knightly deeds in the service of Charlemagne. The "Vita Sancti Willelmi" was written only ca. 1125, shortly before Guillaume's canonization in 1138—i.e., it was written three centuries after the time when he lived, and on this account, it is not altogether reliable as a biography. He is mentioned only three times in the Carolingian annals: in 790 as Louis's adviser, appointed by Charlemagne; in 793 for his bravery in checking the Saracen offensive at Narbonne; and in 802 on the occasion of the siege of Barcelona, as the leader of the attacking army, which drove back the Saracen relief army, leading to the fall of Barcelona. Otherwise, all that is known is that he was the founder of Abbaye de Gellone, Lodève, in the South of France (the nearby village of Saint-Guilhem-le-Désert is named after him). From the deed of founding the monastery at Gellone, it is said that Guillaume was the "youth friend" of Louis the Pious and was his advisor, as well as being the trusted friend of Louis's father, Charlemagne. Following Wolfram's statements in *Willehalm* it can be surmised that (1) the relationship of Charlemagne to Guillaume was like that of a father to his son,[29] and (2) the relationship of Louis to Guillaume was that of brother-in-law, since Loys (or Louis) married his sister [again, since both Louis and his wife were a good 20 years younger than Guillaume, the relationship was probably more akin to uncle and nephew]. The dramatic change in the relationship between Louis the Pious and Count Guillaume de Toulouse may have coincided with the death of Queen Ermengarde de Beaumont (Willehalm's

---

26 Alas, the historical data that was eventually discovered could not support Greub's thesis, "cosmically valid" as it was. —JMP

27 Note that St. Guillaume's last march with Louis the Pious was in 801 to 802 to reclaim Barcelona.

28 This occurred between 804 and 806, when he founded Saint-Guilhem-le-Désert, an abbey in Gellone, France, where he spent the last 7 years or so of his life. How close Herbert Kolb already came, in 1963, to realizing (as Werner Greub subsequently did) the connection between Wolfram's *Parzival* and *Willehalm*, can be seen from the following passage, where Professor Kolb discusses the connection between Queen Anflise and Guillaume: "And there, where the name Anflise appears (in *Parzival*), who is said to be the wife of Foulques, a nephew of Guillaume d'Orange (= Guillaume de Toulouse), perhaps for the first time the whole wide circle of the "Guillaume" epic entered Wolfram's view. It appears that here lies the bridge that leads from the Grail epic to *la chanson de gests* and the Holy Wars in the South of France, and to Guillaume d'Orange especially." Herbert Kolb, *Munsalvaesche, Studien zum Kyot-Problem* (Munich, 1963), p. 23. Thus, through Anflise (mentioned in *Parzival* 76.7; 94.29; 325.27; 406.r) a direct link is forged to Kyot's earlier exoteric life as Willehalm or Guillaume.

29 Charlamagne and Guillaume were actually cousins; Charlemagne was born in 748 and was 5 to 10 years older than his cousin. Their "father–son" relationship probably had more to do with Charlemagne being king and Guillaume his paladin.

sister) on October 3, 818. This might have been the time of transition from "Willehalm" to "Kyot" and the beginning of the drama described in the Grail book *Parzival*.[30]

From the standpoint of Werner Greub's research, a relationship between Wolfram's two books *Willehalm* and *Parzival* can be surmised. Wolfram has two heroes—i.e., Willehalm and Parzival, who are closely connected with one another both in a physical and a spiritual sense. Willehalm is the "preparer of the way" for Parzival, and is at the same time the biographer of the life of Parzival (Wolfram continually asserts that he is writing down only what he "heard" from Kyot). There is a parallel with the relationship between John the Evangelist and Jesus Christ, in that the Evangelist had witnessed many of the events in the life of Jesus Christ and wrote his Gospel according to what he had seen and heard concerning the Messiah. Similarly, Wolfram's book *Parzival* could be described as the "Gospel according to Kyot," an account of the life of a highly evolved spiritual leader of humankind (Parzival), which was written down three centuries later by Wolfram von Eschenbach through direct inspiration from Kyot. Thus, Wolfram's book *Parzival* is no ordinary book but is a kind of Gospel, an account of an enactment of high Christian Mystery, the Grail Mystery, that was fulfilled by Parzival. Wolfram's book *Willehalm* provides a biography of the life of the transmitter of this "Gospel," prior to the beginning of the enactment of the Grail Mystery, and thus *Willehalm* holds the key to the historical authenticity of Wolfram's books, given that the narrative of *Willehalm* is based on the life of Count Guillaume de Toulouse.

Is it possible for this research to go further, to trace the relatives and associates of Count Guillaume de Toulouse, and thereby recover more of the historical background to Wolfram's epics? For those who are interested in Grail research

the answer may well be "yes." But clearly it is not merely a question of locating historical sources. Rather, the success of Grail research depends upon the development of spiritual faculties, especially the ability to "read the book of history," which means the development of Imagination, Inspiration, and Intuition.[31]

Historical sources may be taken as a starting point, accessible to objective (physical) consciousness, but it is only through suprasensory perception that the full reality may be known. The identification of Kyot with Count Guillaume de Toulouse is logically sound, but it is only through suprasensory perception that it can become certain knowledge. The consultation of historical sources offers confirmatory evidence of this identification, but it cannot be conclusive. Thus, although historical sources may confirm spiritually perceived truths, and may themselves be illumined by spiritual research, true Grail research is not possible without the development of higher faculties of perception beyond objective consciousness.

It is especially the faculty of Intuition that is needed to be able to identify the individuality of a historical personality, and the meditation *par excellence* for the development of Intuition is "The Foundation Stone Meditation," given by Rudolf Steiner on Christmas Day in 1923 at the founding of the Anthroposophical Society and the School for Spiritual Science. Intuition requires the development of the power of Love.

Through meditation of the Foundation Stone of Love, which Rudolf Steiner laid in the hearts of the members of the Anthroposophical Society, the faculty of Intuition may be developed. Thereby the ability to "read the book of history" may be acquired. Through the development of Intuition it is possible to begin to penetrate the secrets of the identities of historical personalities. This is the deeper significance of Grail research. The progress of Grail research depends upon the development of spiritual cognition, and especially the faculty of Intuition. Thus, "The Foundation Stone

---

30 In fact, Guillaume died in 812 or 814, years before his sister's death. It is not clear that Ermengarde was Guillaume's sister; this does not appear in the historical record, which states that Ermengarde's father was born around 750, and thus would have been around the same age as Guillaume.

31 Cf. Steiner, *An Outline of Esoteric Science*, ch. 5, for a description of these three faculties of spiritual perception beyond objective consciousness.

Meditation" for developing the faculty of Intuition is at the heart of Grail research. Through this meditation, certainty can be acquired concerning the identity of historical personalities. "The Foundation Stone Meditation" and the esoteric training given in the School for Spiritual Science offer a basis for certainty in Grail research.

Tracing the relatives and associates of Count Guillaume de Toulouse from historical sources is one possible approach to the penetration of the historical background to Wolfram von Eschenbach's books *Willehalm* and *Parzival,* but to read the inner meaning of the Grail book requires spiritual cognition. The Mystery of the Grail can be approached only through the development of spiritual faculties of cognition, and it is this which is the deeper purpose underlying the pursuit of Grail research. It is to be hoped that this brief report will help to awaken further interest in Grail research and, more generally, in the development of spiritual faculties for "reading the book of history."

For helpful comments concerning the mathematical–astronomical details in this report, my thanks are due to Dr. Georg Unger, head of the Mathematical–Astronomical Section at the Goetheanum. My thanks are owing also to Werner Greub and Robert Schmidt for their encouragement and assistance during many discussions on the theme of Grail research.

*To starry realms,*
*To the dwelling places of Gods,*
*Turns the Spirit gaze of my soul.*

*From starry realms,*
*From the dwelling places of Gods,*
*Streams Spirit power into my soul.*

*For starry realms,*
*For the dwelling places of Gods,*
*Lives my Spirit heart through my soul.*

—Rudolf Steiner

# THE PATH FROM PISCES TO AQUARIUS
## AS KEY TO MEETING CHRIST IN THE ETHERIC
### A Modern Reading of the Starry Script

## *Bill Trusiewicz*

*The stars once spoke to the human being.*
*It is world destiny that they are silent now....*
*But in the deepening silence,*
*There grows and ripens*
*What the human being speaks to the stars.*[1]

*Figure 1*

At sunrise on the first day of spring AD 214, our Earth began to receive through the Sun—its cosmic–etheric intermediary—the radiating influence of the spiritual life that springs from Pisces, the Fishes. Behind the Sun dawning that spring morning, the closest edge of the constellation of Pisces came into alignment from the perspective of Earth. Astrosophers know that the cultural age that corresponds to the influence of Pisces did not start immediately, but began 1,199 years later. During this period, the cultural impulse generated by the new starry influence was nurtured by the maternal forces of the planet Venus. In the womb of Venus, the streaming incipient Pisces forces were tenderly mingled as she inscribed a beautiful pentagram one hundred and fifty times, completing one full revolution (fig. 1).

Calculating accordingly, the day that the 150 iterations of the Venus pentagram were completed marked the end of the 4th and the beginning of the 5th post-Atlantean epoch, in AD 1413. It was then that the stars of Pisces began to have a marked influence on the cultural life of humanity, moving away from the previous influence of Aries the Ram. It was the beginning of the cultural age in which we now live, in spiritual–scientific circles called the 5th post-Atlantean cultural epoch.

While the world is mostly unconscious of such astronomical events, those who are aware of their significance have always taken time to reflect upon

them to consider the progress of world evolution in light of zodiacal influences. Such was undoubtedly the case with Christian Rosenkreutz, who in the late 16th century, almost 200 years after the beginning of the 5th cultural epoch, decided to call a conference of the highest initiates in an effort to heal an unhealthy condition of evolution that had been developing since the dawn of the 5th epoch and was beginning to forebode serious future ramifications.[2] The condition we are referring to was the advancing separation of human beings into two groups or types—one group that takes interest exclusively in the material world, surrendering their attention to practical activities on the horizontal plane of world affairs with its many and varied industries that exist to satisfy human physical life, and the second group that would devote their thoughts, feelings, and will to higher worlds—to the vertical dimension of

---

1   Steiner, *Verses and Meditations*, p. 97 (trans. revised).

2   See Steiner, *Esoteric Christianity and the Mission of Christian Rosenkreutz.*

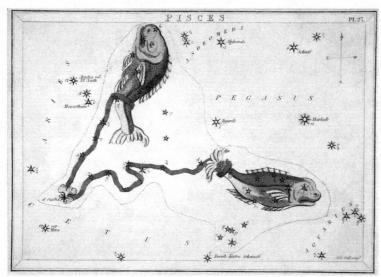

*Figure 2*

existence, the spiritual world—caring little for the physical life.

What came out of that conference of initiates in the 16th century will not concern us here.[3] Instead, we will try to show what may be "read" in the so-called starry script as the Piscean Age eventually gives way to the Aquarian Age. In so doing, we will attempt to formulate ideas that can become a guide to healing the division among human beings, as mentioned, that Christian Rosenkreutz saw—a division partly remediated by the actions implemented by his council, but nevertheless still exists in our time, and can be cured only through an encounter with Christ in the etheric sphere of Earth.

We are now more than six hundred years into the 5th post-Atlantean epoch, the epoch influenced by Pisces, which began in AD 1413 and will last about 2,160 years in all. So, in about 1,554 years, humanity will enter the cultural age corresponding to Aquarius the Waterman, also referred to in Spiritual Science as the 6th cultural, or post-Atlantean, epoch.

As we gaze above us on a good dark night and see the constellation of the Fishes adjacent to Aquarius, we must ask: Is there a living imagination encrypted in these starry constellations that can be deciphered to help us live into the stream of

human evolution in our time in a more profound and meaningful way?

Let us first consider what speaks to us from the stars, and later what we can offer back as a response.

When we contemplate what is imaginatively depicted in Pisces, the Fishes, we can see that it speaks a clear message to modern humanity. The constellation depicts two fishes (fig. 2), one swimming vertically upward and the other swimming horizontally toward the right. One myth connected with the image is this: "The fishes are the goddess Aphrodite and her son Eros (for the Romans, Venus and Cupid). They turned themselves into fish to escape from the monster Typhon, whereupon they connected themselves together with a cord or ribbon in order not to be separated. The constellation is located in an area of the sky known as "the Sea," or "the Water," which is full of water-related constellations."[4] The constellation of Pisces is ruled by Jupiter and Neptune, the gods of the sky and the sea. Venus and Cupid can also represent Love and Desire, which express human longing in two directions, the first toward a higher world, or we might say a more ideal world, and the second, for the experience of fulfillment on the plane of the physical, sense-perceptible world. By rights, both of these should be united in the human breast.

The water and fishes are found in the early Christian identification of Christ with the Greek word for fish: *Ichthyus*. The Bible correspondingly describes Christ as a "fisher of men." And early Christians considered themselves "little fishes," using the *Ichthyus* symbol (fig. 3) as early as the 2nd century, according to historians. Additionally, Christ speaks of himself as the "living water," as we can read in the so-called Water of Life Discourse in John 4:10–26.

The fish are portrayed, in the position of the stars, swimming in different directions to represent the duality often ascribed to Piscean

3   For more about this see "Christian Rosenkreutz and Gautama Buddha," in *The Secret Stream*.

4   See https://web.pa.msu.edu/people/horvatin /Astronomy_Facts/constellation_pages/pisces.htm.

nature, as intimated above, with "Love" swimming upward and "Desire" along the horizontal plane. In addition to this imagination, we should clarify also that "the Sea" or "Water" area of the heavens is key to understanding what is being revealed to us through this starry script. In Spiritual Science we refer to the etheric surrounding the Earth as the sphere of life forces. We recognize that water, as the source of life, the lifeblood of Earth, is the lowest member and functions as a sort of physical body for angelic beings. The science of the spirit speaks of the appearance of Christ (also called the Second Coming) in our time to be a phenomenon "in the Etheric," or life body of the Earth. In the New Testament we read of Christ appearing in "the clouds," a term used numerous times in the Old and New Testaments to mean suprasensory phenomena, whereby "the Lord" appeared in various ways to his people "out of clouds." These "clouds" are watery phenomena, pointing to the special suprasensory nature of water.[5] In a telling way, St. Paul, referring to Christ, directs us in this imagination of fishes swimming in water: "In him we live and move and have our being" (Acts 17:28).

So, we can begin to get a picture in the stars of Pisces displaying two fish swimming in different directions of an archetype of the human condition: human beings separated from one another and also perhaps, as astrologers generally see Pisceans, tending to be divided inwardly. It is a picture of alienation or estrangement of human beings from one another and from ourselves. In Spiritual Science we refer to the Piscean Age as that of the consciousness soul. We understand that, during this particular period of spiritual development, human beings must "find themselves" to use a colloquial term. There is, during this period, the imperative of incarnating the self or ego, a focus on becoming individually conscious, a process that has as its primary challenge: to individualize without losing connection in

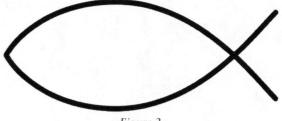

*Figure 3*

the social sphere. We refer here to the process of "individuation" in the field of psychology as early as Arthur Schopenhauer (early 19th century) and popularized by Carl Jung in the early 20th century. In spiritual–scientific parlance, we speak of "incarnating the "I," or more popularly in the self-help realm, "finding oneself." Whatever name it is given, the process is unavoidable in our time; we all confront it continually in the course of our lives, whether consciously or not.

"Finding oneself" is a personal, individual affair that may be compared, in alchemical terms, to being hermetically sealed off from the world. To be hermetically sealed is to be confined or enclosed in a vessel, an alchemical retort, a jar or some such enclosure designed to engender the ferment needed for transformation. The process of discovering the Self is necessarily a lonely affair, since an essential part of the process is separation from others to identify what is different about oneself: to discover our uniqueness, our particular gift or gifts, and to discover our susceptibilities and weaknesses. Both psychological and physical separation might be necessary parts of this process. One must spend time alone to become conscious of one's inner thoughts—to know oneself. The late-nineteenth- and early-twentieth-century initiate Rudolf Steiner referred many times to the experience of loneliness as characteristic of our age—that of the consciousness (or spiritual) soul.

This trend toward independence, a symptom of the age of the consciousness soul toward isolation, has been faithfully recorded by modern artists. One of countless artistic expressions of this loneliness in our time may be seen in *Three Men Walking*, a sculpture by the Italian artist Alberto Giacometti (fig. 4, page 120), in which we see

---

5  The etheric is "at work in the aqueous processes of the Earth...in the sea, in the rivers, rising mists, falling drops, and cloud formations...in all this, etheric currents are working." Steiner, *Anthroposophy and the Inner Life*, p. 73.

*Figure 4*

human independence expressed as alienation from one another.

So much of modern culture, especially as it has developed in the Western world, reflects this process of individuation, the symptoms of which can be seen in the way the fabric of society has been torn into fragments. Families are divided by divorce. Churches divide and divide again into countless denominations. There are *personal* computers for each individual; we each have our own tablets and cell phones; mass transit has long been out of favor since everyone wants to drive in their own personal vehicle. Specialization is another result of the fragmentation that comes with individuation, in which knowledge itself has multiplied and divided in every industry and field of study such that a list of medical doctors—for instance, on MDhealth.com—consists of fifty-three types, while Bioexplorer.net lists sixty types of MDs, whom, presumably, one must see for each of sixty different ailments.

With the Fishes, we see one swimming vertically upward and the other moving horizontally to the right. Aesthetically, we can sense the first fish striving heavenward, and the other preferring to remain on the earthly plane. In so doing, the fish striving upward for higher knowledge leaves the horizontal plane of humanity—the social sphere. Might this upward movement represent the abstract nature of modern thinking, which takes leave of the physical plane of existence, creating ascetic and monastic communities for spiritually inclined individuals? Or in scientific endeavors, does it represent the tendency to weave all sorts of theories based on mathematical conjectures that have a semblance of truth but fail to properly connect to earthly reality? Whereas abstract thinking frees the human imagination for creativity, it doesn't guarantee that its creations are beneficial or respectful to the wise order of growth that looks to nature for guidance on the path to higher knowledge.

Let us consider for a moment how this upwardly swimming fish is closest to Aries the Ram in the zodiacal circle. Aries the Ram is often depicted looking back toward its tail, like Perseus who used a mirror, looking backward to slay Medusa. This gesture represents the evolutionary development of reflective thinking that can look back upon experiences, a step removed from the event, and add a human-derived intellectual element. The position of this upwardly swimming fish suggests, in its rising verticality a new intellectual element bowing in recognition, as it were, to the previous epoch when, through the influence of Aries the Ram, the intellectual soul was developed. During this epoch, abstract thinking capacities were developed, freeing thinking for human creativity, but also making it possible to disconnect from the maternal ground of being, the physical world, through thought. This development could manifest either as polarization of spiritual thought and materialistic thought (the two fishes), or it could manifest in a healthy balance between the two.

Turning our imaginative gaze now to the other fish, the one swimming off on a horizontal plane seems to be oblivious to the first fish; it has its own concerns on the physical plane of existence. Perhaps, as we see the vernal point progressing further through the zodiac toward this second fish (as is now the case), we can read an augur of our current entrenchment in materialism (horizontal fish), following the initial elevation (seen in the upward-swimming fish) that was an aftereffect of the heady flight of the previous intellectual soul age.

In any case, we have the two fishes representing the two primary forces seeking to divert humanity, each to a particular pole—one toward the heavens and the other toward the Earth. Perhaps a reading of the starry script, such as we have done here, is what inspired Christian Rosenkreutz to call the council that met in the 16th century.

Let us now uncover another layer of meaning presented to us on the path of imagination from Pisces to Aquarius. We can begin by asking a question: Why is this happening to humanity, and what is the greater context of forces working here? We see the two oppositional forces—the luciferic and the ahrimanic pulling humanity away from its central task—pulling upward and downward to separate the fishes. *But* the fishes are bound to each other with a cord or a ribbon. They remain united in spite of their separation. There is a "cord" that keeps humanity connected in the social sphere.

What is the cord or ribbon that keeps them connected? There is an unconscious element, an *impulse,* working in the will of human beings. The plane of everyday consciousness was (and is) working in opposition to this impulse, creating a pull from above and below through abstract intellectuality and through an inclination toward all that is earthly. The unconscious impulse referred to here may be seen imaginatively in the water in which the fishes are swimming. It is difficult to be aware of something in which we are wholly immersed—something continuously present, and so present that we don't notice it. Such is the nature of much that invisibly supports our physical and spiritual existence, and of which we are not conscious—such as how our internal organs work. These forces are connected with our will; what works in our will is largely hidden from our awareness, as water is for fish or, in human life, our airy atmosphere permeated by water, which we take for granted. This unconscious impulse expresses itself in our innate longing for community, for companionship with like souls—a longing for soul warmth on an unconscious level. Such is the nature of the Christ impulse, which is especially active in our time, working in the deeply inner will of humanity.

In this inwardness, largely hidden from our awareness, we live and have our being.

As mentioned, the water element, in which the fishes live, refers to the realm of life, *the etheric* in spiritual scientific terms. Recalling again what Saint Paul said—"In him we live and move and have our being," speaking of Christ—we acknowledge this unconscious realm. The space between us, represented by the water and supporting the fishes, is not an inactive, empty space but is permeated by life—a life that human beings have in common.

To grasp the meaning of this more fully and to work through to consciousness of Christ in the etheric, let us examine the evolutionary bridge between Pisces the Fishes and Aquarius the Waterman. The picture we are given by the constellation of the Waterman is that of the god of water (whom the Babylonians called The Great One or Ea), depicted as a bearded man holding a large vessel, a container such as one might use to carry water for drinking, cleaning, and so on. The Great One is the god called Poseidon by ancient Greeks and Neptune by the Romans. In most depictions, he is upright, but also as though seated without a seat and pouring a torrent of water from a large vessel grasped in his right hand. The water falls like a river onto Pisces Australis, the fish below (fig. 5, page 122). In his left hand is a measuring device, a ruler called *Norma Nilotica,* which is to say, "the measure of the water in the Nile river."

What is depicted in the starry script as occurring in the transition from Pisces to Aquarius is that the experience of water has been objectified. In other words, water has been poured into a container so that it may be of use as an impulse in Pisces, in contrast to being ubiquitous and having a mostly unconscious effect. If water is indeed the cosmic script for the etheric (or life) realm, then the significance of the figure of Aquarius (fig. 2, page 122) is strikingly apparent. What surrounds and affects humanity unconsciously can become both conscious and useful.

Let's take this imagination further into the realm of inspiration with the help of Rudolf Steiner's "Twelve Moods of the Zodiac." In the Aquarius mood, we see what is depicted in the artistic

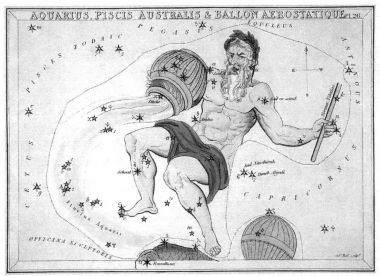

*Figure 2*

rendering of Aquarius that was published in *Urania's Mirror* (fig. 5).[6]

> May what is bounded yield to the boundless.
> What feels the lack of bounds, may it create
> Bounds for itself in its depths;
> May it raise itself in the current,
> As wave, flowing forth, sustaining itself,
> In becoming, shaping itself to existence.
> Set yourself bounds, oh boundless!

Here we see, from above, "what is bounded" in the materialistic age in which we live, when everything is predicated on the boundaries delineated by the physical, sensory world. This "bounded" must yield to the "boundless," the etheric, represented by the sea or ocean in which Pisces and Aquarius are situated in the zodiac. "What feels the lack of bounds" is the "water" of life, the "etheric" element, depicted in Pisces and Aquarius. In Aquarius, with his container of water, it "shapes itself to existence," it set "bounds" for itself. In so doing, the "boundless" is "bound," or taken up in a vessel; it is contained and objectified, so that it may be used, deployed. The etheric Christ therefore comes into

the human realm as an objective experience, depicted with Aquarius holding and pouring the water from his vessel. May we all rise to such an experience! A perfect example of setting yourself "bounds, oh boundless" would be the creation of anthroposophic Spiritual Science by Rudolf Steiner, in which a whole new language was created for the unspeakable mysteries of spirit— "giving bounds to the boundless."

In relation to this, we might also recall what Jesus said after the great day of the feast recorded in the Gospel of John: "'Let anyone who is thirsty come to me and drink. Whoever believes in me, as Scripture has said, rivers of living water will flow from within them.' By this he meant the Spirit..." (7:37–38). And to the woman at the well, after he asked her for a drink of water he said, "Everyone who drinks this water will be thirsty again, but whoever drinks the water I give them will never thirst. Indeed, the water I give them will become in them a spring of water welling up to eternal life." (4:13). Isn't this a picture of the human being becoming a container for the "water of the spirit"—a container for the "boundless" and pouring the "boundless" out of himself—"welling up [within] to eternal life"? It is the answer to our thirst for life; it is what alone can quench that thirst. And aren't these also microcosmic pictures of "the Great One" holding the vessel of water and also pouring it out onto Pisces Australis?

Returning to the artistic depiction of Aquarius, how shall we account for the *Norma nilotica*, the ruler that the Waterman holds in his left hand, which indicates a measuring device for the Nile River? Surely it has some significance, as well. First, let's consider facts about the Nile River. The Nile was the greatest river in the known world; it was viewed as an unequalled watery benefactor to civilization—the lifeblood of Egypt, which depended for its very existence on the fertile black silt that washed onto dry land during the rainy season. The original name of Egypt was *Kemet* (black land),

---

6   Bloxam, *Urania's Mirror: or, A View of the Heavens* (London, 1825), a set of hand-colored cards, designed to accompany Jehoshaphat Aspin's book, *A Familiar Treatise on Astronomy, Explaining the General Phenomena of the Celestial Bodies* (London, 1825).

in honor of the mighty, fertile, lifegiving, black sands of the Nile River. Might not this cosmic picture indicate a blessing of life and fertility (such as that of the Nile) of every sort worldwide—flowing as it does from heaven, from the god of water? The pouring out of the water by the "Great One" augers an age when humanity has matured to the point of conscious awareness and management of the forces of Christ in Earth's etheric sphere.

Spiritual Science indicates something like this during the 6th cultural epoch, in which the second Pentecost is to take place, whereby the spirit is poured out in a greater measure than that experienced by the disciples in Jerusalem. In the *Coenaculum*, or upper room, the spirit came to rest as tongues of fire on each disciple, filling them with the spirit and wisdom to speak a universal language to those "of every nation and tongue" gathered in Jerusalem. With spirit vision, we can see the greater Pentecost being prepared for the 6th epoch, the age of Aquarius the Waterman, in which a community will exist that can be a vessel for unprecedented waves of cosmic wisdom pouring down upon it.

To point toward our own task in light of the foregoing emphasis on water as the bearer of the life forces of the etheric, it is worth mentioning indications found in Homer's prophetic, epic poem *The Odyssey*—indications that have to do with water. In *The Odyssey*, Homer gives us a prophetic view with an accurate account of the current changes of consciousness in his era and their ramifications far into the future. Written near the end of the 8th century BC, at the dawn of the intellectual soul age, it was a time when rational thinking was just starting to play a significant role in humanity, eclipsing the former imaginative clairvoyant capacities through which people naturally felt they were companions of the gods. In one adventure of Odysseus after another, Homer was able to depict humanity's declining state of consciousness, the new possibilities of consciousness for his time, and their ramifications as they develop further in the distant future.

The mission of Odysseus, as portrayed by Homer in *The Odyssey*, was to demonstrate for his contemporaries and for posterity what might be accomplished, as well as what might be encountered as the dangerous pitfalls of employing the new cognitive faculties, often described as "cunning intelligence," which were then beginning to develop and would continue more than two millennia into our own time and beyond. The last task outlined for Odysseus is instructive for us today. The blind prophet Tiresias, who initiated Odysseus, appeared at the gate to the underworld and told Odysseus something like this: "Your task will not be complete until you carry your oar, as a symbol of the power of Neptune, deep into the land, far away from the sea where you will meet those who have lost all connection to the forces over which Neptune rules,[7] and by which he blesses humanity. There the oar that you carry will be mistaken for a wind implement, a device used for fanning air—a winnowing fan. Such will be the mentality of these people; they will consider only Jupiter, who rules the air (representing intellectual thinking forces) and will have lost all appreciation and reverence for the great power of the sea and the forces behind it. You must plant your oar in such a place and speak of Neptune to those people who have long forgotten what blessings come from the sea, from water and from "Ea," the "Water Man," so that *both Jupiter and Neptune together* will be able to be at peace in those people and bring peace and prosperity to their land."

In this regard, we see Odysseus not as an historical personality, but as a mythic character created by Homer, a representative of the offspring of Neptune and Jupiter (the two rulers of Pisces), born into the culture of Greece at the time when the Taurian Age of the Bull was beginning to be overshadowed by the age of Aries the Ram. The name *Odyssey* rightly refers not only to Homer's great epic poem, but also to the remarkable journey that humanity would face for the next few millennia as a result of the new forces of cognition that Odysseus represents. The journey of Odysseus is also *our* journey, the journey of bringing the

---

7  Indicating also a future time and people who would "have lost all connection to the forces over which Neptune rules."

wisdom of Neptune, the sea god, into the land that has forgotten the sea and values only the air—on what can be spun out of human thinking. This is our world; we are fish surrounded by living water that we don't know how to appreciate and rightly acknowledge. Our abstract thinking has blinded us to the gifts that surround us, to which we can gain access by meeting Christ in the etheric sphere surrounding Earth—represented by the "Waterman," the "Fisher of Men" who gives the Water of Life freely—who himself is the Water of Life.

Now that we have deciphered something of the starry script, and the stars have been able to "speak to us," let's deepen our meditation so that we can have something to "speak back to the stars," as Rudolf Steiner adjures us in this article's poetic epigram.

We know that meeting Christ in the etheric in his Second Coming is needed to heal the warring divisions of humanity, the remedy for bringing humanity together and uniting us as a loving human family. Spiritual Science teaches that Christ has returned, that his second coming began in the early twentieth century. Christ is present with us. How do we avail ourselves of his presence—his gifts, his wisdom and love—for healing ourselves and our world? How do we become like the Waterman, who has objectified the very source of life? Who is able to consciously hold the vessel of the blessings of the higher life and pour it out upon humanity?

Christ is already here and powerfully present in the etheric; we need only acknowledge his presence. We have the knowledge of Christ. We feel deeply connected to and motivated by what we know of him. Many of my readers, no doubt, have a conscious relationship with Christ; others may not. Many of us have varying degrees of clairvoyant capacity. If nothing else, we have intellectual clairvoyance, which simply means that the content of our spiritual–scientific investigations and studies lives strongly in our souls—stronger than our sense-based experience. With intellectual clairvoyance, there is an "ironlike" certainty about many

facts we have discovered. Whether or not we have a personal relationship with Christ and a connection to the spiritual world, we can all learn to know him better and to know the spiritual world better. The following is presented to help us to either form a relationship with Christ and the spiritual world or to deepen and strengthen our current relationship. To do this, consider some of the common obstacles to meeting Christ in the etheric, which are really stepping stones to achieving our goal of "speaking once again to the stars."

We will inevitably say (and we hear this, spoken or unspoken, continuously in the outer court of the school of the Archangel Michael): *We lack the clairvoyant vision to see him; we need to have our spiritual eyes opened to recognize his presence; we don't have the requisite faculties to find him. We have sought him; we have meditated; we have studied and we have prayed. Perhaps in a later incarnation we will have the necessary faculties to meet the One for whom we long—to see him. Perhaps in a few more incarnations we will be initiated and be able to perceive the spiritual world and find the etheric Christ.* How many times do we hear ourselves and our companions thinking, if not saying, such things?

This sort of inner (or outer) monologue might sound true, but I tend *not* to believe it. Consider this; the Wisdom of Christ, the Sophia of Christ, has been given to us. We have a pre-Christian tradition of initiation science, the holy scriptures, and the modern language of anthroposophic Spiritual Science, which is the Wisdom of Christ, the Word of God, the language of the etheric Christ—the container for the water! We have the vessel that holds the "water of life"; it is the means to objectify, to take in hand and put to use the water of life. It is directly possible through the inspired words of Spiritual Science to experience Christ in the etheric—Christ who is the Logos, the Word.

What is it that keeps us from a full experience of Christ, which by all accounts we should be able to attain? The great dragon,[8] the accuser, whispers that we are not good enough, that we have

---

8  The "great dragon" is referred to in Revelation 12:10 as "the accuser of the brethren."

not meditated enough, and that we are insufficient for the task. We have absorbed so much spiritual teaching. Why is it that we are so fixed on the material world? Why is it that we don't cross the threshold? The accuser whispers: *You doubt.* We long for the spiritual world; we languish at the threshold. The accuser whispers: *You lack courage. You are afraid.*

If we are listening attentively in the "deepening silence," of which Rudolf Steiner speaks, we will agree that this is what is being spoken; this is the conversation that occurs repeatedly each day and each night as we approach the threshold. Listen carefully; the accuser is helping us. He is helping us to objectify our lower nature. The lesser guardian of the threshold is the mask that Michael wears, as the mask of Anubis the Jackal was worn by Hermes, the great initiator of ancient Egypt.[9] Behind the lesser guardian is Michael, who waits for *our answer* to the guardian's objections before allowing us to cross the threshold to a new experience of Christ in the etheric. What is the answer that is the key to unlock the door of the threshold?

The answer, which must be spoken in all honesty and gravity when the accuser confronts us, is this: *Yes, I am impure and insufficient in myself for the task. Yes, I am inexplicably attached to the material world. Yes, I lack courage. Yes, although I languish at the threshold desirous of entry, I doubt and am afraid to cross.*

If these or similar words can be spoken honestly by us, they can be spoken to the guardian to gain entry, to cross the threshold. But we must answer further, saying something like this: *The desire is nevertheless within me to behold the spirit, to live for the spirit. Although my desire might be feeble, weakened by my fear and doubt, through my inner coldness, I commit the little strength in me, to the best of my ability and with the help of Christ, to change all that is revealed to me about my lower nature, so that I may gain entry to the spiritual world, that I may behold in all clarity,*

*free from illusions, what I so desire and thus overcome myself for the good.*[10]

These are the words that can continue the conversation that the stars have begun with us in presenting the story of Aquarius the Waterman, who is pouring out a great torrent of water upon us "little fishes." The key is that we speak of our insufficiency to the stars and trust Christ to help us along the path to higher knowledge.[11] This can be the beginning of our conversation with the stars, our entry to the cosmic conversation.

Once we begin, something monumental starts to move within us. We become "little fishes"— Eros (desire) wedded to Venus (love), and can receive the great torrent of water, like what we see falling from the Waterman onto Pisces Australis. We can receive the "water of life" and become a container for it; we can be of use to the Waterman, dispensing the water of life to the world. Our purified desire wedded to love, though it is as "small as a mustard seed," can unlock the gate to the spiritual world if we commit without reserve—with the help of Christ and Sophia, through the blessing of "the water of life"—to the tasks incumbent upon us today as friends and servants of Christ and Sophia in the world.

Though such conversation we not only speak back to the stars, but we also *return to the stars.* Through such words, we become not only the fish in the constellation of Pisces, but also the vessel of the Waterman, filled with water. By becoming the vessel, we also become the Waterman, who will continue to pour out torrents of water upon our brothers and sisters, upon humanity out of the living, etheric content we have received from the Waterman. In the Waterman, the Vessel of Water, and the torrent of water we see depicted a threefold activity: the blessing of the "Water of Life" from the Trinity of Father (the Waterman), Son

---

9  For more insight into Anubis and Hermes see the author's article, "Anubis and The Speech of the Threshold: As Key to Meeting Christ in the Etheric," in *Starlight*, vol. 13, no. 1, Pentecost 2013.

10  For another rendering of this threshold scenario see the previous footnote.

11  "You see, there's no need to worry about finding Christ through our own direct experience, for we have found him when we've found ourselves again after the experience of powerlessness—that is, when we fully experience and overcome that powerlessness" ("How Do I Find the Christ?" in Steiner, *Death as Metamorphosis of Life*).

(the Vessel of Water), and Holy Spirit (the torrent of water).

I leave my readers with the Aquarius Mood, for meditation, followed by a fitting remark from Rudolf Steiner:

> May what is bounded yield to the boundless.
> What feels the lack of bounds, may it create
> Bounds for itself in its depths;
> May it raise itself in the current,
> As wave, flowing forth, sustaining itself,
> In becoming, shaping itself to existence.
> Set yourself bounds, oh boundless!

What could give us greater strength for our duties in life than the knowledge that we bear within us the forces pouring from the universe and must prepare ourselves in life that these forces can become active within us...[12]

---

12 Steiner, *Life between Death and Rebirth*, p. 53.

---

## EVENING MEDITATION

In the evening meditate on the Earth as a great radiant green star shining out into the cosmos, and allow the heart to speak:

> *May this prayer from my warm heart unite*
>
> *With the Earth's Light which reveres the Christ–Sun,*
>
> *That I may find Spirit in the Light of the Spirit,*
>
> *Breath of the Soul in the World's Breath,*
>
> *Human Strength in the Life of the Earth.*

Given by Rudolf Steiner, March 9, 1924, to Maud B. Monges
of Spring Valley, New York (translated by R Powell)

# FINDING FUTURE GRAIL SITES
## AN ASTROGEOGRAPHICAL INVESTIGATION

### *Joel Matthew Park*

Since September 2015, Robert Powell has hosted annual Holy Grail retreats. Thus far, these have been pilgrimages to places in Europe that are central to the history of unfolding Grail spirituality. They have also been, in many ways, a journey through time. The first retreat in 2015 centered around Lazarus and Mary Magdalene. A few years after the Resurrection, they were among a group of Christians who were arrested and set adrift on the Mediterranean Sea, with neither oars nor sail. Miraculously, this band of early Christians landed in southern France. This first retreat visited Grans, Provence, in southern France, including many sites in the surrounding areas from the lives of Magdalene and Lazarus.

Magdalene reincarnated as Repanse de Schoye, the Grail Bearer at the time of Parzival. Her brother-in-law was Kyot, a key figure in Wolfram von Eschenbach's stories about the Grail. Historically, Kyot was St. Guilhem, or St. William of Gellone, right hand man of Charlemagne. The 2016 pilgrimage took the participants to Saint-Guilhem-le-Désert, the monastery St. William established for penitent soldiers in AD 806 after he had retired from life as a soldier. This monastery is in Gellone, just east of Marseille, also on the southern border of France.

Then, in 2017, the retreat took the pilgrims to Mont Sainte-Odile near Alsace, France, the home of St. Odile, a visionary and miracle worker who lived in the late 7th to early 8th century. She acted as an inspirer of the Grail stream, both at the time of Parzival and in our own time. After this, the pilgrims went on to the Ermitage forest in Arlesheim, Switzerland, where the original Grail Castle (Munsalvaesche) of Parzival stood more than 1,200 years ago. Finally, the retreat took them to the modern Grail Castle, the second Goetheanum building in Dornach, Switzerland (built in 1928).[1]

The fourth retreat occurred in August 2018 in Kinsau, Germany. Its focus was the mystery of Kaspar Hauser and "what could have been"—or perhaps one could say, what happened despite his death. Rudolf Steiner indicated that had Kaspar Hauser lived, he would have built a modern Grail Castle in southern Germany, and drawn to himself a circle of modern Grail Knights. It seems that to a certain extent King Ludwig II of Bavaria took on this task for his cousin; during this retreat we visited both the Linderhof Palace and Neuschwanstein Castle in Bavaria as Grail Castles of the 19th century. We also visited Ettal Abbey, a Benedictine monastery built by Emperor Ludwig the Bavarian in the 14th century—originally intended to be an exact replica of Parzival's Grail Castle, based on descriptions from Eschenbach's work. Its architectural plan bears a striking similarity to that of the first Goetheanum (see image 1, page 128).

During this retreat, I got to know Natalia Haarahiltunen (now the editor of *Starlight*) and her husband, Markku Maula. They hail from Finland, and had just come from the Scandinavian Sophia retreat. A number of people attending in Kinsau had just come from this event in Sweden, each of them feeling so nourished and transformed by it—the Scandinavian retreat seemed to have a new and different character, something more organic and livelier about it compared to other events.

---

1   For an excellent summary of all three of these events, see Natalia Haarahiltunen's article, "The Stars Are Shining: Three Summers in France," in *Starlight,* Advent 2017 (https://sophiafoundation .org/wp-content/uploads/2017/03/Starlight-Advent -2017-sm2.pdf).

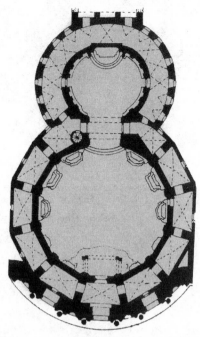

*Image 1: Ground Plan of Ettal Abbey*

As I spent time with Natalia and Markku visiting these different Grail sites over the course of the week, we began to muse about the gesture of the Grail pilgrimages, in terms of what I indicate above: that they were not only journeys to different *places*, but also seemed to be journeys through *time* as well—they had gone to the 1st, 7th, 8th, 14th, 19th, and 20th centuries after Christ, taken all together. But all of these pilgrimages had been journeys into the *past*. We wondered whether there could ever be a Grail retreat to sacred sites of the *future*? Half seriously, I wondered if, using Astrogeography, one could pinpoint those places and visit them, performing cosmic and sacred dance in order to consecrate these sites for their future task. We might run the risk, however, of doing Choreocosmos in someone's backyard!

## Astrogeographia

During this retreat, I was just finishing reading *Astrogeographia* by Robert Powell and David Bowden for the first time. It takes as its point of departure the lecture by Rudolf Steiner from 100 years ago, which we commemorate in this current edition of *Star Wisdom*. The following quote in particular is of key significance:

We are led to the center of the Earth as the polar opposite [of the sphere of the starry heavens].... The counterpart to this star is here, the counterpart to that star is there, and so on. We arrive at a complete counter image in the Earth itself to that which is outside [in the sphere of the starry heavens].... In other words, we can conceive of the active heavenly sphere mirrored in the Earth. We can think of the Earth's mineral realm as a result of this mirroring.[2]

This is a dense and substantial text, full of splendid technical details that bring the Earth's axial tilt, the precession of the equinoxes, and the Earth's surface latitude and longitude into complex connection. It took me a long time to read through and really be able to grasp—to inwardly visualize—what Robert and David were portraying. To put it as briefly and simply as possible, the principle with which they are working is that each star in the heavens acts as a projector of spiritual activity down to a specific location on the Earth. There is a correspondence between the longitudinal axis of a particular star with a longitudinal axis on Earth. For example, the star Alnitak in the constellation Orion has a zodiacal longitude of 29°56' Taurus. This corresponds with an earthly longitude of 31°E12'. The star Alnitak—and any other star above and below it at 29°56' Taurus—projects its influence all along the north–south running meridian of 31°E12'.

But this is not all. Over the course of time, the *latitudinal* projection changes for each star—that is, it projects either further north or south along this *longitudinal* meridian. This phenomenon is related to the precession of the equinoxes.[3] At the Summer Solstice this year (2021), the Sun will be aligned with 4° Gemini. This means that every star along the zodiacal longitude of 4° Gemini will experience its maximum northerly declination in 2021. This will last for the next 72 years. But then, starting around 2093—due to precession—it will

---

2  Steiner, *Interdisciplinary Astronomy: Third Scientific Course*, pp. 158–159 (alternate trans. by R. Powell).

3  This is itself caused by the axial tilt of the Earth; see chap 4, Powell and Bowden, *Astrogeographia*, for a full explanation.

be all the stars along the zodiacal longitude of *3° Gemini* that will experience maximum northerly declination. The stars aligned with 4° Gemini will reach a somewhat lower point in the sky. They will move lower and lower over the course of 12,960 years until they are the stars reaching maximum *southerly* declination at the winter solstice. We can form an image inwardly, of the stars along a certain zodiacal longitude projecting onto a geographic longitude, yet moving the pinpoint focus of their projection *very slowly*—over the course of 25,920 years—north, south, and then north again.

This is all very complicated! In any event, I certainly found it so when I first read of it. I will carry on with my story, and simultaneously give a specific example.

On the flight home from Kinsau, the very next portion that I was set to read in *Astrogeographia* seemed to me like a gift falling into my lap, in response to our somewhat tongue-in-cheek musings about "Grail Sites of the Future." I had been stalled in chapter 8, "Mapping Astrogeographia for the Whole Earth," as it covers quite a bit of material.

Finally, I came to the last section, which is quoted here in full[4]:

## STUDY 2: THE LATITUDE MOVEMENT OF ALNITAK OVER 12,960 YEARS

### *by Robert Powell and David Bowden*

The sine wave formulas can be applied to calculate and draw the timeline for the historical projection of Alnitak as it moves up the continent of Africa over a half precession cycle from 10,574 BC to AD 2386.

The results of the calculations for particular years of interest in the 12960 half precession cycle are shown in the table [page 130], with the corresponding time line projection across the continent of Africa shown in the map.

---

4  Powell and Bowden, *Astrogeographia*, pp. 212–216.

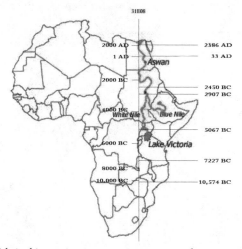

*Alnitak's projection traces out a nonlinear time line on the 31E08 meridian of Africa. The 2,000-year steps show slower movement near the top and bottom, and faster near the middle.*

## *Why Was the Great Pyramid Built at Giza?*

No satisfying answer to this question seems to come from either archaeology or archaeoastronomy. If it is only a matter of the Pyramid's shafts being aligned to certain stars, then the Pyramid does not need to be located at Giza for this. To shed some light on this unanswered riddle we can consider the declination journey of Alnitak as described in the previous section. According to most researchers the Great Pyramid was built around 2450 BC. Much earlier in 10,574 BC (during the last millennia of Atlantis) Alnitak had, on its declination journey, reached its most southerly declination of −48.8°. This journey was a result of the precessional movement of the Earth. It then turned to move north again, and has since been rising upward on the 31E08 meridian of Africa.

The beginning of Alnitak's rise in 10,574 BC can be taken as what the ancient Egyptians called "The First Time." It was then that Orion, a constellation of great significance for them, was at its lowest point in the southern sky, and seen for only a few hours each night. From The First Time onward, the precession of the equinoxes has gradually carried Orion (Osiris) and his consort Sirius (Isis) higher and higher in the sky—in effect a return and resurrection of Osiris. The ancient Egyptians oriented themselves toward the south as the direction of Upper Egypt and the source

| YEAR | DECLINATION | GEOGRAPHIC LATITUDE | ALNITAK |
|---|---|---|---|
| AD 2386 | −1.8° | 29N56 | • closest to Giza, within 3.7 miles (6 km)<br>• most northerly point, turns to move south again<br>• vernal equinox Sun enters Aquarius in AD 2376 |
| AD 33 | −5.6° | 26N13 | • vicinity of Thebes (Luxor) |
| 2450 BC | −16.2° | 15N34 | • building of the Great Pyramid of Giza<br>• 3 miles (150 km) W of Khartoum, Sudan |
| 2907 BC | −18.7° | 13N07 | • beginning of Egyptian cultural age (beginning of Kali Yuga was 3102 BC)<br>• 186 miles (300 km) S of Khartoum, Sudan |
| 5067 BC | −30.8° | 0N57 | • beginning of the Persian cultural age<br>• source of Nile (White Nile meets Lake Victoria) |
| 7227 BC | −41½° | 9S44 | • beginning of the Indian cultural age<br>• Northern Zambia |
| 10574 BC | −48.8° | 17S03 | • most southerly point, turned to move north<br>• the "First Time" of the ancient Egyptians (about 3300 years before the end of Atlantis)<br>• 62 miles (100 km) N of Harare, Zimbabwe<br>• vernal equinox Sun enters Leo in 10,764 BC |

*Historical projection of Alnitak; timeline as it moves up the 31E08 Nilotic meridian of Africa*

of the Nile. And the south was also the direction from which they observed Orion and Sirius ascending in the sky over the centuries. Later in the Egyptian cultural age, the resurrection of Osiris was experienced in the annual cycle as well, as the much awaited heliacal dawn rising (rebirth) of Orion and Sirius from their 70-day annual absence (death) in the night sky. The ancient Egyptians greatly welcomed this yearly return as the sign of the imminent flooding of the Nile and the return of abundant life.

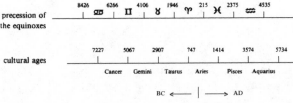

*The astronomical ages based on the precession of the equinoxes; the cultural ages follow 1,199 years later*

The carrying of Orion and Sirius higher in the sky by the precessional movement of the Earth continues into modern times, and is yet to culminate in its full return in AD 2386. It is then that Alnitak will reach its most northerly point in the sky, with a declination of −1.8°. From an astro-geographical perspective, it is remarkable that as the northward journey of Orion and Sirius comes to its end in AD 2386, the projection of Alnitak simultaneously comes into closest alignment with the Great Pyramid, within 3.1 miles (5 km), after a journey of 3,245 miles (5,222 km). This occurrence in AD 2386 is very close to AD 2375, when the vernal equinox Sun leaves the constellation of Pisces and enters the constellation of Aquarius, marking the beginning of the astronomical age of Aquarius (see figure to left). Perhaps these coincidences can bring some new understanding to the riddle of why the Great Pyramid was built at Giza. The riddle could be rephrased as to why the Pyramid was built exactly where the projection of Alnitak comes into full latitude and longitude alignment with it, and just at the time of the beginning of the astronomical Aquarius Age.[5]

---

5  See Powell, *Hermetic Astrology*, vol.1, p. 63.

Rudolf Steiner described how events that occurred during the Egyptian cultural age of Taurus[6] reappear transformed as their fruit or fulfillment[7] in our own cultural age of Pisces. One hypothesis for this riddle could thus be that the Great Pyramid was built to convey a message (as fruit of the Egyptian age) across the millennia to the humanity of AD 2386 in the cultural age of Pisces. This message will proclaim to Piscean humanity that with the full return of Orion and Sirius to their most northerly points in the sky, the great evolutionary work of the Egyptian age of transforming the astral body into sentient soul has come to a certain fulfillment (see the section on the "legend of the Golden Fleece" in this chapter). Then following the entry of the vernal equinox Sun into Aquarius there will be a period of 1,199 years, which is needed for the seed of a new spiritual impulse to come into cultural flourishing. After this gestation period will come the Russian cultural age of Aquarius under the guidance of Sophia. It is during this age that the evolutionary work begun by the Egyptians will continue with the further transformation of sentient soul into spirit self.

A related riddle regarding the Great Pyramid is the question of why it was built next to the Sphinx, which according to some researchers predates it by at least 6,000 years. The Sphinx is the largest monolithic sculpture in the world and has a lion's body and a human head. One hypothesis for this is that the Sphinx was built close to 10,586 BC when the vernal equinox Sun had just entered the constellation of Leo the Lion. This time was very close to "The First Time" of the ancient Egyptians (10,574 BC) mentioned above, when Orion and Sirius began rising from their lowest point in the night sky. Thus the picture arises of the building of the Lion–Sphinx in 10,586 BC at the beginning of the astronomical age of Leo to commemorate The First Time. And then the later building of the Great Pyramid next to the Sphinx in 2450 BC to prefigure what could be called "The Last Time." This will be the time of AD 2386 near the beginning of the astronomical age of Aquarius (as described above), when Alnitak comes into full alignment with the Great Pyramid and, at the same time, Orion and Sirius rise to their most northerly points in the sky. Then will be proclaimed from the heights the fruit and fulfillment of the great evolutionary work of the Egyptian age.

This was exactly the key I needed. To be clear— during the age of Aquarius, the Sun is in the sign of Aquarius at the spring Equinox. It precesses through Aquarius during this time period; therefore, at the start of the age of Aquarius it is at 30° at the Spring Equinox, then 29°, then 28°, etc., for 2,160 years. But this means that, for the entirety of the age of Aquarius, the Sun is in *Taurus* during the summer Solstice. Again, it precesses during this entire age: at 30° Taurus on the Solstice, then 29°, then 28°, etc., for 2,160 years. Therefore, all of the stars in the constellation Taurus will reach their maximum northerly latitude (their "summer Solstice") over the course of the age of Aquarius.

According to Robert and David's research, when looking at the projection of the stars onto planet Earth, it is more or less the continents of Europe and Africa that line up with the stars above within and below Taurus. The implication for me of the previously quoted passage was that as the megastars reach their maximum northerly latitude, it marks a powerful projection of their spiritual force onto the Earth. And it was like the Great Pyramid was built as a gateway to this time— built at the very place on Earth corresponding to the maximum northerly latitude of the megastar

6  Rudolf Steiner describes the first five cultural ages of post-Atlantis: India, Persia, Egypt, Greece–Rome, and Europe as under the signs of Cancer, Gemini, Taurus, Aries and Pisces respectively. See Steiner, *Ancient Myths and the New Isis Mystery*, pp. 80–87.

7  See Steiner, *Egyptian Myths and Mysteries*, pp. 13–14, 20. "Glancing at the immediate implications of our theme, we see a large domain. We see the gigantic pyramids, the enigmatic Sphinx. The souls that belonged to the ancient Indians were also incarnated in Egypt and are again incarnated today. If we follow our general line of thought into detail, we will discover two phenomena that show us how, in superearthly connections, there are mysterious threads between the Egyptian culture and that of today."

Alnitak, quite close to 30° Taurus. Perhaps the Great Pyramid stands uniquely as a marker of the beginning of the age of Aquarius, but hypothetically—so I thought at the time—one could look at the maximum northerly projection of all the most powerful megastars in the Taurian belt and map out a kind of pathway through Aquarius—the places in Europe that hold great spiritual potential as we head into the Aquarian Age.

And so this is what I set out to investigate. At first, I investigated using my own estimates of projection based on what is outlined in *Astrogeographia*. I decided to take a look at the megastars in the earlier degrees of Taurus, to see if there were any that projected onto the Grail sites visited in the pilgrimages over the years. To my surprise and satisfaction, almost immediately I discovered that the only megastar to project its maximum northerly latitude onto mainland western Europe was the star λ at 5°54' Taurus. From what I could tell, it seemed that this megastar projected nearly exactly onto the region of Arlesheim and Dornach—the historical site of Parzival's Grail Castle and the modern site of the Goetheanum! I began to have the impression of the Great Pyramids in the east, and the Goetheanum in the west, both built as monumental gateways to the Aquarius Age. It was after making this initial discovery that I decided to investigate the entire continent of Europe more rigorously, and as I did so I began to see that many of the "future Grail sites" are in Finland—and the inspiration for this idea to seek out future Grail sites had come from my new Finnish friends! It felt like a true synchronicity and confirmation, not a mere coincidence.

And so I decided to investigate the entire continent of Europe even more rigorously and thoroughly, eventually using the Astrogeo and Sinewave programs developed by David Bowden and available through the Sophia Foundation.[8]

### The Method

The first step was to lay out some clear guidelines. There are hundreds of catalogued stars in the

Taurus belt. I wanted to focus my research on only the most powerful. So I used two different standards: primarily, I focused on luminosity, which measures the absolute radiant power emitted from a star (or other light-emitting object). Regardless of how faint these stars may appear in our sky due to their distance from the Earth, they are nonetheless the most powerful in an absolute sense. Luminosity is measured in Ls, one L being equal to the luminosity of our Sun. I focused on stars at least 400 times as powerful as our Sun, i.e., of 400 L or greater.

The other class of stars I looked at were those with a high *apparent* magnitude ($m$). These stars may not be of great power in an absolute sense, but appear very bright geocentrically due to their relative proximity to Earth. Apparent magnitude is measured in reverse, logarithmically; therefore, the lower the number, the brighter the star appears. I focused on stars with an apparent magnitude of 4 or lower.

My second parameter (other than the *power* of the star) was where they projected onto the Earth. I wanted to focus on the European continent in particular. Rudolf Steiner indicated that the era in which we now live is the *European* cultural age, and that it would last from AD 1414 to 3574. This cultural age bridges the transition from the astronomical age of Pisces (ca. 215–2375) to Aquarius (AD 2375–4535). Therefore, I focused on locations that extend from approximately Turkey in the south through the northernmost tip of Scandinavia.

Clearly, there are locations all over the world that might be of equal or greater significance as we pass into the age of Aquarius in 354 years. The entire continent of Africa remains to be "explored" in this mode. Another example is the eastern third of North America, and most of South America, which fall under the sign of Aquarius. One could search for the geographic correspondences in those regions to stars approaching the midpoint of their journey from maximum southerly to maximum northerly latitude over the course of the Age of Aquarius. One could do something similar for the middle third of Russia and much of China, which fall under the sign of Leo, except that here

8 See https://sophiafoundation.org/product/astrogeo -sinewave-software/.

the stars are projecting on to the midpoint of their longitudinal meridians on a journey heading *south* rather than north. Finding correspondences in the Scorpio region of the Earth might be interesting, but at this point in human history, most of this section of the globe is covered by the Pacific Ocean. Here, however, it would be a matter of finding the maximum *southerly* projection of the stars in the Scorpio belt, the opposite of those in the Taurus belt. All of this, however, goes well outside the scope of this small beginning.

## The Results

Using the above parameters, I came to 38 locations in Europe that might be considered "Grail sites"—past, present, and future. I have numbered them here from south to north. In the following list, TA = Taurus, and GE = Gemini.

1. **38°N25', 27°E24': Kemelpasa/Izmir, Turkey.** The Earth projection of Bellatrix in the constellation Orion, in AD 2654. Stellar coordinates = 16°S49', 26°TA12'. (L = 1068; *m* = 1.63)

2. **38°N32', 18°E34': Ionian Sea, between Italy and Greece.** The Earth projection of star 247 in the constellation Orion, in AD 3290. Stellar coordinates = 16°S46', 17°TA22'. (L = 4379, *m* = 3.68)

3. **39°N54', 18°E23': Province of Lecce, Italy.** The Earth projection of Tabit in the constellation Orion, in AD 3303. Stellar coordinates = 15°S23', 17°TA11'. (L = 3, *m* = 3.7)

4. **40°N23', 06°E25': Tyrrhenian Sea, just south of France.** The Earth projection of megastar 897 in the constellation Taurus, in AD 4165. Stellar coordinates = 15°S01', 05°TA13'. (L = 666, *m* = 5.32)

5. **40°N56', 06°E23': Tyrrhenian Sea, just south of France.** The Earth projection of *ν* in the constellation Taurus, in AD 4167. Stellar coordinates = 14°S27', 05°TA11'. (L = 37, *m* = 3.9)

6. **41°N26', 30°E04': Black Sea (Northeast of Istanbul).** The Earth projection of Megastar 530 in the constellation Orion, in AD 2462.

*Image 2: Future Grail sites, all stars*

Stellar coordinates = 13°S48', 28°TA52'. (L = 1394, *m* = 4.4)

7. **41°N51', 30°E10': Black Sea (Northeast of Istanbul).** The Earth projection of Meissa in the constellation Orion, in AD 2455. Stellar coordinates = 13°S22', 28°TA58'. (L = 4019, *m* = 3.39)

8. **42°N09', 30°E12': Black Sea (Northeast of Istanbul).** The Earth projection of megastar 669, in AD 2452. Stellar coordinates = 13°S04', 29°TA00'. (L = 1008, *m* = 5.6)

9. **47°N18', 07°E06': Saint-Brais, Switzerland.** The Earth projection of λ in the constellation Taurus, in AD 4115. Stellar coordinates = 07°S57', 05°TA54'. (L = 485, *m* = 3.45)

10. **48°N43', 19°E28': Ľubietová, Slovakia.** The Earth projection of star 987 in the constellation Taurus, in AD 3225. Stellar coordinates = 06°S30', 18°TA16'. (L = 598, *m* = 6.08)

11. **49°N00', 29°E47': Northwest of Uman', Ukraine.** The Earth projection of megastar 206 in the constellation Taurus, in AD 2477. Stellar coordinates = 06°S13', 28°TA35'. (L = 645, *m* = 5.11)

12. **49°N23', 14°E25': Bernartice, Czech Republic.** The Earth projection of Al Hecka in the constellation Taurus, in the year 3584. Stellar coordinates = 05°S50', 13°TA13'. (L = 79, $m$ = 3.4)

13. **49°N28', 12°E16': Guteneck, Germany.** The Earth projection of Primus Hyadum in the constellation Taurus, in the year 3743. Stellar coordinates = 05°S44', 11°TA04'. (L = 67, $m$ = 3.63)

14. **49°N44', 16°E15': Polička, Czech Republic.** The Earth projection of Aldebaran in the constellation Taurus, in AD 3457. Stellar coordinates = 05°S28', 15°TA03'. (L = 156, $m$ = .86)

15. **50°N23', 29°E51': West of Kiev, Ukraine.** The Earth projection of megastar 206 in the constellation Taurus, in AD 2477. Stellar coordinates = 04°S41', 28°TA39'. (L = 5638, $m$ = 4.38)

16. **50°N28', 30°E10': West of Kiev, Ukraine.** The Earth projection of megastar 489 in the constellation Taurus, in AD 2455. Stellar coordinates = 04°S45', 28°TA58'. (L = 1552, $m$ = 3.39)

17. **51°N13', 13°E20': Lommatzsch, Germany.** The Earth projection of Hyadum II in the constellation Taurus, in AD 3667. Stellar coordinates = 03°S58', 12°TA08'. (L = 60, $m$ = 3.75)

18. **52°N36', 14°E56': Słońsk, Poland.** The Earth projection of Ain in the constellation Taurus, in AD 3551. Stellar coordinates = 02°S34', 13°TA44'. (L = 76, $m$ = 3.53)

19. **53°N01', 31°E15': Chachersk district of Belarus, just west of the Russian border.** The Earth projection of Alheckla in the constellation Taurus, in 2377. Stellar coordinates = 02°S12', 00°GE03'. (L = 924, $m$ = 3.02)

20. **53°N56', 28°E57': Byerazino, Belarus.** The Earth projection of star 114 in the constellation Taurus, in 2542. Stellar coordinates = 01°S17', 27°TA45'. (L = 442, $m$ = 4.87)

21. **54°N01', 24°E23': South of Varėna, Lithuania.** The Earth projection of star 105 in the constellation Taurus, in 2882. Stellar coordinates = 01°S11', 23°TA11'. (L = 402, $m$ = 5.88)

22. **54°N25', 13°E44': Baltic Sea, just north of Sellin, Germany.** The Earth projection of megastar 653, in 3638. Stellar coordinates = 00°S43', 12°TA32'. (L = 1089, $m$ = 5.91)

23. **56°N33', 24°E39': Vecumnieki Parish, Latvia.** The Earth projection of megastar 198, in 2852. Stellar coordinates = 01°N22', 23°TA27'. (L = 5387, $m$ = 5.5)

24. **58°N19', 10°E14': Skagerrak, between Oslo, Norway and Gothenburg, Sweden.** The Earth projection of star 36 in the constellation Taurus, in AD 3890. Stellar coordinates = 03°N16', 09°TA02'. (L = 487, $m$ = 5.47)

25. **58°N55', 06°E49': Sinnes, Norway.** The Earth projection of Atlas in the Pleiades, in AD 4136. Stellar coordinates = 03°N55', 05°TA37'. (L = 423, $m$ = 3.62

26. **59°N02', 06°E27': Flørli, Norway.** The Earth projection of Alcyone in the Pleiades, in AD 4162. Stellar coordinates = 04°N03', 05°TA15'. (L = 802, $m$ = 2.87)

27. **59°N04', 06°E21': Flørli, Norway.** The Earth projection of the entire star cluster of the Pleiades in the constellation Taurus, in AD 4169. Stellar coordinates = 04°N05', 05°TA09'. ($m$ = 1.2)

28. **59°N11', 05°E52': Finnøy, Norway.** The Earth projection of Elektra in the Pleiades, in AD 4204. Stellar coordinates = 04°N12', 04°TA40'. (L = 366, $m$ = 3.7)

29. **59°N23', 06°E08': Jelsa, Norway.** The Earth projection of Maia in the Pleiades, in AD 4185. Stellar coordinates = 04°N24', 04°TA56'. (L = 300, $m$ = 3.87)

30. **60°N35', 29°E02': South of Vyborg, Russia.** The Earth projection of El Nath in the constellation Taurus, in AD 2536. Stellar coordinates = 05°N23', 27°TA50'. (L = 308, $m$ = 1.65)

31. **62°N11', 29°E19': Savonlinna, Finland.**
The Earth projection of megastar 373, in
AD 2516. Stellar coordinates = 06°N59',
28°TA07'. (L = 2320, *m* = 5.71)

32. **64°N06', 30°E37': Muyezersky District,
Republic of Karelia, Russia.** The
Earth projection of megastar 93 in the
constellation Auriga, in AD 2423. Stellar
coordinates = 08°N54', 29°TA21'.
(L = 17775, *m* = 4.71)

33. **65°N35', 23°E06': Bottenviken, south of
Kalix, Sweden.** The Earth projection of
Kabdhilinan in the constellation Auriga,
in AD 2963. Stellar coordinates = 10°N27',
21°TA54'. (L = 1802, *m* = 2.69)

34. **66°N00', 28°E02': Posio, Finland.** The
Earth projection of megastar 169 in the
constellation Auriga, in AD 2608. Stellar
coordinates = 10°N49', 26°TA50'.
(L = 7403, *m* = 5.03)

35. **66°N21', 29°E29': Kuusamo, Finland.** The
Earth projection of megastar 934, in 2504.
Stellar coordinates = 11°N09', 28°TA17'.
(L = 583, *m* = 5.92)

36. **66°N23', 27°E17': Kemijärvi, Finland.** The
Earth projection of megastar 875, in 2662.
Stellar coordinates = 11°N13', 26°TA05'.
(L = 697, *m* = 5.93)

37. **68°N34', 23°E18': North of Hetta, Finland.**
The Earth projection of megastar 55,
in 2949. Stellar coordinates = 13°N27',
22°TA06'. (L = 40335, *m* = 6.07)

38. **69°N27', 26°E17': Utsjoki, Finland.** The
Earth projection of megastar 520, in 2734.
Stellar coordinates = 14°N18', 25°TA05'.
(L = 1346, *m* = 6.03)

There is a lot to take in here—a large haul of
fish! We can treat this current article as only an
introduction, to be continued in a future edition of
*Star Wisdom*. But let's highlight a few key aspects.

First, take a look at the map, and you'll see
certain of the numbers with asterisks (*) next to
them. This indicates that these are the projections
of stars that have great apparent magnitude—
i.e., they look very bright from Earth—but have
a relatively low luminosity—i.e., their absolute
intensity is somewhat low. These are numbers 3,
5, 12, 13, 14, 17, 18, 27, 28, 29, and 30. We might
imagine these sites to be of a different type of
importance vs. the others—they might carry the
outer cultural mantle in a certain sense, while the
spiritual depth and fecundity is nurtured in the
more "luminous" sites.

Notice that a majority of these "bright, but not
powerful" sites are in Central Europe—Germany,
the Czech Republic and Poland primarily, but
also Russia and Norway. This points to the fact
that the outer "center of gravity" for the spiritual
culture of Europe is to be found in these Central
European cultures. However, if we then focus on
the projections of the most *powerful* megastars
rather than the *brightest*—if we, in our mind's
eye, erase all of the central sites (12, 13, 14, 17,
and 18)—we are left with a fascinating result (see
image 3, page 136). We see that, north of Rome,
the focus of these most powerful stars rests pre-
dominantly on Scandinavia and Eastern Europe.
It is not France, Italy, and Germany that have the
greatest spiritual significance for Europe from this
perspective; it is the regions that will build the
bridge to the future Philadelphia culture of Russia. The glaring exception is number 9 in the list
above—Saint-Baire, Switzerland, an hour's drive
from the Goetheanum! One might say that the
Scandinavian/Eastern European representative in
Central and Western Europe is Dornach, the center of Anthroposophy.

Second, notice that the full list of sites has been
arranged in order, from south to north. Now, from
the perspective of Astrogeographia, each of these
sites is "activated" in time from east to west. As
the Sun's vernal equinox travels backward through
Aquarius, so also the stars in the longitudinal segment of Taurus reach their maximum northerly
latitude, beginning with 30° Taurus (in the east)
and ending with 0° Taurus (in the west).

From my own observation and intuition, however, this seems to be beside the point to some
degree. Think about the Great Pyramid—this was
built in the Age of Taurus in order to prepare for
the inauguration of the Age of Aquarius. It isn't as

Image 3: Earthly projections
of the most powerful stars

their greatest cultural flourishing approximately during the so-called Greco–Roman era, from 747 BC through AD 1414. By my estimate, every 1° of latitude north represents a movement through 170 years of time. Giza, which is very close to 30° North latitude, had its flourishing from approximately the 26th century BC through the 4th century BC (when Alexander the Great conquered Egypt). Istanbul (formerly Byzantion and Constantinople) is 41° North latitude, 11° farther north than Giza. This would put its time of cultural flourishing around 11 x 170 = 1,870 years later. And in fact, this is precisely what we see: between the 7th century BC and the 15th to 16th centuries AD was the time of Istanbul's greatest cultural significance.

This puts the other sites in numbers 1–8—sites close to Greece and Italy, and the southern coast of France—in the same time period in terms of their greatest cultural significance. We might look at numbers 4 and 5, which are just south of Toulon and Marseilles—these are the very sites that were of great significance for Mary Magdalene and Lazarus in the 1st century AD, reaching the pinnacle of their significance for the Grail stream in the 15th–16th centuries with the development of the Tarot of Marseilles.

Moving farther north, we come to site number 9, which corresponds to Saint-Brais, Switzerland. This location is very close to Odilienberg, to Arlesheim, and to Dornach. Saint-Brais is 6.28° farther north than Istanbul; 6.28 x 170 = 1067.6 years. Istanbul was founded as Byzantion in 660 BC. This puts the culturally significant time period of Saint-Brais, and the significant Grail sites nearby, in the time period of about AD 408 to 2605. This is the time period within which the lives of St. Odile, Parzival, and Rudolf Steiner took place—and the site will continue to be of great significance for the next 600 years.

Moving farther north, we have a whole grouping of sites close to number 12, the maximum northerly projection of the star Al Hecka in Taurus, the Bull. This projection is very close to the site of Karlstein Castle, constructed by Emperor Charles IV in the 14th century quite deliberately as a Grail temple. The flourishing of this particular

though the site at which the Great Pyramid stands won't become relevant until AD 2375—it has been relevant for thousands of years! It seems that many of these sites that will be the earthly projection of the maximum northerly latitude of the stars in Taurus in several hundred to several thousand years' time are already quite *active* as cultural centers—or will be soon.

For we see with the Great Pyramid, which is at almost exactly 30°N latitude in Giza, that it was active thousands of years ago. On the other hand, look at numbers 1, 6, 7, and 8 above: they are all in the vicinity of Istanbul (formerly Constantinople) about 10° farther north—close to 40°N latitude. This city was founded as Byzantion in 660 BC, and had its greatest importance and cultural influence in the subsequent 2,000 years or so—up through the 15th to 16th centuries AD.

We can imagine that the entire belt containing 1 to 8 in the list above were Grail sites which saw

site and those aligned with it latitudinally more or less corresponds to the late 8th to 29th centuries AD. These are regions, like the Dornach region as well, which transition humanity both out of the Greco–Roman cultural era (747 BC–AD 1414) to the Central European era (in AD 1414), and also from the Age of Pisces to Aquarius (in AD 2375). This special transitional role belongs to sites 9–18, centered in Switzerland, Germany, the Czech Republic, Slovakia, Poland, and Ukraine. Sites number 9 and 16 are the most important from this grouping, as they are the only two that are both particularly *powerful* (i.e., with L > 400) and particularly *bright* (i.e., with $m < 4$). These correspond to Saint-Brais (near Dornach), Switzerland and Kiev, Ukraine. This throws a new light on the high political tensions around the Ukraine—it is understood consciously by guiding forces of both light and darkness that this is a crucial region in the spiritual evolution of Europe.

Finally, looking at an example even closer to our own time, we can consider number 21 in the list above. This site is about 14° further north than Istanbul, which means that the time of its cultural flourishing ought to have begun around the early 18th century, and continue well into the fourth millennium. Notice that this site is very close to Vilnius, Lithuania. It was in the late 17th century that the Discalced Carmelites in Vilnius built a chapel to house and venerate the painting *Our Lady of the Gate of Dawn* (image 4)

More recently, Vilnius was the center of activity for Sister Faustina, a Polish nun who experienced visions of and messages from the Etheric Christ in the 1930s. The Divine Mercy image, a representation of the etheric Christ that he instructed her to have painted and hung in a chapel dedicated to veneration of this image, now has its home in Vilnius at the Sanctuary to the Divine Mercy (see image 5, page 138).[9]

Clearly, Vilnius—which goes by such names as "Jerusalem of Lithuania," "Rome of the North,"

*Image 4: Our Lady of the Gate of Dawn*

"Athens of the North," and "New Babylon"—is a key Grail site both of the present day and on into the future, for the entire 2,500-year age of the Etheric Christ.[10]

So, from one perspective, we see the sites of Europe being "activated" in a movement from east to west as the maximum northerly latitude precesses through the sign of Taurus, which is aligned with the continent of Europe. From another perspective, it seems that these same sites are activated from south to north. This would indicate a particular level of activity in Istanbul in the farthest south, particularly around the time of the Greco–Roman cultural era up through the Lapland region of Finland, in which number 37 and 38 are located, which will be most active around the time of the Russian–Slavic cultural era (AD 3574–5734).

The third and final perspective is more dynamic (image 6). Looking at this image, we see a movement from the horizontal to the vertical. Beginning with Line A, we see that the areas around this line were the focus for the Greco–Roman cultural

---

9  For more on the fascinating story of Sister Faustina and the significance of the Divine Mercy in the time of Christ's Second Coming, see https://sophiafoundation.org/a-special-easter-2020-novena/.

10 On Vilnius, see https://en.wikipedia.org/wiki/Vilnius.

*Image 5: The Divine Mercy*

cultural era (AD 1414–3574), which is the current focal point for world culture.

*Image 6: Europe resurrects*

It is the last two axes, lines D and E, that show us the future. Line D, we might imagine, demarcates the main area of the astronomical age of Aquarius (AD 2375–4535), while line E shows us the places where the Russian–Slavic cultural era (AD 3574–5734) will probably begin. We might imagine this as an image of a human being—the Youth of Nain, or Lazarus—being raised from the dead, moving from the horizontal axis of line A, to the fully upright axis of line E, and then proceeding to walk—heading east, through Russia, over the course of the Russian–Slavic cultural era.

Thus far, the Grail Pilgrimages have focused on locations *below* line C—locations related to the past, up to the present day. Perhaps someday, my Finnish friends and I will organize retreats to sites *above* this line, to the northeast of Europe—focusing on the Uralic, Baltic, and Scandinavian nations—the bridges to the future. In this way, we might play the role of a modern Joseph of Arimathea, who bore the Holy Grail and the blood of Christ to sites all across Europe—ultimately finding his way to Glastonbury—sprinkling Christ's blood to plant the spiritual seeds for the future

era (747 BC–AD 1414), with Spain, France, Italy, Greece and Turkey all along this axis. Moving to Line B, we can see that the sites around this axis are more related to the Age of Pisces (AD 215–2375), with this line moving right through the site of the Munsalvaesche and the Goetheanum, up into the British Isles. Then we come to the third axis, Line C, the midpoint of this movement from horizontal to vertical. Gathered around this line are all of the sites in Germany, the Czech Republic, and Slovakia, with Austria and Hungary close by. This line is the center of gravity for the Central European sacred sites of the coming Christian European culture. It may be that Arimathean journeys are needed to bring about what Rudolf Steiner predicted more than a century ago.

The following are Steiner's remarks made to an esoteric group on March 7, 1914, as remembered by E. A. Karl Stockmeyer (emphasis mine):

As the year 1000 CE approached, European humanity lived in great fear of the expected end of the world. People imagined this, in the physical sense, as a dissolving in smoke and mist. The ahrimanic spirits gave this idea to human beings that something terrible would take place on the physical plane, while, in reality, a number of things took place in the spiritual world. In every millennium the luciferic and ahrimanic spirits gain special power. Humanity does not need to be particularly proud of the decimal system that is predominant today. Every numerical system is brought into the world by specific spirits, and each has the tendency to reveal certain facts and connections more clearly and to obscure others, to let them recede.

The ahrimanic impulses work very strongly in the decimal system. It is evident that with every millennium—thus in the years 1000, 2000, and so on—an especially strong attack by Lucifer and Ahriman, working together, takes place. In the other centuries they keep themselves more in balance. In the centuries that include the number 9, and thus in our own century, when we approach the new millennium, they unite themselves, and together, they influence human beings. This fact lives in the popular belief that Lucifer and Ahriman are bound by chains for a thousand years and then are set free for a short time.

In the millennia before Christ—1000, 2000, and 3000 BC—there was an especially strong influence of the beneficent, progressive powers, which kept this united luciferic–ahrimanic effect in check and let rise out of it a special good. Thus, we see how in 3000 BC the pyramids were built. The year 2000 BC was the age of Abraham and everything that came into being out of that; at the same time it was a high point in Babylonian culture. The year 1000 BC was the age of David. The building of Solomon's temple was prepared at that time. In year zero, Christ appeared. We have often explained how, according to the Gospels and especially the Fifth Gospel, Christ had to take up the battle with Lucifer and Ahriman. In the times after Christ, the good, progressive spirits could not intervene in such a way anymore, and so humanity was left open to the attacks of Lucifer and Ahriman. They managed, in any case, to confuse the thinking of human beings, so that an entry for error was found, the error of the approaching physical end of the world. They are interested in having things be imagined much too spatially and temporally.

At this time [the 11th to 12th centuries AD], there arose for the first time a proof of the existence of God, which the Bishop of Canterbury brought forward, as well as the counterviews of his opponent Roscelin [of Compiègne]. It was also at this time that the popes trod Christian humility under foot and raised themselves to power, so that Kaiser Heinrich had to bow before the pope in Canossa, as the whole exoteric church came to practices that awakened the derisive laughter of ahrimanic spirits.

It is these same ahrimanic spirits that will assert their influence when we near AD 2000. Evolution proceeds like the swing of a pendulum: in the year AD 1000, one expected the end of the world; in the year 2000, one will expect exactly the opposite; and in the year AD 3000 one will again expect the end of the world, but the world will have become such that whole groups of people will long for this end. One can say without sentimentality: European humanity is heading toward terrible times.

Let us take architecture and the influences upon it. In 3000 BC the pyramids were built, in 2000 BC came the hut constructions (Abraham's age). In 1000 BC, Solomon's temple was prepared. In AD 1000, the new element that was meant to arise could not struggle to enter into the world, as a result of the working of the opposing forces of Lucifer and Ahriman. We see the Normans, who spread out from Scandinavia over western and central Europe, and how they tried to express something in their wooden buildings that could not fully develop. Certain lines are suggested there but not worked out further, because the ahrimanic spirits hindered it. Instead, the culture of the Moors appeared on the scene and, with it, the architecture of Cordova and Granada—the horseshoe-shaped pointed arches, which drive out the truly Christian round arch of Romanesque architecture. In the culture of the Moors one can see the anti-Christian element directly in the pointed arches, which should have been round.

That is Ahriman's sign. Thus, Ahriman worked as the Antichrist in architecture, in that he replaced the round Romanesque arch with the horseshoe-shaped or pointed arch. In this way he worked through the Moors and the Turkish people and did not allow the art of the Normans to develop, so that the wooden buildings that they had erected throughout Europe could not impart that which they should have. For that reason, we do not find a flowering of architectural works in AD 1000, as with the turning of earlier millennia. Now the architecture for the next millennium should be created anew. We must express the round lines that Ahriman suppressed in the Norman buildings. If we leave out certain lines that we find in these buildings, we have our Dornach building as a true continuation of the wood buildings of the Normans.

*Terrible times stand before humanity in Europe. We know that when the first third of the century has passed, Christ will be seen in his etheric form and that this will give a powerful impulse over against all the tendencies of decline of this century. In older times, as for instance in AD 1000, human beings had to believe what Lucifer and Ahriman made them believe, because they did not yet have within themselves the conscious Christ impulse. We do not have to believe them anymore; we should freely take in this new Christ impulse so that we can achieve resistance to Lucifer and Ahriman. In the twentieth century, Lucifer and Ahriman will seize hold of the name of Christ. Human beings will call themselves Christians who have no trace of true Christianity in themselves. And they will rage against those who follow the living Christ, who continues to work, and those who hold to what Christ said at one time, according to the tradition of the Gospels: "I am with you always, even unto the end of the ages of Earth."*

Confusion and devastation will reign when the year AD 2000 approaches. At that point, there will be not one piece of wood of our Dornach building resting on the other. All will be destroyed and devastated. We will look down upon this from the spiritual world. However, when the year AD 2086 arrives, one will see all over Europe buildings arise that are dedicated to spiritual goals and which will be reflections of our Dornach building with its two cupolas. That will be the golden age for such buildings in which the spiritual life will flourish.[11]

Perhaps, if we can unite our goodwill with that of the starry heights of the spiritual world, the geographical locations outlined above can become centers of spiritual culture by 2086—the "golden age...in which the spiritual life will flourish."

---

11 Steiner, *Rosicrucianism Renewed*, pp. 224–227.

---

"All fixed land swims, and the stars hold it in position.... The continents swim and do not sit upon anything. They [the continents] upon the Earth are held in place from without by the starry constellations. When the constellations change, the continents change, also. On the old maps and atlases, these relationships between starry constellations and configurations on the Earth's surface were correctly shown, including also the constellations of the zodiac."

—Rudolf Steiner, *Faculty Meetings with Rudolf Steiner,*
April 25, 1923 (trans. rev. by R. Powell)

# THE TREE OF LIFE

## RETURNING TO THE ORIGIN OF THE HOUSES, PART TWO

### *Joel Matthew Park*

In the first part of this series of articles, "Saturn in Cancer,"[1] I hypothesized that Rudolf Steiner, throughout his life, utilized a clockwise house system. Further, from a close reading of the works of Manilius's *Astronomica* (the first text to describe the astrological houses), it seems they were originally conceived as running clockwise, with the 1st house corresponding to the east, the 4th house corresponding to the Ecliptic Zenith, the 7th house corresponding to the west, and the 10th house corresponding to the Ecliptic Nadir. For Manilius, this Cross was the structure upon which the entire phenomenal universe hung, and it emanated eternally from the center of the Earth. Not only were the twelve houses independent realities (i.e., not determined by the movement of the stars above), they comprised the *central* reality, around which all else revolves. Manilius essentially espouses a radical geocentrism.

I ended the first article with a series of questions: When were the astrological houses first perceived and written about? Why at that time in particular? Why has there been confusion as to the particulars of their nature? Is each of the twelve houses simply a temple of mundane fortune, such as health or marriage, or do the houses carry deeper significance? What implications does a fuller understanding of the houses bring in terms of cosmology in general?

Let's look at the first two questions: When were the houses first conceived of, and why then? We notice that Manilius wrote *Astronomica* in the first century AD. Similarly, the first horoscopes that utilized a house system were cast around that time, as well. As Brian Gray points out in his article "Anthroposophic Foundations for a Renewal of Astrology," "…the 'original' house system…arose around the time of the birth of Christ."[2]

The oldest recorded birth charts with 12 houses date back to the period when Jesus was born. According to Deborah Houlding, "Firm evidence for the use of houses in chart judgments has been dated to 22 BC, with the earliest extant book to describe their meaning being the *Astronomica* of Manilius, written in Latin around AD 10."[3]

Could there be any connection between the life of Christ and the perception of the astrological Houses?

Let's take a step back and recall the anthroposophic picture of cosmic evolution. In primal times, the human being was united with the spiritual world (in a dim level of consciousness) in its activity of forming the Earth and in the elements of nature. We could call this primal state "Paradise," in which Father (Primal Essence—Love) and Mother (Primal Substance—Wisdom) are One, acting in total harmony. At the time of the Fall, Lucifer intervened in human evolution. He made the human being independent from Love and Wisdom, from the Father and Mother, necessitating their descent too deeply into matter.

Owing to this complicated series of events, which took place over long stages of time, Father and Mother were separated. Since then, the Father emanated from the heights of the nine hierarchies—Angels, Archangels, Archai, Elohim, Dynamis, Kyriotetes, Thrones, Cherubim, and Seraphim. The Mother and the realm of Paradise (also known as Shambhala in Eastern traditions) descended farther and farther below layers of

---

1 See *Saturn–Mary–Sophia: Star Wisdom*, vol 2.

2 Gray, "Anthroposophic Foundations for a Renewal of Astrology," *Journal for Star Wisdom*, 2012, p. 120.

3 Houlding, *The Houses: Temples of the Sky*, p. 7.

trauma—not just layers of matter, but submatter, what is known in anthroposophic literature as the nine subearthly spheres. Since then, the realm of the Mother—Virginity, or Primal Innocence—has been held captive and guarded by nine virtually impassable spheres of darkness, an inversion of the nine hierarchies above. Father and Mother were divided, one guarded by a kind of blinding Goodness, and the other surrounded by impenetrable Darkness.

Christ's mission was to descend from the heights of the Father down to humanity, and from thence to forge a path to the Mother. This mission took place over the course of long ages. Christ first descended from the realm of the Father into the circle of the zodiac around the time of the ancient Hindu culture, more than 9,000 years ago. The rishis could perceive Christ in his descent and named him *Vishva Karman*. During the time of the ancient Persian culture, he descended from the realm of the fixed stars to the Sun, becoming *Ahura Mazda*, "Aura of the Sun," for Zarathustra. Then, during the ancient Egyptian culture, he became *Osiris*, who died and was divided into fourteen pieces—the fourteen phases from New Moon to Full Moon. Finally, for the ancient Hebrews, he descended all the way into the elemental forces of Earth, appearing as *YHVH*, "I AM that I AM."

Throughout these stages of descent, ancient cosmology (astrology) increasingly took form and clarity as Christ descended lower and lower. By the time of the end of the ancient Egyptian culture, and the start of the Greco–Roman era (747 BC and shortly afterward), ancient Babylonian astrology had become completely codified and systematized.[4] It was as though Christ had brought with him a clear picture of the how, what, when, why, and who of the cosmos, a picture that became crystal clear by the time he united with the elemental aura of Earth in the time of the ancient Hebrews.

Yet, almost unnoticed, a secret corollary to astrology was developing, quite literally under the surface.

## The Veil of Isis

Around 2500 BC,[5] the cult of Osiris and Isis was founded by Hermes Trismegistus, or Thoth as he was known to the Egyptians. Thoth was an initiate who had received the astral body of Zarathustra in a prior incarnation, giving him a vast understanding of the mysteries of space.[6] In addition, he was a kind of mediator between the realm of the heavens above and Earth's interior below. Those who were initiated into the Osiris mysteries came to perceive Christ emanating from the constellation Orion, which is in alignment with the center of the Galaxy. They came to perceive Isis as the Mother, trapped in the subearthly realms below. "I am all that has been and is and shall be; and no mortal has ever lifted my mantle." Such was the inscription on the statues of Isis in ancient Egypt. Isis's veil could not be lifted by a mere human mortal; only Christ could penetrate the nine layers of darkness and open the gateway into the realm of Paradise at the center of the Earth. The Osiris initiation opened up this vista of Christ's future deed to the initiated.

This realm of Isis was a realm of the dead, a realm of shades, formlessness, and chaos. It was to be imbued with the form or essence of Osiris. What is this form of Osiris? It is what we can see in the constellation of Orion. This is an image of the etheric body—form body—of Christ, to be planted in Earth's center, renewing the primal form of Paradise—we might say restoring the Tree of Life.

This cosmic form of Orion was passed on to Moses, who was initiated into the Egyptian mysteries during the first part of his life. During that period in human history, all vestiges of pictorial consciousness were beginning to fade. Mythologies and laws had to be written down, since they could no longer be intuited and perceived directly in the spirit-permeated external world—so, too, with the spiritual reality behind the sense-perceptible constellation of Orion. We could say that Moses and the ancient Hebrews "robbed" the Egyptians of their treasure store of Wisdom. Moses was, in one

---

4  See Robert Powell's work, especially his doctoral thesis *History of the Zodiac*, for a full description of this ancient sidereal astrology.

5  See Powell and Bowden, *Astrogeographia*.

6  See Steiner, *According to Matthew*, lect. 2.

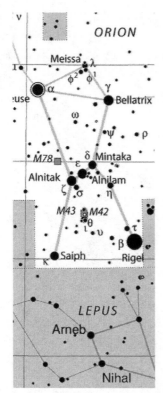

*Image 1: Constellations Orion and Lepus*

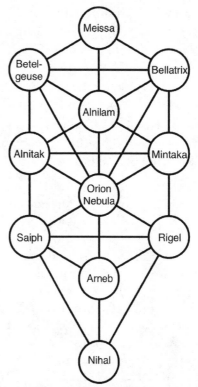

*Image 2: the Sephiroth Tree with stellar correspondences)*

sense, the "last initiate" of ancient Egypt, whose purpose was to preserve this wisdom in a codified, written form among a different culture—the ancient Hebrews. We find this documented formulation of the spiritual reality underlying the constellation Orion in the Sephiroth Tree of the Kabbalah, the esoteric complement to the Torah (see images 1 and 2).[7]

The Sephiroth Tree contains within it all of reality: four planes of existence (corresponding to the spiritual, astral, elemental, and physical levels); ten "Sephira," or modes of expression of God, the qualitative origin of all number; and twenty-two paths of Wisdom running among the ten Sephiroth. These twenty-two paths of Wisdom were the twenty-two letters of the Hebrew alphabet. The essence of Orion, the etheric body of Osiris–Christ,

could now be found in the *Word* of the Hebrew alphabet. It was understood from the beginning that this Sephiroth Tree was none other than the Tree of Life, which had been lost to humanity since the gates of Paradise were closed. The Cherubim Uriel, guarding the gates of Paradise...the veil of Isis that no mere mortal can lift...the mystery of the Sephiroth Tree is that it contains the seed for the Tree of Life, the key to the lost Paradise at the center of the Earth. It was the mission of the Hebrew people to guard and internalize this key through the Word, so that Christ could bring this lost Word back to the Mother in the depths of the Underworld and restore the lost Paradise.

### The Deed of Golgotha

Thus, we have two complementary streams converging at the time of Christ. One was the exoteric astrological cosmology that reaches increasing refinement leading up to Christ's life; indeed, we might say that the three magi represent the apotheosis of that ancient astrology. On the other hand, we have the esoteric mysteries of the "Inner

---

7   The correspondences between Orion and Lepus with the Sephiroth Tree, and the transmission of Egyptian (Hermetic) wisdom into Hebrew esotericism via Moses, is a discovery of Robert Powell's which was brought to my attention in August 2016 in Assisi, Italy.

Earth," passed on from Hermes to Moses and embedded in Kabbalah. What exactly happened at the Deed of Golgotha, when these two streams converged?

Some have come quite close to understanding what took place. For example, consider the words of Dr. Rudolf Hauschka from more than 60 years ago as the expression of a soul who knows that a crucial truth is there, but just out of arm's reach:

> In a lecture held on June 30, 1956 (in the working group of anthroposophic doctors in Witten), Rudolf Hauschka mentioned what had become clear to him in a conversation with Dr. Ita Wegman. "I had always struggled against the idea that astrology should still hold any truth, since it no longer has a cosmic reality underlying it. I was taught otherwise, that indeed a reality exists that is more significant than the constellations visible in the starry heavens—namely, the configuration at the time of the life of Christ. When his blood flowed on Golgotha, the macrocosm imprinted itself into the Earth's aura and is effective since then in the Earth or from the Earth's aura."

Later, in a letter, Dr. Hauschka explained further:

> Then certainly a mysterious perspective will emerge, that one will be able to attribute spiritual significance to these two entities: the constellations and the signs, and one will scarcely abstain, when one sees the effect of the zodiacal *constellations* upon nature, from commemorating here the heavenly and there the earthly offspring of the Elohim. At the Turning Point of Time the representative of the Macrocosm united himself with the Earth and imprinted the stellar constellations into the Earth's aura for all time. Thus, it seems to me that the zodiac *constellations* work upon the physical–etheric side of nature, and the signs have to do with the soul–spiritual constitution."[8]

Here Dr. Hauschka has come to the threshold of the truth, but has been unable to cross over—and indeed, how could he, for the time had not yet come for him to be able to, as we shall see.

We begin to approach a better conception of what occurred at the time of the Death and Resurrection of Christ through Steiner's words 100 years ago this year (emphasis mine):

> ...according to the Ptolemaic paradigm, for example, out there is the blue sphere, and here a point [fig. 1]—we would have to think of a polar point in the center of the Earth. When conceived in a simplified way, every point of the sphere would have its reflected point in the Earth's center. But, of course, it is not to be understood so simply.... The stars, in effect, would be here [fig. 2]. So that, in thinking of the sphere concentrated in the center of the Earth, we would have to think of it in the following way: The polar opposite of this star is here, of this one here, and so on [fig. 2]. We come, then, to a complete mirroring of what is outside in the interior of the Earth.

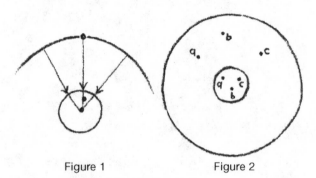

Figure 1          Figure 2

Picturing this in regard to each individual planet, we have, say, Jupiter and then a "polar Jupiter" within the Earth. We come to something that works outward from within the Earth in the way that Jupiter works in the Earth's environment. We arrive at a mirroring (*in reality it is the opposite way 'round*, but I will now describe it like this), a mirroring of what is outside the Earth by the interior of the Earth. And if we think about the effects of this reflection in the forms of the minerals then we must also think about the effects of what works outside in the cosmic sphere itself in forming our capacity to understand the minerals. In other words, *we can think of the whole celestial sphere as being mirrored in the Earth. We conceive the mineral kingdom of the Earth as a result of this reflection, and we conceive that what lives within us, enabling us to understand the mineral kingdom,*

---

8    Quoted in Powell, *The Astrological Revolution*, pp. 131–132 (trans by R. Powell).

*comes from what surrounds us out in the celestial space.* Meanwhile the realities we grasp by means of this faculty of understanding come from within the Earth.[9]

What exactly does Steiner mean by "in reality, it is the opposite way 'round"? Well, notice in the figures that it is not a simple mirroring of "point b" above onto the surface of Earth below. No, there is a total *inversion of the outer into the inner*, a turning inside-out. His words from earlier in the lecture regarding bone structure make this clear:

The inner surface of the tubular bone corresponds morphologically to the outer surface of the cranial bone. The cranial bone can be derived from the tubular bone if we picture it as being inverted, to begin with, in the way that one turns a glove inside-out. In the glove, however, when I turn the outer surface to the inside and the inner to the outside, I get a form similar to the original one. But if in the moment of turning the inside of the tubular bone to the outside, certain tensions come into play and the mutual relationships of the forces change in such a way that the form which was inside and has now been turned outward alters the shape and distribution of its surface, then we obtain, through inversion according to the principle of the turning inside-out of a glove, the outer surface of the cranial bone as derived from the inner surface of the tubular bone. From this you can conclude as follows. The inner space of the tubular bone, this compressed inner space, corresponds with regard to the human cranium to the entire outer world. You must consider the outer universe, forming the outside of the human head, and what works within, tending from within toward the inner surface of the tubular bone, as related in their influence upon the human constitution. You have to see these as belonging together. You have to regard the world on the inside of the tubular bone as a kind of inversion of the world surrounding us outside.[10]

Now we have a key to the Mystery of Golgotha: at his death, Christ descended into the subearthly

spheres, navigating his way back to the Mother in the depths. At this moment, he *pulled along with him* the entirety of the cosmos, so to speak, distilled into the seed of the Tree of Life, his etheric body. He planted that seed in the heart of Shambhala, the lost Paradise. Then, at the moment of his Resurrection, we could say that what he had implanted—the image and distillation of the entire cosmos—was "pulled inside-out"; what was above went below; *what was counterclockwise turned clockwise.* At this moment, what was planted in the center of the Earth began to send out a clearly delineated spiritual radiation, a shining that had never occurred before. Not only were cosmic spiritual forces working from *without* to form the Earth and carry Christ on his mission as they had up until April 5 AD 33; they now also *echoed from the depths* with their own creative, radiating force. A new era in human and cosmic history began—the Turning Point of Time.

And so, in the horoscope of Christ's Resurrection we see the east–west axis is like the pivot around which the entire form of the outer cosmos inverts (see image 3, page 146). The sign just above Aries is Pisces; just below is Taurus. But Aries corresponds to the 1st house (as it does in *every single horoscope*), and just above it is the 2nd house, corresponding to Taurus; just below it is the 12th house (corresponding to Pisces). Whereas the sign of Capricorn is above, the 10th house (corresponding to Capricorn) is below; the sign of Cancer is below, and the 4th house (corresponding to Cancer) is above. A total inversion has now occurred. The fundamental, foundational structure of the universe has been put in place, with the Cross of Golgotha at the center of the Earth, holding in place the movement of the entire cosmos, which had threatened to be torn completely apart due to the temptations of Lucifer and Ahriman.

Now we return to the crucial feature of the houses alluded to in the first article—that the position of the 1st house, corresponding to Aries, is totally dependent on the subjective position on Earth of the person in question. "Aries" as 1st house is *that which is east, what is rising.* Whereas each individual human being has a different rising

---

9  Steiner, *Interdisciplinary Astronomy*, pp. 158–159.
10  Ibid., pp. 151–152.

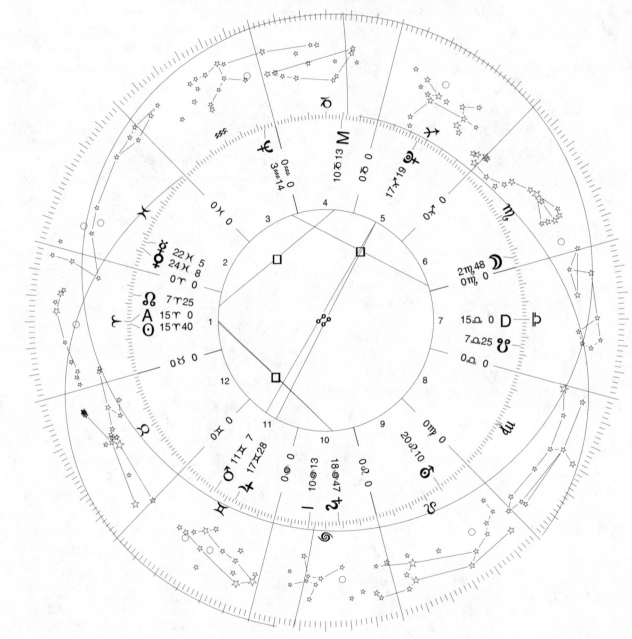

*Image 3: Horoscope of the Resurrection*

sign from the perspective of the cosmos, from the perspective of the houses (that of the Mother in the depths of the underworld), we are all identical. *Our rising sign is exactly the same as what was rising when Christ rose from the dead*—the center of Aries, 15°.

Utilizing the Hermetic Axiom "As Above, So Below," we can conclude from this that the equal house system is the original and accurate one, with each house exactly 30° in length, just as the cosmic signs are exactly 30° in length. Moreover, the eastern horizon marks the *center of the 1st house*, just as it was the center of the sign of Aries that was rising at Christ's Resurrection. And so, we can see that we have a harmonious arrangement when the center of the 1st house (Aries) is the Ascendent; when the center of the 7th house (Libra) is the descendent; when the center of the 4th house (Cancer) is straight above; and when the center of the 10th house (Capricorn) is directly below. All five of the "signs of darkness" (Scorpio, Sagittarius, Capricorn, Aquarius, and Pisces) are submerged completely below the horizon. Meanwhile, at least a portion of all seven "signs of light" (Aries, Taurus, Gemini, Cancer, Leo, Virgo, and Libra) are above the horizon (see image 4).[11]

The research of Brian Gray supports the use of what he refers to as an Earth-centric, equal-house system. In his article "Anthroposophic Foundations for a Renewal of Astrology," he quotes Robert Powell:

> One of the earliest references to the houses is that found on four demotic horoscopes, drawn up on four ostraca from Medinet Habu in Egypt. The horoscopes are dated AD 13, 17, 18, and 35. These horoscopes reveal an early definition of the houses, as originated in Egypt in the hermetic astrology of antiquity. In this early definition each house is simply equated with a sign of the sidereal zodiac: the first house with the rising sign, the second house with the next sign,

*Image 4: Artistic rendering of the horoscope of Resurrection*

> and so on. The houses in this original definition were therefore each 30° long, identical with the zodiacal signs. The first house in this early definition of the houses was the house containing the Ascendent, i.e., the zodiacal sign rising on the eastern horizon at the moment of birth.[12]

Brian then takes the next necessary step after the whole-sign or hermetic house system:

> An advantage of the whole-sign houses is that they are an equal division of the ecliptic into twelve signs of the zodiac. Whole-sign houses nearly align with Rudolf Steiner's picture of the "I" being related to "the perception of the echo of the zodiac." However, they are not yet the *perception* of the echo of the zodiac, since the whole-sign houses *are equivalent with* the signs [of] the zodiac. One further step is required for the whole-sign houses to fulfill the quality of being "the *perception* of the echo of the zodiac"—that is, the "perception of the physical body." ...
>
> This next step naturally leads to 12 equal houses that maintain their relationship to the ecliptic poles but are centered on the horizon and the Earth, that is the *horoscope* or Ascendant....
>
> The Earth-centered equal-house system maintains all the advantages of the whole-sign houses system, in that it is *based in equal*

---

11 Unfortunately, I cannot display a color image in the pages of this publication, but the following is a link to an image on my website TreeHouse. It expresses in color this inversion at the time of the Mystery of Golgotha: https://treehouse.live/2020/08/07/horoscope-of-the-resurrection/.

12 Gray, "Anthroposophic Foundations for a Renewal of Astrology," *Journal for Star Wisdom*, 2012, p. 121.

*divisions of the ecliptic*, as are the signs of the zodiac. The divisions between houses are meridians at right angles to the ecliptic plane, centered at the ecliptic poles. The "top" of the chart is not the MC but the Ecliptic Zenith (EZ), and the "bottom" of the chart is not the IC but the Ecliptic Nadir (EN).

However, the Earth-centered equal-house system has some distinct advantages over the whole-sign house system. In the Earth-centered equal-house system, the Ascendant (the *horoscope*) is always at the *center of the first house*, rather than in an earlier or later degree of a sign in the zodiac straddling the Ascendant. In the Earth-centered equal-house system, the Earth's center is always marked beneath the viewer's feet at the bottom of the chart... aligned with the plane of the ecliptic nadir and ecliptic zenith at 90° angles from the Ascendant–Descendant horizon...

The Earth-centered equal-house system was not invented by the author. A form of it has been used in Vedic astrology for many centuries, and it was apparently (re-)introduced in Europe as the "Vehlow Equal House" system in the nineteenth century by German astrologer Johannes Vehlow. Robert Powell reports that a French astrologer, Maurice Nouvel, wrote a book (in French) about this house system that justifies its use from Nouvel's perspective.

The author "rediscovered" this elegant house system over 30 years ago by naively pondering where to place the "Earth point" within the birth chart. The center of the Earth must be straight down beneath the viewer's feet, at a 90° angle from the horizon plane intersecting the ecliptic at Ascendant and Descendant. With the Earth centered directly "underfoot" (not at the IC), the meanings and clustering of the 12 houses become startlingly evident....

The Earth-centered House system is a ridiculously straightforward and simple temple to "build." Once the *horoscope* or Ascendant has been calculated for the exact time and place of birth, the houses center themselves on the horizon and the center of the Earth without further ado. The boundaries of the 1st house lie on the ecliptic plane 15° to either side of the Ascendant and all 12 houses are 30° in size. The "ruling point" of each house is the center point of that house (such as the Ascendant), not the boundary or "cusp" between houses.

To the mathematician and spherical trigonometer, the Earth-centered equal-house system might seem primitively simple in comparison with the elaborate calculations required to erect the house systems of Placidus or Koch, for example. Most house divisions today begin with the division of the ecliptic into quadrants formed by the horizon and midheaven planes, which are rarely exactly 90° apart. Having worked with quadrant division house systems for many years, the author is painfully aware of their shortcomings. The houses are never equal in size, and two or more signs of the zodiac are often "intercepted"—considered to be "muted" in the birth chart. Defending such irrational house division when reading a birth chart often requires great ingenuity and "hand-waving dismissals" by the astrologer. Unequal houses are clumsy, nonsensical and spiritually barren of meaning and rationale. They are as indefensible as dividing the zodiac into signs of unequal sizes. The Earth-centered equal-house system overcomes the aberrations arising from the faulty assumptions of quadrant division, reestablishing order and coherence and bringing new valid insights to the birth chart.

The beauty of the Earth-centered equal-house system, like that of the whole-sign house system, is that both are *true equal divisions of the ecliptic plane*—the plane of the zodiac, which is the plane of reference for the entire birth chart. Both house systems have meridians at right angles to the ecliptic plane that cross at the *north and south pole of the ecliptic*. On the celestial sphere, the *north pole of the ecliptic* always passes through a point on the Arctic Circle, and the *south pole of the ecliptic* always passes through a point [on] the Antarctic Circle, since the plane of the ecliptic is tilted 23½° off the plane of the equator. The Earth-centered equal-house system and the whole-sign house system can both be erected anywhere on the surface of the Earth with consistency—which is not astronomically true for nearly all quadrant house systems.[13]

---

13 Ibid., pp. 122–123, 127.

Thus, Brian Gray offers us, out of his own experience, as well as a deep familiarity with the history of astrology, a great deal of support—from a very different direction—for the validity of the Earth-centered equal-house system, which is the house system one can derive directly from the event of the Resurrection.

Earlier, I alluded to the fact that, from the perspective of the houses—the perspective of Mother Earth—we all have the same Ascendent of 15° Aries. Can we find deeper reasons as to why this might be? Let's remember Robert Powell's indications regarding the Ascendent in *Hermetic Astrology*, vol. 1:

> …the Ascendent at someone's birth embodies his "mirroring aspect" carried over from cosmic realms.
>
> This "mirroring aspect" of the human being is termed in the Bible the "image." ("God created man in his own image"—*Genesis* 1:27). The connection between the personality—signified by the Ascendant—and the image is indicated by the word *persona*, which has the same root in Latin as the word personality. In the Latin language, *persona* was the term applied to the Roman actor's mask, and Jung used this term to designate the outer expression or public image of the personality. *Persona* signifies the mask or image, i.e., the outer aspect of the personality. The personality itself is bound up with the image, to use the Biblical expression. As the word image indicates, the personality reflects. It is the reflection of something higher. Similarly, the Ascendent—as the significator of the personality in the birth chart—reflects something higher.[14]

At the time of the Fall, the *likeness* of the human being became damaged and was no longer the likeness of God. This "likeness" is the human capacity for virtue and morality. It is carried by one's guardian angel until we have worked to the point of having redeemed this likeness. At the time of the Fall, the *image* remained intact—the image as the accurate mirror that Powell refers to in the quotation, maintaining totally intact both the structural aspect of the physical human form,

and more crucially the capacity for freedom within the human being. The Fall did not violate our fundamental structure of freedom. This "accurate reflection of freedom" is expressed in our individual personalities, the "masks" we present to the outer world.

By the time of the Mystery of Golgotha, it was exactly this image that was now in danger; if intervention did not occur, the fundamental structure of freedom, the individual personality, would be at risk being swept up into the homogenizing activity of Ahriman. So, Christ's deed restored the structural integrity of the image of the human being—the integrity of the free personality, away from ahrimanic sclerosis. From the perspective of the cosmos, of the Father, each human being has a distinct and unique Ascendent, a different portion of the starry heavens rising over the horizon at their birth. Indeed, it is this unique rising sign that is chosen at the Midnight Hour with the aid of the Father.

But what about the Motherly perspective of the houses, emanating from Earth's center? What does the Mother see when we are born? From the Mother's point of view, all human beings *bear the image of the Risen One at birth—15° Aries*. We are *all one* in the eyes of the Mother. From the Father, we become unique personalities; from the Mother, we are reunited into one family, one being. What the Mother perceives, owing to Christ's deed, is our gradual development of the resurrection body. This has a twofold aspect.

When Christ descended to the realm of the Mother, he offered the form-giving seed of his etheric body, restoring Shambhala to its virginal state as mirror image of the cosmos. The Tree of Life was planted anew; the gates to the Garden were thrown open. The redemption of Paradise from chaos enabled the Mother to once again perceive each of her children; it liberated her from her ages-long imprisonment and separation from the Father and her many children.

Simultaneous with his offering of the Tree of Life to the Mother, Christ successfully formed the Resurrection body at the time of the Mystery of Golgotha. It is *this*, as the Immaculate image,

---

14 Powell, *Hermetic Astrology*, vol 1, p. 210.

that the Mother sees in each individual person as a *persona*; to the Mother, all have "put on the Resurrection body," the new body from the New Adam. It is highly illuminating at this point to turn to the words of the anonymous author of *Meditations on the Tarot* in his description of the Resurrection body from the 20th Letter–Meditation on the Judgment:

> ...the resurrection body is that of perfect freedom, i.e., the perfect manifestation of the individuality itself, without impediment on the part of heredity. Thus, it is not an *instrument*...[it] will have nothing mechanical, nothing automatic, about it...[it] will be *magical will*, contracting and expanding. It will be...the synthesis of life and death, i.e., capable of acting here below as a living person and at the same time enjoying freedom from terrestrial links like a deceased person....

> Hermeticism denies the conclusion...that the individual body undergoes complete annihilation at death. Hermeticism advances the thesis that *the body is essentially as immortal as the soul and spirit*—that immortality is threefold and that the *whole* human being is essentially immortal.

> According to Hermeticism, the essence of the body is not the matter of which it is composed nor the energy which is produced in it, but rather the fundamental *will* underlying matter and energy. And it is this will which is indestructible, because it exists prior to the birth of the body—and without it birth...would not be possible.

> Therefore...the body...is the work of the will of the individuality who is descending to incarnation acting hand in hand with the will receiving him below. And it is this united will which constitutes *the indestructible and immortal kernel of the body*. It is the "philosopher's stone," which arranges the matter and energy given by nature in such a way that it is adapted to the individuality—so that it becomes an imprint of it.

> Thus, the resurrection body is prepared during the course of the ages. Each particular human incarnation is effected according to *the law of the cross*, i.e., it is vertical and horizontal at the same time...the process of the growth of the resurrection body is gradual. The resurrection body matures from incarnation to incarnation, although in principle it should be possible for a single incarnation to suffice. In fact, however, it is so that many incarnations are necessary to bring the resurrection body to maturity.

> What is the destiny of the kernel of the indestructible body...after death? Does it ascend with the soul and spirit to the spiritual world, leaving the mortal remains below?

> Death—disincarnation—signifies the separation of the soul and spirit from the physical body, including its indestructible kernel or resurrection body. Whilst the soul and spirit ascend to the spiritual world...the resurrection body descends in the opposite sense, i.e., below, toward the center of the Earth. As it is active will during life, its descent is due to progressive relaxing of the will.[15]

Thus, Rudolf Hauschka's intuition was absolutely correct; an epochal shift occurred at the time of the Mystery of Golgotha that permanently altered Earth's etheric atmosphere, out into the wider cosmos. But it was not in the way that he thought. There is no astrological justification for the tropical zodiac. The Deed of Golgotha did not permanently affix the signs as they were at the time of Christ. Sidereal astrology is still the reality, just as it always has been. But something else *was* established at that time. It is what modern astrologer Gemini Brett is looking for when he refers to an *Earth-strology* in place of an *astro-logy,* which is astrology not determined by the starry heavens.[16] It is what each of us yearns for at one level or another—a way to reconnect concretely and deeply to Mother Earth, in addition to Father Sky.

### The True Meaning of the Houses

And so, we see the true significance of the houses; they reveal to us the workings of the inner Earth in a deceptively simple way. The clockwise

---

15 Anon., *Meditations on the Tarot*, pp. 576–580.

16 See the presentation for Gemini Brett's perspective: https://www.youtube.com/watch?v=UMsrA1JdSYE &feature=youtu.be.

motion of the planets throughout the course of the day in relationship to east and west, above and below, is an indicator or significator of the positions of the "inner planets" in the heart of the Earth—the realm of the Mother. The outer cosmos is found again within the heart of the Earth—an inner zodiac, inner planets, whose movements have consequences for human and cosmic destiny, as the Parzival story makes clear. This is why the concept of houses began to develop only around the time of Christ, owing to the intimation that something new was arising.

Manilius' system was the first detailed and descriptive house system. He descried something that was in a sense still preparing to begin radiating outward to human beings on Earth—a brand new reality. And so, the houses do not deal fundamentally with relatively petty aspects of destiny (romantic or financial propensities, etc.) as has become their commonplace interpretation nowadays. No, there is an entirely new way of approaching the world hidden within them, for they reveal the clock of cosmic timing. As seen in the Parzival story, it makes a great deal of difference whether a planet is directly overhead, directly below, to the west, to the east, and so on in terms of when to attempt a particular action. We might imagine such "cosmic timing" would have unique implications for agriculture, for example.

Consider Steiner's words on January 1, 1912, regarding the activity of the inner Earth:

We can, if we wish, refer to these beings as the group souls of the plants. We can say, when we go beyond what our senses can behold of the plant, that we come to the group souls of the plants, which are related to the single plant as a whole to a part. Altogether there are seven group souls—plant souls—belonging to the Earth, and having in a way the center of their being in the center of the Earth. So that it is not enough to conceive of the Earth as this physical ball, but we have to think of it as penetrated by seven spheres varying in size and all having in the Earth's center their own spiritual center. And then these spiritual beings impel the plants out of the Earth. The root grows toward the center of the Earth, because what it really wants is to reach the center of the Earth, and it is prevented from pushing right through only by all the rest of the earth matter that stands in its way. Every plant root strives to penetrate to the center of the Earth, where the center of the spiritual being is to which the plant belongs.[17]

We might deduce from this that each of the seven "inner planets" is related to one of the seven group souls of plants. Gaining a true understanding of the movements of these inner planets–inner plants (in their diurnal clockwise motion) might have great implications beyond the lunar phases and signs for a field such as biodynamics.

Notice that the movements of these inner planets are not absolute or objective as standard astrology is. If the Sun is in the sign of Aries, it is there for all of us on Earth, regardless whether we can see it or not. No, the positions of the inner planets in regard to the houses (the "inner zodiac") are relative to the point of view of the individual in question, to one's position on Earth. It is an *inner* (trans-subjective) reality, rather than an *outer* (objective) reality.

The 1st house is always due east for any observer, but the portion of the sky due east for me here in Copake, New York, is simultaneously due west for an observer on the other side of the globe. We must bear in mind the nature of the Resurrection body of Christ; it gave him the possibility of being in many places simultaneously. It is a body of absolute freedom, the union of life and death; thus, too, it is for the inner planets. Their positions are intertwined with our own *experiential* position between cosmos and Earth. We are each an individual, mobile center of the inner cosmos, which expresses itself in a dynamic, multivalent way. This demands attunement to *place*—the realization that each place on Earth has its own unique relationship to the movements of the "inner planets."

There are three levels to the study of the stars: *astronomy,* the study of the body of the stars; *astrology,* the study of the soul of the stars; and

---

17 Steiner, *The World of the Senses and the World of the Spirit*, p. 80 (trans. revised).

*astrosophy*, the study of the spirit of the stars. This publication is dedicated primarily to astrosophy. One might say astrosophy is recognized by the fact that it reunites the divided disciplines of astronomy and astrology via an ever-deepening understanding of Christ.

The experiences of the houses takes us not out into the starry heavens, but deep into the heart of the Earth—the 12 houses, or temples, of the Mother. Perhaps a new terminology needs to be adapted to the true nature of this discipline. The Greek word for "house" (as well as "family, property") is *oikos*. This became the prefix *eco-*. We could say perhaps that, whereas humanity has established a study of the body of our house in Economy, and the soul of our house in Ecology, we have yet to establish a discipline for studying the "spirit of our house"—what we might call *Ecosophy*.[18] Economics is the study of productive human activity; ecology is the study of nature's wisdom-filled systems. Perhaps Ecosophy, if properly understood, could reveal to us how these two disciplines might be reconnected via an ever-deepening understanding of the Virgin, the *Shekinah*, the Divine Feminine. The biodynamic movement that arose from Steiner's agricultural lectures in 1924 could be seen as the first practical exercise in Ecosophy.

In the third part of this series of articles, we will continue to investigate the progressive (and sometimes regressive) development of sidereal astrology and the clockwise house system (what will henceforth be called *Ecosophy*) up to the present time; the relationship of this development with Christ's path from the Mystery of Golgotha up to his return in the elemental realm; further examples of the use of Ecosophy in Rudolf Steiner's work; and finally—rather than continuing to appropriate astrological archetypes and terminology—whether Ecosophy has an archetypal language that belongs to it properly, and where this archetypal language can be found today.

---

18  The term *Ecosophy* was used in the past, perhaps most notably by Félix Guattari (Apr. 30, 1930–Aug. 29, 1992), who worked quite closely with fellow continental philosopher and post-structuralist Gilles Deleuze (Jan. 18, 1925–Nov. 4, 1995). This philosophical stream could be seen, in some ways, as a direct continuation of the method laid out by Rudolf Steiner in his *Philosophy of Freedom*. See for example the article by Yeshayahu Ben-Aharon at https://www.rudolfsteiner.org/fileadmin/user_upload/being_human/bh-articles/bh3-Ben-Aharon-Contemporary-Philosophy.pdf.

# WORKING WITH THE
## *STAR WISDOM* CALENDAR

### *Robert Powell, PhD*

In taking note of the astronomical events listed in the Star Calendar, it is important to distinguish between long- and short-term astronomical events. Long-term astronomical events—for example, Pluto transiting a particular degree of the zodiac—will have a longer period of meditation than would the five days advocated for short-term astronomical events such as the New and Full Moon. The following describes, in relation to meditating on the Full Moon, a meditative process extending over a five-day period.

### *Sanctification of the Full Moon*

As a preliminary remark, let us remind ourselves that the great sacrifice of Christ on the Cross—the Mystery of Golgotha—took place at Full Moon. As Christ's sacrifice took place when the Moon was full in the middle of the sidereal sign of Libra, the Libra Full Moon assumes special significance in the sequence of twelve (or thirteen) Full Moons taking place during the cycle of the year. In following this sequence, the Mystery of Golgotha serves as an archetype for *every* Full Moon, since each Full Moon imparts a particular spiritual blessing. Hence the practice described here as *Sanctification of the Full Moon* applies to every Full Moon. Similarly, there is also the practice of *Sanctification of the New Moon*, as described in *Hermetic Astrology, Volume 2: Astrological Biography,* chapter 10.

During the two days prior to the Full Moon, we can consider the focus of one's meditation to extend over these two days as *preparatory days,* immediately preceding the day of the Full Moon. These two days can be dedicated to spiritual reflection and detachment from everyday concerns as one prepares to become a vessel for the in-streaming light and love one will receive at the Full Moon, something that one can then impart further—for example, to help people in need, or to support Mother Earth in times of catastrophe. During these two days, it is helpful to hold an attitude of dedication and service and try to assume an attitude of receptivity that opens to what one's soul will receive and subsequently impart—an attitude conducive to making one a true *servant of the spirit.*

The day of the Full Moon is itself a day of *holding the sacred space.* In doing so, one endeavors to cultivate inner peace and silence, during which one attempts to contact and consciously hold the in-streaming blessing of the Full Moon for the rest of humanity. One can heighten this silent meditation by visualizing the zodiacal constellation–sidereal sign in which the Moon becomes full, since the Moon serves to reflect the starry background against which it appears.

If the Moon is full in Virgo, for example, it reminds us of the night of the birth of the Jesus child visited by the three magi, as described in the Gospel of St. Matthew. That birth occurred at the Full Moon in the middle of the sidereal sign of Virgo, and the three magi, who gazed up that evening to behold the Full Moon against the background of the stars of the Virgin, witnessed the soul of Jesus emerge from the disk of the Full Moon and descend toward Earth. They participated from afar, via the starry heavens, in the Grail Mystery of the holy birth.

By meditating on the Full Moon and opening oneself to receive the in-streaming blessing from the starry heavens, we can exercise restraint by avoiding the formulation of what will happen or what one might receive from the Full Moon. Moreover, we can also refrain from seeking tangible results or effects connected with our attunement to the Full Moon. Even if we observe only the date but not the exact moment when the Moon is full, it is helpful to find quiet time to reflect alone or to use the opportunity for deep meditation on the day of the Full Moon.

We can think of the two days following the Full Moon as a *time of imparting* what we have received from the in-streaming of the Moon's full disk against the background of the stars. It is now possible to turn our attention toward humanity and the world and endeavor to pass on any spiritual blessing we have received from the starry heavens. Thereby we can assist in the work of the spiritual world by transforming what we have received into goodwill and allowing it to flow wherever the greatest need exists.

It is a matter of *holding a sacred space* throughout the day of the Full Moon. This is an important time to still the mind and maintain inner peace. It is a time of spiritual retreat and contact with the spiritual world, of holding in one's consciousness the archetype of the Mystery of Golgotha as a great outpouring of Divine Love that bridges Heaven and Earth. Prior to the day of the Full Moon, the two preceding days prepare the sacred space as a vessel to receive the heavenly blessing. The two days following the day of the Full Moon are a time to assimilate and distribute the spiritual transmission received into the sacred space we have prepared.

One can apply the process described here as a meditative practice in relation to the Full Moon to any of the astronomical events listed in *Star Wisdom*, especially as most of these *remember* significant Christ Events. Take note, however, whether an event is long-term or short-term and adjust the period of meditative practice accordingly.

"*The shadow intellect that is characteristic of all modern culture has fettered human beings to the Earth. They have eyes only for earthly things, particularly when they allow themselves to be influenced by the claims of modern science. In our age it never occurs to someone that their being belongs not to the Earth alone but to the cosmos beyond the Earth. Knowledge of our connection with the cosmos beyond the Earth—that is what we need above all to make our own.... When someone says 'I' to themselves, they experience a force that is working within, and the [ancient] Greek, in feeling the working of this inner force, related it to the Sun;...the Sun and the 'I' are the outer and inner aspects of one being. The Sun out there in space is the cosmic 'I.' What lives within me is the human 'I'.... Human beings are not primarily a creation of Earth. Human beings receive their shape and form from the cosmos. The human being is an offspring of the world of stars, above all of the Sun and Moon.... The Moon forces stream out from a center in the metabolic system....[The] Moon stimulates reproduction.... Saturn works chiefly in the upper part of the astral body....Jupiter has to do with thinking...Mars [has] to do with speech.... The Mercury forces work in the part of the human organism that lies below the region of the heart...in the breathing and circulatory functions.... Venus works preeminently in the etheric body of the human being.*"

—RUDOLF STEINER, *Offspring of the World of Stars*, May 5, 1921

# SYMBOLS USED IN CHARTS

| PLANETS | | ZODIACAL SIGNS | | ASPECTS | |
| --- | --- | --- | --- | --- | --- |
| ⊕ | Earth | ♈ | Aries (Ram) | ☌ | Conjunction 0° |
| ☉ | Sun | ♉ | Taurus (Bull) | ✳ | Sextile 60° |
| ☽ | Moon | ♊ | Gemini (Twins) | ☐ | Square 90° |
| ☿ | Mercury | ♋ | Cancer (Crab) | △ | Trine 120° |
| ♀ | Venus | ♌ | Leo (Lion) | ☍ | Opposition 180° |
| ♂ | Mars | ♍ | Virgo (Virgin) | | |
| ♃ | Jupiter | ♎ | Libra (Scales) | | |
| ♄ | Saturn | ♏ | Scorpio (Scorpion) | | |
| ♅ | Uranus | ♐ | Sagittarius (Archer) | | |
| ♆ | Neptune | ♑ | Capricorn (Goat) | | |
| ♇ | Pluto | ♒ | Aquarius (Water Carrier) | | |
| | | ♓ | Pisces (Fishes) | | |

| OTHER | | | |
| --- | --- | --- | --- |
| ☊ | Ascending (North) Node | ☌ | Sun Eclipse |
| ☋ | Descending (South) Node | ☋ | Moon Eclipse |
| P | Perihelion–Perigee | ☌ | Inferior Conjunction |
| A | Aphelion–Apogee | ☍ | Superior Conjunction |
| ⎍ | Maximum Latitude | ⚷ | Chiron |
| ⎎ | Minimum Latitude | | |

# TIME

The information relating to daily geocentric and heliocentric planetary positions in the sidereal zodiac is tabulated in the form of an ephemeris for each month, in which the planetary positions are given at 0 hours Universal Time (UT) each day.

Beneath the geocentric and heliocentric ephemeris for each month, the information relating to planetary aspects is given in the form of an aspectarian, which lists the most important aspects—geocentric and heliocentric–hermetic—between the planets for the month in question. The day and the time of occurrence of the aspect on that day are indicated, all times being given in Universal Time (UT), which is identical to Greenwich Mean Time (GMT). For example, zero hours Universal Time is midnight GMT. This time system applies in Britain; however, when summer time is in effect, one hour must be added to all times.

**In other time zones, the time has to be adjusted according to whether it is ahead of or behind Britain. For example, in Germany, where the time is one hour ahead of British time, an hour must be added; when summer time is in effect in Germany, two hours have to be added to all times.

Using the calendar in the United States, do the following subtraction from all time indications according to time zone:

- Pacific Time subtract 8 hours
  (7 hours for daylight saving time);
- Mountain Time subtract 7 hours
  (6 hours for daylight saving time);
- Central Time subtract 6 hours
  (5 hours for daylight saving time);
- Eastern Time subtract 5 hours
  (4 hours for daylight saving time).

This subtraction will often change the date of an astronomical occurrence, shifting it back one day. Consequently, since most of the readers of this calendar live on the American Continent, astronomical occurrences during the early hours of day *x* are sometimes listed in the Commentaries as occurring on days *x–1/x*. For example, an eclipse occurring at 03:00 UT on the 12th is listed as occurring on the 11–12th since in America it takes place on the 11th.[1]

## SIMPLIFYING THE PROCEDURE

The preceding procedure can be greatly simplified. Here is an example for someone wishing to know the zodiacal locations of the planets on Christmas Day, December 25, 2018. Looking at the December ephemeris, it can be seen that Christmas Day falls on a Tuesday. In the upper tabulation, the geocentric planetary positions are given, with that of the Sun indicated in the first column, that of the Moon in the second column, and so on. The position of the Sun is listed as 8°07' Sagittarius.

For someone living in London, 8°07' Sagittarius is the Sun's position at midnight, December 24–25, 2017—noting that in London and all of the United Kingdom, the Time Zone applying there is that of Universal Time–Greenwich Mean Time (UT–GMT).

For someone living in Sydney, Australia, which on Christmas Day is eleven hours ahead of UT–GMT, 8°07' Sagittarius is the Sun's position at 11 a.m. on December 25.

For someone living in California, which is eight hours behind UT–GMT on Christmas Day, 8°07' Sagittarius is the Sun's position at 4 p.m. on **December 24**.

For the person living in California, therefore, it is necessary to look at the entries for **December 26** to know the positions of the planets on December 25. The result is:

For someone living in California, which is eight hours behind UT–GMT on Christmas Day, the Sun's position at 4 p.m. on December 25 is 9°08' Sagittarius and, by the same token, the Moon's position on Christmas Day at 4 p.m. on December

---

1 See *General Introduction to the Christian Star Calendar: A Key to Understanding* for an in-depth clarification of the features of the calendar in *Star Wisdom*, including indications about how to work with it.

25 is 24°08' Pisces—these are the positions along-side December 26 at midnight UT–GMT—and eight hours earlier equates with 4 p.m. on December 25 in California.

From these examples it emerges that the **planetary positions as given in the ephemeris** can be utilized, but that according to the Time Zone one is in, **the time of day is different** and also for locations West of the United Kingdom **the date changes** (look at the date following the actual date).

Here is a tabulation in relation to the foregoing example of December 25 (Christmas Day).

### UNITED KINGDOM, EUROPE, AND ALL LOCATIONS WITH TIME ZONES EAST OF GREENWICH

Look at what is given alongside December 25—these entries indicate the planetary positions at these times:

- 12:00 a.m. (midnight December 24–25) in London (UT–GMT)
- 01:00 a.m. in Berlin (CENTRAL EUROPEAN TIME, which is one hour ahead of UT–GMT)
- 11:00 a.m. in Sydney (AUSTRALIAN EASTERN DAYLIGHT TIME, which is eleven hours ahead of UT–GMT)

### CANADA, USA, CENTRAL AMERICA, SOUTH AMERICA, AND ALL LOCATIONS WITH TIME ZONES WEST OF GREENWICH

Look at what is given alongside December 26—these entries indicate the planetary positions at these times:

- 7:00 p.m. in New York (EASTERN STANDARD TIME, which is five hours behind UT–GMT)
- 6:00 p.m. in Chicago (CENTRAL STANDARD TIME, which is six hours behind UT–GMT)
- 5:00 p.m. in Denver (MOUNTAIN STANDARD TIME, which is seven hours behind UT–GMT)

- 4:00 p.m. in San Francisco (PACIFIC STANDARD TIME, which is eight hours behind UT–GMT)
- **IF SUMMER TIME IS IN USE,** add **ONE HOUR—FOR EXAMPLE:**
- 8:00 p.m. in New York (EASTERN DAYLIGHT TIME, which is four hours behind UT–GMT)
- 7:00 p.m. in Chicago (CENTRAL DAYLIGHT TIME, which is five hours behind UT–GMT)
- 6:00 p.m. in Denver (MOUNTAIN DAYLIGHT TIME, which is six hours behind UT–GMT)
- 5:00 p.m. in San Francisco (PACIFIC DAYLIGHT TIME, which is seven hours behind UT–GMT)

Note that in the preceding tabulation, the time given in Sydney on Christmas Day, December 25, is in terms of Daylight Time. Six months earlier, on June 25, for someone in Sydney they would look alongside the entry in the ephemeris for June 25 and would know that this applies (for them) to

- 10:00 a.m. in Sydney (AUSTRALIAN EASTERN TIME, which is ten hours ahead of UT–GMT).

In these examples, it is not just the position of the Sun that is referred to. The same applies to the zodiacal locations given in the ephemeris for *all* the planets, whether geocentric (upper tabulation) or heliocentric (lower tabulation). *All that is necessary to apply this method of reading the ephemeris is to know the Time Zone in which one is and to apply the number of hours difference from UT–GMT.*

The advantage of using the method described here is that it greatly simplifies reference to the ephemeris when studying the **zodiacal positions of the planets.** However, for applying the time indications listed under "Ingresses" or "Aspects" it is still necessary to add or subtract the time difference from UT–GMT as described in the above paragraph denoted.

# COMMENTARIES AND EPHEMERIDES
## JANUARY–DECEMBER 2021

*Commentaries and Ephemerides by Joel Matthew Park,*
*including Monthly Stargazing Previews and*
*Astronomical Sky Watch by Julie Humphreys*

### COMMENTARIES

For the commentaries in this year's edition of *Star Wisdom*, I am continuing the approach I took in volume 2 (2020)—that is, utilizing a "fluid" approach to planetary alignments and noting when planets come within 5° of each other, reach exact alignment, and then begin to drift apart again. This maintains a lively interaction with, and perception of, planetary movements rather than a static one.

This year, however, I am basing my commentaries on a perspective different from what has been customary. Usually the commentaries are about the *geocentric* planetary alignments; occasionally commentary has been offered on *heliocentric* alignments, as well.

This year, I will primarily be approaching the commentaries from the *Tychonic* perspective. What is the Tychonic perspective? In the late 16th and early 17th centuries, two astronomers devised contrasting systems for explaining the movements of the planets in our solar system. Until that time, it was thought that the solar system (indeed, the entire cosmos) is geocentric, having the Earth at its center. Working with this perspective, there were complicated Aristotelian–Ptolemaic explanations for phenomena such as retrograde motion. This all changed with Nicolaus Copernicus and Tycho Brahe.

Copernicus devised the heliocentric model, whereby the Sun was seen as the center of the solar system, and retrograde motion was simply the way the movement of the planets around the Sun *appeared* from the perspective of Earth; it wasn't considered an *actual* back-and-forth motion. This was the chosen model, refined and popularized by Kepler, and the model we are all taught in school. Rudolf Steiner perceived a direct connection between the adoption of the Copernican system and the rise of materialism, as indicated on September 16, 1924, in one of his final lectures:

> The Copernican worldview pictures the universe in a way that, if followed to its logical conclusions, would tend to drive all spirituality out of the cosmos in our concept of it. The Copernican world-picture leads eventually to a mechanical, machine-like concept of the universe in space.... It is, indeed, an entire elimination of spirituality.[1]

Tycho Brahe, on the other hand, devised a more elegant system in which there were *two* centers in the solar system. The Earth was seen as the primary center, with the Sun and Moon orbiting around the Earth. The other five stellar bodies (Uranus, Neptune, and Pluto were unknown at the time) revolved around the Sun, the secondary center. For some time there was competition between the Copernican and Tychonic models, but by the 18th century the Copernican model had won out completely.

Rudolf Steiner indicated the future of the Tychonic system on December 30, 1910:

> The world really knows nothing about [Tycho Brahe] except that he was still "stupid" enough to devise a plan of the cosmos in which the Earth stands still and the Sun, together with the planets, revolve around it. That is what the world in general knows today. The fact that we are dealing here with a significant personality of the 16th century, one who accomplished an

---

1 Steiner, *Karmic Relationships,* vol. 4, lect. 6, pp. 83–84 (trans. revised).

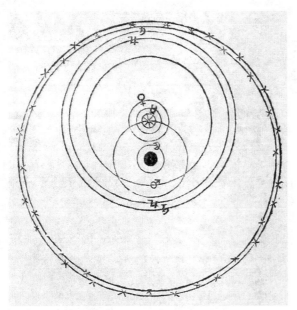

*Riccioli, Almagestum novum*
(*Diagram of the Tychonic system, Bologna, 1651*)

infinite amount that even today is still useful to astronomy, that untold depths of wisdom are contained in what he gave—none of this is usually recorded, for the simple reason that, in presenting the system in detail out of his own deep knowledge, Tycho Brahe saw difficulties that Copernicus did not see. If such a thing dare be said—for it does indeed seem paradoxical—even with the Copernican system the last word has not yet been uttered. And the conflict between the two systems will still occupy the minds of a later humanity. That, however, only by the way; it is too paradoxical for the present age.[2]

What this model encourages is the recognition of *two centers*, the harmonious interaction of Father and Mother, heart and head, spirit and nature. It brings these apparent polarities into a lemniscatory and complex dance.

What this means on a practical level is that we keep track of the *geocentric* positions of the Sun, Moon, Nodes, and Ascendent–Descendent axis. On the other hand, we keep track of the *heliocentric* positions of the other planets—Mercury, Venus, Mars, Jupiter, Saturn, Uranus, Neptune, and Pluto. From this perspective, we are able to become aware of interesting phenomena. For example, if the Sun is *geocentrically* at 3° Leo, and Mars is

*heliocentrically* at 3° Leo, they are considered conjunct—even though they may not appear so from *either* the Earth's or the Sun's perspective.

This requires us to bring to the fore our *external* sensitivity to the positions of the Sun and Moon in particular; while, along with this, we must bring an *internal* (imaginative) sensitivity to the positions of the other planets. The heliocentric positions are not ones we can actually *observe*, we can only recreate them in our mind's eye. This bringing together of external observation with internal *"exakte Phantasie"* (as Goethe termed it), or directed imagination—if worked with consistently—leads to an awakening of the inner life of the stargazer—an awakening to the interweaving of the "inner stars" and outer stars. This is a relatively accessible and quite fruitful path to the experience of Christ in the elemental realms—a path that brings "Christ in me" and "Christ in nature" to the same magical crossing point.[3]

The perceptive reader of last year's commentaries might have noticed that, as the year went on, I progressively relaxed the creation of my own personal commentary, and relied more and more on the words of Anne Catherine Emmerich. Writing the commentaries was a new experience for me last year, and, along with that, such an in-depth reading of Emmerich's visions was also new to me. As I went more deeply into her words, I increasingly began to feel my words as a "clanging cymbal" in comparison to what has arisen from her visionary experiences. It became my desire to expose the reader, as much as possible, to her words—or, should I say, words that are the combined effort of Anne Catherine as visionary, Clemens Brentano as scribe, and Jim Wetmore as translator.

This year, I continue in this same vein—doing my best to bring the reader into a living relationship with Anne Catherine Emmerich's visions. It is very likely that, as of next year's edition (*Star Wisdom* vol. 4, 2022), this portion of the publication will be less of a "commentary" and more of a concordance. Rather than transcribing and quoting so

---

2   Steiner, *Occult History*, p. 79 (trans. revised).

3   See the first five chapters of Powell, *Hermetic Astrology*, vol. 1, for a full explication of the Tychonic system.

much of what is already magnificently compiled in the three volumes of *The Visions of Anne Catherine Emmerich* (published by Angelico Press in 2015), I will direct the reader to the relevant passages. That is, I will do the work of finding out which days in the life of Christ are remembered by next year's alignments, and make note of the passage in *The Visions of Anne Catherine Emmerich* which describes that day. I would strongly recommend, if you have not yet done so, to purchase these three volumes! They are well worth the investment, even if you do not plan to follow along with next year's planetary alignments.

## STARGAZING

Observing the apparent path of the planets (called the ecliptic) before the background of the fixed stars of the zodiac requires denizens of the northern hemisphere to look southward. On the days of our spring and autumn equinoxes, this path will begin directly in the east, arch over the southern horizon, and end directly due west. On the other 363 or 364 days of the year, you'll observe that the planets rise slightly north or south of east, culminate east or west of south, and set south or north of west—however, their east–south–west trajectory remains roughly the same. It is a wonderful exercise throughout the year simply to notice where the planets rise, culminate, and set in reference to one's fixed surroundings—trees, mountains, and so on.

For readers in the southern hemisphere, who look north to view the passage of the planets before the starry background of the zodiac, references here to left and right (and to south and north) will have to be reversed. This year and henceforth, all phenomena will be reported in UTC alone, in accordance with our ephemerides.[4]

One final note: Left and right refer to the perspective of the stargazer, not that of the angels working within the constellations.

---

4  An excellent resource for time zone conversion can be found www.attimeanddate.com. The site also provides important information on meteor showers, as peak nights for viewing differ by location.

# JANUARY 2021

## STARGAZING PREVIEW

We are so blessed to begin the year with the memory of the birth of the Nathan Jesus! At 0720 hours, the Sun will pass through 16°04' Sagittarius; Venus will have just risen, and you'll find the waning gibbous Moon (just above *Praesepe*—also known as the *Beehive*—in the center of Cancer) nearing the western horizon. At sunset on New Year's Day, Mars will be high in the south, overhead, waiting to be joined in the night sky by the rising Moon. Mars sets at 0200.

Other than the Moon and Mars, what might we look for this month? Only dear Venus, and even she will be hidden from us by month's end. A morning star now, she rises more than an hour ahead of the Sun. The remaining classical planets, in Sagittarius and Capricorn, are huddled around the Sun.

On the evening of the 2nd, at 2200 hours, the Moon, having just risen, will pass above *Regulus*, the main star of Leo. Come Tuesday the 5th, when Venus rises, she'll be in Sagittarius, not to visit the Scorpion again until October. The Moon (21° Virgo) reaches its Last Quarter on the 6th; it will rise at midnight as Mars is about to move below the western horizon. In the early dawn hours of the 10th, look to the east to see the Moon alongside *Antares*, the star marking the heart of the Scorpion. *Antares* will appear to be between the Earth and the Moon, reddish and twinkling. Keep an eye out for Venus an hour later, rising to announce the coming daybreak.

With the Moon and Venus so close, it can't be long before they're together! This occurs late on the 11th at 9° Sagittarius, the zodiacal position of the Sun and Pluto during the Last Temptation in the Wilderness. (Indeed, the Sun will conjoin Pluto on the 14th, in the last degree of Sagittarius.) On the morning of the 12th, the Moon, fast approaching New, will rise after Venus.

January's New Moon, at 28° Sagittarius, will occur at 0500 on Wednesday the 13th. During the week that follows, you'll find Venus, still gracing the morning sky, rising an hour ahead of the Sun;

Mars and the Moon will be our only companions in the night sky.

Dusk on the 20th will leave us with Mars and the Moon high in the south, only 7° apart in Aries—you'll see the Moon to the right of and slightly below Mars. Invisible to the naked eye, Uranus occupies the same zodiacal degree (12° Aries) as Mars, despite the fact that they are more than one-and-a-half billion miles apart! The Moon will reach its First Quarter (at 6° Aries) before the three planets set at 0130 the following day.

On the 24th, Mercury, an evening star now, will reach its greatest elongation from the Sun—our best shot at seeing it, as Mercury sets a full ninety minutes after the Sun. When Mercury and the Sun are on the far side of the world, Mars will be high in the southwest, about 30° west (right) of the Moon, now a few degrees past *Aldebaran*, the eye of the Bull.

At sunset on the 27th, the Moon, low in the east, will have passed below *Castor* and *Pollux*, on its way to Cancer. The Full Moon on the following evening will sail above *Praesepe* (from the Latin for "manger") before it reaches culmination at midnight. Mars will share the night sky until 0100, after which time the Full Moon will have it all to itself. By month's end, Orion will be high in the southeast at dusk; he sets at 0500.

## JANUARY COMMENTARIES

Happy New Year, dear reader! As I begin to write these commentaries, the world is in the midst of a bizarre crisis. The perfect storm of media obfuscation and censorship; cherry-picked "scientific" research; materialistic superstition; sociopathic virtue-signaling; and fear of death have combined to bring about the near destruction of the world economy under the heading of "COVID-19."[5] Humanity now comes to the brink of an abyss that we have been pushed closer and closer toward over the past 250 or so years; a choice will now have to be made.

For me, living in Camphill Village Copake, it was a very strange time. We had our last "face to face" meeting during Holy Week, after which the

New York Pause went into effect, enforcing social distancing on all of us. We spent the entirety of Eastertide divided from one another and could meet again only after Ascension. I began to reflect on the play on words *Corona* and *nation…Coronation*.

I began to reflect on the idea that this 40-day period during Eastertide had a twofold significance. On the one hand, it represented the "Coronation," or crowning achievement, of the incarnated Ahriman. It laid out the possibility for a completely technocratic world in which 1) everyone lives in trepidation of meeting other people; 2) the "moral" thing to do is to call out other people who are not social distancing; 3) the government rescinds civil liberties for the sake of health and wellbeing, tracking all citizens and deciding what activities and speech are "safe" or not; 4) technology companies are given full license to spy on all people all the time; 5) the massive pharmaceutical–vaccine industry maximizes profit and control; and 6) rather than an economy based on work, the economy would be based on modern monetary theory and the "printing" of endless amounts of digital currency, so that most people can just stay home. To sum all of this up: 7) *people could put full trust in their authority figures, allowing them to think and make decisions on their behalf.*

On the other hand, I began to reflect on the other side of the situation—that this Coronation had something to do with the Parousia, the Advent of Christ in his elemental form. Perhaps this entire event was something akin to Ebeneezer Scrooge's confrontation with the third and final Spirit—the Ghost of Christmas Future—in Charles Dickens' *Christmas Carol.* Scrooge is given a picture of what will occur if he does not *choose* to change—if he does not *wake up.* I could feel, quite palpably, that the entire world was not sleepwalking into the Ahrimanic "peace." I could feel individuals all over the world waking up and *naming* those who are actively attempting to remove liberty and fraternity and leave only a dreadful equality—individuals such as Bill Gates.

Throughout this whole time period, I have had a deep experience of relief from three spheres. First of all, my children, who, thank God, have

---

5  On COVID, see von Halle, *The Coronavirus Pandemic: Anthroposophical Perspectives.*

been raised in a Waldorf-inspired paradise, blissfully unaware of the heinous "Brave New World" rearing its ugly head. They continued to be themselves, totally unchanged by lockdown. Similarly, certain of my villagers here at Camphill Village Copake, so deep in their authentic character and idiosyncrasies—they, too, were totally *themselves,* totally unchanged by mass hysteria. And finally, the language of nature—increasingly—brought me almost unspeakable joy. She brought me the same comfort that can be found in the words, "Remember you are dust, and to dust you shall return." The chirping of insects, the singing of birds, the wind and the rain—none of this cares an ounce for either side of the myriad arguments stemming from COVID-19. I began to think of Valentin Tomberg's words from 1938 concerning the Second Coming of Christ, when nature herself would begin to speak to human beings and bring them comfort during calamitous times:

> Three years will come, during which nature will radiate goodness. For example, when people are in despair, they will find remarkable consolation in trees. Goodness will flow from plants into human souls. People will have the experience that trees bend before them in goodness and generosity. Goodness will be felt in nature to such a degree that people will not forget it; it will be remembered as a natural marvel. Phenomena such as thunder and lightning will not occur. A breath of goodness will flow from the world of nature, and human nature will feel it as regeneration and healing.[6]

I have no idea whether we have entered this three-year period of which Tomberg speaks in this passage; this is quoted simply to give an impression of nature's effect on me—increasingly, as Whitsun approached—during this period.

Thus, I began to have the image of Christ's appearing at the sound of a trumpet, with a portion of humanity feeling great joy at his coming, and another portion feeling extreme terror—the Right and the Left, the Sheep and the Goats. I began to have this image, because humanity is now at the crossroads—there will be some of us who come out

of this situation ready and willing for technocracy. There are some of us who fear, on a fundamental level, for biophysical security above all else. Indeed, this is the secret behind technocracy—it plays on the human fear of death, and the deeply subconscious craving for material longevity, whatever the cost to all other spheres of human existence. This portion of humanity and of each one of us is ready and willing to sacrifice individual thinking, freedom of speech and movement, and privacy for the sake of longevity. This is the portion who are ready to bow down to experts and authorities who will guide us through challenges that are much too systemic and complicated for us to navigate on our own. It is this fundamental aspect of our nature—within each one of us—that makes straight the way of Ahriman. This portion of humanity trembles at the appearance of the elemental Christ.

On the other hand, there is a portion of us—as individuals and as a human race—striving above all for the heavenly Sophia, for the Woman crowned with stars, clothed in the Sun, with the Moon under her feet, giving birth to a child. We are striving above all for the enlightenment ideal, crowned with truth, clothed with beauty, with goodness under her feet, giving birth to the new world culture of liberty, equality, fraternity. We feel, into our core, the imperishable part of our being—and that an unspeakably greater danger to humanity's survival than any kind of biophysical threat is the removal of our rights to manifest this eternal being on the world stage. We feel *triumphant joy* in the presence of the elemental Christ, for we feel *what is eternal within us becoming stronger.* The child, the developmentally unique, nature—these are three arcana of the same inner indestructible core, and our mission as a human race is to make the entire world an expression of this indestructible core.

And so, the coronation—or crowning achievement, the grand coup—of Ahriman and the Harlot of Babylon occurs simultaneously with the coronation, or advent, of the elemental Christ and heavenly Sophia. As I write these words in May 2020, I feel very strongly that this is our "Crossing of the Threshold" as a human race, and that the Grand

---

6  Tomberg, *Christ and Sophia,* p. 400.

Conjunction of Jupiter and Saturn in Capricorn in November (tychonically–heliocentrically) and December (geocentrically) 2020 marks the time of decision—slavery or freedom, technocracy or enlightenment?

This volume is being published precisely at this time of decision. Where do we now stand? Just as it was the conjunction of Saturn and Pluto that set the tone for all of 2020, as we stand at the threshold to 2021 it is the Great Conjunction of Jupiter and Saturn that sets the tone for the coming year. Tychonically, these two are within 5° of each other from August 3, 2020, through January 31, 2021. Their alignment is exact on **November 3, 2020, 6°49' Capricorn:**

> Finally, we come to the end of the year as Jupiter (the Holy Spirit) unites with Saturn (the Virgin Mary). The image that is created out of the meeting of these two is Whitsuntide [Pentecost], when the Virgin Mary became the vessel through which the Holy Spirit could descend in tongues of fire onto the circle of twelve apostles. In this event, the cosmic unity was divided into twelve. Each apostle contained within him and could bring to expression a completely personal, heartfelt iteration of what up until that point was a transpersonal, lofty spiritual reality.

Historically, the Jupiter–Saturn conjunctions—also known as Great Conjunctions—portend cultural shifts. These occur on a smaller scale, within the approximately 19.86-year rhythm of the conjunctions. More broadly, longer rhythms hold sway. The conjunctions take place for approximately 213.5 years in the earth signs of Capricorn, Virgo, Taurus; then 213.5 years in the air signs of Aquarius, Libra, Gemini; then water, then fire. After approximately 854 years, the cycle starts over again.

At the time of the magi, and the birth of the Solomon Jesus, the Great Conjunction took place in the sign of Pisces. Due to the retrograde movement of Jupiter and Saturn, three such conjunctions occurred over the course of the gestation of the Jesus child in 7 BC (he was born March 5, 6 BC). By the time the magi actually arrived at the house of Mary and Joseph, the child was already over nine months old. The three magi brought their gifts of gold, frankincense, and myrrh on December 26, 6 BC. While the Great Conjunction had occurred the previous year in Pisces, the Sun on the date of the Adoration of the magi was at 6° Capricorn, very close to today's Great Conjunction.

At the time of Christ, the cycle of Great Conjunctions was shifting from water signs to fire signs. A kind of cosmic "changing of water to wine" was taking place, as the clear water of the old law was transformed and fulfilled through the fire of love into new wine. The same transition was taking place at the time of Parzival, who was very likely born close to the Great Conjunction in Pisces on February 15 AD 789, and whose redemption took place in the first half of 810, just after the Great Conjunction in Scorpio in 809.

In our time, however, it is a transition from fire signs into earth signs. All that has been inculcated into humanity from fiery spiritual realms can now begin to come into earthly manifestation. The 20th century was the center of this vortex; heliocentrically, the conjunction of 1901 was in Sagittarius, a fire sign, but then that of 1921 was in Virgo, an earth sign. Subsequently, the conjunctions of 1940 and 1961 were in Aries and Sagittarius, respectively (again, heliocentrically). The 1981 conjunction was in Virgo (earth), but the 2000 conjunction was in Aries (fire). Thus, the entire century wavered back and forth between fire and earth. Beginning with today's conjunction, we have ahead of us our first sequence entirely in earth signs. Capricorn in 2020, Virgo in 2040, and Taurus in 2060. Today is not just a minor cultural shift within a 20-year rhythm; it marks a transition to a greater cycle of over 200 years.

The last time humanity stood at this threshold was in 1106, just prior to the magnificent time of the Knights Templar and the awesome Gothic cathedrals, the Cathars, the School of Chartres, Aquinas and Francis, the troubadours and bards. The time before that was in AD 253, around the time of the rise of Coptic Christianity and the School of Alexandria, of the Neoplatonists such as Plotinus, Porphyry, and Iamblichus, and Manichaeism. Somewhat later came Emperor Constantine, and the concrete institution of Christianity in Constantinople. Prior to this were the earth conjunctions of the 6th century BC, the peak of the Axial Age—Buddha, Pythagoras, and Confucius all taught during this century. This was the time of the Hebrew exile in Babylon, as well as their eventual return.

Prior to that we come to the conjunction of 1516 BC, marking the birth of Moses; before that, the 24th century BC, the height of ancient Egyptian culture and the construction of the pyramids. What we can conclude from this vast [survey] is that the transition out of the fire signs into the earth signs in terms of the cycle of Great Conjunctions marks an entry into a time of outer cultural flourishing, of renaissance and renewal. Under this sign, humanity has amazing prospects to fulfill the destiny laid out for them in the great age of Archangel Michael, which lasts until 2234. The first half of this age (which began in 1879) has been consumed with the struggle of transition from fire to earth; perhaps the second half will consist in humanity properly manifesting a truly Michaelic culture, the new culture of the Holy Grail: *Michael Sophia in Nomine Christi!*[7]

Another alignment that has carried on from last year is the square aspect between Neptune and the Node. This began to take form in September 2020, and was exact on **November 26, 2020: Neptune 24°59' Aquarius square Node 24°59' Taurus.** They remain within 5° of square alignment until March 1, 2021. Neptune and the Node are square—with the Node three signs *advanced* from Neptune—approximately every 17 years. They held a Capricorn–Aries square in 2004; a Sagittarius–Pisces square in 1987; and a Scorpio–Aquarius square in 1970. Robert Powell was first introduced to astrology around 1970; he published *Hermetic Astrology*, vol 1 in 1987; and in 2004 he finished his PhD thesis, published the next year as *History of the Zodiac*. Neptune square Node is a potent time for watching the movements of the stars, and for listening to the harmonies of the spheres. A deeper understanding of Astrosophy is able to come to expression during these times.

Just after Neptune and Node came into exact square alignment, Jupiter and Uranus began to form one as well. They were within 5° of square

on November 27, 2020. This alignment will be exact on February 2 of this year, and will last until April 8. See the February commentaries for more on this alignment.

Between December 30, 2020, and January 2, 2021, Mercury and Saturn conjoin. This conjunction is exact on **December 31, 2020: Mercury conjunct Saturn 8°36' Capricorn.** These two were conjunct opposite this degree on November 29 AD 31. This was less than a week after the sixth archetypal miracle of Christ, the Healing of the Man Born Blind. At this time, too, Neptune and the Node were very close to square alignment, with Neptune straddling the boundary of Capricorn and Aquarius, and Node straddling Aries and Taurus. Additionally, Jupiter and Uranus were square—although Jupiter was in Taurus, and Uranus in Leo. It is remarkable that we end the year 2020 with three very similar alignments that ended in AD 31.

Chapter 10 of the Gospel of John tells of Christ's deeds during this time period:

Then came Hannukah in Jerusalem; it was winter; and Jesus was walking in the Temple, in Solomon's portico; so the Judaeans encircled him and said to him, "For how long are you going to keep a grip on our soul? If you are the Anointed, tell us forthrightly." Jesus replied to them, "I have told you, and you do not have faith; the works that I perform in my Father's name, these testify concerning me; but you do not have faith, because you are not from among my sheep. My sheep hearken to my voice, and I know them, and they follow me, and I give them life in the age, and they most certainly do not perish throughout the age, and no one shall snatch them out of my hand. My Father, who has given them to me, is greater than all, and no one can snatch them out of the Father's hand. I and the Father are one." Again, the Judaeans picked up stones so that they could stone him. Jesus replied to them, "I have displayed to you many good works from the Father; for which work among them do you stone me?" The Judaeans answered him, "We stone you not on account of a good work, but rather on account of blasphemy, and because you who are a man make yourself out to be God." Jesus answered them, "Is it not written in your Law

---

7 Park, *Saturn–Mary–Sophia: Star Wisdom* vol. 2, pp. 217–218.

'I said, "You are gods"'? If he called gods those to whom God's Logos came, and the scripture cannot be dissolved, how is it that, because I have said I am the Son of God, you say, 'You blaspheme,' to one whom the Father sanctified and sent out into the cosmos? If I do not do the works of my Father, do not have faith in me; but if I do, even if you do not have faith in me, have faith in the works, so that you may know and continue to know that the Father is in me and I am in the Father." So, they again sought to seize him; and he slipped out of their hands.[8]

May this admonishing passage be our meditation as we enter the New Year.

**January 1: New Year's configuration.** As in other years, as planets ingress into new signs of the zodiac, we will turn our attention to the relevant line from Rudolf Steiner's *Twelve Cosmic Moods*. But this year will see a major difference: whenever one planet enters a new sign of the zodiac, we will form a verse drawn from the lines of *Twelve Cosmic Moods* that indicates where each planet is at that moment in time. This will provide us with a metamorphosing meditation with which to live throughout the changing year.

We begin with the configuration of planets at the start of the year:

> Growth attains power of existence
>     (*Sun in Sagittarius*)
> In being, experience being
>     (*Venus in Libra*)
> To be strong in the present
>     (*Mercury in Capricorn*)
> Into creative world existence
>     (*Mars in Taurus*)
> May world-being's vigilance grow in power
>     (*Jupiter in Capricorn*)
> And may the might of life's activity flower
>     (*Saturn in Capricorn*)
> Thou glowing light, become strong!
>     (*Moon in Cancer*)[9]

Today, as the Sun commemorates the Nativity from the Luke Gospel, the Jesus Child visited by the Shepherds, the cosmic configuration lays down the above mantra to carry us through the year. There is an emphasis on growth, power, strength, existence. May each of us be imbued with the rejuvenating forces of the spiritual world as we pass through the Holy Nights.

December 31, 2020, to January 3, 2021, Mercury and Jupiter are close to conjunction. The wing-footed messenger, having activated the crown (Saturn—the conscience) a few days ago, now activates the brow (Jupiter—creative vision). This alignment is exact on **January 1: Mercury conjunct Jupiter 11°59' Capricorn.** Mercury was at this degree, square to Jupiter in Aries, on November 7–8 AD 30:

Today Jesus prepared for the Sermon on the Mount that he would deliver the following day. He sent out his disciples to the neighboring places to make it known that he would give instruction on the mountain beyond Gabara. Some sixty disciples, friends, and relatives of Jesus came to Gabara in expectation of this occasion. Among them was Mary Magdalene, who had been persuaded to come by her sister Martha.

Around ten o'clock [the next day] Jesus arrived at the mountain, where there was a teacher's chair. He delivered a powerful discourse, culminating with the words: "Come! Come to me, all who are weary and laden with guilt! Come to me, O sinners! Do penance, believe, and share the kingdom with me!" At these words, Mary Magdalene was deeply moved inwardly, and Jesus, perceiving her agitation, addressed his hearers with some words of consolation—words actually meant for Mary Magdalene—and she was converted. That evening, a Pharisee named Simon Zabulon invited Jesus to a banquet. During the meal, Mary Magdalene entered the room carrying a flask of ointment, with which she anointed Jesus's head. (This scene and the ensuing dispute with Simon Zabulon is described in Luke 7:36–50).[10]

---

8 Hart (tr.), *The New Testament: A Translation.* pp. 194–195.

9 Steiner, *Twelve Cosmic Moods.*

10 Brentano, *The Visions of Anne Catherine Emmerich*, vol. 2, pp. 105, 107.

Jupiter and Mercury were conjunct in Aries, square to today's degree, three weeks later on November 28:

> Jesus and the disciples sailed across the Sea of Galilee. After disembarking, they went to a mountain near Bethsaida–Julias, where many people were gathered to hear Jesus teach. Here began the "Sermon on the Mount" referred to in Matthew 5 and Luke 6. This sermon lasted some fourteen days, but its conclusion was not delivered until three months later.... To begin with, Jesus spoke of the first beatitude (Matt. 5:3). The instruction lasted the whole day.[11]

**January 2:** Venus enters Scorpio.

> Growth attains power of existence
>     (*Sun in Sagittarius*)
> Yet in being, existence endures
>     (*Venus in Scorpio*)
> To be strong in the present
>     (*Mercury in Capricorn*)
> Into creative world existence
>     (*Mars in Taurus*)
> May world-being's vigilance grow in power
>     (*Jupiter in Capricorn*)
> And may the might of life's activity flower
>     (*Saturn in Capricorn*)
> Thou glowing light, become strong!
>     (*Moon in Cancer*)[12]

**January 6: Christian Celebration of Epiphany.** The celebration of Epiphany encapsulates the entirety of the Rosicrucian mantra *Ex Deo nascimur; In Christo morimur; Per Spiritum sanctum revivicimus,* the entirety of the Past, Present and Future of humanity. It honors the Past as it is the celebration of the birth of the Solomon Jesus, the reincarnated Zarathustra, who embodied all of human history and wisdom that had built up to his birth. The three magi, each representing a past cultural age and time period of human development, came to honor him with their gifts of gold (wisdom), frankincense (beauty), and myrrh (goodness).

Epiphany is also a celebration of the "eternal present" of the life of Christ within Jesus. Epiphany honors the descent of the God Christ into the human Jesus of Nazareth at his baptism in the River Jordan by John the Baptist. The life of Christ is the pivot, the Turning Point of Time, upon which all history—past and future—hinges, and out of which all history blossoms.

And finally, Epiphany is the pinnacle, the grand conclusion, to the entire time period of Advent and the Holy Nights, during which we also celebrate our expectation of the Parousia, of the presence of the Future Christ in our midst—a time period that has begun to find its fulfilment since the year 1933 and on into the future.

**January 7:** Mercury enters Aquarius.

> Growth attains power of existence
>     (*Sun in Sagittarius*)
> Yet in being, existence endures
>     (*Venus in Scorpio*)
> Boundaries in its own depths
>     (*Mercury in Aquarius*)
> Into creative world existence
>     (*Mars in Taurus*)
> May world-being's vigilance grow in power
>     (*Jupiter in Capricorn*)
> And may the might of life's activity flower
>     (*Saturn in Capricorn*)
> O soul, know thou beings!
>     (*Moon in Virgo*)[13]

**January 9–18, Venus comes into opposition with Mars.** This alignment is exact on **January 13: Venus 17°45' Scorpio opposite Mars 17°45' Taurus.** Simultaneously, Mercury conjoins Neptune between January 11–14. Their alignment is also exact on **January 13: Mercury conjunct Neptune 25°16' Aquarius.** Both of these alignments occur on the same day as the **New Moon: Sun conjunct Moon 28°11' Sagittarius.** Virtually at the same time as these other configurations, the Sun and Pluto are coming into alignment between January 9–19. Their configuration is exact on **January 14: Sun conjunct Pluto 29°37' Sagittarius.** So, we have a complex arrangement of

---

11 Ibid., p. 162.
12 Steiner, *Twelve Cosmic Moods.*

13 Ibid.

## SIDEREAL GEOCENTRIC LONGITUDES : JANUARY 2021 Gregorian at 0 hours UT

| DAY | ☉ | ☽ | ☊ | ☿ | ♀ | ♂ | ♃ | ♄ | ♅ | ♆ | ♇ |
|---|---|---|---|---|---|---|---|---|---|---|---|
| 1 FR | 15 ♐ 45 | 7 ♋ 43 | 24 ♉ 51R | 22 ♐ 41 | 25 ♏ 23 | 2 ♈ 19 | 7 ♑ 45 | 6 ♑ 36 | 11 ♈ 46R | 23 ♒ 27 | 29 ♐ 9 |
| 2 SA | 16 46 | 20 54 | 24 48 | 24 19 | 26 38 | 2 46 | 7 59 | 6 42 | 11 45 | 23 28 | 29 11 |
| 3 SU | 17 47 | 4 ♌ 18 | 24 44 | 25 57 | 27 53 | 3 12 | 8 12 | 6 49 | 11 45 | 23 29 | 29 13 |
| 4 MO | 18 48 | 17 54 | 24 41 | 27 35 | 29 8 | 3 38 | 8 26 | 6 56 | 11 44 | 23 30 | 29 15 |
| 5 TU | 19 49 | 1 ♍ 41 | 24 39 | 29 13 | 0 ♐ 23 | 4 5 | 8 40 | 7 3 | 11 44 | 23 31 | 29 17 |
| 6 WE | 20 51 | 15 38 | 24 38 | 0 ♑ 52 | 1 39 | 4 32 | 8 54 | 7 10 | 11 43 | 23 33 | 29 19 |
| 7 TH | 21 52 | 29 43 | 24 38D | 2 30 | 2 54 | 5 0 | 9 8 | 7 17 | 11 43 | 23 34 | 29 21 |
| 8 FR | 22 53 | 13 ♎ 56 | 24 39 | 4 9 | 4 9 | 5 27 | 9 22 | 7 24 | 11 42 | 23 35 | 29 23 |
| 9 SA | 23 54 | 28 15 | 24 40 | 5 47 | 5 24 | 5 55 | 9 36 | 7 31 | 11 42 | 23 37 | 29 25 |
| 10 SU | 24 55 | 12 ♏ 36 | 24 42 | 7 26 | 6 39 | 6 23 | 9 50 | 7 38 | 11 42 | 23 38 | 29 27 |
| 11 MO | 25 56 | 26 57 | 24 42R | 9 3 | 7 55 | 6 52 | 10 4 | 7 45 | 11 42 | 23 39 | 29 29 |
| 12 TU | 26 58 | 11 ♐ 12 | 24 41 | 10 41 | 9 10 | 7 20 | 10 18 | 7 52 | 11 41 | 23 41 | 29 31 |
| 13 WE | 27 59 | 25 17 | 24 38 | 12 18 | 10 25 | 7 49 | 10 32 | 7 59 | 11 41 | 23 42 | 29 33 |
| 14 TH | 29 0 | 9 ♑ 9 | 24 34 | 13 54 | 11 40 | 8 18 | 10 46 | 8 6 | 11 41 | 23 44 | 29 35 |
| 15 FR | 0 ♑ 1 | 22 42 | 24 28 | 15 28 | 12 55 | 8 47 | 11 0 | 8 13 | 11 41D | 23 45 | 29 37 |
| 16 SA | 1 2 | 5 ♒ 55 | 24 21 | 17 2 | 14 11 | 9 17 | 11 14 | 8 20 | 11 41 | 23 47 | 29 39 |
| 17 SU | 2 3 | 18 47 | 24 15 | 18 33 | 15 26 | 9 46 | 11 28 | 8 27 | 11 41 | 23 48 | 29 41 |
| 18 MO | 3 4 | 1 ♓ 19 | 24 10 | 20 3 | 16 41 | 10 16 | 11 42 | 8 35 | 11 42 | 23 50 | 29 43 |
| 19 TU | 4 5 | 13 34 | 24 6 | 21 30 | 17 56 | 10 46 | 11 56 | 8 42 | 11 42 | 23 51 | 29 45 |
| 20 WE | 5 7 | 25 36 | 24 4 | 22 53 | 19 12 | 11 16 | 12 11 | 8 49 | 11 42 | 23 53 | 29 47 |
| 21 TH | 6 8 | 7 ♈ 28 | 24 3D | 24 13 | 20 27 | 11 47 | 12 25 | 8 56 | 11 42 | 23 55 | 29 49 |
| 22 FR | 7 9 | 19 18 | 24 4 | 25 29 | 21 42 | 12 17 | 12 39 | 9 3 | 11 43 | 23 56 | 29 51 |
| 23 SA | 8 10 | 1 ♉ 9 | 24 5 | 26 40 | 22 57 | 12 48 | 12 53 | 9 10 | 11 43 | 23 58 | 29 53 |
| 24 SU | 9 11 | 13 6 | 24 7 | 27 45 | 24 12 | 13 19 | 13 8 | 9 17 | 11 44 | 24 0 | 29 55 |
| 25 MO | 10 12 | 25 15 | 24 7R | 28 43 | 25 28 | 13 50 | 13 22 | 9 25 | 11 44 | 24 2 | 29 57 |
| 26 TU | 11 13 | 7 ♊ 39 | 24 6 | 29 33 | 26 43 | 14 21 | 13 36 | 9 32 | 11 45 | 24 3 | 29 59 |
| 27 WE | 12 14 | 20 21 | 24 3 | 0 ♒ 16 | 27 58 | 14 52 | 13 50 | 9 39 | 11 45 | 24 5 | 0 ♑ 1 |
| 28 TH | 13 15 | 3 ♋ 23 | 23 57 | 0 49 | 29 13 | 15 24 | 14 4 | 9 46 | 11 46 | 24 7 | 0 3 |
| 29 FR | 14 16 | 16 43 | 23 50 | 1 12 | 0 ♑ 28 | 15 55 | 14 19 | 9 53 | 11 47 | 24 9 | 0 5 |
| 30 SA | 15 16 | 0 ♌ 21 | 23 41 | 1 25 | 1 43 | 16 27 | 14 33 | 10 0 | 11 48 | 24 11 | 0 7 |
| 31 SU | 16 17 | 14 13 | 23 32 | 1 27R | 2 59 | 16 59 | 14 47 | 10 7 | 11 48 | 24 13 | 0 8 |

### INGRESSES :

| | |
|---|---|
| 2 ☽ → ♌ 16:20 | 20 ☽ → ♈ 8:52 |
| 4 ♀ → ♐ 16:32 | 22 ☽ → ♉ 21:41 |
| ☽ → ♍ 21: 5 | 25 ☽ → ♊ 9:15 |
| 5 ☿ → ♑ 11:22 | 26 ☿ → ♒ 14:31 |
| 7 ☽ → ♎ 0:28 | ♇ → ♑ 15:53 |
| 9 ☽ → ♏ 2:55 | 27 ☽ → ♋ 17:49 |
| 11 ☽ → ♐ 5: 7 | 28 ♀ → ♑ 14:57 |
| 13 ☽ → ♑ 8: 6 | 29 ☽ → ♌ 23:23 |
| 14 ☉ → ♑ 23:37 | |
| 15 ☽ → ♒ 13:11 | |
| 17 ☽ → ♓ 21:27 | |

### ASPECTS & ECLIPSES :

| | | | | |
|---|---|---|---|---|
| 1 ☽ ☍ ♃ 0: 4 | 11 ☿ ☌ ♃ 17:18 | ☽ S ☊ 10:19 | 26 ☉ □ ♅ 12:45 | ☽ ☍ ♆ 17: 8 |
| 4 ☽ ☍ ♆ 9:49 | ☽ ☌ ♀ 20:13 | ♃ □ ♅ 22:42 | ♆ □ ☊ 14:41 | |
| ☽ N ☊ 11:49 | 12 ☿ □ ♅ 14:57 | 20 ♂ ☌ ♅ 20:34 | 27 ☽ ☍ ♀ 15:35 | |
| 5 ☿ ☌ ♇ 0:54 | 13 ☉ ☌ ☽ 4:59 | ☉ □ ☽ 21: 0 | ☽ ☍ ♇ 17:53 | |
| 6 ☉ □ ☽ 9:36 | ☽ ☌ ♇ 7:20 | 21 ☽ ☌ ♅ 8:35 | 28 ☽ ☍ ♄ 11:39 | |
| 7 ☽ ☍ ♂ 9:13 | ♂ □ ♄ 11: 1 | ☽ ☌ ♂ 9: 7 | ♀ ☌ ♇ 16:13 | |
| ☽ ☍ ♅ 20:14 | ☽ ☌ ♄ 22:10 | ☽ ☌ A 13: 1 | ☉ ☍ ☽ 19:15 | |
| 9 ☿ □ ♂ 2:43 | 14 ☽ ☌ ♃ 2:53 | 23 ♂ □ ♃ 7:48 | ☽ ☍ ♃ 19:37 | |
| ☽ ☌ P 15:34 | ☽ ☌ ☿ 9:27 | 24 ☉ ☌ ♄ 3: 0 | 29 ☉ ☌ ♃ 1:38 | |
| 10 ☿ ☌ ♄ 3:16 | ☉ ☌ ♇ 14:13 | ☉ □ Π 6:19 | 30 ☽ ☍ ☿ 1:52 | |
| ☽ ☌ ☋ 20:14 | 17 ☽ ☌ ♆ 9:34 | ☽ ☌ ☊ 21:47 | 31 ☽ N ☊ 15:46 | |

## SIDEREAL HELIOCENTRIC LONGITUDES : JANUARY 2021 Gregorian at 0 hours UT

| DAY | Sid. Time | ☿ | ♀ | ⊕ | ♂ | ♃ | ♄ | ♅ | ♆ | ♇ | Vernal Point |
|---|---|---|---|---|---|---|---|---|---|---|---|
| 1 FR | 6:43:29 | 8 ♑ 45 | 27 ♎ 11 | 15 ♊ 45 | 10 ♉ 58 | 11 ♑ 54 | 8 ♑ 37 | 14 ♈ 20 | 25 ♒ 12 | 29 ♐ 33 | 4 ♓ 58' 1" |
| 2 SA | 6:47:25 | 12 1 | 28 46 | 16 47 | 11 30 | 12 0 | 8 38 | 14 20 | 25 12 | 29 33 | 4 ♓ 58' 1" |
| 3 SU | 6:51:22 | 15 21 | 0 ♏ 22 | 17 48 | 12 2 | 12 5 | 8 40 | 14 21 | 25 12 | 29 33 | 4 ♓ 58' 1" |
| 4 MO | 6:55:18 | 18 45 | 1 58 | 18 49 | 12 33 | 12 10 | 8 42 | 14 22 | 25 13 | 29 34 | 4 ♓ 58' 1" |
| 5 TU | 6:59:15 | 22 14 | 3 33 | 19 50 | 13 5 | 12 15 | 8 44 | 14 22 | 25 13 | 29 34 | 4 ♓ 58' 0" |
| 6 WE | 7: 3:11 | 25 49 | 5 9 | 20 51 | 13 37 | 12 20 | 8 46 | 14 23 | 25 14 | 29 34 | 4 ♓ 58' 0" |
| 7 TH | 7: 7: 8 | 29 29 | 6 45 | 21 52 | 14 8 | 12 26 | 8 48 | 14 24 | 25 14 | 29 34 | 4 ♓ 58' 0" |
| 8 FR | 7:11: 4 | 3 ♒ 14 | 8 20 | 22 53 | 14 40 | 12 31 | 8 49 | 14 24 | 25 14 | 29 35 | 4 ♓ 58' 0" |
| 9 SA | 7:15: 1 | 7 6 | 9 56 | 23 55 | 15 11 | 12 36 | 8 51 | 14 25 | 25 15 | 29 35 | 4 ♓ 58' 0" |
| 10 SU | 7:18:58 | 11 5 | 11 31 | 24 56 | 15 43 | 12 41 | 8 53 | 14 26 | 25 15 | 29 35 | 4 ♓ 58' 0" |
| 11 MO | 7:22:54 | 15 10 | 13 7 | 25 57 | 16 14 | 12 46 | 8 55 | 14 26 | 25 15 | 29 36 | 4 ♓ 58' 0" |
| 12 TU | 7:26:51 | 19 23 | 14 42 | 26 58 | 16 45 | 12 51 | 8 57 | 14 27 | 25 16 | 29 36 | 4 ♓ 58' 0" |
| 13 WE | 7:30:47 | 23 43 | 16 17 | 27 59 | 17 17 | 12 57 | 8 59 | 14 28 | 25 16 | 29 36 | 4 ♓ 57'59" |
| 14 TH | 7:34:44 | 28 12 | 17 53 | 29 0 | 17 48 | 13 2 | 9 0 | 14 28 | 25 16 | 29 36 | 4 ♓ 57'59" |
| 15 FR | 7:38:40 | 2 ♓ 49 | 19 28 | 0 ♋ 2 | 18 19 | 13 7 | 9 2 | 14 29 | 25 17 | 29 37 | 4 ♓ 57'59" |
| 16 SA | 7:42:37 | 7 34 | 21 3 | 1 3 | 18 50 | 13 12 | 9 4 | 14 30 | 25 17 | 29 37 | 4 ♓ 57'59" |
| 17 SU | 7:46:33 | 12 29 | 22 38 | 2 4 | 19 21 | 13 17 | 9 6 | 14 30 | 25 18 | 29 37 | 4 ♓ 57'59" |
| 18 MO | 7:50:30 | 17 32 | 24 13 | 3 5 | 19 52 | 13 23 | 9 8 | 14 31 | 25 18 | 29 38 | 4 ♓ 57'59" |
| 19 TU | 7:54:26 | 22 45 | 25 49 | 4 6 | 20 23 | 13 28 | 9 10 | 14 32 | 25 18 | 29 38 | 4 ♓ 57'59" |
| 20 WE | 7:58:23 | 28 7 | 27 24 | 5 7 | 20 54 | 13 33 | 9 11 | 14 32 | 25 19 | 29 38 | 4 ♓ 57'58" |
| 21 TH | 8: 2:20 | 3 ♈ 37 | 28 59 | 6 8 | 21 25 | 13 38 | 9 13 | 14 33 | 25 19 | 29 39 | 4 ♓ 57'58" |
| 22 FR | 8: 6:16 | 9 17 | 0 ♐ 34 | 7 9 | 21 56 | 13 44 | 9 15 | 14 34 | 25 19 | 29 39 | 4 ♓ 57'58" |
| 23 SA | 8:10:13 | 15 5 | 2 9 | 8 10 | 22 27 | 13 49 | 9 17 | 14 34 | 25 20 | 29 39 | 4 ♓ 57'58" |
| 24 SU | 8:14: 9 | 21 0 | 3 44 | 9 11 | 22 57 | 13 54 | 9 19 | 14 35 | 25 20 | 29 39 | 4 ♓ 57'58" |
| 25 MO | 8:18: 6 | 27 2 | 5 19 | 10 12 | 23 28 | 13 59 | 9 21 | 14 36 | 25 20 | 29 40 | 4 ♓ 57'58" |
| 26 TU | 8:22: 2 | 3 ♉ 10 | 6 54 | 11 13 | 23 58 | 14 4 | 9 22 | 14 36 | 25 21 | 29 40 | 4 ♓ 57'58" |
| 27 WE | 8:25:59 | 9 23 | 8 29 | 12 14 | 24 29 | 14 10 | 9 24 | 14 37 | 25 21 | 29 40 | 4 ♓ 57'57" |
| 28 TH | 8:29:55 | 15 40 | 10 4 | 13 15 | 24 59 | 14 15 | 9 26 | 14 38 | 25 22 | 29 41 | 4 ♓ 57'57" |
| 29 FR | 8:33:52 | 21 59 | 11 39 | 14 16 | 25 30 | 14 20 | 9 28 | 14 38 | 25 22 | 29 41 | 4 ♓ 57'57" |
| 30 SA | 8:37:49 | 28 18 | 13 14 | 15 17 | 26 0 | 14 25 | 9 30 | 14 39 | 25 22 | 29 41 | 4 ♓ 57'57" |
| 31 SU | 8:41:45 | 4 ♊ 37 | 14 49 | 16 18 | 26 31 | 14 30 | 9 32 | 14 40 | 25 23 | 29 41 | 4 ♓ 57'57" |

### INGRESSES :

| |
|---|
| 2 ♀ → ♏ 18:27 |
| 7 ☿ → ♒ 3:23 |
| 14 ☿ → ♓ 9:27 |
| ⊕ → ♋ 23:22 |
| 20 ☿ → ♈ 8:17 |
| 21 ♀ → ♐ 15:25 |
| 25 ☿ → ♉ 11:37 |
| 30 ☿ → ♊ 6:27 |

### ASPECTS (HELIOCENTRIC +MOON(TYCHONIC)) :

| | | | | | |
|---|---|---|---|---|---|
| 1 ☽ ☍ ♄ 1:39 | 6 ☽ □ ♇ 23:44 | ☿ ☌ ♆ 8:22 | 20 ☿ □ ♇ 6:42 | ☿ ☌ ☊ 10:10 | ⊕ □ ♅ 8:49 |
| ☽ ☍ ☿ 2:31 | 7 ☽ □ ♄ 15:21 | ♀ ☍ ♂ 22:17 | ☽ □ ♇ 8: 8 | ☽ ☌ ♂ 20:20 | ☿ □ ♆ 12:51 |
| ☽ ☍ ♃ 7:43 | ☽ □ ♃ 21:34 | ☽ ☌ ♄ 23:45 | ☽ ☌ ☿ 9:22 | 25 ☽ □ ♆ 0:10 | ☿ ☌ ♂ 14:31 |
| ☽ □ ♅ 12: 6 | 8 ☽ ☍ ♅ 0:47 | 14 ☽ ☌ ♃ 6:52 | 21 ☽ □ ♄ 3:32 | ☽ ☍ ♀ 22:21 | 31 ☽ ☍ ♆ 19: 6 |
| ☿ ☌ ♃ 23:51 | 9 ☽ □ ☿ 20:27 | ☽ □ ♅ 9:22 | ☽ □ ♃ 12:36 | 27 ☽ ☍ ♇ 17:14 | ☽ □ ♂ 21:48 |
| 2 ☽ □ ♀ 16: 3 | ☽ ☌ ♀ 21:57 | ⊕ ☍ ♇ 14:13 | ☿ □ ⊕ 13: 5 | 28 ☽ ☍ ♄ 10:59 | |
| ☿ □ ♅ 16:52 | 10 ☿ □ ♀ 4:19 | 16 ♀ ☌ ☋ 11:51 | ☽ ☌ ♅ 14:22 | ♂ □ ♆ 17:36 | |
| 3 ⊕ ☌ P 11: 3 | ☽ ☍ ♂ 5:23 | 17 ☽ □ ♂ 1: 8 | ☿ □ ♄ 23:52 | ☽ ☍ ♃ 19:42 | |
| ☽ □ ♂ 14:14 | ☽ □ ♆ 21:10 | ☽ □ ♀ 8:23 | 22 ☿ □ ♃ 18:43 | ☽ □ ♅ 20:17 | |
| 4 ☽ ☍ ♆ 12:47 | 11 ☿ □ ♂ 7: 1 | ☽ ☌ ♆ 12:24 | ☿ ☌ ♅ 21:55 | 29 ⊕ ☍ ♃ 1:38 | |
| 5 ☿ S ☊ 8:51 | 13 ☽ ☌ ♇ 7:25 | 18 ♀ □ ♆ 16:18 | 24 ⊕ ☍ ♄ 3: 0 | ☿ ☌ P 2:55 | |

a Sun–Moon–Pluto conjunction—which may facilitate insight into the unresolved from our subconscious—along with the focused listening of Mercury conjunct Neptune, and the confrontation of primal masculine and feminine in a Mars–Venus opposition; a challenging time that has the possibility of bearing great fruit.

Venus and Mars were opposed square to their current alignment (in Aquarius and Leo respectively) on October 11 AD 29:

> On the next day Jesus taught in the synagogue, taking again the parable of the sower, alluding to the baptism and the nearness of the kingdom of God. He spoke also of the Feast of Tabernacles and of its celebration here, taking occasion to reprove the people for mixing up pagan customs in their services, for some of the Moabites still dwelt in this place, and with them the Jewish people had intimate relations. When Jesus left the synagogue, he found in the open court numbers of sick who had been borne thither on litters. They cried out as soon as they saw him: "Lord, thou hast been sent from God! Thou canst help us! Help us, Lord!" He cured many. That evening a banquet was prepared in the inn for Jesus and his followers. There were many of the pagan merchants near Jesus when he spoke of the call of the Gentiles, of the star that had appeared in the land of the kings, and of their going to visit the child. Jesus left the place that night alone and went to pray on the mountain.[14]

Mercury was conjunct Neptune in Aquarius on April 11 AD 33. On this day, less than a week after the Resurrection, the apostles and disciples were once again gathered in the Cenacle, where the Last Supper had taken place:

> …they assumed an expression of rapt attention, called up by the approach of the Lord. At the same moment, I saw Jesus in the courtyard. He was resplendent with light, clothed in white garments and a white girdle. He directed his steps to the door of the outer hall, which opened of itself before him and closed behind him. The disciples in the outer hall saw the door opening of itself, and fell back on both sides to make room. But Jesus walked quickly through the hall into the supper room and stepped between Peter and John who, like all the other apostles, fell back on either side.
>
> Jesus did not enter walking properly so called, that is, in the usual way of mortals, and yet it was not a floating along, or hovering, as I have seen spirits doing. It reminded me, as I saw them all falling back, of a priest in his alb passing through a crowded congregation. Everything in the hall appeared to become suddenly large and bright. Jesus was environed with light. The apostles had fallen back from the radiant circle, otherwise they would not have been able to see him.
>
> Jesus's first words were, "Peace be to you!" Then he spoke with Peter and John, and rebuked them for something. They had departed a little from his directions, in order to follow their own ideas about something, and consequently they had not met with success. It related to some of the cures they had sought to effect on their return from Sichar and Thanat–Shiloh. They had not followed Jesus's directions to the letter, and therefore had not been entirely successful. They had done something according to their own ideas. Jesus told them that if it happened again, they should act otherwise. Jesus now stepped under the lamp, and the apostles closed around him. Thomas, very much frightened at the sight of the Lord, timidly drew back. But Jesus, grasping his right hand in his own right hand, took the forefinger and laid the tip of it in the wound of his left hand; then taking the left hand in his own left, he placed the forefinger in the wound of his right hand; lastly, taking again Thomas's right hand in his own right, he put it, without uncovering his breast, under his garment, and laid the fore and middle fingers in the wound of his right side. He spoke some words as he did this. With the exclamation, "My Lord, and my God!" Thomas sank down like one unconscious, Jesus still holding his hand. The nearest of the apostles supported him, and Jesus raised him up by the hand. That sinking down and rising up had some peculiar signification.
>
> When Jesus grasped Thomas's hand, I saw that his wounds were not like bloody marks, but like little radiant suns.[15]

---

14 ACE, vol. 1, p 360.

15 ACE, vol. 3, pp. 399–400.

The Sun and Pluto were conjunct in Sagittarius on December 1 AD 30:

> Jesus preached today concerning the third beatitude. But because the sabbath was approaching, he broke off early and sailed back toward Capernaum. There he taught near the south gate, in a house that Peter had rented. It was here that the healing of the paralytic described in Mark 2:1–2, Luke 5:17–26, and Matthew 9:1–9 occurred. After this, Jesus went to the synagogue, where he taught—this time without disruption. Jairus, whose daughter (Salome) Jesus had raised from the dead on [Nov. 18], was there. As Jesus left, Jairus approached him to ask help for Salome, who was again close to death. Jesus agreed to go. On their way, the message of Salome's death reached them. But they continued on. Then occurred the healing of the widow Enue from Caesarea Philippi, who had been suffering from a flow of blood for twelve years (Matt. 9:20–22, Mark 5:25–34, and Luke 8:43–48). Reaching Jairus's home Jesus then repeated the raising of Salome from the dead (Matt. 9:23–25, Mark 5:35–43, and Luke 8:49–56). Afterward, Jesus left the house. On his way through the streets of Capernaum he was approached by two blind men, whom he healed (Matt. 9:27–30). Following this, Jesus healed Joas the Pharisee, who was possessed (Matt. 9:32–34).[16]

The New Moon in Sagittarius occurred shortly after this, on December 13, during which Christ once again healed a blind man:

> This morning, again, Jesus taught in Hukok. Around midday, he set off in the direction of Bethanat. Not far from the town he was met by an old blind man, named Ctesiphon, led by two youths. Ctesiphon beseeched Jesus to have mercy on him. Jesus led him to a nearby fountain and commanded him to wash his eyes, after which Jesus anointed his forehead, temples, and eyes with oil. Ctesiphon's sight was immediately restored, and he gave profound thanks. Reaching Bethanat, Jesus taught at the synagogue, where he was well received by the people. There were no Pharisees in Bethanat.[17]

My, what a manifold gathering of star memories focused on this third week of 2021! We have themes of rebuke; of healing the blind; of Thomas touching the wounds, and Salome's second raising from the dead. The theme of powerful *release* carries on from the start of the year.

**January 14: Sun enters Capricorn; Mercury enters Pisces.**

> May the future rest upon the past
>     (*Sun in Capricorn*)
> Yet in being, existence endures.
>     (*Venus in Scorpio*)
> In comprehending seek to grasp
>     (*Mercury in Pisces*)
> Into creative world existence
>     (*Mars in Taurus*)
> May world-being's vigilance grow in power
>     (*Jupiter in Capricorn*)
> And may the might of life's activity flower
>     (*Saturn in Capricorn*)
> May the past bear the future!
>     (*Moon in Capricorn*)[18]

**January 14–21, Venus comes into alignment with the Node.** This alignment is exact on **January 17: Venus conjunct South Node 24°10' Scorpio.** Simultaneously, on January 15–21, Venus is square Neptune. This alignment is exact on **January 18: Venus 25°18' Scorpio square Neptune 25°18' Aquarius.** Both clarity and depth of feeling can be heightened during these alignments.

Neptune was conjunct the South Node on November 6 AD 30. On this day Christ healed the son of a Roman officer named Achias:

> In the house in which Paul was born there lived at this period an officer in command of the pagan soldiers of the citadel. He was called Achias. He had a sick son seven years old, to whom he had given the name of Jepthah after the Jewish hero. Achias was a good man. He sighed for help from Jesus, but none of the inhabitants of Gischala would intercede for him with the Lord. The disciples were all engaged, some busy around their Master, others scattered among the harvesters

---

16 ACE, vol. 2, pp. 163–164.
17 Ibid., pp. 179.

18 Steiner, *Twelve Cosmic Moods*.

to whom they were telling of Jesus and repeating his instructions, while some others had already been dispatched as messengers to Capernaum and into the neighboring districts. The townspeople had no liking for the officer, whom they did not care to have so near them. They would have been glad had he fixed his abode elsewhere. They were, besides, not very friendly in disposition, and even showed very little enthusiasm over Jesus himself. They went carelessly on with their work, listening to his words, but taking no lively, active interest. The anxious father therefore made bold to follow Jesus, but at a distance. At last he approached him, stepped before him, bowing, and said, "Master, reject not thy servant! Have pity on my little son lying sick at home!" Jesus replied, "It behooveth to break bread to the children of the household before giving it to the stranger who stands without." Achias responded, "Lord, I believe the Promise. I believe that thou hast said that such as believe in thee are not strangers but thy children. Lord, have pity on my son!" Then said Jesus, "Thy faith hath saved thee!" and followed by some of the disciples, he went into the house in which Paul was born and in which Achias now resided....

Achias conducted Jesus to the interior of the house, and some of the servants carried to him the boy in his bed. The wife of Achias followed veiled. She bowed timidly, and stood somewhat behind the rest in anxious expectation. Achias was radiant with joy. He called in all his domestics who, full of curiosity, were standing at a distance. The boy was a beautiful child of about six years. He had on a long woolen gown and a striped fur around his neck and crossed on the breast. He was without speech and paralyzed, wholly unable to move. But he looked intelligent and affectionate, and cast upon Jesus a most touching glance.

Jesus addressed the parents and all present with words on the vocation of the Gentiles, the nearness of the kingdom, of penance, and of the entrance into the Father's house by baptism. Then he prayed, took the boy from his little bed up in his arms, laid him on his breast, bowed low over him, put his fingers under his tongue, set him down on the floor, and led him to the officer who, with the mother trembling for joy,

rushed forward with heartfelt tears to meet and embrace their child. The little fellow, likewise stretching out his arms toward his parents, cried, "O father! O mother! I can walk, I can speak!" Then Jesus said, "Take the boy! Ye know not what a treasure has been given to you in him. He is now restored to you, but he will one day be demanded of you!" The parents led the child again to Jesus and in tears threw themselves with him at his feet, uttering thanks. Jesus blessed the boy and spoke to him most kindly. The officer begged Jesus to step with him into an adjoining apartment and take some refreshment. This he did along with the disciples. They partook, standing, of bread, honey, small fruits, and some kind of beverage. Jesus again spoke with Achias, telling him that he should go to Capernaum and there receives baptism, and that he might join Zorobabel. Achias and his domestics did this later on. The boy Jephthah after became a very zealous disciple of St. Thomas.[19]

Complementing this star memory is that of Venus square Neptune, which took place on August 26 AD 32. Jesus had recently attended a wedding in Sichar, and made obscure statements a few days earlier about building a house for the newlyweds:

At the Feast of the New Moon just now began, all returned with Jesus to the public house. He knew that, when he said that they should build a house for the newly married pair, many had thought and said to one another, "Perhaps, he has no house of his own, no place of abode. Will he, perhaps, take up his residence with these people?" Therefore, it was that Jesus now told them that he was not going to stay among them, that he had no abiding place on this Earth, that his kingdom was yet to come, that he had to plant his Father's vineyard, and water it with his blood upon Mount Calvary. They could not now comprehend his words, he said, but they would do so after he had watered the vineyard. Then he would come back to them from a dark country. He would send his messengers to call them, and then they would leave this place and follow him. But when he should come again for the third time, he would lead into his Father's kingdom all those who had faithfully labored in

---

19 ACE, vol. 2, pp. 104–105.

the vineyard. Their sojourning here was not to be long, therefore the house they were building was to be a light one, rather a tent that could easily be removed. Jesus next gave a long instruction upon mutual charity. They should, he said, cast their anchor in the heart of their neighbor, that the storms of the world might not separate and destroy them. He spoke again in parables of the vineyard, saying that he would remain only long enough to lay out the vineyard for the newly married pair and teach them to plant the vines, then he would depart in order to cultivate that belonging to his Father. Jesus taught all these things in language so simple, and yet so nicely adapted to the point in question, that his hearers became more and more convinced of its truth, retaining at the same time their simplicity. He taught them to recognize in all nature, in life itself, a law hidden and holy, though now disfigured by sin. The instruction lasted till late into the night.[20]

**January 20: Mercury enters Aries.**

**January 21: Venus enters Sagittarius.**

> May the future rest upon the past
> (*Sun in Capricorn*)
> In existence growth's power dies
> (*Venus in Sagittarius*)
> Lay hold of forces weaving
> (*Mercury in Aries*)
> Into creative world existence
> (*Mars in Taurus*)
> May world-being's vigilance grow in power
> (*Jupiter in Capricorn*)
> And may the might of life's activity flower
> (*Saturn in Capricorn*)
> O shining light, abide!
> (*Moon in Aries*)[21]

**January 21–23, Mercury comes into alignment with Uranus.** This is exact on **January 22: Mercury conjunct Uranus, 14°34' Aries.** Simultaneously, between January 18–28, the Sun and Saturn come into alignment, exact on **January 23: Sun conjunct Saturn, 9°19' Capricorn.** Mercury and Uranus

were last conjunct at this degree on January 2, 1937. Hitler had just created the Hitler Youth; Stalin was consolidating power by taking out the Trotskyists and crafting the Soviet Constitution; the UK was struggling with the King Edward VIII abdication crisis; Franklin D. Roosevelt had just been elected for his second term; and Howard Hughes set a flight record—Los Angeles to New York City in 7 hours, 28 minutes, and 25 seconds.

In the meantime, Willi Sucher was hard at work publishing astrosophical articles under a pseudonym; Valentin Tomberg was writing his meditations on the New Testament; and Karl König was gathering around him a group of young anthroposophists who would become the first Camphill Community in the next few years.

The Sun was in Capricorn opposite Saturn in Cancer on January 10 AD 33. During this time, Jesus was on his way to Jacob's Well in order to reunite with his disciples. He had not seen them for months, as he had gone on a journey south into Egypt with three shepherd youths, Eliud, Silas, and Eremenzear. Sun and Saturn were conjunct in Cancer some months before, in July AD 32, as Christ was slowly making his way to the ill—and eventually deceased—Lazarus. We are in a time of transition. We can keep in mind the planetary mantra from January 20–21, making sure that the future rests upon the past as we take hold of the forces weaving into creative world existence.

**January 24–25: Celebration of the Conversion of St. Paul**—looking ahead to Candlemas and the Feast of Our Lady of Good Success.

Tonight (January 24) is the Eve of the Festival of St. Paul's conversion, when Saul's eyes were blinded by the light of the Risen Christ. After a period of darkness, Saul reemerges, reborn as St. Paul—a brand new creation through the agency of the "Not I, but Christ in me." Tonight, we also have the opportunity of beginning to pray the Novena to Our Lady of Good Success, whose feast is celebrated on February 2 along with Candlemas and the Purification of Mary.[22] Through Christ our

---

20 Ibid., pp. 490–491.
21 Steiner, *Twelve Cosmic Moods.*

22 See https://www.ourladyofgoodsuccess.com/pages /history.

eyes are darkened, so that our ears can be opened to receive inspiration. When our eyes open again, they see differently than they did before. The healing of our sight through darkness opens our eyes to Our Lady of Good Success, who shines the light in the "bleak midwinter" (Feb. 2 is exactly midway between solstice and equinox).

**January 25: Mercury enters Taurus.**

May the future rest upon the past.
   (*Sun in Capricorn*)
In existence growth's power dies
   (*Venus in Sagittarius*)
Weave life's thread
   (*Mercury in Taurus*)
Into creative world existence
   (*Mars in Taurus*)
May world-being's vigilance grow in power
   (*Jupiter in Capricorn*)
And may the might of life's activity flower
   (*Saturn in Capricorn*)
O Sun life, endure!
   (*Moon in Gemini*)[23]

January 16 and February 7, many alignments take shape and fade away. Get ready!

**January 16 and February 3, Mars and the Ascending Node come into alignment**; this is exact on January 26: Mars conjunct Ascending Node 24°6' Taurus.

The Sun and Jupiter come into alignment January 23 and February 3; this is exact on January 28: Sun conjunct Jupiter 14°20' Capricorn.

**January 18 and February 7, Mars is square Neptune**; this is exact on January 28: Mars 25°22' Taurus square Neptune 25°22' Aquarius.

**January 24 and February 3, the Sun is square Uranus**, exact on January 29: Sun 14°39' Capricorn square Uranus 14°39' Aries.

Mercury comes into alignment with the Node on January 28–29, exact on January 29, Mercury conjunct Ascending Node 23°47' Taurus.

**Simultaneously, Mercury** is conjunct Mars between January 28–30, exact on **January 29: Mercury conjunct Mars 25°48' Taurus.** The combination of all of these influences might be best coined as the possibility to know with perfect clarity what we are doing; and to do, with great precision, what we intend.

Mars and Node were conjunct in Taurus on January 28 AD 31. This was one day prior to the fourth and fifth archetypal healing miracles of Christ: The Feeding of the Five Thousand and the Walking on Water. On this day:

Jesus and his party here on the mountain were again surrounded by the immense multitude. The disciples ranged the people in order, and Jesus began again his instructions on the beatitudes and prayer. He again explained the first petition of the Lord's prayer. As the hours flew by, the crowds increased. People came from all the cities around, from Julias, Chorazin, and Gergesa, bringing with them the sick and possessed. Numbers were healed by Jesus and the disciples.

The instructions over, the multitude dispersed.... Jesus with the apostles and disciples then retired higher up the mountain to a shady, solitary spot.

Besides the twelve [apostles], there were with Jesus seventy-two disciples....

Jesus then instructed the disciples upon the work in store for them. He told them that they should take with them neither purse nor money nor bread, but only a staff and a pair of sandals; that wherever they were ungraciously received, they should shake the dust from their shoes. He gave them some general directions for their coming duties as apostles and disciples, called them the salt of the earth, and spoke of the light that must be placed under a bushel, and of the city seated upon a mountain. Still he did not inform them of the full measure of persecution awaiting them.

The main point, however, of this instruction was that by which Jesus drew a definitive line between the apostles and the disciples, the former of whom were set over the latter. To them he said that they should send and call the disciples as he himself sent and called them, namely,

---

23 Steiner, *Twelve Cosmic Moods*.

the apostles. This they were empowered to do by virtue of their own mission. Among the disciples Jesus likewise formed several classes, setting the eldest and best instructed over the younger and more recently received. He arranged them in the following manner, the apostles, two by two, headed by Peter and John. The elder disciples formed a circle around them, and back of these the younger, according to the rank he had assigned them. Then he addressed to them words of earnest and touching instruction, and imposed hands upon the apostles as a ratification of the dignity to which he had raised them; the disciples, he merely blessed. All this was done with the greatest tranquility. The whole scene was deeply impressive. No one offered the least resistance or showed the least sign of discontent.[24]

Here we witness the tranquility and clarity that the Node can offer to the power of the Word that lies within Mars. We can think of the mantra of the Risen Christ that awakens the larynx (Mars) chakra: "Go forth unto all peoples, baptizing them in the name of the Father, the Son, and the Holy Spirit."

Since Neptune is square the Node through March 1, as Mars conjoins the Node, it also comes into square alignment with Neptune. Mars in Taurus was square Neptune in Aquarius for the entirety of November AD 32. According to the research of Robert Powell, the sixth archetypal healing miracle of Christ occurred on November 23 AD 32: the Healing of the Man Born Blind.[25] Shortly after the Feast of St. Paul's Conversion, our attention is once again brought to the transition from blindness to sight.

The Sun and Jupiter conjoin at the same time that Mars is square Neptune. The Sun, close to its position today (Jan. 28) in Capricorn, came into square alignment with Jupiter in Aries on January 5 AD 31:

This evening, at the start of the sabbath, [Jesus] taught in the synagogue. Afterward he healed the sick, but the Pharisees objected to his healing on the sabbath, saying that the sabbath

belonged to God. Jesus replied, "I have no other time and no other measure than the will of the Father in Heaven." Afterward, when Jesus ate a meal with the Pharisees, they reproached him for allowing women of bad repute to follow him. They meant Mary Magdalene, Dinah the Samaritan, and Mara the Suphanite (Luke 8:1–3). Jesus answered, "If you knew me, you would speak differently. I have come out of compassion for sinners."[26]

In the midst of the many different alignments occurring simultaneously at the end of January, we also come to the Full Moon.

**January 28, Full Moon 14°3' Cancer.** The Full Moon occurred very close to this degree on January 4 AD 33, as Jesus was leaving Heliopolis, a city he had not visited since he was an infant fleeing the wrath of Herod with his parents:

When Jesus, escorted by many of the inhabitants, left Heliopolis, he took with him a young man belonging to the city, and who now made his fifth disciple. His name was Deodatus, and that of his mother was Mira. She was that tall old lady who had, on the first evening of Jesus's arrival, been among those that welcomed him under the portico. During Mary's sojourn in Heliopolis, Mira was childless; but on the prayer of the blessed Virgin, this son was afterward given her. He was tall and slender, and appeared to be about eighteen years old. When his escort had returned to the city, I saw Jesus journeying through the desert with his five disciples. He took a direction more to the east than that taken by the holy family on their flight into Egypt.[27]

We reap the fruit of seeds planted by the blessed Virgin long ago, without our knowledge. Our Lady of Good Success continues to carry us.

**On January 29, Sun is square Uranus.** The last time they were square at these degrees was January 28, 1937. We are brought once again to the time of the second inauguration of Franklin D. Roosevelt in the U.S., the execution of Trotskyists in the USSR, and the continued rise of Hitler in Germany.

24 ACE, vol. 2, p. 298.
25 Powell, "The Healing of the Man Born Blind and the Central Sun: Foundations of Star Wisdom (Astrosophy)" in *Journal for Star Wisdom*, 2016.
26 ACE, vol. 2, p. 203.
27 Ibid., p. 519.

On the same day, Mercury comes into conjunction with both the Node and Mars. Mercury was conjunct Node in Taurus on December 4 AD 30:

> In the intervals of his public teaching and curing, Jesus, whenever he found himself alone with his apostles and disciples, prepared them for their mission. Today he led the twelve to a spot near the lake, placed them in the order mentioned in the Gospel, and conferred upon them the power of healing and of casting out devils. To the other disciples he gave only the power to baptize and impose hands. At the same time, he addressed a touching discourse to them in which he promised to be with them always and to share with them all that he possessed. The power to heal and to drive out the devil, Jesus bestowed in the form of a blessing. All wept, and Jesus himself was very much moved. At the close he said that there was still much to be done and then they would go to Jerusalem, for the fullness of time was drawing near. The apostles were glowing with enthusiasm. They expressed their readiness to do all that he would command and to remain true to him. Jesus replied that there were afflictions and hardships in store for them, and that evil would glide in among them. By these words he alluded to Judas. With discourses such as the above, they reached their little boats....
>
> Jesus and his disciples did not at once enter Magdala. Peter's boat was lying near a sandbank to which extended a bridge. As soon as Jesus stepped on shore, several possessed came running toward him with loud cries. They asked what he wanted there, and cried out for him to leave them in peace. This they did of their own accord. Jesus delivered them. They gave thanks, and went into the village. And now others came, bringing with them other possessed. Some of the disciples, Peter, Andrew, John, James and his cousins then went into Magdala, where they delivered the possessed and cured many sick, among others some women attacked by convulsions. They drove out devils and commanded sickness to disappear in the name of Jesus of Nazareth. I heard some of them adding the words, "Whom the storm of the sea obeyed." Some of those that were cured by the disciples went to Jesus to hear his admonitions and instructions. He explained to them and to the disciples why the possessed were so very numerous in these parts. It was because the inhabitants were so intent upon the things of this world and so given up to the indulgence of their passions.[28]

Mercury in Scorpio was opposite Mars in Taurus a month later, on January 14 AD 31:

> ...Jesus visited Zechariah's tomb in company with his disciples and the nephews of the murdered man. It was not like ordinary tombs. It was more like the catacombs, consisting of a vault supported on pillars. It was a most honorable burial place for priests and prophets. It had been determined that John's body should be brought from Machaerus and here buried, therefore the vault was arranged and a funeral couch erected. It was very touching to see Jesus helping to prepare a resting place for his friend. He rendered honor to the remains of Zechariah also.
>
> Elizabeth was not buried here, but on a high mountain, in that cave in which John had sojourned when a boy in the desert.

The overarching themes of these manifold star memories involve the transmission of power from Christ to his followers, the recognition/remembering of key figures from his past (Mary, Zechariah, John the Baptist), and the overcoming of blindness with sight.

### January 30: Mercury enters Gemini.

> May the future rest upon the past
> (*Sun in Capricorn*)
> In existence growth's power dies
> (*Venus in Sagittarius*)
> Embrace joyful striving
> (*Mercury in Gemini*)
> Into creative world existence
> (*Mars in Taurus*)
> May world-being's vigilance grow in power
> (*Jupiter in Capricorn*)
> And may the might of life's activity flower
> (*Saturn in Capricorn*)
> With senses' might, arise!
> (*Moon in Leo*)[29]

---

28 Ibid., pp. 168–169.
29 Steiner, *Twelve Cosmic Moods.*

# FEBRUARY 2021

## STARGAZING PREVIEW

As the month begins, Venus continues her approach toward the Sun, leaving a little over a half hour—very little time!—between her rising and the Sun's (at 0740). The Moon reaches its Last Quarter (at 21° Libra) on the 4th; you'll find it near culmination in the south before sunrise. Mercury and the Sun join in inferior conjunction on the 8th—this is the time to listen for answers to prayers offered when Mercury was last on the far side of the Sun, in December of last year. Saturn and Jupiter rise half an hour before day breaks.

The New Moon on the 11th, at 28° Capricorn, creates a curious heavenly configuration, in which the only planet visible to us at any time that day is Mars. Still in Aries, Mars can be found overhead at sunset. The Moon and Sun are part of a seven planet stellium in Capricorn—Pluto, Saturn, Jupiter, Venus, Mercury, Moon, Sun—reminiscent of the starry script on February 5, 1962, the date of the birth of the Antichrist put forth in Robert Powell's *Prophecy—Phenomena—Hope*.

The Capricorn blockade is broken on the 13th, as Aquarius, always a breath of fresh air, greets the Sun! Sunset on Thursday the 18th bears the gift of the waxing Moon to the right of, and slightly below, Mars. If you're inclined to stay up late, you can watch the Moon surpass Mars just before they sink out of view in the west at 0100.

On the following evening (the 19th), you'll have the chance to observe the First Quarter Moon at 6° Taurus, to the left of Mars. Tonight offers a good opportunity to improve your stargazing by getting a sense of how wide a 20° arc appears from our vantage, for at 2100, the Moon and Mars will be that many degrees apart. How far must you spread your outstretched hand to span this distance? Venus follows the Sun into Aquarius on the 21st; Mars finds Taurus on Tuesday the 23rd. At sunset on the 26th, look to the east to see the Moon move above *Regulus*, its position at the birth of the Nathan Mary! The Moon becomes Full on the 27th; as it rises, Orion will be overhead, high in the south. By the end of the month, Saturn and Jupiter will be visible in the morning for an hour before dawn.

## FEBRUARY COMMENTARIES

**January 31** to **February 3, Mercury and Venus come into opposition**. This alignment is exact on **February 1: Mercury 18°17' Gemini opposite Venus 18°17' Sagittarius.** These two planets were opposed close to these same positions on May 5 AD 33, one month after the Resurrection:

> Jesus communicated with the apostles quite naturally in those last days. He ate and prayed with them, walked with them in many directions, and repeated all that he had before told them. He appeared also to Simon of Cyrene as he was working in a garden between Bethphage and Jerusalem. Jesus, resplendent with light, approached him as if floating in the air. Simon fell on his knees and kissed the ground at Jesus's feet, who signed to him with his hand to keep silence, and then vanished. Some others that were working nearby likewise saw Jesus, and they too fell on their knees like Simon. When Jesus was walking with the apostles around Jerusalem, some of the Jews perceived the apparition, and were terrified. They ran to hide themselves, or to shut themselves up in their houses. Even the apostles and disciples accompanied him with a certain degree of timidity, for there was in him something too spiritual for them. Jesus appeared also in other places, Bethlehem and Nazareth for instance, to those especially with whom he and his blessed Mother had formerly had contact. He scattered blessings everywhere, and they that saw him believed and joined the apostles and disciples.[30]

The planet of movement (Mercury) in the sign of fraternity (Gemini) looks across the sky to the planet of love (Venus) in the sign of focused will (Sagittarius). This is a powerful configuration for the Good.

**February 2: Christian celebration of Candlemas, and the Feast of Purification.** Exact square of Jupiter (14°41' Capricorn) and Uranus (14°41' Aries).

---

30 ACE, vol. 3, p. 409.

We have been looking toward Candlemas since St. Paul's Day on January 25th. Even longer has the square alignment between Jupiter and Uranus been building up; they have been coming into alignment since November 27, around Advent time, and will remain close to square alignment all the way through April 8, close to Easter.

Jupiter and Uranus were square close to these same degrees on March 13, 1938. The Nazi annexation of Austria was announced this day, one day after the *Anschluss*, when German troops began their occupation. A few weeks later, on March 30, Benito Mussolini was granted equal power over the Italian military to the King, becoming First Marshal of the Empire. Earlier in the month, oil was first discovered in Saudi Arabia. In Korea, the predecessor to the company Samsung was founded. *Snow White and the Seven Dwarves*, the first full-length animated film, was released in the United States, as was the first issue of the *Superman* comic books. This is a pivotal time period! The *fuel* is found for the anti-culture (oil); the *methods* are honed for the anti-culture (psychological and physical warfare); and the *media* emerge for the gradual acceptance of the anti-culture (film and entertainment).

At the same time, a proto-culture seemed to be dissolving. Three years prior, the Anthroposophical Society had split, with two of the board members (Ita Wegman and Elizabeth Vreede) being expelled, along with thousands of other Anthroposophists. By 1938, the cracks in the armor had led to a full splintering due to the amping up of World War II. Karl König and his friends (who were all Austrian Jews) were forced to flee from the Nazis—eventually ending up in Scotland, founding the Camphill Movement. Willi Sucher moved out of Germany permanently in 1938 for similar reasons, and also landed in the UK, where he would also work with children with special needs and eventually develop groundbreaking studies in astrosophy. Valentin Tomberg, too, moved in 1938, from Estonia to The Netherlands, where shortly after he would begin his Lord's Prayer Course with a small esoteric group—a seed that has only continued to grow in the 80 years since then.

This is the power of the Good—if you splinter it, it only multiplies. The shattering of the Anthroposophical Society yielded Camphill, the Lord's Prayer course, and astrosophy. This is what we can remember on this Candlemas Day. Candlemas is the first glimmer of the reemergence of the light after the darkness of Christmas, looking toward the Resurrection of Easter. We can have confidence that neither the cold nor the darkness can extinguish the light. Light and warmth overcome cold and darkness. Ultimately, light and heat can be strengthened (thrown into higher contrast) only by the presence of darkness and cold, and never extinguished.

**February 3–4, Mercury is opposite Pluto, exact on February 3: Mercury 29°43' Gemini opposite Pluto 29°43' Sagittarius.** These two were opposed in these degrees on August 15 AD 32, as Jesus was just beginning his journey to Egypt with the shepherd youths:

> ...on account of the great concourse of people, Jesus taught in the open air. He settled many matrimonial affairs, for the people of this place had lost the true conception of the Law on that head. They wanted to espouse two blood relatives in succession, and they questioned Jesus on the matter. He explained to them that it was not allowed by the Mosaic Law, and they promised to refrain from such unions. It was told Jesus also that in one of the neighboring places a certain man was on the point of marrying for the sixth time, his five deceased wives being sisters of the present affianced. Jesus said that he would visit that place. He returned to Kedar for the sabbath, and taught the whole day in the school. He gave decisions upon many questions and doubts concerning the Law and marriage and reconciled some married couples that were at variance.[31]

**February 4: Mercury enters Cancer.**

> May the future rest upon the past
> (*Sun in Capricorn*)
> In existence growth's power dies
> (*Venus in Sagittarius*)
> Warm soul life
> (*Mercury in Cancer*)

---

31 ACE, vol. 2, p. 487.

## SIDEREAL GEOCENTRIC LONGITUDES:     FEBRUARY 2021 Gregorian at 0 hours UT

| DAY | | ☉ | ☽ | ☊ | ☿ | ♀ | ♂ | ♃ | ♄ | ♅ | ♆ | ♇ |
|---|---|---|---|---|---|---|---|---|---|---|---|---|
| 1 | MO | 17 ♑ 18 | 28 ♌ 15 | 23 ♉ 23R | 1 ♒ 17R | 4 ♑ 14 | 17 ♈ 31 | 15 ♑ 1 | 10 ♑ 14 | 11 ♈ 49 | 24 ♒ 14 | 0 ♑ 10 |
| 2 | TU | 18 19 | 12 ♍ 24 | 23 16 | 0 57 | 5 29 | 18 3 | 15 16 | 10 22 | 11 50 | 24 16 | 0 12 |
| 3 | WE | 19 20 | 26 34 | 23 12 | 0 25 | 6 44 | 18 35 | 15 30 | 10 29 | 11 51 | 24 18 | 0 14 |
| 4 | TH | 20 21 | 10 ♎ 44 | 23 9 | 29 ♑ 44 | 7 59 | 19 8 | 15 44 | 10 36 | 11 52 | 24 20 | 0 16 |
| 5 | FR | 21 22 | 24 51 | 23 9D | 28 52 | 9 15 | 19 40 | 15 58 | 10 43 | 11 53 | 24 22 | 0 18 |
| 6 | SA | 22 23 | 8 ♏ 54 | 23 10 | 27 54 | 10 30 | 20 13 | 16 13 | 10 50 | 11 55 | 24 24 | 0 20 |
| 7 | SU | 23 23 | 22 53 | 23 10R | 26 49 | 11 45 | 20 45 | 16 27 | 10 57 | 11 56 | 24 26 | 0 22 |
| 8 | MO | 24 24 | 6 ♐ 47 | 23 9 | 25 40 | 13 0 | 21 18 | 16 41 | 11 4 | 11 57 | 24 28 | 0 24 |
| 9 | TU | 25 25 | 20 34 | 23 6 | 24 29 | 14 15 | 21 51 | 16 55 | 11 11 | 11 58 | 24 30 | 0 25 |
| 10 | WE | 26 26 | 4 ♑ 13 | 23 0 | 23 17 | 15 30 | 22 24 | 17 9 | 11 18 | 12 0 | 24 32 | 0 27 |
| 11 | TH | 27 26 | 17 41 | 22 51 | 22 7 | 16 46 | 22 57 | 17 24 | 11 25 | 12 1 | 24 34 | 0 29 |
| 12 | FR | 28 27 | 0 ♒ 57 | 22 40 | 21 1 | 18 1 | 23 31 | 17 38 | 11 32 | 12 2 | 24 36 | 0 31 |
| 13 | SA | 29 28 | 13 57 | 22 28 | 19 59 | 19 16 | 24 4 | 17 52 | 11 39 | 12 4 | 24 39 | 0 33 |
| 14 | SU | 0 ♒ 28 | 26 41 | 22 16 | 19 3 | 20 31 | 24 37 | 18 6 | 11 46 | 12 5 | 24 41 | 0 35 |
| 15 | MO | 1 29 | 9 ♓ 9 | 22 5 | 18 14 | 21 46 | 25 11 | 18 20 | 11 53 | 12 7 | 24 43 | 0 36 |
| 16 | TU | 2 30 | 21 22 | 21 56 | 17 33 | 23 1 | 25 45 | 18 34 | 12 0 | 12 9 | 24 45 | 0 38 |
| 17 | WE | 3 30 | 3 ♈ 23 | 21 49 | 16 59 | 24 16 | 26 18 | 18 48 | 12 6 | 12 10 | 24 47 | 0 40 |
| 18 | TH | 4 31 | 15 16 | 21 45 | 16 32 | 25 31 | 26 52 | 19 2 | 12 13 | 12 12 | 24 49 | 0 42 |
| 19 | FR | 5 31 | 27 4 | 21 43 | 16 14 | 26 46 | 27 26 | 19 16 | 12 20 | 12 14 | 24 51 | 0 43 |
| 20 | SA | 6 32 | 8 ♉ 54 | 21 43 | 16 3 | 28 2 | 28 0 | 19 30 | 12 27 | 12 16 | 24 54 | 0 45 |
| 21 | SU | 7 32 | 20 50 | 21 43 | 15 59 | 29 17 | 28 34 | 19 44 | 12 33 | 12 17 | 24 56 | 0 47 |
| 22 | MO | 8 33 | 2 ♊ 59 | 21 43 | 16 2D | 0 ♒ 32 | 29 8 | 19 58 | 12 40 | 12 19 | 24 58 | 0 48 |
| 23 | TU | 9 33 | 15 25 | 21 41 | 16 12 | 1 47 | 29 42 | 20 12 | 12 47 | 12 21 | 25 0 | 0 50 |
| 24 | WE | 10 34 | 28 13 | 21 36 | 16 28 | 3 2 | 0 ♉ 17 | 20 26 | 12 53 | 12 23 | 25 2 | 0 52 |
| 25 | TH | 11 34 | 11 ♋ 25 | 21 28 | 16 49 | 4 17 | 0 51 | 20 40 | 13 0 | 12 25 | 25 5 | 0 53 |
| 26 | FR | 12 34 | 25 2 | 21 18 | 17 16 | 5 32 | 1 25 | 20 53 | 13 7 | 12 27 | 25 7 | 0 55 |
| 27 | SA | 13 35 | 9 ♌ 1 | 21 7 | 17 48 | 6 47 | 2 0 | 21 7 | 13 13 | 12 30 | 25 9 | 0 56 |
| 28 | SU | 14 35 | 23 20 | 20 54 | 18 24 | 8 2 | 2 34 | 21 21 | 13 19 | 12 32 | 25 11 | 0 58 |

### INGRESSES:

| | | | | |
|---|---|---|---|---|
| 1 ☽ → ♍ 2:57 | 21 ♀ → ♒ 13:52 | | | |
| 3 ☽ → ♎ 5:48 | ☽ → ♊ 18: 8 | | | |
| ☿ → ♑ 15: 1 | 23 ☽ → ♋ 12:25 | | | |
| 5 ☽ → ♏ 8:46 | 24 ☽ → ♋ 3:17 | | | |
| 7 ☽ → ♐ 12:15 | 26 ☽ → ♌ 8:35 | | | |
| 9 ☽ → ♑ 16:33 | 28 ☽ → ♍ 11: 3 | | | |
| 11 ☽ → ♒ 22:16 | | | | |
| 13 ☉ → ♒ 12:43 | | | | |
| 14 ☽ → ♓ 6:19 | | | | |
| 16 ☽ → ♈ 17:11 | | | | |
| 19 ☽ → ♉ 5:57 | | | | |

### ASPECTS & ECLIPSES:

| | | | |
|---|---|---|---|
| 1 ☉ □ ♂ 10:32 | 10 ☿ □ ♂ 12:14 | 14 ☿ ☌ ♃ 21:38 | ☽ ☍ ♃ 16:39 |
| 3 ☽ ☌ P 19:58 | ☽ ☌ ♄ 12:40 | 17 ☽ ☌ ♅ 17:46 | 26 ☽ ☍ ♀ 19:49 |
| 4 ☽ ☌ ♂ 14:49 | ☽ ☌ ♀ 22: 9 | ♄ □ ♅ 18:47 | 27 ☉ ☍ ☽ 8:16 |
| ☽ ☍ ♂ 14:49 | ☽ ☌ ♃ 23:27 | 18 ☽ ☌ A 10:10 | ☽ ☌ ♊ Ω 20: 1 |
| ☉ □ ☽ 17:36 | 11 ☽ ☌ ☿ 7:21 | 19 ☽ ☌ ♂ 0:46 | 28 ☽ ☍ ♆ 3: 6 |
| 6 ♀ ☌ ♄ 7: 6 | ♀ ☌ ♃ 14:58 | ☉ □ ☽ 18:46 | |
| 7 ☽ ☌ ♅ 0:28 | ☉ ☌ ☽ 19: 4 | ♀ □ ♂ 23: 2 | |
| ♀ □ ♅ 3:30 | 13 ☉ □ ♇ 4:41 | 21 ☽ ☌ ♊ Ω 1:45 | |
| 8 ☉ ☌ ☿ 13:46 | ☿ □ ♀ 7:46 | 24 ☽ ☍ ♇ 4:52 | |
| ☉ □ ♇ 14:13 | ☽ ☌ ♊ Ω 15:44 | 25 ☽ ☍ ♄ 2:51 | |
| 9 ☽ ☌ ♆ 17:20 | ☽ ☌ ♆ 20:10 | ☽ ☍ ☿ 9:55 | |

## SIDEREAL HELIOCENTRIC LONGITUDES:     FEBRUARY 2021 Gregorian at 0 hours UT

| DAY | | Sid. Time | ☿ | ♀ | ⊕ | ♂ | ♃ | ♄ | ♅ | ♆ | ♇ | Vernal Point |
|---|---|---|---|---|---|---|---|---|---|---|---|---|
| 1 | MO | 8:45:42 | 10 ♊ 53 | 16 ♐ 24 | 17 ♋ 19 | 27 ♉ 1 | 14 ♑ 36 | 9 ♑ 33 | 14 ♈ 40 | 25 ♒ 23 | 29 ♐ 42 | 4 ♓ 57'57" |
| 2 | TU | 8:49:38 | 17 5 | 17 59 | 18 20 | 27 31 | 14 41 | 9 35 | 14 41 | 25 23 | 29 42 | 4 ♓ 57'57" |
| 3 | WE | 8:53:35 | 23 12 | 19 34 | 19 21 | 28 1 | 14 46 | 9 37 | 14 42 | 25 24 | 29 42 | 4 ♓ 57'56" |
| 4 | TH | 8:57:31 | 29 13 | 21 8 | 20 21 | 28 32 | 14 51 | 9 39 | 14 42 | 25 24 | 29 43 | 4 ♓ 57'56" |
| 5 | FR | 9: 1:28 | 5 ♋ 7 | 22 43 | 21 22 | 29 2 | 14 56 | 9 41 | 14 43 | 25 24 | 29 43 | 4 ♓ 57'56" |
| 6 | SA | 9: 5:24 | 10 52 | 24 18 | 22 23 | 29 32 | 15 2 | 9 43 | 14 44 | 25 25 | 29 43 | 4 ♓ 57'56" |
| 7 | SU | 9: 9:21 | 16 29 | 25 53 | 23 24 | 0 ♊ 2 | 15 7 | 9 44 | 14 44 | 25 25 | 29 44 | 4 ♓ 57'56" |
| 8 | MO | 9:13:18 | 21 56 | 27 28 | 24 25 | 0 32 | 15 12 | 9 46 | 14 45 | 25 26 | 29 44 | 4 ♓ 57'56" |
| 9 | TU | 9:17:14 | 27 14 | 29 3 | 25 26 | 1 2 | 15 17 | 9 48 | 14 46 | 25 26 | 29 44 | 4 ♓ 57'56" |
| 10 | WE | 9:21:11 | 2 ♌ 22 | 0 ♑ 38 | 26 26 | 1 31 | 15 23 | 9 50 | 14 46 | 25 26 | 29 44 | 4 ♓ 57'56" |
| 11 | TH | 9:25: 7 | 7 20 | 2 12 | 27 27 | 2 1 | 15 28 | 9 52 | 14 47 | 25 27 | 29 45 | 4 ♓ 57'55" |
| 12 | FR | 9:29: 4 | 12 9 | 3 47 | 28 28 | 2 31 | 15 33 | 9 54 | 14 48 | 25 27 | 29 45 | 4 ♓ 57'55" |
| 13 | SA | 9:33: 0 | 16 48 | 5 22 | 29 28 | 3 1 | 15 38 | 9 55 | 14 48 | 25 27 | 29 45 | 4 ♓ 57'55" |
| 14 | SU | 9:36:57 | 21 19 | 6 57 | 0 ♌ 29 | 3 30 | 15 43 | 9 57 | 14 49 | 25 28 | 29 46 | 4 ♓ 57'55" |
| 15 | MO | 9:40:53 | 25 41 | 8 32 | 1 30 | 4 0 | 15 49 | 9 59 | 14 50 | 25 28 | 29 46 | 4 ♓ 57'55" |
| 16 | TU | 9:44:50 | 29 54 | 10 7 | 2 30 | 4 30 | 15 54 | 10 1 | 14 50 | 25 28 | 29 46 | 4 ♓ 57'55" |
| 17 | WE | 9:48:47 | 4 ♍ 0 | 11 42 | 3 31 | 4 59 | 15 59 | 10 3 | 14 51 | 25 29 | 29 47 | 4 ♓ 57'55" |
| 18 | TH | 9:52:43 | 7 59 | 13 16 | 4 31 | 5 29 | 16 4 | 10 5 | 14 52 | 25 29 | 29 47 | 4 ♓ 57'54" |
| 19 | FR | 9:56:40 | 11 50 | 14 51 | 5 32 | 5 58 | 16 10 | 10 6 | 14 52 | 25 30 | 29 47 | 4 ♓ 57'54" |
| 20 | SA | 10: 0:36 | 15 35 | 16 26 | 6 33 | 6 27 | 16 15 | 10 8 | 14 53 | 25 30 | 29 47 | 4 ♓ 57'54" |
| 21 | SU | 10: 4:33 | 19 14 | 18 1 | 7 33 | 6 57 | 16 20 | 10 10 | 14 54 | 25 30 | 29 48 | 4 ♓ 57'54" |
| 22 | MO | 10: 8:29 | 22 47 | 19 36 | 8 33 | 7 26 | 16 26 | 10 12 | 14 54 | 25 31 | 29 48 | 4 ♓ 57'54" |
| 23 | TU | 10:12:26 | 26 15 | 21 11 | 9 34 | 7 55 | 16 30 | 10 14 | 14 55 | 25 31 | 29 48 | 4 ♓ 57'54" |
| 24 | WE | 10:16:22 | 29 37 | 22 46 | 10 34 | 8 25 | 16 36 | 10 15 | 14 56 | 25 31 | 29 49 | 4 ♓ 57'54" |
| 25 | TH | 10:20:19 | 2 ♎ 56 | 24 21 | 11 35 | 8 54 | 16 41 | 10 17 | 14 56 | 25 32 | 29 49 | 4 ♓ 57'53" |
| 26 | FR | 10:24:16 | 6 10 | 25 56 | 12 35 | 9 23 | 16 46 | 10 19 | 14 57 | 25 32 | 29 49 | 4 ♓ 57'53" |
| 27 | SA | 10:28:12 | 9 20 | 27 31 | 13 35 | 9 52 | 16 51 | 10 21 | 14 58 | 25 32 | 29 49 | 4 ♓ 57'53" |
| 28 | SU | 10:32: 9 | 12 27 | 29 6 | 14 35 | 10 21 | 16 57 | 10 23 | 14 58 | 25 33 | 29 50 | 4 ♓ 57'53" |

### INGRESSES:

| | |
|---|---|
| 4 ☿ → ♋ 3: 8 | |
| 6 ♂ → ♊ 22:39 | |
| 9 ☿ → ♌ 12:51 | |
| ♀ → ♑ 14:28 | |
| 13 ⊕ → ♌ 12:29 | |
| 16 ☿ → ♍ 0:32 | |
| 24 ☿ → ♎ 2:42 | |
| 28 ♀ → ♒ 13:43 | |

### ASPECTS (HELIOCENTRIC +MOON(TYCHONIC)):

| | | | |
|---|---|---|---|
| 2 ♃ □ ♅ 0:41 | ☿ ☍ ♃ 18: 0 | 13 ☽ ☍ ☿ 8:17 | 19 ♀ □ ♅ 0:12 | 26 ☽ ☍ ♀ 1:45 |
| ♀ ☌ ♆ 4:40 | 7 ☽ ☌ ♆ 21:40 | ♀ ☌ A 20:55 | 27 ☿ □ ♅ 7:52 |
| ☽ □ ♀ 10:38 | ☽ ☌ ♂ 12:45 | 14 ☽ □ ♂ 13:36 | 20 ♀ ☌ A 5:52 | 28 ☽ ☍ ♆ 3:41 |
| ☽ □ ☿ 14: 1 | 8 ☿ ☌ Ω 7:14 | ☿ ☍ ♆ 22:48 | 21 ☽ □ ♆ 9:16 | ☿ ☍ ♅ 19:51 |
| 3 ☽ □ ♆ 5:18 | ☿ ☌ ⊕ 13:46 | 15 ♀ ☌ ♄ 22:29 | 22 ☽ ☌ ♂ 9: 0 |
| ☽ □ ♄ 22: 9 | 9 ♀ ☌ ♇ 10:29 | 16 ☽ □ ♆ 16:44 | 24 ☿ □ ♀ 1:20 |
| 4 ☽ ☍ ♅ 1:58 | ☽ ☌ ♀ 16: 5 | 17 ♀ □ ♂ 6:41 | ☽ □ ♂ 2:56 |
| ☽ ☍ ♇ 6:45 | ☽ ☌ ♀ 16:49 | ☽ □ ♄ 13:28 | ☽ □ ♀ 3:28 |
| ☽ □ ♃ 7: 2 | 10 ☽ ☌ ♄ 9:58 | ☽ □ ♀ 19:21 | ☽ ☍ ♄ 21:58 |
| 5 ☿ ☍ ♄ 19: 4 | ☽ □ ♅ 18:47 | ☽ ☌ ♅ 23:11 | 25 ☽ □ ♅ 6:16 |
| 6 ☿ □ ♅ 16:27 | | 18 ☽ □ ♃ 1:39 | ☽ ☍ ♃ 9:25 |

Into creative world existence
    (*Mars in Taurus*)
May world-being's vigilance grow in power
    (*Jupiter in Capricorn*)
And may the might of life's activity flower
    (*Saturn in Capricorn*)
O worlds, uphold worlds!
    (*Moon in Libra*)[32]

**February 4–6, Mercury is opposite Saturn. This alignment is exact on February 5: Mercury 9°42' Cancer opposite Saturn 9°42' Capricorn.** Simultaneously, Mercury comes into opposition with Jupiter, between February 5–7. This alignment is exact on **February 6: Mercury 15°6' Cancer opposite Jupiter 15°6' Capricorn.**

Mercury was opposite to Saturn, with Mercury in Capricorn and Saturn in Cancer, on July 16 AD 32:

> Jesus, accompanied by some apostles, returned to the little village where the three holy women were waiting for him. Together they received the news of Lazarus's death. It was here that Jesus spoke the words: "Our friend Lazarus had fallen asleep." (John 11:7–13)[33]

Mercury in Libra was opposite Jupiter in Aries (square to today's alignment) on October 9 AD 30:

> Next morning Jesus went from house to house, exhorting the people to turn away from their avarice and love of gain, and engaging them to attend the instruction to be given in the synagogue. He saluted all with a congratulatory word on the close of the feast. The people of Ophra were so usurious and unpolished that they were held in the same low esteem as the publicans. But they had now improved a little. That afternoon the branches of which the tabernacles had been formed were brought processionally by the boys to the square in front of the synagogue, there piled in a heap, and burned. The Jews watched with interest the rising of the flames, presaging from their various movements good or bad fortune. Jesus preached afterward in the synagogue, taking for his subjects the happiness of Adam, his Fall, the Promise, and

some passages from Joshua. He spoke also of too great solicitude for the things of life, of the lilies that do not spin, of the ravens that do not sow, etc., and brought forward examples in the persons of Daniel and Job. They, he said, were men of piety, engrossed in occupations, but still without worldly solicitude.[34]

Mercury opposite Pluto, Saturn, and Jupiter takes us from Moses's teachings concerning marriage—the alchemical wedding of opposites, with which both Mercury–Hermes and Pluto–Phanes are concerned—to Lazarus's journey to the Mother in the Underworld (Mercury as Lazarus, Saturn as the Mother), and finally to Christ's teachings concerning Adam. There is an open secret in this procession from Moses, to Lazarus, to Adam. Notice that when Christ speaks of Adam, he speaks of the lily and the raven. Adam later reincarnated as Elijah, who was fed by ravens in the wilderness. And juxtaposed to Lazarus–John (who represents the spiritual stream of the Red Rose) is John the Baptist, another incarnation of Adam, who represents the spiritual stream of the White Lily—of the original purity that humanity had in Paradise.

**February 6: Mars enters Gemini.**
May the future rest upon the past
    (*Sun in Capricorn*)
In existence growth's power dies
    (*Venus in Sagittarius*)
Warm soul life
    (*Mercury in Cancer*)
Toward life's mighty weaving
    (*Mars in Gemini*)
May world-being's vigilance grow in power
    (*Jupiter in Capricorn*)
And may the might of life's activity flower
    (*Saturn in Capricorn*)
Being sustains beings!
    (*Moon in Scorpio*)[35]

Starting February 6, the central alignment of the year begins to take shape; Saturn in Capricorn comes into square alignment with Uranus in Aries. They will not be exactly square until October 18.

---

32 Steiner, *Twelve Cosmic Moods.*
33 Ibid., p. 475.

34 Ibid., p. 74.
35 Steiner, *Twelve Cosmic Moods.*

These two planets follow an approximately 45-year cycle; see the "Editorial Foreword" for a more in-depth exploration.

**February 7–9, the Sun is opposite Mercury.** This alignment is exact on **February 8, Sun 24°59' Capricorn opposite Mercury 24°59' Cancer.** Simultaneously, Venus and Pluto come into conjunction, exact on **February 9: Venus conjunct Pluto 29°44' Sagittarius.** Sun and Mercury were opposed in the same signs as they are today on December 24 AD 29:

> Jesus taught again, morning and afternoon, in the synagogue. After the close of the sabbath, Jesus went with his disciples into a little valley near the synagogue. It seemed intended for a promenade or a place of seclusion. There were trees in front of the entrance, as well as in the valley. The sons of Mary Cleophas, of Zebedee, and some others of the disciples were with him. But Philip, who was backward and humble, hung behind, not certain as to whether he should or should not follow. Jesus, who was going on before, turned his head and, addressing Philip, said, "Follow me!" at which words Philip went on joyously with the others. There were about twelve in the little band.
>
> Jesus taught here under a tree, his subject being "Vocation and Correspondence." Andrew, who was full of zeal for his Master's interests, rejoiced at the happy impression made upon the disciples by the teaching of Jesus on the preceding sabbath. He saw them convinced that Jesus was the Messiah, and his own heart was so full that he lost no opportunity to recount to them again and again all that he had seen at Jesus's baptism, also the miracles he had wrought.
>
> I heard Jesus calling Heaven to witness that they should behold still greater things, and he spoke of his mission from his heavenly Father.[36]

Venus was conjunct Pluto in Sagittarius on April 5 AD 30. This was Passover, which Christ and his disciples celebrated at the house of Lazarus:

> The Passover supper was very different from Jesus's last Passover supper, more strictly Judaical. Each here held a staff in his hand, was girded as for a journey, and all ate in haste. Jesus had two staves placed crosswise before him. They chanted psalms and, standing, quickly consumed the paschal lambs. Later on they placed themselves at table in a recumbent position. This supper was different also from that customary among the other Jews at this feast. Jesus explained all to the guests, but omitted the ceremonies that had been added by the Pharisees. He carved the three lambs himself and served at table, saying that he did it as their servant. They remained together far into the night, singing and praying.
>
> Jerusalem was so still and solemn during that whole day. The Jews not engaged in the slaughtering of the lambs remained shut up in their houses, which were ornamented with dark green foliage. The immense multitude of people were, after the slaughtering, so busy in the interior of their homes, and all was so still that it produced upon me quite a melancholy impression.
>
> I saw on that day also where all the paschal lambs for the numerous strangers, of whom many were encamped before the gates, were roasted. Both outside and inside the city, there were built on certain places long, low walls, but so broad that one could walk on them. In these walls were furnace after furnace, and at certain distances lived men who attended to them, and received a small remuneration for their services. At these furnaces travelers and strangers could, at the different feasts, or at any other time, roast their meat and cook any kind of food. The consuming of the fat of the paschal lambs went on in the temple far into the night. After the first watch the altar was purified, and the doors thrown open at a very early hour the next morning.[37]

**February 9: Venus enters Capricorn; Mercury enters Leo.**

> May the future rest upon the past
>     (*Sun in Capricorn*)
> May the past feel the future
>     (*Venus in Capricorn*)
> The essence of feeling beings
>     (*Mercury in Leo*)
> Toward life's mighty weaving
>     (*Mars in Gemini*)

36 ACE, vol. 1, p. 382.

37 Ibid., pp. 422–423.

May world-being's vigilance grow in power
    (*Jupiter in Capricorn*)
And may the might of life's activity flower
    (*Saturn in Capricorn*)
May existence feel existence!
    (*Moon in Sagittarius*)[38]

**February 11: New Moon, 28°15' Capricorn.** A New Moon occurred close to this degree on January 11 AD 31:

> Jesus taught in the synagogue of Hebron on the occasion of a festival celebrated in memory of the expulsion from the Sanhedrin of the Sadducees who, under Alexander Jannaeus, had been the domineering party. There were three triumphal arches erected around the synagogue, and to them vine leaves, ears of corn, and all kinds of floral wreaths were brought. The people formed a procession through the streets, which were strewn with flowers, for it was likewise the beginning of the Feast of the New Moon, that of the sap's rising, and lastly that of the purification of the four-year-old trees. It was on this account that so many arches of leaves and flowers were erected. This Feast of the Expulsion of the Sadducees (who denied the resurrection) coincided very appropriately with that upon which was celebrated the return of the trees to new life.[39]

**February 13: Sun enters Aquarius.**

May the limited yield to the unlimited
    (*Sun in Aquarius*)
May the past feel the future
    (*Venus in Capricorn*)
The essence of feeling beings
    (*Mercury in Leo*)
Toward life's mighty weaving
    (*Mars in Gemini*)
May world-being's vigilance grow in power
    (*Jupiter in Capricorn*)
And may the might of life's activity flower
    (*Saturn in Capricorn*)
Limit thyself, O unlimited!
    (*Moon in Aquarius*)[40]

---

38 Steiner, *Twelve Cosmic Moods.*
39 ACE, vol. 2, p. 209.
40 Steiner, *Twelve Cosmic Moods.*

**February 13–15, Mercury comes into alignment with Neptune.** This is exact on **February 14: Mercury 25°28' Leo opposite Neptune 25°28' Aquarius.** Simultaneously, between February 12–18, Venus comes into alignment with Saturn, exact on **February 15: Venus conjunct Saturn 10°1' Capricorn.**

Mercury and Neptune were opposed in these same signs on August 23 AD 32. This star memory returns us to, and clarifies, the star memory of Venus square Neptune from January 18, when Christ attended a wedding in Sichar:

> …wedding festivities were held in the public house used on such occasions, during which Jesus related many parables, such as that of the prodigal son and the mansions in his Father's house. The bridegroom had no house of his own. He was to make his home in that belonging to the mother of his bride. Jesus told him that, until he should receive a mansion in his Father's house, he should take up his abode under a tent in the vineyard which he himself was going to lay out on the mount of bees.
>
> Then he again taught on marriage, upon which he dwelt for a long time. If married people, he said, would live together modestly and chastely, if they would recognize their state as one of penance, then would they lead their children in the way of salvation, then would their state become not a means of diverting souls from their end, but one that would reap a harvest for those mansions in his Father's house. In this instruction, Jesus called himself the spouse of a bride in whom all those that should be gathered, would be born again. He alluded to the marriage feast of Cana, and told of the changing of water into wine. He always spoke of himself in the third person, as of that man in Judea whom he knew so well, who would be so bitterly persecuted, and who would finally be put to death.
>
> The people heard all this in simple, childlike faith, and the parables were for them real facts. The bridegroom appeared to be a school teacher, for Jesus told him how he should teach by his own example.[41]

Meanwhile, Venus and Saturn were conjunct on June 22 AD 32:

---

41 ACE, vol. 2, p. 490.

Jesus taught again in the village. He said that he had come to bring a sword (Matt. 10:34–36). The disciples were confused by this utterance, but Jesus explained to them that he meant the renunciation of all evil.

Mercury and Neptune working together bring clarity to the depths of one's subconscious emotional life. Venus and Saturn working together bring devotional warmth into the dictates of conscience. These are good aspects for moral development.

### February 15: Mercury enters Virgo.

May the limited yield to the unlimited.
(*Sun in Aquarius*)
May the past feel the future.
(*Venus in Capricorn*)
May the spirit penetrate being
(*Mercury in Virgo*)
Toward life's mighty weaving.
(*Mars in Gemini*)
May world-being's vigilance grow in power
(*Jupiter in Capricorn*)
And may the might of life's activity flower.
(*Saturn in Capricorn*)
May loss be gain in itself!
(*Moon in Pisces*)[42]

### February 16–17: Mardis Gras into Ash Wednesday.
We begin the season of Lent with the meeting of absolute levity (Mardis Gras) and absolute gravity (Ash Wednesday). Mardis Gras invites us into the playful masquerade of the little child, while Ash Wednesday gives us the blessed reminder that becomes ever stronger as we approach old age: "Remember you are Dust, and to Dust you shall return." It is the season to separate the essential from the inessential. Learn what in your life is Dust—the frivolous drama of Mardis Gras—that will pass away with your own physical death. The seeds that remain are what you will carry with you into the heavenly spheres, and cultivate for your next life. Take care, however, as outwardly dust and seeds can be deceptively similar.

February 15–21, Venus comes into square alignment with Uranus. This is exact on **February 18, Venus 14°52' Capricorn square Uranus 14°52' Aries.** Simultaneously, Venus comes into conjunction with Jupiter between February 16–23, exact on **February 19: Venus conjunct Jupiter, 16°14' Capricorn.**

While the Venus–Uranus square, at these degrees, last occurred in June, 1937—just in between the Hindenburg disaster in May and the disappearance of Amelia Earhart in July—Venus conjunct Jupiter in Capricorn reminds us of December 8 AD 30, when Venus at 14° Capricorn was square Jupiter, 14° Aries:

When [Christ] went back to Capernaum, a man mute, blind, and possessed by demons came to meet him, and Jesus cured him instantaneously. This miracle created intense astonishment, for even when approaching Jesus, the man had recovered his speech and cried out: "Jesus, thou Son of David, have mercy on me!" Jesus touched his eyes, and he saw. He was possessed of many devils, having been wholly perverted by the pagans on the other side of the lake. The sorcerers and soothsayers of the land of Gergesa had seized upon him. They dragged him around with them by a cord and exhibited him in other places, where they showed off his strength in all kinds of skillful feats. They showed how he, though blind and mute, still could accomplish everything, could know and understand all, could go everywhere, could bring everything and know everything by virtue of certain incantations, for all this the demon performed in him. These pagan sorcerers from Gergesa, who were ever wandering through the Decapolis and other cities, used the devil by means of that poor creature to help them earn their bread. If they journeyed over the sea, their miserable victim was not allowed to go on board a ship, but at the command of his masters, he was obliged to swim like a dog at its side. No one any longer troubled himself about him, for he was looked upon as forever lost. Most of the time he had no place of shelter. He lay in tombs and caves and endured all manner of ill treatment from his cruel masters. The poor wretch had long been in Capernaum, and yet no one had led

---

42 Steiner, *Twelve Cosmic Moods.*

him to Jesus. Now, however, he went to him himself and was cured.[43]

Our modern day "sorcerers and soothsayers" control us via the modern "cord" of the mobile device, and command the "demon" of mass- and/or social-media saturation. We, too, can ask Christ for mercy.

**February 23: Mercury enters Libra.**

May the limited yield to the unlimited
    (*Sun in Aquarius*)
May the past feel the future
    (*Venus in Capricorn*)
In existing, embrace existence
    (*Mercury in Libra*)
Toward life's mighty weaving
    (*Mars in Gemini*)
May world-being's vigilance grow in power
    (*Jupiter in Capricorn*)
And may the might of life's activity flower
    (*Saturn in Capricorn*)
O Sun life, endure!
    (*Moon in Gemini*)[44]

**February 27: Full Moon, 13°55' Leo.** Solar return of Rudolf Steiner's birthday (Feb. 25, 1861) and Valentin Tomberg's birthday (February 26, 1900).

The Full Moon was in Leo on January 27 AD 31. This star memory returns us to, and further illumines, the star memory we remembered last month when Mars was conjunct the Node (see the entry for January 26, when we remember the events of January 28 AD 31):

During the day Jesus called before him the apostles and disciples, two by two, as he had sent them, and received from them an account of all that had happened to them during their mission. He solved the doubts and difficulties that had arisen in certain circumstances, and instructed them how they should act in the future. He told them again that he would soon give them a new mission. The six apostles who had been laboring in Upper Galilee had been well received. They had found the people well

disposed and had in consequence baptized many. The others, who had gone to Judea, had not baptized any, and here and there had experienced contradiction.

The crowd around the house becoming greater and greater, Jesus and his followers slipped away secretly. The stars shed their light down upon the little party as they hurried along the bypaths to Peter's boat. They ferried across the lake and landed between Matthew's custom house and little Chorazin.[45]

**February 26 and March 2, Mercury is opposite Uranus.** Their alignment is exact on **February 28: Mercury 14°59' Libra opposite Uranus 14°59' Aries.** These two were last aligned at these degrees in February 1937—most of the aspects involving Uranus in Aries will draw our gaze back to this tragic and pivotal time period. Simultaneously with this aspect, **Venus enters Aquarius:**

May the limited yield to the unlimited
    (*Sun in Aquarius*)
What lacks boundaries should
    (*Venus in Aquarius*)
In existing, embrace existence
    (*Mercury in Libra*)
Toward life's mighty weaving
    (*Mars in Gemini*)
May world-being's vigilance grow in power
    (*Jupiter in Capricorn*)
And may the might of life's activity flower
    (*Saturn in Capricorn*)
O soul, know thou beings!
    (*Moon in Virgo*)[46]

# MARCH 2021

## STARGAZING PREVIEW

Sunset on the 3rd will bring the beautiful sight of Mars just below the *Pleiades*, at 5° Taurus; he'll be just past culmination, in the southwest. As

43 Ibid., p. 174.
44 Steiner, *Twelve Cosmic Moods.*
45 ACE, vol. 2, p. 297.
46 Steiner, *Twelve Cosmic Moods.*

the Last Quarter Moon (21° Scorpio) rises at 0200 on the 6th, look for Leo high in the south, ruling all that he can see. The Moon will have the night sky to itself until 0530, when Saturn rises, followed by Jupiter twenty minutes later. It might be possible to see Mercury as well, rising concurrently with Jupiter—as it has again reached its greatest elongation from the Sun. Good luck!

It might be worth your while to rise early on the 10th, as you'll be able to see Saturn, the Moon, and Jupiter (all in Capricorn) rise in a tight cluster, beginning at 0530. Don't forget to look to the southeast for the Scorpion; if the sky is very clear, you might even be able to see the Milky Way weaving between Scorpio and the risen planets, its stars sprinkled throughout Sagittarius—the Archer.

How appropriate that March's New Moon, at 28° Aquarius, marks its position at the end of Christ's Forty Days in the Wilderness, when the angels ministered to him—for it is Aquarius that teaches us of the communion that we might have with our angel. The New Moon will occur on the 13th, leaving Mars alone to the night sky until 0500, when Saturn and Jupiter rise. The Sun reaches Pisces on the 15th, whence streams magnanimous love for all that lives.

Be sure to mark your calendars for the evening of the 19th: you'll be able to view the Moon move below Mars just as it sails atop *Aldebaran*, the star marking the eye of the Bull—and all before 2015! At 0937 the following morning, spring will be announced as the Sun reaches the Vernal Equinox. Are we listening?

Dusk on Sunday the 21st will be the start of a lovely evening; the Lion will have just risen in the east, while the First Quarter Moon (6° Gemini) will be visible high in the southern sky. Over the next few nights, the waxing Moon will weave its way under *Pollux* (Gemini), over the *Beehive* (Cancer) and above *Regulus* (Leo) as it makes its way around the zodiacal circle. The early hours of the 26th will celebrate the superior conjunction of the Sun and Venus, after which she'll be an evening star again. Hallelujah!

March's Full Moon (13° Virgo) rises on the 28th; at that time, Mars will be high in the southwest, to

*Aldebaran*'s left by fewer than 5°. At the close of the month, Saturn and Jupiter rise two hours and ninety minutes, respectively, ahead of the Sun. At dusk, you'll find Orion and Mars high in the southwest; they set at midnight.

## MARCH COMMENTARIES

February 28 and March 10, the Sun is square the Node. This alignment is exact on **March 5: Sun 20°19' Aquarius square Node 20°19' Taurus.** This same aspect, at 19° Aquarius and Taurus, occurred on February 7 AD 31:

> On this journey Jesus further instructed the twelve and the disciples exactly how to proceed in the future when healing the sick and exorcising the possessed, as he himself did in such cases. He imparted to them the power and the courage always to effect, by imposition of hands and anointing with oil, what he himself could do. This communication of power took place without the imposition of hands, though not without a substantial transmission. They stood around Jesus, and I saw rays darting toward them of different colors, according to the nature of the gifts received and the particular disposition of each recipient. They exclaimed: "Lord, we feel ourselves imbued with strength! Thy words are truth and life!" And now each knew just what he had to do in every case in order to effect a cure. There was no room left for either choice or reflection.[47]

The Sun in dynamic alignment with the Node brings an enormous clarity from our Higher Self, imbuing us with new strength of will.

**March 5: Mercury enters Scorpio.**

> May the limited yield to the unlimited
> > (*Sun in Aquarius*)
> What lacks boundaries should find
> > (*Venus in Aquarius*)
> In activity growth disappears
> > (*Mercury in Scorpio*)
> Toward life's mighty weaving
> > (*Mars in Gemini*)

---

47 ACE, vol. 2, p. 307.

May world-being's vigilance grow in power
   (*Jupiter in Capricorn*)
And may the might of life's activity flower
   (*Saturn in Capricorn*)
Being sustains beings
   (*Moon in Scorpio*)[48]

**March 5–15, the Sun and Neptune conjoin**, exact on **March 10: Sun and Neptune 25°37' Aquarius.** Simultaneously, Venus and Node come into square alignment. They are within 5° of each other from March 9 until March 15, exact on **March 12: Venus 19°33' Aquarius square Node 19°33' Taurus.** During this same time period, Mercury is conjunct the Descending Node from March 11–14, exact on **March 12: Mercury and South Node 19°32' Scorpio.**

The Sun and Neptune were conjunct in Aquarius on January 19 AD 33. Christ had only recently returned, with the three shepherd youths, from his journeys in Egypt:

On the journey from Shechem to Ephron it was very foggy, and quantities of rain fell. Jesus did not confine himself to the straight route. He went to different localities, different towns and houses, consoling the inhabitants, healing the sick, and exhorting all to follow him. The apostles and disciples likewise did not take the direct road to the places to which they were sent, but turned off into the farms and houses lying along their way in order to announce Jesus's coming. It was as if all who sighed after salvation were to be again stirred up, as if the sheep that had strayed in the forest because their shepherd had gone away were, now that he had come back, to be gathered again by the shepherd servants into one herd. When, toward evening, Jesus with the three disciples arrived at Ephron, he went into the houses, cured the sick, and called upon all to follow him to the school. This place had a large synagogue, consisting of two halls, one above and the other below. A crowd of people, men and women, some from Ephron and some from neighboring places, flocked to the instruction. The synagogue was crowded. Jesus directed a chair to be placed in the center of the hall whence he taught first the men and then the women. The latter were standing back, but the men gave place to them. Jesus taught upon the necessity of following him, upon his approaching end, and upon the chastisement that would fall on all that would not believe. Murmuring arose in the crowd, for there were many wicked souls among them.[49]

Venus was square the Node very close to the same degree as it is on the 12th on January 1 AD 31. This was one day prior to the beheading of John the Baptist:

In the morning Jesus healed the brother and two sisters of the child whom he had cured yesterday. All three were feebleminded.... He performed the cure by the imposition of hands. When restored to sense, the children appeared to be perfectly amazed, and as if awaking from a dream. They had always thought that people wanted to kill them, and had in particular a great dread of fire. When on the day before Jesus healed the elder boy, he told (very unusual for him) the father to go out and relate to all what had taken place. The consequence was a great concourse of people, among them numbers of sick, and that morning I saw Jesus instructing the people on the street, and curing and blessing many of the children.

After that I saw him with Peter and John journeying rapidly the whole day and night through the plain of Esdrelon in the direction of Ginea. They seldom paused to rest. I heard Jesus saying on the way that John's end was approaching, and after that, his enemies would begin their pursuit of himself. But it was not lawful to expose one's self to one's enemies. I think I understood that they were going to Hebron, to console John's relatives and prevent any imprudent manifestation.[50]

There is a deep and mysterious connection between John the Baptist and the developmentally challenged in our time. His literal beheading—a private entertainment for the elite—occurred just after Christ very publicly returned the "spiritual head" to these children.

---

48 Steiner, *Twelve Cosmic Moods*.

49 ACE, vol. 2, p. 523.
50 Ibid., p. 197.

## SIDEREAL GEOCENTRIC LONGITUDES : MARCH 2021 Gregorian at 0 hours UT

| DAY | ☉ | ☽ | ☊ | ☿ | ♀ | ♂ | ♃ | ♄ | ♅ | ♆ | ♇ |
|---|---|---|---|---|---|---|---|---|---|---|---|
| 1 MO | 15 ♒ 35 | 7 ♍ 50 | 20 ♉ 42R | 19 ♑ 4 | 9 ♒ 17 | 3 ♉ 9 | 21 ♑ 35 | 13 ♑ 26 | 12 ♈ 34 | 25 ♒ 14 | 0 ♑ 59 |
| 2 TU | 16 35 | 22 26 | 20 33 | 19 49 | 10 32 | 3 43 | 21 48 | 13 32 | 12 36 | 25 16 | 1 1 |
| 3 WE | 17 35 | 7 ♎ 1 | 20 25 | 20 37 | 11 47 | 4 18 | 22 2 | 13 39 | 12 38 | 25 18 | 1 2 |
| 4 TH | 18 36 | 21 28 | 20 21 | 21 28 | 13 1 | 4 53 | 22 15 | 13 45 | 12 41 | 25 20 | 1 4 |
| 5 FR | 19 36 | 5 ♏ 44 | 20 20 | 22 23 | 14 16 | 5 28 | 22 29 | 13 51 | 12 43 | 25 23 | 1 5 |
| 6 SA | 20 36 | 19 48 | 20 19 | 23 20 | 15 31 | 6 2 | 22 42 | 13 57 | 12 45 | 25 25 | 1 7 |
| 7 SU | 21 36 | 3 ♐ 38 | 20 19 | 24 20 | 16 46 | 6 37 | 22 56 | 14 4 | 12 48 | 25 27 | 1 8 |
| 8 MO | 22 36 | 17 16 | 20 18 | 25 23 | 18 1 | 7 12 | 23 9 | 14 10 | 12 50 | 25 29 | 1 10 |
| 9 TU | 23 36 | 0 ♑ 43 | 20 14 | 26 29 | 19 16 | 7 47 | 23 22 | 14 16 | 12 53 | 25 32 | 1 11 |
| 10 WE | 24 36 | 13 58 | 20 8 | 27 36 | 20 31 | 8 22 | 23 36 | 14 22 | 12 55 | 25 34 | 1 12 |
| 11 TH | 25 36 | 27 2 | 19 58 | 28 46 | 21 46 | 8 58 | 23 49 | 14 28 | 12 58 | 25 36 | 1 14 |
| 12 FR | 26 36 | 9 ♒ 56 | 19 46 | 29 58 | 23 1 | 9 33 | 24 2 | 14 34 | 13 0 | 25 38 | 1 15 |
| 13 SA | 27 36 | 22 37 | 19 32 | 1 ♒ 11 | 24 15 | 10 8 | 24 15 | 14 40 | 13 3 | 25 41 | 1 16 |
| 14 SU | 28 36 | 5 ♓ 7 | 19 18 | 2 27 | 25 30 | 10 43 | 24 28 | 14 46 | 13 6 | 25 43 | 1 17 |
| 15 MO | 29 35 | 17 24 | 19 5 | 3 44 | 26 45 | 11 19 | 24 41 | 14 51 | 13 8 | 25 45 | 1 19 |
| 16 TU | 0 ♓ 35 | 29 31 | 18 54 | 5 3 | 28 0 | 11 54 | 24 54 | 14 57 | 13 11 | 25 48 | 1 20 |
| 17 WE | 1 35 | 11 ♈ 27 | 18 46 | 6 24 | 29 15 | 12 29 | 25 7 | 15 3 | 13 14 | 25 50 | 1 21 |
| 18 TH | 2 35 | 23 18 | 18 41 | 7 46 | 0 ♓ 29 | 13 5 | 25 20 | 15 8 | 13 17 | 25 52 | 1 22 |
| 19 FR | 3 34 | 5 ♉ 5 | 18 38 | 9 10 | 1 44 | 13 40 | 25 32 | 15 14 | 13 19 | 25 54 | 1 23 |
| 20 SA | 4 34 | 16 53 | 18 37 | 10 35 | 2 59 | 14 16 | 25 45 | 15 19 | 13 22 | 25 57 | 1 24 |
| 21 SU | 5 34 | 28 48 | 18 37D | 12 2 | 4 13 | 14 51 | 25 58 | 15 25 | 13 25 | 25 59 | 1 26 |
| 22 MO | 6 33 | 10 ♊ 55 | 18 37R | 13 30 | 5 28 | 15 27 | 26 10 | 15 30 | 13 28 | 26 1 | 1 27 |
| 23 TU | 7 33 | 23 19 | 18 36 | 14 59 | 6 43 | 16 3 | 26 23 | 15 35 | 13 31 | 26 3 | 1 28 |
| 24 WE | 8 32 | 6 ♋ 5 | 18 33 | 16 30 | 7 57 | 16 38 | 26 35 | 15 41 | 13 34 | 26 6 | 1 29 |
| 25 TH | 9 32 | 19 18 | 18 27 | 18 3 | 9 12 | 17 14 | 26 47 | 15 46 | 13 37 | 26 8 | 1 30 |
| 26 FR | 10 31 | 2 ♌ 59 | 18 19 | 19 36 | 10 27 | 17 50 | 27 0 | 15 51 | 13 40 | 26 10 | 1 31 |
| 27 SA | 11 30 | 17 8 | 18 10 | 21 11 | 11 41 | 18 25 | 27 12 | 15 56 | 13 43 | 26 12 | 1 31 |
| 28 SU | 12 30 | 1 ♍ 40 | 17 59 | 22 48 | 12 56 | 19 1 | 27 24 | 16 1 | 13 46 | 26 14 | 1 32 |
| 29 MO | 13 29 | 16 31 | 17 49 | 24 26 | 14 10 | 19 37 | 27 36 | 16 6 | 13 49 | 26 17 | 1 33 |
| 30 TU | 14 28 | 1 ♎ 30 | 17 41 | 26 5 | 15 25 | 20 13 | 27 48 | 16 11 | 13 52 | 26 19 | 1 34 |
| 31 WE | 15 28 | 16 29 | 17 35 | 27 45 | 16 39 | 20 49 | 28 0 | 16 16 | 13 55 | 26 21 | 1 35 |

### INGRESSES :

| | |
|---|---|
| 2 ☽ → ♎ 12:26 | 21 ☽ → ♊ 2:24 |
| 4 ☽ → ♏ 14:18 | 23 ☽ → ♋ 12:39 |
| 6 ☽ → ♐ 17:39 | 25 ☽ → ♌ 18:50 |
| 8 ☽ → ♑ 22:43 | 27 ☽ → ♍ 21:15 |
| 11 ☽ → ♒ 5:28 | 29 ☽ → ♎ 21:36 |
| 12 ☿ → ♒ 0:47 | 31 ☽ → ♏ 21:51 |
| 13 ☽ → ♓ 14: 7 | |
| 15 ☉ → ♓ 9:53 | |
| 16 ☽ → ♈ 0:58 | |
| 17 ♀ → ♓ 14:35 | |
| 18 ☽ → ♉ 13:39 | |

### ASPECTS & ECLIPSES :

| | | | |
|---|---|---|---|
| 2 ☽ ☌ P 4:57 | 11 ☉ ☌ ♆ 0: 9 | 21 ☉ □ ☽ 14:39 | 28 ☉ ☍ ☽ 18:47 |
| 3 ☽ ☍ ♅ 9:20 | ☽ ☌ ☿ 3:30 | 23 ☽ ☍ ♇ 15:24 | ☽ ☍ ♀ 19:53 |
| 4 ☽ ☍ ♂ 23:30 | 12 ☽ □S ☊ 18:14 | 24 ☿ □ ♂ 3:25 | 30 ☿ ☌ ♆ 3:28 |
| 5 ☿ ☌ ♃ 3:26 | 13 ☽ ☌ ♀ 3:28 | ☽ ☍ ♄ 17:37 | ☽ ☌ P 6: 1 |
| ☉ □ ☊ 17:29 | ☽ ☌ ♆ 5:51 | 25 ☿ □ ☊ 5:56 | ☽ ☍ ♅ 19:52 |
| 6 ☽ ☌ ☋ 0:54 | ☉ ☌ ☽ 10:20 | ☽ ☍ ♃ 13:26 | |
| ☉ □ ☽ 1:29 | 14 ♀ ☌ ♆ 4:14 | 26 ☉ S☌ ♀ 6:56 | |
| 9 ☽ ☌ ♇ 0:50 | 17 ☽ ☌ ♅ 3:35 | ♂ ☌ ☊ 15:47 | |
| ♀ □ ☊ 17:15 | 18 ☽ ☌ A 4:46 | 27 ☽ N□ ☊ 1:42 | |
| 10 ☽ ☌ ♄ 0:43 | 19 ☽ ☌ ♂ 18:24 | ☽ ☍ ☿ 7:36 | |
| ☽ ☌ ♃ 17:56 | 20 ☽ ☌ ☊ 3:30 | ☽ ☍ ♆ 15: 4 | |

## SIDEREAL HELIOCENTRIC LONGITUDES : MARCH 2021 Gregorian at 0 hours UT

| DAY | Sid. Time | ☿ | ♀ | ⊕ | ♂ | ♃ | ♄ | ♅ | ♆ | ♇ | Vernal Point |
|---|---|---|---|---|---|---|---|---|---|---|---|
| 1 MO | 10:36: 5 | 15 ♎ 30 | 0 ♒ 41 | 15 ♌ 36 | 10 ♊ 50 | 17 ♑ 2 | 10 ♑ 25 | 14 ♈ 59 | 25 ♒ 33 | 29 ♐ 50 | 4 ♓ 57'53" |
| 2 TU | 10:40: 2 | 18 31 | 2 16 | 16 36 | 11 19 | 17 7 | 10 27 | 14 59 | 25 34 | 29 50 | 4 ♓ 57'53" |
| 3 WE | 10:43:58 | 21 29 | 3 51 | 17 36 | 11 48 | 17 12 | 10 28 | 15 0 | 25 34 | 29 51 | 4 ♓ 57'53" |
| 4 TH | 10:47:55 | 24 24 | 5 26 | 18 36 | 12 17 | 17 17 | 10 30 | 15 1 | 25 34 | 29 51 | 4 ♓ 57'52" |
| 5 FR | 10:51:51 | 27 17 | 7 1 | 19 36 | 12 46 | 17 23 | 10 32 | 15 1 | 25 35 | 29 51 | 4 ♓ 57'52" |
| 6 SA | 10:55:48 | 0 ♏ 9 | 8 36 | 20 36 | 13 15 | 17 28 | 10 34 | 15 2 | 25 35 | 29 52 | 4 ♓ 57'52" |
| 7 SU | 10:59:45 | 2 59 | 10 11 | 21 36 | 13 43 | 17 33 | 10 36 | 15 3 | 25 35 | 29 52 | 4 ♓ 57'52" |
| 8 MO | 11: 3:41 | 5 47 | 11 46 | 22 36 | 14 12 | 17 38 | 10 38 | 15 3 | 25 36 | 29 52 | 4 ♓ 57'52" |
| 9 TU | 11: 7:38 | 8 35 | 13 21 | 23 36 | 14 41 | 17 44 | 10 39 | 15 4 | 25 36 | 29 52 | 4 ♓ 57'52" |
| 10 WE | 11:11:34 | 11 21 | 14 56 | 24 36 | 15 10 | 17 49 | 10 41 | 15 5 | 25 36 | 29 53 | 4 ♓ 57'52" |
| 11 TH | 11:15:31 | 14 7 | 16 31 | 25 36 | 15 38 | 17 54 | 10 43 | 15 5 | 25 37 | 29 53 | 4 ♓ 57'52" |
| 12 FR | 11:19:27 | 16 52 | 18 7 | 26 36 | 16 7 | 17 59 | 10 45 | 15 6 | 25 37 | 29 53 | 4 ♓ 57'51" |
| 13 SA | 11:23:24 | 19 36 | 19 42 | 27 36 | 16 35 | 18 5 | 10 47 | 15 7 | 25 38 | 29 54 | 4 ♓ 57'51" |
| 14 SU | 11:27:20 | 22 21 | 21 17 | 28 36 | 17 4 | 18 10 | 10 49 | 15 7 | 25 38 | 29 54 | 4 ♓ 57'51" |
| 15 MO | 11:31:17 | 25 6 | 22 52 | 29 36 | 17 32 | 18 15 | 10 50 | 15 8 | 25 38 | 29 54 | 4 ♓ 57'51" |
| 16 TU | 11:35:14 | 27 51 | 24 28 | 0 ♍ 36 | 18 1 | 18 20 | 10 52 | 15 9 | 25 39 | 29 54 | 4 ♓ 57'51" |
| 17 WE | 11:39:10 | 0 ♐ 36 | 26 3 | 1 36 | 18 29 | 18 26 | 10 54 | 15 9 | 25 39 | 29 55 | 4 ♓ 57'51" |
| 18 TH | 11:43: 7 | 3 23 | 27 38 | 2 35 | 18 57 | 18 31 | 10 56 | 15 10 | 25 39 | 29 55 | 4 ♓ 57'51" |
| 19 FR | 11:47: 3 | 6 10 | 29 13 | 3 35 | 19 26 | 18 36 | 10 58 | 15 11 | 25 40 | 29 55 | 4 ♓ 57'50" |
| 20 SA | 11:51: 0 | 8 58 | 0 ♓ 49 | 4 35 | 19 54 | 18 41 | 11 0 | 15 11 | 25 40 | 29 56 | 4 ♓ 57'50" |
| 21 SU | 11:54:56 | 11 47 | 2 24 | 5 34 | 20 22 | 18 47 | 11 1 | 15 12 | 25 40 | 29 56 | 4 ♓ 57'50" |
| 22 MO | 11:58:53 | 14 38 | 3 59 | 6 34 | 20 51 | 18 52 | 11 3 | 15 13 | 25 41 | 29 56 | 4 ♓ 57'50" |
| 23 TU | 12: 2:49 | 17 31 | 5 35 | 7 33 | 21 19 | 18 57 | 11 5 | 15 13 | 25 41 | 29 57 | 4 ♓ 57'50" |
| 24 WE | 12: 6:46 | 20 26 | 7 10 | 8 33 | 21 47 | 19 2 | 11 7 | 15 14 | 25 42 | 29 57 | 4 ♓ 57'50" |
| 25 TH | 12:10:43 | 23 23 | 8 46 | 9 32 | 22 15 | 19 8 | 11 9 | 15 15 | 25 42 | 29 57 | 4 ♓ 57'50" |
| 26 FR | 12:14:39 | 26 23 | 10 21 | 10 32 | 22 43 | 19 13 | 11 11 | 15 15 | 25 42 | 29 57 | 4 ♓ 57'49" |
| 27 SA | 12:18:36 | 29 25 | 11 57 | 11 31 | 23 11 | 19 18 | 11 12 | 15 16 | 25 43 | 29 58 | 4 ♓ 57'49" |
| 28 SU | 12:22:32 | 2 ♑ 30 | 13 32 | 12 30 | 23 39 | 19 23 | 11 14 | 15 17 | 25 43 | 29 58 | 4 ♓ 57'49" |
| 29 MO | 12:26:29 | 5 39 | 15 8 | 13 30 | 24 7 | 19 29 | 11 16 | 15 17 | 25 43 | 29 58 | 4 ♓ 57'49" |
| 30 TU | 12:30:25 | 8 51 | 16 43 | 14 29 | 24 35 | 19 34 | 11 18 | 15 18 | 25 44 | 29 59 | 4 ♓ 57'49" |
| 31 WE | 12:34:22 | 12 7 | 18 19 | 15 28 | 25 3 | 19 39 | 11 20 | 15 19 | 25 44 | 29 59 | 4 ♓ 57'49" |

### INGRESSES :

5 ☿ → ♏ 22:43
15 ⊕ → ♍ 9:39
16 ☿ → ♐ 18:44
19 ♀ → ♓ 11:43
27 ☿ → ♑ 4:33

### ASPECTS (HELIOCENTRIC +MOON(TYCHONIC)) :

| | | | | |
|---|---|---|---|---|
| 1 ☽ □ ♂ 5: 6 | 8 ☽ ☌ ♇ 22:29 | 15 ☽ □ ♂ 0:16 | ☽ ☌ ♂ 20: 1 | ☽ □ ♇ 21:33 |
| ☿ □ ♃ 12:29 | 9 ☽ ☌ ♄ 18: 1 | ☿ □ ♆ 4:43 | 23 ☽ ☍ ♇ 12:33 | 30 ☽ □ ☿ 15: 1 |
| 2 ☽ □ ♇ 12:10 | 10 ☽ □ ♅ 2: 1 | 16 ☽ □ ♇ 0:47 | 24 ☽ ☍ ♄ 9:15 | ☽ □ ♄ 15:42 |
| 3 ☽ □ ♄ 5:44 | ☽ ☌ ♃ 7: 4 | ♀ ☌ ♆ 17:58 | ☿ ☍ ♂ 13: 3 | ☿ ☌ ♄ 18:13 |
| ☽ ☍ ♅ 13:14 | 11 ⊕ ☍ ♆ 0: 9 | ☽ □ ♄ 22:52 | ☽ □ ♅ 16:43 | ☽ ☍ ♅ 22: 7 |
| ☿ ☌ ☋ 16:57 | 12 ☽ □ ☿ 16:41 | 17 ☽ ☌ ♅ 7:29 | ☽ ☍ ♃ 23:41 | 31 ☽ □ ♃ 5: 7 |
| ☽ □ ♃ 17: 0 | ☽ ☌ ♀ 17:38 | ☿ □ ⊕ 13:21 | 26 ♀ ☍ ⊕ 6:56 | ☿ □ ♅ 23: 5 |
| 4 ☽ ☌ ☿ 6: 9 | 13 ☿ □ ♀ 1:50 | ☽ □ ♃ 14:12 | 27 ☿ ☌ ♇ 4:15 | |
| 5 ☽ □ ♀ 2:26 | ☽ ☌ ♆ 5:44 | 20 ☽ □ ♆ 17:43 | ☽ ☍ ♆ 14:14 | |
| 6 ☽ □ ♆ 9:59 | 14 ☿ ☌ A 3:29 | 21 ☽ □ ♀ 8:16 | 28 ☽ ☍ ♀ 21:30 | |
| 7 ☽ ☍ ♂ 18:22 | ♀ □S ☊ 8:20 | 22 ☽ ☍ ☿ 9:29 | 29 ☽ □ ♂ 12:34 | |

Mercury was conjunct the South Node in Scorpio on October 22 AD 30:

A fast day commemorative of the putting out of Zedekiah's eyes by Nebuchadnezzar having begun, Jesus preached in the fields among the shepherds, also at Abraham's well. He spoke of the kingdom of god, declaring that it would pass from the Jews to the Gentiles, the latter of whom would even attain preeminence over the former. Obed afterward remarked to Jesus that if he preached to the Gentiles in that strain, they might possibly become proud. Jesus replied very graciously, and explained that it was just on account of their humility that they should reach the first place. He warned Obed and his people against the feeling of conscious rectitude and self-complacency to which they were predisposed. They in a measure distinguished themselves from their neighbors, and on account of their well-regulated life, their temperance, and the fruits of salvation amassed thereby, they esteemed themselves good and pleasing in the sight of God. Such sentiments might very easily end in pride. To guard against such a consequence, Jesus related the parable of the day laborers. He instructed the women also in their own separate pleasure garden, in which was a beautiful bower. To them he related the parable of the wise and foolish virgins. While so engaged, Jesus stood, and they sat around him in a terraced circle, one above another. They sat on the ground with one knee slightly raised, and on it resting their hands. All the women on such occasions wore long mantles or veils that covered them completely; the rich had fine, transparent ones, while those of the poor were of coarse, thick stuff. At first these veils were worn closed, but during the sermon they were opened for the sake of comfort.

About thirty men were here baptized. Most of them were servants and people from a distance who had come hither after John's imprisonment.

Jesus took a walk with the people through the vineyards, the fruits of which were ripening for the second time that year.[51]

**March 13: New Moon 28°2' Aquarius.** An Aquarian New Moon occurred on February 10 AD 31:

Jesus continued to teach in the synagogue, urging both Jews and unbelievers to become baptized. Again, the Pharisees reproached him, this time saying that his disciples did not fast regularly. Jesus replied: "The disciples eat after long labor, and then only if others are supplied. But if these latter are hungry, they give them what they have, and God blesses it." Here Jesus was referring to the feeding of the five thousand, where the disciples had given bread and fish to the hungry multitude. Then Jesus and the disciples left the town and made their way northwestward. On the way, he gave instruction concerning prayer, referring especially to the Lord's Prayer.[52]

Over the course of a very short time, the Sun, Moon, Mercury, Venus, Node *and* Neptune all aspecting each other in the fixed signs! The presence of Venus, Neptune, the Node, and the New Moon—a time of the "opening of the spiral," the possibility for the infusion of something totally new—make this an extremely potent time.

**March 15: Sun enters Pisces.**

**March 16: Mercury enters Sagittarius.**

> In losing, may loss be found
>    (*Sun in Pisces*)
> What lacks boundaries should find
>    (*Venus in Aquarius*)
> Attainment concludes joyful striving
>    (*Mercury in Sagittarius*)
> Toward life's mighty weaving
>    (*Mars in Gemini*)
> May world-being's vigilance grow in power
>    (*Jupiter in Capricorn*)
> And may the might of life's activity flower
>    (*Saturn in Capricorn*)
> O shining light, abide!
>    (*Moon in Aries*)[53]

**March 13–19, Venus conjoins Neptune.** The two are exactly aligned on **March 16: Venus and Neptune 25°39' Aquarius.** These two are signifiers of

---

51  Ibid., pp. 82–83.

52  Ibid., p. 307.
53  Steiner, *Twelve Cosmic Moods.*

Love and Mystical Depth, but also Jealousy and Intrigue. The two were also conjunct (albeit in Capricorn) on December 16 AD 30:

Next morning numbers of very sick persons, some of them aged, were brought and ranged in the courtyard before the house in which Jesus was stopping. It had cost their friends no little trouble to bring them from the pathless, mountainous city. Jesus began to cure them one after another. Some were deaf; others blind, palsied, lame; in a word, there were sick of all kinds among them. Jesus made use of prayer, the imposition of hands, consecrated oil, and in general of more ceremonies than usual. He spoke with the disciples, taught them to make use of this manner of curing, and exhorted the sick according to their various needs.

The Pharisees and Sadducees from Jerusalem were very much scandalized at all that they saw. They wanted to send away some of the newly arrived sick, and they began to quarrel. They would by no means tolerate such disturbance on the sabbath, and so great a tumult arose that Jesus, turning to them, inquired what they wanted. And now they began a dispute with him on the subject of his teaching, especially of his constant reference to the Father and the Son. "But," they said, "we know well whose son thou art!" Jesus replied that whoever does the will of the Father is the son of the Father. But that he who does not keep the commandments has no right to raise his voice in judgment upon others; he should rather rejoice at not being cast out of the house as an intruder. But they continued to allege all sorts of objections against his cures, to accuse him of not having washed before the meal of the preceding evening, and to repudiate his charge against them of not keeping the Law. They went so far that Jesus, to their exceedingly great terror, began to write on the wall of the house, and in letters that they alone could decipher, their secret sins and transgressions. Then he asked them whether they wanted the writing to remain upon the wall and become publicly known, or whether, effacing it, they would permit him to continue his work in peace. The Pharisees were thoroughly frightened. They rubbed out the writing and slunk away, leaving Jesus to continue his cures. These Pharisees

had been guilty of embezzlement of the public funds. Legacies and donations intended for the foundation of homes for widows and orphans they had used for the erection of all kinds of magnificent buildings. Saphet was rich in such establishments, and yet there were to be found in it numbers of poor, miserable creatures.

That evening Jesus closed the instructions in the synagogue, and passed the night in the same house. There was a fountain near the synagogue. The mountain of Saphet was beautiful and green, covered with numerous trees and gardens. The roads were bordered by sweet-scented myrtles. High up on the plateau were large, four-cornered houses and solid foundations around which could be erected tent habitation. This city was largely engaged in the manufacture of vestments for the priests, and it was full of students and learned men.[54]

**March 19: Venus enters Pisces.**

> In losing, may loss be found
>     (*Sun in Pisces*)
> Feel growth's power
>     (*Venus in Pisces*)
> Attainment concludes joyful striving
>     (*Mercury in Sagittarius*)
> Toward life's mighty weaving
>     (*Mars in Gemini*)
> May world-being's vigilance grow in power
>     (*Jupiter in Capricorn*)
> And may the might of life's activity flower
>     (*Saturn in Capricorn*)
> O radiant being, appear!
>     (*Moon in Taurus*)[55]

**March 22–26, Mercury and Mars come into opposition,** exact on **March 24: Mercury 22°2' Sagittarius opposite Mars 22°2' Gemini.** Beginning even earlier, and lasting longer, Sun and Venus conjoin, from March 17 through April 3. This alignment is exact on **March 26: Sun and Venus 10°48' Pisces.** These two alignments bookend the second major Marian festival of the year, on **March 25: The Feast of the Annunciation,** during which we seek to

---

54 ACE, vol. 2, p. 182.

55 Steiner, *Twelve Cosmic Moods.*

embody the formula of sacred magic as realized by the Virgin Mary—*Ecce ancilla Domini; mihi fiat secundum verbum tuum* ("Behold, I am the hand-maid of the Lord; let it be to me according to your word"—Luke 1:38).

Mercury and Mars were opposed exactly square to their opposition on the 24th (in Pisces and Virgo respectively) on December 7 AD 29:

> From Bethabara Jesus, with three disciples, went up through the valley to Dibon, where he had lately been for the Feast of Tabernacles. He taught in some houses, also in the synagogue, which was somewhat distant from the city on the road running through the valley. Jesus did not enter Dibon itself. He stayed overnight at a poor, retired inn which indeed was little more than a shed where the field laborers from the country around obtained food and lodging. It was now seed time on the sunny side of the valley, the crops of which were to ripen about Passover. They had to dig the ground here, for it was made up of soil, sand, and stone. They could not use the implement generally employed in breaking up the ground. Part of the standing-out harvest was now gathered in for the first time. The inhabitants of this valley, which was about three hours in length, were good people, of simple habits, and well inclined toward Jesus.
>
> In the synagogue, as also among the field laborers, Jesus related and explained the parable of the sower. He did not always explain his parables. He often related them to the Pharisees without an explanation.[56]

Here we see the sowers needing to find a creative solution (Mercury) to engage in their activities (Mars), breaking up the rocky ground (Mars) in order to cultivate life (Mercury). The Parable of the Sower is a proper meditation for this time—especially as, in many parts of the Northern Hemisphere, we have just entered Spring, a time of sowing and cultivating both inner and outer seeds.

Sun and Venus were conjunct, also exactly square (in Gemini) to their position on the 26th (in Pisces) on June 1 AD 32. This was one day after Christ and his apostles ate with Zacchaeus:

> The sabbath over, Jesus went with his apostles to Zacchaeus's dwelling outside Jericho. None of the disciples accompanied him. The woman so desirous of help for her daughter again followed Jesus on the road out to Zacchaeus's. He laid his hand on her to free her from her own bad disposition, and told her to return home, for her child was cured. During the meal, which consisted of honey, fruit, and a lamb, Zacchaeus served at table, but whenever Jesus spoke, he listened devoutly. Jesus related the parable of the fig tree in the vineyard which for three years bore no fruit, and for which the vinedresser implored one more year of indulgence. When uttering this parable, Jesus addressed the apostles as the vineyard; of himself he spoke as the owner; and of Zacchaeus as the fig tree. It was now three years since the relatives of the last-named had abandoned their dishonorable calling and followed Jesus, while he all this time had still carried on the same business, on which account he was looked upon with special contempt by the disciples. But Jesus had cast upon him a look of mercy when he called him down from the tree. Jesus spoke also of the sterile trees that produce many leaves, but no fruit. The leaves, he said, are exterior works. They make a great rustling, but soon pass away leaving no seed of good. But the fruits are that interior, efficacious reality in faith and action, with their capability of reproduction, and the prolongation of the tree's life stored away in the kernel. It seems to me that Jesus, in calling Zacchaeus down from the tree, did the same as to engage him to renounce the noise and bustle of the crowd, for Zacchaeus was like the ripe fruit which now detached itself from the tree that for three years had stood unfruitful in the vineyard. Jesus spoke, likewise, of the faithful servants who watched for the coming of their lord, and who suffered no noise that could prevent them from hearing his knock.[57]

Both of these star memories, especially in conjunction with the Feast of the Annunciation, bring us into a realm of great humility for the sake of cultivating the great Garden.

**March 25–28, Mercury is conjunct Pluto**, exact on **March 26: Mercury and Pluto 29°58' Sagittarius.**

---

56 ACE, vol. 1, p. 375.

57 ACE, vol. 2, p. 472.

The two were conjunct in this same sign on October 3 AD 32. Christ and the three shepherd youths had just arrived at the encampment of Azarias, the nephew of Mensor (the Gold King). Here he healed Azarias's sick wife:

> Jesus asked for a basin of water, but bade them not bring it from their sacred fountain. He wanted only ordinary water, nor would he use their holy water sprinkler. They had to bring him a fresh branch with fine, narrow leaves. They had likewise to cover their idols, which they did with fine, white tapestry embroidered in gold. Jesus placed the water on the altar. The three disciples stood around him, one at either side, right and left, and the third behind him. One of them handed him a metal box from the wallet that they always carried with them. Several such boxes of oil and cotton were placed one above the other.
>
> In that which the disciple handed to Jesus, there was a fine, white powder, which appeared to me to be salt. Jesus sprinkled some of it on the water, and bent low over it. He prayed, blessed it with his hand, dipped the branch into it, sprinkled the water over all around him, and extended his hand to the woman with the command to rise. She obeyed instantly, and rose up cured. She threw herself on her knees and wanted to embrace his feet, but he would not suffer her to touch him.[58]

Just after conjoining Pluto, **Mercury enters Capricorn:**

> In losing, may loss be found
>> (*Sun in Pisces*)
> Feel growth's power
>> (*Venus in Pisces*)
> To be strong in the present
>> (*Mercury in Capricorn*)
> Toward life's mighty weaving
>> (*Mars in Gemini*)
> May world-being's vigilance grow in power
>> (*Jupiter in Capricorn*)
> And may the might of life's activity flower
>> (*Saturn in Capricorn*)

> With senses' might, arise!
>> (*Moon in Leo*)[59]

**March 28: Palm Sunday. Full Moon, 13°18' Virgo.**
The Full Moon was 14° Virgo on March 4 AD 33:

> Next day when Jesus was going from Bethany to the temple, whither his disciples had preceded him to make ready the lecture hall, a blind man cried after him on the road and implored him to cure him, but Jesus passed him by. The disciples were dissatisfied at this. In his discourse, Jesus referred to the incident, and gave his reasons for acting as he did. The man, he said, was blinder in his soul than in the eyes of his body. His words were very earnest. He said that there were many present who did not believe in him and who ran after him only through curiosity. They would abandon him in the critical hour of trial. They were like those that followed him as long as he fed them with the bread of the body, but when that was over, they scattered in different directions. Those present, he added, should now decide. During this speech I saw many going away, and only some few over a hundred remaining around the Lord. I saw Jesus weeping over this defection on his return to Bethany.[60]

Today's Full Moon is the first after the Spring Equinox, meaning Easter is soon upon us. Each day bears an archetypal memory of the Holy Week:

> **Sunday:** The Triumphant Entry into Jerusalem
> **Monday:** Cleansing the Temple
> **Tuesday:** Enmity of the Pharisees
> **Wednesday:** Magdalene's Anointing Christ with Oil
> **Thursday:** The Last Supper
> **Friday:** The Passion
> **Saturday:** Descent into Hell
> **Sunday:** Resurrection

The star memory brought by today's Full Moon reminds us of the stark contrast between Palm Sunday and Good Friday, when virtually the entire crowd that praised Christ's entry to Jerusalem turned on him, demanding his crucifixion

58 Ibid., p. 512.

59 Steiner, *Twelve Cosmic Moods.*
60 ACE, vol. 3, p. 2.

from Pilate. Practicing true fidelity is easier said than done.

**March 28 to April 1, Mercury and Saturn conjoin, exact on March 30: Mercury and Saturn 11°15' Capricorn.** Mercury was opposite to Saturn in Cancer, close to today's degree, July 16–17 AD 32. It was during these days that Jesus, some of the apostles, and three of the holy women (including the Virgin Mary) received word that Lazarus had died. It was at this time that Christ spoke the words of John 11:11: "Our friend Lazarus has fallen asleep; but I am going so that I might awaken him." This week we too are asleep with Christ, until the victorious awakening of the Resurrection on Easter Sunday.

# APRIL 2021

## STARGAZING PREVIEW

April is a big month for looking up! After dusk on the 1st, Mars will be aligned with *Rigel*—as the Sun was at the Ascension—the star marking the left foot of Orion (the one on the right from the stargazer's perspective). They can be found in the southwest, approximately a third of the distance between culmination (due south) and setting (due west). As the waning Moon rises at midnight, it will have a companion: nearby you'll see *Antares*, the star at the heart of the Scorpion. Saturn and Jupiter will have risen by 0420, at which time the Lion will be low in the west.

The Moon reaches its Last Quarter on the 4th, at 20° Sagittarius. If you're up between 0330 and 0400 on the 6th, you'll see the Moon rise ahead of Saturn and Jupiter; at the same time on the 7th, the Moon will be between them; on the 8th, the Moon will rise last.

Jupiter moves into its "Aquarius year" on the 10th: *As a flowing wave self-sustaining* (Jupiter spends a little less than one year in each sign of the zodiac). April's New Moon will occur on the 12th, at 27° Pisces. That evening, as you gaze into the moonless night, you'll find Mars above Orion,

aligned with *Alnilam*, the star that marks the center of his belt. Wednesday the 14th is the day that the Sun finds Aries and begins its zodiacal journey anew!

The Moon passes Mars (1° Gemini) from below on the 17th, recalling the position of Mars as Jesus rode a donkey into the Old City through the Golden Gate on March 19 AD 33. As you say your prayers on the evening of the 18th, be aware that Mercury will be on the far side of the Sun before daybreak! The superior conjunction of Mercury presents a special opportunity to offer our prayers to the angels. It is at the next inferior conjunction (on June 11) that we must turn our consciousness to their response.

On the 20th the Moon reaches its First Quarter at 5° Cancer. After sunset, the waxing crescent will preside over the night sky from the south, between Gemini and Leo. The night spanning the 22nd and 23rd will be the peak of the Lyrid meteor showers, which originate from the northern constellation *Lyra* (though they can be seen anywhere in the night sky). *Lyra*'s brightest star, *Vega*, is part of the Summer Triangle (along with *Deneb* and *Altair*), and will be our North Star in approximately 12,000 years' time. (To orient yourself to its location, look above you for the Northern Cross, also known as the Swan—the Milky Way runs right through it—and imagine that you are looking at the cross right side up. *Lyra* is slightly above the level of the bottom of the cross, and a bit to your right). At the start of the evening, the Moon, nearing Full, will have passed above *Regulus*. Because our luminous satellite sets at 0300, the predawn hours will offer the best opportunity for seeing the meteor showers.

Our April 27 Full Moon is a Supermoon, and a special one indeed, as the Sun (12° Aries) and Moon (12° Libra) are just 1° shy of their positions at the Crucifixion. *It is fulfilled.*

## APRIL COMMENTARIES

The month of April is dominated by the opposition of Mars and Pluto. This is already coming into formation on March 30, and lasts until April 21. It is exact on April 10 (see commentary below).

March 31 to April 3, Mercury is conjunct Jupiter. This alignment is exact April 2.

**April 2, Good Friday: Mercury conjunct Jupiter 19°51' Capricorn.** Mercury was at the same degree on February 6 AD 31, in square alignment to Jupiter. This occurred very close to the star memory of February 7 (see the commentary for Sun square Node on March 5), as well as that of February 5:

> While they were walking this morning in the neighborhood of Gischala, Jesus revealed to the twelve the disposition and character of each, and arranged them correspondingly in three groups or rows: in the first row—Peter, Andrew, John, James the Greater and Matthew; in the second row—Judas Thaddeus, Bartholomew, and James the Less; and in the third row—Thomas, Simon, Philip, and Judas Iscariot. Joseph Barsabbas stood at the head of the remaining disciples, nearest to the twelve, and Jesus then placed him in the second row together with Thaddeus, Bartholomew and James.[61]

In addition to the Mercury–Jupiter alignment, today **Pluto enters Capricorn.** It has been traversing Sagittarius since 2006; the last time it ingressed into Capricorn was May 6, 1773. See Julie Humphreys' article in this same volume, "The Bellows of Ahriman: Pluto Reaches Capricorn," for valuable insight into this rare transition—one that we will not experience again in this lifetime.

Good Friday begins the Novena to the Divine Mercy, leading up to the Festival of the Divine Mercy, a moveable feast which always occurs one week after Easter Sunday. This is the official Holy Catholic Feast to Christ in His Second Coming, first celebrated informally in 1935, and as an officially sanctioned Feast in the year 2000.[62] May Christ, in his unfathomable mercy, reveal to each of us our disposition and character, and guide us to the place in the circle we are meant to hold.

**April 4: Easter Sunday. Mercury enters Aquarius.**

---

61 ACE, vol. 2, p. 306.

62 For more information, see the following: https://sophiafoundation.org/a-special-easter-2020-novena/.

In losing, may loss be found
  (*Sun in Pisces*)
Feel growth's power
  (*Venus in Pisces*)
Found boundaries in its own depths
  (*Mercury in Aquarius*)
Toward life's mighty weaving
  (*Mars in Gemini*)
May world-being's vigilance grow in power
  (*Jupiter in Capricorn*)
And may the might of life's activity flower
  (*Saturn in Capricorn*)
May existence feel existence!
  (*Moon in Sagittarius*)[63]

Today we celebrate the triumph of Life over Death, of the magical marriage of life and death in the Resurrection Body, born of Christ's deed on April 5 AD 33. Our New Year's verse revolved around finding our *strength*; Easter's verse is about *growth* and *life*. The combination of Venus in Pisces, Mercury in Aquarius, and Mars in Gemini yields a potent mantra for Christ's victory on Easter Sunday: *Feel growth's power found boundaries in its own depths, toward life's might weaving.* There is a gesture conjured in these words of growth—an activity moving ever upward and outward—binding and anchoring itself in the impossibly finite center of the deep. This maximum tension of point and periphery, rather than tearing in two, allows the perfect medium for "life's mighty weaving," the string upon which the song of life can be played. We can think of Christ attaining absolute zero on Holy Saturday, only to counterbalance this with infinite expansion on Easter Sunday. Christ was then, is now, and ever will be the measure of all things (Cosmos and Humanity): the string upon which the Eternal Song is playing.

**April 1–10, Venus comes into square alignment with Mars,** exact on **April 5: Venus 27°48' Pisces square Mars 27°48' Gemini.** Venus and Mars were conjunct in Gemini on March 8 AD 31:

> Argob was for the most part inhabited by Jews. The few pagans in it were poor and worked for

---

63 Steiner, *Twelve Cosmic Moods.*

| SIDEREAL GEOCENTRIC LONGITUDES : APRIL 2021 Gregorian at 0 hours UT | | | | | | | | | | | |
|---|---|---|---|---|---|---|---|---|---|---|---|
| DAY | ☉ | ☽ | ☊ | ☿ | ♀ | ♂ | ♃ | ♄ | ♅ | ♆ | ♇ |
| 1 TH | 16 ♓ 27 | 1 ♏ 19 | 17 ♉ 31R | 29 ♒ 27 | 17 ♓ 54 | 21 ♉ 24 | 28 ♑ 12 | 16 ♑ 20 | 13 ♈ 58 | 26 ♒ 23 | 1 ♑ 36 |
| 2 FR | 17 26 | 15 54 | 17 30 | 1 ♓ 11 | 19 8 | 22 0 | 28 23 | 16 25 | 14 2 | 26 25 | 1 36 |
| 3 SA | 18 25 | 0 ♐ 10 | 17 31D | 2 55 | 20 23 | 22 36 | 28 35 | 16 29 | 14 5 | 26 28 | 1 37 |
| 4 SU | 19 24 | 14 6 | 17 32 | 4 41 | 21 37 | 23 12 | 28 46 | 16 34 | 14 8 | 26 30 | 1 38 |
| 5 MO | 20 23 | 27 42 | 17 31R | 6 29 | 22 52 | 23 48 | 28 58 | 16 38 | 14 11 | 26 32 | 1 39 |
| 6 TU | 21 23 | 11 ♑ 0 | 17 30 | 8 18 | 24 6 | 24 24 | 29 9 | 16 43 | 14 14 | 26 34 | 1 39 |
| 7 WE | 22 22 | 24 2 | 17 26 | 10 9 | 25 21 | 25 0 | 29 20 | 16 47 | 14 18 | 26 36 | 1 40 |
| 8 TH | 23 21 | 6 ♒ 49 | 17 19 | 12 0 | 26 35 | 25 36 | 29 32 | 16 51 | 14 21 | 26 38 | 1 40 |
| 9 FR | 24 20 | 19 24 | 17 11 | 13 54 | 27 49 | 26 12 | 29 43 | 16 55 | 14 24 | 26 40 | 1 41 |
| 10 SA | 25 19 | 1 ♓ 48 | 17 1 | 15 49 | 29 4 | 26 49 | 29 54 | 16 59 | 14 28 | 26 42 | 1 41 |
| 11 SU | 26 17 | 14 2 | 16 51 | 17 45 | 0 ♈ 18 | 27 25 | 0 ♒ 5 | 17 3 | 14 31 | 26 44 | 1 42 |
| 12 MO | 27 16 | 26 8 | 16 42 | 19 43 | 1 32 | 28 1 | 0 15 | 17 7 | 14 34 | 26 46 | 1 42 |
| 13 TU | 28 15 | 8 ♈ 5 | 16 34 | 21 42 | 2 47 | 28 37 | 0 26 | 17 11 | 14 38 | 26 48 | 1 43 |
| 14 WE | 29 14 | 19 57 | 16 29 | 23 42 | 4 1 | 29 13 | 0 37 | 17 15 | 14 41 | 26 50 | 1 43 |
| 15 TH | 0 ♈ 13 | 1 ♉ 45 | 16 25 | 25 44 | 5 15 | 29 49 | 0 47 | 17 18 | 14 44 | 26 52 | 1 44 |
| 16 FR | 1 12 | 13 31 | 16 24 | 27 47 | 6 30 | 0 ♊ 26 | 0 57 | 17 22 | 14 48 | 26 54 | 1 44 |
| 17 SA | 2 10 | 25 20 | 16 24D | 29 51 | 7 44 | 1 2 | 1 8 | 17 25 | 14 51 | 26 56 | 1 44 |
| 18 SU | 3 9 | 7 ♊ 15 | 16 25 | 1 ♈ 56 | 8 58 | 1 38 | 1 18 | 17 29 | 14 54 | 26 58 | 1 45 |
| 19 MO | 4 8 | 19 22 | 16 27 | 4 2 | 10 12 | 2 15 | 1 28 | 17 32 | 14 58 | 27 0 | 1 45 |
| 20 TU | 5 6 | 1 ♋ 44 | 16 28 | 6 9 | 11 26 | 2 51 | 1 38 | 17 35 | 15 1 | 27 2 | 1 45 |
| 21 WE | 6 5 | 14 27 | 16 28R | 8 17 | 12 40 | 3 27 | 1 48 | 17 38 | 15 5 | 27 4 | 1 45 |
| 22 TH | 7 3 | 27 35 | 16 26 | 10 25 | 13 55 | 4 4 | 1 57 | 17 41 | 15 8 | 27 6 | 1 46 |
| 23 FR | 8 2 | 11 ♌ 11 | 16 22 | 12 33 | 15 9 | 4 40 | 2 7 | 17 44 | 15 12 | 27 8 | 1 46 |
| 24 SA | 9 0 | 25 16 | 16 18 | 14 40 | 16 23 | 5 16 | 2 16 | 17 47 | 15 15 | 27 9 | 1 46 |
| 25 SU | 9 59 | 9 ♍ 48 | 16 12 | 16 48 | 17 37 | 5 53 | 2 26 | 17 50 | 15 18 | 27 11 | 1 46 |
| 26 MO | 10 57 | 24 42 | 16 7 | 18 54 | 18 51 | 6 29 | 2 35 | 17 52 | 15 22 | 27 13 | 1 46 |
| 27 TU | 11 55 | 9 ♎ 51 | 16 3 | 21 0 | 20 5 | 7 5 | 2 44 | 17 55 | 15 25 | 27 15 | 1 46 |
| 28 WE | 12 54 | 25 3 | 16 0 | 23 4 | 21 19 | 7 42 | 2 53 | 17 57 | 15 29 | 27 16 | 1 46R |
| 29 TH | 13 52 | 10 ♏ 11 | 15 59 | 25 7 | 22 33 | 8 18 | 3 2 | 18 0 | 15 32 | 27 18 | 1 46 |
| 30 FR | 14 50 | 25 4 | 15 59D | 27 8 | 23 47 | 8 55 | 3 10 | 18 2 | 15 36 | 27 20 | 1 46 |

INGRESSES :

| | | | | | |
|---|---|---|---|---|---|
| 1 | ☿ → ♓ | 7:39 | 17 | ☿ → ♈ | 1:42 |
| 2 | ☽ → ♐ | 23:43 | | ☽ → ♊ | 9:25 |
| 5 | ☽ → ♑ | 4: 6 | 19 | ☽ → ♋ | 20:40 |
| 7 | ☽ → ♒ | 11: 9 | 22 | ☽ → ♌ | 4:19 |
| 9 | ☽ → ♓ | 20:29 | 24 | ☽ → ♍ | 7:53 |
| 10 | ♃ → ♒ | 14: 0 | 26 | ☽ → ♎ | 8:25 |
| | ♀ → ♈ | 18: 9 | 28 | ☽ → ♏ | 7:49 |
| 12 | ☽ → ♈ | 7:45 | 30 | ☽ → ♐ | 8: 3 |
| 14 | ☉ → ♈ | 18:45 | | | |
| | ☽ → ♉ | 20:27 | | | |
| 15 | ♂ → ♊ | 7: 0 | | | |

ASPECTS & ECLIPSES :

| | | | | | | | | | | | |
|---|---|---|---|---|---|---|---|---|---|---|---|
| 2 | ☽ ☌ ☋ | 2:40 | | ♀ □ ♇ | 3:15 | 21 | ☽ ☍ ♄ | 5:54 | | ☽ ☌ P | 15:25 |
| | ☽ ☍ ♂ | 10:39 | | ☽ ☌ ♀ | 12: 5 | 22 | ☽ ☍ ♃ | 7:53 | | ☽ ☍ ♀ | 17:34 |
| 4 | ☉ □ ☽ | 10: 1 | 13 | ☽ ☌ ♅ | 13:16 | 23 | ♀ ☌ ♅ | 0:59 | | ☽ ☍ ☿ | 20:22 |
| 5 | ☽ ☌ ♇ | 7: 3 | 14 | ☽ ☌ A | 17:46 | | ☽ N□ ☊ | 8:52 | 29 | ☽ ☌ ☋ | 9:17 |
| 6 | ☽ ☌ ♄ | 10:31 | 16 | ☽ ☌ ☊ | 5:51 | 24 | ☽ ☍ ♆ | 3: 9 | 30 | ☉ ☌ ♅ | 19:51 |
| 7 | ☽ ☌ ♃ | 10: 3 | | ☉ □ ♇ | 13:20 | | ☿ ☌ ♅ | 6:40 | | ☽ ☍ ♂ | 23:49 |
| 8 | ☽ □S ☊ | 19:46 | 17 | ☽ ☌ ♂ | 12: 7 | 25 | ♀ □ ♄ | 4:20 | | | |
| 9 | ☽ ☌ ♆ | 14: 3 | | ☿ □ ♇ | 21:45 | | ☿ □ ♄ | 11:57 | | | |
| | ♂ □ ♆ | 19:33 | 19 | ☉ S☌ ☿ | 1:48 | | ☿ ☌ ♀ | 22:18 | | | |
| 11 | ☽ ☌ ☿ | 8:44 | 20 | ☽ ☍ ♇ | 0: 2 | 27 | ☉ ☍ ☽ | 3:30 | | | |
| 12 | ☉ ☌ ☽ | 2:29 | | ☉ □ ☽ | 6:57 | | ☽ ☍ ♅ | 8:50 | | | |

| SIDEREAL HELIOCENTRIC LONGITUDES : APRIL 2021 Gregorian at 0 hours UT | | | | | | | | | | | |
|---|---|---|---|---|---|---|---|---|---|---|---|
| DAY | Sid. Time | ☿ | ♀ | ⊕ | ♂ | ♃ | ♄ | ♅ | ♆ | ♇ | Vernal Point |
| 1 TH | 12:38:18 | 15 ♑ 27 | 19 ♓ 55 | 16 ♍ 28 | 25 ♊ 31 | 19 ♑ 44 | 11 ♑ 22 | 15 ♈ 19 | 25 ♒ 44 | 29 ♐ 59 | 4 ♓ 57'49" |
| 2 FR | 12:42:15 | 18 52 | 21 30 | 17 27 | 25 59 | 19 50 | 11 23 | 15 20 | 25 45 | 29 59 | 4 ♓ 57'48" |
| 3 SA | 12:46:12 | 22 21 | 23 6 | 18 26 | 26 26 | 19 55 | 11 25 | 15 21 | 25 45 | 0 ♑ 0 | 4 ♓ 57'48" |
| 4 SU | 12:50: 8 | 25 55 | 24 42 | 19 25 | 26 54 | 20 0 | 11 27 | 15 21 | 25 46 | 0 0 | 4 ♓ 57'48" |
| 5 MO | 12:54: 5 | 29 35 | 26 17 | 20 24 | 27 22 | 20 5 | 11 29 | 15 22 | 25 46 | 0 0 | 4 ♓ 57'48" |
| 6 TU | 12:58: 1 | 3 ♒ 21 | 27 53 | 21 23 | 27 50 | 20 11 | 11 31 | 15 23 | 25 46 | 0 1 | 4 ♓ 57'48" |
| 7 WE | 13: 1:58 | 7 13 | 29 29 | 22 22 | 28 17 | 20 16 | 11 33 | 15 23 | 25 47 | 0 1 | 4 ♓ 57'48" |
| 8 TH | 13: 5:54 | 11 12 | 1 ♈ 5 | 23 21 | 28 45 | 20 21 | 11 35 | 15 24 | 25 47 | 0 1 | 4 ♓ 57'48" |
| 9 FR | 13: 9:51 | 15 18 | 2 40 | 24 20 | 29 13 | 20 26 | 11 36 | 15 25 | 25 47 | 0 2 | 4 ♓ 57'48" |
| 10 SA | 13:13:47 | 19 31 | 4 16 | 25 19 | 29 40 | 20 32 | 11 38 | 15 25 | 25 48 | 0 2 | 4 ♓ 57'47" |
| 11 SU | 13:17:44 | 23 51 | 5 52 | 26 18 | 0 ♋ 8 | 20 37 | 11 40 | 15 26 | 25 48 | 0 2 | 4 ♓ 57'47" |
| 12 MO | 13:21:41 | 28 20 | 7 28 | 27 17 | 0 35 | 20 42 | 11 42 | 15 27 | 25 48 | 0 2 | 4 ♓ 57'47" |
| 13 TU | 13:25:37 | 2 ♓ 57 | 9 4 | 28 16 | 1 3 | 20 47 | 11 44 | 15 27 | 25 49 | 0 3 | 4 ♓ 57'47" |
| 14 WE | 13:29:34 | 7 43 | 10 40 | 29 15 | 1 30 | 20 53 | 11 46 | 15 28 | 25 49 | 0 3 | 4 ♓ 57'47" |
| 15 TH | 13:33:30 | 12 38 | 12 16 | 0 ♎ 13 | 1 58 | 20 58 | 11 47 | 15 29 | 25 50 | 0 3 | 4 ♓ 57'47" |
| 16 FR | 13:37:27 | 17 42 | 13 52 | 1 12 | 2 25 | 21 3 | 11 49 | 15 29 | 25 50 | 0 4 | 4 ♓ 57'47" |
| 17 SA | 13:41:23 | 22 54 | 15 28 | 2 11 | 2 53 | 21 8 | 11 51 | 15 30 | 25 50 | 0 4 | 4 ♓ 57'46" |
| 18 SU | 13:45:20 | 28 16 | 17 4 | 3 10 | 3 20 | 21 14 | 11 53 | 15 31 | 25 51 | 0 4 | 4 ♓ 57'46" |
| 19 MO | 13:49:16 | 3 ♈ 47 | 18 40 | 4 8 | 3 47 | 21 19 | 11 55 | 15 31 | 25 51 | 0 4 | 4 ♓ 57'46" |
| 20 TU | 13:53:13 | 9 27 | 20 16 | 5 7 | 4 15 | 21 24 | 11 57 | 15 32 | 25 51 | 0 5 | 4 ♓ 57'46" |
| 21 WE | 13:57:10 | 15 15 | 21 52 | 6 5 | 4 42 | 21 29 | 11 58 | 15 33 | 25 52 | 0 5 | 4 ♓ 57'46" |
| 22 TH | 14: 1: 6 | 21 10 | 23 29 | 7 4 | 5 9 | 21 35 | 12 0 | 15 33 | 25 52 | 0 5 | 4 ♓ 57'46" |
| 23 FR | 14: 5: 3 | 27 13 | 25 5 | 8 2 | 5 36 | 21 40 | 12 2 | 15 34 | 25 52 | 0 6 | 4 ♓ 57'46" |
| 24 SA | 14: 8:59 | 3 ♉ 21 | 26 41 | 9 1 | 6 4 | 21 45 | 12 4 | 15 35 | 25 53 | 0 6 | 4 ♓ 57'45" |
| 25 SU | 14:12:56 | 9 34 | 28 17 | 9 59 | 6 31 | 21 51 | 12 6 | 15 35 | 25 53 | 0 6 | 4 ♓ 57'45" |
| 26 MO | 14:16:52 | 15 51 | 29 54 | 10 58 | 6 58 | 21 56 | 12 8 | 15 36 | 25 54 | 0 7 | 4 ♓ 57'45" |
| 27 TU | 14:20:49 | 22 10 | 1 ♉ 30 | 11 56 | 7 25 | 22 1 | 12 9 | 15 37 | 25 54 | 0 7 | 4 ♓ 57'45" |
| 28 WE | 14:24:45 | 28 29 | 3 6 | 12 54 | 7 52 | 22 6 | 12 11 | 15 37 | 25 54 | 0 7 | 4 ♓ 57'45" |
| 29 TH | 14:28:42 | 4 ♊ 47 | 4 43 | 13 53 | 8 19 | 22 12 | 12 13 | 15 38 | 25 55 | 0 7 | 4 ♓ 57'45" |
| 30 FR | 14:32:39 | 11 4 | 6 19 | 14 51 | 8 46 | 22 17 | 12 15 | 15 39 | 25 55 | 0 8 | 4 ♓ 57'45" |

INGRESSES :

| | | |
|---|---|---|
| 3 | ♇ → ♑ | 18:31 |
| 5 | ☿ → ♒ | 2:38 |
| 7 | ♀ → ♈ | 7:48 |
| 10 | ♂ → ♋ | 17:11 |
| 12 | ☿ → ♓ | 8:43 |
| 14 | ⊕ → ♎ | 18:30 |
| 18 | ☿ → ♈ | 7:34 |
| 23 | ☿ → ♉ | 10:56 |
| 26 | ♀ → ♉ | 1:36 |
| 28 | ☿ → ♊ | 5:45 |

ASPECTS (HELIOCENTRIC +MOON(TYCHONIC)) :

| | | | | | | | | | | | | | | |
|---|---|---|---|---|---|---|---|---|---|---|---|---|---|---|
| 2 | ☿ ☌ ♃ | 6:52 | 8 | ☽ ☌ ☿ | 12:16 | | ⊕ □ ♇ | 19:50 | | ☽ ☍ ♄ | 19:22 | | ☽ □ ♂ | 20: 3 |
| | ☽ □ ♆ | 16:30 | 9 | ☽ ☌ ♆ | 12:19 | 17 | ♀ ☌ ♅ | 0:30 | 21 | ☿ ☌ ♅ | 1:12 | 27 | ☿ ☌ P | 2:14 |
| 3 | ☿ □S ☊ | 8: 6 | 10 | ♂ ☍ ♇ | 18:59 | | ☽ □ ♆ | 1: 1 | | ☽ □ ♅ | 2: 1 | | ☽ □ ♄ | 3:39 |
| 4 | ☽ □ ♀ | 21: 8 | 11 | ☿ ☌ ♆ | 10:31 | 18 | ☿ □ ♇ | 7:53 | | ☽ □ ☿ | 2:41 | | ⊕ □ ♄ | 5:40 |
| | ☽ ☍ ♂ | 23:22 | 12 | ☽ □ ♇ | 7:50 | | ⊕ □ ♂ | 7:58 | | ☽ ☍ ♃ | 13: 2 | | ☽ ☍ ♅ | 9: 6 |
| 5 | ☽ ☌ ♇ | 4: 7 | | ☽ □ ♂ | 9:17 | | ☿ □ ♂ | 23:59 | | ☽ □ ♀ | 15:33 | | ☿ □ ♆ | 14:12 |
| | ♀ □ ♂ | 22:47 | 13 | ☽ ☌ ♀ | 2:17 | 19 | ☿ ☍ ⊕ | 1:48 | 22 | ☿ □ ♃ | 1:38 | | ☽ □ ♃ | 19:18 |
| 6 | ☽ ☌ ♄ | 0:56 | | ☽ □ ♄ | 7:22 | | ☽ ☍ ♇ | 20:49 | | ☿ ☌ ☊ | 9:28 | 28 | ☽ ☍ ♀ | 14:15 |
| | ☽ □ ♅ | 8: 1 | | ☽ ☌ ♅ | 14:54 | 20 | ☽ ☌ ♂ | 4:58 | | ☿ ☌ ♀ | 12:31 | 30 | ☽ □ ♆ | 1:22 |
| | ☽ ☌ ♃ | 16:58 | 14 | ☽ □ ♃ | 1:54 | | ☿ □ ♄ | 10:26 | 24 | ☽ ☍ ♆ | 1: 1 | | ⊕ ☍ ♅ | 19:51 |
| 7 | ♀ □ ♇ | 8: 3 | | ♀ □ ♄ | 16:42 | | ♀ □ ♃ | 17:56 | 26 | ☽ □ ♇ | 8:36 | | | |

them. Cotton goods were manufactured here, women, children, and men being engaged in spinning and weaving. The place suffered from want of water, which had to be carried up to the city in leathern bottles, and then poured into the cisterns. Jesus taught in a public square, healed some of the sick, and visited in their own homes some old and infirm people, whom he cured and consoled. Almost all the inhabitants had been baptized, and there were no Pharisees among them. A very distant view could be commanded from Argob. They could see far over into Upper Galilee, the Mount of Beatitudes rose before them, and the prospect down into Bethsaida–Julias was remarkably beautiful.[64]

May Venus and Mars grant us an equally wide vista of the "Mount of Beatitudes" during this glorious Eastertide.

Simultaneous with her alignment with Mars, Venus comes into square alignment with Pluto. This is taking shape from April 3–10, and is exact on the 7th.

**April 7: Venus 0°1' Aries square Pluto 0°1' Capricorn.** These two planets were square, also in Aries and Capricorn, just before the death and Assumption of the Virgin Mary, on August 15 AD 44:

As the blessed Virgin felt her end approaching, in accordance with the directions of her divine Son, she called the apostles to her by prayer. She was now in her sixty-third year. At the time of Christ's birth, she was in her fifteenth. Before his ascension Jesus had made known to his most holy mother what she should say at the end of her earthly career to the apostles and some of the disciples who should be with her. He told her also that she should bless them, and that it would conduce very much to their welfare and eternal salvation. He entrusted to her also certain spiritual labors for the general good, which being accomplished, her longing after Heaven was to be realized. Jesus had at the same time made known to Magdalene that she was to live concealed in the wilderness, and that Martha was to establish a community of women. He added that he himself would always be with them.

At the prayer of the blessed Virgin, the apostles received, through angels, an admonition to repair to her at Ephesus.[65]

**April 7: Venus enters Aries.**

**April 10: Mars enters Cancer.**

> In losing, may loss be found
>     (*Sun in Pisces*)
> Take hold of growth's being
>     (*Venus in Aries*)
> Found boundaries in its own depths
>     (*Mercury in Aquarius*)
> To gain strength in test of trial
>     (*Mars in Cancer*)
> May world-being's vigilance grow in power
>     (*Jupiter in Capricorn*)
> And may the might of life's activity flower
>     (*Saturn in Capricorn*)
> May loss be gain in itself!
>     (*Moon in Pisces*)[66]

Also on **April 10: Mars 0°2' Cancer opposite Pluto 0°2' Capricorn.** Mars was in Cancer and Pluto in Capricorn for the weeks leading up to the Assumption of Mary. This is a strong star memory this month:

Peter, Andrew, and John were the first to reach the blessed Virgin's house. She was already near death. She was lying calmly on her couch in her sleeping place. I saw the maidservant looking very sorrowful in this and that corner of the house, also outdoors, where she prayed prostrate with outstretched arms. I saw also two of Mary's sisters and five disciples coming together to the house. All looked tired and exhausted. They carried staves of various kinds, each according to his rank. They wore, under their hooded mantles of white wool, long albs of the same material fastened all the way down the front with little leather straps slit in the middle over little rolls like buttons. Both mantle and alb were girded high when traveling. Some had a pouch hanging from their girdle at the side. They embraced each other tenderly when they met. Many wept

---

64 ACE, vol. 2, p. 321.

65 ACE, vol. 3, p. 424.

66 Steiner, *Twelve Cosmic Moods*.

from mingled feelings of joy and sorrow at meeting on such an occasion. On entering the house, they laid aside their mantles, staves, pouches, and girdles; allowed their white robes to fall in broad folds down to their feet, and each put on a wide girdle inscribed with letters, which he had brought with him. Then with deep emotion they drew near Mary's couch to salute her, though she could now say only a few words....

I saw that the first to arrive prepared in the front apartment of the house a place suitable for prayer and offering the holy sacrifice. There was an altar covered with a red and over that a white cloth, and on it stood a crucifix, white like mother of pearl, and in shape like a Maltese cross. The cross could be opened. It contained five compartments, likewise cross-shaped. The middle one held the most blessed sacrament, while the others were intended respectively for chrism, oil, cotton, and salt. It was not quite a span, or nine inches, in length. Each of the apostles when traveling carried one like it on his breast. It was in this cross that Peter took to Mary the holy communion, during the reception of which the apostles stood bowing low, ranged in two rows from the altar down to her couch.[67]

**April 10–12, Mercury comes into conjunction with Neptune,** exact on **April 11, Divine Mercy Sunday: Mercury conjunct Neptune 25°48' Aquarius.** These two were conjunct in Aquarius on April 11 AD 33, when Thomas placed his fingers in the wounds of Christ. Five days later, on April 16, Mercury reached 24° Aquarius, when the Risen One appeared to a crowd of 500 people. Today is also the **New Moon, 27°23' Pisces.**

The Full Moon that set our sights on Easter Sunday took place two weeks ago, on Palm Sunday. And now today, we celebrate the Etheric Christ on Divine Mercy Sunday with a Pisces New Moon that remembers the *original* Palm Sunday (when the New Moon was 29° Pisces) on March 19 AD 33. The triumphant entry in Jerusalem; the appearances of the Risen One; and the Divine Mercy—truly a day for jubilation and rejoicing!

**April 12: Mercury enters Pisces.**

**April 14: Sun enters Aries.**

> Arise, O shining light
>> (*Sun in Aries*)
> Take hold of growth's being
>> (*Venus in Aries*)
> In comprehending seek to grasp
>> (*Mercury in Pisces*)
> To gain strength in test of trial
>> (*Mars in Cancer*)
> May world-being's vigilance grow in power
>> (*Jupiter in Capricorn*)
> And may the might of life's activity flower
>> (*Saturn in Capricorn*)
> O shining light, abide!
>> (*Moon in Aries*)[68]

**April 11–17, Venus and Saturn come into square alignment.** This is exact on **April 14: Venus 11°41' Aries square Saturn 11°41' Capricorn.** These two planets were square in the signs opposite those of today (Libra and Cancer) on April 5 AD 33—the original Resurrection Sunday, when Love (Venus) conquered Death (Saturn). Simultaneous with this alignment, the Sun is square to Pluto April 9–19, exact on the 14th.

**April 14: Sun 0°3' Aries square Pluto 0°3' Capricorn.** The Sun was at this degree on March 20 AD 33, during which a number of the events honored during Holy Week took place: Christ cursing the fig tree that bore no fruit; turning over the tables of the vendors in the temple; and Magdalene anointing Christ's head with precious oil, driving Judas to make a bargain with the Pharisees to betray him.

Also during this time, the Sun and Mars are square from April 8–27—an even longer portion of the month—exact on the 18th.

**April 18: Sun 3°29' Aries square Mars 3°29' Cancer.** Again, we are brought to the time leading up to Easter, as these two were square in the same signs on March 27 AD 33:

> Jesus and the apostles and disciples returned to the Mount of Olives early in the morning. Jesus spoke of the destruction of Jerusalem and of

---

67 ACE, vol. 3, pp. 424–425.

68 Steiner, *Twelve Cosmic Moods.*

the end of the world (Matt. 24:15–31), referring, by way of analogy, to a fig tree standing there (Matt. 24:32–35). He also referred to his betrayal, saying that the Pharisees were longing to see the betrayer again. Judas listened with a smile. Jesus also warned the apostles not to be burdened with worldly cares. Later, he taught in the temple, employing the parables of the ten virgins (Matt. 25:1–13) and of the talents (Matt. 25:14–30). He also repeated his words to the Pharisees concerning the shedding of the blood of the prophets (Matt. 23:29–39). Jesus then spent the night at a place at the foot of the Mount of Olives.[69]

Now that we have entered Eastertide, having celebrated the Resurrection two weeks ago, it seems that the star memories carry us on a retrospective back through the Lenten period we have just left behind—perhaps we can process the events and conversations we experienced leading up to Easter in a new light during these days.

Finally, on April 13–19, Venus comes into conjunction with Uranus. These two are exactly aligned on the 16th.

**April 16: Venus and Uranus 15°30' Aries.** Besides the memories of the original Passiontide, we are brought to another time period the stars keep returning to: Venus was in Aries, nearly exactly opposite to Uranus in Libra, on August 15/16, during the death and Assumption of the Virgin. Two pivotal moments in human evolution are recalled all through this month: the redemption of fallen nature through the Mystery of Golgotha, and the perfection of unfallen (virginal) nature in the Assumption.

**April 18: Mercury enters Aries.**

Arise, O shining light
  (*Sun in Aries*)
Take hold of growth's being
  (*Venus in Aries*)
Lay hold of forces weaving
  (*Mercury in Aries*)

To gain strength in test of trial
  (*Mars in Cancer*)
May world-being's vigilance grow in power
  (*Jupiter in Capricorn*)
And may the might of life's activity flower
  (*Saturn in Capricorn*)
O Sun life, endure!
  (*Moon in Gemini*)[70]

April 17–19, Sun and Mercury come into alignment, exact on the 18th.

**April 18: Sun conjunct Mercury 4°12' Aries.** These two were conjunct in Libra, opposite their position today, on October 9 AD 30:

That afternoon the branches of which the tabernacles [of the Feast of Tabernacles, celebrated the day before] had been formed were brought processionally by the boys to the square in front of the synagogue, there piled in a heap, and burned. The Jews watched with interest the rising of the flames, presaging from their various movements good or bad fortune. Jesus preached afterward in the synagogue, taking for his subjects the happiness of Adam, his Fall, the Promise, and some passages from Joshua. He spoke also of too great solicitude for the things of life, of the lilies that do not spin, of the ravens that do not sow, etc., and brought forward examples in the person of Daniel and Job. They, he said, were men of piety, engrossed in occupations, but still without worldly solicitude.[71]

Shortly after this alignment, Venus is square Jupiter, April 17–24, exact on the 20th.

**April 20: Venus 21°28' Aries square Jupiter 21°28' Capricorn.** These two were square, but with Venus in Capricorn and Jupiter in Aries, on December 8 AD 30 (see commentary for February 19). April 21–23, Mercury and Venus come into conjunction, exact on the 22nd.

**April 22: Mercury and Venus 24°19' Aries.** These two were conjunct opposite Aries, in Libra, on October 4 AD 30, during the Feast of Tabernacles already referenced:

69 ACE, vol. 3, pp. 14–15.

70 Steiner, *Twelve Cosmic Moods.*
71 ACE, vol. 2, p. 74.

...Jesus made the rounds of the city, visited all the tabernacles, and gave instructions here and there. The people observed many customs particular to this festival; for instance, they took only a mouthful in the morning, the rest of the repast being reserved for the poor. Their employment during the day was interrupted by canticles and prayers, and instructions were given by the elders. These instructions were now delivered by Jesus. On his coming and going he was received and escorted by little boys and girls carrying around him garlands of flowers. This, too, was one of their customs.[72]

Already starting on April 20, and extending through May 2, the Sun and Saturn are square. This is exact on the 27th.

**April 23: Mercury enters Taurus.**

**April 25: Venus enters Taurus.**

> Arise, O shining light
>     (*Sun in Aries*)
> Feel growth's power
>     (*Venus in Taurus*)
> Weave life's thread
>     (*Mercury in Taurus*)
> To gain strength in test of trial
>     (*Mars in Cancer*)
> May world-being's vigilance grow in power
>     (*Jupiter in Capricorn*)
> And may the might of life's activity flower
>     (*Saturn in Capricorn*)
> O soul, know thou beings!
>     (*Moon in Virgo*)[73]

**April 25–26, Mercury is conjunct the Ascending Node, exact on April 25: Mercury conjunct Node 16°57' Taurus.** These two were conjunct very close to this degree on December 4 AD 30—see the star memory for January 29.

**April 26: Full Moon 12°4' Libra.** A Libra Full Moon occurred on April 3 AD 33, during the Passion of Christ. The full lunar glow of intellectual materialism held judgment over the radiant, solar heart of the Lamb. Every Libra Full Moon can bring us into a deep awareness of the mystery of the redemption of Death, which is simultaneously the redemption of the intellect and matter. The Moon was exactly full (opposite the Sun) at around 5:15 p.m. local time on that day, while Christ's body was being prepared for burial:

> While all were kneeling around the Lord's body, taking leave of it with many tears, a touching miracle was exhibited before their eyes: the entire form of Jesus's sacred body with all its wounds appeared, as if drawn in brown and reddish colors, on the cloth that covered it. It was as if he wished gratefully to reward their loving care of him, gratefully to acknowledge their sorrow, and leave to them an image of himself imprinted through all the coverings that enveloped him. Weeping and lamenting, they embraced the sacred body, and reverently kissed the miraculous portrait. Their astonishment was so great that they opened the outside wrapping, and it became still greater when they found all the linen bands around the sacred body white as before and only the uppermost cloth marked with the Lord's figure.[74]

May we be likewise imprinted by today's Full Moon.

**April 27: Sun 12°10' Aries square Saturn 12°10' Capricorn.** This recalls more or less the entire time period from Good Friday (April 3) up through April 15 AD 33 (when the miraculous draught of fish occurred). During this time period, Sun was in Aries square to Saturn in Cancer. The planetary configurations continue to strongly recall the time of Easter.

**April 28: Mercury enters Gemini.**

> Arise, O shining light
>     (*Sun in Aries*)
> Feel growth's power
>     (*Venus in Taurus*)
> Embrace joyful striving
>     (*Mercury in Gemini*)

72 Ibid., p. 71.

73 Steiner, *Twelve Cosmic Moods.*

74 ACE, vol. 3, p. 318.

To gain strength in test of trial
    (*Mars in Cancer*)
May world-being's vigilance grow in power
    (*Jupiter in Capricorn*)
And may the might of life's activity flower
    (*Saturn in Capricorn*)
O worlds, uphold worlds!
    (*Moon in Virgo*)[75]

**April 25** and May 5, the Sun comes into conjunction with Uranus, exact on **April 30: Sun and Uranus conjunct 15°39' Aries.** This is a very powerful configuration. The Sun was at this degree on the Resurrection, the most miraculous occurrence in history. And the Sun and Uranus were conjunct, albeit in Leo, on August 3 AD 30, during the second archetypal healing miracle of Christ, the Healing of the Nobleman's Son. A powerful foundation and inspiration for renewal is created during this time period—strive to bring it to fulfillment!

# MAY 2021

## STARGAZING PREVIEW

After Sunset on Monday the 3rd, the waning crescent Moon will pass below Saturn and reach its Last Quarter (19° Capricorn)—however, we won't catch sight of them until they rise (Saturn first) just before 0200. Twenty minutes later, it will be Jupiter that pulls up the Moon from below the eastern horizon. If by some chance you think you'll be asleep at this time, try rising at 0430 to watch Saturn, Jupiter, and the Moon overhead, due south, before dawn!

The night of May 4–5 offers the best chance to see the Eta–Aquarid meteor showers. Arising from Halley's comet, they can typically be seen in both the southern and northern hemispheres. Moonlight often interferes with our ability to enjoy any meteor shower, and tonight is no exception; your best viewing opportunity will be to look toward the northeast before the 0200 moonrise. Brilliant Jupiter will rise first, just a degree from the Moon.

---

75 Steiner, *Twelve Cosmic Moods*.

May's New Moon (26° Aries) occurs on the 11th. That night, between the setting of Mars (at 2340) and the rising of Saturn in the early hours of the 12th, the stars will have the sky to themselves.

On Saturday the 15th, the Sun is greeted by angels of Taurus: *Become bright, radiant being!* During the last hour of this day, the Moon will set slightly below and to the right of Mars. Sundown on the 17th will give you another chance to see Mercury, as it will set a full two hours after the Sun. Wednesday the 19th marks the First Quarter Moon at 4° Leo, its position at the Raising of Lazarus. At sunset, it will be at culmination, moments from passing above *Regulus*. What a show! Saturn begins its yearly retrograde movement on the 23rd, so it will appear to be moving backward through the zodiac until October.

Yes, it's another Supermoon this month (on the 26th at 1115), this time at 10° Scorpio! More amazing still is the Total Lunar Eclipse that will result! This is a Pacific eclipse that will be experienced in eastern Asia, Australia, and the Americas. Steiner said that those seeking evil thoughts can easily find them during a lunar eclipse—let us all, therefore, wherever we may live, think only of the good, the true, and the beautiful while the Earth's shadow moves across the face of the Full Moon. As the Moon rises that evening, you might also be able to see *Antares* by its side. On the final day of May, the Moon and Saturn will rise together at midnight. Mars sets with *Pollux* at 2300.

## MAY COMMENTARIES

The opposition of Mars and Pluto set the tone for most of the month of April, as did the square alignments of the Sun with Pluto, Mars, and Saturn (in that order). Now, as we enter the month of May, it is the opposition of Mars and Saturn that carries through most of the month, from April 26 through May 20. This alignment is exact on **May 8: Mars 12°30' Cancer opposite Saturn 12°30' Capricorn.** The other dominant aspect for the first part of the month of May is Sun square Jupiter, from May 2–13. They, too, come into exact alignment on **May 8: Sun 23°1' Aries square Jupiter 23°1' Capricorn.** At the beginning of the month, however, fleet-footed

Mercury aspects several planets—we will address Mercury specifically before investigating the star memories of these longer lasting aspects involving Mars, Saturn, Sun, and Jupiter...

**May 3: Mercury enters Cancer.**

> Arise, O shining light
>> (*Sun in Aries*)
> Feel growth's power
>> (*Venus in Taurus*)
> Warm soul life
>> (*Mercury in Cancer*)
> To gain strength in test of trial
>> (*Mars in Cancer*)
> May world-being's vigilance grow in power
>> (*Jupiter in Capricorn*)
> And may the might of life's activity flower
>> (*Saturn in Capricorn*)
> May the past bear the future!
>> (*Moon in Capricorn*)[76]

May 2–3, Mercury opposes Pluto, exact on **May 3: Mercury 0°9' Cancer opposite Pluto 0°9' Capricorn.** Then, between May 3–5, Mercury conjoins Mars, exact on the 4th.

**May 4: Mercury conjunct Mars 11°1' Cancer.** After this, Mercury opposes Saturn between May 4–5, exact on **May 5: Mercury 12°25' Cancer opposite Saturn 12°25' Capricorn.** Finally, on May 6–7, Mercury opposes Jupiter, exact on **May 6: Mercury 22°55' Cancer opposite Jupiter 22°55' Capricorn.** The Messenger has *a lot* to communicate this week!

Mercury was ingressing Cancer on December 23 AD 29, during which "...Jesus taught in the synagogue. Many friends and relatives were in attendance, including the holy Virgin Mary. In connection with the lighting of the candles at the Feast of Dedication, Jesus spoke of the light that should not be hidden under a bushel (Matt. 5:7)."[77] Mercury and Pluto were opposed in Gemini and Sagittarius respectively on December 8 AD 30—once again we return to the star memory from February 19 (see the entry for Venus conjunct Jupiter for commentary).

As to Mercury and Mars, the former (in Cancer) opposed the latter (in Capricorn) over the course of Good Friday through the day after Easter Sunday. This opposition was exact on Sunday evening, during which the disciples and the holy women hosted the first Agape Love Feast after the resurrection of Christ. This was a solemn, and yet very joyful and intimate occasion.

Mercury opposite Saturn once again recalls to us July 16 AD 32, shortly after Lazarus had died (see the commentary for February 5).

At the same time Mercury is coming into opposition with Saturn, Venus aligns with the Node. On May 2–8, they are conjunct, and exact on the 5th.

**May 5: Venus and Node 16° Taurus.** These two were conjunct very close to this degree on February 23 AD 31:

> The publicans distributed the greater part of their wealth. On the place upon which Jesus had taught, they heaped up great quantities of corn which they afterward measured out to the poor. They likewise bestowed fields and gardens upon poor day laborers and slaves, and repaired all the wrong they had done.
>
> When Jesus was again teaching at the custom house before the pagans and Jews, some strangers arrived, Pharisees, to celebrate here the sabbath. They reproached Jesus for lodging among the publicans and for having familiar communications with them and the pagans.[78]

Mercury and Jupiter were conjunct 21° Aries a few days later, on February 25, each of them square to their positions on May 6 of this year:

> Jesus taught in the schools, and went with some of the inhabitants and the apostles into the homes of the shepherds around the lake. John the Baptist had once sojourned in this region.
>
> From this place, Jesus with John, Bartholomew, and a disciple went three hours southward to Nobah, a city of Decapolis. The inhabitants were pagans and Jews. they dwelt apart, the city being divided into two quarters, each of which had a somewhat different name. All the cities of this part of the country were built of black, glimmering stone. Jesus taught in Nobah

---

76 Steiner, *Twelve Cosmic Moods.*
77 ACE, vol. 1, p. 382.
78 ACE, vol. 2, p. 315.

## SIDEREAL GEOCENTRIC LONGITUDES : MAY 2021 Gregorian at 0 hours UT

| DAY | ☉ | ☽ | ☊ | ☿ | ♀ | ♂ | ♃ | ♄ | ♅ | ♆ | ♇ |
|---|---|---|---|---|---|---|---|---|---|---|---|
| 1 SA | 15 ♈ 49 | 9 ♐ 37 | 16 ♉ 0 | 29 ♈ 6 | 25 ♈ 1 | 9 ♊ 31 | 3 ♒ 19 | 18 ♑ 4 | 15 ♈ 39 | 27 ♒ 21 | 1 ♑ 46R |
| 2 SU | 16 47 | 23 46 | 16 2 | 1 ♉ 2 | 26 15 | 10 8 | 3 27 | 18 6 | 15 43 | 27 23 | 1 46 |
| 3 MO | 17 45 | 7 ♑ 30 | 16 3 | 2 55 | 27 28 | 10 44 | 3 36 | 18 8 | 15 46 | 27 25 | 1 46 |
| 4 TU | 18 43 | 20 51 | 16 3R | 4 45 | 28 42 | 11 21 | 3 44 | 18 10 | 15 50 | 27 26 | 1 45 |
| 5 WE | 19 41 | 3 ♒ 50 | 16 2 | 6 32 | 29 56 | 11 57 | 3 52 | 18 12 | 15 53 | 27 28 | 1 45 |
| 6 TH | 20 39 | 16 30 | 16 0 | 8 16 | 1 ♉ 10 | 12 34 | 4 0 | 18 14 | 15 56 | 27 29 | 1 45 |
| 7 FR | 21 38 | 28 55 | 15 57 | 9 56 | 2 24 | 13 10 | 4 8 | 18 16 | 16 0 | 27 31 | 1 45 |
| 8 SA | 22 36 | 11 ♓ 7 | 15 53 | 11 33 | 3 38 | 13 47 | 4 15 | 18 17 | 16 3 | 27 32 | 1 45 |
| 9 SU | 23 34 | 23 9 | 15 49 | 13 6 | 4 52 | 14 23 | 4 23 | 18 19 | 16 7 | 27 34 | 1 44 |
| 10 MO | 24 32 | 5 ♈ 5 | 15 46 | 14 35 | 6 5 | 15 0 | 4 30 | 18 20 | 16 10 | 27 35 | 1 44 |
| 11 TU | 25 30 | 16 56 | 15 43 | 16 1 | 7 19 | 15 37 | 4 37 | 18 21 | 16 14 | 27 37 | 1 44 |
| 12 WE | 26 28 | 28 44 | 15 41 | 17 23 | 8 33 | 16 13 | 4 44 | 18 22 | 16 17 | 27 38 | 1 43 |
| 13 TH | 27 26 | 10 ♉ 31 | 15 41 | 18 41 | 9 47 | 16 50 | 4 51 | 18 23 | 16 20 | 27 40 | 1 43 |
| 14 FR | 28 24 | 22 20 | 15 41D | 19 54 | 11 0 | 17 27 | 4 58 | 18 24 | 16 24 | 27 41 | 1 42 |
| 15 SA | 29 21 | 4 ♊ 13 | 15 41 | 21 4 | 12 14 | 18 3 | 5 5 | 18 25 | 16 27 | 27 42 | 1 42 |
| 16 SU | 0 ♉ 19 | 16 14 | 15 43 | 22 10 | 13 28 | 18 40 | 5 11 | 18 26 | 16 31 | 27 43 | 1 41 |
| 17 MO | 1 17 | 28 25 | 15 44 | 23 11 | 14 41 | 19 17 | 5 17 | 18 27 | 16 34 | 27 45 | 1 41 |
| 18 TU | 2 15 | 10 ♋ 50 | 15 45 | 24 8 | 15 55 | 19 53 | 5 24 | 18 27 | 16 37 | 27 46 | 1 40 |
| 19 WE | 3 13 | 23 33 | 15 46 | 25 1 | 17 9 | 20 30 | 5 30 | 18 28 | 16 41 | 27 47 | 1 40 |
| 20 TH | 4 11 | 6 ♌ 38 | 15 46R | 25 49 | 18 22 | 21 7 | 5 35 | 18 28 | 16 44 | 27 48 | 1 39 |
| 21 FR | 5 8 | 20 7 | 15 46 | 26 33 | 19 36 | 21 43 | 5 41 | 18 28 | 16 47 | 27 49 | 1 38 |
| 22 SA | 6 6 | 4 ♍ 2 | 15 45 | 27 13 | 20 49 | 22 20 | 5 46 | 18 29 | 16 51 | 27 51 | 1 38 |
| 23 SU | 7 4 | 18 23 | 15 44 | 27 48 | 22 3 | 22 57 | 5 52 | 18 29 | 16 54 | 27 52 | 1 37 |
| 24 MO | 8 1 | 3 ♎ 6 | 15 43 | 28 18 | 23 16 | 23 34 | 5 57 | 18 29R | 16 57 | 27 53 | 1 36 |
| 25 TU | 8 59 | 18 7 | 15 42 | 28 44 | 24 30 | 24 10 | 6 2 | 18 29 | 17 1 | 27 54 | 1 36 |
| 26 WE | 9 57 | 3 ♏ 18 | 15 42 | 29 4 | 25 43 | 24 47 | 6 7 | 18 28 | 17 4 | 27 55 | 1 35 |
| 27 TH | 10 54 | 18 28 | 15 42D | 29 21 | 26 57 | 25 24 | 6 11 | 18 28 | 17 7 | 27 56 | 1 34 |
| 28 FR | 11 52 | 3 ♐ 29 | 15 42 | 29 32 | 28 10 | 26 1 | 6 16 | 18 28 | 17 10 | 27 57 | 1 33 |
| 29 SA | 12 49 | 18 14 | 15 42 | 29 39 | 29 24 | 26 37 | 6 20 | 18 27 | 17 14 | 27 58 | 1 33 |
| 30 SU | 13 47 | 2 ♑ 35 | 15 43 | 29 41R | 0 ♊ 37 | 27 14 | 6 24 | 18 27 | 17 17 | 27 58 | 1 32 |
| 31 MO | 14 44 | 16 30 | 15 43 | 29 38 | 1 50 | 27 51 | 6 28 | 18 26 | 17 20 | 27 59 | 1 31 |

## SIDEREAL HELIOCENTRIC LONGITUDES : MAY 2021 Gregorian at 0 hours UT

| DAY | Sid. Time | ☿ | ♀ | ⊕ | ♂ | ♃ | ♄ | ♅ | ♆ | ♇ | Vernal Point |
|---|---|---|---|---|---|---|---|---|---|---|---|
| 1 SA | 14:36:35 | 17 ♊ 16 | 7 ♉ 55 | 15 ♎ 49 | 9 ♋ 13 | 22 ♑ 22 | 12 ♑ 17 | 15 ♈ 39 | 25 ♒ 55 | 0 ♑ 8 | 4 ♓ 5′45″ |
| 2 SU | 14:40:32 | 23 23 | 9 32 | 16 47 | 9 40 | 22 27 | 12 19 | 15 40 | 25 56 | 0 8 | 4 ♓ 5′44″ |
| 3 MO | 14:44:28 | 29 24 | 11 8 | 17 46 | 10 7 | 22 33 | 12 20 | 15 41 | 25 56 | 0 9 | 4 ♓ 5′44″ |
| 4 TU | 14:48:25 | 5 ♋ 17 | 12 45 | 18 44 | 10 34 | 22 38 | 12 22 | 15 41 | 25 56 | 0 9 | 4 ♓ 5′44″ |
| 5 WE | 14:52:21 | 11 2 | 14 21 | 19 42 | 11 1 | 22 43 | 12 24 | 15 42 | 25 57 | 0 9 | 4 ♓ 5′44″ |
| 6 TH | 14:56:18 | 16 38 | 15 58 | 20 40 | 11 28 | 22 49 | 12 26 | 15 43 | 25 57 | 0 9 | 4 ♓ 5′44″ |
| 7 FR | 15: 0:14 | 22 5 | 17 35 | 21 38 | 11 55 | 22 54 | 12 28 | 15 44 | 25 58 | 0 10 | 4 ♓ 5′44″ |
| 8 SA | 15: 4:11 | 27 23 | 19 11 | 22 36 | 12 22 | 22 59 | 12 30 | 15 44 | 25 58 | 0 10 | 4 ♓ 5′44″ |
| 9 SU | 15: 8: 8 | 2 ♌ 30 | 20 48 | 23 34 | 12 49 | 23 4 | 12 32 | 15 45 | 25 58 | 0 10 | 4 ♓ 5′43″ |
| 10 MO | 15:12: 4 | 7 29 | 22 25 | 24 32 | 13 16 | 23 10 | 12 33 | 15 45 | 25 59 | 0 11 | 4 ♓ 5′43″ |
| 11 TU | 15:16: 1 | 12 17 | 24 1 | 25 30 | 13 43 | 23 15 | 12 35 | 15 46 | 25 59 | 0 11 | 4 ♓ 5′43″ |
| 12 WE | 15:19:57 | 16 56 | 25 38 | 26 28 | 14 10 | 23 20 | 12 37 | 15 47 | 25 59 | 0 11 | 4 ♓ 5′43″ |
| 13 TH | 15:23:54 | 21 27 | 27 15 | 27 26 | 14 36 | 23 25 | 12 39 | 15 47 | 26 0 | 0 12 | 4 ♓ 5′43″ |
| 14 FR | 15:27:50 | 25 48 | 28 52 | 28 24 | 15 3 | 23 31 | 12 41 | 15 48 | 26 0 | 0 12 | 4 ♓ 5′43″ |
| 15 SA | 15:31:47 | 0 ♍ 2 | 0 ♊ 29 | 29 22 | 15 30 | 23 36 | 12 43 | 15 49 | 26 0 | 0 12 | 4 ♓ 5′43″ |
| 16 SU | 15:35:43 | 4 7 | 2 6 | 0 ♏ 20 | 15 57 | 23 41 | 12 44 | 15 49 | 26 1 | 0 12 | 4 ♓ 5′42″ |
| 17 MO | 15:39:40 | 8 6 | 3 42 | 1 18 | 16 23 | 23 47 | 12 46 | 15 50 | 26 1 | 0 13 | 4 ♓ 5′42″ |
| 18 TU | 15:43:37 | 11 57 | 5 19 | 2 16 | 16 50 | 23 52 | 12 48 | 15 51 | 26 2 | 0 13 | 4 ♓ 5′42″ |
| 19 WE | 15:47:33 | 15 42 | 6 56 | 3 13 | 17 17 | 23 57 | 12 50 | 15 51 | 26 2 | 0 13 | 4 ♓ 5′42″ |
| 20 TH | 15:51:30 | 19 20 | 8 33 | 4 11 | 17 43 | 24 2 | 12 52 | 15 52 | 26 2 | 0 14 | 4 ♓ 5′42″ |
| 21 FR | 15:55:26 | 22 53 | 10 10 | 5 9 | 18 10 | 24 8 | 12 54 | 15 53 | 26 3 | 0 14 | 4 ♓ 5′42″ |
| 22 SA | 15:59:23 | 26 21 | 11 48 | 6 7 | 18 37 | 24 13 | 12 55 | 15 53 | 26 3 | 0 14 | 4 ♓ 5′42″ |
| 23 SU | 16: 3:19 | 29 44 | 13 25 | 7 4 | 19 3 | 24 18 | 12 57 | 15 54 | 26 3 | 0 14 | 4 ♓ 5′41″ |
| 24 MO | 16: 7:16 | 3 ♎ 2 | 15 2 | 8 2 | 19 30 | 24 24 | 12 59 | 15 55 | 26 4 | 0 15 | 4 ♓ 5′41″ |
| 25 TU | 16:11:12 | 6 16 | 16 39 | 9 0 | 19 56 | 24 29 | 13 1 | 15 55 | 26 4 | 0 15 | 4 ♓ 5′41″ |
| 26 WE | 16:15: 9 | 9 26 | 18 16 | 9 57 | 20 23 | 24 34 | 13 3 | 15 56 | 26 4 | 0 16 | 4 ♓ 5′41″ |
| 27 TH | 16:19: 6 | 12 33 | 19 53 | 10 55 | 20 50 | 24 39 | 13 5 | 15 57 | 26 5 | 0 16 | 4 ♓ 5′41″ |
| 28 FR | 16:23: 2 | 15 36 | 21 30 | 11 52 | 21 16 | 24 45 | 13 6 | 15 57 | 26 5 | 0 16 | 4 ♓ 5′41″ |
| 29 SA | 16:26:59 | 18 36 | 23 8 | 12 50 | 21 43 | 24 50 | 13 8 | 15 58 | 26 6 | 0 17 | 4 ♓ 5′41″ |
| 30 SU | 16:30:55 | 21 34 | 24 45 | 13 47 | 22 9 | 24 55 | 13 10 | 15 59 | 26 6 | 0 17 | 4 ♓ 5′41″ |
| 31 MO | 16:34:52 | 24 30 | 26 22 | 14 45 | 22 36 | 25 1 | 13 12 | 15 59 | 26 6 | 0 17 | 4 ♓ 5′40″ |

and in some of the little places around. John and Bartholomew were with him, the other apostles and disciples being scattered throughout the neighboring country. They stayed in an inn frequented by Pharisees.[79]

And now, we come to the events recalled by Mars and Saturn on May 8, which shine vividly through the first few weeks of the month. They were aligned in the opposite degrees (Mars in Capricorn and Saturn in Cancer) on May 17 AD 32, during which the events of Matthew 19 took place:

Then the small children were brought to him, that he might lay hands upon them and pray. But the disciples rebuked them. But Jesus said, "Leave the little children be and do not prevent them from coming to me; for of such is the Kingdom of the heavens." And, laying hands upon them, he departed from there.

And look: Someone approaching him said, "Teacher, what good thing may I do in order that I may have the life of the Age?" And he said to him, "Why do you question me concerning the good? One there is who is good. But if you wish to enter into life keep the commandments." He said to him, "Which ones?" And Jesus said, "You shall not murder, you shall not commit adultery, you shall not steal, you shall not bear false witness, honor your father and mother, and love your neighbor as yourself." The young man said to him, "All of these I have kept; what am I still lacking?" Jesus said to him, "If you wish to be perfect, go sell your possessions and give to the poor, and you shall have a treasury in the heavens, and come follow me." But the young man, hearing the counsel, went away in sorrow, for he was someone who had many possessions. And Jesus said to his disciples, "Amen, I tell you that it will be hard for a rich man to enter into the Kingdom of the heavens. And again, I tell you, it is easier for a camel to enter in through the eye of a needle than for a rich man to enter into the Kingdom of God." But on hearing this the disciples were greatly astonished, saying, "Can any of them then be saved?" And, looking directly at them, Jesus said to them, "For men this is impossible, but for God all things are possible." Then, in reply, Peter said to him, "Look: We gave up

all things and followed you; what then will there be for us?" And Jesus said to them, "Amen, I tell you, in the Regeneration, when the Son of Man sits upon the throne of his glory, you who have followed me will yourselves sit also upon twelve thrones, judging the twelve tribes of Israel. And everyone who gave up houses or brothers or sisters or father or mother or children or fields for my name's sake will receive many times as much and will inherit life in that Age. But many who are first will be last, and the last first."[80]

At the same time that Mars and Saturn are exactly opposed on the 8th, the Sun is square Jupiter. These two were square, albeit with Sun in Capricorn and Jupiter in Aries, on January 5 AD 31:

The Pharisees had invited him to dinner, and when they found him so tardy in coming, they went to call him. All things, they said, had their time and so had these cures. The sabbath belonged to God, and he had now done enough. Jesus responded: "I have no other time and no other measure than the will of the heavenly Father." When he had finished curing, he accompanied the disciples to the dinner.

During the meal the Pharisees addressed to him all kinds of reproaches; among others that he allowed women of bad repute to follow him about. These men had heard of the conversion of Magdalene, of Mara the Suphanite, and of the Samaritan. Jesus replied: "If ye knew me, ye would speak differently. I am come to have pity on sinners." He contrasted external ulcers, which carry off poisonous humors and are easily healed, with internal ones which, though full of loathsome matter, do not affect the appearance of the individual so afflicted.[81]

In addition to Mars opposite Saturn and Sun square Jupiter, another dominant aspect over the course of May is Mars square Uranus. These two are in alignment from May 4–24, nearly three weeks. The exact alignment is not until May 15—see further down for commentary.

**May 8: Mercury enters Leo.**

79 Ibid., p. 316.

80 Hart, David Bentley, *The New Testament: A Translation*; Matt. 19:13–30.

81 ACE, vol. 2, p. 204.

Arise, O shining light
   (*Sun in Aries*)
Feel growth's power
   (*Venus in Taurus*)
Feeling being's essence
   (*Mercury in Leo*)
To gain strength in test of trial
   (*Mars in Cancer*)
May world-being's vigilance grow in power
   (*Jupiter in Capricorn*)
And may the might of life's activity flower
   (*Saturn in Capricorn*)
May loss be gain in itself!
   (*Moon in Pisces*)[82]

**May 11: New Moon 26°15' Aries.** There was a New Moon at 21° Aries on April 10 AD 31:

> Jesus went into some of the houses to visit the old people, and he cured some sick. On the market square of the place in front of the synagogue, he delivered a long discourse first to the children, whom he caressed and blessed, then to the youths and maidens who, on account of the general festival, were present with their teachers. After they had gone home, he taught successively several groups of men and women, making use of all kinds of similitudes. His subject was marriage, which he treated in very beautiful and deeply significant terms. He began by saying that in human nature much evil is mixed with good, but that by prayer and renunciation the two must be separated and the evil subdued. He who follows his unbridled passions works mischief. Our works follow us and they will at some future day rise up against their author. Our body is an image of the Creator, but Satan aims at destroying that image in us. All that is superfluous brings with it sin and sickness, becomes deformity and abomination. Jesus exhorted his hearers to chastity, moderation, and prayer. Continence, prayer, and discipline have produced holy men and prophets. Jesus illustrated all this by similitudes referring to the sowing of the grain, to the clearing out of stones and weeds from the field, to its lying fallow, and to the blessing of God upon land justly acquired. In speaking of the married state, he

borrowed his similitudes from the planting of the vine and the pruning of the branches. He spoke of noble offspring, of pious families, of improved vineyards... [83]

May 8–15, Venus enters square alignment with Neptune, exact on the 12th.

**May 12: Venus 25°59' Taurus square Neptune 25°59' Aquarius.** These two were square, with Venus in Scorpio and Neptune in Aquarius, in the days just after Easter Sunday (exact on April 9 AD 33). Mercury comes into opposition with Neptune at the same time as this square alignment, exact on the 13th.

**May 13: Ascension Thursday, Mercury 26° Leo opposite Neptune 26° Aquarius.** Mercury opposite Neptune once again recalls the events and teachings of August 23 AD 32 (see commentary for Feb. 14). Today we celebrate Christ's journey through the nine hierarchies back to the Father, perhaps acutely experiencing the loss of the presence of the Risen Christ. We can experience this over the course of the next ten days as a sort of fast, preparing us for the gift of the tongues of flame through the Mediatrix, the Virgin Mary–Sophia, on Whitsun.

**May 14: Venus enters Gemini; Mercury enters Virgo.**

**May 15: Sun enters Taurus.**

Become bright, radiant being
   (*Sun in Taurus*)
Set repose in movement
   (*Venus in Gemini*)
May the spirit penetrate being
   (*Mercury in Virgo*)
To gain strength in test of trial
   (*Mars in Cancer*)
May world-being's vigilance grow in power
   (*Jupiter in Capricorn*)
And may the might of life's activity flower
   (*Saturn in Capricorn*)
O Sun life, endure!
   (*Moon in Gemini*)[84]

---

82 Steiner, *Twelve Cosmic Moods.*

83 ACE, vol. 2, p. 346.
84 Steiner, *Twelve Cosmic Moods.*

**May 15: Mars 15°49' Cancer square Uranus 15°49' Aries.** Mars was at this degree on April 15 AD 33, ten days after the Resurrection. This was the morning that Christ appeared to the apostles at the Sea of Galilee, when upon his direction they miraculously caught 153 fish after a whole night coming up empty:

> While the apostles were on the sea fishing, I saw the Savior floating out of the valley of Jehosaphat and surrounded by many souls of the ancient patriarchs whom he had freed from Limbo, also by others who had been banished to different places, caves, swamps, and deserts. During the whole period of these forty days, I saw Jesus, when not among the disciples, with the holy souls. They were principally from Adam and Eve down to Noah, Abraham, and other ancient leaders of the people. He went over all places remarkable in his life, showing them all things, and instructing them upon what he had done and suffered for them, whereby they became indescribably quickened and through gratitude purified. He taught them, in a certain measure at this time, the mysteries of the New Testament, by which they were released from their fetters. I saw him with them in Nazareth, in the crib cave and Bethlehem, and in every place in which anything remarkable had happened to him.... I saw them in long, narrow garments that fell around them in shining folds, and floated behind in a long train. Their hair did not look like ordinary hair, but like rays of light, each of which signified something. The beards of the men were composed of similar rays. Though not distinguished by any external sign, yet I recognized the kings, and especially the priests to do with the Ark of the Covenant. In the journeys of the Savior I always saw them floating around him, so that here too the spirit of order reigned in everything. The movements of these apparitions were exceedingly graceful and dignified. They seemed to float along, not exactly in an upright position, but inclining gently forward. They did not touch the earth-like bodies that have weight, but appeared to hover just above the ground.
>
> I saw the Lord arrive at the sea in company with these souls while the apostles were still fishing. Back of a little mound on the shore there was a hollow in which was a covered fireplace, for the use of the shepherds, perhaps. I did not see Jesus kindling a fire, catching a fish, or getting one in any other way. Fire and fish and everything necessary appeared at once in the presence of the souls as soon as ever it entered into the Lord's mind that a fish should here be prepared for eating. How it happened, I cannot say.
>
> The spirits of the patriarchs had a share in this fish and in its preparation. It bore some signification relative to the Church Suffering, to the souls undergoing purification. They were in this meal bound to the Church Militant by visible ties. In the eating of this fish, Jesus gave the apostles an idea of the union existing between the Church Suffering and the Church Militant. Jonah in the fish was typical of Jesus's stay in the lower world. Outside the hut was a beam that served for a table.[85]

**May 23: Pentecost; Mercury enters Libra.**

> Become bright, radiant being
>     (*Sun in Taurus*)
> Set repose in movement
>     (*Venus in Gemini*)
> In existing embrace existence
>     (*Mercury in Libra*)
> To gain strength in test of trial
>     (*Mars in Cancer*)
> May world-being's vigilance grow in power
>     (*Jupiter in Capricorn*)
> And may the might of life's activity flower
>     (*Saturn in Capricorn*)
> O soul, know thou beings!
>     (*Moon in Virgo*)[86]

Today we celebrate the coming into being of the living zodiac of apostles, with the Virgin Mary in their midst—the archetypal social phenomenon of conversation raised to its highest niveau. At the same time we feel Mercury ingressing into Libra. In one sense, Mercury is related to the fifth major arcanum, the Pope, and Libra, is related to the eighth major arcanum, Justice. The Pope represents to us the monk's vow of poverty, while Justice represents the corollary to poverty in the knight's

---

85 ACE, vol. 3, p. 401.
86 Steiner, *Twelve Cosmic Moods*.

vows: justice, righteousness, self-mastery. In the interplay of poverty and righteousness is the secret to the first sacrifice of Archangel Jesus and Christ in the early ages of human incarnation. During this time, the Archangel Jesus sacrificed his "I" to facilitate Christ's harmonizing of the human physical body. This resulted in both *uprightness* (the vertical orientation of the human form) and *sensory integration,* or harmonization of the twelve senses. We can imagine today's Whitsun as a similar organization of the social body—a sacrifice on the part of Jesus and Christ to give us collective uprightness, as well as a harmonization of the twelve "social senses," the twelve conceptual languages of worldview that are always active, but rarely harmonized, in the body social.

### May 26: Full Moon 10°23' Scorpio.

A Scorpio Full Moon took place on April 25 AD 31. In the evening, Jesus Christ and his disciples set sail for Cyprus from Ornithopolis:

It was by starlight that Jesus, accompanied by all the travelers, went down to the harbor and embarked. The night was clear, and the stars looked larger than they do to us. There was quite a little fleet ready to receive the travelers.... Five of these galleys were fastened with ropes to the front and sides of the burden ship, which they drew forward after them. The remaining five formed an outer circle to these. Each of these vessels had, like Peter's boat on the Sea of Galilee, benches for the rowers raised around the mast and below these little cabins. Jesus stood near the mast of the ships that were fastened to the large one and, as they pushed off, he blessed both land and sea. Shoals of fishes swarmed after the flotilla, among them some very large ones with remarkable-looking mouths. They sported around and stretched their heads out of the water, as if hearkening to the instructions given by Jesus during the voyage.[87]

May 26–29, Mercury is opposite Uranus, exact on the 27th.

### May 27: Mercury 15°57' Libra opposite Uranus 15°57' Aries.

Mercury was at this degree the day before the Transfiguration, April 3 AD 31. We can imagine the long and arduous journey to the summit of Mt. Tabor during this time.

May 26 through June 6, the Sun is conjunct the Node, exact on the 31st.

### May 31: The Feast of the Visitation, Sun conjunct Node 15°43' Taurus.

These two were together at 19° Taurus on May 10 AD 31:

When Jesus was afterward taking dinner with the elders, three blind boys about ten to twelve years old were led in to him by some other children. The former were playing on flutes and another kind of instrument which they held to the mouth and touched at the same time with the fingers. It was not a fife, and it made a buzzing, humming sound like the Jew's harp. At intervals also they sang in a very agreeable manner. Their eyes were open, and it seemed as if a cataract had obscured the sight. Jesus asked them whether they desired to see the light, in order to walk diligently and piously in the paths of righteousness. They answered most joyously: "Lord, do thou help us! Help us, Lord, and we will do whatever thou commandest!" Then Jesus said, "Put down your instruments!" and he stood them before him, put his thumbs to his mouth, and passed them one after the other from the corner of the eyes to the temple above. Then he took up a dish of fruit from the table, held it before the boys, said, "Do ye see that?" blessed them, and gave them its contents. They stared around in joyful amazement, they were intoxicated with delight, and at last cast themselves weeping at Jesus's feet. The whole company were deeply touched; joy and wonder took possession of all. The three boys, full of joy, hurried with their guides out of the hall and through the streets to their parents. The whole city was in excitement. The children returned with their relatives and many others to the forecourt of the hall, singing songs of joy and playing upon their instruments, in order thus to express their thanks. Jesus took occasion from this circumstance to give a beautiful instruction on gratitude. He said, "Thanksgiving is a prayer which attracts new favors, so good is the heavenly Father."[88]

---

87 ACE, vol. 2, p. 354.

88 Ibid., p. 374.

What a wonderful imagination to carry with us as we celebrate the third major Marian festival of the year, when Mary visited her cousin Elizabeth. Jesus and John, though physically blind to each other in their mother's wombs, were nevertheless clearly visible to each other spiritually.

# JUNE 2021

## STARGAZING PREVIEW

As the month begins, you'll have more than an hour to view Venus (now in Gemini) in the evening sky; her only visible companion will be Mars, in the last degree of the Twins. Over the next six weeks, if you can manage stepping out after sunset, you'll be able to observe Venus drawing nearer to Mars, in advance of their meeting in Cancer next month. Saturn, Jupiter, and the Moon—all in the Waterman—will rise by 0100 on the 2nd, hours before the Moon reaches its Last Quarter (17° Aquarius). Mars enters Cancer on the 3rd, helping us *to gain strength in test of trial.*

The Taurus New Moon on the 10th will result in an Annular Solar Eclipse—lasting nearly four minutes—to those of us in the far north (Canada, Greenland, and Russia). Before daybreak the following morning, Mercury will have joined the Sun for another inferior conjunction. Have your prayers been answered?

Once the Sun has set on Friday the 11th, watch the waxing crescent Moon drawing Venus toward the western horizon; they set at 2130. On the 15th, the Sun moves into Gemini, which bestows clarity to our thinking when we seek a connection to what is *above*. The evening of the 13th brings the glorious sight of the Moon surpassing Mars before they set!

The Moon (2° Virgo) reaches its First Quarter on the 18th; after sunset, you'll be able to see it high in the south, fewer than 20° to the right of Spica, while Venus and Mars hover close to the western horizon. Jupiter begins its yearly retrograde movement on this day as well, reversing into Capricorn (from our perspective) in September.

The Sun makes a particularly spectacular entrance on the 21st, as it will have just reached its highest latitude of the year. In other words, dawn brings to us the Summer Solstice! That evening, Venus will travel below *Pollux*. During the early hours of the 23rd, Venus joins Mars (in Cancer), entreating us to *create life warmth*. The year's last Supermoon will occur on the 24th, at 8° Sagittarius. May the skies be clear so that we may gaze upon it!

## JUNE COMMENTARIES

**June 1: Mercury enters Scorpio.**

**June 2: Venus enters Cancer.**

> Become bright, radiant being
>     (*Sun in Taurus*)
> Create life warmth
>     (*Venus in Cancer*)
> In activity growth disappears
>     (*Mercury in Scorpio*)
> To gain strength in test of trial
>     (*Mars in Cancer*)
> May world-being's vigilance grow in power
>     (*Jupiter in Capricorn*)
> And may the might of life's activity flower
>     (*Saturn in Capricorn*)
> Limit thyself, O unlimited!
>     (*Moon in Aquarius*)[89]

May 30–June 5, Venus and Pluto come into opposition. This is exact on **June 2: Venus 0°18' Cancer opposite Pluto 0°18' Capricorn.** Venus was close to this degree on December 28 AD 29:

> Today, on the third day after Jesus's arrival in Cana, the marriage ceremony took place at about nine o'clock in the morning. Afterward, the guests left the synagogue and assembled for the wedding banquet. Jesus had taken responsibility for arranging the banquet. However, when Mary saw that there was no wine, she said to him: "They have no wine." There then followed the sequence of events that culminated in the miracle of the transformation of water into wine (John 2:4–11). This miracle gave

---

89 Steiner, *Twelve Cosmic Moods.*

## SIDEREAL GEOCENTRIC LONGITUDES : JUNE 2021 Gregorian at 0 hours UT

| DAY | ☉ | ☽ | ☊ | ☿ | ♀ | ♂ | ♃ | ♄ | ♅ | ♆ | ♇ |
|---|---|---|---|---|---|---|---|---|---|---|---|
| 1 TU | 15 ♉ 42 | 29 ♑ 58 | 15 ♉ 43R | 29 ♉ 31R | 3 ♊ 4 | 28 ♊ 28 | 6 ♒ 32 | 18 ♑ 25R | 17 ♈ 23 | 28 ♒ 0 | 1 ♑ 30R |
| 2 WE | 16 39 | 13 ♒ 1 | 15 43 | 29 20 | 4 17 | 29 5 | 6 36 | 18 24 | 17 26 | 28 1 | 1 29 |
| 3 TH | 17 37 | 25 41 | 15 42 | 29 5 | 5 30 | 29 42 | 6 39 | 18 23 | 17 29 | 28 2 | 1 28 |
| 4 FR | 18 34 | 8 ♓ 3 | 15 43D | 28 46 | 6 44 | 0 ♋ 18 | 6 42 | 18 22 | 17 32 | 28 2 | 1 27 |
| 5 SA | 19 32 | 20 10 | 15 43 | 28 23 | 7 57 | 0 55 | 6 45 | 18 21 | 17 35 | 28 3 | 1 26 |
| 6 SU | 20 29 | 2 ♈ 7 | 15 43 | 27 58 | 9 10 | 1 32 | 6 48 | 18 20 | 17 38 | 28 4 | 1 25 |
| 7 MO | 21 27 | 13 57 | 15 44 | 27 30 | 10 23 | 2 9 | 6 51 | 18 18 | 17 41 | 28 4 | 1 24 |
| 8 TU | 22 24 | 25 44 | 15 44 | 26 59 | 11 37 | 2 46 | 6 53 | 18 17 | 17 44 | 28 5 | 1 23 |
| 9 WE | 23 21 | 7 ♉ 32 | 15 45 | 26 27 | 12 50 | 3 23 | 6 56 | 18 15 | 17 47 | 28 5 | 1 22 |
| 10 TH | 24 19 | 19 22 | 15 45R | 25 54 | 14 3 | 4 0 | 6 58 | 18 14 | 17 50 | 28 6 | 1 21 |
| 11 FR | 25 16 | 1 ♊ 17 | 15 45 | 25 21 | 15 16 | 4 37 | 7 0 | 18 12 | 17 53 | 28 6 | 1 20 |
| 12 SA | 26 14 | 13 19 | 15 44 | 24 47 | 16 30 | 5 14 | 7 2 | 18 10 | 17 56 | 28 7 | 1 19 |
| 13 SU | 27 11 | 25 31 | 15 43 | 24 14 | 17 43 | 5 51 | 7 3 | 18 8 | 17 59 | 28 7 | 1 18 |
| 14 MO | 28 8 | 7 ♋ 53 | 15 41 | 23 42 | 18 56 | 6 28 | 7 4 | 18 6 | 18 2 | 28 8 | 1 17 |
| 15 TU | 29 6 | 20 29 | 15 39 | 23 12 | 20 9 | 7 5 | 7 6 | 18 4 | 18 5 | 28 8 | 1 15 |
| 16 WE | 0 ♊ 3 | 3 ♌ 20 | 15 38 | 22 45 | 21 22 | 7 42 | 7 7 | 18 2 | 18 7 | 28 8 | 1 14 |
| 17 TH | 1 0 | 16 27 | 15 36 | 22 19 | 22 35 | 8 19 | 7 7 | 18 0 | 18 10 | 28 9 | 1 13 |
| 18 FR | 1 57 | 29 54 | 15 36 | 21 57 | 23 48 | 8 56 | 7 8 | 17 58 | 18 13 | 28 9 | 1 12 |
| 19 SA | 2 55 | 13 ♍ 41 | 15 36D | 21 39 | 25 1 | 9 33 | 7 8 | 17 55 | 18 16 | 28 9 | 1 11 |
| 20 SU | 3 52 | 27 48 | 15 37 | 21 24 | 26 14 | 10 10 | 7 9 | 17 53 | 18 18 | 28 9 | 1 9 |
| 21 MO | 4 49 | 12 ♎ 15 | 15 38 | 21 14 | 27 27 | 10 47 | 7 9R | 17 50 | 18 21 | 28 10 | 1 8 |
| 22 TU | 5 46 | 26 58 | 15 39 | 21 7 | 28 40 | 11 24 | 7 9 | 17 47 | 18 24 | 28 10 | 1 7 |
| 23 WE | 6 44 | 11 ♏ 52 | 15 39 | 21 5D | 29 53 | 12 1 | 7 8 | 17 45 | 18 26 | 28 10 | 1 6 |
| 24 TH | 7 41 | 26 50 | 15 39R | 21 8 | 1 ♋ 6 | 12 38 | 7 8 | 17 42 | 18 29 | 28 10 | 1 4 |
| 25 FR | 8 38 | 11 ♐ 44 | 15 38 | 21 15 | 2 19 | 13 15 | 7 7 | 17 39 | 18 31 | 28 10 | 1 3 |
| 26 SA | 9 35 | 26 27 | 15 35 | 21 28 | 3 31 | 13 52 | 7 6 | 17 36 | 18 34 | 28 10R | 1 2 |
| 27 SU | 10 33 | 10 ♑ 50 | 15 32 | 21 44 | 4 44 | 14 29 | 7 5 | 17 33 | 18 36 | 28 10 | 1 0 |
| 28 MO | 11 30 | 24 50 | 15 29 | 22 6 | 5 57 | 15 7 | 7 3 | 17 30 | 18 38 | 28 10 | 0 59 |
| 29 TU | 12 27 | 8 ♒ 24 | 15 25 | 22 33 | 7 10 | 15 44 | 7 2 | 17 27 | 18 41 | 28 10 | 0 58 |
| 30 WE | 13 24 | 21 32 | 15 23 | 23 4 | 8 22 | 16 21 | 7 0 | 17 24 | 18 43 | 28 10 | 0 56 |

### INGRESSES :

1 ☽ → ♒ 0: 3
3 ☽ → ♓ 8:18
♂ → ♋ 12: 0
5 ☽ → ♈ 19:43
8 ☽ → ♉ 8:40
10 ☽ → ♊ 21:25
13 ☽ → ♋ 8:44
15 ☽ → ♌ 17:49
☉ → ♊ 22:47
18 ☽ → ♍ 0:10
20 ☽ → ♎ 3:40
22 ☽ → ♏ 4:54
23 ♀ → ♋ 2:22
24 ☽ → ♐ 5: 5
26 ☽ → ♑ 5:52
28 ☽ → ♒ 9: 2
30 ☽ → ♓ 15:53

### ASPECTS & ECLIPSES :

1 ☉ ☌ ☊ 0:21
☽ ☌ ♃ 12: 2
2 ☽ S☊ ☊ 5: 3
☉ □ ☽ 7:23
3 ☽ ☌ ♆ 4:30
5 ☿ □ ♆ 18:42
♂ ☍ ♇ 19:36
7 ☽ ☌ ♅ 7:38
8 ☽ ☌ A 2:11
9 ☽ ☌ ☊ 16:40
10 ☉ ● A 10:40
☉ ☌ ☽ 10:51
☽ ☌ ☿ 12:36
11 ☉ ☌i ☿ 1:11
12 ☽ ☌ ♀ 6:58
13 ☽ ☍ ♇ 11:14
☽ ☌ ♂ 21: 6
☉ □ ♆ 23:48
14 ☽ ☍ ♄ 19:27
♄ □ ♅ 22:20
16 ☽ ☍ ♃ 6:58
☽ N☊ ☊ 22:27
17 ☽ ☍ ♆ 20:54
18 ☉ □ ☽ 3:53
21 ☽ ☍ ♅ 10: 1
23 ☽ ☌ ☋ 6: 5
☽ ☌ P 10: 3
☽ ☍ ☿ 14:49
♀ ☍ ♇ 23:34
24 ☉ ☍ ☽ 18:38
26 ☽ ☌ ♇ 7:34
☽ ☍ ♀ 12:48
27 ☽ ☍ ♂ 6:28
☽ ☌ ♄ 11:22
28 ☽ ☌ ♃ 21:32
29 ☽ S☊ ☊ 12:40
30 ☽ ☌ ♆ 12:24

## SIDEREAL HELIOCENTRIC LONGITUDES : JUNE 2021 Gregorian at 0 hours UT

| DAY | Sid. Time | ☿ | ♀ | ⊕ | ♂ | ♃ | ♄ | ♅ | ♆ | ♇ | Vernal Point |
|---|---|---|---|---|---|---|---|---|---|---|---|
| 1 TU | 16:38:48 | 27 ♎ 23 | 28 ♊ 0 | 15 ♍ 42 | 23 ♋ 2 | 25 ♑ 6 | 13 ♑ 14 | 16 ♈ 0 | 26 ♒ 7 | 0 ♑ 17 | 4 ♓ 57'40" |
| 2 WE | 16:42:45 | 0 ♏ 15 | 29 37 | 16 40 | 23 29 | 25 11 | 13 16 | 16 1 | 26 7 | 0 17 | 4 ♓ 57'40" |
| 3 TH | 16:46:41 | 3 4 | 1 ♋ 14 | 17 37 | 23 55 | 25 16 | 13 18 | 16 1 | 26 7 | 0 18 | 4 ♓ 57'40" |
| 4 FR | 16:50:38 | 5 53 | 2 52 | 18 35 | 24 21 | 25 22 | 13 19 | 16 2 | 26 8 | 0 18 | 4 ♓ 57'40" |
| 5 SA | 16:54:35 | 8 40 | 4 29 | 19 32 | 24 48 | 25 27 | 13 21 | 16 3 | 26 8 | 0 18 | 4 ♓ 57'40" |
| 6 SU | 16:58:31 | 11 27 | 6 6 | 20 30 | 25 14 | 25 32 | 13 23 | 16 3 | 26 8 | 0 19 | 4 ♓ 57'40" |
| 7 MO | 17: 2:28 | 14 12 | 7 44 | 21 27 | 25 41 | 25 38 | 13 25 | 16 4 | 26 9 | 0 19 | 4 ♓ 57'39" |
| 8 TU | 17: 6:24 | 16 57 | 9 21 | 22 25 | 26 7 | 25 43 | 13 27 | 16 5 | 26 9 | 0 19 | 4 ♓ 57'39" |
| 9 WE | 17:10:21 | 19 42 | 10 59 | 23 22 | 26 34 | 25 48 | 13 29 | 16 5 | 26 10 | 0 19 | 4 ♓ 57'39" |
| 10 TH | 17:14:17 | 22 27 | 12 36 | 24 19 | 27 0 | 25 54 | 13 30 | 16 6 | 26 10 | 0 20 | 4 ♓ 57'39" |
| 11 FR | 17:18:14 | 25 11 | 14 14 | 25 17 | 27 26 | 25 59 | 13 32 | 16 7 | 26 10 | 0 20 | 4 ♓ 57'39" |
| 12 SA | 17:22:10 | 27 56 | 15 51 | 26 14 | 27 53 | 26 4 | 13 34 | 16 7 | 26 11 | 0 20 | 4 ♓ 57'39" |
| 13 SU | 17:26: 7 | 0 ♐ 42 | 17 29 | 27 12 | 28 19 | 26 9 | 13 36 | 16 8 | 26 11 | 0 21 | 4 ♓ 57'39" |
| 14 MO | 17:30: 4 | 3 28 | 19 6 | 28 9 | 28 45 | 26 15 | 13 38 | 16 8 | 26 11 | 0 21 | 4 ♓ 57'38" |
| 15 TU | 17:34: 0 | 6 15 | 20 44 | 29 6 | 29 12 | 26 20 | 13 40 | 16 9 | 26 12 | 0 21 | 4 ♓ 57'38" |
| 16 WE | 17:37:57 | 9 4 | 22 21 | 0 ♐ 3 | 29 38 | 26 25 | 13 41 | 16 10 | 26 12 | 0 22 | 4 ♓ 57'38" |
| 17 TH | 17:41:53 | 11 53 | 23 59 | 1 1 | 0 ♌ 4 | 26 31 | 13 43 | 16 10 | 26 12 | 0 22 | 4 ♓ 57'38" |
| 18 FR | 17:45:50 | 14 44 | 25 36 | 1 58 | 0 31 | 26 36 | 13 45 | 16 11 | 26 13 | 0 22 | 4 ♓ 57'38" |
| 19 SA | 17:49:46 | 17 37 | 27 14 | 2 55 | 0 57 | 26 41 | 13 47 | 16 12 | 26 13 | 0 22 | 4 ♓ 57'38" |
| 20 SU | 17:53:43 | 20 32 | 28 51 | 3 53 | 1 23 | 26 47 | 13 49 | 16 12 | 26 13 | 0 23 | 4 ♓ 57'38" |
| 21 MO | 17:57:39 | 23 29 | 0 ♌ 29 | 4 50 | 1 49 | 26 52 | 13 51 | 16 13 | 26 14 | 0 23 | 4 ♓ 57'37" |
| 22 TU | 18: 1:36 | 26 29 | 2 6 | 5 47 | 2 16 | 26 57 | 13 53 | 16 14 | 26 14 | 0 23 | 4 ♓ 57'37" |
| 23 WE | 18: 5:33 | 29 31 | 3 44 | 6 44 | 2 42 | 27 2 | 13 54 | 16 14 | 26 15 | 0 24 | 4 ♓ 57'37" |
| 24 TH | 18: 9:29 | 2 ♑ 37 | 5 22 | 7 42 | 3 8 | 27 8 | 13 56 | 16 15 | 26 15 | 0 24 | 4 ♓ 57'37" |
| 25 FR | 18:13:26 | 5 45 | 6 59 | 8 39 | 3 34 | 27 13 | 13 58 | 16 16 | 26 15 | 0 24 | 4 ♓ 57'37" |
| 26 SA | 18:17:22 | 8 58 | 8 37 | 9 36 | 4 1 | 27 18 | 14 0 | 16 16 | 26 16 | 0 24 | 4 ♓ 57'37" |
| 27 SU | 18:21:19 | 12 14 | 10 14 | 10 33 | 4 27 | 27 24 | 14 2 | 16 17 | 26 16 | 0 25 | 4 ♓ 57'37" |
| 28 MO | 18:25:15 | 15 34 | 11 52 | 11 30 | 4 53 | 27 29 | 14 4 | 16 18 | 26 16 | 0 25 | 4 ♓ 57'37" |
| 29 TU | 18:29:12 | 18 59 | 13 29 | 12 28 | 5 19 | 27 34 | 14 5 | 16 18 | 26 17 | 0 25 | 4 ♓ 57'36" |
| 30 WE | 18:33: 8 | 22 28 | 15 6 | 13 25 | 5 46 | 27 40 | 14 7 | 16 19 | 26 17 | 0 26 | 4 ♓ 57'36" |

### INGRESSES :

1 ☿ → ♏ 21:56
2 ♀ → ♋ 5:42
12 ☿ → ♐ 17:55
15 ⊕ → ♐ 22:32
16 ♂ → ♌ 20: 6
20 ♀ → ♌ 16:52
23 ☿ → ♑ 3:43

### ASPECTS (HELIOCENTRIC +MOON(TYCHONIC)) :

2 ♀ ☍ ♆ 10: 1
3 ☽ ☌ ♆ 0:50
4 ♂ N☊ ☊ 17:46
5 ☽ □ ♇ 20:21
6 ☽ □ ♀ 9:21
♂ ☍ ♃ 20:26
☽ □ ♄ 22:54
7 ☽ ☌ ♅ 4:17
☽ □ ♃ 23:56
8 ☽ □ ♂ 0:47
10 ☿ ☌ A 2:40
☽ ☍ ☿ 8: 5
♀ ☍ ♄ 13:36
☽ □ ♆ 13:43
11 ☿ ☌ ⊕ 1:11
☿ □ ♆ 8:34
⊕ □ ♆ 22:30
12 ♀ □ ♅ 3:57
♀ ☌ P 14:21
13 ☽ ☍ ♇ 9:25
14 ☽ ☍ ♄ 11: 1
☽ □ ♅ 15:47
15 ☽ ☌ ♀ 0:32
☽ ☍ ♃ 11: 4
☽ ☌ ♂ 16:54
17 ☽ ☍ ♆ 17:28
18 ♀ ☍ ♃ 15:30
19 ☽ □ ☿ 8:30
20 ☽ □ ♆ 4:18
21 ☽ □ ♄ 2:37
☽ ☍ ♅ 6:30
☽ □ ♃ 23:58
22 ♀ ☌ ♂ 3: 6
☽ □ ♂ 8:49
☽ □ ♀ 9:19
23 ☿ ☌ ♇ 6:48
☽ □ ♆ 23: 3
26 ☽ ☌ ♇ 6:33
27 ☽ ☌ ☿ 3: 3
☽ ☌ ♄ 5:24
☽ ☌ ♅ 9:15
☿ ☌ ♄ 13: 7
28 ☽ ☌ ♃ 4:38
☿ □ ♅ 5:12
☽ ☍ ♂ 18:17
29 ☽ ☍ ♀ 10:28
30 ☿ S☊ ☊ 7:16
☽ ☌ ♆ 8:52

interior strength to all those present who drank of the wine. All became convinced of Jesus's power and of the lofty nature of his mission. Faith entered their hearts, and they became inwardly united as a community. Here, for the first time, Jesus was in the midst of his community. He wrought this miracle on their behalf. This was his first miraculous sign, which found its octave subsequently in the last miracle, that of the Last Supper, at which the apostles received inner strength for their mission. After the banquet, the bridegroom Nathaniel had a private conversation with Jesus in which he expressed his desire to lead a life of continence. His bride came to Jesus with the same wish. Kneeling before Jesus, they took a vow to live as brother and sister for a period of three years. He bestowed his blessing upon them.[90]

Venus (Mother Nature) opposite Pluto (the Chthonic depths), remembering this first archetypal miracle of Christ is a powerful aspect under which to begin the month.

Already on May 23, one of the major aspects of the month of June begins to form: Mars opposite Jupiter. These two are opposed until June 20, with their alignment exact on the 6th.

**June 6: Mars 25°37' Cancer opposite Jupiter 25°37' Capricorn.** Mars was at this degree on September 7, 21 BC, at the birth of the Solomon Mary: the reincarnation of Eve, the mother of all humanity (Jupiter was also in Capricorn, but not exactly opposite). This wise woman's son (the reincarnated Zarathustra) died around the age of 17, his ego having entered into the pure body of the Nathan Jesus. After the death of her son, the Solomon Mary's husband died; after the great change that took place in the Nathan Jesus (who had barely expressed words at all, let alone wisdom, and now had become suddenly brilliant), his mother, the pure Nathan Mary died. The Solomon Mary wed Joseph, the Nathan Jesus's father, and took the other Jesus as her own son—as indeed he was inwardly! Later, just before the Baptism in the Jordan, Jesus poured out his soul—quite literally—to his mother. The "I" of Zarathustra departed, making way for Christ to

enter in. At the same time, due to this conversation, the pure immaculate soul of the Nathan Mary united with the Solomon Mary. She once again became the Virgin Mary. This composite being never died—she was "assumed" into Heaven some 15 years later, on August 16 AD 44. Mars was once again close to today's degree—24° Cancer—at the Assumption of the Virgin Mary. Mars at this degree marks both the birth and death of this holy being.

June 5–9, Mercury conjoins the Descending Node. This alignment is exact on the 7th.

**June 7: Mercury conjunct Descending Node 15°44' Scorpio.** Mercury was at this degree on April 13 AD 31:

> After the evening sabbath sermon in the synagogue, Jesus accepted the invitation of a well-to-do Pharisee to dine with him at his house. Here took place the healing of a man with edema, which scandalized the Pharisees (Luke 14:1–14). Jesus then told the parable of the great feast (Luke 14:15–24) and asked that the poor be invited to join with them in their meal.[91]

As this alignment is becoming exact, another begins to take shape: Venus is opposite Saturn June 7–13, exact on the 10th.

**June 10: Venus 13°31' Cancer opposite Saturn 13°31' Capricorn.** Venus was close to this degree on March 30 AD 31:

> Jesus and the disciples left Thanat–Shiloh and went on to Ataroth, where Jesus taught on a hill outside of the town and healed the sick. Later, after the sabbath had begun, Jesus taught in the synagogue. During the course of the evening, he healed a widow crippled at the waist for eighteen years. She was used to going bent double, almost touching the ground. Jesus summoned her to him and laid his hand on her back, saying: "Woman, be freed from your infirmity!" She rose up straightway and gave thanks to God. An aged Pharisee, who was also a cripple and for this reason had not gone to Jerusalem, presided over the synagogue. When the healing of the crippled widow took place, he turned to the people and said, "There are six days upon which

---

90 ACE, vol. 1, p. 386.

91 ACE, vol. 2, p. 346.

we may work. Come then and be healed, but not on the sabbath." Jesus replied: "You hypocrite! Does not everyone loose his ox or ass from the manger on the sabbath and lead it to water? And shall not this woman, a daughter of Abraham, be loosed from the bond in which Satan as bound her for eighteen years?" (Luke 13:10–17).[92]

At the same time, Mercury is opposed the Sun from June 8–13, also exact on the 10th.

**June 10: Mercury 25°19' Scorpio opposite Sun 25°19' Taurus.** The Sun at this degree brings us once again to the blessing of the children on May 17 AD 32 (see commentary for May 8). Mercury was close to this degree on January 19 AD 31, during which Christ performed the third archetypal healing miracle, the Healing of the Paralyzed Man—a man who, like the crooked woman above, had waited for many years to be healed. The burial of the remains of John the Baptist, who had died over two weeks prior, also occurred on that day.

With the overarching aspect between Mars and Jupiter, along with aspects between Venus and Saturn, and Mercury with both the Sun and Node, this is a very dynamic time period. Our attention is brought to Mary, to doing what is right in the face of self-righteous disdain, of burying the dead, and bringing movement to those who have been paralyzed for long, long years. Along with all these aspects, we also have a New Moon, during which there is an opening in the spiral, and new influences are able to enter and break us out of worn-out cycles.

**June 10: New Moon 24°45' Taurus.** A Taurus New Moon occurred on May 10 AD 31, when the Sun was also conjunct the Node. See the commentary for May 31 for the star memory of this day, when three blind boys were miraculously healed.

There are two other aspects occurring during this same time period in the first half of the month. One is Sun square Neptune; this occurs from June 6–17, exact on the 11th.

**June 11: Sun 26°11' Taurus square Neptune 26°11' Aquarius.** This once again brings us to the Assumption of the Virgin Mary, as Neptune was almost exactly at this same degree on that day. Meanwhile,

June 8–15, Venus is square Uranus, also exact on **June 11: Venus 16°7' Cancer square Uranus 16°7' Aries.** Venus was at this same degree on August 19 AD 30:

> Jesus went again to the synagogue in Capernaum to teach. It was the sabbath. And there took place the scene, described in Mark 1:23–27 and Luke 4:31–36, where Jesus healed a man who was possessed. After further healings, around midday, Jesus went to Peter's house in Bethsaida where he healed Peter's mother-in-law, who had a raging fever. She rose immediately from her bed and helped the other women serve the next meal (Luke 4:38–39; Matt. 8:14–15; Mark 1:29–31). Jesus then healed many more people who were brought to him at Peter's house (Mark 1:32–34). Later, after teaching again in the synagogue, Jesus withdrew to a lonely place where he spent the night in prayer.[93]

Virtually every single starry body (and the Node) is aspecting another during these first two weeks of June. This may be an exhausting time. Perhaps the right course of action here, midway through the month, is also to withdraw to a lonely place to spend time in prayer.

**June 12: Mercury enters Sagittarius.**

**June 15: Sun enters Gemini.**

**June 16: Mars enters Leo.**

> Reveal thyself, Sun life
>     (*Sun in Gemini*)
> Create life warmth
>     (*Venus in Cancer*)
> Attainment concludes joyful striving
>     (*Mercury in Sagittarius*)
> To firmly willed existence
>     (*Mars in Leo*)
> May world-being's vigilance grow in power
>     (*Jupiter in Capricorn*)
> And may the might of life's activity flower
>     (*Saturn in Capricorn*)
> With senses' might, arise!
>     (*Moon in Leo*)[94]

---

92  Ibid., p. 335.

93  Ibid., p. 21.

94  Steiner, *Twelve Cosmic Moods*.

The pause that we have taken after the over-whelming wash of influences from the starry heavens has yielded might, firm will, and fulfilled striving. The dominant aspect in the middle of the month is the opposition of Venus and Jupiter, from June 15–21. This alignment is exact on the 18th.

**June 18: Venus 26°39' Cancer opposite Jupiter 26°39' Capricorn.** Jupiter was at this degree at the conception of John the Baptist on September 9, 3 BC, while Venus was at this same degree on September 23 AD 29—the Baptism of Christ by John in the River Jordan. We feel here a strong resonance with the John individuality, with both his being called down from spiritual heights as well as the fulfilment of his mission—calling down Christ—being remembered today. We can consider the baptism of Christ as a kind of conception; the three-and-a-half-year ministry of Christ is a gestation; and Christ's descent into the depths of the Earth and Resurrection are the birth of the New Adam. The mysterious activity of conception—of John the Baptist physically (the reincarnation of the Old Adam) and of Christ spiritually (the New Adam)—also deserves the attention of our meditative life during these days.

**June 20: Venus enters Leo.**

**June 23: Mercury enters Capricorn.**

> Reveal thyself, Sun life
>   (*Sun in Gemini*)
> Existing ground of worlds
>   (*Venus in Leo*)
> To be strong in the present
>   (*Mercury in Capricorn*)
> To gain strength in test of trial
>   (*Mars in Leo*)
> May world-being's vigilance grow in power
>   (*Jupiter in Capricorn*)
> And may the might of life's activity flower
>   (*Saturn in Capricorn*)
> Being sustains beings
>   (*Moon in Scorpio*)[95]

For a good part of the month, Mars and Jupiter have been in opposition; later, and more briefly,

Venus and Jupiter were opposite each other. Mars and Jupiter recalled the Virgin Mary (the reincarnated Eve), while Venus and Jupiter recalled John (the reincarnated Adam). Isn't it remarkable that Venus, the archetypal Feminine, conjures Adam, while Mars, the archetypal Masculine, conjures Eve? What might this be drawing our attention to?

Now, after both have aspected Jupiter, Venus and Mars align. They conjoin from June 17–26, exact on the 22nd.

**June 22: Venus and Mars 2°19' Leo.** This occurs just one day after the Summer Solstice, the brightest and longest day of the year in the northern hemisphere. An opposition occurred between these two, with Venus in Leo and Mars in Aquarius, on July 15 AD 32: the death of Lazarus. Lazarus's health had been declining for months; he had become utterly disenchanted with the material plane, harboring a yearning for the spiritual world that he could find no way to meet on Earth. His sister, Mary Magdalene, attempted to heal his spiritual illness by performing an Egyptian death rite—an initiation—on her brother. But neither of them was adequately prepared for this (no longer appropriate) activity, leading to her brother's death. Mars and Jupiter lead us to the Virgin Mary (Eve); Venus and Jupiter to John the Baptist (Adam); and here, Venus and Mars lead us to Lazarus—the reincarnated Cain—and Magdalene—the reincarnated Abel. The primal family lives vividly in the heart and imagination during this month.

During the time of this conjunction, Mercury aligns with Pluto from June 21–24. This is exact on the 23rd.

**June 23: Mercury and Pluto 0°24' Capricorn.** Mercury was at this degree on April 2 AD 33, the morning before the Last Supper. Our attention is drawn to the Holy Grail:

> [Peter and John] got from Veronica all kinds of table service, which was carried by the disciples in covered baskets to the Cenacle. They took from here also the chalice of which Jesus made use in the institution of the blessed sacrament.
>
> This chalice was a very wonderful and mysterious vessel that had lain in the temple for a

---

95 Ibid.

long time among other old and precious things, whose use and origin even had been forgotten, just as with us many ancient, holy treasures have through the lapse of time fallen into oblivion. Frequently at the temple ancient vessels and precious ornaments whose use was no longer known were reset, made over anew, or sold. It was in this way, and by God's permission, that holy vessel (whose unknown material prevented its being melted down, although frequent attempts had been made to do so) had been found by the young priests in the treasury of the temple. It was stowed away in a chest along with other objects no longer of use, and when discovered was sold to some antiquaries. The chalice and all the vessels belonging to it were afterward bought by Veronica. It had several times been made use of by Jesus in the celebration of festivals, and from today it became the exclusive possession of the holy community of Jesus Christ. It was not always the same as when used at the Last Supper. I no longer remember when the parts that composed it were put together; perhaps it was on the occasion of the Lord's using it at the Last Supper. It was now, however, along with all that was necessary for the institution of the blessed sacrament, put up in one portable case.

On a flat surface out of which a little board, or tablet, could be drawn, stood the large chalice surrounded by six small beakers. The chalice itself contained another smaller vase. I cannot remember whether the tablet held the holy thing or not. A little plate was laid upon the chalice, and over the whole was a convex cover. In the foot of the chalice was a place for keeping a spoon, which could be easily drawn out. All these vessels in fine linen coverings were protected by a cap, or case of leather, I think, which had a knob on top. The large chalice consisted of the cup and the foot, which latter must have been added at a later period, for it was of different material. The cup was pear-shaped, and of a brownish, highly polished metal, overlaid with gold. It had two small handles, by which it could be raised when its contents rendered it tolerably heavy. The foot was elaborately wrought of dark virgin gold, the edge encircled by a serpent. It was ornamented with a little bunch of grapes, and enriched with precious stones. The small spoon was concealed in the foot.

The large chalice was left to the Church of Jerusalem under the care of James the Less. I see it still carefully preserved somewhere. It will again come to light as it did once before. The smaller cups that stood around it were distributed among the other churches: one to Antioch, another to Ephesus. These vessels enriched seven churches. The small beakers once belonged to the patriarchs, who drank some mysterious beverage out of them when they received or imparted the Blessing, as I have seen and already explained.

The large chalice once belonged to Abraham. Melchizedek brought it from the land of Semiramis, where it was lying neglected, to the land of Canaan, when he began to mark off settlements on the site afterward occupied by Jerusalem. He had used it at the sacrifice of bread and wine offered in Abraham's presence, and he afterward gave it to him. This same chalice was even in Noah's possession. It stood in the upper part of the ark. Moses also had it in his keeping. The cup was massive like a bell. It looked as if it had been shaped by nature, not formed by art. I have seen clear through it. Jesus alone knew of what it was made.[96]

### June 24: Feast of St. John. Full Moon 6°25' Sagittarius. A Sagittarius Full Moon occurred on June 12 AD 32:

Not far from the village were ten lepers in a tent. Jesus healed them, but only one ran after Jesus to thank him (Luke 17:11–19). The leper who ran after Jesus later became a disciple. Shortly afterward, as they passed along, a man came out of a shepherd settlement and begged Jesus to come because his daughter had just died. Jesus, accompanied by Peter, James, and John went with the shepherd to his house. His daughter, who was about seven years old, lay dead. Looking up to Heaven, Jesus placed one hand on her head and the other on her breast and prayed. The child then rose up, alive. Jesus told the apostles that—in his name—they should do as he did.[97]

### June 25–28, Mercury conjoins Saturn, exact on the 27th.

---

96 ACE, vol. 3, pp. 73–74.
97 ACE, vol. 2, p. 473.

**June 27: Mercury and Saturn 14°3' Capricorn.** Mercury at this degree recalls August 12 AD 30:

> Jesus taught again in the synagogue at Nazareth and sharply reproached the Pharisees for their misinterpretation of the Law. At midday, he dined with an Essene family. He then returned to teach at the synagogue again (Luke 4:23–28). At the close of the sabbath, when Jesus came out of the synagogue, he was immediately surrounded by about twenty Pharisees. They began to lead him out of the town toward a nearby hill, for they intended to cast him down from the brow of the hill. Suddenly, however, Jesus stopped, stood still, and with the help of angelic beings passed—as if invisible—through the midst of the crowd to his escape (Luke 4:29–30).[98]

From June 26 through to July 3, Venus is square the Node. This alignment is exact on the 29th.

**June 29: Venus 15°22' Leo square Node 15°22' Taurus.** These two were square, at almost exactly the same degrees, on April 18 AD 31:

> It was toward ten o'clock the next day when Jesus appeared upon the mountain. The disciples had put the people in order and indicated to them how they should in certain numbers exchange places from time to time, in order to hear Jesus's discourse, for the multitude was far greater than could be accommodated within hearing distance of the teacher's chair. The people were under tents, those from the same district camping together. Each district had its own camp, the entrance to which was adorned with an arch formed of the fruits peculiar to that district and surmounted by a crown made of the most magnificent specimens. Some had grapevines and corn; others, cotton plants, sugar cane, aromatic herbs, and all kinds of fruits and berries. Every district had its own distinctive sign, adorned with flowers and beautifully arranged. The whole produced a very pleasing effect. Numbers of birds, among them pigeons and quails, had taken up their quarters in the camp and were busy picking up the scattered crumbs. They had grown so familiar, so tame, that the people fed them from their hands.[99]

---

98 Ibid., p. 12.
99 Ibid., p. 348.

# JULY 2021

## STARGAZING PREVIEW

July opens and closes with a Last Quarter Moon! On the first day of the month, the Moon will be at 15° Pisces, a degree from the position of the Sun at both the birth of the Solomon Jesus and the conception of the Nathan Jesus. It sets at noon. Also on this day, Mars (Cancer) opposes Saturn (Capricorn), so those with an unobstructed horizon will be able to see Saturn rise at 2200, as Mars sets in the west. Venus reaches exact opposition to Saturn on Wednesday the 7th.

This month's New Moon will happen during the early hours of the 10th, at 23° Gemini. By the evening of the 12th, after the sun sets at 2000, you will be graced with a heavenly sight, as Venus, Mars, and the Moon (in a 5° arc, in Cancer) disappear below the western horizon together.

Tuesday the 13th will be a special day indeed, as Venus and Mars meet at 25° Cancer. Not only is it so satisfying to see the lovers together—it doesn't happen every year—but this zodiacal degree is one at which the life of the Nathan Mary can be particularly remembered. For this is the degree of her natal Sun, as well as the Moon (1° away, at 24° Cancer) and Mars at her death. Ave Maria!

An hour after the Crab welcomes the Sun on the 17th, the Moon (0° Libra) finds its First Quarter; it will be high in the south at dusk. Later that evening, Venus finds the warmth of Leo; with the planet of love only 5° from *Regulus*, can compassion be far behind? Mars follows Venus into Leo on the evening of the 21st. At 2100 on the 22nd, Venus, now beside the star marking the heart of the Lion, will set precisely as Jupiter (5° Aquarius) rises.

The 24th is the day of our July Full Moon, now at 6° Capricorn, less than a degree from its position at the birth of Valentin Tomberg; how lovely it will be to see it full and shining from there! The best night to view the Delta Aquarid meteor showers is the 27th–28th. As the name suggests, they originate from the direction of the constellation of Aquarius; unfortunately, this is also the location of the still-bright Moon. But it is July, after all, and those in the balmy northern hemisphere might enjoy a meteor quest despite suboptimal visibility.

The 31st is the day of July's second Last Quarter Moon, which will shine from the center of Aries. As it rises around 2300, Saturn and Jupiter will be high in the southern sky, as Scorpio is about to set. Orion is visible again, but only for a few hours before daybreak. He'll be in the southeast as the Sun rises.

## JULY COMMENTARIES

The month begins with Mercury conjunct Jupiter from June 29 through July 2. Their alignment is exact on the 1st.

**July 1: Mercury conjunct Jupiter 27°47' Capricorn.** Mercury was at this degree, square Jupiter in Aries, on May 7 AD 31. On this day Christ was teaching at an apiary in the land of Kythria:

> The Rechabites spoke with Jesus about Malachi, for whom they entertained great veneration. They told Jesus that they esteemed him an angel of God, that he had come as a child to certain pious people, that he had frequently disappeared for a time, and that no one knew whether he was now really dead or not. They dwelt at length on his prophecies of the Messiah and his new sacrifice, which Jesus explained as relating to the present and the near future....
>
> From thirty to forty pagan women and maidens and about ten Jewish girls were assembled at the entrance of the gardens to do Jesus honor. They were playing on flutes and singing canticles of praise; they wore flowery wreaths and strewed green branches in the way. Here and there also they spread mats on the road over which Jesus was to pass, inclined low before him, and offered him presents of wreaths, flowers, aromatic shrubs, and little flasks of perfume. Jesus thanked them, and addressed to them some words. They followed him to the courtyard of Barnabas's house, and set their gifts down in the assembly hall. They had adorned everything with flowers and garlands. This reception, though rural and less noisy, was something similar to that tendered Jesus on Palm Sunday. His escort soon returned to their homes, for it was evening.[100]

**July 2: Mercury enters Aquarius.**

> Reveal thyself, Sun life
> (*Sun in Gemini*)
> Existing ground of worlds
> (*Venus in Leo*)
> Found boundaries in its own depths
> (*Mercury in Aquarius*)
> To gain strength in test of trial
> (*Mars in Leo*)
> May world-being's vigilance grow in power
> (*Jupiter in Capricorn*)
> And may the might of life's activity flower
> (*Saturn in Capricorn*)
> May loss be gain in itself!
> (*Moon in Pisces*)[101]

**July 2–5,** Mercury and Mars are in opposition, exact on the 3rd.

**July 3: Mercury 7°32' Aquarius opposite Mars 7°32' Leo.** A kind of impish boldness can accompany such an aspect, as seen on September 1 AD 29, when these two planets were in almost exactly the same positions as today. Jesus of Nazareth was being hosted by the Pharisees in Chisloth for dinner, during which they hoped to trip him up in his speech:

> In this city there must have been an ancient custom commanding the poor—of whom there were numbers dwelling in the greatest abandonment—to be invited; for as soon as Jesus sat down at table, he turned to the Pharisees asking where were the poor, and whether it was not their right to take part in the feast. The Pharisees were embarrassed, and they answered that the custom had long fallen into disuse. Then Jesus commanded his disciples Arastaria and Cocharia, the sons of Maraha, and Kolaya, the son of the widow Lea, to go gather together the poor of the city and bring them to the feast. The Pharisees were highly displeased at the command, for it gave rise to much comment throughout the city. Many of the poor were already in bed and asleep. I saw the disciples rousing them. Numerous and varied were the joyous scenes I then witnessed in the huts and haunts of the poor. At last they arrived and were received and welcomed by

---

100   Ibid., p. 372.

101 Steiner, *Twelve Cosmic Moods.*

## SIDEREAL GEOCENTRIC LONGITUDES : JULY 2021 Gregorian at 0 hours UT

| DAY | | ☉ | ☽ | ☊ | ☿ | ♀ | ♂ | ♃ | ♄ | ♅ | ♆ | ♇ |
|---|---|---|---|---|---|---|---|---|---|---|---|---|
| 1 | TH | 14 ♊ 21 | 4 ♓ 16 | 15 ♉ 21R | 23 ♉ 40 | 9 ♋ 35 | 16 ♋ 58 | 6 ♒ 58R | 17 ♑ 20R | 18 ♈ 45 | 28 ♒ 10R | 0 ♑ 55R |
| 2 | FR | 15 19 | 16 39 | 15 21D | 24 20 | 10 48 | 17 35 | 6 56 | 17 17 | 18 48 | 28 9 | 0 54 |
| 3 | SA | 16 16 | 28 46 | 15 21 | 25 6 | 12 0 | 18 13 | 6 54 | 17 13 | 18 50 | 28 9 | 0 52 |
| 4 | SU | 17 13 | 10 ♈ 41 | 15 23 | 25 55 | 13 13 | 18 50 | 6 52 | 17 10 | 18 52 | 28 9 | 0 51 |
| 5 | MO | 18 10 | 22 30 | 15 24 | 26 50 | 14 26 | 19 27 | 6 49 | 17 6 | 18 54 | 28 9 | 0 49 |
| 6 | TU | 19 7 | 4 ♉ 17 | 15 26 | 27 48 | 15 38 | 20 4 | 6 46 | 17 3 | 18 56 | 28 8 | 0 48 |
| 7 | WE | 20 5 | 16 6 | 15 26R | 28 51 | 16 51 | 20 41 | 6 43 | 16 59 | 18 58 | 28 8 | 0 47 |
| 8 | TH | 21 2 | 28 2 | 15 25 | 29 59 | 18 3 | 21 19 | 6 40 | 16 55 | 19 0 | 28 8 | 0 45 |
| 9 | FR | 21 59 | 10 ♊ 6 | 15 23 | 1 ♊ 10 | 19 16 | 21 56 | 6 36 | 16 52 | 19 2 | 28 7 | 0 44 |
| 10 | SA | 22 56 | 22 20 | 15 19 | 2 26 | 20 28 | 22 33 | 6 33 | 16 48 | 19 4 | 28 7 | 0 42 |
| 11 | SU | 23 53 | 4 ♋ 47 | 15 13 | 3 46 | 21 41 | 23 11 | 6 29 | 16 44 | 19 6 | 28 6 | 0 41 |
| 12 | MO | 24 51 | 17 27 | 15 7 | 5 10 | 22 53 | 23 48 | 6 25 | 16 40 | 19 8 | 28 6 | 0 40 |
| 13 | TU | 25 48 | 0 ♌ 21 | 15 0 | 6 38 | 24 6 | 24 25 | 6 21 | 16 36 | 19 10 | 28 5 | 0 38 |
| 14 | WE | 26 45 | 13 27 | 14 54 | 8 10 | 25 18 | 25 3 | 6 17 | 16 32 | 19 12 | 28 5 | 0 37 |
| 15 | TH | 27 42 | 26 48 | 14 49 | 9 45 | 26 30 | 25 40 | 6 12 | 16 28 | 19 13 | 28 4 | 0 35 |
| 16 | FR | 28 40 | 10 ♍ 21 | 14 46 | 11 25 | 27 43 | 26 18 | 6 8 | 16 24 | 19 15 | 28 3 | 0 34 |
| 17 | SA | 29 37 | 24 7 | 14 44 | 13 8 | 28 55 | 26 55 | 6 3 | 16 20 | 19 17 | 28 3 | 0 32 |
| 18 | SU | 0 ♋ 34 | 8 ♎ 7 | 14 44D | 14 54 | 0 ♌ 7 | 27 33 | 5 58 | 16 15 | 19 18 | 28 2 | 0 31 |
| 19 | MO | 1 31 | 22 19 | 14 45 | 16 44 | 1 19 | 28 10 | 5 53 | 16 11 | 19 20 | 28 1 | 0 29 |
| 20 | TU | 2 29 | 6 ♏ 42 | 14 46 | 18 36 | 2 32 | 28 47 | 5 48 | 16 7 | 19 21 | 28 1 | 0 28 |
| 21 | WE | 3 26 | 21 13 | 14 46R | 20 32 | 3 44 | 29 25 | 5 42 | 16 3 | 19 23 | 28 0 | 0 27 |
| 22 | TH | 4 23 | 5 ♐ 49 | 14 44 | 22 29 | 4 56 | 0 ♌ 2 | 5 37 | 15 58 | 19 24 | 27 59 | 0 25 |
| 23 | FR | 5 20 | 20 24 | 14 40 | 24 29 | 6 8 | 0 40 | 5 31 | 15 54 | 19 26 | 27 58 | 0 24 |
| 24 | SA | 6 18 | 4 ♑ 51 | 14 34 | 26 31 | 7 20 | 1 17 | 5 26 | 15 50 | 19 27 | 27 57 | 0 22 |
| 25 | SU | 7 15 | 19 4 | 14 27 | 28 35 | 8 32 | 1 55 | 5 20 | 15 45 | 19 28 | 27 57 | 0 21 |
| 26 | MO | 8 12 | 2 ♒ 58 | 14 18 | 0 ♋ 39 | 9 44 | 2 33 | 5 13 | 15 41 | 19 30 | 27 56 | 0 19 |
| 27 | TU | 9 10 | 16 30 | 14 10 | 2 45 | 10 56 | 3 10 | 5 7 | 15 36 | 19 31 | 27 55 | 0 18 |
| 28 | WE | 10 7 | 29 38 | 14 2 | 4 51 | 12 7 | 3 48 | 5 1 | 15 32 | 19 32 | 27 54 | 0 17 |
| 29 | TH | 11 4 | 12 ♓ 23 | 13 57 | 6 58 | 13 19 | 4 25 | 4 54 | 15 28 | 19 33 | 27 53 | 0 15 |
| 30 | FR | 12 2 | 24 47 | 13 53 | 9 4 | 14 31 | 5 3 | 4 48 | 15 23 | 19 34 | 27 52 | 0 14 |
| 31 | SA | 12 59 | 6 ♈ 54 | 13 51 | 11 11 | 15 43 | 5 41 | 4 41 | 15 19 | 19 35 | 27 51 | 0 12 |

### INGRESSES :

3 ☽ → ♈ 2:29
5 ☽ → ♉ 15:16
8 ☿ → ♊ 0:30
☽ → ♊ 3:56
10 ☽ → ♋ 14:48
12 ☽ → ♌ 23:21
15 ☽ → ♍ 5:42
17 ☉ → ♋ 9:41
☽ → ♎ 10: 7
♀ → ♌ 21:35
19 ☽ → ♏ 12:51
21 ☽ → ♐ 14:26
♂ → ♌ 22:27
23 ☽ → ♑ 15:55
25 ☿ → ♋ 16:25
☽ → ♒ 18:48
28 ☽ → ♓ 0:40
30 ☽ → ♈ 10:16

### ASPECTS & ECLIPSES :

1 ♂ ☍ ♄ 13: 7
☉ □ ☽ 21: 9
4 ♂ □ ♅ 1:36
☽ ☌ ♅ 16:39
5 ☽ ☌ A 14:34
6 ☿ □ ♆ 7:47
☽ ☌ ☊ 22:38
7 ♀ ☍ ♄ 2:35
8 ☽ ☌ ☿ 4:18
♀ □ ♅ 19:23
10 ☉ ☌ ☽ 1:15
☽ ☍ ♇ 16: 8
11 ☽ ☍ ♄ 22:31
12 ☽ ☌ ♀ 11:12
☽ ☌ ♂ 12:28
13 ☽ ☍ ♃ 10:59
♀ ☌ ♂ 13:31
14 ☽ N□ ☊ 2:35
15 ☽ ☍ ♆ 2:16
17 ☉ □ ☽ 10: 9
☉ ☍ ♇ 22:40
18 ☽ ☍ ♅ 18:58
20 ☽ ☌ ☋ 13:21
21 ☽ ☌ P 10:30
22 ♀ ☍ ♃ 12:43
23 ☽ ☍ ☿ 7:52
☽ ☌ ♇ 16:32
24 ☉ ☍ ☽ 2:35
☽ ☌ ♄ 18:23
25 ☿ ☍ ♇ 20:11
☽ ☍ ♂ 23:12
26 ☽ ☌ ♃ 3:54
☽ ☍ ♀ 13: 2
☽ □S ☊ 19:50
27 ☽ ☌ ♆ 20:46
29 ♀ □ ☊ 11:48
♂ ☍ ♃ 15:49
31 ☉ □ ☽ 13:14

## SIDEREAL HELIOCENTRIC LONGITUDES : JULY 2021 Gregorian at 0 hours UT

| DAY | | Sid. Time | ☿ | ♀ | ⊕ | ♂ | ♃ | ♄ | ♅ | ♆ | ♇ | Vernal Point |
|---|---|---|---|---|---|---|---|---|---|---|---|---|
| 1 | TH | 18:37: 5 | 26 ♑ 3 | 16 ♌ 44 | 14 ♐ 22 | 6 ♌ 12 | 27 ♑ 45 | 14 ♑ 9 | 16 ♈ 20 | 26 ♒ 17 | 0 ♑ 26 | 4 ♓ 57'36" |
| 2 | FR | 18:41: 2 | 29 43 | 18 21 | 15 19 | 6 38 | 27 50 | 14 11 | 16 20 | 26 18 | 0 26 | 4 ♓ 57'36" |
| 3 | SA | 18:44:58 | 3 ♒ 29 | 19 59 | 16 16 | 7 4 | 27 55 | 14 13 | 16 21 | 26 18 | 0 27 | 4 ♓ 57'36" |
| 4 | SU | 18:48:55 | 7 21 | 21 36 | 17 14 | 7 31 | 28 1 | 14 15 | 16 22 | 26 19 | 0 27 | 4 ♓ 57'36" |
| 5 | MO | 18:52:51 | 11 20 | 23 14 | 18 11 | 7 57 | 28 6 | 14 16 | 16 22 | 26 19 | 0 27 | 4 ♓ 57'36" |
| 6 | TU | 18:56:48 | 15 26 | 24 51 | 19 8 | 8 23 | 28 11 | 14 18 | 16 23 | 26 19 | 0 27 | 4 ♓ 57'35" |
| 7 | WE | 19: 0:44 | 19 39 | 26 28 | 20 5 | 8 49 | 28 17 | 14 20 | 16 24 | 26 20 | 0 28 | 4 ♓ 57'35" |
| 8 | TH | 19: 4:41 | 24 0 | 28 6 | 21 2 | 9 15 | 28 22 | 14 22 | 16 24 | 26 20 | 0 28 | 4 ♓ 57'35" |
| 9 | FR | 19: 8:37 | 28 29 | 29 43 | 22 0 | 9 42 | 28 27 | 14 24 | 16 25 | 26 20 | 0 28 | 4 ♓ 57'35" |
| 10 | SA | 19:12:34 | 3 ♓ 7 | 1 ♍ 20 | 22 57 | 10 8 | 28 33 | 14 26 | 16 26 | 26 21 | 0 29 | 4 ♓ 57'35" |
| 11 | SU | 19:16:31 | 7 53 | 2 57 | 23 54 | 10 34 | 28 38 | 14 28 | 16 26 | 26 21 | 0 29 | 4 ♓ 57'35" |
| 12 | MO | 19:20:27 | 12 48 | 4 34 | 24 51 | 11 0 | 28 43 | 14 29 | 16 27 | 26 21 | 0 29 | 4 ♓ 57'35" |
| 13 | TU | 19:24:24 | 17 52 | 6 12 | 25 49 | 11 26 | 28 49 | 14 31 | 16 28 | 26 22 | 0 29 | 4 ♓ 57'34" |
| 14 | WE | 19:28:20 | 23 5 | 7 49 | 26 46 | 11 53 | 28 54 | 14 33 | 16 28 | 26 22 | 0 30 | 4 ♓ 57'34" |
| 15 | TH | 19:32:17 | 28 27 | 9 26 | 27 43 | 12 19 | 28 59 | 14 35 | 16 29 | 26 23 | 0 30 | 4 ♓ 57'34" |
| 16 | FR | 19:36:13 | 3 ♈ 58 | 11 3 | 28 40 | 12 45 | 29 5 | 14 37 | 16 30 | 26 23 | 0 30 | 4 ♓ 57'34" |
| 17 | SA | 19:40:10 | 9 38 | 12 40 | 29 37 | 13 11 | 29 10 | 14 39 | 16 30 | 26 23 | 0 31 | 4 ♓ 57'34" |
| 18 | SU | 19:44: 6 | 15 26 | 14 17 | 0 ♑ 35 | 13 37 | 29 15 | 14 40 | 16 31 | 26 24 | 0 31 | 4 ♓ 57'34" |
| 19 | MO | 19:48: 3 | 21 22 | 15 54 | 1 32 | 14 4 | 29 21 | 14 42 | 16 32 | 26 24 | 0 31 | 4 ♓ 57'34" |
| 20 | TU | 19:52: 0 | 27 24 | 17 31 | 2 29 | 14 30 | 29 26 | 14 44 | 16 32 | 26 24 | 0 32 | 4 ♓ 57'33" |
| 21 | WE | 19:55:56 | 3 ♉ 33 | 19 8 | 3 26 | 14 56 | 29 31 | 14 46 | 16 33 | 26 25 | 0 32 | 4 ♓ 57'33" |
| 22 | TH | 19:59:53 | 9 46 | 20 45 | 4 24 | 15 22 | 29 37 | 14 48 | 16 34 | 26 25 | 0 32 | 4 ♓ 57'33" |
| 23 | FR | 20: 3:49 | 16 3 | 22 21 | 5 21 | 15 48 | 29 42 | 14 50 | 16 34 | 26 25 | 0 32 | 4 ♓ 57'33" |
| 24 | SA | 20: 7:46 | 22 21 | 23 58 | 6 18 | 16 15 | 29 47 | 14 52 | 16 35 | 26 26 | 0 33 | 4 ♓ 57'33" |
| 25 | SU | 20:11:42 | 28 41 | 25 35 | 7 16 | 16 41 | 29 52 | 14 53 | 16 36 | 26 26 | 0 33 | 4 ♓ 57'33" |
| 26 | MO | 20:15:39 | 4 ♊ 59 | 27 11 | 8 13 | 17 7 | 29 58 | 14 55 | 16 36 | 26 27 | 0 33 | 4 ♓ 57'33" |
| 27 | TU | 20:19:35 | 11 15 | 28 48 | 9 10 | 17 33 | 0 ♒ 3 | 14 57 | 16 37 | 26 27 | 0 34 | 4 ♓ 57'33" |
| 28 | WE | 20:23:32 | 17 27 | 0 ♎ 25 | 10 7 | 17 59 | 0 8 | 14 59 | 16 38 | 26 27 | 0 34 | 4 ♓ 57'32" |
| 29 | TH | 20:27:29 | 23 34 | 2 1 | 11 5 | 18 26 | 0 14 | 15 1 | 16 38 | 26 28 | 0 34 | 4 ♓ 57'32" |
| 30 | FR | 20:31:25 | 29 34 | 3 38 | 12 2 | 18 52 | 0 19 | 15 3 | 16 39 | 26 28 | 0 34 | 4 ♓ 57'32" |
| 31 | SA | 20:35:22 | 5 ♋ 27 | 5 14 | 13 0 | 19 18 | 0 24 | 15 4 | 16 40 | 26 28 | 0 35 | 4 ♓ 57'32" |

### INGRESSES :

2 ☿ → ♒ 1:49
9 ♀ → ♍ 4:14
☿ → ♓ 7:55
15 ☿ → ♈ 6:48
17 ⊕ → ♑ 9:26
20 ☿ → ♉ 10:10
25 ☿ → ♊ 5: 1
26 ♃ → ♒ 9:53
27 ♀ → ♎ 17:53
30 ☿ → ♋ 1:44

### ASPECTS (HELIOCENTRIC +MOON(TYCHONIC)) :

1 ☿ ☌ ♃ 11:28
3 ☽ □ ♇ 3:22
4 ☿ ☍ ♂ 1: 3
♀ N□ ☊ 3:24
☽ □ ♄ 7:14
☽ ☌ ♅ 11:31
5 ⊕ ☌ A 2:13
☽ □ ♃ 11:29
6 ☽ □ ♂ 8:39
♀ ☍ ♆ 21:52
7 ☽ □ ☿ 11:14
☽ □ ♆ 20:36
8 ☽ □ ♀ 0: 9
☿ ☌ ♆ 12:34
9 ☿ ☍ ♀ 9:56
10 ☽ ☍ ♇ 15:44
11 ☽ ☍ ♄ 18:24
☽ □ ♅ 22: 6
12 ☽ ☍ ♃ 21: 8
♂ ☌ A 22:43
13 ☽ ☌ ♂ 21: 1
14 ☿ □ ⊕ 20: 4
☽ ☍ ♆ 23:15
15 ☿ □ ♇ 8:59
16 ☽ ☌ ♀ 1:23
17 ☽ □ ♇ 11: 0
☿ □ ♄ 20:51
⊕ ☌ ♇ 22:23
18 ☿ ☌ ♅ 4:25
☽ □ ♄ 11: 9
☽ ☍ ♅ 14:15
☽ ☍ ☿ 21:15
19 ☿ ☌ ☊ 8:43
☽ □ ♃ 11:49
20 ☿ □ ♃ 8: 4
☽ □ ♂ 13:18
21 ☽ □ ♆ 8:32
22 ☿ □ ♂ 23: 1
23 ☽ □ ♀ 3:38
☽ ☌ ♇ 16:49
24 ☿ ☌ P 1:30
☿ □ ♆ 15:29
☽ ☌ ♄ 16:52
☽ □ ♅ 19:47
25 ☽ ☌ ♃ 18:43
27 ☽ ☍ ♂ 1:57
☽ ☌ ♆ 18: 7
28 ♀ □ ♇ 2:18
30 ☿ ☍ ♇ 4: 3
☽ □ ♇ 11:24
☽ □ ☿ 18:22
☽ ☍ ♀ 20: 9
☿ □ ♀ 22:45
31 ☽ □ ♄ 16:26
☽ ☌ ♅ 19:37

Jesus and his disciples. The latter served them while Jesus addressed to them a very beautiful instruction. The Pharisees, though greatly irritated, had not a word to say, for Jesus was in the right, and at this the people rejoiced. Great excitement prevailed in the city. After partaking plentifully of the various good things, the poor people departed, taking with them a supply for their friends at home. Jesus had blessed the food for them, prayed with them, and exhorted them to go to John's baptism. He would not tarry longer in the city, and left that night with his followers. Many of the latter, however, discouraged partly by his exhortations, left him for their homes while others went to prepare for John's baptism.[102]

Around the same time as the Mercury/Mars opposition, Venus comes into alignment with Neptune on July 3–9. This is exact on the 6th.

**July 6: Venus 26°20' Leo opposite Neptune 26°20' Aquarius.** Neptune continues to remember the Assumption of the Virgin Mary in AD 44. Venus, on the other hand, was at 21° Leo during both the birth of the Nathan Jesus on December 6, 2 BC, as well as at the death of Lazarus on July 15 AD 32. Here we have the mystery of birth, death, and—rather than Resurrection—Assumption. Especially in relation to the pure soul of the Nathan Jesus, we can consider the difference between Resurrection, which is a transformation of *death* and *evil* into higher forms of *life* and *goodness*, and Assumption, which is a return to the Origin, an absolutely pure and virginal state brought to its highest and eternal octave (see the 20th Letter–Meditation on The Judgment in *Meditations on the Tarot*).

Next, Mercury aspects Neptune, continuing the cosmic recall of the Assumption. These two conjoin on July 7–9, exact on the 8th.

**July 8: Mercury conjunct Neptune 26°20' Aquarius.** Mercury was at this degree on November 19 AD 30:

After being present for the baptism of a number of people this morning, Jesus taught from the banks of the Sea of Galilee. As the throng of people grew, Jesus and some of his disciples climbed

aboard a ship placed at his disposal, and Jesus taught from there. The other disciples boarded Peter's ship. This then hooked up Jesus's ship, towing it across the lake while Jesus continued to teach on the way. Around four o'clock that afternoon they reached the eastern shore and went to a nearby place of tax collectors where Matthew (then called Levi) lived. He cast himself down before Jesus. Jesus said, "Levi (Matthew), arise, and follow me!" (Matt. 9:9). That night, Jesus stayed at an inn in the town of Bethsaida–Julias.[103]

According to tradition, St. Matthew and his Gospel represent the Angel (St. Luke, the Bull; St. John, the Eagle; St. Mark, the Lion). This Angel of the four Holy Creatures is the same as Aquarius, the Waterbearer, the Watcher in the North, where Mercury and Neptune are currently meeting. Perhaps today is a good day to turn our meditative life to the Gospel of St. Matthew.

**July 9: Venus enters Virgo; Mercury enters Pisces.**

Reveal thyself, Sun life
　　(*Sun in Gemini*)
May the soul fathom worlds
　　(*Venus in Virgo*)
In comprehending seek to grasp
　　(*Mercury in Pisces*)
To gain strength in test of trial
　　(*Mars in Leo*)
May world-being's vigilance grow in power
　　(*Jupiter in Capricorn*)
And may the might of life's activity flower
　　(*Saturn in Capricorn*)
O Sun life, endure!
　　(*Moon in Gemini*)[104]

Mercury and Venus have been drawing ever closer to opposition since the month began. They are within 5° of alignment from July 7–10, exact on the 9th.

**July 9: Mercury 0°23' Pisces opposite Venus 0°23' Virgo.** Venus was at 2° Virgo, square Mercury in Sagittarius, on February 3–4 AD 30:

102 ACE, vol. 1, p. 311.

103 ACE, vol. 2, p. 152.
104 Steiner, *Twelve Cosmic Moods*.

I saw Jesus going from house to house at Ono. At first I knew not for what reason, but later I heard that it was on account of the tithes, to the paying of which he was urging the people. He reminded them also of the alms which it was customary to give on the feast of fruit trees now beginning. That evening he celebrated the sabbath in the synagogue, where he taught....

After that began the preparations for the new year's fruit festival. Throughout the day, Jesus taught in Ono concerning the threefold meaning of the approaching feast: firstly, it commemorated the rising of the sap in the trees; secondly, because today tithes of all the fruits were offered; and lastly, it was a feast of thanksgiving for the fertility of the soil.[105]

Today is a good day for honoring the land. **July 9: New Moon, 22°59' Gemini.** While Mercury and Venus face each other in Pisces and Virgo, Sun and Moon are together in Gemini. The mutable signs are very active right now—be ready for change. A Gemini New Moon occurred on June 8 AD 31, during which Christ was teaching in Nain. He had harsh words and hard truths to deliver to the Pharisees there, who treated him with disdain and spite. The enmity of the Pharisees is a recurring theme this month.

**July 15: Mercury enters Aries.**

**July 17: Sun enters Cancer.**

Thou resting, glowing light
   (*Sun in Cancer*)
May the soul fathom worlds
   (*Venus in Virgo*)
Lay hold of forces weaving
   (*Mercury in Aries*)
To gain strength in test of trial
   (*Mars in Leo*)
May world-being's vigilance grow in power
   (*Jupiter in Capricorn*)
And may the might of life's activity flower
   (*Saturn in Capricorn*)
O soul, know thou beings!
   (*Moon in Virgo*)[106]

Sun opposes Pluto July 12–22, exact on the 17th.

**July 17: Sun 0°31' Cancer opposite Pluto 0°31' Capricorn.** The Sun was at this degree on June 22 AD 31; once again, Christ disputes with the Pharisees:

This morning Jesus ate with his mother. In the afternoon, he taught the apostles and disciples. Then they all went together to the synagogue in Capernaum for the sabbath. Here he taught concerning Korah and Abiram (Num. 16) and spoke of Samuel's resigning from his judicial office (1 Sam. 12). The Pharisees reproached Jesus for his disciples' failure to observe the Law. At this, Jesus again delivered a severe discourse against the Pharisees. He was interrupted by a young Pharisee suddenly crying out in a loud voice: "Truly this is the Son of God! The Holy One of Israel! He is more than a prophet!" A great commotion arose, and two Pharisees ejected the young man from the synagogue. Later, as Jesus was leaving, the young Pharisee cast himself down at his feet and begged to become a disciple. Jesus assented and introduced him to some of his disciples.[107]

At the same time, Mercury and Uranus conjoin July 17–18, exact on the 18th.

**July 18: Mercury conjunct Uranus 16°31' Aries.** For quite some time this month, since July 10 and lasting until the 29th, Mars has been square the Node. This alignment is exact on **July 20: Mars 14°46' Leo square Node 14°46' Taurus.** Mercury was 16° Aries and Mars was 14° Leo on September 15 AD 29, as Jesus of Nazareth was travelling with Eliud, the elderly mystic:

I saw Jesus journeying with Eliud in a southwesterly direction from Nazareth, but not exactly on the high road. He wanted to go to Chim, a leper settlement. They reached it at daybreak, and I saw that Eliud tried to restrain Jesus from entering it, that he might not be defiled; for, as Eliud urged, if it were discovered that he had been there, he would not be allowed to go to the baptism. But Jesus replied that he knew his mission, that he would enter, for there was in it a good man who was sighing for his coming. They had to cross the Kishon. The leper settlement lay near a brook formed by the waters of the Kishon which flowed into a little pond in which the lepers

---

105 ACE, vol. 1, p. 401.

106 Steiner, *Twelve Cosmic Moods*.

107 ACE, vol. 2, p. 405.

bathed. The water thus used did not return into the Kishon. This settlement was perfectly isolated; no one ever approached it. The lepers dwelt in scattered huts. There were no others in the place, excepting those that attended the infected. Eliud remained at a distance and waited for the Lord. Jesus entered one of the most remote huts wherein lay stretched on the ground a miserable creature entirely enveloped in sheets. He was a good man. I have forgotten how he contracted leprosy. Jesus addressed him. He raised himself, and appeared to be deeply touched at the Lord's deigning to visit him. Jesus commanded him to rise and stretch himself in a trough of water that stood near the hut. He obeyed, while Jesus held his hands extended over the water. The rigid limbs of the leper relaxed, and he was made clean. He then resumed his ordinary dress, and Jesus commanded him not to speak of his cure until he should have returned from the baptism. He accompanied Jesus and Eliud along the road till Jesus ordered him to go back.[108]

Later that evening, Eliud experienced the "little Transfiguration": a prefiguring on the part of Jesus of Nazareth (who had not yet been baptized and united with the Christ Spirit) of the full Transfiguration that would occur a year and seven months later before John, Peter, and James.

### July 20: Mercury enters Taurus.

Thou resting, glowing light
(*Sun in Cancer*)
May the soul fathom worlds
(*Venus in Virgo*)
Weave life's thread
(*Mercury in Taurus*)
To gain strength in test of trial
(*Mars in Leo*)
May world-being's vigilance grow in power
(*Jupiter in Capricorn*)
And may the might of life's activity flower
(*Saturn in Capricorn*)
Being sustains beings!
(*Moon in Scorpio*)[109]

---

108 ACE, vol. 1, p. 321.
109 Steiner, *Twelve Cosmic Moods*.

### July 21–23, Mercury conjoins the Node. This alignment is exact on the 22nd.

### July 22: Mercury and Node 14°41' Taurus. These were conjunct at the same degree on May 28 AD 31:

> Jesus…delivered a farewell discourse after which he went around to some huts and cured several invalids who had begged him to do so. He had already set out on his return journey to Mallep when an old peasant implored him to go to his house and take pity on his blind son. There were in the house three families of twelve persons, the grandparents, two married sons, and their children. The mother, veiled, brought the blind boy to Jesus in her arms, although it could both speak and walk. Jesus took the child into his arms, with a finger of his right hand anointed its eyes with his own saliva, blessed it, put it down on the ground, and held something before its eyes. The child grasped after it awkwardly, ran at the sound of its mother's voice, then turned to the father, and so from the arms of one to those of the other. The parents led it to Jesus, and weeping thanked him on their knees. Jesus pressed the child to his bosom and gave it back to the parents with the admonition to lead it to the true light, that its eyes, which now saw, might not be closed in darkness deeper than before. He blessed the other children also, and the whole family. The people shed tears and followed him with acclamations of praise.
>
> In the house used for such purposes at Mallep, a feast was given, in which all took part. The poor were fed, and presents were given them. Jesus, finally, delivered a grand discourse on the word "Amen," which, he said, was the whole summary of prayer. Whoever pronounces it carelessly, makes void his prayer. Prayer cries to God; binds us to God; opens to us His mercy, and, with the word "Amen," rightly uttered, we take the asked-for gift out of His hands. Jesus spoke most forcibly of the power of the word "Amen." He called it the beginning and the end of everything. He spoke almost as if God had by it created the whole world. He uttered an "Amen" over all that he had taught them, over his own departure from them, over the accomplishment of his own mission, and ended his discourse by

a solemn "Amen." Then he blessed his audience, who wept and cried after him.[110]

Mercury and Node conjoined so close to Aldebaran bear the power of the AUMEYN.

**July 23: Full Moon 6°24' Capricorn.** The Capricorn Full Moon takes us to June 23 AD 31, the day after the dispute with the Pharisees remembered during the Sun/Pluto opposition on July 17. The battle with the Pharisees carries on:

> Jesus taught in Bethsaida this morning. In the afternoon he returned to Capernaum, where he and the disciples went to the synagogue before the close of the sabbath. Jesus taught of the need to be awake at the coming of the Son of Man (Luke 12:35–40). Then, in answer to Peter's question as to whether he spoke for everyone or only for the disciples, Jesus replied as in Luke 12:41–59. After the close of the sabbath, Jesus and some disciples were invited to dine with the Pharisees. Here, again, a dispute broke out (Luke 11:37–52). Afterward, Jesus was approached by a young man from Nazareth who had often sought to become a disciple. Then the exchange about the good Samaritan recounted in Luke 10:25–37 took place.[111]

**July 25: Mercury enters Gemini.**

**July 26: Jupiter enters Aquarius.**

**July 27: Venus enters Libra.**

> Thou resting, glowing light
>     (*Sun in Cancer*)
> In being experience being
>     (*Venus in Libra*)
> Embrace joyful striving
>     (*Mercury in Gemini*)
> To gain strength in test of trial
>     (*Mars in Leo*)
> As a flowing wave self-sustaining
>     (*Jupiter in Aquarius*)
> And may the might of life's activity flower
>     (*Saturn in Capricorn*)
> Limit thyself, O unlimited!
>     (*Moon in Aquarius*)[112]

July 24–31, Venus square Pluto and exact on the 27th.

**July 27: Venus 0°34' Libra square Pluto 0°34' Capricorn.** Venus had just ingressed into Libra on February 21 AD 30:

> From Jezreel, Jesus went one hour and a half southward to a field in a valley, two hours long and as many broad, wherein were numerous orchards surrounded by low hedges. It was an uncommonly productive and charming fruit region. There were numerous tents here standing in couples at different intervals, and occupied by people from Shunem who guarded and gathered in the fruit. I think it was a kind of service that they were obliged to take turns in rendering. About four occupied one tent. The women dwelt together apart from the men, for whom they did the cooking. Jesus instructed these people under a tent. There were here most beautiful springs and abundant streams, which flowed into the Jordan. The principal source came from Jezreel. It formed in the valley a charming spring, over which a kind of chapel was built. From this spring house the stream divided into several others throughout the valley, united with other waters, and at last emptied into the Jordan. There were about thirty custodians whom Jesus instructed, the women remaining at some distance. He taught of the slavery of sin, from which they should free themselves. They were inexpressibly rejoiced and touched that he had come to them. He was so loving and courteous to these poor people that I had to shed tears myself over it. They set before Jesus and the disciples fruit, of which they ate. In some parts of the valley the fruit was already ripe, in others the trees were only in blossom. There were some brown fruits like figs, but growing in clusters like grapes, also yellow plants from which they prepared a kind of pap. In this valley rises Mount Gilboa, and here also was Saul slain in battle against the Philistines.[113]

---

110 ACE, vol. 2, p. 390.
111 Ibid., p. 405.
112 Steiner, *Twelve Cosmic Moods.*

---

113 ACE, vol. 1, p. 407.

**July 30: Mercury enters Cancer.**

> Thou resting, glowing light
> > (*Sun in Cancer*)
> In being experience being
> > (*Venus in Libra*)
> Warm soul life
> > (*Mercury in Cancer*)
> To gain strength in test of trial
> > (*Mars in Leo*)
> As a flowing wave self-sustaining
> > (*Jupiter in Aquarius*)
> And may the might of life's activity flower
> > (*Saturn in Capricorn*)
> May loss be gain in itself!
> > (*Moon in Pisces*)[114]

The month closes with **Mercury opposite Pluto from July 29–31.** This alignment is exact on the 30th.

**July 30: Mercury 0°34' Cancer opposite Pluto 0°34' Capricorn.** Mercury had just ingressed into Cancer on March 22 AD 30:

> Accompanied by Lazarus and Saturnin, he visited the homes of several poor, pious sick people of the working class in Bethany, and cured about six of them. Some were lame, some dropsical, and others afflicted with melancholy. Jesus commanded those that he cured to go outdoors and sit in the Sun. Up to this time there was very little excitement about Jesus in Bethany, and even these cures produced none. The presence of Lazarus, for whom they felt great reverence, kept the enthusiasm of the people in check.
>
> That evening, upon which began the first day of the month Nisan, there was a feast celebrated in the synagogue. It appeared to be the Feast of the New Moon, for there was a kind of illumination in the synagogue. There was a disc like the moon, which, during the recitation of prayers, shone with ever-increasing brilliancy, owing to the lights lit one after another by a man behind it.[115]

---

114 Steiner, *Twelve Cosmic Moods.*
115 ACE, vol. 1, p. 418.

# AUGUST 2021

## STARGAZING PREVIEW

August opens with a bang as Mercury moves beyond the Sun for another superior conjunction. On Monday the 2nd, Saturn will be at its brightest—in exact opposition to the Sun—and will therefore rise at dusk. As the Sun is now nearer to Mars, there will be less than an hour to see him after sunset. Venus, still an evening star, sets at 2040.

This month's New Moon (22° Cancer) occurs on the 8th. There will be a brief moment in time that evening, at around 2000, when, if you look to the west, Mars and Venus will be visible close to the horizon; look east and you'll see Saturn and Jupiter, just risen. The waxing Leo Moon sets between Mars and Venus on the 10th—by the following evening, the Moon, now in Virgo, will set last. Venus enters Virgo on the 12th, conferring to those born under it a particular love of nature.

The night of the 12th–13th will offer your best opportunity to view the beloved Perseid meteor showers, which are best viewed from the northern hemisphere. The Sun sets at 1930, followed by the Virgo Moon ninety minutes later; if the weather cooperates as well, this should be a great night for viewing. For most of the night, *Perseus* will be visible (the apparent radiant of the showers) in the southeastern sky. Our hero *Perseus* can be found above Aries and Taurus, and below and to the right of Cassiopeia (when seen as a right side up "W").

The Moon, at 28° Libra, reaches its First Quarter on the 15th. On the following evening, at about 2030, you'll be able to watch the waxing Moon pass above *Antares*; the three stars marking the Scorpion's claws will be above them and to their right. On the 17th the Sun enters Leo—the zodiacal sign it calls home!

Jupiter will be at its brightest on Friday the 20th, as it opposes the Sun; the Great Benefic rises at 1900, at which time the Moon and Saturn will be close together in the southeast. By the next evening, the Moon will have passed below Saturn, well on its way to Jupiter. The Full Moon (5°

Aquarius) on the evening of the 22nd rises just ten minutes after Jupiter.

August's Last Quarter Moon will occur on the 30th, at 12° Taurus. This is the point on the zodiacal circle aligned with the *Hyades*, the five-star cluster to the right of *Aldebaran*. As the Moon rises at 2300, Orion will have just begun his journey across the night sky.

## AUGUST COMMENTARIES

We begin the month of August with the Sun and Mercury opposite Saturn. Sun and Mercury conjoin, and Mercury opposes Saturn, July 31 and August 2. These alignments are exact on the 1st.

**August 1: Sun conjunct Mercury 14°30' Cancer; Mercury 15°8' Cancer opposite Saturn 15°8' Capricorn.** At the same time, July 27 through August 7, the Sun opposes Saturn, exact on August 2: Sun 15°9' Cancer opposite Saturn 15°9' Capricorn.

These three planets aligned in the cardinal signs during significant time periods in the last year of Christ's ministry. July 7–20 AD 32, as Lazarus died and entered into the subearthly spheres, Sun and Saturn conjoined in Cancer while Mercury opposed them in Capricorn. Then, October 11–15, as Christ and the three shepherd youths visited Ur, the birthplace of Abraham, and then set out on their long journey to Heliopolis, the Sun was in Libra square Saturn in Cancer opposite Mercury in Capricorn once again. Later, on January 10 AD 33, Sun and Mercury conjoined in Capricorn opposite Saturn in Cancer just as Christ and the shepherd youths were returning from their long pilgrimage and about to rejoin the apostles and holy women at Jacob's Well. Finally, April 7–15, the Sun in Aries was once again square Mercury in Capricorn opposite Saturn in Cancer. These were the days that saw the Risen Christ's miraculous appearance to the twelve when Thomas placed his hands in Christ's wounds, and of Christ's appearance at the Sea of Galilee and the miraculous catch of 153 fish.

Can we feel a gesture woven through these three time periods: death of Lazarus—journey *to* Egypt—return *from* Egypt—Resurrected Christ? Can we feel an analogy between the underworld in which Lazarus became entrapped and Egypt, the land of bondage?

**August 4: Mercury enters Leo.**

> Thou resting, glowing light
>    (*Sun in Cancer*)
> In being experience being
>    (*Venus in Libra*)
> Feeling being's essence
>    (*Mercury in Leo*)
> To gain strength in test of trial
>    (*Mars in Leo*)
> As a flowing wave self-sustaining
>    (*Jupiter in Aquarius*)
> And may the might of life's activity flower
>    (*Saturn in Capricorn*)
> O Sun life, endure!
>    (*Moon in Gemini*)[116]

August 3–5, Mercury is opposite Jupiter. This alignment is exact on the 4th.

**August 4: Mercury 0°49' Leo opposite Jupiter 0°49' Aquarius.** At the same time, Venus is square Saturn August 2–9, exact on the 6th.

**August 6: Venus 15°16' Libra square Saturn 15°16' Capricorn.** August 3–10, Venus opposes Uranus, also exact on **August 6: Venus 16°44' Libra opposite Uranus 16°44' Aries.** While Mercury and Jupiter bring activity into our thought life, Venus is playing the role of an emollient in the ever-tightening square between solid, conservative Saturn and bright, revolutionary Uranus.

Mercury was at 1° Leo on May 14 AD 33, during the Ascension of Christ. Venus was between 15–16° Libra on March 30–31 AD 33. On March 30:

> …Jesus went with the disciples to Jerusalem. In the temple, he spoke of union and separation. He used the analogy of fire and water, which are inimicable. When water does not overpower fire, the flames become greater and more powerful. He spoke of persecution and martyrdom. By the flames of fire, he was referring to those disciples who would remain true to him, and by water he meant those who would leave him and seek the

---

116 Steiner, *Twelve Cosmic Moods*.

## SIDEREAL GEOCENTRIC LONGITUDES : AUGUST 2021 Gregorian at 0 hours UT

| DAY | ☉ | ☽ | ☊ | ☿ | ♀ | ♂ | ♃ | ♄ | ♅ | ♆ | ♇ |
|---|---|---|---|---|---|---|---|---|---|---|---|
| 1 SU | 13 ♋ 56 | 18 ♈ 50 | 13 ♉ 51 | 13 ♋ 16 | 16 ♌ 54 | 6 ♌ 18 | 4 ♒ 34R | 15 ♑ 14R | 19 ♈ 36 | 27 ♒ 50R | 0 ♑ 11R |
| 2 MO | 14 54 | 0 ♉ 39 | 13 52 | 15 22 | 18 6 | 6 56 | 4 28 | 15 10 | 19 37 | 27 49 | 0 10 |
| 3 TU | 15 51 | 12 28 | 13 52R | 17 26 | 19 18 | 7 34 | 4 21 | 15 5 | 19 38 | 27 47 | 0 8 |
| 4 WE | 16 49 | 24 20 | 13 51 | 19 29 | 20 29 | 8 11 | 4 13 | 15 1 | 19 39 | 27 46 | 0 7 |
| 5 TH | 17 46 | 6 ♊ 20 | 13 49 | 21 31 | 21 41 | 8 49 | 4 6 | 14 56 | 19 39 | 27 45 | 0 5 |
| 6 FR | 18 44 | 18 33 | 13 44 | 23 32 | 22 52 | 9 27 | 3 59 | 14 52 | 19 40 | 27 44 | 0 4 |
| 7 SA | 19 41 | 1 ♋ 0 | 13 37 | 25 31 | 24 4 | 10 5 | 3 52 | 14 47 | 19 41 | 27 43 | 0 3 |
| 8 SU | 20 39 | 13 44 | 13 27 | 27 29 | 25 15 | 10 43 | 3 44 | 14 43 | 19 41 | 27 42 | 0 1 |
| 9 MO | 21 36 | 26 45 | 13 17 | 29 26 | 26 26 | 11 21 | 3 37 | 14 39 | 19 42 | 27 40 | 0 0 |
| 10 TU | 22 34 | 10 ♌ 1 | 13 5 | 1 ♌ 21 | 27 38 | 11 58 | 3 29 | 14 34 | 19 43 | 27 39 | 29 ♐ 59 |
| 11 WE | 23 31 | 23 30 | 12 55 | 3 15 | 28 49 | 12 36 | 3 21 | 14 30 | 19 43 | 27 38 | 29 57 |
| 12 TH | 24 29 | 7 ♍ 11 | 12 46 | 5 7 | 0 ♍ 0 | 13 14 | 3 14 | 14 25 | 19 43 | 27 36 | 29 56 |
| 13 FR | 25 26 | 21 1 | 12 39 | 6 58 | 1 11 | 13 52 | 3 6 | 14 21 | 19 44 | 27 35 | 29 55 |
| 14 SA | 26 24 | 4 ♎ 57 | 12 35 | 8 47 | 2 22 | 14 30 | 2 58 | 14 17 | 19 44 | 27 34 | 29 54 |
| 15 SU | 27 22 | 18 59 | 12 34 | 10 35 | 3 33 | 15 8 | 2 51 | 14 12 | 19 44 | 27 32 | 29 52 |
| 16 MO | 28 19 | 3 ♏ 5 | 12 34D | 12 21 | 4 44 | 15 46 | 2 43 | 14 8 | 19 45 | 27 31 | 29 51 |
| 17 TU | 29 17 | 17 15 | 12 34R | 14 6 | 5 55 | 16 24 | 2 35 | 14 4 | 19 45 | 27 30 | 29 50 |
| 18 WE | 0 ♌ 15 | 1 ♐ 26 | 12 33 | 15 49 | 7 6 | 17 2 | 2 27 | 14 0 | 19 45 | 27 28 | 29 49 |
| 19 TH | 1 12 | 15 38 | 12 30 | 17 31 | 8 17 | 17 40 | 2 19 | 13 56 | 19 45 | 27 27 | 29 48 |
| 20 FR | 2 10 | 29 48 | 12 24 | 19 12 | 9 28 | 18 18 | 2 11 | 13 51 | 19 45 | 27 25 | 29 46 |
| 21 SA | 3 8 | 13 ♑ 51 | 12 15 | 20 51 | 10 38 | 18 56 | 2 3 | 13 47 | 19 45R | 27 24 | 29 45 |
| 22 SU | 4 6 | 27 43 | 12 4 | 22 28 | 11 49 | 19 34 | 1 56 | 13 43 | 19 45 | 27 22 | 29 44 |
| 23 MO | 5 3 | 11 ♒ 21 | 11 52 | 24 4 | 13 0 | 20 13 | 1 48 | 13 39 | 19 45 | 27 21 | 29 43 |
| 24 TU | 6 1 | 24 41 | 11 40 | 25 39 | 14 10 | 20 51 | 1 40 | 13 35 | 19 45 | 27 19 | 29 42 |
| 25 WE | 6 59 | 7 ♓ 41 | 11 29 | 27 13 | 15 21 | 21 29 | 1 32 | 13 31 | 19 44 | 27 18 | 29 41 |
| 26 TH | 7 57 | 20 21 | 11 20 | 28 45 | 16 31 | 22 7 | 1 24 | 13 28 | 19 44 | 27 16 | 29 40 |
| 27 FR | 8 55 | 2 ♈ 42 | 11 13 | 0 ♍ 15 | 17 41 | 22 45 | 1 17 | 13 24 | 19 44 | 27 15 | 29 39 |
| 28 SA | 9 53 | 14 49 | 11 10 | 1 45 | 18 51 | 23 24 | 1 9 | 13 20 | 19 43 | 27 13 | 29 38 |
| 29 SU | 10 51 | 26 44 | 11 8 | 3 13 | 20 2 | 24 2 | 1 1 | 13 16 | 19 43 | 27 12 | 29 37 |
| 30 MO | 11 49 | 8 ♉ 33 | 11 7 | 4 39 | 21 12 | 24 40 | 0 54 | 13 13 | 19 43 | 27 10 | 29 36 |
| 31 TU | 12 47 | 20 22 | 11 7 | 6 4 | 22 22 | 25 19 | 0 46 | 13 9 | 19 42 | 27 9 | 29 35 |

### INGRESSES :

| | |
|---|---|
| 1 ☽ → ♉ 22:39 | ☽ → ♐ 21:34 |
| 4 ☽ → ♊ 11:22 | 20 ☽ → ♑ 0:21 |
| 6 ☽ → ♋ 22: 4 | 22 ☽ → ♒ 3:59 |
| 9 ♇ → ♐ 0:41 | 24 ☽ → ♓ 9:45 |
| ☽ → ♌ 5:55 | 26 ☽ → ♈ 18:41 |
| ☿ → ♌ 7: 3 | ☿ → ♍ 19:53 |
| 11 ☽ → ♍ 11:25 | 29 ☽ → ♉ 6:36 |
| ♀ → ♍ 23:57 | 31 ☽ → ♊ 19:27 |
| 13 ☽ → ♎ 15:29 | |
| 15 ☽ → ♏ 18:45 | |
| 17 ☉ → ♌ 17:54 | |

### ASPECTS & ECLIPSES :

| | | | |
|---|---|---|---|
| 1 ☽ ☌ ♅ 1:33 | 9 ☽ ☌ ☿ 5:44 | 16 ☿ □ ☊ 2:54 | 24 ☽ ☍ ☿ 2: 1 |
| ☉ ☋S ☿ 14: 6 | ☽ ☍ ♃ 12:21 | ☽ ☌ ☋ 16: 4 | ☽ ☌ ♆ 4:49 |
| ☿ ☍ ♄ 21:49 | 10 ♀ ☍ ♆ 0:26 | 17 ☽ ☌ P 9:10 | 25 ☿ ☍ ♆ 1:18 |
| 2 ☉ ☍ ♄ 6:13 | ☽ ☌ ♂ 3:41 | 19 ☿ ☌ ♂ 3:26 | ☽ ☍ ♀ 15:55 |
| ☽ ☌ A 7:25 | ☽ ⊓N ☊ 5:25 | ☽ ☌ ♇ 23:57 | 28 ☽ ☌ ♅ 9:50 |
| 3 ☽ ☌ ☊ 2:51 | 11 ☿ ☍ ♃ 1:18 | 20 ☉ ☍ ♃ 0:27 | 29 ☉ □ Π 1:59 |
| 4 ☿ □ ♅ 1:55 | ☽ ☍ ♆ 7:15 | ☽ ☌ ♄ 23:54 | ☉ □ ☊ 7: 2 |
| 6 ☽ ☍ ♇ 22:10 | ♂ □ ☊ 9:13 | 22 ☽ ☌ ♃ 7:17 | 30 ☽ ☌ A 2:14 |
| ☉ □ ♅ 23:54 | ☽ ☌ ♀ 10:14 | ☉ ☍ ☽ 12: 0 | ☽ ☌ ☊ 5:12 |
| 8 ☽ ☍ ♄ 1:48 | 15 ☽ ☍ ♅ 1:17 | 23 ☽ ⊓S ☊ 0:54 | ☉ □ ☽ 7:12 |
| ☉ ☌ ☽ 13:49 | ☉ □ ☽ 15:18 | ☽ ☍ ♂ 16:41 | |

## SIDEREAL HELIOCENTRIC LONGITUDES : AUGUST 2021 Gregorian at 0 hours UT

| DAY | Sid. Time | ☿ | ♀ | ⊕ | ♂ | ♃ | ♄ | ♅ | ♆ | ♇ | Vernal Point |
|---|---|---|---|---|---|---|---|---|---|---|---|
| 1 SU | 20:39:18 | 11 ♋ 12 | 6 ♎ 50 | 13 ♑ 57 | 19 ♌ 44 | 0 ♒ 30 | 15 ♑ 6 | 16 ♈ 40 | 26 ♒ 29 | 0 ♑ 35 | 4 ♓ 57'32" |
| 2 MO | 20:43:15 | 16 48 | 8 27 | 14 54 | 20 11 | 0 35 | 15 8 | 16 41 | 26 29 | 0 35 | 4 ♓ 57'32" |
| 3 TU | 20:47:11 | 22 15 | 10 3 | 15 52 | 20 37 | 0 40 | 15 10 | 16 42 | 26 29 | 0 36 | 4 ♓ 57'32" |
| 4 WE | 20:51: 8 | 27 32 | 11 39 | 16 49 | 21 3 | 0 46 | 15 12 | 16 42 | 26 30 | 0 36 | 4 ♓ 57'31" |
| 5 TH | 20:55: 4 | 2 ♌ 39 | 13 16 | 17 47 | 21 29 | 0 51 | 15 14 | 16 43 | 26 30 | 0 36 | 4 ♓ 57'31" |
| 6 FR | 20:59: 1 | 7 37 | 14 52 | 18 44 | 21 56 | 0 56 | 15 15 | 16 44 | 26 31 | 0 36 | 4 ♓ 57'31" |
| 7 SA | 21: 2:58 | 12 25 | 16 28 | 19 42 | 22 22 | 1 2 | 15 17 | 16 44 | 26 31 | 0 37 | 4 ♓ 57'31" |
| 8 SU | 21: 6:54 | 17 4 | 18 4 | 20 39 | 22 48 | 1 7 | 15 19 | 16 45 | 26 31 | 0 37 | 4 ♓ 57'31" |
| 9 MO | 21:10:51 | 21 34 | 19 40 | 21 37 | 23 15 | 1 12 | 15 21 | 16 46 | 26 32 | 0 37 | 4 ♓ 57'31" |
| 10 TU | 21:14:47 | 25 56 | 21 16 | 22 34 | 23 41 | 1 18 | 15 23 | 16 46 | 26 32 | 0 38 | 4 ♓ 57'31" |
| 11 WE | 21:18:44 | 0 ♍ 9 | 22 52 | 23 32 | 24 7 | 1 23 | 15 25 | 16 47 | 26 32 | 0 38 | 4 ♓ 57'30" |
| 12 TH | 21:22:40 | 4 14 | 24 28 | 24 29 | 24 34 | 1 28 | 15 27 | 16 48 | 26 33 | 0 38 | 4 ♓ 57'30" |
| 13 FR | 21:26:37 | 8 12 | 26 4 | 25 27 | 25 0 | 1 34 | 15 28 | 16 48 | 26 33 | 0 39 | 4 ♓ 57'30" |
| 14 SA | 21:30:33 | 12 3 | 27 39 | 26 25 | 25 26 | 1 39 | 15 30 | 16 49 | 26 33 | 0 39 | 4 ♓ 57'30" |
| 15 SU | 21:34:30 | 15 48 | 29 15 | 27 22 | 25 53 | 1 44 | 15 32 | 16 50 | 26 34 | 0 39 | 4 ♓ 57'30" |
| 16 MO | 21:38:27 | 19 26 | 0 ♏ 51 | 28 20 | 26 19 | 1 50 | 15 34 | 16 50 | 26 34 | 0 39 | 4 ♓ 57'30" |
| 17 TU | 21:42:23 | 22 59 | 2 27 | 29 18 | 26 45 | 1 55 | 15 36 | 16 51 | 26 35 | 0 40 | 4 ♓ 57'30" |
| 18 WE | 21:46:20 | 26 27 | 4 2 | 0 ♒ 15 | 27 12 | 2 0 | 15 38 | 16 52 | 26 35 | 0 40 | 4 ♓ 57'30" |
| 19 TH | 21:50:16 | 29 49 | 5 38 | 1 13 | 27 38 | 2 6 | 15 39 | 16 52 | 26 35 | 0 40 | 4 ♓ 57'29" |
| 20 FR | 21:54:13 | 3 ♎ 7 | 7 13 | 2 11 | 28 5 | 2 11 | 15 41 | 16 53 | 26 36 | 0 41 | 4 ♓ 57'29" |
| 21 SA | 21:58: 9 | 6 21 | 8 49 | 3 8 | 28 31 | 2 16 | 15 43 | 16 54 | 26 36 | 0 41 | 4 ♓ 57'29" |
| 22 SU | 22: 2: 6 | 9 31 | 10 24 | 4 6 | 28 57 | 2 22 | 15 45 | 16 54 | 26 36 | 0 41 | 4 ♓ 57'29" |
| 23 MO | 22: 6: 2 | 12 38 | 12 0 | 5 4 | 29 24 | 2 27 | 15 47 | 16 55 | 26 37 | 0 41 | 4 ♓ 57'29" |
| 24 TU | 22: 9:59 | 15 41 | 13 35 | 6 2 | 29 50 | 2 32 | 15 49 | 16 56 | 26 37 | 0 42 | 4 ♓ 57'29" |
| 25 WE | 22:13:56 | 18 41 | 15 11 | 7 0 | 0 ♍ 17 | 2 38 | 15 51 | 16 56 | 26 37 | 0 42 | 4 ♓ 57'29" |
| 26 TH | 22:17:52 | 21 39 | 16 46 | 7 57 | 0 43 | 2 43 | 15 52 | 16 57 | 26 38 | 0 42 | 4 ♓ 57'28" |
| 27 FR | 22:21:49 | 24 35 | 18 21 | 8 55 | 1 10 | 2 48 | 15 54 | 16 58 | 26 38 | 0 43 | 4 ♓ 57'28" |
| 28 SA | 22:25:45 | 27 28 | 19 57 | 9 53 | 1 36 | 2 54 | 15 56 | 16 58 | 26 39 | 0 43 | 4 ♓ 57'28" |
| 29 SU | 22:29:42 | 0 ♏ 19 | 21 32 | 10 51 | 2 3 | 2 59 | 15 58 | 16 59 | 26 39 | 0 43 | 4 ♓ 57'28" |
| 30 MO | 22:33:38 | 3 9 | 23 7 | 11 49 | 2 29 | 3 5 | 16 0 | 17 0 | 26 39 | 0 44 | 4 ♓ 57'28" |
| 31 TU | 22:37:35 | 5 58 | 24 42 | 12 47 | 2 56 | 3 10 | 16 2 | 17 0 | 26 40 | 0 44 | 4 ♓ 57'28" |

### INGRESSES :

| |
|---|
| 4 ☿ → ♌ 11:28 |
| 10 ☿ → ♍ 23: 8 |
| 15 ♀ → ♏ 11:13 |
| 17 ⊕ → ♒ 17:40 |
| 19 ☿ → ♎ 1:18 |
| 24 ♂ → ♍ 8:42 |
| 28 ☿ → ♏ 21:17 |

### ASPECTS (HELIOCENTRIC +MOON(TYCHONIC)) :

| | | | | |
|---|---|---|---|---|
| 1 ☿ ☍ ⊕ 14: 6 | ☽ ☍ ♇ 23:14 | 12 ♀ □ ⊕ 0:59 | 20 ⊕ ☌ ♃ 0:12 | 26 ☿ ☌ ☋ 15:30 |
| ☿ ☍ ♄ 16:45 | 7 ♀ ☍ ♅ 4: 9 | 13 ☽ □ ♇ 16:35 | ☽ ☌ ♇ 1:30 | ☽ □ ♇ 20: 5 |
| ☿ □ ♅ 23:29 | 8 ☽ ☍ ♄ 2:57 | 14 ☽ □ ♄ 18: 5 | ☽ □ ☿ 7:21 | 28 ☽ □ ♄ 2:14 |
| ☽ □ ♃ 23:51 | ☽ □ ♅ 5:36 | ☽ ☍ ♅ 20:18 | 21 ☽ ☌ ♄ 3:13 | ☽ ☌ ♅ 4:19 |
| 2 ⊕ ☌ ♄ 5:58 | ☽ □ ♀ 9:10 | 15 ☽ ☌ ♀ 19:42 | ☽ □ ♅ 5:15 | 29 ♀ ☌ ☋ 4:33 |
| 3 ☿ ⊓N ☊ 5:50 | 9 ☽ ☍ ♃ 8:10 | ☽ □ ♃ 21:50 | 22 ☽ ☌ ♃ 8:10 | ☽ ☍ ☿ 9:33 |
| ☽ □ ♂ 17: 9 | ☿ ☌ ♂ 10: 8 | 16 ♂ ☍ ♆ 14: 0 | 23 ☽ □ ♀ 1:18 | ☽ □ ♃ 12:46 |
| ⊕ □ ♅ 21: 8 | 10 ☿ ☍ ♆ 3:24 | ♀ □ ♃ 15:37 | 24 ☿ □ ♄ 1: 1 | ☿ □ ♃ 23:19 |
| 4 ☽ □ ♆ 4:21 | 11 ☽ ☌ ♂ 1: 7 | 17 ☽ □ ♆ 15:47 | ☽ ☌ ♆ 3:32 | 31 ☽ ☍ ♀ 10: 8 |
| ☿ ☍ ♃ 15:19 | ☽ ☍ ♆ 5:21 | ☽ □ ♂ 16:36 | ☽ ☍ ♂ 9:47 | ☽ □ ♆ 12:44 |
| 6 ♀ □ ♄ 6: 2 | ☽ ☌ ☿ 16:41 | 19 ☿ □ ♇ 6: 9 | ☿ ☍ ♅ 9:55 | |

abyss. He spoke also of the mingling of milk and water; this symbolizes an inner union which cannot be separated. With this he meant his union with them. He referred to the mild and nourishing power of milk. He also spoke of the union of human beings in marriage. He said that there are two kinds of marriage: that of the flesh, where the couple become separated at death; and that of the spirit, where they remain united beyond death. He spoke also of the bridegroom and of the church as his bride and went on to refer to the union with them through the Last Supper, which union could never be dissolved. He spoke also of the baptism of John, which would be replaced by the baptism of the Holy Spirit, whom he would send, and gave instructions to the disciples to baptize all who came to them to be baptized. That evening he returned to Bethany.[117]

And on March 31:

...Jesus taught for the last time in the temple. He spoke of the truth and of the necessity of fulfilling what one teaches. He wished to bring his teaching to fulfillment. It was not enough to believe; one must also practice one's faith. Thus, he would bring his teaching to fulfillment by going to the Father. Before leaving his disciples, however, he wished to bestow on them all that he had; not money and property, which he did not have, but his power and his forces. These he wanted to give them, and also to found an intimate union with them to the end of the world, a more perfect union than the present one. He asked them to become united with one another as limbs of one body. By this, Jesus referred to that which was to be accomplished through the Last Supper, but without mentioning it. He also said that his mother, the holy Virgin, would remain with them for a number of years after his ascension to the Father. As he left the temple that evening, he took leave of it, saying that he would never enter it again in this body. This was so moving that the apostles and disciples cast themselves down on the ground and wept. Jesus also wept. It was dark as he made his way back to Bethany.[118]

Later, the fulfillment of these words came as Venus (still in Libra) entered square alignment with

Saturn—albeit in Cancer, opposite its position today—April 5 (Easter Sunday) and April 6, when the Risen One appeared to Luke and Cleophas on the road to Emmaus.

**August 8: New Moon 21°12' Cancer.** A Cancer New Moon occurred on July 8 AD 31, as Jesus traveled from Thantia to Datheman, where there was a ruined citadel used in the war of the Maccabees:

Near it was the mountain that had been chosen by Jephthah's daughter upon which to mourn with her twelve young companions [Jud. 11:29–40]. Upon it were prophets and hermits, something like the Essenes. It was on this same mountain that Balaam was tarrying in solitude and meditation when summoned by the Moabite king to appear before him [Num. 22:4–5]. He was of noble origin, his family very wealthy. From early youth, he had been filled with the spirit of prophecy, and he belonged to that nation that was ever on the lookout for the promised star, among whom were the ancestors of the three holy kings. Though a reprobate, Balaam was no sorcerer. He served the true God only, like the enlightened of other nations, but in an imperfect manner, mingling many errors with the truth. He was very young when he retired into the solitude of the mountains, and upon this one in particular he dwelt a long time. I think he had around him some other prophets, or pupils. When he returned from the Moabite king, Balak, he wished to take up his abode upon this mountain, but was prevented by divine interposition. By his scandalous counsel to the Moabites, he fell from grace, and now he wandered in despair around the desert in which at last he miserably perished.[119]

**August 9: August 7–10, Mercury conjoins Mars, exact on the 9th, Mercury conjunct Mars 23°26' Leo.** Simultaneously, August 8–11, Mercury opposes Neptune. This alignment is also exact on **August 9: Mercury 26°32' Leo opposite Neptune 26°32' Aquarius.** Notice that Mars and Neptune are gradually coming into opposition. This alignment builds from August 4 and lasts through August 27; it is exact on August 16 (see commentary below).

---

117 ACE, vol. 3, pp. 16–17.-
118 Ibid., p. 18.

119 ACE, vol. 2, p. 467.

Mercury and Mars were conjunct at 24° Leo on October 7 AD 29:

> …Jesus departed with his disciples, followed by the crowd that had gathered around him. They wended their way toward the Jordan, distant from this point at least three hours. The Jordan flows through a broad valley that rises on either bank for the distance of about half an hour. The stone in the enclosed space whereon the Ark of the Covenant had rested, and where the recent festival was celebrated, was about an hour's distance from John's place of baptism, that is, taking it in a straight line toward Jerusalem. John's hut near the twelve stones was in direction of Beth–Arabah and somewhat more to the south than the stone of the Ark of the Covenant. The twelve stones lay one-half hour from the place of baptism and in the direction of Gilgal. Gilgal was on a gentle slope on the west side of the mountain.
>
> From John's baptismal pool the view up both the shores, which were very fertile, was most lovely. The most delightful region, however, rich in fruits and teeming with abundance, was around the Sea of Galilee. But here, and also around Bethlehem, there were broader meadowlands, more husbandry, and a greater abundance of dhurra, garlic, and cucumbers.
>
> Jesus had already passed the memorial stone of the Ark of the Covenant and was about one quarter of an hour beyond John's tent, before which the latter stood teaching. A gap in the valley disclosed this scene to the distant traveler, and Jesus in passing was for not longer than a couple of minutes visible to the Baptist. John was seized by the Spirit and, pointing to Jesus, he cried out: "Behold the Lamb of God, who bears the sins of the world!" Jesus passed, preceded and followed by his disciples in groups, the multitude lately gathered around him in the rear. It was early morning. The people crowded forward at the words of John, but Jesus had already disappeared. They called after him in acclamations of praise, but he was out of hearing.[120]

John the Baptist lives strongly in these star memories, as Mercury was 26° Leo on June 4, 2 BC, the birthday of John.

**August 10: Mercury enters Virgo.**

> Thou resting, glowing light
>    (*Sun in Cancer*)
> In being experience being
>    (*Venus in Libra*)
> May the spirit penetrate being
>    (*Mercury in Virgo*)
> To gain strength in test of trial
>    (*Mars in Leo*)
> As a flowing wave self-sustaining
>    (*Jupiter in Aquarius*)
> And may the might of life's activity flower
>    (*Saturn in Capricorn*)
> With senses' might, arise!
>    (*Moon in Leo*)[121]

For a good part of the month, from August 4–19, the Sun is in square alignment with Venus. The two are exactly square on August 11.

**August 11: Sun 24°29' Cancer square Venus 24°29' Libra.** These two planets were nearly exactly square (with Sun in Capricorn rather than Cancer) on January 15 AD 1, at the Purification of the Virgin Mary and Christ's Presentation in the Temple:

> I saw the festival of the Purification celebrated also in the spiritual church. It was filled with angelic choirs and in the center above them I saw the most holy Trinity and in it something like a void. In the middle of the church stood an altar and on it a tree with broad, pendent leaves, similar to the tree in Paradise by which Adam fell.
>
> I saw the blessed Virgin with the child Jesus in her arms floating up from the earth to the altar, while the tree on the same inclined low before her and began to wither. A magnificent angel in priestly garments, a halo round his head, approached Mary. She gave him the child, and he laid it upon the altar. At that instant I saw the most holy Trinity as ever before in its fullness. I saw the angel give to Mary a little shining ball whereon was the figure of a swathed child, and I saw her with this gift hovering over the altar. From all sides, I saw crowds of poor people approaching Mary with

120 ACE, vol. 1, p. 356.

121 Steiner, *Twelve Cosmic Moods*.

lights. She reached those lights to the child on the ball into which they seemed to pass, and then to reappear. I saw that all these lights united into one, which spread over Mary and the child, and illuminated all things. Mary had extended her wide mantle over the whole Earth. And now there was a festival.

I think that the withering of the Tree of Knowledge at Mary's appearance and the offering of the child to the most holy Trinity signified the reuniting of the human race with God, and through Mary those scattered lights become one light in the light of Jesus, and illumined all things.[122]

**August 15:** Venus enters Scorpio—Feast of the Assumption.

> Thou resting, glowing light
> > (*Sun in Cancer*)
> Yet in being existence endures
> > (*Venus in Scorpio*)
> May the spirit penetrate being
> > (*Mercury in Virgo*)
> To gain strength in test of trial
> > (*Mars in Leo*)
> As a flowing wave self-sustaining
> > (*Jupiter in Aquarius*)
> And may the might of life's activity flower
> > (*Saturn in Capricorn*)
> O worlds, uphold worlds!
> > (*Moon in Libra*)[123]

**August 16: Mars 26°34' Leo opposite Neptune 26°34' Aquarius.** These two planets have been close to opposition since the 4th, and will be until the 27th. Mars and Neptune were opposed in the same signs (albeit at 1° rather than 26°) on May 21 AD 33, in the midst of the ten days between the Ascension and Pentecost:

The apostles and disciples now felt themselves alone. They were at first restless and like people forsaken. But by the soothing presence of the blessed Virgin they were comforted, and putting entire confidence in Jesus's words that she

would be to them a mediatrix, a mother, and an advocate, they regained peace of soul.

A certain fear stole over the Jews in Jerusalem. I saw many closing doors and windows, others gathering together in groups. During the last days, they had experienced some peculiar feelings of alarm, which today were greatly intensified.

On the following days I saw the apostles always together and the blessed Virgin with them in the house of the Last Supper. At the last repast of Jesus, and ever after, I saw Mary when at prayer and the breaking of bread always opposite Peter, who now took the Lord's place in the prayer circle and at meals. I received at the time the impression that Mary now held a position of high importance among the apostles, and that she was placed over the church.

The apostles kept themselves very much aloof. I saw no one out of the great crowd of Jesus's followers going to them into the house of the Last Supper. They guarded more against persecution from the Jews and gave themselves up to more earnest and well-regulated prayer than did the disciples in bands throughout the other apartments of the same house. The latter went in and out more freely. I saw many of them also very devoutly traversing the way of the Lord by night.[124]

Considering the fact that Neptune's position continues to remember the Assumption of the Virgin Mary—one day after the annual celebration of the Feast of the Assumption on August 15—we can devote our thoughts and prayers strongly to the Holy Virgin during the whole of this month.

At the same time, in the middle of August, Venus is square Jupiter. The alignment takes shape August 13–19, and is also exact on August 16.

**August 16: Venus 1°53' Scorpio square Jupiter 1°53' Aquarius.** Venus was at today's position on October 23 AD 30, when Bartholomew and Simon recommended that Christ accept Judas Iscariot as a disciple:

Judas Iscariot may have been at that time twenty-five years old. He was of middle height and by no means ugly. His hair was of a deep

---

122 ACE, vol. 1, pp. 217–218.

123 Steiner, *Twelve Cosmic Moods.*

124 ACE, vol. 3, p. 412.

black, his beard somewhat reddish. In his attire he was perfectly neat and more elegant than the majority of Jews. He was affable in address, obliging, and fond of making himself important. He talked with an air of confidence of the great or of persons renowned for holiness, affecting familiarity with such when he found himself among those that did not know him. But if anyone who knew better convicted him of untruth, he retired confused. He was avaricious of honors, distinctions, and money. He was always in pursuit of good luck, always longing for fame, rank, a high position, wealth, though not seeing clearly how all this was to come to him. The appearance of Jesus in public greatly encouraged him to hope for a realization of his dreams. The disciples were provided for; the wealthy Lazarus took part with Jesus, of whom everyone thought that he was about to establish a kingdom; he was spoken of on all sides as a king, as the Messiah, as the prophet of Nazareth. His miracles and wisdom were on every tongue. Judas consequently conceived a great desire to be numbered as his disciple and to share his greatness which, he thought, was to be that of this world. For a long time previously he had picked up, wherever he could, information of Jesus and had in turn carried around tidings of him. He had sought the acquaintance of several of the disciples, and was now nearing the object of his desires. The chief motive that influenced him to follow Jesus was the fact that he had no settled occupation and only a half-education. He had embarked on trade and commerce, but without success, and had squandered the fortune left him by his natural father. Lately he had been executing all kinds of commissions, carrying on all kinds of business and brokerage for other people. In the discharge of such affairs he showed himself both zealous and intelligent. A brother of his deceased father, named Simeon, was engaged in agriculture in Iscariot, the little place of about twenty houses that belonged to Meroz and from which it lay only a short distance toward the east. His parents had lived there a long time, and even after their death he had generally made it his home, hence his appellation of Iscariot. His parents at one time led a wandering life, for his mother was a public dancer and singer. She was of the race of Jephthah, or rather that of his wife, and from

the land of Tob. She was a poetess. She composed songs and anthems, which she sang with harp accompaniment. She taught young girls to dance, and carried with her from place to place all sorts of feminine finery and new fashions. Her husband, a Jew, was not with her; he lived at Pella. Judas was an illegitimate child whose father was an officer in the army near Damascus. He was born at Ascalon on one of his mother's professional journeys, but she soon freed herself from the encumbrance by exposing the child. Shortly after his birth, he was abandoned on the water's edge. But being found by some rich people with no children of their own, they cared for the child and bestowed upon him a liberal education. Later on, however, he turned out to be a bad boy, and through some kind of knavery, fell again to the care of his mother, who assumed the charge for pay. It is in my mind that the husband of his mother, becoming acquainted with the boy's origin, had cursed him. Judas received some wealth from his illegitimate father. He was possessed of much wit. After the death of his parents, he lived mostly in Iscariot with his uncle Simeon, the tanner, and helped him in his business. He was not as yet a villain, but loquacious, greedy for wealth and honor, and without stability. He was neither a profligate nor a man without religion, for he adhered strictly to all the prescriptions of the Jewish Law. He comes before me as a man that could be influenced as easily to the best things as to the worst. With all his cleverness, courteousness, and obligingness, there was a shade of darkness, of sadness, in the expression of his countenance, proceeding from his avarice, his ambition, his secret envy of even the virtues of others.

He was not, however, exactly ugly. There was something bland and affable in his countenance, though at the same time, something abject and repulsive. His father had something good in him, and thence came that possessed by Judas. When as a boy he was returned to his mother, and she on his account was embroiled in a quarrel with her husband, she cursed him. Both she and her husband were jugglers. They practiced all kinds of tricks; they were sometimes in plenty and as often in want.[125]

---

125 ACE, vol. 2, p. 85.

**August 17: Sun enters Leo.**

**August 19: Mercury enters Libra**.

> Irradiate with senses' might
>> (*Sun in Leo*)
> Yet in being existence endures
>> (*Venus in Scorpio*)
> In existing embrace existence
>> (*Mercury in Libra*)
> To gain strength in test of trial
>> (*Mars in Leo*)
> As a flowing wave self-sustaining
>> (*Jupiter in Aquarius*)
> And may the might of life's activity flower
>> (*Saturn in Capricorn*)
> May existence feel existence!
>> (*Moon in Sagittarius*)[126]

August 14–25, the Sun opposes Jupiter, exact on August 19. August 19: Sun 2°11' Leo opposite Jupiter 2°11' Aquarius. Simultaneously, Venus conjoins the South Node August 19–25, exact on August 22: Venus conjunct South Node 11°53' Scorpio.

The Sun was at 2° Leo during the final archetypal healing miracle of Christ, the Raising of Lazarus, on July 26 AD 32—the miracle that includes and summarizes the preceding six, which in their turn include and summarize all the miracles performed by Christ during his ministry. Today is a day for the miraculous—i.e., the purely *creative and intentional deed*, as opposed to the mechanical, the instinctual, the automatic.

Venus was at 11° Scorpio on April 15 AD 33, during the miraculous catch of fish. It was also here on the night of October 29–30 AD 30:

> After a journey of about five hours, and night having set in, Jesus and the disciples arrived at a lonely inn where only sleeping accommodations were to be found. Nearby was a well that owed its origin to Jacob. The disciples gathered wood and made a fire. On the way Jesus had had a long conversation with them, intended principally for the instruction of Thomas, Simon, Manahem, "Little Cleophas," and the others newly received. He spoke of their following him, and through the deep conviction of the worthlessness of

earthly goods, of their leaving their relatives without regret and without looking back. He promised that what they had left should be restored to them in his kingdom a thousandfold. But they should reflect maturely whether or not they could break their earthly ties.

> To some of the disciples, and especially to Thomas, Judas Iscariot was not particularly pleasing. He did not hesitate to say plainly to Jesus that he did not like Judas because he was too ready to say yes and no. Why, he asked, had he admitted that man among his disciples, since he had been so difficult to please in others. Jesus answered evasively that from eternity it was decreed by God for Judas, like all the others, to be of the number of his disciples.[127]

Venus and the South Node conjoined in Scorpio a week later, on November 6 AD 30, when Christ healed the mute and paralyzed son of a Roman officer.

**August 22: Full Moon 4°34' Aquarius.** The Full Moon in Aquarius occurred on August 2 AD 30, one day prior to the second archetypal healing miracle, the Healing of the Nobleman's Son:

> I saw this man not as invested with the royal commission, but as himself the father of the sick boy. He was the chief officer of the centurion of Capernaum. The latter had no children, but had long desired to have one. He had, consequently, adopted as his own a son of this his confidential servant and his wife. The boy was now fourteen years old. The man came in quality of messenger, though he was himself the true father and almost indeed the master. I saw the whole affair, all the circumstances were clear to me. It was perhaps on account of them that Jesus permitted the man to importune him so long. The details I have just given were not publicly known.[128]

Hidden motivations are not always malicious. The Aquarius Full Moon can contribute to intuitive insight into the true needs and intentions of others.

**August 22–25,** Mercury comes into opposition with Uranus. Their alignment is exact on **August**

---

126 Steiner, *Twelve Cosmic Moods*.

127 ACE, vol. 2, p. 94.
128 Ibid., p. 1.

**24: Mercury 16°56' Libra opposite Uranus 16°56' Aries.** Mercury was at this degree on Holy Saturday, April 4 AD 33, as Christ was reintegrating the subearthly spheres, opening the path to the Mother.

August 24: Mars enters Virgo.

**August 28: Mercury enters Scorpio.**

> Irradiate with senses' might
> (*Sun in Leo*)
> Yet in being existence endures
> (*Venus in Scorpio*)
> In activity growth disappears
> (*Mercury in Scorpio*)
> Work with powers of life
> (*Mars in Virgo*)
> As a flowing wave self-sustaining
> (*Jupiter in Aquarius*)
> And may the might of life's activity flower
> (*Saturn in Capricorn*)
> O shining light, abide!
> (*Moon in Aries*)[129]

**August 24** and September 3, the Sun is square the Node. This alignment is exact on **August 29: Sun 11°8' Leo square Node 11°8' Taurus.** The Sun was at this degree the day after the healing of the nobleman's son:

> When Jesus approached the environs of Capernaum, several possessed began to rage outside the gate and to call into the city: "The prophet is coming! What does he want here? What business has he with us?" But when he reached the city, they ran away. A tent had been erected outside. The centurion and the father of the boy came out to meet Jesus, the child walking between them. They were followed by the entire family, all the relatives, servants, and slaves. These last were pagans who had been sent to Zorobabel by Herod. It was a real procession, and all cast themselves down before Jesus giving thanks. They washed his feet and offered him a little luncheon, a mouthful to eat and a glass of wine. Jesus spoke some words of admonition to the boy, laying his hand on his head as he knelt before him. He now received the name of Jesse, whereas he had before been called Joel.

The centurion's name was Zorobabel. He earnestly besought Jesus to stay with him while at Capernaum and to accept a feast in his honor. But Jesus refused, still reproaching him with his desire to see a miracle in order to vex others. He said, "I should not have cured the boy, had not the faith of the messenger been so strong and urgent." And thereupon Jesus went on his way.[130]

# SEPTEMBER 2021

## STARGAZING PREVIEW

On Sunday September 5th, the Sun sets at 1830, followed quickly by Mars, now hidden within the Sun's radiance. This evening will offer your last opportunity to see Venus in Virgo until September of next year. Planets interpret and "speak for" the constellations; it is when Venus moves before the stars of Virgo that Sophia might resound more readily within our souls. Tonight, she and *Spica*, the brightest star of the constellation of Virgo, set at 1940. Retrograde Jupiter leaves Aquarius on the 6th, joining Saturn in Capricorn. Also, on this day, Venus enters Libra, one of the two zodiacal signs (along with Taurus) that she rules.

The September New Moon (19° Leo) will be exact during the first hour of the 7th. By 0700, Mars, rising less than an hour after the Sun and Moon, enters Virgo; how comforting it is that she has his protection, and that our aggressions might be tempered by her tenderness! The Moon and Venus set together (at 1930) on the 9th. Venus sets before the Moon on the 10th, after their exact conjunction earlier in the day.

The First Quarter Moon appears on the evening of the 13th, not far from *Lesath*, the star of the Scorpion's stinger. They can be spotted high in the south at sunset (1810). For another half hour or so, it may also be possible to see Mercury, now nearly 27° from the Sun; Mercury sets at 1900.

During the evening of the 16th, you'll find the Moon in the southeastern sky, to the right of Saturn.

---

129 Steiner, *Twelve Cosmic Moods.*

130 ACE, vol. 2, pp. 2–3.

A day later—the day on which the Sun moves into Virgo— the Moon will be directly between Saturn and Jupiter. Once the Virgo Sun sets on the 18th, the Moon, waxing toward Full, will have passed them both. Watch for September's Full Moon on Monday the 20th, at 3° Pisces—its degree at the miracle of Turning of Water into Wine!

Take note that the 22nd marks the Autumnal Equinox, the start of our long inhalation toward winter's quietude.

The Moon finds its Last Quarter (11° Gemini) on the 29th, the degree from which it shone at the second conversion of Mary Magdalene. Jesus had commanded the devils to flee from all those who sought freedom from possession. Magdalene fell unconscious several times as the devils that she had sheltered departed from her.

By month's end, Orion will rise in the east at 2100.

## September Commentaries

The month of September begins with two alignments taking shape: the first is Venus square Neptune, from August 28 through September 4. This alignment is exact on the 1st.

**September 1: Venus 26°40' Scorpio square Neptune 26°40' Aquarius.** At the same time, Mercury conjoins the South Node, between August 30 and September 3, exact on September 1: **Mercury conjunct South Node 11°4' Scorpio.**

Venus was at this degree on the morning of November 8 AD 30, as Christ began to deliver a powerful discourse that would culminate with the first conversion of Mary Magdalene:

About ten o'clock, Jesus ascended the mountain with his disciples, followed by the Pharisees, the Herodians, and the Sadducees, and took the teacher's chair. The disciples were on one side, the Pharisees on the other, forming a circle around him. Several times during his discourse Jesus made a pause to allow his hearers to exchange places, the more distant coming forward, the nearest falling back, and he likewise repeated the same instructions several times. His auditors partook of refreshments in the intervals, and Jesus himself once took a mouthful to eat

and a little drink. This discourse of Jesus was one of the most powerful that he had yet delivered. He prayed before he began, and then told his hearers that they should not be scandalized at him if he called God his Father, for whosoever does the will of the Father in Heaven, he is his son, and that he really accomplished the Father's will, he clearly proved. Hereupon he prayed aloud to his Father and then commenced his austere preaching of penance after the manner of the ancient prophets. All that had happened from the time of the first Promise, all the figures and all the menaces, he introduced into his discourse and showed how, in the present and in the near future, they would be accomplished. He proved the coming of the Messiah from the fulfillment of the prophecies. He spoke of John, the precursor and preparer of the ways, who had honestly fulfilled his mission, but whose hearers had remained obdurate. Then he enumerated their vices, their hypocrisy, their idolatry of sinful flesh; painted in strong colors the Pharisees, Sadducees, and Herodians; and spoke with great warmth of the anger of God and the approaching judgment, of the destruction of Jerusalem and the temple, and of the diverse woes that hung over their country. He quoted many passages from the prophet Malachi, explaining and applying them to the precursor, to the Messiah, to the pure oblation of bread and wine of the New Law (which I plainly understood to signify the Holy Sacrifice of the Mass), to the judgment awaiting the godless, to the second coming of the Messiah on the last day, and spoke of the confidence and consolation those that feared God would then experience. He added, moreover, that the grace taken from them would be given to the pagans.[131]

Mercury was 11° Scorpio on April 12 AD 31:

The country around Julias was extraordinarily charming, fertile, solitary, and verdant, full of grazing asses and camels. It was like a zoological garden, the abode of all kinds of birds and animals. Serpentine footpaths wound down to the harbor, and springs were abundant. The noonday sun shone full upon it and flashed on the mirrorlike surface of the lake. The high road to Julius ran nearer to the Jordan, but the

---

131 Ibid., p. 107.

country of which I speak was a solitude. Jesus and the disciples recrossed the Jordan and proceeded to Bethsaida and Capernaum. In the latter place, Jesus taught in the synagogue, for it was the sabbath. The scripture assigned for the day were passages from Moses, treating of the annual sacrifice of expiation, of that offered before the tabernacle, of the prohibition to eat the blood of animals, and of the degrees of kindred in which marriage could not be solemnized. Passages were read from Ezekial, also, upon the sins of the city of Jerusalem.[132]

And on the next day, Mercury conjoined the South Node at 14° Scorpio:

After the evening sabbath sermon in the synagogue, Jesus accepted the invitation of a well-to-do Pharisee to dine with him at his house. Here took place the healing of a man with edema, which scandalized the Pharisees (Luke 14:1–14). Jesus then told the parable of the great feast (Luke 14:15–24) and asked that the poor be invited to join with them in their meal.[133]

**September 3:** Venus enters Sagittarius.

> Irradiate with senses' might
>     (*Sun in Leo*)
> In existence growth's power dies
>     (*Venus in Sagittarius*)
> In activity growth disappears
>     (*Mercury in Scorpio*)
> Work with powers of life
>     (*Mars in Virgo*)
> As a flowing wave self-sustaining
>     (*Jupiter in Aquarius*)
> And may the might of life's activity flower
>     (*Saturn in Capricorn*)
> Thou glowing light, become strong!
>     (*Moon in Cancer*)[134]

September 2–11, Venus is square Mars; this is exact on the 6th.

**September 6: Venus 6°8' Sagittarius square Mars 6°8' Virgo.** Venus was at this same degree on

November 14 AD 30, the day after the raising of the Youth of Nain from the dead. Mars was at 6° Virgo on December 26, 6 BC, at the Adoration of the magi.

The three magi were Mensor (the Gold King), Sair (the Myrrh King), and Theokeno (the Frankincense King). Sair (traditionally Balthasar) represented the ancient Indian culture, and offered strength of *willing* sacrifice (myrrh) to Jesus; Theokeno (traditionally known as Caspar) represented the ancient Persian culture, and offered the gift of devotional and reverent *feeling* (frankincense) to the Jesus child. Mensor (traditionally Melchior) represented the ancient Egyptian culture, offering pure wisdom (gold). The three ancient cultures which prepared the way for the incarnation of Christ offered the distillation and accumulation of their spiritual treasures to the Solomon Jesus, the reincarnated Zarathustra, at this Turning Point of Time.

Rudolf Steiner indicates that there were three individuals raised by Christ who are the counterbalance to these three kings. Salome, the daughter of Jairus (who was raised *twice* from the dead) represents the future Anglo–American culture, which will be the resurrection of the ancient Indian culture. Lazarus is the representative of the future Russo–Slavic culture, which will be the counterbalance to the ancient Persian culture. And the Youth of Nain (who later incarnated as Mani and Parzival) is the representative of the current Central-European culture, in particular in its role as christening and resurrection of ancient Egyptian (Hermetic) culture.

Today we can meditate on the incarnational, masculine impulse proceeding from the end of the Age of Atlantis toward the Mystery of Golgotha (Mars in Virgo) dissolving and resolving into the excarnational, feminine impulse proceeding from the Mystery of Golgotha into the Sixth Epoch (Venus in Sagittarius).

**September 6: New Moon 19°35' Leo.** While Venus recalls the raising of the Youth of Nain (the modern day "Gold King"), the Leo New Moon remembers the seventh archetypal miracle, the Raising of Lazarus (the modern day "Frankincense King"). Sun and Moon conjoined July 26 AD 32 at 3° Leo, aligned with the megastar Eta Leonis.

---

132 Ibid., p. 346.
133 Ibid., p. 346.
134 Steiner, *Twelve Cosmic Moods.*

## SIDEREAL GEOCENTRIC LONGITUDES : SEPTEMBER 2021 Gregorian at 0 hours UT

| DAY | ☉ | ☽ | ☊ | ☿ | ♀ | ♂ | ♃ | ♄ | ♅ | ♆ | ♇ |
|---|---|---|---|---|---|---|---|---|---|---|---|
| 1 WE | 13 ♌ 45 | 2 ♊ 15 | 11 ♉ 6R | 7 ♍ 28 | 23 ♍ 32 | 25 ♌ 57 | 0 ♒ 38R | 13 ♑ 6R | 19 ♈ 41R | 27 ♒ 7R | 29 ♐ 34R |
| 2 TH | 14 43 | 14 19 | 11 3 | 8 50 | 24 42 | 26 35 | 0 31 | 13 2 | 19 41 | 27 5 | 29 33 |
| 3 FR | 15 41 | 26 37 | 10 58 | 10 11 | 25 51 | 27 14 | 0 24 | 12 59 | 19 40 | 27 4 | 29 32 |
| 4 SA | 16 39 | 9 ♋ 13 | 10 51 | 11 30 | 27 1 | 27 52 | 0 16 | 12 55 | 19 39 | 27 2 | 29 31 |
| 5 SU | 17 37 | 22 10 | 10 41 | 12 47 | 28 11 | 28 31 | 0 9 | 12 52 | 19 39 | 27 0 | 29 30 |
| 6 MO | 18 35 | 5 ♌ 29 | 10 29 | 14 3 | 29 20 | 29 9 | 0 2 | 12 49 | 19 38 | 26 59 | 29 29 |
| 7 TU | 19 34 | 19 6 | 10 17 | 15 17 | 0 ♎ 30 | 29 48 | 29 ♑ 55 | 12 46 | 19 37 | 26 57 | 29 28 |
| 8 WE | 20 32 | 3 ♍ 1 | 10 5 | 16 29 | 1 39 | 0 ♍ 26 | 29 48 | 12 43 | 19 36 | 26 56 | 29 28 |
| 9 TH | 21 30 | 17 7 | 9 55 | 17 40 | 2 49 | 1 5 | 29 41 | 12 40 | 19 35 | 26 54 | 29 27 |
| 10 FR | 22 28 | 1 ♎ 21 | 9 48 | 18 48 | 3 58 | 1 44 | 29 35 | 12 37 | 19 34 | 26 52 | 29 26 |
| 11 SA | 23 27 | 15 38 | 9 44 | 19 55 | 5 7 | 2 22 | 29 28 | 12 34 | 19 33 | 26 51 | 29 25 |
| 12 SU | 24 25 | 29 53 | 9 42 | 20 59 | 6 16 | 3 1 | 29 22 | 12 31 | 19 32 | 26 49 | 29 25 |
| 13 MO | 25 23 | 14 ♏ 5 | 9 42D | 22 1 | 7 25 | 3 40 | 29 15 | 12 28 | 19 31 | 26 47 | 29 24 |
| 14 TU | 26 22 | 28 12 | 9 42R | 23 0 | 8 34 | 4 18 | 29 9 | 12 26 | 19 30 | 26 46 | 29 23 |
| 15 WE | 27 20 | 12 ♐ 13 | 9 41 | 23 57 | 9 43 | 4 57 | 29 3 | 12 23 | 19 29 | 26 44 | 29 23 |
| 16 TH | 28 19 | 26 7 | 9 39 | 24 51 | 10 52 | 5 36 | 28 57 | 12 21 | 19 27 | 26 42 | 29 22 |
| 17 FR | 29 17 | 9 ♑ 54 | 9 33 | 25 42 | 12 0 | 6 15 | 28 51 | 12 19 | 19 26 | 26 41 | 29 22 |
| 18 SA | 0 ♍ 16 | 23 32 | 9 25 | 26 30 | 13 9 | 6 54 | 28 46 | 12 16 | 19 25 | 26 39 | 29 21 |
| 19 SU | 1 14 | 6 ♒ 59 | 9 15 | 27 14 | 14 17 | 7 32 | 28 40 | 12 14 | 19 23 | 26 37 | 29 21 |
| 20 MO | 2 13 | 20 14 | 9 4 | 27 55 | 15 25 | 8 11 | 28 35 | 12 12 | 19 22 | 26 36 | 29 20 |
| 21 TU | 3 12 | 3 ♓ 15 | 8 53 | 28 31 | 16 34 | 8 50 | 28 30 | 12 10 | 19 20 | 26 34 | 29 20 |
| 22 WE | 4 10 | 16 0 | 8 42 | 29 4 | 17 42 | 9 29 | 28 25 | 12 8 | 19 19 | 26 32 | 29 19 |
| 23 TH | 5 9 | 28 29 | 8 34 | 29 31 | 18 49 | 10 8 | 28 20 | 12 6 | 19 17 | 26 31 | 29 19 |
| 24 FR | 6 8 | 10 ♈ 44 | 8 27 | 29 53 | 19 57 | 10 47 | 28 15 | 12 5 | 19 16 | 26 29 | 29 18 |
| 25 SA | 7 6 | 22 47 | 8 24 | 0 ♎ 10 | 21 5 | 11 26 | 28 10 | 12 3 | 19 14 | 26 28 | 29 18 |
| 26 SU | 8 5 | 4 ♉ 40 | 8 23 | 0 21 | 22 12 | 12 5 | 28 6 | 12 2 | 19 12 | 26 26 | 29 18 |
| 27 MO | 9 4 | 16 28 | 8 23D | 0 26 | 23 20 | 12 44 | 28 2 | 12 0 | 19 11 | 26 24 | 29 17 |
| 28 TU | 10 3 | 28 16 | 8 23 | 0 24R | 24 27 | 13 23 | 27 58 | 11 59 | 19 9 | 26 23 | 29 17 |
| 29 WE | 11 2 | 10 ♊ 9 | 8 24R | 0 15 | 25 34 | 14 3 | 27 54 | 11 57 | 19 7 | 26 21 | 29 17 |
| 30 TH | 12 1 | 22 12 | 8 23 | 29 ♍ 58 | 26 41 | 14 42 | 27 50 | 11 56 | 19 5 | 26 19 | 29 17 |

### INGRESSES :

| | |
|---|---|
| 3 ☽ → ♋ 6:30 | 18 ☽ → ♒ 11:29 |
| 5 ☽ → ♌ 14:11 | 20 ☽ → ♓ 17:58 |
| 6 ♃ → ♑ 7: 0 | 23 ☽ → ♈ 2:56 |
| ♀ → ♎ 13:40 | 24 ☿ → ♎ 8:47 |
| 7 ♂ → ♍ 7:35 | 25 ☽ → ♉ 14:32 |
| ☽ → ♍ 18:49 | 28 ☽ → ♊ 3:31 |
| 9 ☽ → ♎ 21:43 | 29 ☿ → ♍ 22: 8 |
| 12 ☽ → ♏ 0:11 | 30 ☽ → ♋ 15:17 |
| 14 ☽ → ♐ 3: 4 | |
| 16 ☽ → ♑ 6:44 | |
| 17 ☉ → ♍ 17:32 | |

### ASPECTS & ECLIPSES :

| | | | |
|---|---|---|---|
| 2 ♂ ☍ ♆ 17:56 | 11 ☽ ☍ ♅ 6:35 | ☉ ☍ ☽ 23:53 | ♀ □ ♃ 23:30 |
| 3 ☽ ☍ ♇ 5:35 | ☽ ☌ P 9:50 | 21 ☽ ☍ ♂ 11: 1 | |
| 4 ☽ ☍ ♄ 6:53 | 12 ☽ ☌ ☋ 16:34 | 22 ☿ □ ♇ 13: 0 | |
| 5 ☽ ☍ ♃ 14:20 | 13 ☉ □ ☽ 20:38 | 23 ☽ ☍ ☿ 2: 3 | |
| 6 ♀ □ ♇ 3: 1 | 14 ☉ ☍ ♆ 9:29 | ♀ ☍ ♅ 9:38 | |
| ☽ □N ☊ 8:45 | 16 ☽ ☌ ♇ 5:38 | 24 ☽ ☌ ♅ 16:54 | |
| 7 ☉ ☌ ☽ 0:50 | 17 ☽ ☌ ♄ 4:12 | ☽ ☍ ♀ 20:14 | |
| ☽ ☍ ♆ 13:33 | ♀ □ ♄ 6:13 | 26 ☽ ☌ ☊ 7:31 | |
| ☽ ☌ ♂ 19:22 | 18 ☽ ☌ ♃ 9:13 | ☽ ☌ A 21:49 | |
| 9 ☽ ☌ ☿ 0:59 | 19 ☽ □S ☊ 4: 1 | 29 ☉ □ ☽ 1:56 | |
| 10 ☽ ☌ ♀ 4:46 | 20 ☽ ☌ ♆ 11:39 | 30 ☽ ☍ ♇ 13:52 | |

## SIDEREAL HELIOCENTRIC LONGITUDES : SEPTEMBER 2021 Gregorian at 0 hours UT

| DAY | Sid. Time | ☿ | ♀ | ⊕ | ♂ | ♃ | ♄ | ♅ | ♆ | ♇ | Vernal Point |
|---|---|---|---|---|---|---|---|---|---|---|---|
| 1 WE | 22:41:31 | 8 ♏ 45 | 26 ♏ 17 | 13 ♒ 45 | 3 ♍ 23 | 3 ♒ 15 | 16 ♑ 4 | 17 ♈ 1 | 26 ♒ 40 | 0 ♑ 44 | 4 ♓ 57'28" |
| 2 TH | 22:45:28 | 11 31 | 27 53 | 14 43 | 3 49 | 3 21 | 16 5 | 17 2 | 26 40 | 0 44 | 4 ♓ 57'27" |
| 3 FR | 22:49:25 | 14 17 | 29 28 | 15 41 | 4 16 | 3 26 | 16 7 | 17 2 | 26 41 | 0 45 | 4 ♓ 57'27" |
| 4 SA | 22:53:21 | 17 2 | 1 ♐ 3 | 16 40 | 4 42 | 3 31 | 16 9 | 17 3 | 26 41 | 0 45 | 4 ♓ 57'27" |
| 5 SU | 22:57:18 | 19 47 | 2 38 | 17 38 | 5 9 | 3 37 | 16 11 | 17 4 | 26 41 | 0 45 | 4 ♓ 57'27" |
| 6 MO | 23: 1:14 | 22 31 | 4 13 | 18 36 | 5 36 | 3 42 | 16 13 | 17 4 | 26 42 | 0 46 | 4 ♓ 57'27" |
| 7 TU | 23: 5:11 | 25 16 | 5 48 | 19 34 | 6 2 | 3 47 | 16 15 | 17 5 | 26 42 | 0 46 | 4 ♓ 57'27" |
| 8 WE | 23: 9: 7 | 28 1 | 7 23 | 20 32 | 6 29 | 3 53 | 16 16 | 17 6 | 26 43 | 0 46 | 4 ♓ 57'27" |
| 9 TH | 23:13: 4 | 0 ♐ 47 | 8 58 | 21 31 | 6 56 | 3 58 | 16 18 | 17 6 | 26 43 | 0 46 | 4 ♓ 57'26" |
| 10 FR | 23:17: 0 | 3 33 | 10 33 | 22 29 | 7 22 | 4 3 | 16 20 | 17 7 | 26 43 | 0 47 | 4 ♓ 57'26" |
| 11 SA | 23:20:57 | 6 20 | 12 8 | 23 27 | 7 49 | 4 9 | 16 22 | 17 8 | 26 44 | 0 47 | 4 ♓ 57'26" |
| 12 SU | 23:24:54 | 9 8 | 13 43 | 24 26 | 8 16 | 4 14 | 16 24 | 17 8 | 26 44 | 0 47 | 4 ♓ 57'26" |
| 13 MO | 23:28:50 | 11 58 | 15 18 | 25 24 | 8 43 | 4 19 | 16 26 | 17 9 | 26 44 | 0 48 | 4 ♓ 57'26" |
| 14 TU | 23:32:47 | 14 49 | 16 53 | 26 22 | 9 10 | 4 25 | 16 28 | 17 10 | 26 45 | 0 48 | 4 ♓ 57'26" |
| 15 WE | 23:36:43 | 17 42 | 18 28 | 27 21 | 9 36 | 4 30 | 16 29 | 17 10 | 26 45 | 0 48 | 4 ♓ 57'26" |
| 16 TH | 23:40:40 | 20 37 | 20 2 | 28 19 | 10 3 | 4 35 | 16 31 | 17 11 | 26 45 | 0 48 | 4 ♓ 57'26" |
| 17 FR | 23:44:36 | 23 35 | 21 37 | 29 18 | 10 30 | 4 41 | 16 33 | 17 12 | 26 46 | 0 49 | 4 ♓ 57'25" |
| 18 SA | 23:48:33 | 26 34 | 23 12 | 0 ♓ 16 | 10 57 | 4 46 | 16 35 | 17 12 | 26 46 | 0 49 | 4 ♓ 57'25" |
| 19 SU | 23:52:29 | 29 37 | 24 47 | 1 15 | 11 24 | 4 52 | 16 37 | 17 13 | 26 47 | 0 49 | 4 ♓ 57'25" |
| 20 MO | 23:56:26 | 2 ♑ 42 | 26 22 | 2 13 | 11 51 | 4 57 | 16 39 | 17 14 | 26 47 | 0 50 | 4 ♓ 57'25" |
| 21 TU | 0: 0:23 | 5 51 | 27 57 | 3 12 | 12 18 | 5 2 | 16 40 | 17 14 | 26 47 | 0 50 | 4 ♓ 57'25" |
| 22 WE | 0: 4:19 | 9 3 | 29 32 | 4 11 | 12 45 | 5 8 | 16 42 | 17 15 | 26 48 | 0 50 | 4 ♓ 57'25" |
| 23 TH | 0: 8:16 | 12 20 | 1 ♑ 6 | 5 9 | 13 12 | 5 13 | 16 44 | 17 16 | 26 48 | 0 51 | 4 ♓ 57'25" |
| 24 FR | 0:12:12 | 15 40 | 2 41 | 6 8 | 13 39 | 5 18 | 16 46 | 17 16 | 26 48 | 0 51 | 4 ♓ 57'24" |
| 25 SA | 0:16: 9 | 19 5 | 4 16 | 7 7 | 14 6 | 5 24 | 16 48 | 17 17 | 26 49 | 0 51 | 4 ♓ 57'24" |
| 26 SU | 0:20: 5 | 22 35 | 5 51 | 8 6 | 14 33 | 5 29 | 16 50 | 17 18 | 26 49 | 0 51 | 4 ♓ 57'24" |
| 27 MO | 0:24: 2 | 26 10 | 7 26 | 9 4 | 15 0 | 5 34 | 16 52 | 17 18 | 26 49 | 0 52 | 4 ♓ 57'24" |
| 28 TU | 0:27:58 | 29 50 | 9 1 | 10 3 | 15 27 | 5 40 | 16 53 | 17 19 | 26 50 | 0 52 | 4 ♓ 57'24" |
| 29 WE | 0:31:55 | 3 ♒ 36 | 10 36 | 11 2 | 15 54 | 5 45 | 16 55 | 17 20 | 26 50 | 0 52 | 4 ♓ 57'24" |
| 30 TH | 0:35:52 | 7 29 | 12 11 | 12 1 | 16 21 | 5 50 | 16 57 | 17 20 | 26 51 | 0 53 | 4 ♓ 57'24" |

### INGRESSES :

3 ♀ → ♐ 8: 9
8 ☿ → ♐ 17:14
17 ⊕ → ♓ 17:17
19 ☿ → ♑ 3: 1
22 ♀ → ♑ 7:10
28 ☿ → ♒ 1: 4

### ASPECTS (HELIOCENTRIC +MOON(TYCHONIC)) :

| | | | | |
|---|---|---|---|---|
| 1 ☽ □ ♂ 2:19 | ☽ □ ☿ 13:18 | 15 ☽ ☌ ☿ 11:57 | 23 ☽ □ ♇ 4:34 | ☿ ☌ ♃ 13:41 |
| ♀ □ ♆ 5:43 | 8 ☽ ☌ ♂ 6: 7 | ☽ ☌ ♀ 12: 8 | ☽ □ ♀ 5:50 | 30 ☽ ☍ ♇ 16:59 |
| 3 ☽ ☍ ♇ 7:56 | ☽ □ ♀ 8:24 | ☿ ☌ ♀ 13:37 | 24 ☿ ☌ ♄ 7:51 | |
| ☿ □ ⊕ 18:58 | 9 ☽ □ ♇ 23: 1 | 16 ☽ ☌ ♇ 8: 8 | ☿ □ ♅ 11:22 | |
| 4 ☽ ☍ ♄ 12:57 | 11 ☽ □ ♄ 1:14 | 17 ☽ ☌ ♄ 11:42 | ☽ □ ♄ 12: 0 | |
| ☽ □ ♅ 14:35 | ☽ ☍ ♅ 2:31 | ☽ □ ♅ 12:49 | ☽ ☌ ♅ 12:59 | |
| 5 ☽ ☍ ♃ 20:48 | ☿ □ ♂ 15: 7 | 18 ☽ ☌ ♃ 20: 9 | ☽ □ ☿ 13:37 | |
| 6 ☿ ☌ A 2: 0 | 12 ☽ □ ♃ 7:22 | 19 ☿ ☌ ♇ 9:27 | 26 ☽ □ ♃ 1:40 | |
| 7 ♀ □ ♂ 5: 3 | 13 ☽ □ ♆ 21:31 | 20 ☽ ☌ ♆ 12: 1 | ☿ □S ☊ 6:32 | |
| ☿ □ ♆ 12:34 | 14 ⊕ ☌ ♆ 9:13 | 21 ☽ ☍ ♂ 17:36 | 27 ☽ □ ♆ 21: 5 | |
| ☽ ☍ ♆ 13:10 | ☽ □ ♂ 19:22 | 22 ♀ ☌ ♇ 19:57 | 29 ☽ □ ♂ 11:58 | |

In Valentin Tomberg's *Lord's Prayer Course,* he writes of seven levels of communion, related to the seven archetypal miracles ascending through the seven lotuses:

| | | |
|---|---|---|
| **Root** | Changing of Water into Wine | Wine |
| **Sacral** | Healing of the Nobleman's Son | Honey |
| **Solar Plexus** | Healing of the Paralyzed Man | Milk |
| **Heart** | Feeding of the Five Thousand | Bread |
| **Larynx** | Walking on Water | Fish |
| **Brow** | Healing of the Man Born Blind | Oil |
| **Crown** | Raising of Lazarus | Frankincense |

Note the relationship of Frankincense with Lazarus, indicating from another avenue this individuality's relationship to the resurrection of the ancient Persian culture. Tomberg writes of this miracle:

Lazarus languishes on account of his devotion to the Spirit. He loves the pure Light, only that which is absolutely pure. He elevates himself, and all streams within him go more and more up to the Light. But correspondingly all his life functions grow weaker and weaker. He, so to say, "fades away."

His interest in earthly things grows less and, eventually, he fades away completely. Then one pictures the cave where Lazarus is lying entombed, and in front all the human beings, also Christ, weeping. What is this weeping?

It is the pleading prayer of the Earth that he may not depart, this human being who is able to bring Light. It is an unaccomplished mission that is being mourned. It is not at all Lazarus who is being mourned, for it is known that he will be fine in the life after death. Rather, it is for the Earth that the tears are shed, out of compassion for the Earth. And the tears are a pleading prayer in the name of the Mother. With the thundering wrath of the Father there comes the answer, which resounds in the commanding call of Christ: "Lazarus, come forth!"

He says this in the name of the Father. So, the wrath of the Father concerning the faithlessness toward His work comes like a blast of thunder upon Lazarus. Pleading with tears and commanding with wrath can enliven the heart again. Through prayer and command, through pleading and ordering, the heart awakens. It is awakened and pierced by compassion and wrath; by the incense of tears and by the wrath of the Father.

Earlier, he writes:

The *seventh element* is all resins. Incense, which ascends, is an outer symbol of this. In human beings, tears correspond to resins. Tears have the power to keep the deceased living in the etheric body. Mary Magdalene wept; Christ appeared to her. Through the tears she attracted him to her (too soon, he was not yet quite ready). Thus, Christ said, "Do not touch me, for I have not yet ascended to the Father." Thus, also, Christ wept at the tomb of Lazarus.

Through his tears he could call him back. The *mystery of tears* was also known in the Egyptian Mysteries. There was the service performed of weeping for the dead. The Jews adopted this without knowing about the reality of this service. One could establish an entire *healing science* based on knowledge of these seven elements and of the seven lotus flowers of the human being. *All this must come one day.*[135]

**September 8: Mercury enters Sagittarius.**

> Irradiate with senses' might
>     (*Sun in Leo*)
> In existence growth's power dies
>     (*Venus in Sagittarius*)
> Attainment concludes joyful striving
>     (*Mercury in Sagittarius*)
> Work with powers of life
>     (*Mars in Virgo*)
> As a flowing wave self-sustaining
>     (*Jupiter in Aquarius*)
> And may the might of life's activity flower
>     (*Saturn in Capricorn*)
> O soul, know thou beings!
>     (*Moon in Virgo*)[136]

---

135 Quotations from weeks 187 and 288 of *The Lord's Prayer Course*, available in installments through the Sophia Foundation (http://www.sophiafoundation .org); soon to be published as a complete volume.

136 Steiner, *Twelve Cosmic Moods.*

September 9–19, the Sun opposes Neptune. This alignment is exact on the 14th.

**September 14: Sun 26°45' Leo opposite Neptune 26°45' Aquarius.** Simultaneously, Mercury conjoins Venus September 11–18, exact on the 18th.

**September 17: Sun enters Virgo.**

**September 18: Mercury conjunct Venus 19°21' Sagittarius.** The Sun was 26° Leo on August 19 AD 30, at the healing of Peter's mother-in-law:

Jesus now went without delay with the disciples out of the city gate and along the mountain to Peter's in Bethsaida. They had urged him to do so, for they thought that Peter's mother-in-law was dying. Her sickness had very much increased, and now she had a raging fever. Jesus went straight into her room. He was followed by some of the family; I think Peter's daughter was among them. He stepped to that side of the bed to which the sick woman's face was turned, and leaned against the bed, half standing, half sitting, so that his head approached hers. He spoke to her some words, and laid his hand upon her head and breast. She became perfectly still. Then standing before her, he took her hand and raised her into sitting posture, saying: "Give her something to drink!" Peter's daughter gave her a drink out of a vessel in the form of a little boat. Jesus blessed the drink and commanded the invalid to rise. She obeyed and arose from her low couch. Her limbs were bandaged, and she wore a wide nightdress. Disengaging herself from the bandages, she stepped to the floor and rendered thanks to the Lord, the entire household uniting with her.

At the meal that followed, she helped with the other women and, perfectly recovered, served at table. After that, Jesus, with Peter, Andrew, James, John, and several of the other disciples, went to Peter's fishery on the lake. In the instruction he gave them, he spoke principally of the fact that they would soon give up their present occupations and follow him. Peter became quite timid and anxious. He fell on his knees before Jesus, begging him to reflect upon his ignorance and weakness, and not to insist on his undertaking anything so important, that he was entirely unworthy, and quite unable to instruct others.

Jesus replied that his disciples should have no worldly solicitude, that he who gave health to the sick would provide for their subsistence and furnish them with ability for what they had to do. All were perfectly satisfied, excepting Peter who, in his humility and simplicity, could not comprehend how he was for the future to be, not a fisherman, but a teacher of men. This, however, is not the call of the apostles related in the Gospel. That had not yet taken place.[137]

This official "call of the apostles" took place when Venus was close to today's degree (18° Sagittarius), on November 21 AD 30:

Next morning, when Jesus went to the lake, which was about a quarter of an hour distant from Matthew's dwelling, Peter and Andrew were upon the point of launching out on the deep to let down their nets. Jesus called to them: "Come and follow me! I will make you fishers of men!" They instantly abandoned their work, hove to their boat, and came on shore. Jesus went on a little farther up the shore to the ship of Zebedee, who with his sons James and John was mending his nets on the ship. Jesus called the two sons to come to him. They obeyed immediately and came to land, while Zebedee remained on the ship with his servants.[138]

Mercury was 19° Sagittarius two months later, on January 27 AD 31:

This morning, at Peter's house, the twelve and the other disciples reported their experiences from their missionary travels since Kislev 25 [Dec. 10 AD 30] (Mark 6:30). Jesus listened to their doubts and to the problems they had encountered, giving practical instructions for the future.[139]

**September 19: Mercury enters Capricorn.**

Behold worlds, O soul!
 (*Sun in Virgo*)
In existence growth's power dies
 (*Venus in Sagittarius*)

---

137 ACE, vol. 2, p. 23.
138 Ibid., p. 155.
139 Ibid., p. 297.

To be strong in the present
    (*Mercury in Capricorn*)
Work with powers of life
    (*Mars in Virgo*)
As a flowing wave self-sustaining
    (*Jupiter in Aquarius*)
And may the might of life's activity flower
    (*Saturn in Capricorn*)
Limit thyself, O unlimited!
    (*Moon in Aquarius*)[140]

September 17–20, Mercury conjoins Pluto, exact on the 19th: **Mercury conjunct Pluto 0°49' Capricorn.** This conjunction once again draws our attention to the morning before the Last Supper, on April 2 AD 33 (see commentary for June 23).

**September 20: Full Moon 3°11' Pisces.** The Pisces Full Moon fell close to the same degree (8° Pisces) on August 31 AD 30:

Jesus taught in an inn outside the city, the first of those erected for his and the disciples' accommodation that he had met on his journey since leaving Bethany. It was in the charge of a pious, upright man, who went out to meet the travelers, washed their feet and gave them refreshments, after which Jesus entered the city. The superintendents of the school came out into the street to receive him, and he visited several houses and cured the sick....

The married couple who directed the inn at Bezek were good, devout people. They observed continence by virtue of a vow, although they were not Essenes. They were distant relatives of the holy family. During his stay here, Jesus had several private interviews with these good people.

All the friends and disciples ate and slept with Jesus in the newly erected inn. They found ready for them, thanks to the forethought of Lazarus and the holy women, table furniture, covers, carpets, beds, screens, and even sandals and other articles of clothing. Martha had near the desert of Jericho a house full of women whom she kept busy preparing all these things. She had gathered together many poor widows and penniless girls, who were striving to lead a good life. There they lived and worked together. All was carried on quietly and unknown to the public. It was no little thing to provide for so many inns and so many people and to superintend them constantly—above all, to send messengers around to them, or give them personal attention.[141]

**September 22: Autumn Equinox—Venus enters Capricorn.**

Behold worlds, O soul!
    (*Sun in Virgo*)
May the past feel the future
    (*Venus in Capricorn*)
To be strong in the present
    (*Mercury in Capricorn*)
Work with powers of life
    (*Mars in Virgo*)
As a flowing wave self-sustaining
    (*Jupiter in Aquarius*)
And may the might of life's activity flower
    (*Saturn in Capricorn*)
May loss be gain in itself!
    (*Moon in Pisces*)[142]

From September 19–25, it is now Venus's turn to conjoin Pluto. Their alignment is exact on the 22nd: **Venus conjunct Pluto 0°50'.** Venus was at this same degree on November 29–30 AD 30:

On the following day he continued his preaching [concerning the second beatitude] on the mountain. Mary Cleophas, Maroni of Nain, and two other women were present. When Jesus with the apostles and disciples went back to the lake, he spoke of their vocation in these words: "Ye are the light of the world!" He illustrated by the similitude of the city seated on a mountain, the light on the candlestick, and the fulfilling of the Law [Matt. 5:14–20]. Then he rowed to Bethsaida, and put up at Andrew's.

Among the neophytes whom Saturnin baptized on those days near Capernaum were some Jews from Achaia whose ancestors had fled thither at the time of the Babylonian Captivity.

---

140 Steiner, *Twelve Cosmic Moods*.

141 ACE, vol. 2, p. 39.
142 Steiner, *Twelve Cosmic Moods*.

The recently built city of Bethsaida–Julius was inhabited mostly by pagans. There were, however, some Jews, and the city possessed a famous school in which all kinds of knowledge were taught. Jesus had not yet visited it, but the inhabitants went out to the instruction and also to Capernaum, where their sick were cured. Bethsaida–Julius was beautifully situated in the narrow valley of the Jordan, built a little up on the eastern side of the mountain, one-half hour from the point where the river flows into the lake. One hour northward, a stone bridge spanned the Jordan.

[The following day] Jesus continued to teach on the second beatitude. He also explained many teachings of the prophets.

While going down from the mountain whereon he had been teaching, Jesus again instructed the disciples, and spoke of the sufferings and sharp persecutions in store for them. He slept that night in Peter's boat.[143]

On the next day, December 1 AD 30, Christ performed the miracle of raising Salome, the daughter of Jairus, from the dead for the second and last time.

Around the same time that Venus and Pluto conjoin, Mercury and Saturn also come into conjunction. This lasts from September 22–26, and is exact on the 24th.

**September 24: Mercury conjunct Saturn 16°47' Capricorn.** Mercury was at this degree on November 9 AD 30, a few days before the raising of Martialis (the Youth of Nain) from the dead:

From Gabara, Jesus went to the estate of the officer Zorobabel [the high-ranking official whose son Jesus had healed on Aug, 3 AD 30] near Capernaum. The two lepers whom at this last visit to Capernaum he had healed, here presented themselves to return him thanks. The steward, the domestics, and the cured son of Zorobabel also were here. They had already been baptized. Jesus taught and cured many sick. In the dusk of the evening, after his disciples had separated and gone to their respective families, Jesus proceeded along the valley of Capernaum to the house of his mother. All the holy women were here assembled, and there was great joy. Mary and the women

renewed their petition to Jesus that he would cross to the other side of the lake early next morning because the committee of the Pharisees was so irritated against him. Jesus calmed their fears. Mary interceded for the sick slave of the centurion Cornelius, who was, she said, a very good man. Although a pagan, he had, through affection for the Jews, built them a synagogue. She begged him likewise to cure the sick daughter of Jairus, the elder of the synagogue, who lived in a little village not far from Capernaum.[144]

**September 28: Mercury enters Aquarius.**

Behold worlds, O soul!
  (*Sun in Virgo*)
May the past feel the future
  (*Venus in Capricorn*)
Boundaries in its own depths
  (*Mercury in Aquarius*)
Work with powers of life
  (*Mars in Virgo*)
As a flowing wave self-sustaining
  (*Jupiter in Aquarius*)
And may the might of life's activity flower
  (*Saturn in Capricorn*)
O radiant being, appear!
  (*Moon in Taurus*)[145]

September 28–30, Mercury is conjunct Jupiter. This is exact on the 29th.

**September 29: Michaelmas—Mercury conjunct Jupiter, 5°48' Aquarius.** Mercury was at 5° Aquarius on November 27 AD 29, during the first temptation of Christ in the wilderness. This is a perfect star memory upon which to meditate on Michaelmas, when we must summon the Cosmic Intelligence to aid us in overcoming dead, materialistic thinking:

Satan seized him fiercely by the shoulders, and flew with him over the desert toward Jericho. While standing on the tower, I noticed twilight in the western sky. This second flight appeared to me longer than the first. Satan was filled with rage and fury. He flew with Jesus now high, now low, reeling like one who would vent his rage if he could. He bore him to the same mountain,

143 ACE, vol. 2, p. 163.

144 Ibid., p. 136.
145 Steiner, *Twelve Cosmic Moods*.

seven hours from Jerusalem, upon which he had commenced his fast.

I saw that Satan carried Jesus low over an old pine tree on the way. It was a large and still vigorous tree that had stood long ago in the garden of one of the ancient Essenes. Elijah had once lived a short time in its vicinity.

The tree was behind the grotto and close by the rugged precipice. Such trees used to be pierced three times in one season, and each time they yielded a little turpentine.

Satan flew with the Lord to the highest peak of the mountain, and set him upon an over-hanging, inaccessible crag much higher than the grotto. It was night, but while Satan pointed around, it grew bright, revealing the most wonderful regions in all parts of the world. The devil addressed Jesus in words something like these: "I know that thou art a great teacher, that thou art now about to gather disciples around thee and promulgate thy doctrines. Behold, all these magnificent countries, these mighty nations! Compare them with poor, little Judea lying yonder! Go rather to these. I will deliver them over to thee, if kneeling down thou wilt adore me!" By adoration the devil meant that obeisance common among the Jews, and especially among the Pharisees, when supplicating favors from kings and great personages. This temptation of Satan was similar to that other one in which, under the guise of one of Herod's officers, he had sought to lure Jesus to take up his abode in the castle of Jerusalem, and had offered to assist him in his undertaking. It was similar in kind, though more distinct until, at last, they seemed to be in the immediate vicinity. One looked down upon all their details, every scene, every nation differing in customs and manners, in splendor and magnificence.

Satan pointed out in each the features of special attraction. He dwelt particularly upon those of a country whose inhabitants were unusually tall and magnificent looking. They were almost like giants. I think it was Persia. Satan advised Jesus to go there above all to teach. He showed him Palestine, but as a poor, little, insignificant place. This was a most wonderful vision, so extended, so grand, and magnificent!

The only words uttered by Jesus were, "The Lord thy God shalt thou adore and him only shalt thou serve! Depart from me, Satan!" Then I saw Satan in an inexpressibly horrible form rise from the rock, cast himself into the abyss, and vanish as if the earth had swallowed him.[146]

# OCTOBER 2021

## STARGAZING PREVIEW

Venus begins the month in Libra, and spends its last few hours in Sagittarius! On the 2nd, she finds Scorpio, which she'll call home for most of October. The month's New Moon (18° Virgo) occurs on Wednesday the 6th; by sunset, the Sun, Mars, Moon, and Mercury will set together within a 5° arc of the Virgin. Look for Venus high in the southwest, Saturn climbing toward culmination from the east, and the stars of the Milky Way sweeping between them.

If you made a note of your dreams and prayers on August 1st, the date of the last superior conjunction of Mercury and the Sun, you'll want to be aware of any response that might accompany the inferior conjunction on the 9th of this month. The evening sky on Saturday the 9th will feature the crescent Moon setting moments ahead of Venus, 30 minutes in advance of their conjunction at 7° Scorpio. Having hovered in the 12th° of Capricorn for about a month, Saturn stations direct on the 11th.

October's first Quarter Moon (25° Sagittarius) will be high in the south at sunset on the 13th, below and to the right of Saturn. By the following evening, on its way to Jupiter, the Moon will have passed Saturn from below. On the 18th, the Sun enters Libra. We might now ask: *What dissatisfactions stand in the way of our enjoyment of all we see before us?* October's Full Moon will shine on the 20th from 2° Aries.

The Orionid Meteor Shower peaks during the night of October 21–22. Typically, they can be observed from both hemispheres, but the large waning Moon will make this more difficult. As you will have guessed by now, Orion is the apparent radiant of the showers. Look for him high in the

---

146 ACE, vol. 1, pp. 369–370.

south at midnight and close to the western horizon before dawn. Mercury, a morning star now, will rise at 0500, ninety minutes before the Sun, so today might be the day you catch a glimpse of the swift fellow. The Archangel Michael (Mars) finds the Scales (Libra) on the 23rd.

You'll find the last Quarter Moon, at 11° Cancer, on the 28th. It rises at 2230, opposite Saturn, as Saturn joins the sunlit half of the globe. Venus is a full 47° from the Sun on the 29th, giving us all more than two hours to watch her after sunset. She finds Sagittarius on the 31st, when Orion will be visible throughout the night.

## OCTOBER COMMENTARIES

While the dominant aspect for the first part of October is Sun square Mars (from September 28 through October 17; see entry for October 8 below), the month begins with two Venus alignments. The first is a conjunction of Venus and Saturn, from September 29 through October 6, exact on the 3rd.

**October 3: Venus and Saturn 17°3' Capricorn.** Over the course of the exact same time period, Venus and Uranus come into square alignment, also exact on October 3: **Venus 17°22' Capricorn square Uranus 17°22' Aries.** We are coming ever closer to the exact square of Saturn and Uranus that has been building up all year.

Venus was at 17° Capricorn on December 10 AD 30, at the first of his disciples Jesus sent forth:

Jesus afterward left Capernaum, accompanied by the twelve and by thirty disciples. They directed their steps northward. Crowds of people were journeying along the same way. Jesus frequently paused to instruct sometimes this, sometimes that crowd, who then turned off in the direction of their homes. In this way he arrived at about three in the afternoon at a beautiful mountain, three hours from Capernaum and not quite so far from the Jordan. Five roads branched out from it, and about as many little towns lay around it. The people who had followed Jesus thus far now took their leave, while he with his own party, having first taken some refreshment at the foot of the mountain, began to ascend the height. There was a teacher's chair

upon it, from which he again instructed the apostles and disciples upon their vocation. He said that now they should show forth what they had learned. They should proclaim the advent of the kingdom, that the last chance for doing penance had arrived, that the end of John's life was very near. They should baptize, impose hands, and expel demons. He taught them how they should conduct themselves in discussions, how to recognize true from false friends, and how to confound the latter. He told them that now none should be greater than the others. In the various places to which their mission called them, they should go among the pious, should live poorly and humbly, and be burdensome to none. He told them also how to separate and how again to unite. Two apostles and some disciples should go on ahead to gather together the people and announce the coming of the former. The apostles, he said, should carry with them little flasks of oil, which he taught them how to consecrate and how to use in effecting cures. Then he gave them all the other instructions recorded in the Gospels on the occasion of their mission. He made allusion to no special danger in store for them, but said only; "Today ye will everywhere be welcomed, but a time will come wherein they will persecute you!"[147]

Saturn was opposite today's degree on September 1 AD 32, as Christ was traveling to Egypt with the shepherd youths:

About one hour to the east of Sichar stood the dwelling of a rich herd proprietor. The house was surrounded by a moat. The owner had died suddenly in a field not far from his house, and his wife and children were in great affliction. The remains were ready for interment, and the family had sent messengers into the city to beg the Lord and some others to come to the funeral. Jesus went, accompanied by his three disciples, Salathiel and his wife, and several others—about thirty in all. The corpse, ready for the grave, was placed in a broad avenue of trees before the house. The man had been struck dead in punishment of his sins, for he had seized upon part of the possessions of some shepherds who, owing to his oppressive treatment, were obliged

---

147 ACE, vol. 2, p. 176.

| DAY | ☉ | ☽ | ☊ | ☿ | ♀ | ♂ | ♃ | ♄ | ♅ | ♆ | ♇ |
|---|---|---|---|---|---|---|---|---|---|---|---|
| 1 FR | 13♍0 | 4♋30 | 8♉21R | 29♍35R | 27♎48 | 15♍21 | 27♑47R | 11♑55R | 19♈4R | 26♒18R | 29♐17R |
| 2 SA | 13 59 | 17 9 | 8 16 | 29 3 | 28 55 | 16 0 | 27 43 | 11 54 | 19 2 | 26 16 | 29 16 |
| 3 SU | 14 58 | 0♌11 | 8 10 | 28 24 | 0♏2 | 16 40 | 27 40 | 11 53 | 19 0 | 26 15 | 29 16 |
| 4 MO | 15 57 | 13 38 | 8 2 | 27 38 | 1 8 | 17 19 | 27 37 | 11 53 | 18 58 | 26 13 | 29 16 |
| 5 TU | 16 56 | 27 29 | 7 54 | 26 44 | 2 14 | 17 58 | 27 35 | 11 52 | 18 56 | 26 12 | 29 16 |
| 6 WE | 17 55 | 11♍43 | 7 45 | 25 45 | 3 20 | 18 38 | 27 32 | 11 51 | 18 54 | 26 10 | 29 16 |
| 7 TH | 18 54 | 26 12 | 7 39 | 24 40 | 4 26 | 19 17 | 27 30 | 11 51 | 18 52 | 26 9 | 29 16D |
| 8 FR | 19 53 | 10♎52 | 7 34 | 23 32 | 5 32 | 19 57 | 27 28 | 11 51 | 18 50 | 26 7 | 29 16 |
| 9 SA | 20 53 | 25 34 | 7 31 | 22 21 | 6 38 | 20 36 | 27 26 | 11 50 | 18 48 | 26 6 | 29 16 |
| 10 SU | 21 52 | 10♏12 | 7 30 | 21 10 | 7 43 | 21 16 | 27 24 | 11 50 | 18 46 | 26 4 | 29 16 |
| 11 MO | 22 51 | 24 41 | 7 31D | 20 1 | 8 48 | 21 55 | 27 22 | 11 50 | 18 44 | 26 3 | 29 16 |
| 12 TU | 23 51 | 8♐58 | 7 32 | 18 55 | 9 53 | 22 35 | 27 21 | 11 50D | 18 41 | 26 1 | 29 16 |
| 13 WE | 24 50 | 23 0 | 7 33 | 17 55 | 10 58 | 23 14 | 27 20 | 11 50 | 18 39 | 26 0 | 29 17 |
| 14 TH | 25 49 | 6♑48 | 7 32R | 17 2 | 12 3 | 23 54 | 27 19 | 11 51 | 18 37 | 25 59 | 29 17 |
| 15 FR | 26 49 | 20 21 | 7 30 | 16 18 | 13 7 | 24 34 | 27 18 | 11 51 | 18 35 | 25 57 | 29 17 |
| 16 SA | 27 48 | 3♒40 | 7 26 | 15 44 | 14 11 | 25 14 | 27 18 | 11 51 | 18 32 | 25 56 | 29 17 |
| 17 SU | 28 48 | 16 45 | 7 20 | 15 20 | 15 15 | 25 53 | 27 17 | 11 52 | 18 30 | 25 55 | 29 18 |
| 18 MO | 29 47 | 29 38 | 7 14 | 15 7 | 16 19 | 26 33 | 27 17 | 11 52 | 18 28 | 25 53 | 29 18 |
| 19 TU | 0♎47 | 12♓17 | 7 7 | 15 6D | 17 22 | 27 13 | 27 17D | 11 53 | 18 26 | 25 52 | 29 18 |
| 20 WE | 1 46 | 24 45 | 7 1 | 15 15 | 18 25 | 27 53 | 27 17 | 11 54 | 18 23 | 25 51 | 29 19 |
| 21 TH | 2 46 | 7♈5 | 6 56 | 15 35 | 19 28 | 28 33 | 27 18 | 11 55 | 18 21 | 25 49 | 29 19 |
| 22 FR | 3 46 | 19 5 | 6 53 | 16 5 | 20 31 | 29 13 | 27 19 | 11 56 | 18 19 | 25 48 | 29 19 |
| 23 SA | 4 45 | 1♉2 | 6 51 | 16 44 | 21 33 | 29 53 | 27 19 | 11 57 | 18 16 | 25 47 | 29 20 |
| 24 SU | 5 45 | 12 52 | 6 51D | 17 32 | 22 35 | 0♎33 | 27 20 | 11 58 | 18 14 | 25 46 | 29 20 |
| 25 MO | 6 45 | 24 39 | 6 53 | 18 27 | 23 37 | 1 13 | 27 22 | 12 0 | 18 11 | 25 45 | 29 21 |
| 26 TU | 7 45 | 6♊26 | 6 54 | 19 29 | 24 38 | 1 53 | 27 23 | 12 1 | 18 9 | 25 44 | 29 21 |
| 27 WE | 8 44 | 18 18 | 6 56 | 20 37 | 25 39 | 2 33 | 27 25 | 12 3 | 18 6 | 25 42 | 29 22 |
| 28 TH | 9 44 | 0♋20 | 6 57 | 21 50 | 26 40 | 3 13 | 27 27 | 12 4 | 18 4 | 25 41 | 29 23 |
| 29 FR | 10 44 | 12 36 | 6 58R | 23 8 | 27 40 | 3 53 | 27 29 | 12 6 | 18 2 | 25 40 | 29 23 |
| 30 SA | 11 44 | 25 11 | 6 57 | 24 29 | 28 40 | 4 33 | 27 31 | 12 8 | 17 59 | 25 39 | 29 24 |
| 31 SU | 12 44 | 8♌10 | 6 55 | 25 54 | 29 40 | 5 14 | 27 33 | 12 10 | 17 57 | 25 38 | 29 25 |

**INGRESSES :**

```
 2 ♀ → ♏ 23:26      22 ☽ → ♉ 21:54
   ☽ → ♌ 23:40         ♂ → ♎  4:29
 5 ☽ → ♍  4:16      25 ☽ → ♊ 10:54
 7 ☽ → ♎  6:13      27 ☽ → ♋ 23:20
 9 ☽ → ♏  7:15      30 ☽ → ♌  8:59
11 ☽ → ♐  8:53      31 ♀ → ♐  8: 9
13 ☽ → ♑ 12: 7
15 ☽ → ♒ 17:20
18 ☽ → ♓  0:41
   ☉ → ♎  5: 8
20 ☽ → ♈ 10:14
```

**ASPECTS & ECLIPSES :**

```
 1 ☽☍♄ 14: 8    9 ☉ ⚷ ☿ 16:17   ☽☍♆ 16:59   28 ☉□☽ 20: 4
   ♀□☊ 14:34      ♀□☊ ...  23: 1  19 ☽ ... 5:24      ☽ ... ☊ 23: 1
 2 ☽☍♃ 19:27      ☽☌☊ 19:33   20 ☽☍♂  6:27   30 ☽☍♃  4:22
 3 ☽ ⛢ ☊ 14:12    ☽☌♀ 19:35   21 ☽☌♅ 22:26      ☉□☽  9:52
 4 ☽☍♆ 21:47   13 ☉☌☽  3:24   22 ☽□♆  4:10
 6 ☉☌☽ 11: 4      ☽☌♀ 10:51   23 ☽☌☊ 11:47
   ☽☌♂ 12: 2   14 ☽☌♄  8:53   24 ☽☌A 15:27
   ☽☌☿ 21:38   15 ☽☌♃ 12:28      ☽☍♀ 21:41
 8 ☉☌♂  4: 0   16 ☽ ☌ ☊  6:48  27 ♀□♆  1:14
   ☽☌♂ 12:58   17 ☉□♆ 12: 6      ☽☍♇ 22: 6
   ☽☌P 17:23
```

| DAY | Sid. Time | ☿ | ♀ | ⊕ | ♂ | ♃ | ♄ | ♅ | ♆ | ♇ | Vernal Point |
|---|---|---|---|---|---|---|---|---|---|---|---|
| 1 FR | 0:39:48 | 11♒28 | 13♑45 | 13♓0 | 16♍48 | 5♒56 | 16♑59 | 17♈21 | 26♒51 | 0♑53 | 4♓57'23" |
| 2 SA | 0:43:45 | 15 34 | 15 20 | 13 59 | 17 16 | 6 1 | 17 1 | 17 22 | 26 51 | 0 53 | 4♓57'23" |
| 3 SU | 0:47:41 | 19 48 | 16 55 | 14 58 | 17 43 | 6 7 | 17 3 | 17 22 | 26 52 | 0 53 | 4♓57'23" |
| 4 MO | 0:51:38 | 24 9 | 18 30 | 15 57 | 18 10 | 6 12 | 17 4 | 17 23 | 26 52 | 0 54 | 4♓57'23" |
| 5 TU | 0:55:34 | 28 38 | 20 5 | 16 56 | 18 37 | 6 17 | 17 6 | 17 24 | 26 52 | 0 54 | 4♓57'23" |
| 6 WE | 0:59:31 | 3♓16 | 21 40 | 17 56 | 19 5 | 6 23 | 17 8 | 17 24 | 26 53 | 0 54 | 4♓57'23" |
| 7 TH | 1: 3:27 | 8 2 | 23 15 | 18 55 | 19 32 | 6 28 | 17 10 | 17 25 | 26 53 | 0 55 | 4♓57'23" |
| 8 FR | 1: 7:24 | 12 57 | 24 50 | 19 54 | 19 59 | 6 33 | 17 12 | 17 26 | 26 53 | 0 55 | 4♓57'22" |
| 9 SA | 1:11:21 | 18 2 | 26 25 | 20 53 | 20 27 | 6 39 | 17 14 | 17 26 | 26 54 | 0 55 | 4♓57'22" |
| 10 SU | 1:15:17 | 23 15 | 28 0 | 21 52 | 20 54 | 6 44 | 17 16 | 17 27 | 26 54 | 0 56 | 4♓57'22" |
| 11 MO | 1:19:14 | 28 38 | 29 35 | 22 51 | 21 22 | 6 49 | 17 17 | 17 28 | 26 55 | 0 56 | 4♓57'22" |
| 12 TU | 1:23:10 | 4♈9 | 1♒10 | 23 51 | 21 49 | 6 55 | 17 19 | 17 28 | 26 55 | 0 56 | 4♓57'22" |
| 13 WE | 1:27: 7 | 9 49 | 2 45 | 24 51 | 22 16 | 7 0 | 17 21 | 17 29 | 26 55 | 0 56 | 4♓57'22" |
| 14 TH | 1:31: 3 | 15 38 | 4 20 | 25 50 | 22 44 | 7 6 | 17 23 | 17 30 | 26 56 | 0 57 | 4♓57'22" |
| 15 FR | 1:35: 0 | 21 34 | 5 55 | 26 49 | 23 12 | 7 11 | 17 25 | 17 30 | 26 56 | 0 57 | 4♓57'22" |
| 16 SA | 1:38:56 | 27 36 | 7 30 | 27 49 | 23 39 | 7 16 | 17 27 | 17 31 | 26 56 | 0 57 | 4♓57'21" |
| 17 SU | 1:42:53 | 3♉45 | 9 5 | 28 48 | 24 7 | 7 22 | 17 29 | 17 32 | 26 57 | 0 58 | 4♓57'21" |
| 18 MO | 1:46:50 | 9 58 | 10 40 | 29 48 | 24 34 | 7 27 | 17 30 | 17 32 | 26 57 | 0 58 | 4♓57'21" |
| 19 TU | 1:50:46 | 16 15 | 12 15 | 0♈47 | 25 2 | 7 32 | 17 32 | 17 33 | 26 57 | 0 58 | 4♓57'21" |
| 20 WE | 1:54:43 | 22 34 | 13 50 | 1 47 | 25 30 | 7 38 | 17 34 | 17 34 | 26 58 | 0 58 | 4♓57'21" |
| 21 TH | 1:58:39 | 28 53 | 15 25 | 2 47 | 25 57 | 7 43 | 17 36 | 17 34 | 26 58 | 0 59 | 4♓57'21" |
| 22 FR | 2: 2:36 | 5♊11 | 17 1 | 3 46 | 26 25 | 7 49 | 17 38 | 17 35 | 26 59 | 0 59 | 4♓57'21" |
| 23 SA | 2: 6:32 | 11 27 | 18 36 | 4 46 | 26 53 | 7 54 | 17 40 | 17 36 | 26 59 | 0 59 | 4♓57'20" |
| 24 SU | 2:10:29 | 17 39 | 20 11 | 5 46 | 27 21 | 7 59 | 17 42 | 17 36 | 26 59 | 1 0 | 4♓57'20" |
| 25 MO | 2:14:25 | 23 45 | 21 46 | 6 45 | 27 49 | 8 5 | 17 43 | 17 37 | 27 0 | 1 0 | 4♓57'20" |
| 26 TU | 2:18:22 | 29 46 | 23 21 | 7 45 | 28 17 | 8 10 | 17 45 | 17 38 | 27 0 | 1 0 | 4♓57'20" |
| 27 WE | 2:22:19 | 5♋38 | 24 57 | 8 45 | 28 45 | 8 15 | 17 47 | 17 38 | 27 0 | 1 0 | 4♓57'20" |
| 28 TH | 2:26:15 | 11 23 | 26 32 | 9 45 | 29 12 | 8 21 | 17 49 | 17 39 | 27 1 | 1 1 | 4♓57'20" |
| 29 FR | 2:30:12 | 16 58 | 28 7 | 10 45 | 29 40 | 8 26 | 17 51 | 17 40 | 27 1 | 1 1 | 4♓57'20" |
| 30 SA | 2:34: 8 | 22 25 | 29 43 | 11 45 | 0♎8 | 8 32 | 17 53 | 17 40 | 27 1 | 1 1 | 4♓57'19" |
| 31 SU | 2:38: 5 | 27 42 | 1♓18 | 12 45 | 0 37 | 8 37 | 17 54 | 17 41 | 27 2 | 1 2 | 4♓57'19" |

**INGRESSES :**

```
 5 ☿ → ♓  7: 9
11 ☿ → ♈  6: 1
   ♀ → ♒  6:23
16 ☿ → ♉  9:23
18 ⊕ → ♈  4:54
21 ☿ → ♊  4:14
26 ☿ → ♋  0:58
29 ♂ → ♎ 16:43
30 ♀ → ♓  4:21
31 ☿ → ♌ 10:43
```

**ASPECTS (HELIOCENTRIC + MOON(TYCHONIC)) :**

```
 1 ☽☍♀ 20: 7    7 ☽□♅  7:43   13 ☽☌♂ 13:45      ☽☌♆ 18:58   24 ☽□♀ 17:12   ☽□♅  9:44
   ☽☍♄ 23:45      ☽□♄ 10:21   14 ☿□♄  7:11   18 ☿□♀  3:34   25 ♀⚷☊  0:56   ☽☍♄ 10: 6
 2 ☽□♅  0:24      ☽☌♅ 10:43      ☿☌♅  7:36   19 ⊕□♆  4:20      ☽□♆  4:46   ☽☌☿ 14:53
   ♀☌A 22:33      ☽□♀ 18:45      ☽☌♀  7:55      ☽□♆ 17:31   26 ☽☌P  5: 2   ☽☌♄  0:49
 3 ☽☌♀  1:55    8 ⊕☌♂  4: 0   15 ☽□☿  3:54   20 ☿☌P  0:43      ☽□⊕ 15:39
   ♀□♂  6:54      ☽□♄ 10:43      ☽☌♀  1:31   27 ♀□♆  ...   31 ♂□♆ 21:39
   ☽☍♃ 10:44    9 ♀☌♀  1:33   16 ☽☌♀  7:56      ☽□♆ 12: 9
 4 ☽☌♆ 14:39      ☽□☿ 18:55   17 ☿□♃ 14:10   21 ☽□♄ 21: 4
   ☽☍♆ 22:56   11 ♀□♄ 12:56                     ☽☌♀ 20:59
 5 ☽☍♂  2:53   12 ☽□♂ 22:42                  23 ☽☌♃ 14: 0
 6 ☽☌♂ 12:38
```

to leave that section of the country. Shortly after the commission of this sin, he had fallen dead upon the very ground that he had unjustly appropriated. Standing in front of the corpse, Jesus spoke of the deceased. He asked of what advantage was it to him now that he had once pampered and served his body, that house which his soul had now to leave. He had, on account of that body, run his soul into debt which he neither had and which he never could discharge....

The wife had addressed these words to Jesus: "Lord, thou speakest as if thou thyself wert the king of the Jews!" But Jesus had motioned her to be silent. When now those others, whom he knew to be weaker in faith, had retired, Jesus told the family that if they would believe in his doctrine, if they would follow him, and if they would keep silence upon the matter, he would raise the dead man to life, for his soul was not yet judged, it was still tarrying in the field, the scene of its injustice as well as of its separation from the body. The family promised with all their heart both obedience and silence, and Jesus went with them to the field in which the man had died. I saw the state in which the soul of the deceased was. I saw it in a circle, in a sphere above the spot upon which he had died. Before it passed pictures of all its transgressions with their temporal consequences, and the sight consumed it with sorrow. I saw, too, all the punishments it was to undergo, and it was vouchsafed a view of the redemptive Passion of Jesus. Torn with grief, it was about to enter upon its punishment, when Jesus prayed, and called it back into the body by pronouncing the name *Nazor,* the name of the deceased. Then turning to the assistants, he said, "When we return, we shall find Nazor sitting up and alive!" I saw the soul at Jesus's call floating toward the body, becoming smaller, and disappearing through the mouth, at which moment Nazor rose to a sitting posture in his coffin. I always see the human soul reposing above the heart from which numerous threads run to the head.[148]

A week later, just as Christ and the shepherds reached the first tent city of star worshippers, Venus and Uranus were square (albeit in Scorpio and Leo respectively).

October 3–5, Mercury and Neptune conjoin, exact on the 4th.

**October 4, Mercury conjunct Neptune 26°52' Aquarius.** Mercury was at this degree on November 19 AD 30:

A great crowd of pagans who had been at Cornelius's feast were here assembled. Jesus was instructing them and, as the throng became very great, he with some of his disciples went on board his little boat, while the rest of them and the publican's went on Peter's boat. And now from the boat he instructed the pagans on the strand, making use of the parables of the sower and the tares in the field. The instruction over, they struck out across the lake, the disciples in Peter's boat plying the oars. Jesus's boat was fastened to Peter's, and the disciples took turns to row. Jesus sat on a raised seat near the mast, the others around him and on the edge of the boat. They interrogated him upon the meaning of the parable and asked why he spoke in similitudes. Jesus gave them a satisfactory explanation. They landed at a point between the valley of Gerasa and Bethsaida–Julias. A road ran from the shore to the houses of the tax collectors, and into it the four who were with Jesus turned. Jesus, meanwhile, with the disciples continued along the shore to the right, thus passing Matthew's residence, though at a distance. A side path ran from this road to his custom office, and along it Jesus bent his steps, the disciples timidly remaining behind. Servants and publicans were out in front of the custom house, busied with all kinds of merchandise. When Matthew, from the top of a little eminence, beheld Jesus and the disciples coming toward him, he became confused and withdrew into his private office. But Jesus continued to approach, and from the opposite side of the road called him. Then came Matthew hurrying out, prostrated with his face on the ground before Jesus, protesting that he did not esteem himself worthy that Jesus should speak with him. But Jesus said, "Matthew, arise, and follow me!" Then Matthew arose, saying that he would instantly and joyfully abandon all things and follow him.[149]

---

148 Ibid., p. 493.

149 Ibid., p. 154.

**October 5: Mercury enters Pisces.**

Behold worlds, O soul!
(*Sun in Virgo*)
May the past feel the future
(*Venus in Capricorn*)
In comprehending seek to grasp
(*Mercury in Pisces*)
Work with powers of life
(*Mars in Virgo*)
As a flowing wave self-sustaining
(*Jupiter in Aquarius*)
And may the might of life's activity flower
(*Saturn in Capricorn*)
O soul, know thou beings!
(*Moon in Virgo*)[150]

**October 6: New Moon, 18°22' Virgo.** The Virgo New Moon was at 17° Virgo on the day of the conception of John the Baptist (Sept. 9, 3 BC):

In the days of Herod, king of Judaea, there was a certain priest, Zacharias by name, from the priestly order of Abijah, and his wife came from the daughters of Aaron, and her name was Elizabeth. And both were upright before God, conducting themselves impeccably in all the commandments and ordinances of the Lord. And they had no child, because Elizabeth was barren, and both were well advanced in their days. Now it happened that, when it was his order's turn in the presence of God, and as he was serving as priest, it fell to him by lot—as was the custom of the priesthood—to enter the sanctuary of the Lord and burn incense. And all the main body of the people was outside praying during the hour of the incense. And an angel of the Lord appeared to him, standing to the right of the altar of the incense. And seeing him Zacharias was alarmed, and fear descended upon him. But the angel said to him, "Do not be afraid, Zacharias, for your supplication has been heard, and your wife Elizabeth will bear you a son, and you shall declare his name to be John; and for you there will be joy and delight, and many will rejoice at his birth. For he will be great in the Lord's eyes; and he must not drink wine or fermented drink, and he will be filled with a Holy Spirit even from his mother's womb, and he will turn many of the sons of Israel to the Lord their God; and he will go forth in his presence, in the spirit and power of Elijah, to turn the hearts of fathers to their children and to turn the wayward to the wisdom of the upright, to prepare a people made ready for the Lord." And Zacharias said to the angel, "In what way shall I know this? For I am old and my wife is well advanced in her days." And in reply the angel said to him, "I am Gabriel, who stand before the presence of God, and I was sent to speak to you and announce these good tidings to you; see then: You shall be silent and unable to speak till the day these things take place, because you did not trust my words, which will be fulfilled at their proper time." Now the people were waiting for Zacharias, and they were amazed that he was taking so much time in the sanctuary. And when he came out, he was unable to speak to them and they knew he had seen a vision in the sanctuary; and he was gesturing to them, and remained mute. And it happened that when the days of his service were completed, he departed to his house. And after these days his wife Elizabeth conceived, and kept herself concealed, saying, "Thus the Lord has done for me, in the days when he looked to remove the censure that is mine among men."[151]

September 29 to October 17 (more than half of the month), the Sun and Mars are within 5° of each other. Their alignment is exact on the 8th.

**October 8: Sun conjunct Mars 20°4' Virgo.** Mars was at this degree on December 2 AD 29, just a few days after Christ finished with his forty days' temptation in the wilderness:

Jesus went with the disciples from Bethabara to a group of houses that stood near the river ferry. Here he taught in the presence of a small audience. After that he crossed the river and taught in a little village of about twenty houses, distant perhaps one hour from Jericho. Crowds of neophytes and John's disciples kept coming and going, to hear his words and report them to the Baptist. It was near midday when Jesus taught here.

After the sabbath Jesus commissioned several of the disciples to cross the Jordan and go up

---

150 Steiner, *Twelve Cosmic Moods.*

151 Hart, *The New Testament*, Luke 5:1–25, pp. 103–104.

the river to the distance of about one hour from Bethabara, there to prepare a pool for baptism. The site chosen by Jesus was that upon which John, when going down from Ainon, had baptized before he had crossed to the west bank of the river opposite Bethabara.[152]

Sun was square Mars (27° Sagittarius and Virgo respectively) a few weeks later, on December 17 AD 29:

Kibzaim was a solitary place hidden away in a corner of the mountain. The inhabitants subsisted chiefly by the cultivation of fruits. The manufacture of tents and carpets was also carried on, and many were engaged in sandal making. Jesus spent the sabbath here, and cured several sick persons by a word of command. Some were dropsical and others simpletons. They were brought on litters to Jesus and set down in front of the school.[153]

October 8–10, **Mercury opposes Mars**, exact on the 9th.

**October 9: Mercury 20°41' Pisces opposite Mars 20°41' Virgo.** Mercury and Sun are opposed at the same time, also exact on the 9th; **Sun 21°33' Virgo opposite Mercury 21°33' Pisces.** Mercury was in Pisces square Sun in Virgo on December 6 AD 29, and was opposite Mars in Virgo the next day. These star memories are from the same time period as yesterday's: in between the end of the forty days' temptation and the first healing miracle at the wedding at Cana:

Jesus and his disciples left Ophra and returned to Bethabara. On the way they separated, Andrew and the greater number being sent on ahead by the same route by which they had come; while Jesus with Saturnin and Joseph of Arimathea's nephews went on toward John's place of baptism, taking the same road as at the time upon which John rendered to him the first public testimony after his baptism. On the way he entered some of the houses, taught their occupants, and exhorted them to baptism. They reached Bethabara in the afternoon, where Jesus again delivered an instruction at the place of baptism.

Andrew and Saturnin baptized the crowds that succeeded on another. Jesus's teaching was generally the same; that is, that to all that did penance and were baptized his heavenly Father had said, "This is my beloved Son," and that, in truth, all then became God's children.

Many of those who now received baptism were under the jurisdiction of the Tetrarch Philip, who was a good man. His people were tolerably happy, and therefore had thought little about receiving baptism....

[The next day] Jesus, with three disciples, went up through the valley to Dibon, where he had lately been for the Feast of Tabernacles. He taught in some houses, also in the synagogue, which was somewhat distant from the city on the road running through the valley. Jesus did not enter Dibon itself. He stayed overnight at a poor, retired inn which indeed was little more than a shed where the field laborers from the country around obtained food and lodging. It was now seed time on the sunny side of the valley, the crops of which were to ripen about Passover. They had to dig the ground here, for it was made up of soil, sand, and stone. They could not use the implement generally employed in breaking up the ground. Part of the standing-out harvest was now gathered in for the first time. The inhabitants of this valley, which was about three hours in length, were good people, of simple habits, and well inclined toward Jesus.

In the synagogue, as also among the field laborers, Jesus related and explained the parable of the sower. He did not always explain his parables. He often related them to the Pharisees without an explanation.[154]

**October 11: Mercury enters Aries; Venus enters Aquarius.**

Behold worlds, O soul!
　(*Sun in Virgo*)
What lacks boundaries should
　(*Venus in Aquarius*)
Lay hold of forces weaving
　(*Mercury in Aries*)
Work with powers of life
　(*Mars in Virgo*)

---

152 ACE, vol. 1, p. 373.
153 Ibid., p. 378.

---

154 Ibid., p. 375.

As a flowing wave self-sustaining
   (*Jupiter in Aquarius*)
And may the might of life's activity flower
   (*Saturn in Capricorn*)
Being sustains beings!
   (*Moon in Scorpio*)[155]

October 13–14, **Mercury conjoins Uranus**, exact on the 14th.

**October 14: Mercury and Uranus 17°30' Aries.** These two were conjunct in Leo close to the time of our recent star memories—December 30–31 AD 29, just after the Changing of Water to Wine at the wedding at Cana:

On the sabbath spent at Cana, Jesus taught twice in the synagogue. He alluded to the wedding feast and to the obedience and pious sentiments of the bridal couple. On leaving the synagogue, he was accosted by the people, who threw themselves at his feet and implored him to cure their sick.

Jesus performed here two wonderful cures. A man had fallen from a high tower. He was taken up dead, all his limbs broken. Jesus went to him, placed the limbs in position, touched the fractures, and then commanded the man to rise and go to his home. The man arose, thanked Jesus, and went home. He had a wife and children. Jesus was next conducted to a man possessed by the devil, and whom he found chained to a great stone. Jesus freed him. He was next led to a woman, a sinner, who was afflicted by an issue of blood. He cured her, as also some others sick of edema. He healed seven in all. The people had not dared to crowd around him during the marriage festivities; but now that it was rumored that he was going away after the sabbath, they could no longer be restrained. Since the miracle of the marriage feast, the priests did not interfere with Jesus. They allowed him to do all that he wished. The miracles, the cures just related happened in their presence alone, for the disciples were not there.[156]

October 12–18, Venus conjoins Jupiter, exact on the 15th.

---

155 Steiner, *Twelve Cosmic Moods.*
156 Ibid., p. 390.

**October 15: Venus and Jupiter 7°16' Aquarius.** Simultaneously, Venus is square the Node, also exact on October 18: **Venus 7°26' Aquarius square Node 7°26' Taurus.** Venus reached this degree on December 22–23 AD 30, when Christ taught in Abram on marriage and attended a wedding ceremony of several couples simultaneously:

Next day Jesus assisted with two of the disciples at the marriage ceremony of the young couples. He even acted as witness. They were married facing the chest that contained the Law and under the open heavens, for they had opened the cupola of the synagogue. I saw that both parties allowed some drops of blood from the ring finger to fall into a glass of wine, which they then drank. They exchanged rings and went through other ceremonies. After the religious rites came the celebration of the nuptials, beginning with dance and banquet and merrymaking, to all of which Jesus and the disciples were invited. The festivities took place in the beautiful public hall, which was supported by a colonnade. The bridal couples were not all from the city, but from the neighboring localities. They celebrated their nuptials here together, according to an agreement they had made to that effect when the news of Jesus's coming was announced. Some of them, indeed, had been present with their parents at his instructions in Capernaum. The people of this region were particularly good natured and sociable. The weddings of the poorer were now celebrated with those of the rich, greatly to the advantage of the former....

The feast began with a bridal dance in slow and measured step. The brides were veiled. The couples stood facing one another, and each bridegroom danced once with each bride. They never touched one another, but grasped the ends of the scarf that they held in their hands. The dance lasted one hour, because each groom danced once with all the brides separately, and then all danced together. Besides this, the step was very slow.

Then followed the banquet, at which the men and women were, as usually, separated. The musicians were children, little boys and girls, with crowns of wool on their heads and wreaths of the same on their arms. They played on flutes, little twisted horns, and other instruments. The banqueting tables were so placed that the guests could hear without seeing one another. Jesus went to that of the brides and related a parable, something in the styles of the ten wise and the ten foolish virgins. He explained it in quite a homey way adapted to the occasion, though at the same time his words were full of spiritual signification. He told each how she should acquit herself of the duties of her new, domestic position and what provisions she should lay up for that. His instructions contained a spiritual sense, and were suited to the particular character and shortcomings of the one to whom they were addressed.

The banquet over, then came the game of riddles. The enigmas written on slips of paper were thrown on a board that was full of holes, through which they fell into bags. Everyone had to solve the particular enigma that had fallen into his or her bag, or else pay a forfeit. The unsolved riddles were again and again thrown onto the board, and the one that was so fortunate as to solve them at last, could claim all that had been previously lost on their account. Jesus looked on during the game, making happy and instructive applications of all that took place.[157]

**October 16: Mercury enters Taurus.**

Behold worlds, O soul!
 (*Sun in Virgo*)
What lacks boundaries should
 (*Venus in Aquarius*)
Weave life's thread
 (*Mercury in Taurus*)
Work with powers of life
 (*Mars in Virgo*)
As a flowing wave self-sustaining
 (*Jupiter in Aquarius*)
And may the might of life's activity flower
 (*Saturn in Capricorn*)
Limit thyself, O unlimited!
 (*Moon in Aquarius*)[158]

Since September 16, Jupiter and the Node have been coming into square alignment, which will last until December 4. It is exact on October 16; Jupiter

7°21′ Aquarius square Node 7°21′ Taurus. The exact alignment is virtually coincidental with the Venus–Jupiter conjunction and Venus–Node square.

The last time these two planets were square in these same signs was in 1891. Protests and labor strikes were occurring in countries across the world, circumstances that led to Pope Leo XIII issuing *Rerum novarum,* or *Rights and Duties of Capital and Labor.* This encyclical laid the foundation for modern Catholic social teaching. This was also a time of massive innovations in technological development: railroads, telephones, and electricity. Thomas Edison and Nikola Tesla were in a race to out-innovate the other. On June 21, the first long-distance transmission of alternating current was made.

This year also saw the first appearance of the stories of *Sherlock Holmes*—stories that hinged on the use of precise sensory observation and sharp, deductive reasoning. Paradoxically, these stories were written by Sir Arthur Conan Doyle, a man who devoted much of his life to spiritualism, seances, and trying to capture photos of (material–sensory) fairies.

In the midst of this confusion of religion, politics, science, and spiritism, a young Rudolf Steiner was busy writing his doctoral dissertation (later published as *Truth and Science*) at Rostock University—the same university at which Tycho Brahe had studied more than 300 years earlier. This time period was for Steiner the first step to re-enlivening and harmonizing these seemingly disparate disciplines—a first step which relied on laying the epistemological foundations for *knowing* Truth. If only there could be a wider recognition of this almost entirely forgotten first step to attaining certainty in knowledge! Unfortunately, a work such as *Truth and Science* is merely prosaic to some, and unreadable to many. And yet what is the use of technological development, of protests and worker's rights, of religious renewal, if we are unable to assess—experientially, not conceptually—whether they have any authentic relationship to Truth? If you've never taken the time to do so, make time to read *Truth and Knowledge* or any of Steiner's pre-Theosophical, epistemological work—e.g., his

---

157 ACE, vol. 2, pp. 186–187.
158 Steiner, *Twelve Cosmic Moods.*

writings on Goethean science, or *The Philosophy of Freedom* (now published as *Intuitive Thinking as a Spiritual Path*).

October 16–18, **Mercury conjoins the Node**, exact on the 17th.

**October 17; Mercury and Node 7°17' Taurus.** These two were conjunct in Taurus February 28 to March 1 AD 31:

> From Nobah, Jesus went to Golan. The road wound westwardly round a high mountain chain for a span of four hours. Golan was inhabited by both Jews and pagans and was a couple of hours distant from the Jordan. Jesus tarried here only a few hours teaching and healing. Continuing his journey, he passed the city of Argob, built at a high elevation on a mountain ridge, and arrived late that night at the stronghold Regaba. He rested with his companions on the grass of a solitary place outside the city, and awaited the other apostles and disciples, fifteen in number. When these arrived, they all went with their Master to the inn established here for their accommodation. Regaba belonged to the Gergesean district. It was the most northerly of their towns, and one of the best disposed. Golan was a frontier town of the tetrarch Philip....
>
> Most of the inhabitants, both Jews and pagans, were already baptized, and their sick had been healed on the Mount of Beatitudes. Jesus spent the whole day in teaching, consoling, and strengthening souls in faith, often in their homes.[159]

October 13–24, **Sun is square Pluto**, exact on the 18th.

**October 18: Sun 0°58' Libra square Pluto 0°58' Capricorn.** Today the Sun remembers the event that perhaps marks the overall *raison d'être* of the Adam—Elijah—John the Baptist individuality— the Baptism of Christ in the River Jordan, the start of Christ's three-and-half-year ministry:

> The baptismal well lay in a gently inclined, octangular basin the bottom of which was encircled by a similarly shaped rim connected with the Jordan by five subterranean canals.

The water surrounded the whole basin, filling it through incisions made in the rim, three in the northern side serving as inlets, and two on the southern acting as outlets. The former were visible, the latter covered, for at this point were the place of action and the avenue of entrance. For this reason, the water did not here surround the well. From this south side, sodded steps led down into it by an inclination of about three feet in depth.

> In the water off the southern shore was a red, triangular, sparkling stone sunk close to the margin of the basin, the flat side toward the center of the well, the point toward the land. This side of the well, upon which were the steps leading down into it, was somewhat higher than the opposite one. This latter, that is, the north side, was the one with the three in-flowing canals. On the southwestern side was a step leading to the somewhat deeper part of the margin and on this side only was there access to the well. In the well, in front of the triangular stone, there stood a green tree which had a slender trunk.
>
> The island was not quite level. It was rather elevated toward the center and in some parts rocky. It was covered with moss and in the middle of it was the wide-spreading tree connected with which were the tops of the twelve trees planted around the edge of the island. Between every two of the trees, was a hedge of several small shrubs....
>
> And now Jesus descended into the well, and stood in the water up to his breast. His left arm encircled the tree, his right hand was laid on his breast, and the loosened ends of the white, linen binder floated out on the water. On the southern side of the well stood John, holding in his hand a shell with a perforated margin through which the water flowed in three streams. He stooped, filled the shell, and then poured the water in three streams over the head of the Lord, one on the back of the head, one in the middle, and the third over the forepart of the head and on the face.
>
> I do not now clearly remember John's words when baptizing Jesus, but they were something like the following: "May Yahweh through the ministry of his cherubim and seraphim, pour out his blessing over thee with wisdom, understanding, and strength!" I cannot say for certain

---

159 ACE, vol. 2, p. 318.

whether these last three words were really those that I heard; but I know that they were expressive of three gifts, for the mind, the soul, and the body respectively. In them was contained all that was needed to convert every creature, renewed in mind, in soul, and in body, to the Lord.

While Jesus ascended from the depths of the baptismal well, Andrew and Saturnin, who were standing to the right of the Baptist around the triangular stone, threw about him a large linen cloth with which he dried his person. They then put on him a long, white baptismal robe. After this Jesus stepped onto the red triangular stone that lay to the right of the descent into the well, Andrew and Saturnin each laid one hand upon his shoulder, while John rested his upon his head.

This part of the ceremony over, they were just mounting the steps when the Voice of God came over Jesus, who was still standing alone and in prayer upon the stone. There came from Heaven a great, rushing wind like thunder. All trembled and looked up. A cloud of white light descended, and I saw over Jesus a winged figure of light as if flowing over him like a stream. The heavens opened. I beheld an apparition of the heavenly Father in the figure in which he is usually depicted and, in a voice of thunder, I heard the words, "This is my beloved Son, in whom I am well pleased."[160]

## October 19: Saturn 17°33' Capricorn square Uranus 17°33' Aries.

This alignment has been building since February 6, and the two of them will remain within 5° of alignment all the way through June 27, 2022.[161]

Saturn was opposite today's degree on September 8 AD 32. Christ and the shepherd youths were about forty days into their journey to Egypt, and on September 9, they came to the first tent city of star worshippers:

When Jesus with the three youths left Kedar, Nazor, the ruler of the synagogue (who traced his origin up to Tobias), Salathiel, Eliud, and the youth Titus accompanied him a good part of the way. They crossed the river and passed through the pagan quarter of the city, in which just at that time a pagan feast was being celebrated and sacrifice was being offered in front of the temple. The road ran first eastward and then to the south through a plain that lay between two high mountain ridges, sometimes over heaths, again over yellow or white sand, and sometimes over white pebbles. At last they reached a large, open tract of country covered with verdure, in which stood a great tent among the palm trees, and around it many smaller ones. Here Jesus blessed and took leave of his escort, and then continued his journey awhile longer toward the tent city of the star worshippers. The day was on its decline when he arrived at a beautiful well in a hollow. It was surrounded by a low embankment, and near it was a drinking ladle. The Lord drank, and then sat down by the well. The youths washed his feet and he, in turn, rendered them the same service. All was done with childlike simplicity, and the sight was extremely touching. The plain was covered with palm trees, meadows, and at a considerable distance apart there were groups of tents. A tower, or terraced pyramid of pretty good size, still not higher than an ordinary church, arose in the center of the district. Here and there some people made their appearance and from a distance gazed at Jesus in surprise not unmingled with awe, but no one approached him.[162]

What a peaceful star memory to accompany the longest-lasting aspect of the year. Perhaps we too, after an analogous forty days' wandering, can have a respite in the oasis of the "tent city of star worshippers."

## October 20: Full Moon 2°23' Aries.

There was an Aries Full Moon on October 7 AD 32, one month later into Christ's journey to Egypt:

On the evening of the second day of their departure from Sikdor, I saw Jesus and the disciples drawing near to a city outside of which rose a hill covered with circular gardens. Most of them had a fountain in the center and were planted with fine ornamental trees and shrubbery. The way taken by the Lord ran toward the south:

---

160 ACE, vol. 1, pp. 343–344.
161 See the "Editorial Foreword" to the current volume for a more in-depth picture of the Saturn–Uranus cycle.

162 ACE, vol. 2, p. 495.

Babylon lay to the north. It seemed as if one would have to descend a mountainous country to reach Babylon, which lay far below. The city was built on the river Tigris, which flowed through it. Jesus entered quietly and without pausing at the gates. It was evening, but few of the inhabitants were to be seen, and no one troubled himself about him. Soon, however, I saw several men in long garments, like those worn by Abraham, and with scarfs wound round their head, coming to meet him and inclining low before him. One of them extended toward him a short, crooked staff. It was made of reed, something like that afterward presented to Christ in derision, and was called the staff of peace. The others, two by two, held across the street a strip of carpet upon which Jesus walked. When he stepped from the first to the second, the former was raised and spread before the latter to be again in readiness for use, and so on. In this way they reached a courtyard, over whose grated entrance with its idols waved a standard upon which was represented the figure of a man holding a crooked staff like that presented to Jesus. The standard was the standard of peace. They led the Lord through a building from whose gallery floated another standard. It appeared to be the temple, for all around the interior stood veiled idols and in the center was another veiled in the same way, the veil being gathered above it form a crown. The Lord did not pause here, but proceeded through a corridor, on either side of which were sleeping apartments. At last he and his attendants reached a little enclosed garden planted with delicate bushes and aromatic shrubs, its walks paved in ornamental figures with different kinds of colored stone. In the center rose a fountain under a little temple open on all sides, and here the Lord and the disciples sat down. In answer to Jesus's request, the idolators brought some water in a basin. The Lord first blessed it, as if to annul the pagan benediction, and then the disciples washed his feet and he theirs, after which they poured what remained into the fountain. The pagans then conducted the Lord into an open hall adjoining, in which a meal had been prepared: large yellow, ribbed apples and other kinds of fruit; honeycombs; bread in the form of thin cakes, like waffles; and something else in little, square morsels. The

table upon which they were spread was very low. The guests ate standing. Jesus's coming had been announced to these people by the priests of the neighboring city. They had in consequence expected him the whole day and at last received him with so much solemnity. Abraham also had received a staff of welcome such as had been presented to Jesus.[163]

### October 21: Mercury enters Gemini.

Worlds sustain worlds
    (*Sun in Libra*)
What lacks boundaries should
    (*Venus in Aquarius*)
Embrace joyful striving
    (*Mercury in Gemini*)
Work with powers of life
    (*Mars in Virgo*)
As a flowing wave self-sustaining
    (*Jupiter in Aquarius*)
And may the might of life's activity flower
    (*Saturn in Capricorn*)
O shining light, abide!
    (*Moon in Aries*)[164]

### October 26: Mercury enters Cancer.

Worlds sustain worlds
    (*Sun in Libra*)
What lacks boundaries should
    (*Venus in Aquarius*)
Warm soul life
    (*Mercury in Gemini*)
Work with powers of life
    (*Mars in Virgo*)
As a flowing wave self-sustaining
    (*Jupiter in Aquarius*)
And may the might of life's activity flower
    (*Saturn in Capricorn*)
O sun life, endure!
    (*Moon in Gemini*)[165]

October 25–26, **Mercury is opposite Pluto**, exact on the 26th.

---

163 Ibid., pp. 514–515.
164 Steiner, *Twelve Cosmic Moods*.
165 Steiner, *Twelve Cosmic Moods*.

**October 26: Mercury 1°0' Cancer opposite Pluto 1°0' Capricorn.** Mercury was at this degree on December 24 AD 29, at the summons of the apostle Philip:

Jesus taught again, morning and afternoon, in the synagogue. After the close of the sabbath, Jesus went with his disciples into a little valley near the synagogue. It seemed intended for a promenade or a place of seclusion. There were trees in front of the entrance, as well as in the valley. The sons of Mary Cleophas, of Zebedee, and some others of the disciples were with him. But Philip, who was backward and humble, hung behind, not certain as to whether he should or should not follow. Jesus, who was going on before, turned his head and, addressing Philip, said, "Follow me!" at which words Philip went on joyously with the others. There were about twelve in the little band.[166]

October 24–31, **Venus conjoins Neptune,** the two of them exactly aligned on the 28th.

**October 28: Venus and Neptune 27°1' Aquarius.** Simultaneously, Mercury opposes Saturn October 28–29, exact on the 29th.

**October 29: Mercury 17°51' Cancer opposite Saturn 17°51' Capricorn. Mars enters Libra.** Mercury was at this same degree just a few days after the summons of Philip, on December 27 AD 29. This was the day before the wedding ceremony in Cana which saw the first healing miracle of the Changing of Water into Wine:

Long ago had Jesus, in his twelfth year at the children's feast held in the house of St. Anne upon his return from the temple, addressed to the bridegroom words full of mysterious significance on the subject of bread and wine. He had told him that at some future day he would be present at his marriage. Jesus's participation in this marriage, like every other action of his earthly career, had, besides its high, mysterious signification, its exterior, apparent, and ordinary motives. More than once had Mary sent messengers to Jesus begging him to be present at it. The friends and relatives of the holy family,

judging from a human view, were making such speeches as these: "Mary, the mother of Jesus, is a lone widow. Jesus is roaming the country, caring little for her or his relatives, etc., etc." It was on this account, therefore, that Mary was anxious that her son should honor his friends by his presence at the marriage. Jesus entered into Mary's views and looked upon the present as a fitting opportunity to disabuse them of their erroneous ideas. He undertook also to supply one course of the feast, and so Mary went to Cana before the other guests and helped in the various preparations. Jesus had engaged to supply all the wine for the feast, wherefore it was that Mary so anxiously reminded him that the wine failed. Jesus had also invited Lazarus and Martha to Cana. Martha assisted, with Mary, in the preparations, and it was Lazarus who defrayed (a circumstance known only to Jesus and Mary) all the expenses assumed by Jesus at the feast. Jesus had great confidence in Lazarus, and willingly received everything from him, while Lazarus was only too happy to give to Jesus. He was up to the last like the treasurer of the community. During the whole feast, he was treated by the bride's father as a person of special distinction, and he even personally busied himself in his service. Lazarus was very refined in his manners, his whole demeanor earnest, quiet, and marked by a dignified affability; he spoke little, and his bearing toward Jesus was full of loving devotedness.[167]

Venus was at 27° Aquarius on January 4 AD 31, at the healing of Michol, the daughter of Ozias:

Jesus spoke with the invalid, prayed, breathed into her face, and motioned to the mother to kneel down opposite him. She obeyed. Then Jesus poured some oil that he carried with him upon the palm of his hand and, with the first two fingers of his right hand, anointed the sick maiden's forehead and temples, then the joints of both hands, allowing his own hand to rest for one moment upon them. Then he directed the mother to open Michol's long garment over the region of the stomach, which too he anointed with the oil. After that the mother raised the edge of the coverlet from her daughter's feet, and

166 ACE, vol. 1, p. 382.

167 Ibid., pp. 384–85.

they also received the unction. Then Jesus said, "Michol, give me thy right hand and thy mother thy left!" At this command, the maiden, for the first time, raised both hands and stretched them out. Jesus continued: "Stand up, Michol!" and the pale, haggard child arose to a sitting posture and then to her feet, tottering in the unaccustomed position. Jesus and the mother led her into the open arms of the father. The mother also embraced her. They wept for joy, and all three fell at Jesus's feet.[168]

**October 30: Venus enters Pisces.**

**October 31: Mercury enters Leo.**

> Worlds sustain worlds
> 　　(*Sun in Libra*)
> In winning may gain be lost
> 　　(*Venus in Pisces*)
> Feeling being's essence
> 　　(*Mercury in Leo*)
> And being effects being
> 　　(*Mars in Libra*)
> As a flowing wave self-sustaining
> 　　(*Jupiter in Aquarius*)
> And may the might of life's activity flower
> 　　(*Saturn in Capricorn*)
> With senses' might, arise!
> 　　(*Moon in Leo*)[169]

## NOVEMBER 2021

### STARGAZING PREVIEW

Thursday the 4th is the day of this year's Libra New Moon; at 18°, it recalls its position at the Assumption of Mary. After sunset, Venus, Saturn, and Jupiter will be the only wanderers in the night sky; after midnight, only the stars will remain. If you watch the sky each evening at 1800 during the week beginning Sunday the 7th, you'll be able to see the waxing Moon weave its way above Venus

and below Saturn and Jupiter. It reaches its First Quarter (24° Capricorn) on the 11th.

The Sun is greeted by Scorpio on the 17th; it is easy to forget that hidden behind the stinger and the claws lies a most sensitive heart! The evening of the 17th will also offer your best opportunity to see the Leonid meteor showers, despite the Moon's swift approach to Full. As the Sun is now in Scorpio, Leo, the apparent radiant of the showers, will be due north (and below the horizon) at sunset. If you're up at midnight, watch for Leo as it rises in the east following the setting of Jupiter in the west.

Our Full Moon this month, at 2° Taurus, graces the night sky on Friday the 19th, creating a Partial Lunar Eclipse over the Americas, the Pacific, Australia, and East Asia; it will be most dramatic throughout North America. As the Full Moon rises at 1600—now aligned with the *Pleiades*—Venus, Saturn, and Jupiter will be high in the southwest.

On the 26th, the waning Moon will rise at 2300, very close indeed to *Regulus*. The following evening brings us the Last Quarter Moon at 10° Leo, recalling the Sun's degree at the Healing of the Nobleman's Son. As it rises at midnight—behold! Jupiter returns to its Aquarius year on the 28th, after having retrogressed into Capricorn in September: *As a flowing wave self-sustaining*. It will be in the southwestern evening sky until 2200.

Mercury (12° Scorpio) moves to the far side of the Sun on the 29th, blessing us with another superior conjunction of the two light bearers. Orion, now opposite the Sun, is up all night!

### NOVEMBER COMMENTARIES

The month of November begins with several alignments taking shape simultaneously. From October 31 to November 3, Mercury opposes Jupiter, exact on the 2nd.

**November 2: Mercury 8°49' Leo opposite Jupiter 8°49' Aquarius.** October 30–November 9, Sun is opposite Uranus, exact on

**November 4: Sun 17°44' Libra opposite Uranus 17°44' Aries.** The New Moon also occurs on November 4: **New Moon 17°37' Libra.** October 30

---

168 ACE, vol. 2, p. 202.
169 Steiner, *Twelve Cosmic Moods*.

to November 10, Sun is square Saturn, exact on the 5th.

**November 5: Sun 18°4' Libra square Saturn 18°4' Capricorn**. Finally, November 4–7, Mercury opposes Neptune, exact on the 6th.

**November 6: Mercury enters Virgo.**

> Worlds sustain worlds
>    (*Sun in Libra*)
> In winning may gain be lost
>    (*Venus in Pisces*)
> Work with powers of life
>    (*Mercury in Virgo*)
> And being effects being
>    (*Mars in Libra*)
> As a flowing wave self-sustaining
>    (*Jupiter in Aquarius*)
> And may the might of life's activity flower
>    (*Saturn in Capricorn*)
> Being sustains beings!
>    (*Moon in Scorpio*)[170]

November 6: **Mercury 27°4' Leo opposite Neptune 27°4' Aquarius.** We have a New Moon opposite Uranus square Saturn, and Mercury opposite Jupiter and Neptune. Mercury was at Jupiter's current position on November 15 AD 30:

> Jesus took for the subject of his discourse his own reply to John's disciples. He spoke of how they should use the benefits received from God, and exhorted to penance and a change of life. As he knew that some of the Pharisees present had taken occasion—from the brevity of his reply to John's messengers—to say to the people that he, Jesus, made little account of John and was willing enough to see him ruined in public estimation (that he himself might be exalted), he explained the answer he had given as well as what he had said on the score of penance. He also recalled to them what they themselves had heard John say of him. Why, he asked, were they always doubting? What did they expect from John? He said: "What went ye out to see when ye went to John? Did ye go to see a reed shaken in the wind? Or a man effeminately and magnificently clothed? Listen! They that are clothed sumptuously and who live delicately are in the palaces of kings. But what did ye desire to see when ye went in quest of him? Was it to see a prophet? Yea, I tell ye, ye saw more than a prophet when ye saw him. This is he of whom it is written: 'Behold, I send my angel before thy face, who shall prepare thy way before thee.' Amen, I say to you there hath not risen among them that are born of women a greater prophet than John the Baptist, and yet he that is least in the Kingdom of Heaven is greater than he. And from the days of John the Baptist until now the Kingdom of Heaven suffereth violence, and the violent bear it away. For all the prophets and the Law prophesied of it until John; and if ye will receive it, he is Elijah that is to come again. He that hath ears to hear, let him hear!"[171]

The Sun opposed Uranus (albeit in Aquarius and Leo respectively) January 31 to February 1 AD 31, when Christ delivered the teaching of the Bread of Life (see John 6:25–51). This star memory is enhanced by the Libra New Moon, which also occurred on September 23 AD 32, when Christ visited with Magi Mensor and Theokeno:

> The kings had some knowledge of Abraham and David; and when Jesus spoke of his ancestors, they produced some old books and searched in them to see whether they too could not claim descent from the same race. The books were in the form of tablets opening out in a zigzag form, like sample patterns. These pagans were so childlike, so desirous of doing all that they were told. They knew that circumcision had been prescribed to Abraham, and they asked the Lord whether they, too, should obey this part of the Law. Jesus answered that it was no longer necessary, that they had already circumcised their evil inclinations, and that they would do so still more. Then they told him that they knew something of Melchizadek and his sacrifice of bread and wine, and said that they too had a sacrifice of the same kind, namely, a sacrifice of little leaves and some kind of a green liquor. When they offered it they spoke some words like these: "Whoever eats me and is devout, shall have all kinds of felicity." Jesus told them that Melchizadek's sacrifice was a type of the most

---

170 Steiner, *Twelve Cosmic Moods.*

171 ACE, vol. 2, p. 146.

## SIDEREAL GEOCENTRIC LONGITUDES : NOVEMBER 2021 Gregorian at 0 hours UT

| DAY | ☉ | ☽ | ☊ | ☿ | ♀ | ♂ | ♃ | ♄ | ♅ | ♆ | ♇ |
|---|---|---|---|---|---|---|---|---|---|---|---|
| 1 MO | 13 ♎ 44 | 21 ♌ 35 | 6 ♉ 53R | 27 ♍ 21 | 0 ♐ 39 | 5 ♎ 54 | 27 ♑ 36 | 12 ♑ 12 | 17 ♈ 54R | 25 ♒ 37R | 29 ♐ 25 |
| 2 TU | 14 44 | 5 ♍ 27 | 6 50 | 28 50 | 1 38 | 6 34 | 27 39 | 12 14 | 17 52 | 25 36 | 29 26 |
| 3 WE | 15 44 | 19 45 | 6 47 | 0 ♎ 21 | 2 36 | 7 15 | 27 42 | 12 16 | 17 49 | 25 35 | 29 27 |
| 4 TH | 16 44 | 4 ♎ 26 | 6 44 | 1 54 | 3 34 | 7 55 | 27 45 | 12 19 | 17 47 | 25 34 | 29 28 |
| 5 FR | 17 44 | 19 22 | 6 42 | 3 28 | 4 32 | 8 35 | 27 49 | 12 21 | 17 44 | 25 34 | 29 29 |
| 6 SA | 18 45 | 4 ♏ 25 | 6 42 | 5 3 | 5 29 | 9 16 | 27 52 | 12 24 | 17 42 | 25 33 | 29 29 |
| 7 SU | 19 45 | 19 27 | 6 42D | 6 39 | 6 25 | 9 56 | 27 56 | 12 26 | 17 39 | 25 32 | 29 30 |
| 8 MO | 20 45 | 4 ♐ 19 | 6 43 | 8 15 | 7 21 | 10 37 | 28 0 | 12 29 | 17 37 | 25 31 | 29 31 |
| 9 TU | 21 45 | 18 55 | 6 44 | 9 51 | 8 17 | 11 18 | 28 4 | 12 32 | 17 34 | 25 30 | 29 32 |
| 10 WE | 22 46 | 3 ♑ 11 | 6 45 | 11 28 | 9 12 | 11 58 | 28 9 | 12 35 | 17 32 | 25 30 | 29 33 |
| 11 TH | 23 46 | 17 4 | 6 45 | 13 5 | 10 6 | 12 39 | 28 13 | 12 38 | 17 29 | 25 29 | 29 34 |
| 12 FR | 24 46 | 0 ♒ 36 | 6 45R | 14 42 | 11 0 | 13 20 | 28 18 | 12 41 | 17 27 | 25 28 | 29 35 |
| 13 SA | 25 47 | 13 46 | 6 45 | 16 19 | 11 53 | 14 0 | 28 23 | 12 44 | 17 25 | 25 28 | 29 36 |
| 14 SU | 26 47 | 26 38 | 6 44 | 17 56 | 12 46 | 14 41 | 28 28 | 12 47 | 17 22 | 25 27 | 29 37 |
| 15 MO | 27 47 | 9 ♓ 14 | 6 43 | 19 32 | 13 37 | 15 22 | 28 33 | 12 50 | 17 20 | 25 26 | 29 38 |
| 16 TU | 28 48 | 21 37 | 6 42 | 21 9 | 14 29 | 16 3 | 28 39 | 12 54 | 17 17 | 25 26 | 29 40 |
| 17 WE | 29 48 | 3 ♈ 48 | 6 41 | 22 45 | 15 19 | 16 44 | 28 44 | 12 57 | 17 15 | 25 25 | 29 41 |
| 18 TH | 0 ♏ 49 | 15 51 | 6 40 | 24 22 | 16 8 | 17 24 | 28 50 | 13 1 | 17 12 | 25 25 | 29 42 |
| 19 FR | 1 49 | 27 47 | 6 39 | 25 58 | 16 57 | 18 5 | 28 56 | 13 5 | 17 10 | 25 24 | 29 43 |
| 20 SA | 2 50 | 9 ♉ 37 | 6 39D | 27 34 | 17 45 | 18 46 | 29 2 | 13 8 | 17 8 | 25 24 | 29 44 |
| 21 SU | 3 50 | 21 25 | 6 40 | 29 9 | 18 32 | 19 27 | 29 8 | 13 12 | 17 5 | 25 24 | 29 45 |
| 22 MO | 4 51 | 3 ♊ 13 | 6 40 | 0 ♏ 45 | 19 18 | 20 8 | 29 15 | 13 16 | 17 3 | 25 23 | 29 47 |
| 23 TU | 5 51 | 15 3 | 6 40 | 2 20 | 20 3 | 20 50 | 29 21 | 13 20 | 17 1 | 25 23 | 29 48 |
| 24 WE | 6 52 | 26 58 | 6 40R | 3 56 | 20 48 | 21 31 | 29 28 | 13 24 | 16 58 | 25 23 | 29 49 |
| 25 TH | 7 53 | 9 ♋ 1 | 6 40 | 5 31 | 21 31 | 22 12 | 29 35 | 13 29 | 16 56 | 25 23 | 29 51 |
| 26 FR | 8 53 | 21 16 | 6 40 | 7 5 | 22 13 | 22 53 | 29 42 | 13 33 | 16 54 | 25 22 | 29 52 |
| 27 SA | 9 54 | 3 ♌ 48 | 6 39 | 8 40 | 22 54 | 23 34 | 29 50 | 13 37 | 16 52 | 25 22 | 29 53 |
| 28 SU | 10 55 | 16 40 | 6 39D | 10 15 | 23 34 | 24 16 | 29 57 | 13 42 | 16 49 | 25 22 | 29 55 |
| 29 MO | 11 56 | 29 56 | 6 40 | 11 49 | 24 13 | 24 57 | 0 ♒ 5 | 13 46 | 16 47 | 25 22 | 29 56 |
| 30 TU | 12 56 | 13 ♍ 38 | 6 40 | 13 23 | 24 50 | 25 38 | 0 12 | 13 51 | 16 45 | 25 22 | 29 58 |

### INGRESSES :

1 ☽ → ♍ 14:40
2 ☿ → ♎ 18:23
3 ☽ → ♎ 16:48
5 ☽ → ♏ 16:57
7 ☽ → ♐ 16:59
9 ☽ → ♑ 18:35
11 ☽ → ♒ 22:55
14 ☽ → ♓ 6:21
16 ☽ → ♈ 16:28
17 ☉ → ♏ 4:39
19 ☽ → ♉ 4:29
21 ☿ → ♏ 12:41
☽ → ♊ 17:27
24 ☽ → ♋ 6: 5
26 ☽ → ♌ 16:46
28 ♃ → ♒ 9:26
29 ☽ → ♍ 0: 7

### ASPECTS & ECLIPSES :

1 ☽ ☍ ♆ 7: 4
2 ☿ □ ♇ 9:35
3 ☽ ☌ ☿ 19:25
4 ☽ ☌ ♂ 5:54
☉ ☌ ☽ 21:13
☽ ☍ ♅ 21:24
☉ ☍ ♅ 23:55
5 ☽ ☌ P 22: 9
6 ☽ ☌ ☋ 3:37
8 ☽ ☌ ♀ 5:17
9 ☽ ☌ ♇ 17:49
10 ☿ ☌ ♂ 12:55
☽ ☌ ♄ 16:13
☿ □ ♄ 17: 3
♂ □ ♄ 23:13
11 ☉ □ ☽ 12:44
☽ ☌ ♃ 19:51
12 ☽ □(S) ☊ 11: 8
13 ☿ ☍ ♅ 15:54
☽ ☌ ♆ 21:45
15 ☉ □ ♃ 19:57
17 ♂ ☍ ♅ 17:20
18 ☽ ☌ ♅ 2:43
☽ ☍ ♂ 3:19
☽ ☍ ☿ 19:46
19 ☉ ☍ ☽ 8:56
☽ •–• P 9: 2
☽ ☌ ☊ 17:58
20 ☿ □ ♃ 23:41
21 ☽ ☌ A 2:35
23 ☽ ☍ ♀ 10:47
☉ ☍ ☊ 19: 9
24 ☽ ☍ ♇ 5:44
25 ☽ ☍ ♄ 8:50
☿ ☍ ☊ 17:27
26 ☽ ☍ ♃ 16:22
27 ☽ □(N) ☊ 5:22
☉ □ ☽ 12:26
28 ☽ ☍ ♆ 15:49
29 ☉ ☋(S) ☿ 4:38

## SIDEREAL HELIOCENTRIC LONGITUDES : NOVEMBER 2021 Gregorian at 0 hours UT

| DAY | Sid. Time | ☿ | ♀ | ⊕ | ♂ | ♃ | ♄ | ♅ | ♆ | ♇ | Vernal Point |
|---|---|---|---|---|---|---|---|---|---|---|---|
| 1 MO | 2:42: 1 | 2 ♌ 49 | 2 ♓ 53 | 13 ♈ 45 | 1 ♎ 5 | 8 ♒ 42 | 17 ♑ 56 | 17 ♈ 42 | 27 ♒ 2 | 1 ♑ 2 | 4 ♓ 57'19" |
| 2 TU | 2:45:58 | 7 46 | 4 29 | 14 45 | 1 33 | 8 48 | 17 58 | 17 42 | 27 3 | 1 2 | 4 ♓ 57'19" |
| 3 WE | 2:49:54 | 12 34 | 6 4 | 15 45 | 2 1 | 8 53 | 18 0 | 17 43 | 27 3 | 1 3 | 4 ♓ 57'19" |
| 4 TH | 2:53:51 | 17 13 | 7 40 | 16 45 | 2 29 | 8 58 | 18 2 | 17 44 | 27 3 | 1 3 | 4 ♓ 57'19" |
| 5 FR | 2:57:48 | 21 42 | 9 15 | 17 45 | 2 57 | 9 4 | 18 4 | 17 44 | 27 4 | 1 3 | 4 ♓ 57'19" |
| 6 SA | 3: 1:44 | 26 4 | 10 51 | 18 45 | 3 26 | 9 9 | 18 6 | 17 45 | 27 4 | 1 3 | 4 ♓ 57'18" |
| 7 SU | 3: 5:41 | 0 ♍ 16 | 12 26 | 19 45 | 3 54 | 9 15 | 18 7 | 17 46 | 27 4 | 1 4 | 4 ♓ 57'18" |
| 8 MO | 3: 9:37 | 4 22 | 14 2 | 20 46 | 4 22 | 9 20 | 18 9 | 17 46 | 27 5 | 1 4 | 4 ♓ 57'18" |
| 9 TU | 3:13:34 | 8 19 | 15 37 | 21 46 | 4 51 | 9 25 | 18 11 | 17 47 | 27 5 | 1 4 | 4 ♓ 57'18" |
| 10 WE | 3:17:30 | 12 10 | 17 13 | 22 46 | 5 19 | 9 31 | 18 13 | 17 48 | 27 5 | 1 5 | 4 ♓ 57'18" |
| 11 TH | 3:21:27 | 15 54 | 18 48 | 23 47 | 5 48 | 9 36 | 18 15 | 17 48 | 27 6 | 1 5 | 4 ♓ 57'18" |
| 12 FR | 3:25:23 | 19 33 | 20 24 | 24 47 | 6 16 | 9 41 | 18 17 | 17 49 | 27 6 | 1 5 | 4 ♓ 57'18" |
| 13 SA | 3:29:20 | 23 5 | 22 0 | 25 47 | 6 45 | 9 47 | 18 19 | 17 50 | 27 7 | 1 5 | 4 ♓ 57'18" |
| 14 SU | 3:33:17 | 26 33 | 23 35 | 26 48 | 7 13 | 9 52 | 18 20 | 17 50 | 27 7 | 1 6 | 4 ♓ 57'17" |
| 15 MO | 3:37:13 | 29 55 | 25 11 | 27 48 | 7 42 | 9 58 | 18 22 | 17 51 | 27 7 | 1 6 | 4 ♓ 57'17" |
| 16 TU | 3:41:10 | 3 ♎ 13 | 26 47 | 28 48 | 8 10 | 10 3 | 18 24 | 17 52 | 27 8 | 1 6 | 4 ♓ 57'17" |
| 17 WE | 3:45: 6 | 6 27 | 28 23 | 29 49 | 8 39 | 10 8 | 18 26 | 17 52 | 27 8 | 1 7 | 4 ♓ 57'17" |
| 18 TH | 3:49: 3 | 9 37 | 29 58 | 0 ♉ 49 | 9 8 | 10 14 | 18 28 | 17 53 | 27 8 | 1 7 | 4 ♓ 57'17" |
| 19 FR | 3:52:59 | 12 43 | 1 ♈ 34 | 1 50 | 9 37 | 10 19 | 18 30 | 17 54 | 27 9 | 1 7 | 4 ♓ 57'17" |
| 20 SA | 3:56:56 | 15 46 | 3 10 | 2 50 | 10 5 | 10 25 | 18 32 | 17 54 | 27 9 | 1 7 | 4 ♓ 57'17" |
| 21 SU | 4: 0:52 | 18 47 | 4 46 | 3 51 | 10 34 | 10 30 | 18 33 | 17 55 | 27 9 | 1 8 | 4 ♓ 57'16" |
| 22 MO | 4: 4:49 | 21 44 | 6 22 | 4 51 | 11 3 | 10 35 | 18 35 | 17 56 | 27 10 | 1 8 | 4 ♓ 57'16" |
| 23 TU | 4: 8:46 | 24 40 | 7 58 | 5 52 | 11 32 | 10 41 | 18 37 | 17 56 | 27 10 | 1 8 | 4 ♓ 57'16" |
| 24 WE | 4:12:42 | 27 33 | 9 34 | 6 53 | 12 1 | 10 46 | 18 39 | 17 57 | 27 11 | 1 9 | 4 ♓ 57'16" |
| 25 TH | 4:16:39 | 0 ♏ 24 | 11 10 | 7 53 | 12 30 | 10 52 | 18 41 | 17 58 | 27 11 | 1 9 | 4 ♓ 57'16" |
| 26 FR | 4:20:35 | 3 14 | 12 46 | 8 54 | 12 59 | 10 57 | 18 43 | 17 58 | 27 11 | 1 9 | 4 ♓ 57'16" |
| 27 SA | 4:24:32 | 6 2 | 14 22 | 9 55 | 13 28 | 11 2 | 18 44 | 17 59 | 27 12 | 1 10 | 4 ♓ 57'16" |
| 28 SU | 4:28:28 | 8 50 | 15 58 | 10 55 | 13 57 | 11 8 | 18 46 | 18 0 | 27 12 | 1 10 | 4 ♓ 57'15" |
| 29 MO | 4:32:25 | 11 36 | 17 34 | 11 56 | 14 26 | 11 13 | 18 48 | 18 0 | 27 12 | 1 10 | 4 ♓ 57'15" |
| 30 TU | 4:36:21 | 14 21 | 19 10 | 12 57 | 14 56 | 11 18 | 18 50 | 18 1 | 27 13 | 1 10 | 4 ♓ 57'15" |

### INGRESSES :

6 ☿ → ♍ 22:25
15 ☿ → ♎ 0:35
17 ⊕ → ♉ 4:25
18 ♀ → ♈ 0:24
24 ☿ → ♏ 20:35

### ASPECTS (HELIOCENTRIC +MOON(TYCHONIC)) :

1 ☽ ☍ ♆ 9:32
☽ ☍ ♀ 22: 8
2 ☿ ☍ ♃ 5:10
3 ☽ □ ♇ 18:31
☽ ☌ ♂ 20:45
4 ☽ ☍ ♅ 21:24
☽ □ ♄ 21:55
⊕ ☌ ♅ 23:39
5 ⊕ □ ♄ 7:40
6 ☿ ☍ ♆ 5:40
☽ □ ♃ 7:35
7 ☽ □ ♆ 12:16
8 ☽ □ ☿ 0: 5
☽ □ ♀ 17:51
9 ☽ ☌ ♇ 20:25
10 ☽ □ ♂ 3:46
11 ☽ □ ♅ 1:17
☽ ☌ ♄ 2: 4
12 ☿ ☍ ♀ 10:23
☽ ☌ ♃ 16:37
14 ☽ ☌ ♆ 0:53
15 ☿ □ ♇ 8:33
16 ☽ ☌ ♀ 11:39
☽ □ ♇ 18:39
17 ☽ ☍ ☿ 7: 7
☽ ☍ ♂ 10: 1
☿ ☌ ♂ 19:39
18 ☽ ☌ ♅ 4: 5
☽ □ ♄ 5:15
♀ □ ♇ 17:12
20 ☽ □ ♃ 1:36
☿ ☍ ♅ 17: 3
☿ □ ♄ 22:12
21 ☽ □ ♆ 11:40
22 ☿ ☌ ☋ 14:48
24 ☽ ☍ ♇ 8:22
25 ☽ □ ♀ 4:52
☽ □ ♂ 7: 9
☽ □ ♅ 17:34
☽ ☍ ♄ 19: 0
26 ♀ ☍ ♂ 4:48
27 ☽ □ ☿ 5:24
☽ ☍ ♃ 13:40
28 ⊕ □ ♃ 5:18
☽ ☍ ♆ 19: 7
☿ □ ♃ 20:35
29 ☿ ☍ ⊕ 4:38
♀ ☌ ♅ 6:39
♀ □ ♄ 18:57

holy Sacrifice, and that he himself was the Victim. Thus, though plunged in darkness, these pagans had preserved many forms of truth.

Either the night that preceded Jesus's coming or that which followed, I cannot now say which, all the paths and avenues to a great distance around the tent castle were brilliantly illuminated. Transparent globes with lights in them were raised on poles, and every globe was surmounted by a little crown that glistened like a star.[172]

Sun and Saturn were square in the other two cardinal signs (Aries and Cancer respectively) on April 15 AD 33. This star memory enhances those related to the Bread of Life, as this was the day the Risen One shared the Fish Communion with seven of his apostles by the seashore:

Of the fish that the apostles caught, none were used at that meal. When Jesus said that they should bring them ashore, Peter threw them in rows at Jesus's feet, that they might be numbered. By this is was acknowledged that they had caught the fish not by themselves and for themselves, but by his miraculous power and for him. When the fish were deposited on the shore, Jesus said to the apostles: "Come and eat!" and conducted them over the little hill, or mound, where the sea could no longer be seen, to the mud hut over the furnace. Jesus did not at once place himself at table, but went to the pan and brought to each a portion of fish on a piece of bread. He blessed the portions and they shone with light. The honey cakes were not in the pan. They were already prepared, and lay in a pile one above the other. Jesus distributed them, and when all were served, he too ate with them. There was only one fish in the pan, but it was larger than any they had caught. There was some mystery connected with this meal. The presence of the souls of the patriarchs and others, their participation in the preparation of the meal, and the subsequent call of Peter, gave me to understand that in this spiritual meal the Church Suffering, the holy souls, should be committed to Peter's care, should be incorporated with the Church Militant, and the Church Triumphant, in short, that they should occupy a third place in the church as a whole. I cannot explain how this

was to be done, but I had in vision this intimate conviction. It was in reference to this also that Jesus closed with the prophecy of Peter's death and John's future.[173]

Mercury and Neptune were opposed (with Mercury in Cancer and Neptune in Capricorn) on December 28 AD 29 at the first healing miracle—the Changing of Water into Wine at the wedding in Cana. These first ten days of November work to draw our hearts and minds to the mystery of communion—of fish, bread, wine, honey, with both the living and the dead.

November 9–14, **Mercury and Venus come into opposition**. This alignment is exact on the 12th.

**November 12: Mercury 21°5' Virgo opposite Venus 21°5' Pisces.** Mercury was at this degree the morning after the "nighttime conversation" between Christ and Nicodemus, April 9 AD 30. The two of them journeyed together to Lazarus's house on Mt. Zion:

Here came Joseph of Arimathea also to see Jesus. He conversed with them. They humbled themselves before him, telling him that they did indeed discern that he was more than human, and they pledged him lasting fidelity. Jesus commanded them to secrecy, and they begged him to remember them kindly.

Venus was at 21° Pisces on December 26, 6 BC, when the magi visited the Jesus child, and on January 19 AD 31. This latter date saw both the third healing miracle, the Healing of Paralyzed Man at the Pool of Bethesda, as well as the burial of the body of John the Baptist.

The alignment of these two planets therefore calls up very strongly the karmic stream related to the Holy Grail. For example: Joseph of Arimathea later incarnated as Trevrizent; Nicodemus, as the wounded King Anfortas; and Mensor, the "Gold King," as Kyot. The other magi, Lazarus, and (in a spiritual sense) both the Master Jesus and John the Baptist were also involved in the Holy Grail mysteries.

On the other hand, the work of Robert Powell on the behalf of the reincarnated John the Baptist

---

172 Ibid., p. 504.

173 ACE, vol. 3, p. 403.

individuality could be seen as an expression of the third healing miracle of the Etheric Christ in our time—the equivalent of the Healing of the Paralyzed Man, which was a healing of movement and of karma.[174] Robert's work has centered around *movement* (eurythmy, cosmic and sacred dance) as well as *karma research*—and is intimately connected with the karmic stream of the Holy Grail.

**November 15: Mercury enters Libra.**

**November 17: Sun enters Scorpio.** November 15–21, **Mercury and Mars conjoin**, exact on the 17th. **Mercury and Mars 9°2' Libra.** Mercury at this degree recalls the events of January 3 AD 31:

> This morning, Jesus taught in the synagogue. Afterward, some people from Jerusalem told him of the sudden collapse of a wall and a tower in Jerusalem two days before. As a result, a crowd of laborers, including eighteen master workers sent by Herod, had been buried beneath the falling debris (Luke 13:4). Herod's workmen had engineered the accident to stir up the people against Pontius Pilate. But their plan had backfired, resulting in their own deaths. Jesus expressed his compassion for the innocent laborers, but added that the sin of the master workers was not greater than that of the Pharisees, Sadducees, and others who labored against the kingdom of God. These later would also be buried one day under their own treacherous structures. After healing the sick, Jesus and the disciples made their way to Antipatris, where they stayed overnight in an inn. That night, during the festivities to celebrate Herod's birthday at Machaerus, John the Baptist was beheaded at the request of Herodias's daughter, Salome. After witnessing the spectacle of Salome dancing before him, Herod had said to her: "Ask what you will, and I will give it to you. Yes, I swear, even if you ask for half my kingdom, I shall give it to you." Salome hurriedly conferred with her mother, who told her to ask for the head of John the Baptist on a dish (Mark 6:17–29).[175]

Mars was close to this degree both at the birth of the Nathan Jesus (December 6, 2 BC, conjunct Mercury at 9° Libra two days later) as well as the flight of the family of the Solomon Jesus to Egypt, to avoid the wrath of Herod the Great. It was Herod's the Great's son, Herod Antipas, who reigned during the ministry of Christ, and committed the atrocities outlined in the above vision of Anne Catherine Emmerich. Today's star memories bring vividly to our mind's eye representatives of innocence and purity, and what they suffer at the hands of the treacherous.

November 15–21, **Venus and Pluto enter square alignment**, exact on the 18th.

**November 18: Venus 1°7' Aries square Pluto 1°7' Capricorn.**

> Existence consumes being
>     (*Sun in Scorpio*)
> Take hold of growth's being
>     (*Venus in Aries*)
> In existing embrace existence
>     (*Mercury in Libra*)
> And being effects being
>     (*Mars in Libra*)
> As a flowing wave self-sustaining
>     (*Jupiter in Aquarius*)
> And may the might of life's activity flower
>     (*Saturn in Capricorn*)
> O shining light, abide!
>     (*Moon in Aries*)[176]

Venus was at this degree on January 25–26 AD 31, when Christ was in Capernaum:

> Capernaum was full of visitors who had come from afar to hear Jesus. In addition, a group of sixty-four Pharisees had also gathered, having come from all around to investigate the carpenter's son from Nazareth. Jesus visited the homes of Zorobabel, Cornelius, and Jairus. Jairus had lost his position as chief elder at the synagogue and had been persecuted because of his contact with Jesus. Now Jairus committed himself wholly to the service of Jesus. Jesus then began healing and continued to heal throughout the morning. Around midday, he withdrew to a

---

174 See here for further explication: https://treehouse.
    live/2017/06/14/the-seven-miracles-part-2.
175 ACE, vol. 2, p. 200.

176 Steiner, *Twelve Cosmic Moods.*

hall to preach. Then, as the sabbath began, he went to the synagogue. He had to make his way through a great crowd before he could begin to teach. When the Pharisees asked him if it was allowed to heal on the sabbath, he answered by healing a man with a withered hand (Matt. 12:9) and by driving out a devil from one who was deaf, mute, and possessed, and whose hearing and speech were immediately restored. Witnessing this, the Pharisees accused Jesus of being in league with the devil (Matt. 9:32–34). Jesus, however, defended himself with the words spoken in Matthew 12:33–37. Amid the uproar, Jesus and the disciples withdrew.[177]

At the time as this alignment there is a Full Moon on the 19th.

**November 19: Full Moon 2°12' Taurus.** A Taurus Full Moon occurred October 29–30 AD 30:

After a journey of about five hours, and night having set in, Jesus and the disciples arrived at a lonely inn where only sleeping accommodations were to be found. Nearby was a well that owed its origin to Jacob. The disciples gathered wood and made a fire. On the way Jesus had had a long conversation with them, intended principally for the instruction of Thomas, Simon, Manahem, "Little Cleophas," and the others newly received. He spoke of their following him, and through the deep conviction of the worthlessness of earthly goods, of their leaving their relatives without regret and without looking back. He promised that what they had left should be restored to them in his kingdom a thousandfold. But they should reflect maturely whether or not they could break their earthly ties.[178]

Jesus held this conversation with the new disciples after they had earlier that day discovered that John the Baptist had been arrested. A good day for self-reflection, especially in regard to our commitments.

November 18–22, **Mercury aligns with Uranus,** exact on the 20th.

**November 20: Mercury 17°55' Libra opposite Uranus 17°55' Aries.** Mercury was at exactly this

degree during the Transfiguration of Christ on Mt. Tabor, which began around midnight on April 4 AD 31, lasting into the early hours of the morning:

Jesus began again his instructions, and along with the angelic apparitions flowed alternate streams of delicious perfumes, of celestial delights and contentment over the apostles. Jesus meantime continued to shine with ever-increasing splendor, until he became as if transparent. The circle around them was so lighted up in the darkness of night that each little plant could be distinguished on the green sod as if in clear daylight. The three apostles were so penetrated, so ravished that, when the light reached a certain degree, they covered their heads, prostrated on the ground, and there remained lying.

It was about twelve o'clock at night when I beheld this glory at its height. I saw a shining pathway reaching from Heaven to Earth, and on it angelic spirits of different choirs, all in constant movement. Some were small, but of perfect form; others were merely faces peeping forth from the glancing light; some were in priestly garb, while others looked like warriors. Each had some special characteristic different from that of the others, and from each radiated some special refreshment, strength, delight, and light. They were in constant action, constant movement.[179]

November 18–28, **the Sun conjoins the Descending Node,** exact on the 23rd.

**November 23: Sun and Descending Node 6°40' Scorpio.** The Sun was at this degree on October 29 AD 30—see the commentary above for the Full Moon. We continue to be offered clarity around our reflections in regard to commitments.

**November 24: Mercury enters Scorpio.**

Existence consumes being
  (*Sun in Scorpio*)
Take hold of growth's being
  (*Venus in Aries*)
In activity growth disappears
  (*Mercury in Scorpio*)
And being effects being
  (*Mars in Libra*)

---

177 Ibid., p. 223.
178 Ibid., p. 94.

179 Ibid., p. 339.

As a flowing wave self-sustaining
> (*Jupiter in Aquarius*)
And may the might of life's activity flower
> (*Saturn in Capricorn*)
Thou glowing light, become strong!
> (*Moon in Cancer*)[180]

November 21–30, **Venus aligns with Mars**, exact on the 26th.

**November 26: Venus 13°5' Aries opposite Mars 13°5' Libra.** Venus was at this degree on February 2 AD 31, when Christ taught on his being the Bread of Life—we return to meditations with which the month began. Venus was also here at the Assumption of the Virgin Mary on August 16 AD 44, a star memory that Neptune recalls for the entire year. As Mars in Libra continues to remember both the birth of the Nathan Jesus as well as the flight into Egypt, our thoughts can be drawn to the essential roles of the Nathan Mary (mother of the Nathan Jesus) and the Solomon Mary (who fled to Egypt with the Solomon Jesus)—and the Assumption of their unified and perfected being as the Most Holy Virgin.

The month ends as it began—with a series of alignments occurring in close proximity. Mercury and Descending Node align November 25–28, exact on the 27th.

**November 27: Mercury and Descending Node 6°39' Scorpio.** Sun and Jupiter are square November 22 to December 3; they are exactly aligned on the 28th.

**November 28: Sun 11°9' Scorpio square Jupiter 11°9' Aquarius.** November 26 and December 2, **Sun and Mercury conjoin**, exact on the 29th: **Sun and Mercury 12°7' Scorpio.** Venus and **Uranus conjoin** November 25 and December 2, also exact on the 29th.

**November 29: Venus and Uranus 18°0' Aries.** Finally, Venus and Saturn are square November 26 to December 2, also exact on November 29: **Venus 18°50' Aries square Saturn 18°50' Capricorn.** Sun, **Descending Node**, and Mercury are all together square Jupiter, while Venus opposes Uranus square Saturn.

---

180 Steiner, *Twelve Cosmic Moods.*

This intense grouping ushers us into the Advent Season, which begins with the first Sunday of Advent on November 28. This first week we honor the mineral kingdom; the Platonic virtue of Justice (i.e., Righteousness, Severity); and the Christian virtue of Hope—directed toward the Appearance (Advent) of Christ in his Second Coming.

Mercury conjoined the Descending Node on January 17 AD 31. This was two days prior to the Healing of the Paralyzed Man, which occurred on the same day that the remains of John the Baptist were buried. January 17 was the day during which Saturnin and some other disciples made the hazardous journey to Herod's castle and were miraculously aided by the spirit of Elizabeth, John's mother, in retrieving his remains from the grounds—all but his head, which had been tossed into a rubbish heap. This would be retrieved by the holy women months later.

The Sun was at 11° Scorpio on November 2 AD 30, as Jesus was visiting relatives in Debrath:

> Joseph's brother…was called Elia. He had had five sons—of whom one named Jesse, now an old man, dwelt in that house. His wife was still living, and they had a family of six children, three sons and three daughters. Two of the sons were already between eighteen and twenty years old. Their names were Caleb and Aaron. Their father begged Jesus to receive them as disciples, which he did. They were to join the band when he should again pass through that part of the country. Jesse collected the taxes destined for the support of the Levites. He superintended also a cloth factory in which the wool that he purchased was cleansed, spun, and woven. Fine cloth was manufactured there, and a whole street was in Jesse's employ. He had also, in a long building, a machine for expressing the juice from various herbs, some of which were found on Tabor, and others were brought hither from a distance. The juice of some was used in dyeing; others, for beverages; and others, again, were made into perfumes. I saw hollow cylinders standing in troughs, in which the herbs were pressed by means of a heavy pounder. The pipes through which the expressed juice flowed ran outside of the building and were provided with spigots. When the pounders were not in

use, they were kept in place by means of wedges. They prepared also the oil of myrrh. Jesse and his whole family were very pious. His children went daily, and he often accompanied them, to pray on Tabor.[181]

The Sun and Mercury conjoined in Scorpio (8° rather than 12°) shortly after Christ began the forty-days' temptation in the wilderness, which lasted from October 21 to November 30 AD 29. The time between Advent and Christmas can also be a time of trials; in the first week, we may be confronted with the ahrimanic temptation to "turn stones into bread," to mineralize what is living. Particularly in our modern consumer culture, it becomes more and more difficult to enter the Holy Silence of this time of year.

Venus was conjunct Uranus (in Leo, rather than Aries) at the death of Lazarus, the result of a failed "temple sleep" enacted on him by his sister Mary Magdalene in the hope of appeasing his ever-growing hunger for a purely spiritual world. While we must avoid the temptation of base consumerism, we must avoid flipping to the other extreme of asceticism and total withdrawal from the world.

Venus and Saturn were square, opposite to today's degrees (Venus in Libra and Saturn in Cancer) April 5–6 AD 33. Here they give us the hope of the Resurrection, and the visitation that is possible through the healing conversation and burning hearts of Luke and Cleophas on the Road to Emmaus.

# DECEMBER 2021

## STARGAZING PREVIEW

As December begins, Venus, Saturn, and Jupiter will still be shining from the southwest as night falls. After Jupiter disappears in the west at 2200, the night sky will be without visible planets until Mars rises at 0600, our only morning star this month. The New Moon (17° Scorpio) on Saturday the 4th will create a Total Solar Eclipse over

Antarctica and the South Pacific; Australia, east Asia, and the Americas will experience it to a lesser degree.

Scorpio welcomes Mars, its classical ruler, on the 6th, just fifteen minutes after it crests the eastern horizon. The Moon passes beneath Venus, Saturn, and Jupiter on the 7th, 8th, and 9th, respectively. On the 10th, as Venus enters Capricorn, we are reminded to maintain the continuity between past and future.

The Moon finds its First Quarter (24° Aquarius) on Saturday the 11th. The night of the 13th–14th will be the peak of the glorious Geminid Meteor Shower, visible from both hemispheres. Gemini, the apparent radiant of the shower, rises around 1800, but at this time the waxing Moon will be high in the south. When the Moon leaves the night sky at 0300, take a look to the south for your best chance of seeing shooting stars sparkling before the Twins, flanked by Taurus on the right and Leo on the left. Good luck!

The 16th is the day that the Sun enters Sagittarius; can we not all imagine the magnificent chords of the Egmont Overture resounding from the heavens? Beethoven lovers among us will also cherish the 19th, the day on which the Sun, closely aligned with the Galactic Center, reaches its position at the birth of the great composer. On this same day, across the zodiac, December's Full Moon will shine upon us from 2° Gemini—the Sun's position at Pentecost! Winter's silence commences on Tuesday the 21st, marking (for the northern hemisphere) the longest night of the year. Sleep well.

If you're up before sunrise on Christmas Eve, you'll see the waning Moon in the southwest, just above *Regulus*. As the Moon continues to draw nearer to the Sun, it finds its Last Quarter (11° Virgo) on the 27th, recalling its zodiacal degree at the Walking on the Water. Look for it high in the southeast as Mars and *Antares* rise at 0600.

## DECEMBER COMMENTARIES

Already at the end of November an alignment between Mars and Uranus is taking shape; it lasts from November 25 through December 16. Their opposition is exact on December 6. Simultaneously,

November 27 and December 19, Mars is square Saturn, exact on December 8. See commentaries for both further on.

**December 4: New Moon 17°19' Scorpio.**

**December 5: Second Sunday of Advent.** There was a New Moon in Scorpio on October 24, 18 BC, at the conception of the Nathan Mary. The mother of the Nathan Jesus was, like him, a soul that had never incarnated before, the sister soul of Eve (who incarnated as the Solomon Mary, mother of the reincarnated Zarathustra). After the mysterious transformation of her son at the age of 12, the Nathan Mary died. Her husband married the Solomon Mary—whose son and husband had both died after the Union in the Temple—and so the reincarnated Eve adopted the Nathan Jesus, now with the ego of Zarathustra residing in his soul. Some seventeen years later, just prior to the Baptism in the Jordan, Jesus poured out his heart to his mother Mary. In doing so, the Zarathustra "I" left him, making room for the entry of Christ—and the soul of the Nathan Mary united with that of the Solomon Mary. It was at this point that she became the Most Holy Virgin, Eve restored to her pre-fallen state as Regina, Queen of the Angels. In four days we will celebrate the Feast of the Immaculate Conception—a celebration of one of only two *ex cathedra* (i.e., infallible) declarations made by the Pope (the other being the Assumption of the Virgin Mary)—see commentary for December 8. And in fact, the date of conception of the Solomon Mary coincides with the chosen date of the feast day: December 8, 22 BC.

Last week we celebrated the mineral element, the solid structure and foundation of all manifest reality. As we enter the second Sunday of Advent, we honor the plant kingdom, and the force of growth in all that lives in the cosmos. We strive to cultivate the Platonic virtue of *Temperance* in the face of the luciferic–ahrimanic temptation to "cast ourselves down from the pinnacle"—i.e., to "vegetize" the soul life, to be *in*temperate. We center our focus on the Christian virtue of *Faith* and the voices of the prophets—particularly John the Baptist—in preparing the way for the incarnation of the Logos.

**December 5: Mercury enters Sagittarius.**

**December 6: Venus enters Taurus.**

> Existence consumes being
> (*Sun in Scorpio*)
> Feel growth's power
> (*Venus in Taurus*)
> Attainment concludes joyful striving
> (*Mercury in Sagittarius*)
> And being effects being
> (*Mars in Libra*)
> As a flowing wave self-sustaining
> (*Jupiter in Aquarius*)
> And may the might of life's activity flower
> (*Saturn in Capricorn*)
> May existence feel existence!
> (*Moon in Sagittarius*)[182]

**December 6: Mars 18°5' Libra opposite Uranus 18°5' Aries.**

**December 8: Mars 19°6' Libra square Saturn 19°6' Capricorn.** Feast of the Immaculate Conception. Last month it was the New Moon and Venus who joined the Saturn–Uranus square, the former at the start of the month, the latter at the end. Now Mars joins them: Archangel Michael (Mars) redeeming Lucifer (Uranus) for the Virgin Mary–Sophia (Saturn). Mars was at these degrees of Libra January 30–31 AD 30:

> Jesus, from a teacher's chair and out in the open air, prepared the people for baptism, which the disciples administered. The baptismal basin was placed over a cistern into which the neophytes stepped, and which was filled with water to a certain height. The disciples had brought with them the baptismal robes, rolled up and wrapped around their person, which were put on the neophytes during the ceremony. They floated around them on the water. After the baptism a kind of little mantle was placed on their shoulders. At John's baptism, it was something like a stole and as wide as a hand towel, but at the baptism of Jesus it was more like a real little mantle on which was fastened a stole like a lappet trimmed with fringe. Among the

---

182 Steiner, *Twelve Cosmic Moods*.

## SIDEREAL GEOCENTRIC LONGITUDES : DECEMBER 2021 Gregorian at 0 hours UT

| DAY | ☉ | ☽ | ☊ | ☿ | ♀ | ♂ | ♃ | ♄ | ⛢ | ♆ | ♇ |
|---|---|---|---|---|---|---|---|---|---|---|---|
| 1 WE | 13 ♏ 57 | 27 ♍ 46 | 6 ♉ 41 | 14 ♏ 58 | 25 ♐ 26 | 26 ♎ 20 | 0 ♒ 20 | 13 ♑ 55 | 16 ♈ 43R | 25 ♒ 22R | 29 ♐ 59 |
| 2 TH | 14 58 | 12 ♎ 21 | 6 41 | 16 32 | 26 1 | 27 1 | 0 28 | 14 0 | 16 41 | 25 22D | 0 ♑ 1 |
| 3 FR | 15 59 | 27 16 | 6 42 | 18 6 | 26 34 | 27 43 | 0 36 | 14 5 | 16 39 | 25 22 | 0 2 |
| 4 SA | 17 0 | 12 ♏ 26 | 6 42R | 19 40 | 27 6 | 28 24 | 0 45 | 14 10 | 16 37 | 25 22 | 0 4 |
| 5 SU | 18 1 | 27 40 | 6 42 | 21 14 | 27 37 | 29 6 | 0 53 | 14 15 | 16 35 | 25 22 | 0 5 |
| 6 MO | 19 2 | 12 ♐ 50 | 6 41 | 22 48 | 28 6 | 29 48 | 1 2 | 14 20 | 16 33 | 25 22 | 0 7 |
| 7 TU | 20 2 | 27 45 | 6 39 | 24 22 | 28 33 | 0 ♏ 29 | 1 11 | 14 25 | 16 31 | 25 22 | 0 8 |
| 8 WE | 21 3 | 12 ♑ 19 | 6 37 | 25 56 | 28 58 | 1 11 | 1 20 | 14 30 | 16 29 | 25 23 | 0 10 |
| 9 TH | 22 4 | 26 26 | 6 36 | 27 30 | 29 22 | 1 53 | 1 29 | 14 35 | 16 27 | 25 23 | 0 12 |
| 10 FR | 23 5 | 10 ♒ 6 | 6 34 | 29 5 | 29 44 | 2 34 | 1 38 | 14 41 | 16 25 | 25 23 | 0 13 |
| 11 SA | 24 6 | 23 19 | 6 34 | 0 ♐ 39 | 0 ♑ 4 | 3 16 | 1 47 | 14 46 | 16 23 | 25 23 | 0 15 |
| 12 SU | 25 7 | 6 ♓ 8 | 6 34D | 2 13 | 0 22 | 3 58 | 1 57 | 14 51 | 16 21 | 25 24 | 0 17 |
| 13 MO | 26 8 | 18 38 | 6 35 | 3 47 | 0 38 | 4 40 | 2 6 | 14 57 | 16 20 | 25 24 | 0 18 |
| 14 TU | 27 9 | 0 ♈ 51 | 6 37 | 5 21 | 0 51 | 5 22 | 2 16 | 15 2 | 16 18 | 25 24 | 0 20 |
| 15 WE | 28 10 | 12 52 | 6 39 | 6 56 | 1 3 | 6 4 | 2 26 | 15 8 | 16 16 | 25 25 | 0 22 |
| 16 TH | 29 11 | 24 46 | 6 40 | 8 30 | 1 12 | 6 46 | 2 36 | 15 14 | 16 15 | 25 25 | 0 24 |
| 17 FR | 0 ♐ 12 | 6 ♉ 35 | 6 41R | 10 4 | 1 19 | 7 28 | 2 46 | 15 19 | 16 13 | 25 26 | 0 25 |
| 18 SA | 1 13 | 18 22 | 6 40 | 11 39 | 1 24 | 8 10 | 2 56 | 15 25 | 16 12 | 25 26 | 0 27 |
| 19 SU | 2 14 | 0 ♊ 11 | 6 38 | 13 13 | 1 26 | 8 52 | 3 6 | 15 31 | 16 10 | 25 27 | 0 29 |
| 20 MO | 3 15 | 12 2 | 6 35 | 14 48 | 1 26R | 9 34 | 3 17 | 15 37 | 16 9 | 25 28 | 0 31 |
| 21 TU | 4 17 | 23 59 | 6 30 | 16 22 | 1 24 | 10 16 | 3 27 | 15 43 | 16 7 | 25 28 | 0 32 |
| 22 WE | 5 18 | 6 ♋ 1 | 6 25 | 17 56 | 1 18 | 10 59 | 3 38 | 15 49 | 16 6 | 25 29 | 0 34 |
| 23 TH | 6 19 | 18 13 | 6 19 | 19 30 | 1 11 | 11 41 | 3 48 | 15 55 | 16 4 | 25 30 | 0 36 |
| 24 FR | 7 20 | 0 ♌ 35 | 6 14 | 21 4 | 1 1 | 12 23 | 3 59 | 16 1 | 16 3 | 25 30 | 0 38 |
| 25 SA | 8 21 | 13 10 | 6 10 | 22 37 | 0 48 | 13 6 | 4 10 | 16 7 | 16 2 | 25 31 | 0 40 |
| 26 SU | 9 22 | 26 1 | 6 8 | 24 10 | 0 33 | 13 48 | 4 21 | 16 13 | 16 1 | 25 32 | 0 42 |
| 27 MO | 10 23 | 9 ♍ 10 | 6 7 | 25 42 | 0 16 | 14 30 | 4 33 | 16 19 | 15 59 | 25 33 | 0 44 |
| 28 TU | 11 24 | 22 40 | 6 8D | 27 14 | 29 ♐ 56 | 15 13 | 4 44 | 16 26 | 15 58 | 25 34 | 0 45 |
| 29 WE | 12 25 | 6 ♎ 34 | 6 9 | 28 44 | 29 34 | 15 55 | 4 55 | 16 32 | 15 57 | 25 35 | 0 47 |
| 30 TH | 13 27 | 20 51 | 6 10 | 0 ♑ 14 | 29 9 | 16 38 | 5 7 | 16 38 | 15 56 | 25 36 | 0 49 |
| 31 FR | 14 28 | 5 ♏ 30 | 6 11R | 1 42 | 28 43 | 17 21 | 5 18 | 16 45 | 15 55 | 25 37 | 0 51 |

### INGRESSES :

| | | | | | |
|---|---|---|---|---|---|
| 1 | ☽ → ♎ | 3:42 | 16 | ☽ → ♉ | 10:37 |
| | ♇ → ♑ | 12:25 | | ☉ → ♐ | 19: 8 |
| 3 | ☽ → ♏ | 4:20 | 18 | ☽ → ♊ | 23:38 |
| 5 | ☽ → ♐ | 3:40 | 21 | ☽ → ♋ | 12: 1 |
| 6 | ♂ → ♏ | 7: 8 | 23 | ☽ → ♌ | 22:52 |
| 7 | ☽ → ♑ | 3:39 | 26 | ☽ → ♍ | 7:20 |
| 9 | ☽ → ♒ | 6:11 | 27 | ♀ → ♐ | 19: 6 |
| 10 | ☿ → ♐ | 14: 8 | 28 | ☽ → ♎ | 12:44 |
| | ♀ → ♑ | 19:13 | 29 | ☿ → ♑ | 20:16 |
| 11 | ☽ → ♓ | 12:25 | 30 | ☽ → ♏ | 15: 3 |
| 13 | ☽ → ♈ | 22:19 | | | |

### ASPECTS & ECLIPSES :

| | | | | | | | | | | | |
|---|---|---|---|---|---|---|---|---|---|---|---|
| 2 | ☽ ☍ ⛢ | 7: 0 | | ♂ □ ♃ | 6:19 | 18 | ☽ ☌ A | 2:19 | 27 | ☉ □ ☽ | 2:22 |
| 3 | ☽ ☌ ♂ | 0:44 | 9 | ☽ ☌ ♃ | 8:51 | 19 | ☉ ☍ ☽ | 4:34 | 29 | ☿ ☌ ♀ | 10:26 |
| | ☽ ☌ ☋ | 14:57 | | ☽ □S ☊ | 17:44 | 20 | ☽ ☍ ☿ | 6:24 | | ☽ ☍ ⛢ | 15:50 |
| 4 | ☉ ● T | 7:32 | 11 | ☉ □ ☽ | 1:34 | 21 | ☽ ☍ ♇ | 13: 8 | 30 | ☿ ☌ ♇ | 9:49 |
| | ☉ ☌ ☽ | 7:41 | | ☽ ☌ ♆ | 3:49 | | ☽ ☍ ♀ | 14:42 | 31 | ☽ ☌ ☋ | 1: 6 |
| | ☽ ☌ P | 10: 2 | | ♀ ☌ ♇ | 16:12 | 22 | ☽ ☍ ♄ | 19:27 | | ☽ ☌ ♂ | 19:59 |
| | ☽ ☌ ☿ | 12:41 | 12 | ☉ □ ♆ | 6:29 | 24 | ☽ ☍ ♃ | 6:38 | | | |
| 7 | ☽ ☌ ♀ | 1:20 | 15 | ☽ ☌ ⛢ | 6:49 | | ♄ □ ⛢ | 7: 1 | | | |
| | ☽ ☌ ♇ | 3:54 | | ♂ ☍ ☊ | 20:37 | | ☽ □N ☊ | 10:46 | | | |
| | ☿ □ ♆ | 15:20 | 17 | ☽ ☌ ☊ | 0:11 | 25 | ♀ ☌ ♇ | 12:15 | | | |
| 8 | ☽ ☌ ♄ | 3:41 | | ☽ ☍ ♂ | 1:54 | | ☽ ☍ ♆ | 23: 7 | | | |

## SIDEREAL HELIOCENTRIC LONGITUDES : DECEMBER 2021 Gregorian at 0 hours UT

| DAY | Sid. Time | ☿ | ♀ | ⊕ | ♂ | ♃ | ♄ | ⛢ | ♆ | ♇ | Vernal Point |
|---|---|---|---|---|---|---|---|---|---|---|---|
| 1 WE | 4:40:18 | 17 ♏ 7 | 20 ♈ 46 | 13 ♉ 58 | 15 ♎ 25 | 11 ♒ 24 | 18 ♑ 52 | 18 ♈ 2 | 27 ♒ 13 | 1 ♑ 11 | 4 ♓ 57'15" |
| 2 TH | 4:44:15 | 19 51 | 22 22 | 14 59 | 15 54 | 11 29 | 18 54 | 18 2 | 27 13 | 1 11 | 4 ♓ 57'15" |
| 3 FR | 4:48:11 | 22 36 | 23 58 | 15 59 | 16 24 | 11 35 | 18 56 | 18 3 | 27 14 | 1 11 | 4 ♓ 57'15" |
| 4 SA | 4:52: 8 | 25 21 | 25 35 | 17 0 | 16 53 | 11 40 | 18 57 | 18 4 | 27 14 | 1 12 | 4 ♓ 57'15" |
| 5 SU | 4:56: 4 | 28 6 | 27 11 | 18 1 | 17 22 | 11 45 | 18 59 | 18 4 | 27 15 | 1 12 | 4 ♓ 57'15" |
| 6 MO | 5: 0: 1 | 0 ♐ 51 | 28 47 | 19 2 | 17 52 | 11 51 | 19 1 | 18 5 | 27 15 | 1 12 | 4 ♓ 57'14" |
| 7 TU | 5: 3:57 | 3 38 | 0 ♉ 23 | 20 3 | 18 21 | 11 56 | 19 3 | 18 6 | 27 15 | 1 12 | 4 ♓ 57'14" |
| 8 WE | 5: 7:54 | 6 25 | 2 0 | 21 4 | 18 51 | 12 2 | 19 5 | 18 6 | 27 16 | 1 13 | 4 ♓ 57'14" |
| 9 TH | 5:11:50 | 9 13 | 3 36 | 22 5 | 19 21 | 12 7 | 19 7 | 18 7 | 27 16 | 1 13 | 4 ♓ 57'14" |
| 10 FR | 5:15:47 | 12 3 | 5 12 | 23 6 | 19 50 | 12 12 | 19 9 | 18 8 | 27 16 | 1 13 | 4 ♓ 57'14" |
| 11 SA | 5:19:44 | 14 54 | 6 49 | 24 7 | 20 20 | 12 18 | 19 10 | 18 8 | 27 17 | 1 14 | 4 ♓ 57'14" |
| 12 SU | 5:23:40 | 17 47 | 8 25 | 25 8 | 20 50 | 12 23 | 19 12 | 18 9 | 27 17 | 1 14 | 4 ♓ 57'14" |
| 13 MO | 5:27:37 | 20 42 | 10 2 | 26 9 | 21 19 | 12 29 | 19 14 | 18 10 | 27 17 | 1 14 | 4 ♓ 57'13" |
| 14 TU | 5:31:33 | 23 39 | 11 38 | 27 10 | 21 49 | 12 34 | 19 16 | 18 10 | 27 18 | 1 14 | 4 ♓ 57'13" |
| 15 WE | 5:35:30 | 26 39 | 13 15 | 28 11 | 22 19 | 12 39 | 19 18 | 18 11 | 27 18 | 1 15 | 4 ♓ 57'13" |
| 16 TH | 5:39:26 | 29 42 | 14 51 | 29 12 | 22 49 | 12 45 | 19 20 | 18 12 | 27 19 | 1 15 | 4 ♓ 57'13" |
| 17 FR | 5:43:23 | 2 ♑ 47 | 16 28 | 0 ♊ 13 | 23 19 | 12 50 | 19 22 | 18 12 | 27 19 | 1 15 | 4 ♓ 57'13" |
| 18 SA | 5:47:19 | 5 56 | 18 5 | 1 14 | 23 49 | 12 56 | 19 23 | 18 13 | 27 19 | 1 16 | 4 ♓ 57'13" |
| 19 SU | 5:51:16 | 9 9 | 19 41 | 2 15 | 24 19 | 13 1 | 19 25 | 18 14 | 27 20 | 1 16 | 4 ♓ 57'13" |
| 20 MO | 5:55:13 | 12 25 | 21 18 | 3 16 | 24 49 | 13 6 | 19 27 | 18 14 | 27 20 | 1 16 | 4 ♓ 57'12" |
| 21 TU | 5:59: 9 | 15 46 | 22 55 | 4 17 | 25 20 | 13 12 | 19 29 | 18 15 | 27 20 | 1 17 | 4 ♓ 57'12" |
| 22 WE | 6: 3: 6 | 19 11 | 24 31 | 5 18 | 25 50 | 13 17 | 19 31 | 18 16 | 27 21 | 1 17 | 4 ♓ 57'12" |
| 23 TH | 6: 7: 2 | 22 41 | 26 8 | 6 19 | 26 20 | 13 23 | 19 33 | 18 16 | 27 21 | 1 17 | 4 ♓ 57'12" |
| 24 FR | 6:10:59 | 26 16 | 27 45 | 7 20 | 26 50 | 13 28 | 19 35 | 18 17 | 27 21 | 1 17 | 4 ♓ 57'12" |
| 25 SA | 6:14:55 | 29 56 | 29 22 | 8 22 | 27 21 | 13 33 | 19 36 | 18 18 | 27 22 | 1 18 | 4 ♓ 57'12" |
| 26 SU | 6:18:52 | 3 ♒ 43 | 0 ♊ 59 | 9 23 | 27 51 | 13 39 | 19 38 | 18 18 | 27 22 | 1 18 | 4 ♓ 57'12" |
| 27 MO | 6:22:48 | 7 35 | 2 36 | 10 24 | 28 22 | 13 44 | 19 40 | 18 19 | 27 23 | 1 18 | 4 ♓ 57'11" |
| 28 TU | 6:26:45 | 11 35 | 4 12 | 11 25 | 28 52 | 13 50 | 19 42 | 18 20 | 27 23 | 1 19 | 4 ♓ 57'11" |
| 29 WE | 6:30:42 | 15 41 | 5 49 | 12 26 | 29 23 | 13 55 | 19 44 | 18 20 | 27 23 | 1 19 | 4 ♓ 57'11" |
| 30 TH | 6:34:38 | 19 55 | 7 26 | 13 27 | 29 54 | 14 0 | 19 46 | 18 21 | 27 24 | 1 19 | 4 ♓ 57'11" |
| 31 FR | 6:38:35 | 24 16 | 9 3 | 14 28 | 0 ♏ 24 | 14 6 | 19 48 | 18 22 | 27 24 | 1 19 | 4 ♓ 57'11" |

### INGRESSES :

| | | |
|---|---|---|
| 5 | ☿ → ♐ | 16:34 |
| 6 | ♀ → ♉ | 18:11 |
| 16 | ☿ → ♑ | 2:21 |
| | ⊕ → ♊ | 18:54 |
| 25 | ☿ → ♒ | 0:25 |
| | ♀ → ♊ | 9:27 |
| 30 | ♂ → ♏ | 5: 3 |

### ASPECTS (HELIOCENTRIC +MOON(TYCHONIC)) :

| | | | | | | | | | | | | | | |
|---|---|---|---|---|---|---|---|---|---|---|---|---|---|---|
| 1 | ☽ □ ♇ | 5:40 | 7 | ☽ ☌ ♇ | 5:38 | | ♀ □ ♃ | 14:40 | | ☿ □ ⛢ | 17:34 | | ☽ □ ♀ | 10:24 |
| 2 | ☽ ☌ ♂ | 5:57 | 8 | ☽ □ ⛢ | 9:45 | 15 | ☽ ☌ ⛢ | 10:42 | 22 | ☿ ☌ ♄ | 2:21 | 28 | ☿ ☌ ♃ | 13:32 |
| | ☽ ☍ ⛢ | 9:12 | | ☽ □ ♂ | 11:24 | | ☽ □ ♄ | 12:58 | 23 | ☽ □ ⛢ | 0: 6 | | ☽ □ ♇ | 15: 0 |
| | ☽ □ ♄ | 10:36 | | ☽ ☌ ♄ | 11:26 | | ☽ ☍ ♂ | 19:53 | | ☽ ☍ ♄ | 2:36 | 29 | ☽ ☍ ⛢ | 19:50 |
| | ☽ ☍ ♀ | 18: 6 | | ♂ □ ♄ | 12: 3 | 16 | ☿ ☌ ♇ | 12: 7 | | ☿ □S ☊ | 5:52 | | ☽ □ ♄ | 22:11 |
| 3 | ☿ ☌ A | 1:20 | 9 | ☽ □ ♀ | 14: 9 | 17 | ☽ □ ♃ | 12:49 | | ☽ ☍ ☿ | 12:13 | 30 | ☽ ☌ ♂ | 15:25 |
| | ☽ □ ♃ | 22:47 | 10 | ☽ ☌ ♃ | 3:48 | | ☽ ☌ ♀ | 23:18 | | ☽ □ ♂ | 16:28 | 31 | ☽ □ ♃ | 13:56 |
| 4 | ☿ □ ♆ | 16:32 | 11 | ☽ ☌ ♆ | 7:20 | 18 | ☽ □ ♆ | 18:12 | | ♀ □ ♆ | 18: 9 | | ☿ ☌ ♆ | 16:49 |
| | ☽ □ ♆ | 23:19 | 13 | ☽ □ ☿ | 5:19 | 19 | ♂ ☌ ☋ | 17:10 | 24 | ☿ □ ♂ | 4:27 | | | |
| 5 | ☽ ☌ ☿ | 0:48 | 14 | ☽ □ ♇ | 0:46 | 20 | ♀ ☌ ☊ | 7:55 | 25 | ☽ ☍ ♃ | 0:44 | | | |
| 6 | ♂ ☍ ⛢ | 10:51 | | ⊕ □ ♆ | 3: 8 | 21 | ☽ ☍ ♇ | 14:34 | 26 | ☽ ☍ ♆ | 2:30 | | | |

newly baptized were mostly tender youths and very old men, for many of the middle-aged were postponed until they should become less unworthy. Jesus healed many sick of fevers and many dropsical who had been carried thither on litters. The possessed among the pagans were not so numerous as among the Jews.

Jesus blessed also the drinking water, which was not good here. It was muddy and brackish. It was collected among the rocks whence it was brought in bottles and poured into a reservoir. Jesus blessed it crosswise, and rested his hand upon several different points of the surface....

On their return journey [the next day] to the inn outside Ono, Jesus and the disciples spent the greater part of the day on the road, only one hour long, from Nebo to the Jordan ferry. Jesus taught the whole way. The road was bordered by huts and tents in which the people from Nebo sold to travelers fruit and distilled wine. It was these vendors that Jesus instructed. Before evening he returned with the disciples to his inn at the place of baptism.[183]

December 7–13: **Venus joins the Node**, exact on the 10th.

**December 10: Venus conjunct Node 6°34' Taurus.** Venus was at this degree on February 17 AD 31:

After visiting a school in Ornithopolis this morning, Jesus and the disciples set off for Sarepta, the town where the widow had dwelt at the time of Elijah (1 Kings 17:10). Arriving at the Jewish settlement on the outskirts of Sarepta, they were given a joyful reception. The apostles brought bread and clothing from Sarepta to be distributed to the poor Jews in the settlement.[184]

Less than a week later, Venus and Node were conjunct at 17° Taurus:

Today, the tax collectors with whom Jesus was staying distributed their wealth to the poor and needy. They were moved to do so by Jesus's teaching. Jesus taught at the tax collectors' custom house before a crowd of both Jews and pagans. Some Pharisees, who were visiting Gessur for the sabbath, criticized Jesus for mixing with tax collectors and pagans. That evening, he taught at the synagogue. Again, a dispute arose with the Pharisees.[185]

Our capacity for generosity, which ought to be heightened at this time of year but sometimes suffers under the weight of anxiety, is given a needed boost by Venus today. Tomorrow, December 11, we celebrate the Feast of Santa Lucia, further encouraging this mood of generosity. The next day, December 12, is the third Sunday of Advent: traditionally this third week of Advent is a break from the fast that typically lasts from the first Sunday of Advent (or even Martinmas) all the way to Christmas. It is a week during which we honor the animal kingdom, the psyche within all ensouled beings. We cultivate the Platonic virtue of *Fortitude,* or Courage, in the face of the luciferic temptation to bow down in order to gain earthly power. And the Christian virtue this week is *Joy*—the joy experienced by the shepherds in the fields, as the Angels proclaimed to them:

Glory to God in the Highest Places
And Peace on Earth
Among men of Good Will[186]

We can perhaps experience this as a transformation of the Hermetic Axiom "As Above, So Below"—and in our time, a further transformation of this injunction from the Angels in the form of "The Foundation Stone Meditation," given at Christmas 98 years ago:

O Light Divine
O Sun of Christ
Warm Thou our Hearts
Enlighten Thou our Heads
That Good may become
What from our Hearts we would found
And from our Heads direct
With single Purpose.[187]

---

183 ACE, vol. 1, pp. 399, 401.
184 ACE, vol. 2, p. 313.
185 Ibid., p. 314.
186 Adapted from Hart, *The New Testament: A Translation,* Luke 2:14, p. 108.
187 Steiner, *The Christmas Conference for the Foundation of the General Anthroposophical Society 1923/1924.*

December 9–19: **Sun is square Neptune**, exact on the 14th.

**December 14: Sun 27°18' Scorpio square Neptune 27°18' Aquarius.** Simultaneously, Venus is square Jupiter December 11–17, also exact on the 14th: **Venus 12°37' Taurus square Jupiter 12°37' Aquarius.** What a soulful group—Sun, Venus, Jupiter, Neptune—to have in the fixed signs at this time of year. The Sun was at this degree on November 18 AD 30 at the first raising of the daughter of Jairus, Salome:

The mother did not please me. She was cold and wanting in confidence. The father, too, was not a warm friend of Jesus. He would not willingly do anything to displease the Pharisees. It was anxiety and necessity alone that had driven him to Jesus. He was actuated by a double motive. If Jesus cured his child, she would be restored to him; if not, he would have prepared a triumph for the Pharisees. Still, the cure of Cornelius's servant had greatly impressed him and awakened in him a feeling of confidence. The little daughter was not tall, and she was very much wasted. At most, I should say she was eleven years old, and even at that small for her age, for the Jewish girls of twelve are usually fully grown. She lay on the couch enveloped in a long garment. Jesus raised her lightly in his arms, held her on his breast, and breathed upon her. Then I saw something wonderful. Near the right side of the corpse was a luminous figure in a sphere of light. When Jesus breathed upon the little girl, that figure entered her mouth as a tiny human form of light. Then he laid the body down upon the couch, grasped one of the wrists, and said: "Damsel, arise!" The girl sat up in her bed. Jesus still held her by the hand. Then she stood up, opened her eyes, and supported by the hand of Jesus, stepped from the couch to the floor. Jesus led her, weak and tremulous, to the arms of her parents. They had watched the progress of the event at first coldly, though anxiously, then trembling with agitation, and now they were out of themselves for very joy. Jesus bade them give the child to eat and to make no unnecessary noise over the affair. After receiving the thanks of the father, he went down to the city. The mother was confused and stupefied. Her words of thanks were few. The news soon spread through the mourners that the maiden was alive. They immediately returned, some confused at their former incredulity, others still uttering vulgar pleasantries, and went into the house, where they saw the damsel eating.[188]

Venus was at 12° Taurus on November 28 AD 29, during the second temptation of Christ—the dual temptation of Lucifer and Ahriman to cast himself down from the pinnacle of the temple:

Toward evening of the following day, I saw Satan in the form of a majestic angel sweeping down toward Jesus with a noise like the rushing wind. He was clad in a sort of military dress such as I have seen St. Michael wear. But in the midst of his greatest splendor, one might detect something sinister and horrible. He addressed boasting words to Jesus, something in this strain: "I will show thee who I am, and what I can do, and how the angels bear me up in their hands. Look yonder, there is Jerusalem! Behold the temple! I shall place thee upon its highest pinnacle. Then do thou show what thou canst do, and see whether the angels will carry thee down." While Satan thus spoke and pointed out Jerusalem and the temple, I seemed to see them both quite near, just in front of the mountain. But I think that it was only an illusion. Jesus made no reply, and Satan seized him by the shoulders and bore him through the air. He flew low toward Jerusalem, and placed Jesus upon the highest point of one of the four towers that rose from the four corners of the temple, and which I had not before noticed. The tower to which Satan bore Jesus was on the west side toward Zion and opposite the citadel Antonia. The mount upon which the temple stood was very steep on that side. The towers were like prisons, and in one of them were kept the costly garments of the high priest. The roofs of these towers were flat, so that one could walk on them; but from the center rose a hollow, conical turret capped by a large sphere, upon which there was standing room for two. From that position, one could view the whole temple below.

It was on the loftiest point of the tower that Satan placed Jesus, who uttered no word. Then Satan flew to the ground, and cried up to him:

---

188 ACE, vol. 2, p. 151.

"If thou art the Son of God, show thy power and come down also, for it is written: 'He has given his angels charge over thee, and in their hands shall they bear thee up, lest perhaps thou dash thy foot against a stone.'" Jesus replied: "It is written again: Thou shalt not tempt the Lord, thy God."[189]

**December 16:** Mercury enters Capricorn; Sun enters Sagittarius.

> Growth attains power of existence
>     (*Sun in Sagittarius*)
> Feel growth's power
>     (*Venus in Taurus*)
> To be strong in the present
>     (*Mercury in Capricorn*)
> And being effects being
>     (*Mars in Libra*)
> As a flowing wave self-sustaining
>     (*Jupiter in Aquarius*)
> And may the might of life's activity flower
>     (*Saturn in Capricorn*)
> O radiant being, appear!
>     (*Moon in Taurus*)[190]

December 14–17, **Mercury conjoins Pluto**, exact on the 16th: **Mercury and Pluto 1°15' Capricorn.** Mercury was at this degree on April 2 AD 33, as Christ and his apostles were on their way to the Cenacle, the upper room in which the Last Supper—and first Holy Eucharist—would take place later that evening:

> Jesus and his companions walked here and there around the Mount of Olives, through the valley of Jehosaphat, and even as far as Mount Calvary. During the whole walk, Jesus gave uninterrupted instructions. Among other things he told the apostles that until now he had given them his bread and his wine, but that today he would give them his flesh and his blood. He would bestow upon them, he would make over to them, all that he had. While uttering these words, the countenance of the Lord wore a touching expression, as if he were pouring his whole soul out, as if he were languishing with love to give himself to humanity. His

disciples did not comprehend his words—they thought that he was speaking of the paschal lamb. No words can say how affectionate, how patient Jesus was in his last instructions both at Bethany and on his way to Jerusalem.[191]

**December 19: Full Moon 2°26' Gemini**, aligned with the Galactic Center. Fourth Sunday of Advent. Today marks the day that we honor the Human Being, the microcosmic summary of the macrocosm—from the deepest depths of subnature up to the highest heights of the Luminous Holy Trinity. The Platonic virtue we cultivate, in the face of the "fourth temptation" of megalomania is *Wisdom*— that Wisdom which is the harmony of Obedience, Chastity and Poverty in deed, feeling, and thought. The Christian virtue we cultivate this week is *Love*—and our focus is the Christ Child and the Virgin Mary. Considering the Full Moon's alignment with the Galactic Center, perhaps the best meditation for today as we turn our gaze to Christmas in six days' time, is the Gabrielic imagination, appropriate to this time of year—the imagination of the fifth apocalyptic seal, the heavenly Sophia:

> And a great sign was seen in heaven: a woman garbed with the sun, and the moon beneath her feet, and on her head a chaplet of twelve stars, and she was pregnant, and she cries out, enduring birth pangs, and in an agony to give birth. And another sign was seen in heaven, and look: a great flame-hued dragon who had seven heads and ten horns and on his heads seven diadems, and his tail drags along one third of the stars of heaven, and he cast them onto the Earth. And the dragon stood before the woman who was about to give birth so that, when she should give birth, he might devour her child. And she bore a son, a male child, who is about to shepherd all the gentiles with a rod of iron, and her child was seized away to God and to his throne. And the woman fled into the wilderness, there where she has a place prepared by God, so that they might nourish her for twelve hundred and sixty days.[192]

---

189 ACE, vol. 1, p. 369.
190 Steiner, *Twelve Cosmic Moods.*

---

191 ACE, vol. 3, p. 74.
192 Hart, *The New Testament: A Translation.* Rev. 12:1–6, p. 514.

December 21–23, **Mercury conjoins Saturn,** exact on the 22nd.

**December 22: Mercury and Saturn 19°31' Capricorn.** At the same time, **Venus is square Neptune** December 20–26, exact on the 23rd.

**December 23: Venus 27°21' Taurus square Neptune 27°21' Aquarius.** August to October AD 32, Christ traveled with three (eventually four) shepherd youths mainly northeast toward Ur and Babylonia, the Tigris and Euphrates, to visit the tent city of the Mensor the Gold King. After visiting them, they spent over two months traveling across the desert southwest to Heliopolis in Egypt. They set out for this journey on October 13 AD 32, when Mercury was 18° Capricorn opposite Saturn 18° Cancer:

> Today Jesus and the four youths set off on the long journey to Egypt, traveling westward through the Arabian desert....
>
> From the castle of the idols, Jesus's route now lay toward the west. He traveled quickly with his four companions, pausing nowhere, but ever hurrying on. First, they crossed a sandy desert, toiled slowly up a steep mountain ridge, pursued their way over a country covered with vegetation, then through low bushes like juniper bushes, whose branches, meeting overhead, formed a covered walk. After that they came to a stony region overrun with ivy, thence through meadows and woods until they reached a river, not rapid, but deep, over which they crossed on a raft of beams.[193]

December 21 was the winter solstice, the shortest day of the year in the northern hemisphere. We enter into the time of the Earth's wakefulness, when we must go into the wilderness, like the heavenly Sophia or Christ and the shepherds—yet despite the fact that winter is a wilderness, a place of nourishment has been prepared for us. It is our time of inner renewal, of cultivating the light and fire within, so that we have the strength for good deeds by the time we reach St. John's in six months.

Venus was 28° Taurus on March 6, 2 BC, at the conception of the Nathan Jesus—the birth of whom we celebrate on December 25. This is the Nativity described in the Gospel of Luke, the child born in a cave used as a barn, and laid in a manger for a crib. In esoteric lore, this being is known as the sole incarnation of a being with many names: the sister soul of Adam, Krishna, Apollo. He is a magical blend of purity, innocence, and simplicity with the stature of the warrior (both Apollo and Krishna are associated with charioteers). And radiating into the astral body of this baby, via the angelic host above, is Gautama Buddha—a being of purest compassion. How can we learn to blend these three: militant stature—awakened compassion—childlike simplicity? *Michael Sophia in Nomine Christi.*

**December 25: Christmas Day: Mercury enters Aquarius; Venus enters Gemini.**

> Growth attains power of existence
> (*Sun in Sagittarius*)
> Set repose in movement
> (*Venus in Gemini*)
> Found boundaries in its own depths
> (*Mercury in Aquarius*)
> And being effects being
> (*Mars in Libra*)
> As a flowing wave self-sustaining
> (*Jupiter in Aquarius*)
> And may the might of life's activity flower
> (*Saturn in Capricorn*)
> With senses' might, arise!
> (*Moon in Leo*)[194]

Today we discover the fulfillment of Advent, and embark on the "thinnest" time of the year: the twelve Holy Nights. Each of these nights plants the seed for the coming year; December 24–25 lays the foundation for the Sun's journey through Sagittarius (Dec. 16–Jan. 14, 2022), the next evening Capricorn (Jan. 14–Feb. 13, 2022), and so on. It is good practice to bring clear intentions and prayers into the night, and to keep a record of one's dreams or first waking impressions. These can be of great value as the year carries on.

December 27–29, **Mercury conjoins Jupiter,** exact on the 28th.

---

193 ACE, vol. 2, p. 517.

194 Steiner, *Twelve Cosmic Moods.*

**December 28: Mercury and Jupiter 13°53' Aquarius.** Mercury was at this degree on November 29 AD 29, the day of the ahrimanic temptation to turn stones into bread. It was also at this degree on February 12 AD 31:

In the company of Peter, John, and James the Greater, Jesus healed the sick at many homes in Dan. He was followed by an old pagan woman from Ornithopolis, who was crippled on one side. Jesus seemed to ignore her, for he was concerned solely with healing the Jews. Nevertheless, she begged him to come and heal her daughter, who was possessed. Jesus replied that it was not yet time, that he wanted to avoid giving offence, and that he would not help the pagans before the Jews. Later that afternoon, the Syrophoenician woman from Ornithopolis approached Jesus and again begged him to drive the unclean spirit out of her daughter. There then followed the exorcism of her daughter, as described in Matthew 15:21–28. Jesus asked her whether she herself wished to be healed, but the Syrophoenician woman replied that she was not worthy, and that she asked only for her daughter's cure. Then Jesus laid one hand upon her head, the other on her side, and said, "Straighten up! May it be done to you as you also will it to be done! The devil has gone out of your daughter." The woman stood upright and cried out: "O Lord, I see my daughter lying in bed well and at peace!"[195]

Perhaps this can be our meditation through the Holy Nights, and for all of the coming year: "Straighten up!"—all will be made well.

**December 30: Mars enters Scorpio.**

Growth attains power of existence
   (*Sun in Sagittarius*)
Set repose in movement
   (*Venus in Gemini*)
Found boundaries in its own depths
   (*Mercury in Aquarius*)

In growth activity persists
   (*Mars in Scorpio*)
As a flowing wave self-sustaining
   (*Jupiter in Aquarius*)
And may the might of life's activity flower
   (*Saturn in Capricorn*)
Being sustains beings!
   (*Moon in Scorpio*)[196]

With this, we come to the mantra that will hold good through New Year's Eve, the configuration with which we will begin 2022. There is perhaps a bit more sobriety and equanimity in this mantra in contrast that with which we began the year. Whereas 2021 seemed to be a year to be met with enthusiasm and vigor, 2022 is asking for calm persistence.

We can end our meditations for the year with the reminder from the final configuration on the 31st.

**December 31: Mercury conjunct Neptune 27°24'**—once more our gaze is drawn to the Assumption of the Virgin Mary. Let us no longer ignore our need for the Divine Feminine—she who is Silence to counterbalance the Word, Stillness in counterpoise to Movement, Death as the companion to Life:

It is said that "nature has a horror of emptiness" (*horror vacui*). The spiritual counter-truth here is that, "the Spirit has a horror of fullness." It is necessary to create a natural emptiness—and this is what renunciation achieves—in order for the spiritual to manifest itself.... Revelation presupposes emptiness—space put at its disposal—in order to manifest itself.[197]

This void, this absolute emptiness, is made possible for us only through the agency of *Kore Kosmu*—the Virgin of Perfect Night.

---

195 Ibid., p. 308.

196 Steiner, *Twelve Cosmic Moods*.

197 Anonymous, *Meditations on the Tarot*. (Brooklyn, NY: Angelico Press, 2019) p. 79.

"The stars are the expression of love in the cosmic ether.... To see a star means to feel a caress that has been prompted by love.... To gaze at the stars is to become aware of the love proceeding from divine spiritual beings.... The stars are signs and tokens of the presence of gods in the universe." (*Karmic Relationships*, vol. 7, June 8, 1924)

"We must see in the shining stars the outer signs of colonies of spirits in the cosmos. Wherever a star is seen in the heavens, there—in that direction—is a colony of spirits." (*Karmic Relationships*, vol. 6, June 1, 1924)

"They looked up above all to what is represented by the zodiac. And they regarded what the human being bears within as the spirit in connection with the constellations, the glory of the fixed stars, the spiritual powers whom they knew to be there in the stars." (*Karmic Relationships*, vol. 4, Sept. 12, 1924)

# GLOSSARY

This glossary of entries relating to Esoteric Christianity lists only some of the specialized terms used in the articles and commentaries of *Star Wisdom*. Owing to limited space, the entries are very brief, and the reader is encouraged to study the foundational works of Rudolf Steiner for a more complete understanding of these terms.

**Ahriman**: An adversarial being identified by the great prophet Zarathustra during the ancient Persian cultural epoch (5067–2907 BC) as an opponent to the Sun God *Ahura Mazda* (obs.; "Aura of the Sun"). Also called Satan, Ahriman represents one aspect of the Dragon. Ahriman's influence leads to materialistic thinking devoid of feeling, empathy, and moral conscience. Ahriman helps inspire science and technology, and works through forces of subnature such as gravity, electricity, magnetism, radioactivity—forces that are antithetical to life. The influence of Ahriman's activity upon the human being limits human cognition to what is derived from sense perception, hardens thinking (materialistic thoughts), attacks the etheric body by way of modern technology (electromagnetic radiation, etc.), and hardens hearts (cold and calculating).

**ahrimanic beings**: Spiritual beings who have become agents of Ahriman's influences.

**Angel Jesus**: A pure immaculate Angelic being who sacrifices himself so that the Christ may work through him. This Angelic being is actually of the status of an Archangel, who has descended to work on the Angelic level to be closer to human beings and to assist them on the path of confrontation with evil.

**Ascension**: An unfathomable process at the start of which, on May 14 AD 33, Christ united with the etheric realm that surrounds and permeates the Earth with Cosmic Life. Thus began his cosmic ascent to the realm of the heavenly Father, with the goal of elevating the Earth spiritually and opening pathways between the Earth and the spiritual world for the future.

**astral body**: Part of the human being that is the bearer of consciousness, passion, and desires, as well as idealism and the longing for perfection.

**Asuras**: Fallen Archai (Time Spirits) from the time of Old Saturn, whose opposition to human evolution comes to expression through promoting debauched sexuality and senseless violence among human beings. So low is the regard that the Asuras have for the sacredness of human life, that as well as promoting extreme violence and debauchery (for example, through the film industry), they do not hold back from the destruction of the physical body of human beings. In particular, the activity of the Asuras retards the development of the consciousness soul.

**bodhisattva**: On the human level a bodhisattva is a human being far advanced on the spiritual path, a human being belonging to the circle of twelve great teachers surrounding the Cosmic Christ. One who incarnates periodically to further the evolution of the Earth and humanity, working on the level of an angelic, archangelic, or higher being in relation to the rest of humanity. Every 5,000 years, one of these great teachers from the circle of bodhisattvas takes on a special mission, incarnating repeatedly to awake a new human faculty and capacity. Once that capacity has been imparted through its human bearer, this bodhisattva then incarnates upon the Earth for the last time, ascending to the level of a Buddha to serve humankind from spirit realms. See also Maitreya Bodhisattva.

**Central Sun**: Heart of the Milky Way, also called the Galactic Center. Our Sun orbits this Central Sun over a period of approximately 225 million years.

**chakra**: One of seven astral organs of perception through which human beings develop higher levels of cognition such as clairvoyance, telepathy, and so on.

**Christ:** The eternal being who is the second member of the Trinity. Also called the "Divine 'I AM,'" the Son of God, the Cosmic Christ, and the Logos–Word. Christ began to fully unite with the human vessel (Jesus) at the Baptism in the Jordan, and for 3½ years penetrated as the *Divine I AM* successively into the astral body, etheric body, and physical body of Jesus, spiritualizing each member. Through the Mystery of Golgotha Christ united with the Earth, kindling the spark of Christ consciousness (*Not I, but Christ in me*) in all human beings.

**consciousness soul:** The portion of the human soul in which "I" consciousness is awaking not only to its own sense of individuality and to the individualities of others, but also to its higher self—spirit self (Sanskrit: *manas*). Within the consciousness soul, the "I" perceives truth, beauty, and goodness; within the spirit self, the "I" becomes truth, beauty, and goodness.

**crossing the threshold:** a term applicable to our time, as human beings are increasingly encountering the spiritual world—in so doing, crossing the threshold between the sense-perceptible realm and non-physical realms of existence. To the extent that spiritual capacities have not been cultivated, this encounter with non-physical realms beyond the sense world signifies a descent into the subconscious (for example, through drugs) rather than an ascent to knowledge of higher worlds through the awaking of higher levels of consciousness.

**decan:** The zodiac of 360° is divided into twelve signs, each of 30°. A decan is 10°, thus one third of one sign or $1/36$ of the zodiac.

**devil:** Another term for Lucifer.

**dragon:** As used in the Apocalypse of John, there are different appearances of the dragon, each one representing an adversarial being opposed to Michael, Christ, and Sophia. For example, the great red dragon of chapter 12 opposes Sophia, the woman clothed with the Sun (Sophia is the pure Divine-Cosmic Feminine Soul of the World). The imagery from chapter 12 of Revelation depicts the woman clothed with the Sun as pregnant and that the great red dragon attempts to devour her child as soon as it is born. The child coming to birth from the woman clothed with the Sun represents the Divine-Cosmic "I AM" born through the assistance of the pure Divine Feminine Soul of the World. The dragon is cast down from the heavenly realm by the mighty Archangel Michael. Cast down to the Earth, the dragon continues with attempts to devour the cosmic child (the Divine-Cosmic "I AM") coming to birth among humankind.

**ego:** The soul sheath through which the "I" begins to incarnate and to experience life on Earth (to be distinguished from the term *ego* used in Freudian and Jungian psychology). The terms *"I,"* and *soul* are sometimes used interchangeably in Spiritual Science. The ego maintains threads of integrity and continuity through memory, while experiencing new sensations and perceptions through observation and thinking, feeling, and willing. The ego is capable of moral discernment and also experiences temptation. Thus, it is often stated that the "I" comprises both a higher nature and the lower nature ("ego").

**Emmerich, Anne Catherine** (also "Sister Emmerich"): A Catholic stigmatist (1774–1824) whose visions depicted the daily life of Jesus, beginning some weeks before the event of the descent of Christ into the body of Jesus at the Baptism in the River Jordan and extending for a period of several weeks after the Crucifixion.

**Ephesus:** The area in Asia Minor (now Turkey) to which the Apostle John (also called John Zebedee, the brother of James the Greater) accompanied the Virgin Mary approximately three years after the death of Jesus Christ. Ephesus was a very significant ancient mystery center where cosmic mysteries of the East found their way into the West. Initiates at Ephesus were devoted to the goddess Artemis, known as "Artemis of Ephesus," whose qualities are more those of a Mother goddess than is the case with the Greek goddess Artemis, although there is a certain degree of overlap between Artemis and Artemis of Ephesus with regard to many of their respective characteristics. A magnificent Ionic mystery temple was built in honor of Artemis of Ephesus at a location close to the Aegean Sea. Mary's house, built by John, was located high up above, on the nearby hill known as Mount Nightingale, about six miles from the temple of Artemis at Ephesus.

**etheric body:** The body of life forces permeating and animating the physical body. The etheric body was formed during ancient Sun evolution. The etheric body's activity is expressed in the seven life processes permeating the seven vital organs. The etheric body is related to the movements of the seven visible planets.

**Fall, The:** A fall from oneness with spiritual worlds. The Fall, which took place during the Lemurian period of Earth evolution, was a time of dramatic transition in human evolution when the soul descended from "Paradise" into earthly existence. Through the Fall the human soul began to incarnate into a physical body upon the Earth and experience the world from "within" the body, perceiving through the senses.

**Fifth Gospel:** The writings and lectures of Rudolf Steiner based on new spiritual perceptions and insights into the mysteries of Christ's life on Earth, including the Second Coming of Christ—his appearance in the etheric realm in our time, beginning in the twentieth century.

**Golgotha, Mystery of:** Rudolf Steiner's designation for the entire mystery of the coming of Christ to the Earth. Sometimes this term is used more specifically to refer to the events surrounding the Crucifixion and Resurrection. In particular, the Crucifixion—the sacrifice on the cross—marked the birth of Christ's union with the Earth. Also referred to as the "Turning Point of Time," whereby at the Crucifixion Christ descended from the sphere of the Sun and became the "Spirit of the Earth."

**Grail:** An etheric chalice into which Christ can work to transform earthly substance into spiritual substance. The term *Grail* has many deep levels of meaning and refers on the one hand to a spiritual stream in service of Christ, and on the other hand to the means by which the human "I" penetrates and transforms evil into good. The power of transubstantiation expresses something of this process of transformation of evil into good.

**Grail Knights:** Those trained to confront evil and transform it into something good, in service of Christ. Members of a spiritual stream that existed in the past and continues to exist—albeit in metamorphosed form—in the present. Every human being striving for the good can potentially become a Grail Knight.

**I AM:** One's true individuality, that—with few exceptions—never fully incarnates but works into the developing "I" and its lower bodies (astral, etheric, and physical). The **Cosmic I AM** is the "I AM" of Christ, through which—on account of the Mystery of Golgotha—we are all graced with the possibility of receiving a divine spark therefrom.

**Jesus** (see Nathan Jesus and Solomon Jesus): The pure human being who received the Christ at the Baptism in the River Jordan.

**Jesus Christ:** The Divine-Human being; the God-Man; the union of the Divine with the Human. The presence of the Cosmic Christ in the physical body of the human being called the Nathan Jesus during the 3½ years of the ministry.

**Jesus of Nazareth:** The name of the human being whose birth is celebrated in the Gospel of Luke, also referred to as the Nathan Jesus. When Jesus of Nazareth reached the age of twelve, the spirit of the Solomon Jesus (Gospel of Matthew) united with the body and sheaths of the pure Nathan Jesus. This union lasted for about 18 years, until the Baptism in the River Jordan. During these eighteen years, Jesus of Nazareth was a composite being comprising the Nathan Jesus and the spirit ("I") of the Solomon Jesus. Just before the Baptism, the spirit of the Solomon Jesus withdrew, and at the Baptism Jesus became known as "Jesus Christ" through the union of Christ with the sheaths of Jesus.

**Jezebel:** Wife of King Ahab, approximately 900 BC, who worked through the powers of black magic against the prophet Elijah.

**Kali Yuga:** Yugas are ages of influence referred to in Hindu cosmography, each yuga lasting a certain numbers of years in length (always a multiple of 2,500). The Kali Yuga is also known as the Dark Age, which began with the death of Krishna in 3102 BC (-3101). Kali Yuga lasted 5,000 years and ended in AD 1899.

**Kingly Stream:** Biblically, the line of heredity from King David into which the Solomon Jesus (Gospel of Matthew) was born. The kings (the three magi) were initiates who sought to bring the cosmic will of the heavenly Father to expression on the Earth through spiritual forces working from spiritual beings dwelling in the stars. The minds of the wise kings were enlightened by the coming of Jesus Christ.

**Krishna:** A cosmic-human being, the sister soul of Adam that over-lighted Arjuna as described in the Bhagavad Gita. The over-lighting by Krishna of Arjuna could be described as an incorporation of Krishna into Arjuna. An incorporation is a partial incarnation. The cosmic-human being known as Krishna later fully incarnated as Jesus of Nazareth (Nathan Jesus—Gospel of Luke).

**Lazarus:** The elder brother of Mary Magdalene, Martha, and Silent Mary. At his raising from the dead, Lazarus became the first human being to be fully initiated by Christ (see Lazarus–John).

**Lazarus–John:** At the raising of Lazarus from the dead by Christ, the spiritual being of John the Baptist united with Lazarus. The higher spiritual members of John (spirit body, life spirit, spirit self) entered into the members of Lazarus, which were developed to the level of the consciousness soul.

**Lucifer:** The name of a fallen spiritual being, also called the Light-Bearer, who acts as a retarding force within the human astral body and also in the sentient soul. Lucifer inflames egoism and pride within the human being, often inspiring genius and supreme artistry. Arrogance and self-importance are stimulated, without humility or sacrificial love. Lucifer stirs up forces of rebellion, but cannot deliver true freedom—just its illusion.

**luciferic beings:** Spiritual beings who have become agents of Lucifer's influences.

**magi:** Initiates in the mystery school of Zarathustra, the Bodhisattva who incarnated as Zoroaster (Zaratas, Nazaratos) in the sixth century BC and who, after he came to Babylon, became a teacher of the Chaldean priesthood. At the time of Jesus, the magi were still continuing the star-gazing tradition of the school of Zoroaster. The task of the magi was to recognize when their master would reincarnate. With their visit to the newborn Jesus child in Bethlehem (Gospel of Matthew), to this child who was the reincarnated Zarathustra–Zoroaster, they fulfilled their mission. The three magi are the "priest kings from the East" referred to in the Gospel of Matthew.

**Maitreya Bodhisattva:** The bodhisattva individuality that is preparing to become the successor of Gautama Buddha and will be known as the Bringer of the Good. This bodhisattva was incarnated in the second century BC as Jeshu ben Pandira, the teacher of the Essenes, who died about 100 BC. Rudolf Steiner indicated that Jeshu ben Pandira reincarnated at the beginning of the twentieth century as a great bodhisattva individuality to fulfill the lofty mission of proclaiming Christ's coming in the etheric realm, beginning around 1933: "He will be the actual herald of Christ in his etheric form" (lecture about Jeshu ben Pandira held in Leipzig on November 4, 1911). There are differing points of view as to who this individuality actually was in his twentieth century incarnation.

**manas:** Also called the spirit self; the purified astral body, lifted into full communion with truth and goodness by becoming the true and the good within the essence of the higher self of the human being. Manas is the spiritual source of the "I," and as it is the eternal part of the human being that goes from life to life, manas bears the human being's true "eternal name" through its union with the Holy Spirit. The "eternal name" expresses the human being's true mission from life to life.

**Mani:** The name of a lofty initiate who lived in Babylon in the third century AD. The founder of the Manichean stream, whose mission is the transformation of evil into goodness through compassion and love. Mani reincarnated as Parzival in the ninth century AD. Mani–Parzival is one of the leading initiates of our present age—the age of the consciousness soul (AD 1414–3574). One of the highest beings ever to incarnate upon the Earth, he will become the future Manu beginning in the astrological age of Sagittarius. This future Manu will oversee the spiritual evolution of a sequence of seven ages, comprising the seven cultural epochs of the Sixth Great Age of Earth evolution from the Age of Sagittarius to the Age of Gemini—lasting a total of 7 x 2,160 years (15,120 years), since each zodiacal age lasts 2,160 years.

**Manu:** Like the word Buddha, the word Manu is a title. A Manu has the task of spiritually overseeing one Great Age of Earth evolution, comprising seven astrological ages (seven cultural epochs)—lasting a total of 7 x 2,160 years (15,120 years), since each zodiacal age lasts 2,160 years. The present Age of Pisces (AD 215–2375)—with its corresponding cultural epoch (AD 1414–3574)—is the fifth epoch during the Fifth Great Age of Earth evolution. (Lemuria was the Third Great Age, Atlantis the Fourth Great Age, and since the great flood that destroyed Atlantis, we are now in the Fifth Great Age.) The present Manu is the exalted Sun-initiate who guided humanity out of Atlantis during the ancient flooding that destroyed the continent of Atlantis formerly in the region of the Atlantic Ocean—the Flood referred to in the Bible in connection with Noah. He is the overseer of the seven cultural epochs corresponding to the seven astrological ages from the Age of Cancer to the Age of Capricorn, following the sequence: Cancer, Gemini, Taurus, Aries, Pisces, Aquarius, Capricorn. The present Manu was the teacher of the Seven Holy Rishis who were the founders of the ancient Indian cultural epoch (7227–5067 BC) during the Age of Cancer. He is known in the Bible as Noah, and in the Flood story belonging to the Gilgamesh epic he is called Utnapishtim. Subsequently this Manu appeared to Abraham as Melchizedek and offered Abraham an agape ("love feast") of bread and wine. Jesus "was designated by God to be high priest in the order of Melchizedek" (Heb. 5:10).

**Mary:** Rudolf Steiner distinguishes between the Nathan Mary and the Solomon Mary (see corresponding entries). The expression "Virgin Mary" refers to the Solomon Mary, the mother of the child Jesus whose birth is described in the Gospel of Matthew.

**Mary Magdalene:** Sister of Lazarus, whose soul was transformed and purified as Christ cast out seven demons who had taken possession of her. Christ thus initiated Mary Magdalene. Later, she anointed Jesus Christ. And she was the first to behold the Risen Christ in the Garden of the Holy Sepulcher on the morning of his resurrection.

**megastar:** Stars with a luminosity greater than 10,000 times that of our Sun.

**Nain, Youth of:** Referred to in the Gospel of Luke as the son of the widow of Nain. The Youth of Nain—at the time he was twelve years old—was raised from the dead by Jesus. The Youth of Nain later reincarnated as the Prophet Mani (third century AD) and subsequently as the Grail King Parzival (ninth century AD).

**Nathan Jesus:** From the priestly line of David, as described in the Gospel of Luke. An immaculate and pure soul whose one and only physical incarnation was as Jesus of Nazareth (Nathan Jesus).

**Nathan Mary:** A pure being who was the mother of the Nathan Jesus. The Nathan Mary died in AD 12, but her spirit united with the Solomon Mary at the time of the Baptism of Jesus in the River Jordan. From this time on, the Solomon Mary—spiritually united with the Nathan Mary—was known as the Virgin Mary.

**New Jerusalem:** A spiritual condition denoting humanity's future existence that will come into being as human beings free themselves from the *maya* of the material world and work together to bring about a spiritualized Earth.

**Osiris:** *Osiris* and *Isis* are names given by the Egyptians to the preincarnatory forms of the spiritual beings who are now known as Christ and Sophia.

**Parzival:** Son of Gahmuret and Herzeloyde in the epic *Parzival* by Wolfram von Eschenbach. Although written in the thirteenth century, this work refers to actual people and events in the ninth century AD, one of whom (the central figure) bore the name Parzival. After living a life of dullness and doubt, Parzival's mission was to seek the Castle of the Grail and to ask the question "What ails thee?" of the Grail King, Anfortas—moreover, to ask the question without being bidden to do so. Parzival eventually became the new Grail King, the successor of Anfortas. Parzival was the reincarnated prophet Mani. In the incarnation preceding that of Mani, he was incarnated as the Youth of Nain (Luke 7:11–15). Parzival is a great initiate responsible for guiding humanity during the Age of Pisces, which has given birth to the cultural epoch of the development of the consciousness soul (AD 1414–3574).

**Pentecost:** Descent of the Holy Spirit fifty days after Easter, whereby the cosmic "I AM" was birthed among the disciples and those individuals close to Christ. They received the capacity to develop manas, or spirit self, within the community of striving human individuals, whereby the birth of the spirit self is facilitated through the soul of the Virgin Mary. See also World Pentecost.

**phantom body:** The pure spiritual form of the human physical body, unhindered by matter.

The far-distant future state of the human physical body when it has become purified and spiritualized into a body of transformed divine will.

**Presbyter John:** Refers to Lazarus–John who moved to Ephesus about twenty years after the Virgin Mary had died there. In Ephesus he became a bishop. He is the author of the book of Revelation, the Gospel of St. John, and the Letters of John.

**Risen One:** The initial appearance of Christ in his phantom body (resurrection body), beginning with his appearance to Mary Magdalene on Easter Sunday morning. Christ frequently appeared to the disciples in his phantom body during the forty days leading from Easter to Ascension.

**Satan:** The traditional Christian name for Ahriman.

**Serpent:** Another name for Lucifer, but sometimes naming a combination of Lucifer and Ahriman: "The great dragon was hurled down—that ancient serpent called the devil, or Satan, who leads the whole world astray" (Rev. 12:9).

**Shepherd Stream:** Biblically, the genealogical line from David the shepherd through his son Nathan. It was into this line that the Nathan Jesus was born, whose birth is described in the Gospel of Luke. Rudolf Steiner describes the shepherds, who—according to Luke—came to pay homage to the newborn child, as those servants of pure heart who perceive the goodwill streaming up from Mother Earth. The hearts of the shepherds were kindled with the fire of Divine Love by the coming of the Christ. The shepherds can be regarded as precursors of the heart stream of humanity that now intuits the being of Christ as the spirit of the Earth.

**Solomon Jesus:** Descended from the genealogical line from David through his son Solomon. This line of descent is described in the Gospel of Matthew. The Solomon Jesus was a reincarnation of Zoroaster (sixth century BC). In turn, Zoroaster was a reincarnation of Zarathustra (6000 BC), the great prophet and founder of the ancient Persian religion of Zoroastrianism. He was a bodhisattva who, as the founder of this new religion that focused on the Sun Spirit Ahura Mazda, helped prepare humanity for the subsequent descent into incarnation of Ahura Mazda, the cosmic Sun Spirit, as Christ.

**Solomon Mary:** The wise mother of the Solomon Jesus, who adopted the Nathan Jesus after the death of the Nathan Mary. At the time of the Baptism of Jesus in the River Jordan, the spirit of the Nathan Mary united with the Solomon Mary. Usually referred to as the Virgin Mary or Mother Mary, the Solomon Mary bore witness at the foot of the cross to the Mystery of Golgotha. She died in Ephesus eleven years after Christ's Ascension.

**Sophia:** Part of the Divine Feminine Trinity comprising the Mother (counterpart of the Father), the Daughter (counterpart of the Son), and the Holy Soul (counterpart of the Holy Spirit). Sophia, also known as the Bride of the Lamb, is the Daughter aspect of the threefold Divine Feminine Trinity. To the Egyptians Sophia was known as Isis, who was seen as belonging to the starry realm surrounding the Earth. In the Book of Proverbs, attributed to King Solomon, Sophia's temple has seven pillars (Proverbs 9:1). The seven pillars in Sophia's temple represent the seven great stages of Earth evolution (from ancient Saturn to future Vulcan).

**Sorath:** The great enemy of Christ who works against the "I" in the human being. Sorath is identified with the two-horned beast that rises up from the depths of Earth, as described in the book of Revelation. Sorath is the Sun Demon, and is identified by Rudolf Steiner as the Antichrist. According to the book of Revelation, his number is 666.

**Sun Demon:** Another name for Sorath.

**Transfiguration:** The event on Mt. Tabor where Jesus Christ was illumined with Divine Light raying forth from the purified etheric body of Jesus, which the Divine "I AM" of Christ had penetrated. The Gospels of Matthew and Luke describe the Transfiguration. The Sun-like radiance that shone forth from Jesus Christ on Mt. Tabor was an expression of the purified etheric body that had its origin during the Old Sun period of Earth evolution.

**Transubstantiation:** Sacramental transformation of physical substance—for example, the transubstantiation of bread and wine during the Mass to become the body and blood of Christ. During the Holy Eucharist the bread and wine are transformed in such a way that the substances of bread and wine are infused with the life force (body) and light (blood) of Christ. Thereby the bread and wine are reunited with their divine archetypes and are no longer "merely" physical substances, but are bearers on the physical level of a spiritual reality.

**Turning Point of Time**: Transition between involution and evolution, as marked by the Mystery of Golgotha. The descending stream of involution culminated with the Mystery of Golgotha. With the descent of the Cosmic Christ into earthly evolution, through his sacrifice on Golgotha an ascending stream of evolution began. This sacrifice of Christ was followed by the events of his Resurrection and Ascension, which were followed in turn by Whitsun (Pentecost)—all expressing the ascending stream of evolution. This path of ascent was also opened up to all human beings by way of the power of the divine "I AM" bestowed—at least, potentially—on all humanity by Christ through his sacrifice on the cross.

**Union in the Temple:** The event of the union of the spirit of the Solomon Jesus with the twelve-year-old Nathan Jesus. This union of the two Jesus children signified the uniting of the priestly (Nathan) line and the kingly (Solomon) line—both lines descended from King David.

**Whitsun:** "White Sunday"; Pentecost.

**World Pentecost** is the gradual event of cosmic revelation becoming human revelation as a signature of the end of the Dark Age (Kali Yuga). Anthroposophy (Spiritual Science) is a language of spiritual truth that could awake a community of striving human beings to the presence of the Holy Spirit and the founding of the New Jerusalem.

**Zarathustra:** The great teacher of the ancient Persians in the sixth millennium BC (around 6000 BC). In the sixth century BC, Zarathustra reincarnated as Zoroaster. He then reincarnated as the Solomon Jesus (6 BC–AD 12), whose birth is described in the Gospel of Matthew.

**Zoroaster:** An incarnation of Zarathustra. Zarathustra–Zoroaster was a Bodhisattva. Zoroaster lived in the sixth century BC. He was a master of wisdom. Among his communications as a teacher of wisdom was his specification as to how the zodiac of living beings in the heavens comes to expression in relation to the stars comprising the twelve zodiacal constellations. Zoroaster subsequently incarnated as the Solomon Jesus, whose birth is described in the Gospel of Matthew, to whom the three magi came from the East bearing gifts of gold, frankincense, and myrrh.

"It became clearer and clearer to me—as the outcome of many years of research—that in our epoch there is really something like a resurrection of the astrology of the third epoch [the Egyptian–Babylonian period], but permeated now with the Christ Impulse. Today, we must search among the stars in a way different from the old ways. The stellar script must once more become something that speaks to us."

—RUDOLF STEINER (*Christ and the Spiritual World and the Search for the Holy Grail*, p. 106)

"In Palestine during the time that Jesus of Nazareth walked on Earth as Jesus Christ—during the three years of his life, from his thirtieth to his thirty-third year—the entire being of the cosmic Christ was acting uninterruptedly upon him, and was working into him. The Christ stood always under the influence of the entire cosmos; he made no step without this working of the cosmic forces into and in him.... It was always in accordance with the collective being of the whole universe with whom the Earth is in harmony, that all which Jesus Christ did took place."

—RUDOLF STEINER (*Spiritual Guidance of Man and Humanity*, p. 66)

# BIBLIOGRAPHY AND RELATED READING

*See "Literature" on page 10 for an annotated list of books on Astrosophy.*

Andreev, Daniel. *The Rose of the World*. Great Barrington, MA: Lindisfarne Books, 1997.

Anonymous. *Meditations on the Tarot: A Journey into Christian Hermeticism*. New York: Putman, 2002.

Aspin, Jehoshaphat. *A Familiar Treatise on Astronomy: Explaining the General Phenomena of the Celestial Bodies*. London, 1825.

Bloxam, Richard R. *Urania's Mirror: or, A View of the Heavens* (a set of illustrated cards). London, 1825.

Cox, Christopher. *Sonic Flux: Sound, Art, and Metaphysics*. Chicago: University of Chicago, 2018.

Dionysius the Areopagite, *Mystical Theology and the Celestial Hierarchies*. Fintry, UK: Shrine of Wisdom, 1965.

Dorsan, Jacques. *The Clockwise House System: A True Foundation for Sidereal and Tropical Astrology*. Great Barrington, MA: Lindisfarne Books, 2011.

Dutt, Romesh C. *The Ramayana and the Mahábhárata: Condensed into English Verse*. London–New York: Everyman's Library, 1972.

Emerson, Ralph Waldo. *Essays and Lectures*. New York: The Library of America, 1983.

Emmerich, Anne Catherine. *Visions of the Life of Christ* (3 vols.). Kettering, OH: Angelico Press, 2015.

Eno, Brian. *A Year with Swollen Appendices: Brian Eno's Diary* (2nd ed.). New York: Faber & Faber, 2021.

Godwin, Joscelyn (ed.). *Cosmic Music: Musical Keys to the Interpretation of Reality*. Rochester, VT: Inner Traditions, 1989.

Hamilton, Alexander. *Writings*. New York: Library of America Founders Collection, 2001.

Hart, David Bentley. *The New Testament: A Translation*. New Haven, CT: Yale, 2017.

Hickey, Isabel M. *Astrology: A Cosmic Science: The Classic Work on Spiritual Astrology*. Sebastopol, CA: CRCS, 1992.

Houlding, Deborah. *The Houses: Temples of the Sky*. Bournemouth, UK: The Wessex Astrologer, 2006.

Huxley, Aldous. *Brave New World*. New York: Harper Perennial, 2006.

Isaacson, Estelle. *Through the Eyes of Mary Magdalene*, 3 vols. Taos, NM: LogoSophia, 2012–2015.

LaBelle, Brandon. *Background Noise: Perspectives on Sound Art*. London: Bloomsbury, 2015.

McCullough, David. *John Adams*. New York: Simon and Schuster, 2001.

McLaren Lainson, Claudia. *The Circle of Twelve and the Legacy of Valentin Tomberg*. Boulder: Windrose Academy, 2015.

Michael, Emily. *Sealed by the Sun: Life between Rudolf Steiner and Peter Deunov*. Varna, Bulgaria: Self-published, 2014.

Pagan, Isabel M. *Astrological Key to Character: The Twelve Zodiacal Types*. Whitefish, MT: Literary Licensing, 2011.

Powell, Robert. *The Christ Mystery*. Fair Oaks, CA: Rudolf Steiner College, 1999.

——. *Christian Hermetic Astrology: The Star of the Magi and the Life of Christ*. Great Barrington, MA: Lindisfarne Books, 2009.

——. *Chronicle of the Living Christ: The Life and Ministry of Jesus Christ: Foundations of Cosmic Christianity*. Hudson, NY: Anthroposophic Press, 1996.

——. *Cultivating Inner Radiance and the Body of Immortality: Awakening the Soul through Modern Etheric Movement*. Great Barrington, MA: Lindisfarne Books, 2012.

——. *Elijah Come Again: A Prophet for Our Time: A Scientific Approach to Reincarnation*. Great Barrington, MA: Lindisfarne Books, 2009.

——. *Hermetic Astrology*, vols. 1 and 2. San Rafael, CA: Sophia Foundation Press, 2006.

——. *History of the Zodiac*. San Rafael, CA: Sophia Academic Press, 2007.

——. *The Most Holy Trinosophia: The New Revelation of the Divine Feminine*. Great Barrington, MA: SteinerBooks, 2000.

——. *The Mystery, Biography, and Destiny of Mary Magdalene: Sister of Lazarus–John and Spiritual Sister of Jesus*. Great Barrington, MA: Lindisfarne Books, 2008.

——. *Prophecy-Phenomena-Hope: The Real Meaning of the year 2012*. Great Barrington, MA: SteinerBooks, 2011.

——. *The Sign of the Son of Man in Heaven*. San Rafael, CA: Sophia Foundation, 2007.

——. *The Sophia Teachings: The Emergence of the Divine Feminine in Our Time*. Great Barrington, MA: Lindisfarne Books, 2007.

Powell, Robert, and David Bowden. *Astrogeographia: Correspondences between the Stars and Earthly Locations: Earth Chakras and the*

*Bible of Astrology*. Great Barrington, MA: SteinerBooks, 2012.

Powell, Robert, and Kevin Dann. *The Astrological Revolution: Unveiling the Science of the Stars as a Science of Reincarnation and Karma*. Great Barrington, MA: SteinerBooks, 2010.

———. *Christ and the Maya Calendar: 2012 and the Coming of the Antichrist*. Great Barrington, MA: SteinerBooks, 2009.

Powell, Robert, and Estelle Isaacson. *Gautama Buddha's Successor: A Force for Good in our Time*. Great Barrington, MA: SteinerBooks, 2013.

———. *The Mystery of Sophia: Bearer of the New Culture: The Rose of the World*. Great Barrington, MA: SteinerBooks, 2014.

Powell, Robert, and Lacquanna Paul. *Cosmic Dances of the Planets*. San Rafael, CA: Sophia Foundation Press, 2006.

Powell, Robert, and Peter Treadgold. *The Sidereal Zodiac*. Tempe, AZ: AFA, 1985.

Renold, Maria. *Intervals, Scales, Tones: And the Concert Pitch c = 128 Hz*. Forest Row, UK: Temple Lodge, 2015.

Richmond, M. Temple. *Sirius*. Raleigh, NC: Manasadeva Press, 1997.

Schlesinger, Kathleen. *The Greek Aulos: A Study of Its Mechanism and of Its Relation to the Modal System of Ancient Greek Music*. N. Yorkshire, UK: Methuen, 1939.

Selg, Peter. *Elisabeth Vreede: Adversity, Resilience, and Spiritual Science*. Great Barrington, MA: SteinerBooks, 2017.

Smigel, Eric. *Alchemy of the Avant-garde: David Tudor and the New Music of the 1950s* (doctoral disertation). Los Angeles: USC, 2003.

Spaulding, Rick, and Maurice York. *A Sanctuary for the Rights of Mankind: The Founding Fathers and the Temple of Liberty*. Chicago: Wrightwood, 2008.

Stebbing, Lionel. *Music: Its Occult Basis and Healing Value*. Lancaster, UK: New Knowledge, 1974.

Steiner, Rudolf. *According to Matthew: The Gospel of Christ's Humanity*. Great Barrington, MA: Anthroposophic Press, 2002.

———. *Ancient Myths and the New Isis Mystery* (rev. 2nd ed.). Great Barrington, MA: SteinerBooks, 2018.

———. *Anthroposophical Leading Thoughts: Anthroposophy as a Path of Knowledge: The Michael Mystery*. London: Rudolf Steiner Press, 1973.

———. *Anthroposophy (a Fragment): A New Foundation for the Study of Human Nature*. Hudson, NY: Anthroposophic Press, 1996.

———. *Anthroposophy and the Inner Life: An Esoteric Introduction*. Forest Row, UK: Rudolf Steiner Press, 1983.

———. *The Arts and Their Mission*. Hudson, NY: Anthroposophic Press, 1986.

———. *Astronomy and Astrology: Finding a Relationship to the Cosmos*. Forest Row, UK: Rudolf Steiner Press, 2009.

———. *The Bhagavad Gita and the West: The Esoteric Meaning of the Bhagavad Gita and Its Relation to the Letters of St. Paul*. Great Barrington, MA: SteinerBooks, 2008.

———. *Building Stones for an Understanding of the Mystery of Golgotha: Human Life in a Cosmic Context*. Forest Row, UK: Rudolf Steiner Press, 2015.

———. *Christ and the Spiritual World and the Search for the Holy Grail*. Forest Row, UK: Rudolf Steiner Press, 1963.

———. *The Child's Changing Consciousness: As the Basis of Pedagogical Practice*. Hudson, NY: Anthroposophic Press, 1996.

———. *The Christmas Conference for the Foundation of the General Anthroposophical Society 1923/1924: The Laying of the Foundation Stone, Lectures and Addresses, Discussions of the Statutes*. Hudson, NY: Anthroposophic Press, 1990.

———. *Constitution of the School of Spiritual Science* (G. Adams, ed.). Forest Row, UK: Rudolf Steiner Press, 2013.

———. *Death as Metamorphosis of Life: Including "What Does the Angel Do in our Astral Body?" and "How Do I Find Christ?"* Great Barrington, MA: SteinerBooks, 2008.

———. *Egyptian Myths and Mysteries*. Hudson, NY: Anthroposophic Press, 1971.

———. *Esoteric Christianity and the Mission of Christian Rosenkreutz*. Forest Row, UK: Rudolf Steiner Press, 2001.

———. *An Esoteric Cosmology: Evolution, Christ, and Modern Spirituality*. Great Barrington, MA: SteinerBooks, 2008.

———. *Founding a Science of the Spirit*. Forest Row, UK: Rudolf Steiner Press, 1999.

———. *Freemasonry and Ritual Work: The Misraim Service*. Great Barrington, MA: SteinerBooks, 2007.

———. *The Inner Nature of Music and the Experience of Tone*. Hudson, NY: Anthroposophic Press, 1983.

———. *Interdisciplinary Astronomy: Third Scientific Course*. Great Barrington, MA: SteinerBooks, 2003.

———. *Karmic Relationships: Esoteric Studies*, vol. 1. Forest Row, UK: Rudolf Steiner Press, 2012.

———. *Karmic Relationships: Esoteric Studies*, vol. 4. Forest Row, UK: Rudolf Steiner Press, 2017.

———. *Die Konstitution der Allgemeinen Anthroposophischen Gesellschaft und der Freien Hochschule für Geisteswissenschaft. Der Wiederaufbau des Goetheanum.* Basel: Rudolf Steiner Verlag, 1987.

———. *Life between Death and Rebirth.* Hudson, NY: Anthroposophic Press, 1975.

———. *Occult History: Historical Personalities and Events in the Light of Spiritual Science.* New York: Anthroposophic Press, 1957.

———. *Occult Science, an Outline.* London: Rudolf Steiner Press, 1969.

———. *An Outline of Esoteric Science.* Hudson, NY: Anthroposophic Press, 1997.

———. *Rosicrucianism Renewed: The Unity of Art, Science, and Religion.* Great Barrington, MA: SteinerBooks, 2007.

———. *Secret Brotherhoods: And the Mystery of the Human Double.* Forest Row, UK: Rudolf Steiner Press, 2004.

———. *The Secret Stream: Christian Rosenkreutz and Rosicrucianism.* Great Barrington, MA: Anthroposophic Press, 2000.

———. *Spiritual Beings in the Heavenly Bodies and in the Kingdoms of Nature.* Great Barrington, MA: SteinerBooks, 2011.

———. *Truth and Knowledge: Introduction to the Philosophy of Spiritual Activity.* Spring Valley, NY: Anthroposophic Press, 1981.

———. *Twelve Moods.* Spring Valley, NY: Mercury Press, 1984.

———. *Verses and Mediations.* Forest Row, UK: Rudolf Steiner Press, 2014.

Sucher, Willi. *Cosmic Christianity and the Changing Countenance of Cosmology: An Introduction to Astrosophy: A New Wisdom of the Stars.* Hudson, NY: Anthroposophic Press, 1993.

———. *The Drama of the Universe.* Larkfield, UK: Landvidi Research Centre, 1958.

———. *Isis Sophia I: Introducing Astrosophy.* Meadow Vista, CA: Astrosophy Research Center, 1999.

———. *Isis Sophia II: An Outline of a New Star Wisdom.* Meadow Vista, CA: Astrosophy Research Center, 1985.

———. *Star Journals II: Toward New Astrosophy.* Meadow Vista, CA: Astrosophy Research Center, 2006.

Sullivan, Erin. *Retrograde Planets: Traversing the Inner Landscape.* York, ME: Samuel Weiser, 2000.

Tomberg, Valentin. *Christ and Sophia: Anthroposophic Meditations on the Old Testament, New Testament, and Apocalypse.* Great Barrington, MA: SteinerBooks, 2006.

———. *Studies on the Foundation Stone Meditation.* San Rafael, CA: LogoSophia, 2010.

Tommasini, Anthony. *The Indispensable Composers: A Personal Guide.* New York: Penguin, 2018.

Tresemer, David, and Robert Schiappacasse. *Star Wisdom and Rudolf Steiner: A Life Seen through the Oracle of the Solar Cross.* Great Barrington, MA: SteinerBooks, 2006.

van Wingerden, Sebastian. *The Northern Moon Node: The Message from Beyond; Spiritual Astrology,* vol. 1. Amsterdam: Lillalith, 2017.

von Eschenbach, Wolfram. *Parzival: A Romance of the Middle Ages* (trans. H. Mustard and C. Passage). New York: Vintage Classics, 1961.

von Halle, Judith. *The Coronavirus Pandemic: Anthroposophical Perspectives.* Forest Row, UK: Rudolf Steiner Press, 2021.

von Keyserlingk, Adalbert Graf. *The Birth of a New Agriculture: Koberwitz 1924 and the Introduction of Biodynamics.* Forest Row, UK: Temple Lodge, 1999.

Vreede, Elisabeth. *Astronomy and Spiritual Science: The Astronomical Letters of Elisabeth Vreede.* Great Barrington, MA: SteinerBooks, 2007.

Warm, Hartmut. *Signature of the Celestial Spheres: Discovering Order in the Solar System.* Forest Row, UK: Sophia Books, 2010.

West, M. L. *Ancient Greek Music.* Oxford, UK: Oxford University, 1992.

Zeylmans van Emmichoven, J. E. *Who Was Ita Wegman: A Documentation, Volume 2: 1925 until 1943.* Spring Valley, NY: Mercury Press, 2005.

# ABOUT THE CONTRIBUTORS

**KRISZTINA CSERI** graduated as an economist and worked in the production and financial controlling field at various companies for twelve years. She started to work with astrology in 2002 and attended a course from 2004 until 2007. She became a student of Anthroposophy at Pentecost 2009, when a friend invited her to the anniversary celebration of Rudolf Steiner's "Budapest-lectures." Owing to the impact of that event, she soon left her financial career. She first encountered the work of Willi Sucher and Robert Powell in 2010. With her husband, she founded the Hungarian Sophia Foundation in 2012. They have a small publishing company and translate and distribute books on spiritual themes. Krisztina translated six books written by Robert Powell (and Kevin Dann) into Hungarian and finished translating *Meditations on the Tarot* into Hungarian in 2020. She is a mother of two little children and lives with her family in a village near Budapest.

**JULIE HUMPHREYS** is a graduate of Stanford and a former pediatric nurse and Waldorf mom. An early interest in astrology lay dormant for more than three decades until she was introduced to the sidereal system, the works of Robert Powell, and the visions of Anne Catherine Emmerich. She has taken great joy in researching astrological phenomena for the *Journal for Star Wisdom*. Julie lives in Carmel, California, where shooting stars and the Milky Way are often visible.

**JOEL MATTHEW PARK** is a Hermeticist based in Copake, New York. From 2011 to 2019, he was a life-sharing coworker at Plowshare Farm (a Camphill affiliate), farming and candlemaking with people from a variety of countries, ages, and developmental backgrounds. During this time he earned a certification in Social Therapy from the School of Spiritual Science through the Camphill Academy. He is now, along with his wife Molly, householding in Ita Wegman, an elder-care house in Camphill Village Copake. Joel has been a student of Anthroposophy since 2008 and a Christian Hermeticist since 2010. In 2015, he joined the Grail Knighthood, a group spiritual practice offered through the Sophia Foundation. Through this, he met Robert Powell, whose work he had been studying since 2009. Since then, Joel has been actively working with him to continue the karma research Robert began in 1977, and exemplified in works such as *Hermetic Astrology,* volumes 1 and 2, and *Elijah, Come Again.* Joel has led two retreats on "Tarot and the Art of Hermetic Conversation" (2017 and 2019), and given talks on the karmic biography of Anfortas, the three essentials of Camphill, and the ideal social organism. Most recently he led courses on Astrological Biography and an exploration of Dieter Brull's "Creating Social Sacraments." His first contribution was to the *Journal for Star Wisdom* 2018, after which he became editor of the continuation of the journal, the *Star Wisdom* series. The first volume of this series was published in November 2018. A selection of his writings can be found on his website, "TreeHouse": www.treehouse.live.

**ROBERT POWELL**, PhD, is an internationally known lecturer, author, eurythmist, and movement therapist. He is founder of the Choreocosmos School of Cosmic and Sacred Dance, and cofounder of the Sophia Foundation of North America. He received his doctorate for his thesis *The History of the Zodiac,* available as a book from Sophia Academic Press. His published works include *The Sophia Teachings,* a six-tape series (Sounds True Recordings), as well as *Elijah Come Again: A Prophet for Our Time; The Mystery, Biography, and Destiny of Mary Madgalene; Divine Sophia—Holy Wisdom; The Most Holy Trinosophia and the New Revelation of the Divine Feminine; Chronicle of the Living Christ; Christian Hermetic Astrology; The Christ Mystery; The Sign of the Son of Man in the Heavens; Cultivating Inner Radiance and the Body of Immortality;* and the yearly *Journal for Star Wisdom* (previously *Christian Star Calendar*). He translated the spiritual classic *Meditations on the Tarot* and co-translated Valentin Tomberg's *Lazarus, Come Forth!* Robert is coauthor with David Bowden of *Astrogeographia: Correspondences between the Stars and Earthly Locations* and coauthor with Estelle Isaacson of *Gautama Buddha's Successor* and *The Mystery of Sophia.* Robert is also coauthor with Kevin Dann of *The Astrological Revolution: Unveiling the Science of the Stars as a Science of Reincarnation and Karma* and *Christ and the Maya Calendar: 2012 and the Coming of the Antichrist;* and coauthor with Lacquanna Paul of *Cosmic Dances of the Zodiac* and *Cosmic Dances of the Planets.* He teaches a gentle form of healing movement: the sacred dance of eurythmy, as well as the Cosmic Dances of the Planets and signs of the zodiac. Through the Sophia Grail Circle, Robert facilitates sacred celebrations dedicated to the Divine Feminine. He offers workshops in Europe and Australia, and with Karen Rivers, cofounder of the Sophia Foundation, leads pilgrimages to the world's sacred sites: Turkey, 1996; the Holy Land, 1997; France, 1998; Britain, 2000; Italy, 2002; Greece, 2004; Egypt, 2006; India, 2008; Turkey, 2009; the Grand Canyon, 2010; South Africa, 2012; Peru, 2014; the Holy Land, 2016; and Bali, 2018. Visit www.sophiafoundation.org and www.astrogeographia.org.

**BILL TRUSIEWICZ:** *Et ignotas animum dimittit in artes naturamque nouat.* Bill takes this Latin phrase from Ovid's *Metamorphoses* as his motto to identify his modus operandi. He translates it: "And his mind he addresses to unknown arts advancing the laws of nature." It was written of Daedalus the legendary inventor of the famed labyrinth that housed the illegitimate son of the Cretan King Minos. As Daedalus held the keys to the Labyrinthine path leading to the Minotaur, Bill seeks to help others on their journey to conquer their own Minotaurs. And as Daedalus created wings for himself and his son Icarus, to fly from his imprisonment in Minoan Crete back to his homeland in Greece, so Bill endeavors, through art, to create wings for himself and others "to fly from lesser horizons." Although Bill is an inveterate student with wide interests, love of beauty and experience and observation of LIFE have been his primary teachers. On this basis, he writes articles on spiritual topics, with an emphasis on the experiential, often related to language, Anthroposophy, Rosicrucianism, esoteric Christianity, Sophiology, and the Divine Feminine. His goal is to create a body of writing that is initiatory and allows readers to grow beyond themselves. Bill lives happily with his wife of 45 years in a small hill town between the Catskills of the Hudson Valley, New York, and the Berkshire Mountains of western Massachusetts. Bill's published articles may be found at https://independent.academia.edu/BillTrusiewicz.

**AMBER WOLFE ROUNDS** is a second-generation astrologer with 15 years of experience. She provides astrology services, including predictive forecasting, natal charts for individuals, composite readings for couples or groups, and workshops. Amber composes and performs musical scores from astrology with Zizia. She earned a Waldorf Certificate and an MEd from Antioch University New England after submitting her thesis, *Tone Art: Anthroposophy, Astrology, Music.*

NOTE: These symbols are used at the
start of each project:

= easy

= moderate

# Table of Contents

## One-Strand Bracelets 2

## Memoir Bracelets 4

## Hardware Store Bracelets 7

## The Charming Bracelets 10

## Vintage Button Bracelets 12

## Woven Bracelets 15

## Techniques 18

# One-Strand Bracelets

These one-strand bracelets are so easy to make that you'll find yourself dreaming up new combinations every time you stop by the bead store or take an old necklace apart. They make a fun gift, too—customize them to be as elegant, as cute, or as sleek as you like.

## TECHNIQUES

- **Bead stringing**
- **Crimp beads**
  Row of Ovals

- **Knotting**
  Bronze Knotted

## Row of Ovals One-Strand Bracelet

*This colorful, simple piece combines multihued ovals with blue and lime green cubes.*

*Length: 7½ inches*

**TIP** Try to keep your bracelet design balanced. Using beads similar in size or weight will ensure it's not always falling to one side as you wear it. If you use identical beads, you'll create a sleeker piece, even if they're bright and eye-catching, too.

## Row of Ovals One-Strand Bracelet

**YOU'LL NEED**

- Tape
- Pliers
- Soft Flex wire
- Seven 16mm oval beads (O)
- 4 small glass cube beads (SC)
- 4 larger glass cube beads (LC)
- Seed beads (s)
- 2 crimp beads
- Clasp

**1.** Cut a 15-inch piece of wire and double a piece of tape 4 inches from one end.

**2.** String beads in this pattern: s-SC-s-O-s-LC-s-O-s-SC-s-O-s-LC-s-<u>O</u>-s-SC-s-O-s-LC-s-O-s-SC-s-O-s-LC-s.

**3.** Add one crimp bead and thread the wire through the clasp then back through the crimp bead. Slip the wire tail inside the first four beads and pull it taut. Securely flatten the crimp bead with your flat-nose pliers.

**4.** Remove the tape from the other end of the wire and add a crimp bead. Attach the other half of the clasp following step 3.

**5.** Trim both wire tails closely.

# Key to My Heart Hardware Store Bracelet

*An industrial brass chain paired with a single key is striking in its simplicity.*

*Length: 8½ inches*

**YOU'LL NEED**

- Pliers
- 20-gauge craft wire
- An antique or new key
- 8 inches of heavy brass chain
- 16-gauge brass wire

**1.** Using 20-gauge wire, form a double-wrapped loop to connect your key to the chain—I added my key three links from one end.

**2.** Make a modified hook clasp with the 16-gauge wire. Be sure that the hook is flush with the bracelet. Add the clasp to the opposite end of the chain.

# Memoir Bracelets

Memoir bracelets, which are strung on memory wire, retain their circular shape perfectly. Try a combination of large beads with tiny seed beads, a mix of delicate pieces, or even an assortment of charms for a modern "charm bangle."

## TECHNIQUES

- Memory wire
- Briolette-style wrapping and/or jump rings
  Charm Bangle

**TIP** When selecting beads make sure they aren't too heavy for this style. If you use larger, more substantial beads, try cutting your memory wire rounds about 1 to 2 inches longer so the two ends overlap for added stability.

## Lucky Blue Memoir Bracelet

*This bracelet features blue oval beads with a lucky eye bead.*

*Length: 7 inches (adjustable)*

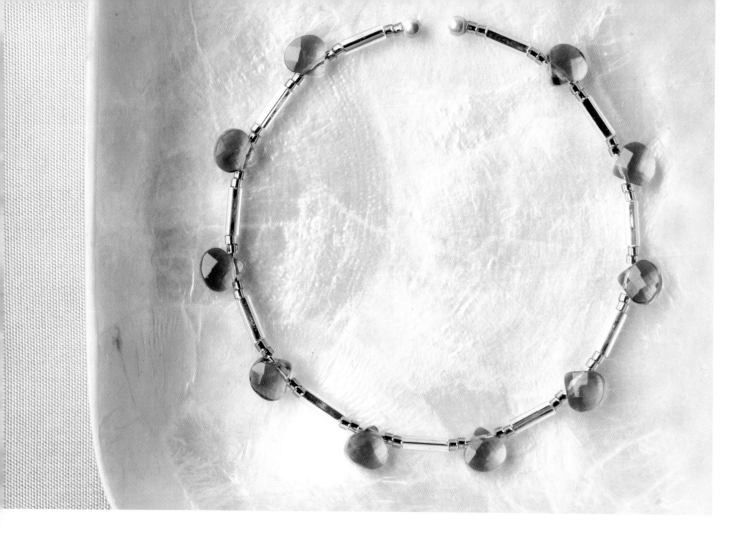

## YOU'LL NEED

• Glue

• Pliers

• One 7-inch round of memory wire

• 2 round bead ends

• Eleven 10mm glass oval beads (G)

• Seed beads in a coordinating color (s)

• 1 small lucky charm on a jump or soldered ring (C)

**1.** Glue one tip onto the end of your memory wire and let dry completely.

**2.** String your beads on in this pattern: G-s-C-s-G-s-s-G-s-s-G-s-s-G-s-s-<u>G</u>-s-s-G-s-s-G-s-s-G-s-s-G-s-s-G. Continue until you have 11 oval beads on the wire. You'll start and end with an oval bead.

**3.** Carefully glue the second bead end onto the tail. Let it dry completely.

# Delicate Briolettes Memoir Bracelet

*This bracelet mixes translucent amethyst glass briolettes with tiny silver beads. Length: 7 inches (adjustable)*

## YOU'LL NEED

• Pliers

• Glue

• 10 small briolettes (BR)

• 12 bugle beads (B)

• Delica seed beads (s)

• 7 inches of memory wire

• 2 bead ends

Follow the instructions for the Lucky Blue Memoir Bracelet (at left) using this pattern:

s-s-B-s-s-BR-s-s-B-s-s-BR (repeat 10 more times).

# Charm Bangle
# Memoir Bracelet

*This modern combination is striking and easy to wear.*

*Length: 7 inches (adjustable)*

**YOU'LL NEED**

- Pliers
- Glue
- 9 charms (C)
- Jump rings and/or 24-gauge wire
- Eight ⅝-inch pieces of plastic tubing (P)
- Two ⅛-inch pieces of plastic tubing (SP)
- 7-inch round of memory wire
- 2 bead ends

Make this bracelet the same way as the Lucky Blue, but the charms will be neatly separated by pieces of tubing. Form briolette-style drops (or use jump rings) to suspend each charm, and simply slide each one on through its loop. Follow this pattern:

SP-C-P-C-P-C-P-C-P-C-P-C-P-C-P-C-SP.

# Hardware Store Bracelets

These simple bracelets use hardware store materials for a fun, unexpected, and inexpensive design. They're all flexible ideas—use different combinations of "charms" or embellishments to make yours ultra-personalized.

## TECHNIQUES

- **Jump rings**
  So So

- **Double-wrapped loops**
  So So

**TIP** You can find a great variety of colors and sizes of ball chain at hardware stores. Look for interesting link chains, too—they're usually in brass or silver. Both types are available by the foot pretty inexpensively. Be sure to get the heaviest chains cut to the lengths you need at the store, instead of ruining your own wire cutters.

## So So Hardware Store Bracelet

*A super-stylish piece, this bracelet features washers and S-hooks on silver-colored ball chain.*

*Length: 7 inches*

### YOU'LL NEED

• Pliers
• 20-gauge wire
• 7 inches of ball chain and clasp
• 4 S-hooks
• 5 washers
• 4 jump rings

**1.** Cut five 4-inch pieces of wire and make the first half of a double-wrapped loop around each washer.

**2.** Lay your ball chain out in a straight line, and arrange your S-hooks and washers, alternating them. Space them out evenly—for my bracelet, I added one every fourth link.

**3.** Beginning on the left side, put one washer charm on after the fifth link in to complete the top half of the loop.

**4.** Open all four jump rings and set all but one aside. Slip one ring onto an S-hook and place it next to the first washer.

**5.** Continue adding washers and S-hooks to the ball chain, alternating so they are evenly spaced four links apart until you reach the other end.

# Gone Fishin' Hardware Bracelet

AlternaCrafts *author Jessica Vitkus says, "One day I drifted into the bait and tackle section and found these intriguing little guys called snap swivels, which come in different metals, sizes, and colors. I like the idea of using something like sports gear to make something delicate. Add beads and link the swivels together into jewelry in less than an hour."*

**TIP** Play with scale by trying different swivel sizes and metals, different beads, or even charms.

### YOU'LL NEED

- Pliers (optional)
- 6–8 size 10 snap swivels
  (from the fishing tackle section or store)
- Several dozen glass seed beads
  (make sure you have extras)

**1.** Take your first snap swivel and open it with your fingers or pliers. This involves unhooking the bowed side from the straight side.

**2.** String several seed beads onto the snap swivel in one of two ways. You can pour a few beads into the palm of your hand and poke them with the open wire end. Or you can hold one bead between your thumb and forefinger and place it on the open end of the snap swivel.

**NOTE:** Not every seed bead will fit around the swivel's hook, so you will have to fish (sorry!) for the skinnier ones. This is why you need extras.

**3.** When you are happy with the beads on your first swivel, take the next snap swivel and hook it on so the two swivels lie head-to-tail as shown.

**4.** Shut the first snap swivel with your fingers or pliers.

**5.** Repeat steps 1 to 4 on the second swivel.

**6.** Continue until you are happy with the size. Link the head of the last swivel to the tail of the first.

**BONUS:** To make the larger-scale bracelet, use six snap swivels in size 130 pound. I beaded them with brass, silver, and copper *hishi* from Ethiopia.

# The Charming Bracelets

The traditional charm bracelet gets a fresh new interpretation in glossy gold and a flurry of blues. Put your own spin on it in the combination you like best!

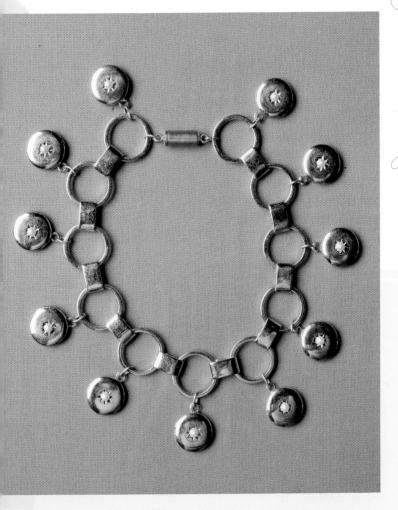

### TECHNIQUES

- **Jump rings**
  Little Lockets

- **Wrapped loops**
  Tangled Up in Blues

**TIP** Try using all kinds of things to make charm bracelets—beads, lockets, charms, found bits and pieces. Also, to save time, open all your jump rings before you start attaching each piece.

## Little Lockets Charming Bracelet

*A collection of gold lockets hang from a round gold chain.*

*Length: 7 inches*

# Tangled Up in Blues Charming Bracelet

*This happily jumbled collection includes blue vintage and new pieces on chain.*

*Length: 7 inches*

### YOU'LL NEED

- Pliers
- 24-gauge wire
- Assortment of 30 beads in the same color family—different shades and shapes
- Headpins
- Medium-size chain
- 2 jump rings
- Clasp

**1.** Cut one 3-inch piece of wire for each briolette-style wrap you will make. Form briolette wraps above any teardrop-shaped bead (I used five), and form the first half of a wrapped loop above each one.

**2.** Take one headpin and add a seed bead, one anchor bead, and another seed bead. Form the first half of a wrapped loop above the beads and set it aside. Repeat until all your beads are on wire.

**3.** Cut a 6½-inch piece of chain and lay it out flat. Choose one bead at random, slip it onto the first link, and complete the wrap.

**4.** Continue adding beads, one per link, in a random mix until you reach the other end of the chain.

**5.** Use jump rings to attach your clasp.

### YOU'LL NEED

- Pliers
- Oversize circle chain
- 13 jump rings
- 11 small vintage lockets
- Magnetic clasp

**1.** Cut your chain to 6½ inches long. Open up 11 jump rings and set all but one aside.

**2.** Place the first ring on the first link of chain and add a locket, making sure it's facing up. Close the ring securely.

**3.** Add a locket to each link of chain until you reach the other end.

**4.** Use a jump ring to attach the clasp at each end of the chain.

# Vintage Button Bracelets

Dip into your button box to make these cute, simple bracelets—whether you use heirloom pieces from your great-aunt or a handful you picked up at an estate sale, your wrist will be adorned with plenty of style.

## TECHNIQUES

• **Hand-stitching**
Red Sparkles

• **Gluing**
Red Sparkles

• **Wire wrapping**
Cute as a Button

**TIP** If you're stitching your buttons onto elastic, your bracelet will be much stretchier if you knot each button as you go instead of keeping the thread intact. If you want to sew them on with one continuous strand, just make your bracelet a little longer so it slips on over your hand easily without breaking the thread (as I did my first time out).

# Red Sparkles Vintage Button Bracelet

*This bracelet is a flashy mix of red buttons and rhinestones.*

*Length: 7½ inches*

### YOU'LL NEED

- Sewing needle
- Marker in the color of your buttons (optional)
- Fray Check
- Craft glue
- Buttons of your choice (I used 16 ⅜-inch red flowered buttons)
- 1 foot of ⅛-inch elastic
- Thread in a coordinating color
- Small rhinestones (one for each button)

**1.** Thread your needle and tie a double knot at one end. If you want to disguise the white of your elastic, you can color it in with marker to match the buttons.

**2.** Hold your first button in place over the elastic (about 1 inch in from one end) and stitch it on, reinforcing it three times. Once your first button is in place, you can either knot the thread and cut it off, or simply bring your needle up through the elastic to stitch on the second button.

**3.** Arrange the second button so that it's touching but not overlapping the first one and stitch it on the same way. Add the next buttons the same way until your bracelet is about 1 inch from being finished. Try it on for fit.

**4.** Finish the bracelet by stitching the last two buttons through both thicknesses of elastic: trim the elastic ends to the right length, keeping in mind they will overlap exactly, and put a drop of Fray Check™ on each end. Make a few quick basting stitches to hold the double layer in place, then stitch on the last two buttons. Tie a strong knot at the end of the sewing and add a drop of Fray Check to seal it.

**5.** Use a drop of craft glue to add a rhinestone to each button, covering the stitches in the buttonholes. Let it dry for several hours or until the glue is set.

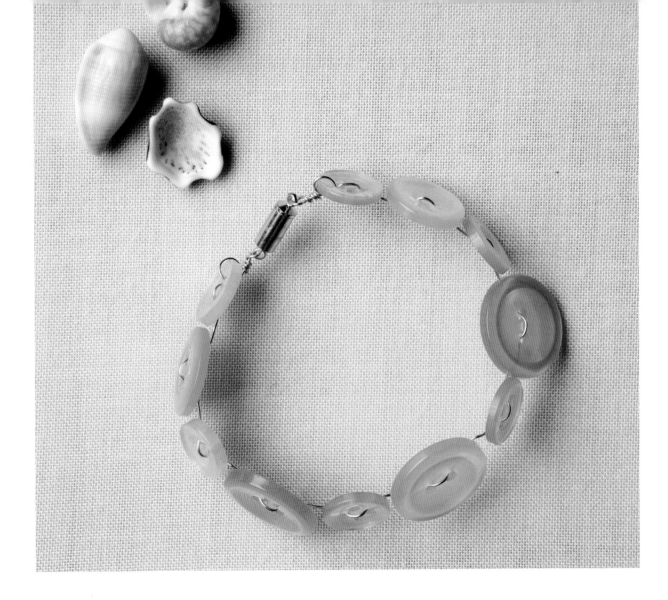

# Cute as a Button Bracelet

*These pink buttons on wire have a classic and beautiful look.*

*Length: 6¾ inches*

**YOU'LL NEED**

- Pliers
- An assortment of buttons in the same color family (I used 11 pink buttons ranging from ⅜ to ¾ inch across)
- 18 inches of 24-gauge gold craft wire
- Clasp

**1.** Arrange your buttons in a row so you like the mix of colors and sizes. (I alternated larger with smaller and darker with lighter.) Slip the wire through one of the holes of your first button, and place it about 6 inches from one end of the wire. Next, feed it through the opposite hole and pull it taut so that the button "sits" where you've placed it.

**2.** Add the next button in the same way, and secure it so it's close to the first one. Add more buttons until you have a section of wired buttons about 6 inches long. Clip the wire ends so they're each 5 to 6 inches long.

**3.** Feed one of the wire ends back into the outer hole of the last button, looping it through to reinforce it. Form the first half of a wrapped loop with the wire but don't close it. Repeat on the other side.

**4.** Slip half of a magnetic clasp onto each open loop, then complete the wrap to close them.

# Woven Bracelets

These bracelets take a simple woven pattern in very different directions—try including your favorite beads as the centers so they really stand out. Flip ahead to the bead-weaving techniques on pp. 27 and 29 for reference as you go.

## TECHNIQUES

• **Bead weaving**
  All

**TIP** Use long, vertical beads as your "ladder rungs" for a wide cuff style or narrow/wider beads for a cool, streamlined version. This is such a versatile design once you have the basic pattern down—have fun with it!

## Ice Cube Deluxe Woven Bracelet

*These clear glass cubes are woven together to form an elegant statement.*

*Length: 7 inches*

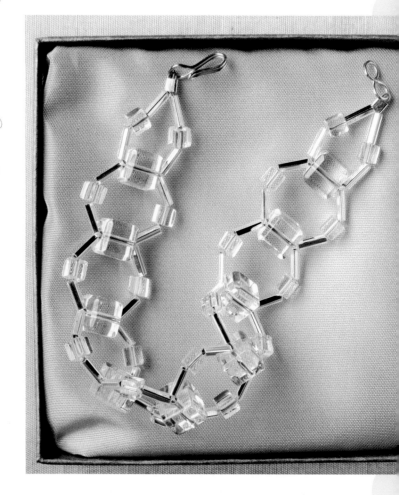

### Ice Cube Deluxe Woven Bracelet

**YOU'LL NEED**

- Pliers
- Tape
- Soft Flex wire
- Clasp or chain
- 2 large crimp beads
- Glass bugle beads, ¼ inch long (b)
- 20 small glass cubes, about 4mm (g)
- 9 large glass cubes, about 8 mm (these will be the connectors) (G)

**1.** Cut a 3-foot piece of beading wire and slip the clasp (or the last link in a piece of chain, to make it adjustable necklace-style) onto it. Add a large crimp bead over both wire tails, and slip it all the way down the wire so it is just over the clasp or chain. Crimp it closed. You now have two 1½-foot wire tails extending out of the crimp bead to work with.

**2.** Think of the tail that is currently upper as A and the other as B. Begin your pattern by adding several beads to each strand to form the sides. For this piece, string a bugle, a small cube, and another bugle on each strand.

**3.** Next, add a large cube to A and then slip B through it, coming in the side that A exited. Pull the two tails tight so that the large cube is neatly holding the first few beads in place. A will now be lower and B upper since they have crossed inside the large cube.

**4.** Add a bugle, a small cube, and another bugle on each strand, then slip both wires through a large cube as you did in steps 2 and 3.

**5.** Continue until you have nine large cubes strung. Add a bugle/small cube/bugle to each strand, then add a crimp bead over both strands.

**6.** Slip the other half of your clasp (or the last link of a second piece of chain) onto each wire, and bring the wires back through the crimp bead. Slip one piece of wire through each of the beaded strands, and pull the tail through so the design is taut and symmetrical. Crimp the bead closed, then trim each of the wire tails.

**PATTERN:** identical upper and lower (both strands pass through <u>G</u> each time):

b-g-b-<u>G</u>-b-g-b-<u>G</u>-b-g-b-<u>G</u>-b-g-b-<u>G</u>-b-g-b-<u>G</u>-b-g-b-<u>G</u>-b-g-b-<u>G</u>-b-g-b-<u>G</u>-b-g-b

## Perfectly Pink Woven Bracelet

*This sparkly-pearly bracelet has a sweet vintage feel.*

*Length: 7 inches*

**YOU'LL NEED**

- Pliers
- Tape
- 3 feet of Soft Flex wire
- 2 large crimp beads
- 9 large pink pearl rounds, approximately 10mm (these will be the connectors) (P)
- 40 pink faceted Lucite rounds, approximately 8mm (p)

**FOLLOW** the same technique for Ice Cube Deluxe using this pattern: identical upper and lower (both strands pass through <u>P</u> each time):

p-p-<u>P</u>-p-p-<u>P</u>-p-p-<u>P</u>-p-p-<u>P</u>-p-p-<u>P</u>-p-p-<u>P</u>-p-p-<u>P</u>-p-p-<u>P</u>-p-p-<u>P</u>-p-p

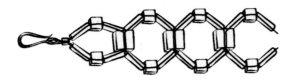

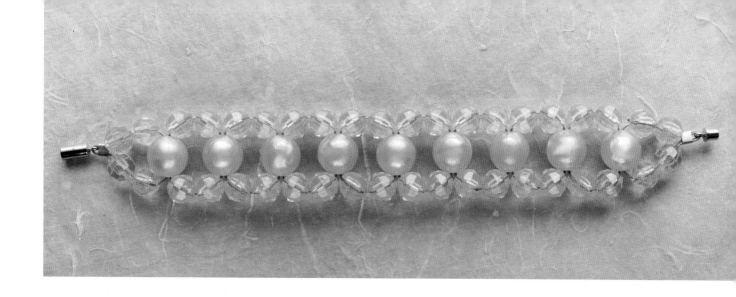

# Glossy Black Woven Bracelet

*This version is sleek and eye-catching.*

*Length: 7 inches*

**YOU'LL NEED**

- Pliers
- Tape
- 3 feet of Soft Flex wire
- 2 large crimp beads
- 7 large black ovals (mine were about 20mm long; these will be the connectors) (B)
- Thirty-two 6mm black rounds (b)
- Black seed beads

Follow the Ice Cube Deluxe technique using this pattern: identical upper and lower (both strands pass through <u>B</u> each time):

**NOTE:** Each black round (b) has a seed bead on each side of it.

b-b-<u>B</u>-b-b-<u>B</u>-b-b-<u>B</u>-b-b-<u>B</u>-b-b-<u>B</u>-b-b-<u>B</u>-b-b-<u>B</u>-b-b

# Techniques

Here are the techniques you'll use to create every design in this booklet. You may need to practice some of them a few times before trying them out on a project, but they get much easier with a little trial and error. If you need help, there are short videos of many of these on beadsimple.com for reference, too.

## Bead Stringing

Bead stringing is the most basic way to construct a piece of jewelry like a necklace or bracelet—just thread a needle or pick up a piece of flexible wire, secure the end, and add beads one after another. Depending on what you're using materials-wise and your own taste, there are several ways to construct your piece of jewelry.

### Needle beading

**1.** Before you begin, you may want to add a bead tip (see facing page) to add your clasp or end component.

**2.** Thread a needle with your thinner material (like elastic, silk cord, or nylon thread), and tie a knot or cover the end with a doubled piece of tape.

**3.** Add your beads one (or more) at a time, and continue beading until you reach the desired length.

**4.** Finish with a bead tip or durable knotting (if no clasp is required).

## Needle Beading

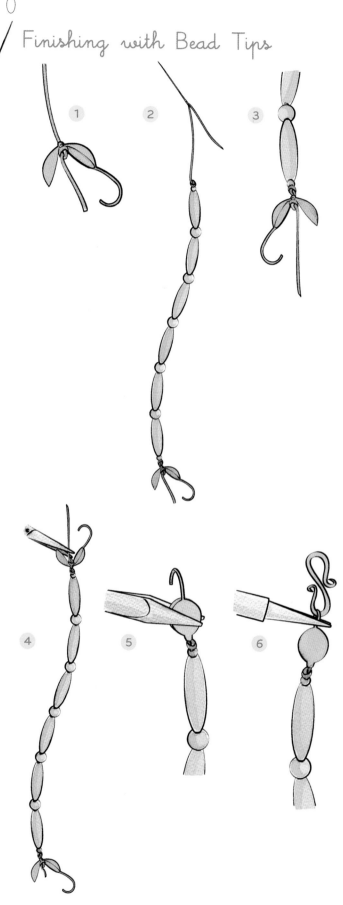

## Finishing with Bead Tips

### Finishing with bead tips

Bead tips cover a knot at each end of the cord securely, and the curved hook attaches to a finding. See complete instructions for knotting on p. 29.

**1.** Tie a knot near the beginning of your cord and slip one bead tip onto it, with the two cupping halves facing and enveloping the knot (as shown). Knot again directly above the bead tip to keep it in place.

**2.** String or knot your beads as you go until you're finished with your piece. Tie a knot at the end.

**3.** Add a bead tip with the halves facing outward, away from the beads and toward the needle. Using your knotting tweezers to pinpoint the spot, tie a knot inside the tip and pull it taut.

**4.** Add a drop of glue or Fray Check (I often use Fray Check, then glue), and snip the cord ends away just above each knot.

**5.** Using your flat-nose pliers, press the tips closed around the knots.

**6.** Using your round-nose pliers, curve the hook around a jump ring or clasp loop.

### Flexible beading wire

This thin, durable wire is easy to bead with. Use good-quality materials—it's so worth it! I highly recommend Soft Flex wire, since inexpensive tiger-tail wire kinks and ages poorly.

**1.** Cut a piece of wire at least 4 to 6 inches longer than the finished length of the piece you're making. Add a doubled piece of clear tape near the end of your wire to hold your design as you string your pieces—it's easy to take off when you're ready to

## Flexible Beading Wire

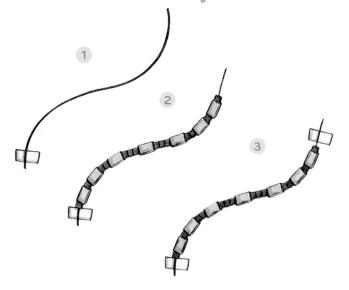

finish the ends but won't kink or untie itself as a knot often does.

**2.** Begin creating your design from one end, or construct the middle section and move outward—it's up to you. Beads will slip right onto your wire, so you don't need a needle. Just add them in the desired pattern, and remember, you can always tape the working end and switch back to the other side if you want to change your design—it's very flexible.

## Crimp Beads

**3.** If you need to take a break or don't finish the project right away, just tape both ends of the wire to hold the pattern.

### Crimp beads

Finish a Soft Flex or a ribbon piece with crimp beads—small metal cylinders that hold a doubled cord securely when you flatten or crimp them with pliers. They can also be used to hold a bead or piece in place on a single wire or cord, like the Row of Ovals One-Strand Bracelet (p. 2).

I recommend sterling or gold-filled cylinder-shaped crimp beads, which are easy to work with and finish smoothly. Base metal crimps can be rough at the edge, scratching your skin or cutting through the wire itself.

**1.** Finish stringing your piece. Place a single crimp bead on the end of the strand and add a clasp.

**2.** Slip the wire tail back through the crimp bead then through the next several beads.

**3.** Tug the wire so it's taut, with no gaps between beads or at the end.

**4.** Firmly crimp the bead closed with your flat-nose pliers.

**5.** Clip off the end of the wire close to the beads so the end tucks back in and won't scratch your skin.

**TIP** Use an oversize crimp bead if you are crimping more than two strands at a time, especially if it's a thicker Soft Flex wire.

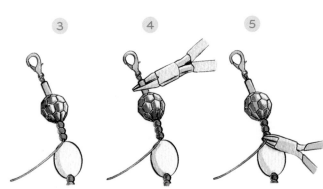

## Crimp clasps

You'll attach all-in-one crimp/clasp pieces similarly. Just use your flat-nose pliers to securely flatten the metal crimp around the cord or ribbon. Crimp one side at a time if it's a flap style or the entire thing if it's a cylinder style. You may want to add a drop of glue to your cord before slipping it into the crimp clasp for extra hold.

## Double crimp variation

You can also use special crimping pliers to make a double crimp with a tighter, cleaner finish.

**1.** Follow steps 1–3 for crimp beads, but instead of pressing the crimp bead flat in one motion as in step 4, position it inside the first notch of the crimping pliers (closest to the handles) and gently squeeze it, forming a curved U shape.

**2.** Place the curved crimp bead into the second notch (closer to the tips), rotate it 90 degrees, and squeeze again, tightening the U shape closed.

**3.** Finally, flatten the doubled crimp bead completely using the tip of the pliers.

## Memory wire

Here's how to start—and finish—a necklace or bracelet made with memory wire.

**1.** Cut the memory wire round to the length you want it to be. Take a ball- or cube-shaped tip and use a small drop of glue to attach it to the end of the

memory wire round on one side. Once it's completely dry, start adding beads.

**2.** When you finish your bead stringing, you should have a short "tail" of memory wire at the open end. Gripping the tail with your flat-nose pliers, gently shake the memory wire so the beads fall into place with no gaps between them. Place the tip on the end to see if there's any open space once it's on. If there

Memory Wire

Double Crimp

is, cut the tail more closely (you may need to take off a few beads, cut it, and put them back on) or add another seed bead.

**3.** Glue the last seed bead in place, then carefully glue the second tip onto the tail. Let it dry completely. Note: If you'd rather not glue your last bead, just glue the tip on the end of the wire.

# Wirework

These basic techniques—forming plain loops and wrapped loops with your pliers—are easy steps that transform a simple piece of wire into a custom eyepin, earwire, chain link, or pendant. Plain and wrapped loops are the knit and purl stitches of jewelry making—they're invaluable for making just about anything, from simple drop earrings to elaborate wire masterpieces. Once you learn these basics, you'll be able to repair or alter jewelry and create and embellish new pieces.

In these diagrams, the flat-nose pliers are shown with blue handles, the round-nose pliers have red handles, and the wire cutters have black handles.

## Plain loops

**1.** Cut a 4-inch piece of craft wire, then use your flat-nose pliers to bend it at a neat 90-degree angle about ¼ to ½ inch from the end. The longer the wire bend, the larger the loop.

**2.** Holding the longer part of the wire with your flat-nose pliers, grasp the end of the shorter wire bend with the tip of your round-nose pliers.

**3.** Twist your wrist so you begin to bring the very end of the wire around to meet the bend, forming a neat circle. You'll essentially be rolling the pliers toward you. It can be easier to do this in two steps, letting go of the wire about halfway through and then grasping it again with your pliers to finish bringing it around. You can adjust or finish the loop after you curve the wire so it's perfectly round.

**4.** The finished loop should look like a lollipop. If there is any excess wire extending beyond the circle, trim it with wire cutters and gently tweak it back into shape. If your loops are misshapen or crooked, just clip them off and start again.

## Wrapped loops

**1.** Place a bead on the eyepin you've just created. Grasp the wire just above the bead with your round-nose pliers, and make another neat 90-degree angle bend above and over the tips, holding the wire tail with your flat-nose pliers.

**2.** Next, adjust the round-nose pliers so they are gripping on either side of the wire bend, above and below it. Use your flat-nose pliers to pull the wire tail over the end of the round-nose pliers and all the way around, creating a circle with an extra tail of wire still extending beyond it.

**3.** Use the flat-nose pliers to hold the circle while you grip the end of the wire tail with your round-nose pliers.

**4.** Wrap the wire tail around the space above the bead, working from top to bottom to create a neat

Plain Loops

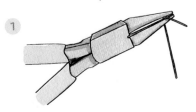

## Wrapped Loops

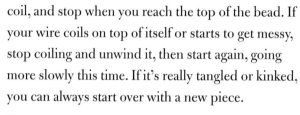

coil, and stop when you reach the top of the bead. If your wire coils on top of itself or starts to get messy, stop coiling and unwind it, then start again, going more slowly this time. If it's really tangled or kinked, you can always start over with a new piece.

**5.** Clip the end of the wire flush with the coil. Make sure the sharp edge isn't sticking out—if it does, use your flat-nose pliers to flatten and smooth it into the coil.

**TIP** Practice with inexpensive craft wire until your loops are nice and even.

**TIP** Plain loops work best with thick wire (such as 20 gauge), while the more secure wrapped loops are good for thinner wire (24 gauge).

**BASIC DANGLE** Creating a plain loop below a bead and a wrapped loop above it transforms the bead into a dangling charm as illustrated at right.

Alternate way: Use a headpin or eyepin for the base instead of forming the plain loop.

**DOUBLE-LOOPED BEAD CONNECTOR** Use this process to link a bead into a longer chain or design. Just cut a piece of wire and make a wrapped loop or a plain loop on each side, being sure to join the loops to the chain or design before you close them completely. As always, you'll use a wrapped loop

## Flat-Front Plain Loop Variation

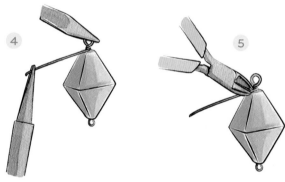

For this variation, the plain loop looks like a "P"—the curve of the loop is to the back of, say, a drop pendant. To do this, skip step 1 and grasp the end of the wire. Simply curve it into a loop. The wire will still look straight and smooth in front instead of obviously curved.

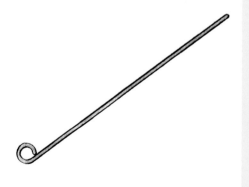

## Double-Looped Connectors

## Briolette Wrapping

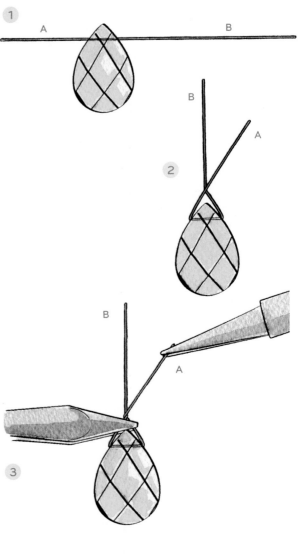

with a thinner-gauge wire (24 and up) and have the option of doing a plain loop with a heavier-gauge wire (20 and below). See the illustrations above.

## Briolette wrapping

This technique is great for creating a handmade "hanger" for both horizontally drilled briolettes and pieces with a space in the middle. It's essentially a variation on the double-wrapped loop on the facing page.

**1.** Cut a 4-inch piece of wire and run it through a briolette, side to side, so one-third of the wire is on one side (A) and two-thirds on the other (B).

**2.** Fold one then the other wire up into a triangle, following the lines of the bead. The wires will look like an X.

**3.** Form a sharp angle in wire B so it extends straight above the bead.

**4.** Grip the wires below the X with flat-nose pliers, and wrap wire A in a coil around wire B. Stop after three coils and clip the wire.

**5.** Form a loop above the coil. Grip it with flat-nose pliers, using round-nose pliers to make a new coil starting at the top and moving downward.

**6.** Bring the wire tail around to the side of the coil where the tail from step 4 is and clip it closely. Use your flat-nose pliers to make sure the wire clipping is flush with the coil. This side will be the back of the finished piece, so the neat coiling shows continuously and the raw edges are hidden behind it.

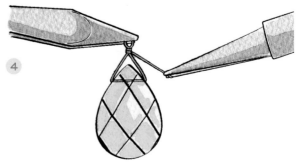

## Variation: Side-to-side briolette

Use this version to connect a single briolette to chain or cord on both sides, instead of making a drop to suspend from one strand. Cut a piece of wire and make a wrapped loop on one side, slipping it through the last link of a piece of chain before completing the wrap. Slip the briolette onto the wire and form a second wrapped loop on its other side, again adding it to a last link of chain before completing the wrap (see the drawing above).

You may also want to curve the loops upward.

## Double-wrapped loop

This dual loop wraps around (or through) a charm or piece and the chain or cord to form a double connector or hanger. It's made the same way as a double-looped bead connector without the bead in the middle of the coils.

**1.** Cut a piece of wire and form a briolette-style hanger around or through the piece, front to back, leaving the top loop open after forming the first half. You'll wrap the coil using the back wire tail, going around the front piece.

**2.** Slip the open loop onto a chain or cord and complete the wrap, making sure the wire ends are tucked to the back of the coil so they don't show. As you wind the top wrap, the coil will stay neater if you bring the wire around on the opposite side from the first wrap.

## Wire looping

This technique is simple—just use wire to go through a bead once, back to front, bring it around to the back again, and slip it through a second time. It's great for securing small beads or holding larger ones.

**1.** Slip the bead onto the wire.

**2.** Bring the wire tail around and through the bead again.

**3.** Pull it tight so the wire hugs the bead.

Wire Looping

## Jump rings

Use jump rings—small circles of wire with an opening—to attach clasps, suspend charms, or form a simple chain.

**1.** Open a jump ring by gripping the ring on each side with a pair of pliers. Separate the ring by tilting the right side toward you and the left side away from you—don't pull the ring open into a U shape.

**2.** Close the ring by reversing step 1. The ring should close neatly with no gap where the ends meet. If it doesn't meet neatly on the first try, gently tilt the two sides back and forth past the closed position a few times until the ring "clicks" shut. You can also make sure it's secure by squeezing it shut with the flat-nose pliers.

Jump Rings

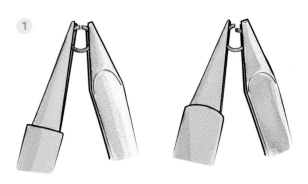

Basic Earring Wires

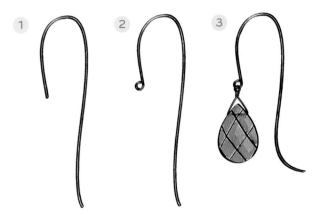

To attach a clasp to a chain, simply slip both the last link in the chain and the clasp (or its ring) onto the open jump ring in step 1. Close it to connect the two, as in step 2.

To attach a charm to a chain, choose the link you want to use and open a jump ring. Slip the charm or dangle onto the ring, then slip one end of the open ring through the link you've chosen. Close it securely.

To create a simple chain, just join a series of jump rings into a long row. Start with two: Open one, join it to the other, and close it. Add a third the same way, and so on until your chain is the desired length.

**TIP** If your jump ring becomes misshapen or dented from pliers marks, just throw it away and start over with a new one.

## Basic earring wires

**1.** Cut a 2½-inch piece of 22-gauge or 24-gauge wire, and form a large, round curve starting about ¾ inch in from the end. If the wire has a natural curve, follow it.

**2.** Next, create a small flat-front plain loop at the short end. This will be the loop of the earring wire.

**3.** Use your pliers to make a neat bend on the long end of the wire.

## Eyepins

These are ultra-simple—just take a 1-inch to 4-inch piece of straight wire and form a plain loop at one end. That's it!

## Clasps

Use your round-nose pliers to bend wire into clasp shapes, much like heavier-gauge versions of the earring wires. Pair these handmade clasps with soldered rings.

**TIP** Make different sizes of clasps by changing the length of the wire piece you work with. A 1½-inch wire will make an approximately ⅝-inch hook clasp, for example, and a 2-inch wire will make a ¾-inch S-clasp.

## Hooks

**1.** Cut a 1½-inch to 2-inch piece of 16-gauge or 18-gauge wire. Following the natural curve of the wire, bend a curve into it just before the halfway point.

**2.** Form a small or medium-size plain loop at the shorter end, curving the wire out into a circle. This will be the hook end.

**3.** Now form a larger plain loop at the longer end. This loop will connect to the cord, chain, or jump ring.

**4.** Open the larger plain loop just as you would open a jump ring to attach it to your finding or chain.

## S-clasp

**1.** Cut a 2-inch piece of 16-gauge or 18-gauge half-hard wire. Hold the wire about one-third of the way in on one side and make a curve in it, following the natural curve of the wire.

**2.** Make a second curve about one-third of the way in from the other side. Now you have a basic S shape (as shown).

**3.** Form a small plain loop at first one end of the S (the flat-front variation is fine, since the thicker wire will be harder to bend) and then the other.

**4.** Use your pliers to adjust the wire so one side is closed and the other is slightly open—this side will be the hook, and the closed side will be the connector.

## Basic Bead Weaving

The Woven Bracelet projects (pp. 15–17) use this pretty, but very basic, bead-weaving pattern. Once you get the pattern down, it's surprisingly easy: You'll create a repetitive design with beads mirroring each other, and the two wires you weave with will pass through central beads that look like rungs on a ladder.

Hooks

S-Clasp

The main difference between the two projects is that the bracelets are symmetrical, while the necklaces have embellishments on the lower scallops. The necklace sits like a collar, so these projects have an adjustable chain back instead of a simple clasp. Always string this pattern on Soft Flex instead of stiffer wire. For very lightweight beads, you could also use silk or nylon cord with bead tips instead of crimp beads.

## Basic Bead Weaving

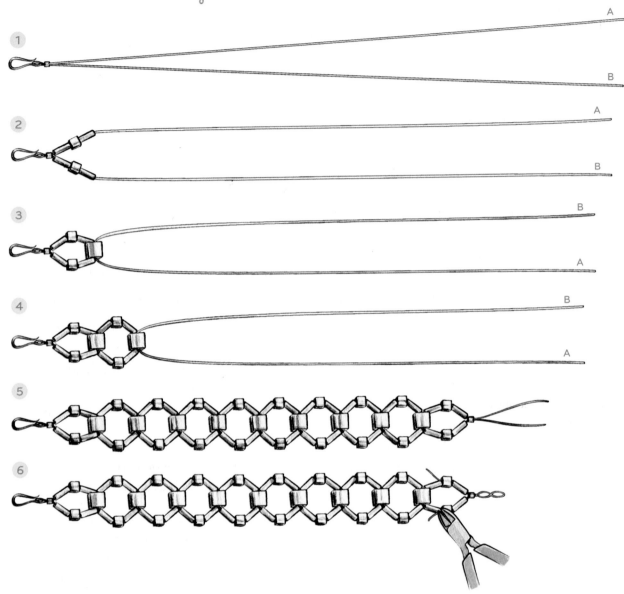

## Bracelet/symmetrical style

**1.** Cut a 3-foot piece of beading wire and slip the clasp onto it. Add a crimp bead over both wire tails, and slip it all the way down the wire so it is just over the clasp or chain. Crimp it closed. You now have two 1½-foot wire tails extending out of the crimp bead to work with.

**2.** Think of the tail that is currently upper as A and the one that's currently lower as B. Begin your pattern by adding several beads to each strand to form the sides. For this sample pattern, string a bugle, a small bead, and another bugle on each strand.

**3.** Add a large central bead to A and then slip B through it, coming in the side that A exited. Pull the two tails tight so that the central bead is neatly holding the first few beads in place. A will now be lower and B upper since they have crossed inside the large bead.

**4.** Add a bugle, a small bead, and another bugle on each strand, then slip both wires through a large bead as you did in steps 2 and 3.

**5.** Continue until you have nine large beads strung. Add a bugle/small bead/bugle to each strand, then slip a crimp bead over both strands.

**6.** Slip the other half of your clasp onto both wires, and bring the wires back through the crimp bead. Slip one piece of wire through each of the beaded strands, and pull the tail through so the design is taut and symmetrical. Crimp the bead closed, then trim each of the wire tails.

## Necklace/asymmetrical version

This method is very similar to the bracelet, with one major difference: The lower scallops have a drop or embellishment and the upper ones are simpler. There are two things to remember: First, since your wires will weave back and forth, the embellishments will not be strung on the same strand but alternate between A and B. Second, you'll need to balance your embellishments with beads above that have similar width so the pattern hangs well. Follow the same basic directions for making a bracelet style, but construct the necklace with chain on each side so it's adjustable in length, and use a drop ornament on all the odd-numbered segments and a small bead on the evens.

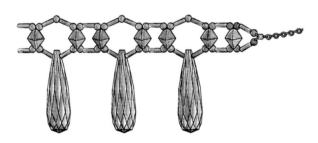

## Knotting

Knotting between beads is easy—especially when you use narrow tweezers to pinpoint exactly where you want your knot to go. Use knotting to separate beads or to create spaces on a cord.

**1.** Choose where you want your knot to be, and grip that spot firmly with tweezers.

Knotting

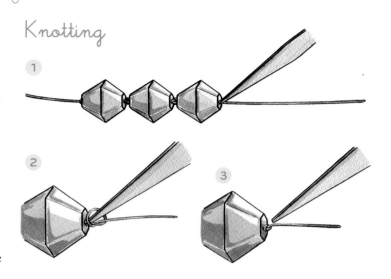

**2.** Bring your working cord around and over to tie a simple square knot over the tip of the tweezers.

**3.** Move the tweezers away just as you tighten the knot closed.

You can also use a row of knots to hold a larger piece.

## Stitching

You can stitch beads, buttons, and charms onto fabric and ribbons as easily as threading a needle.

TIP If you are stitching your beads on with sewing thread (especially nice when you want to match your garment or ribbon's unusual color exactly), be sure to use 100 percent polyester thread instead of cotton, which is much less durable. For added resilience, cut your thread, run it through beeswax twice, and give it a quick iron (on the synthetic setting) to seal it. This process will strengthen your thread considerably. Match your bead weight to the fabric or ribbon you're embellishing—a thin material will sag with heavy beads attached, so use lighter-weight or smaller ones instead.

## Bead Stitching

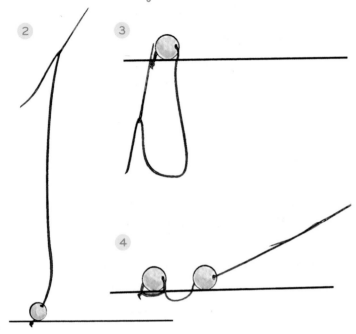

### Bead stitching

**1.** Thread a needle with your thread or cord and double the thread tail. Tie a knot at the end.

**2.** Choose where you want to place your first bead, then bring the needle up from the wrong side of the fabric there to hide the knot. Slip the bead onto the needle and all the way down the thread. Let the bead lie flat on the fabric, and bring the needle back through the fabric to hold it in place.

**3.** Bring the thread through the bead twice more for security, always pulling the thread taut as you sew.

**4.** Place the second bead in your design, and repeat steps 2 and 3 to stitch it down. Continue until all your beads are in place, then knot securely on the back of your work.

## Running stitch

This simple forward stitch is the easiest way to join two pieces of fabric or make a broken-line design.

**1.** Thread a needle and bring it up from the back (wrong side) of your fabric through to the front so the knot is on the underside.

**2.** Next, just stitch ahead, moving your needle forward as shown in the drawing on the facing page, following the pattern of your choice—straight, curved, or angled. You can easily vary the length or distance between your stitches to change the look of them.

## Backstitch

This method is a bit more involved, but it creates a much more durable join since it is reinforced by doubling back with each stitch. The stitches on the front of your fabric will look as neat as a running stitch, while the back will have overlapping longer stitches showing.

**1.** Thread a needle and bring it up from the back (wrong side) of your fabric through to the front so the knot is on the underside.

**2.** Bring your needle back into the fabric *behind* where it emerged (as shown on the facing page)—you'll double back instead of stitching forward. To begin the second one, bring the needle well out in front of the completed first stitch, then double back again the same way. You can also vary the length or placement of your stitches as with the running stitch, but it works best for a straight line rather than any curve or elaborate pattern.

## Running Stitch

## Backstitch

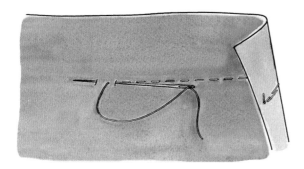

# Jewelry Repair

Let's face it—jewelry can be fragile. Whether it's a new or vintage piece, you can often repair or rework a break or damaged section. Another option is to rework the best of the existing piece into a whole new design—be creative in recycling a single earring or broken brooch into the centerpiece or highlight of an updated piece.

## Mending a chain

To mend a broken chain, you'll first need to cut away the damaged links. Sometimes it's easiest to just start over with a new length of chain and add the clasp and other components to it to rebuild your piece. You can often match a jump ring to your chain links for a subtle fix. Another option is to connect your chain using a linked coordinating bead— you can add them symmetrically so the join isn't as obvious once you've added to the design in more than one place.

## Replacing a jump ring

This is an easy repair. When a jump ring has deteriorated, simply cut it loose and replace it with a similar new one. If your piece has many (a link bracelet or necklace, for example), carefully examine the others to make sure that they're still in good shape. It's easy to replace one before it gets worn out instead of doing a fix on the fly while you're out and about wearing your jewelry.

## Reknotting

Unfortunately, this is a complete do-over; you'll have to cut your beads free and reknot them on a new cord from scratch. If you lost any beads in the shuffle and they're hard to match, try adding extras on both sides of the piece so they're less obvious.

bead simple

150 designs
for earrings,
necklaces, bracelets,
embellishments,
and more

susan beal

essential techniques for making jewelry just the way you want it

**Look for these other *Threads* Selects booklets at www.taunton.com and wherever crafts are sold.**

**Baby Beanies**
Debby Ware
EAN: 9781621137634
8 ½ x 10 ⅞, 32 pages
Product# 078001
$9.95 U.S., $11.95 Can.

**Fair Isle Flower Garden**
Kathleen Taylor
EAN: 9781621137702
8 ½ x 10 ⅞, 32 pages
Product# 078008
$9.95 U.S., $11.95 Can.

**Fair Isle Hats, Scarves, Mittens & Gloves**
Kathleen Taylor
EAN: 9781621137719
8 ½ x 10 ⅞, 32 pages
Product# 078009
$9.95 U.S., $11.95 Can.

**Lace Socks**
Kathleen Taylor
EAN: 9781621137894
8 ½ x 10 ⅞, 32 pages
Product# 078012
$9.95 U.S., $11.95 Can.

**Colorwork Socks**
Kathleen Taylor
EAN: 9781621137740
8 ½ x 10 ⅞, 32 pages
Product# 078011
$9.95 U.S., $11.95 Can.

**DIY Bride Cakes & Sweets**
Khris Cochran
EAN: 9781621137665
8 ½ x 10 ⅞, 32 pages
Product# 078004
$9.95 U.S., $11.95 Can.

**DIY Bride Beautiful Bouquets**
Khris Cochran
EAN: 9781621137672
8 ½ x 10 ⅞, 32 pages
Product# 078005
$9.95 U.S., $11.95 Can.

**Bead Necklaces**
Susan Beal
EAN: 9781621137641
8 ½ x 10 ⅞, 32 pages
Product# 078002
$9.95 U.S., $11.95 Can.

**Drop Earrings**
Susan Beal
EAN: 9781621137658
8 ½ x 10 ⅞, 32 pages
Product# 078003
$9.95 U.S., $11.95 Can.

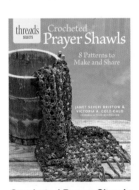

**Crocheted Prayer Shawls**
Janet Severi Bristow &
Victoria A. Cole-Galo
EAN: 9781621137689
8 ½ x 10 ⅞, 32 pages
Product# 078006
$9.95 U.S., $11.95 Can.

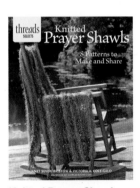

**Knitted Prayer Shawls**
Janet Severi Bristow &
Victoria A. Cole-Galo
EAN: 9781621137696
8 ½ x 10 ⅞, 32 pages
Product# 078007
$9.95 U.S., $11.95 Can.

**Shawlettes**
Jean Moss
EAN: 9781621137726
8 ½ x 10 ⅞, 32 pages
Product# 078010
$9.95 U.S., $11.95 Can.